JOHNSON O'CONNOR
ENGLISH VOCABULARY
BUILDER

BOOKS BY

JOHNSON O'CONNOR

BORN THAT WAY
PSYCHOMETRICS
UNSOLVED BUSINESS PROBLEMS
TOO MANY APTITUDE WOMAN
STRUCTURAL VISUALIZATION
APTITUDES AND THE LANGUAGES
IDEAPHORIA
THE UNIQUE INDIVIDUAL
ENGLISH VOCABULARY BUILDER, VOL. I, II
SCIENCE VOCABULARY BUILDER

JOHNSON O'CONNOR

ENGLISH VOCABULARY

BUILDER

VOLUME III

BOSTON

HUMAN ENGINEERING LABORATORY

1974

PRINTED IN THE UNITED STATES
BY THOMAS TODD COMPANY · BOSTON

JOHNSON O'CONNOR RESEARCH FOUNDATION INCORPORATED
11 East 62nd Street New York New York 10021
JOHNSON O'CONNOR RESEARCH FOUNDATION INCORPORATED
121 Second Street N. E. Washington D. C. 20002
JOHNSON O'CONNOR RESEARCH FOUNDATION INCORPORATED
47 E. Adams Avenue Detroit Michigan 48226
JOHNSON O'CONNOR RESEARCH FOUNDATION INCORPORATED
Box 3521 Baytown Texas 77520
JOHNSON O'CONNOR RESEARCH FOUNDATION INCORPORATED
Suite 520 Pershing Point Plaza
1371 Peachtree Street N. E. Atlanta Georgia 30309
HUMAN ENGINEERING LABORATORY INCORPORATED
347 Beacon Street Boston Massachusetts 02116
HUMAN ENGINEERING LABORATORY
2012 Delancey Place Philadelphia Pennsylvania 19103
HUMAN ENGINEERING LABORATORY
1349 West Fifth Street Los Angeles California 90017
HUMAN ENGINEERING LABORATORY
906 South Cheyenne Tulsa Oklahoma 74119
HUMAN ENGINEERING LABORATORY
161 East Erie Street Chicago Illinois 60611
HUMAN ENGINEERING LABORATORY
657 Fifth Avenue Fort Worth Texas 76104
HUMAN ENGINEERING LABORATORY
3004 Sixth Avenue San Diego California 92103
JOHNSON O'CONNOR RESEARCH FOUNDATION
(an Ontario Corporation)
FUNDACIÓN DE INVESTIGACIONES JOHNSON O'CONNOR A. C.
Calle Enrique Wallon 417-201, Polanco
Mexico 5 D. F. Mexico

INTRODUCTION

This book, Volume III in the series of Vocabulary Builders, is the final published work of Johnson O'Connor. He devoted an energetic and prolific lifetime to forming an approach to understanding human behavior through the measurement of aptitudes. He created and sustained a nationwide organization of testing and research centers, the Johnson O'Connor Research Foundation and Human Engineering Laboratory. From insights gained in more than fifty years of testing, measuring specific traits and comparing the test performance of individuals with subsequent success in chosen vocations, Johnson O'Connor determined that the vocabulary level of the examinee is the best indicator of his or her career advancement. The aptitude measurements serve to point the individual in the proper direction, to put him on the right path; but it is the knowledge possessed and obtained, represented by the English vocabulary score, that propels one along, determining the distance on the career path one can travel. The issue of success and what will predict it had long engaged Johnson O'Connor as well as many others seeking answers to the riddles of human ability, motivation and achievement. The introduction to the English Vocabulary Builder, Volume I, treats this at length, as have other publications of the Laboratory.

In counseling those who take the aptitude worksamples, the Laboratory puts great emphasis on vocabulary. Whatever a person's pattern of aptitudes, if he fails in precise articulation of ideas, he is likely to be considered less competent to perform a task than is the person who, although perhaps not naturally as adept, has a better vocabulary and is thus able to express himself more convincingly. This superior word knowledge does not necessarily cause a frequent verbal flaunting of unusual words, rather such words reflect a good thinking vocabulary, well-honed tools for thought.

Eminent authors, practiced public speakers, celebrated critics seek the turn of phrase, the droll line that says so much, so well, so succinctly. Much is made of word placement, clustering of thoughts, ironies, hidden or implied extensions of meaning. These skills are perhaps unobtainable for the majority of mortals. Yet appreciation of fine writing style hinges not on the ability to duplicate originality of expression, but on comprehending the essence of what is expressed. Many rich layers of meaning may co-exist in a Robert Frost poem or a Shakespeare soliloquy, yet the primal communication of thought in most verbal exchange is transmitted and received by a precise understanding of the words therein. This Vocabulary Builder is dedicated to instilling a sense of exact meaning and a heightened awareness of the words found in better writing, words often pivotal to a proper interpretation of the communicator's intent. The book is firmly rooted in tradition. Johnson O'Connor has wisely clung to the history and roots of words as a way to extend our time and thoughts into the past so that we may draw out from the evolution of language the optimum expressiveness for the future.

Just as literature may be read and understood on different levels, so varying purposes may be served by this book. Wordsmiths may absorb every insight into esoteric words and dwell on every obscure citation provided in the word descriptions. Pragmatic businessmen may wish basic improvement of verbal ability as a precision tool for commercial undertakings. Young students may realize the limitations inherent in a vocabulary not yet suited to appreciating literature or erudite non-fiction, nor even sure enough to cope with the standardized placement tests which figure in admission decisions at colleges and graduate schools. Most people are too busy in their chosen livelihoods to linger on each word as might a poet, who will sift and sort each word to find the most suitable. Some of these people in taking our tests have confused INFERIOR and INEXPENSIVE (see #13), which could cause overspending or waste for professional buyers and retail store owners. Those who might confuse INJUNCTION and SETTLEMENT (#273) or who misread PRUDENTLY to mean QUICKLY (#61) may suffer in day to day life. The injunction which may delay an organized resistance does not necessarily signify that an amicable settlement will result. The hasty action is unlikely to be carefully considered and will seldom satisfy.

This volume spans the full range of most student and adult vocabularies. Statistically, the first words will be known by all, but fewer than one in one hundred will be familiar with any of the topic words in the closing pages. Thus everyone should be able to find old friends as well as obscurities through perusing the topic words. Some of these words may be fading from active use in our language and may be unsuited for self-initiated use. Johnson O'Connor suggests firmly that although INSPISSATE (#1062) may be used correctly instead of THICKEN, it should not be. The more familiar word can often be the better choice. As our language evolves, some words seem too effete or lacking in appeal, too wanting in vigor to endure. The EDACIOUS (#1275) tooth of time gnaws on even this time-honored word. Yet EDACIOUS or other unknowns may be encountered. It enlarges one's world view to recognize and share rare words with others. In a book of advice for examinees, Johnson O'Connor mentions the skeptical educator who balked at the unfamiliar GLABROUS (VB II #2060) when faced with marking one of five misleads on a vocabulary test to approximate its meaning; he thought the word of dubious relevance. Yet in the month following his confrontation with this improbable word, the same man stumbled upon GLABROUS on three occasions: in reading a newspaper, a magazine, and in a technical reference to its biological usage. This lost word stood out in bold relief in unanticipated places. We may lose sight of less well-known words, words beyond our border of knowledge. But with a systematic study of such words, we may readily push back this frontier and expand our knowledge; knowledge not restricted to definitions alone, but to a richer comprehension of the many facets of human endeavor symbolized by those words.

This stress on vocabulary may be felt by some as an obsession with the pieces of language but not the process, with the building bricks but not the construction techniques. A mason, well supplied with bricks and mortar, will attend to his task of laying the bricks, applying the mortar, aligning the wall: the process of building. The process in language: syntax, grammar, style, tend to dominate the writing craftman's professional thoughts in much the same manner as he builds the phrases, sentences, paragraphs in shaping his verbal structure — whether poem, drama, essay or whatever.

Yet if the brick mason, sure and deft in setting his line of bricks, is limited to poorly made, misshapen building materials, all the style and deliberate process in laying these imperfect bricks cannot prevent the structure's collapse. Neither the house put together with inferior bricks nor the sentence strung with inappropriate words can stand firmly on its own. Clear expression of ideas begins with a clear understanding of words.

From studies of vocabulary test performances, three principles have been isolated by Johnson O'Connor. They indicate the nature of vocabulary knowledge and acquisition for native English-speaking persons. They are formulated as the three laws of learning, which help in guiding one's self-study of words.

First: it is possible to arrange words in order of difficulty, from easy to hard, an order inherent in words themselves, or more probably in the ideas which the words convey.

Second: each person knows all, or practically all, of these words in order of difficulty, up to a point where his knowledge becomes doubtful, and knows practically no words beyond this point. Try it for yourself. The first topic words are easy. How many words are you not familiar with out of the first 150? How many words do you find too difficult to use correctly from the last 150? The border of your vocabulary is somewhere between.

Third: the rate of learning is greatest just at the border of one's vocabulary.

An exception to the second and third laws is the situation for someone whose native tongue provides a different vocabulary base. An English-speaking Italian native may know words of Latin derivation common to his first language but may be unfamiliar with a common Anglo-Saxon word such as WRANGLE (#14). As you may sense by scanning this book, the topic words are listed in their order of difficulty, from the familiar to the unknown.

In the past, the Human Engineering Laboratory advised a person to page through the Vocabulary Builder until stumbling upon a few vaguely familiar words, words recognized and sensed but not clearly definable. As stated in the third law of learning, it is at this frontier of knowledge, the edge of one's vocabulary, where the rate of learning will be at its greatest. Obviously, studying single words which are already known will not increase vocabulary. Perhaps less self-evident, difficult words — well beyond the upper fringe of one's vocabulary — will not find company among known words and will slip away. Although the rate of learning for acquiring a sure grasp of the topic words is at a maximum somewhere beyond the first easy words and well before the difficult later words, the Laboratory now advises plunging in at the very beginning. For here, even in the discussion of so familiar a word as EXUBER-ANTLY, appear related words sharing similar connotations or implications and also others, opposite in meaning, which are not always so certainly understood. The words used in the discussion to illuminate the topic word often run the gamut of difficulty.

Mr. O'Connor thought of his discussion of a topic word as more than a dictionary definition. The attendant commentary serves as a stimulus to a host of associated words, meanings and thoughts. By careful reading of the commentary, the student will be enriched by exposure to the exact meanings of words. Following this study, one will not be likely to think an AT-TESTED (#500) record is a DISPUTED document. To contest a statement is to dispute; to attest to one is to certify, affirm. Confusion of a word with its opposite, often the final step in learning a word, indicates a closing in on the word in question, but can lead to misunderstanding in a friendly discussion, a business deal, or an important political issue. Read the discussion of COMMENCE (#3) for an exposition of the four steps of learning, from initial familiarity to confusion of opposites. In using this book, read over the doubted word description carefully. A re-reading will uncover additional terms and comparisons. A third reading, before advancing to the next, will help anchor the topic word firmly in one's mind alongside its synonyms and antonyms.

The study of one set of words, either a section of topic words from this book, or words given on Vocabulary Building Machines (programmed electronic teaching devices in use at some of our aptitude testing centers), has actually led to an increase in vocabulary level for individuals tested after using the teaching materials. Although the test words were not those discussed in the lessons, the exposure to vocabulary building itself stimulated a greater awareness of words and resulted in higher vocabulary scores. The reader will not, then, simply learn the words here in print, but will develop a pattern of thought conducive to absorbing new words wherever encountered. Reading alone will not build vocabulary. The Laboratory has found that the level of difficulty of the words at the border of knowledge may be such that the words scarcely appear in even one million printed words. If one attempts to read at an unusually high level of word use in a particularly esoteric article, or a book replete with recondite words and smothered in obfuscations, of what value can it be? Words totally unkown and well beyond the upper range of knowledge are not readily retained even if looked up and carefully noted. Better to elevate reading interests gradually, to find new words occasionally in conjunction with old friends, affording a context for interpretation. But for the limitations of time, this approach of increased reading at gradually more rigorous levels would be beneficial. However, if one wants to enhance vocabulary immediately, the problem must be attacked directly. Study words for the sake of learning words. Reading a dictionary or attempting word games can help, but the words are not approached in a systematic fashion. Studying new words and words almost but not quite known in their order of difficulty as arranged in this Vocabulary Builder will expose one much more rapidly to the right words than can leisurely reading alone, and will keep the reader on an even course along the cutting edge of vocabulary knowledge without the risk of being mired in dictionary oddities and crossword strangers.

In Laboratory Bulletins and meetings with educators the Laboratory has expressed a parallel concern for teaching and measuring vocabulary comprehension. If, as a compromise, words for school lessons and testing instruments are selected to suit the middle range of knowledge, the top students will easily recognize the test words and become complacent, easily bored; while those with a very much smaller word awareness will fail to gain anything positive by being immersed in lessons beyond their border of understanding. As stated in the third law of learning, vocabulary should be studied and built upon in a sequence corresponding to the order of difficulty.

Lacking even the levels of vocabulary mastered by the average student, the low scoring student needs an opportunity to have his current level of understanding properly measured. A study lesson using only words of this demonstrated level should be provided, without the encumbrance of a multitude of more difficult words. To find each and every individual's level of vocabulary, and the optimum point on the ascending scale of words ranked by difficulty, we strongly recommend starting everyone with the easiest vocabulary list available. The students with rich and varied vocabularies can race through such a list of easy words, while those already reaching into the unfamiliar can deliberate over the misleads with some hope of success. They will be able to gain the same feeling of challenge and exposure to learning as is regularly experienced by the more advanced student. When schools reach down to help those with the lowest vocabulary level, each student can find his or her proper point of departure for word study. Building from this base, even the lower vocabulary student can learn to assimilate increasingly difficult words.

As a guide to the level of difficulty of the topic words in this book, there is a runner at the top of each page giving the percentage of persons not knowing the words listed on that page. These percentages are approximations derived from norms for the vocabulary tests from which these topic words have been taken. The values are computed for a twenty-five-year-old. If younger, the percentages should be increased somewhat, that is, the words are even less well known. For the more mature adult, the percentages overstate the case somewhat. In the text, specific percentages of persons missing a word on a vocabulary test are calculated from varying samples of examinees, with a broad range of age and vocabulary level. Thus these textual percentages vary sometimes substantially from the runner figures. Although ABHOR (#69) may be a word at or beyond the fringe of understanding for only three per cent of twenty-five-year-olds, on the specific sample of test takers cited in the discussions some 19 per cent erred, misconstruing the word to suggest SUSPECT. This higher percentage represents a group of younger examinees. Differing samples have been utilized to provide the data given in the word discussions, as these topic words come from diverse vocabulary tests given throughout the country to individuals from early adolescence to full maturity. The textual percentages will aid the reader in understanding how a word may be misunderstood. Indeed, a valuable adjunct to the word discussion is the tangential description provided for these erroneous misleads.

All words cited in a definition of a topic word, including some which are themselves defined in the discussion, are listed in the index. Topic words are capitalized. The page references are listed by order of the relative importance of the coverage given the indexed word, so that the most significant material on the given word may be readily found when there are multiple references. In the text of the topic word discussions, references to words treated as topic words in the earlier Vocabulary Builders, Volume I and Volume II, are provided to help the reader in finding a full discussion of these words.

Ruth Davis Memorial Library

Many laboratory staff members, including this writer, have had the fascinating experience in recent years of sitting with Johnson O'Connor before his hearth, the ever-present fire consuming seasoned birch, to debate a research point or converse on yet another esoteric word or etymological detail. In rooms surrounded by dictionaries of every sort, from rare tomes such as the progenitor Bailey's or the seminal work of Samuel Johnson, the delightful Ephraim Chambers, to utilitarian modern Webster's and his favorite Century, Johnson O'Connor held sway over a rich assortment of treatises on the English language.

His collection of dictionaries constitutes a prominent part of a memorial library of the Johnson O'Connor books at the Boston Laboratory. This library is dedicated to the memory of his first wife, Ruth Davis, and open to all alumni of the laboratory testing program and serious students of the concerns with human ability and knowledge pursued over a dynamic lifetime by Johnson O'Connor.

The brief list below highlights some of the dictionaries owned and consulted by Johnson O'Connor in preparation of this and earlier Vocabulary Builders and now part of the Ruth Davis library collection.

1658   Cowell, John
       The interpreter: or book containing the signification of words.

1673   Cotgrave, Randle
       A French and English dictionary. The fourth edition. (First edition 1611.)

1678   Phillips, Edward
       The new world of words, or a general English dictionary.

1690   A new dictionary of the terms ancient and modern of the canting crew. Facsimile of the 1690 edition. No date for facsimile. By B. E., gent.

1705   Solleysel, Sieur de
       The gentleman's dictionary. In three parts. Abridged from the folio. Done into English by Sir William Hope.

1726   Altieri, F.
       Dizionario Italiano ed Englese.

1726   Bailey, N. (Nathan)
       A universal etymological English dictionary. The third edition, with large addition.

1735   Bayle, Peter
       Dictionary historical and critical of Mr. Peter Bayle.

1737 Bailey, N. (Nathan)
      The universal etymological English dictionary. The third
      edition with many additions. Volume II.

1755 Johnson, Samuel
      Dictionary of the English language in which the words
      are deduced from their originals. Two volumes, folio.

1771 Dyche, Thomas
      A new general English dictionary. Originally begun by
      the late Reverend Mr. Thomas Dyche and finished by
      the late William Pardon, Gent.

1775 Ash, John
      A new and complete dictionary of the English language.
      In two volumes.

1777 Perry, William
      The Royal standard dictionary.

1778 Diderot, Denis
      Encyclopédie ou dictionnaire raisonné des sciences, des
      arts et des métiers, par une société de gens de lettres.
      Mis en ordre et publié par M. Diderot, et quant à la
      partie mathématique, par M. D'Alembert. Edition exact-
      ement conforme à celle de Pellet, in-quarto. A Lausanne-
      chez la société typographique.

1778 Johnson, Samuel
      A dictionary of the English language . . . abstracted from
      the folio edition by the author. To which is prefixed a
      grammar of the English language. J*Cheere. Sixth edi-
      tion, corrected by the author. In two volumes.

1786 Chambers, E.
      Cyclopaedia or an universal dictionary of arts and sci-
      ences . . . with the supplement and modern improve-
      ments incorporated in one alphabet by Abraham Rees.
      In four volumes, with volume five of cuts.

1786 Dictionnaire de l'Académie Françoise. Nouvelle édition.
      Two volumes. A Nismes. Chez Pierre Beaume.

1790 Sheridan, Thomas
A complete dictionary of the English language both with regard to sound and meaning. The fourth edition, revised, corrected and enlarged by the author.

1792 Newbery, E.
Newbery's new spelling dictionary of the English language.

1804 Walker, John
A critical pronouncing dictionary and expositor of the English language. Abridged and adapted to the use of the citizens of the United States.

1813 Good, John Mason
Pantologia. By John Mason Good, Esq., F. R. S., Olinthus Gregory, LL.D., and Mr. Newton Bosworth. In twelve volumes.

1818 Johnson, Samuel
A dictionary of the English language. In four volumes. First American from the eleventh London edition. To which are added Walker's principles of English pronunciation.

1828 Webster, Noah
An American dictionary of the English language. Volume I.

1833 Crabb, George
Universal technological dictionary or familiar explanation of the terms used in all art and sciences . . . Enlarged edition, in two volumes.

1864 Liddell, Henry George and Robert Scott
A Greek-English lexicon. Fifth edition. Revised and augmented.

1873 Littré, E.
Dictionnaire de la langue Française . . . In four volumes. Libraire Hachette et Companie.

1874   Worcester, Joseph E.
        A dictionary of the English language.

1882   Skeat, Rev. Walter W.
        An etymological dictionary of the English language.

1888-   Murray, James A. H. (Ed.)
1928   A new English dictionary on historical principles; found-
        ed mainly on the material collected by the Philological
        Society. Ten volumes bound as twelve.

1889   The Century dictionary. An encyclopedic lexicon of
1891   the English language. Prepared under the superintend-
        ence of William Dwight Whitney. In six volumes (two
        sets).

1914   The Century dictionary. As above, but revised and en-
        larged under the superintendence of Benjamin E. Smith.

1914   Phyfe, W. H. P.
        Eighteen thousand words often mispronounced. Hand-
        book of difficulties in English pronunciation. Sixth edi-
        tion.

1927   Fowler, H. W.
        A dictionary of modern English usage.

1937   The Encyclopaedia Britannica. A new survey of uni-
        versal knowledge. The fourteenth edition. In twenty-
        four volumes.

1956   Velàquez de la Cadena, Mariano
        A new pronouncing dictionary of the Spanish and Eng-
        lish languages. Compiled by Mariano Velàzquez de la
        Cadena . . . and Edward Gray. With supplement of new
        words by Carlos Toral.

1969   Random House dictionary of the English language. Jess
        Stein, Editor-in-chief.

Ever the guiding light and prime mover in the conceiving and realizing of the Vocabulary Builder, Johnson O'Connor nevertheless was not alone in carrying out the many difficult tasks of seeing this book to completion. The late author finished the manuscript and major proofreading of his own work before his death in July, 1973. Subsequent proofreading and index preparation have been carried out in Boston. Special tribute should go to Joseph Wallace, Director of the Los Angeles Laboratory, for the many hours of careful collating and editing necessary to organize the words from disparate vocabulary tests preparatory to the initial writing of the book. In Boston, Anne Graham has used thousands of cards, working many hours in organizing the index; Richard Bowker has employed his sure sense of Greek and Latin as well as his extremely high vocabulary in proofreading and editing the final proofs. Any errors which may have slipped through into this published edition, however, may well be the error of this writer in his stints of proofreading. Other laboratory staff members (included in the list of senior staff of the Laboratory) have supplied research assistance, expert guidance and material support. Thomas McAveeney, Director of the Boston Laboratory, has overseen the staff working here, and Richard Krill, President of the Human Engineering Laboratory, has insured the fulfillment of this project.

But most of all, a warm word of praise and acknowledgement must go to Eleanor Manning O'Connor, late wife of Johnson O'Connor, who died with him in July, 1973, in Mexico. She accompanied him on all his travels, participated in all his writing, worked tirelessly to transcribe, notate, and organize the material generated by Johnson O'Connor for his books. An accomplished architect and an esteemed teacher as well, she served as an inspiration for the staff of the Laboratory.

DAVID RANSOM
Boston, Spring 1974

SUGGESTED METHOD FOR SUCCESSFUL VOCABULARY STUDY

Irvin Shambaugh, a senior staff member, has researched and developed an effective study program for using this English Vocabulary Builder. Diligent application of this method has helped many individuals.

DISCIPLINE — Study vocabulary every day; do not skip a day. Spend a set amount of time each day, perhaps fifteen minutes, but a definite uniform time period daily. You will find it better to plan your quota for study in terms of time instead of the number of word discussions covered. The length of the discussion varies; you may have to reread one paragraph several times before understanding it. If your study quota is ten words per day, the temptation is to read them too quickly in order to go on to other activities you find more pleasurable. If you know you must spend a full quarter-hour, you are more likely to spend your time in earnest study. Just as an athlete's conditioning suffers from lack of regular exercise, vocabulary building is hurt by irregular effort.

REPETITION — We recommend repeating each group of fifty words. In reading a discussion you do not learn everything contained in it. Also, if you rush through the book without repeating, you will almost certainly get ahead of the borderline of your vocabulary and your rate of improvement will decrease. We suggest fifty words for two reasons. First, it is an easy number to remember. Second, by the time you have covered fifty words about a week has passed. Thus, when you repeat the discussion, you should recognize the parts of it that you understood from the first reading. Hence, on the second reading you can concentrate on the parts you did not learn before. If you feel it is necessary, you may decide to read each group more than twice.

REVIEW — Perhaps once a month, leaf casually through the parts of the book which you have already studied. Cover up the discussion of a word with your hand or a piece of paper. Think about the word and try to define it as accurately as you can. Then uncover the answer to see if you were correct. Several people have reported that when they do this, the following situation may occur: A person has read up to word 1000; in reviewing, he begins to find words around word 900 which he does not know; in fact, when he reads the discussions, he can scarcely believe he has read that passage twice before. It seems totally unfamiliar. This person has been reading faster than the advance of his borderline of vocabulary. His rate of reading has slipped ahead of his rate of learning and retention. By word 900, this gap in learning has become large enough to diminish his rate of learning to almost zero. When you study words which are too difficult for your present vocabulary, it is almost impossible to retain their meanings permanently. If this happens when you review, go back to the level at which you start to make mistakes and continue the program from there, reading those sections for a third or fourth time.

Remember: Rates of improvement seem to be related less to how fast you cover the material and more to how thoroughly you study the material step-by-step in order of difficulty.

PRONUNCIATION

In this book no attempt has been made to give exact vowel sounds. In addition to the accent only two phonetic marks have been used, the long and the short. This book does not replace a dictionary; it is not primarily a reference book, but is an attempt to answer a few specific questions with which the general reader is frequently faced.

ă	CAP (kăp), FAT (făt), BLACK (blăk)
ā	MAKE (māk), CAGE (kāj), DAY (dā)
ĕ	MET (mĕt), TEN (tĕn), BELL (bĕl)
ē	DEEP (dēp), NEAT (nēt), SEEM (sēm)
ĭ	DIP (dĭp), IT (ĭt), THIS (thĭs)
ī	FIVE (fīv), LIKE (līk), FLY (flī)
ŏ	LOG (lŏg), ON (ŏn), TOP (tŏp)
ō	BONE (bōn), ROLL (rōl), NO (nō)
ŭ	UP (ŭp), SUN (sŭn), TUB (tŭb)
ū	TUNE (tūn), DUKE (dūk), USE (ūz)
ah	FAR (fahr), STAR (stahr), FATHER (fah'-ther)
aw	LAW (law), SAW (saw), CAUGHT (kawt)
er	HER (her), TURN (tern), DIRT (dert)
or	FOR (for), ORDER (or'-der), HORSE (hors)
oo	SCHOOL (skool), FOOD (food), BOOT (boot)
o͝o	BOOK (bo͝ok), LOOK (lo͝ok), FOOT (fo͝ot)

Only one accent mark (') has been used; the secondary accent, when it occurs, having been omitted. LESSON (lĕs'-sŏn); RAILROAD (rāl'-rōd); ELEPHANT (ĕl'-ĕ-fănt); EVERLASTING (ĕv-er-lăs'-tĭng).

1. *EXUBERANTLY*, exuberantly (ĕks-ū'-ber-ănt-lĭ) *adv.*
Abundantly, copiously, plentifully, luxuriantly, profusely, amply, superabundantly.

EXUBERANCE, an overflowing supply, superabundance, is the noun, as, from James Fergusson, who made a fortune manufacturing indigo in India, and then retired to write on architecture: 'An EXUBERANCE of fancy, scorning restrain'. EXUBERANT is the adjective, modifying, qualifying the noun, as: 'EXUBERANT vitality'. This phrase leads EXUBERANTLY, as applied to human beings, to mean enthusiastically, vivaciously. EXUBERANTLY is the adverb, modifying the verb, the action, as: 'To grow EXUBERANTLY'. The word comes from the Latin *exuberare*, to come forth in quantity, a combination of *ex*, out, and *uberare*, to be fruitful, from the Latin word for udder.

To 6 per cent of those who have tried this relatively easy form of the vocabulary worksamples, EXUBERANTLY means ROUGHLY, rudely, violently, boisterously. This is the 6 per cent who punish a child for his ROUGHNESS, when in reality it is EXUBERANCE, an overflowing of spirits, superabundance of energy, which motivates the child's behavior.

2. *CHARIOT*, chariot (chă'-rĭ-ŏt) *n.* A two-wheeled vehicle, drawn by two or more horses side by side, used by both the Greeks and the Romans, in war, in racing, and in processions. The word CHARIOT comes from the French *chariot*, the diminutive of *char*, the source of the English CAR.

A CHARIOT is thought by 6 per cent to be a ROMAN BARGE. A BARGE was at one time any boat with sails, but in ancient times was an elegant vessel with two banks of oars. Both BARGES and CHARIOTS were used by the Romans in war and in celebrations. A BARGE is large, and carries many persons; a CHARIOT, as the word is used here, is for one or two. A BARGE goes by water; a CHARIOT, by land.

3. *COMMENCE*, commence (kŏm-mĕns') *v.* To begin, start, initiate, originate.

COMMENCE comes from the Latin *com-*, together, and, though it is difficult to see how, *initiare*, to begin, the source of INITIATE, with the same meaning.

To 13 per cent COMMENCED, began, started, means ENDED, stopped, halted. This confusion of a word with its exact opposite is the fourth and final step in learning, and will occur repeatedly throughout this book. First comes learning the sound of a word, with no attempt at its meaning. Then using the word in the correct situation, as CHARIOT and BARGE, both conveyances, one by land and the other by water. Third, narrowing, refining, sharpening the meaning, as EXUBERANTLY and ROUGHLY, two interpretations of the same outward act. Finally confusing a word with its exact opposite, COMMENCE and END, begin and stop.

H. W. Fowler says: 'BEGIN is the word always thought,' though 'it is translated sometimes into COMMENCE'. The Oxford English Dictionary describes COMMENCE as: 'Precisely equivalent to the native BEGIN'.

4. *MEAGER*, meager ($mē'$-ger) *adj*. Scanty (v. b. 182), barely enough, slender, limited, restricted, niggardly, parsimonious, jejune (v. b. 2098), really insufficient, inadequate, poor, mean, deficient in quantity; also: thrifty (v. b. 164), chary, frugal (v. b. 1122); of a person: thin, lean, spare, lank, emaciated (v. b. 1191), cadaverous (v. b. 1245).

To 14 per cent of those tested MEAGER means STRICT, almost correct, except that given a choice between STRICT and SCANT, as synonyms of MEAGER, 97 per cent of high-vocabulary examinees select SCANT. STRICT is literally drawn tight and, although sometimes defined as narrowly limited, exacting, severe, rigorously enforced, STRICT in this sense applies to rules and regulations. To RESTRICT is to hold within limits, restrain, curb, and so suggests scantiness, MEAGERNESS, confined within limits.

From Tombs, Temples, and Ancient Art, by Joseph Lindon Smith, a book for everyone interested in archaeology and Egyptian excavations, comes: 'In the rear straggled the needy in the hope of supplementing their customary MEAGER diet from the ceremonial offerings'.

Of the choice in spelling between MEAGRE and MEAGER, H. W. Fowler in his English Usage says: 'The American usage (-ER) is more consistent. The prophecy may be hazarded that we shall conform in time, one word in -RE after another changing to -ER; but we prefer in England to break with our illogicalities slowly'.

5. *SPRIGHTLY*, sprightly (*sprīt'-lĭ*) *adj.* Brisk, lively, vivacious, gay, cheerful, spirited, nimble, animated, exuberant.
SPRIGHTLY comes from SPRITE, spirit, originally the breath of life, now an elf, fairy, goblin, supernatural being, plus one of the two -LY endings, this one added to a noun to make an adjective. Walter W. Skeat, in his Etymological Dictionary, says: 'The common spelling SPRIGHTLY is wholly wrong; GH is a purely English combination, whereas the present word is French. The mistake was due to the very common false spelling SPRIGHT, for SPRITE, a spirit, a doublet of SPIRIT.' Despite the historic error, SPRIGHTLY is properly spelt in English with -GH-, and SPRITE without it.
SPRIGHTLY is thought by 11 per cent to mean ATTRACTIVE. SPRIGHTLY, and most of its synonyms: LIVELY, VIVACIOUS, SPIRITED, are ATTRACTIVE words.

6. *CELESTIAL*, celestial (*sĕ-lĕs'-tĭal*) *adj.* Heavenly, belonging to the sky, of great excellence.
CELESTIAL, which goes back to Chaucer, 1390, comes from the Latin *caelestis*, of heaven, from *caelum*, heaven, sky, canopy, the source also of CEILING.
To 8 per cent CELESTIAL means SUPPORTING; and to another 6 per cent POWERFUL, the last closely associated with CELESTIAL in two lines from John Dryden:

> Desire of POWER, on earth a vicious weed,
> Yet sprung from high is of CELESTIAL seed.

7. *DESPICABLE*, despicable (*dĕs'-pĭk-ă-bl*) *adj.* Contemptible, worthless, mean, low, base, vile, to be despised.
DESPICABLE comes from the Latin *despicere*, to look down upon, a combination of *de-*, down, and *specere*, to see, look at. From *specere* come SPECTACLES, eyeglasses, for seeing, INSPECTION, and RESPECTABLE (*rē-spĕk'-tă-bl*), with the suggestion of worth looking back at, an opposite of DESPICABLE, a strong word, stronger even than CONTEMPTIBLE.
DESPERATE (*dĕs'-pĕ-răt*), from the Latin *sperare*, to hope, somewhat like DESPICABLE in sound, may be defined as characterized by the RECKLESSNESS of despair, and this may lead 20 per

cent to select RECKLESS as the meaning of DESPICABLE. RECKLESS
is foolhardy, rash, venturesome, bold without judgment.

The verb to DESPISE is to scorn, disdain. The adjectives SCORN-
FUL and DISDAINFUL apply to the person who looks down; while
DESPICABLE characterizes the individual who is looked down
upon.

8. *DIMINUTION*, diminution (*dĭ-mĭ-nū'-shŏn*) *n.* Lessening,
   reduction, decrease, ensmallment, process of diminishing.
The English MINOR, from the Latin *minor*, the comparative,
meaning less, smaller, appears in music, as: MINOR intervals; or
as a noun to mean a young person, a MINOR. From MINOR comes
MINORITY, the smaller, lesser of two political groups, or any
group small in comparison with another. MINIMUM is the
superlative, smallest, the opposite of MAXIMUM. From the Latin
minor comes MINUS, less, as: one number MINUS another. From
minus comes the verb *minuere*, to make smaller, the source of
MINUTE (*mĭ-nūt'*), extremely small, little, trifling; and so finally
deminuere, to diminish, the initial *de-* adding little. DIMINUTION
is the noun, as: a DIMINUTION of wealth.

The only mislead, selected by 5 per cent, is BUILD-UP, used as
a noun, and accented on the first syllable, an exact opposite, an
increase, addition, augmentation. LESSENING is Anglo-Saxon;
DIMINUTION is Latin. Use the Anglo-Saxon LESSENING.

9. *IMPRECISION*, imprecision (*ĭm-prē-sĭ'-shŏn*) *n.* Without
   accuracy, lacking precision, carelessness, slovenliness, inex-
actness, incorrectness.
PRECISE comes from the Latin *praecisus*, cut short, brief, from
the verb *praecidere*, to cut short, abridge, diminish, cut off in
front. This in turn is a combination of *prae*, before, and *caedere*,
to cut. PRECISE means measured, cut to the right length, neither
more nor less, definite, accurate, exact, just, with no error.

CONCISE, from the same Latin verb, means brief and comprehensive, much in a few words. Someone wrote: 'If I had more
time, I would write less'. It consumes time to be CONCISE. It
demands constant care and attention to be PRECISE.

No scientific figure is exact. Many are ACCURATE to within
known limits of error, and PRECISE enough to use practically.

PRECISION is the corresponding noun. The initial IM- stands for IN-, not, which becomes IM- before B, M, or P. The meaning of IMPRECISION is marked correctly by almost everyone who has taken the more difficult form of vocabulary test in which this word appears, very few select EXACTNESS, an opposite.

10. *DISJUNCT,* disjunct (*dĭs-jŭnkt'*) *adj.* Separated, disjoined, not connected, dissevered, detached, disunited, dissociate, disengaged, sundered, parted.

DISJUNCT is an adjective formed from the verb DISJOIN, to disunite, dissolve, undo. This comes from the Latin *disjungere,* a combination of *dis,* apart, and *jungere,* to join.

The only mislead, sometimes marked, is WELL-WORN. DEFUNCT is deceased, dead, extinct, and might conceivably suggest WELL-WORN to an occasional person. A CONJUNCTION is a word which joins another word or phrase to a sentence. An ADJUNCT is something added to something else. A JUNCTION is a place where two railway lines join. DISJUNCT means not joined.

11. *ACCENTUATE,* accentuate (*ăk-sĕn'-tū-āt*) *v.* To pronounce with an accent, lay stress upon, emphasize, give prominence to, mark as important.

An ACCENT may be the manner of pronouncing a word, as a foreign ACCENT, or it may be the stress placed on one syllable, the force with which that syllable is uttered in comparison with others. It is in this last sense that the word appears in ACCENTUATE.

ACCENTUATE comes from the Latin *accentus,* accent, tone, from the verb *accinere,* to sing, a combination of *ad,* to, and *canere,* to sing, the source of CHANT, to sing, which comes to English from French.

To nearly 10 per cent ACCENTUATE means CLARIFY. One may ACCENTUATE a word or a phrase in order to CLARIFY one's meaning; but CLARIFY means make clear, ACCENTUATE is to stress.

12. *MONOPODE,* monopode (*mŏn'-ō-pōd*) *adj.* One footed, with a single leg.

MONOPODE, though rarely in print and seldom heard in conversation, is thus far answered correctly by every person who has tried, and this despite the Greek origin of both parts.

Mono-, from the Greek μόνος (*monos*), single, one, alone, appears in a score or more of English words, many of frequent occurrence. Thus, a MONOPOLY (*mŏ-nŏp'-ō-lē*) is the right, privilege, or power, of a single person or entity to sell, barter, or carry on a business. A MONOLOGUE is a talk, a speaking, by one person alone. A MONOGRAM is, by derivation, a single letter; while a MONOGRAPH is a writing on a single subject.

A TRIPOD, again directly from the Greek τρίπους (*tripous*), from πούς (*pous*), ποδός (*podos*), foot, is something with three feet; and OCTOPUS (*ŏk'-tō-pŭs*), an eight-footed animal.

Pliny the Elder, noted Roman author, described MONOPODES as a race of one-footed men who shaded themselves from the sun with the lone foot.

13. *INFERIOR*, inferior (*ĭn-fē'-rĭ-ŏr*) *adj.* Lower in quality, subordinate (v. B. 818), less valuable, underneath in position. The Latin ending *-ior*, added to a Latin adjective, makes the comparative, as: *latior*, wider, from *latus*, wide; *fortior*, braver, from *fortis*, brave; *interior*, inner, from *inter*, within; *exterior*, outer, from *exterus*, outward, really from *ex-*, out; and the Latin comparative *inferior*, from *inferus*, low, underground, down, beneath, nether, low in position, poor in quality.

INFERIOR is thought by a clear majority of the low-vocabulary group, and by 17 per cent of students in general, to mean IN-EXPENSIVE, costing little. To EXPEND, from the Latin *ex-*, out, and *pendĕre*, to weigh, is to pay out, disburse, spend. Those readers who wonder why successful men and women score high English vocabulary should picture a purchasing agent EXPENDING money, confident that the more he spends the higher the quality of what he buys. An effective high-vocabulary purchasing agent endeavors to buy materials of high quality INEXPENSIVELY, without over-paying. To do this he must distinguish cost and quality. Yet many purchasing agents, spending large sums annually, score low enough in vocabulary to confuse the words INEXPENSIVE and INFERIOR, and the basic ideas cost and quality.

From Wisdom and Destiny by Maurice Maeterlinck, perhaps too seldom read in this commercially-minded age, comes: 'No man of upright soul should go forth in a region INFERIOR to his noblest hours'.

14. *WRANGLE*, wrangle (*răng'-gl*) *v*. To dispute, argue
    noisily, quarrel, squabble, brawl, bicker, spar, jangle, carry
on an altercation.

Like most words beginning with WR-, such as WRONG, WRINKLE,
WRIST, and WRITE, WRANGLE goes back through Middle English
to an Anglo-Saxon word akin to WRING, to twist, compress.

BRAWLS, BROILS, WRANGLES, and SQUABBLES are all noisy; but,
unlike a SCUFFLE, none of them involve any sort of physical
struggle. A BRAWL is between two participants, a BROIL requires
several. BRAWLS and BROILS are over points which seem to both
sides to be serious. A WRANGLE is severe but unreasoning, over
nothing of consequence. A SQUABBLE is a minor undignified
WRANGLE. A WRANGLE could hardly exist without GESTURES, arm
waving, and GESTURE is the mislead chosen by 10 per cent.

15. *GYRATE*, gyrate (*jī'-rāt*) *v*. To whirl, rotate, wheel, spin,
    turn around.

The corresponding noun GYRE (*jīr*), a ring, turn, from the
same Greek source, is more difficult, perhaps in this case because
it is so seldom used, for the idea is no harder to grasp than
GYRATE, to turn. GYRATE comes from the Latin *gyratus*, the past
participle of *gyrare*, through *gyrus*, from the Greek γῦρος
(*gyros*), a circle, ring.

GYRO- belongs in the technical term GYROCOMPASS, an instrument with no needle pointing north but instead a small heavy
rapidly turning wheel which points always in the same direction, no matter how much the ship or airplane under it turns or
pitches. In conversation and in most writing use TURN or WHIRL
instead of GYRATE.

16. *RENAISSANCE*, renaissance (*rĕn-ā-sawns'*) *n*. Revival, re-
    birth, rising anew, springing up again.

Spelt with a capital, the RENAISSANCE, directly from the French,
was the spirit of classical art between the medieval and modern
worlds, at the end of the 15th century, the late 1400's, and the
early 1500's, represented by Lorenzo de Medici, Michelangelo,
Leonardo da Vinci, and Raphael.

Matthew Arnold says: 'I have ventured to give to the foreign
word RENAISSANCE, an English form RENASCENCE (*rĕ-năs'-sĕns*)'.

Both words come from the Latin *renasci*, to be born again, grow, rise, spring up again, from *re-*, again, and *nasci*, to be born.

Of these, H. W. Fowler remarks in his delightful manner: 'RENAISSANCE was so far established as the English word before it was latinized or anglicized into RENASCENCE that it is still the more intelligible of the two, and may well be left in possession.'

17. *EJACULATION*, ejaculation (*ē-jă-kū-lā'-shŏn*) *n.* Exclamation, utterance, interjection, outcry.

EJACULATION comes from the Latin, *e*, out, and *jaculari*, to throw, from *jacere*, to throw, through *jaculum*, a dart, missile.

EJACULATION is one of the few words from *jacere*, to throw, spelt with the A of the original, after the J. INJECT, literally to throw in; EJECT, to throw out; REJECT, to throw back; DEJECTED and ABJECT, depressed, all come from the past participle of an early word, though all go back through *jacere*, to throw.

EJACULATION is thought by 22 per cent to mean VIOLENCE, suggested perhaps by the derivation from *jacere*, to throw, which enters such words as PROJECTILE, something thrown. Today an EJACULATION is an expression thrown out, something said briefly.

18. *EDICT*, edict (*ē'-dĭkt*) *n.* A decree, order, command, proclamation, ordinance, law, mandate, manifesto, injunction.

EDICT, INTERDICT, and VERDICT, all come from the Latin *dicere*, to speak, the source of DICTUM, manner of speaking, and BENEDICTION, the only mislead thus far marked. A VERDICT, originally two words, *vere*, true, and DICTUM, saying, is by derivation a true saying, now a decision, the final pronouncement of a judge or jury. An INTERDICT, starting with the Latin *inter-*, between, is a prohibition, order to stop. An EDICT, from the Latin *edictum*, a proclamation, the neuter of *edictus*, the past participle of *edicere*, to proclaim, is a speaking out. An EDICT is a decree, order, command, issued by a ruler on his own authority.

EDICTS and DECREES are not legislative, do not come from a law-making group, but are executive, management acts. EDICTS are commands of a sovereign, an autocrat, an individual in control. A DECREE is the order of an executive body, a management group.

19. *GOURD*, gourd (*gŏŏrd*) *n.* Originally a fruit belonging
   to the same family as the melons, pumpkins, and squashes,
now used in a more restricted sense.
GOURDS are thought by 10 per cent to be COINS; but the four
wrong choices are almost equally marked, which means that
selecting COINS is luck and not a popular misinterpretation.
Curiously, however, GOURDE, spelt with an E at the end, was once
used in Cuba, Haiti, and Louisiana for a dollar.
   The word GOURD seems to go back to the Latin *cucurbita* (*kū-
ker'-bĭ-tah*), a group of plants including the pumpkin and
squashes. GOURDS are best known in the form of their hard,
dry, brightly colored shells, sometimes with brilliant green and
orange stripes, sometimes with a cultivated neck or handle as
much as three feet in length.

20. *PLEASANTRY*, pleasantry (*plĕ'-zăn-trĭ*) *n.* Nice remark,
   witticism, humorousness, jest; also facetiousness, drollery,
sport, fun, jocoseness.
The adjective PLEASANT comes from the Latin *placens, placentis*,
pleasing, charming, the present participle of the verb *placere*,
to please.
   Although PLEASANTRY has been used to mean cheerfulness,
good humor, PLEASANTNESS is now used for this, and PLEASANTRY
reserved for a pleasant saying.

21. *AQUARIUM*, aquarium (*ă-kwā'-rĭ-ŭm*) *n.* A vessel filled
   with water, perhaps with rocks and growing plants, in
which aquatic animals are kept, goldfish bowl.
   AQUARIUM, marked correctly by everyone, is a Latin word
meaning a watering place for cattle. It is the neuter of AQUARIUS,
a water carrier, also the name of a group of stars, one of the
signs of the zodiac, from the Latin *aqua*, water, the source of
the adjective AQUATIC, connected with water, like water; AQUE-
DUCT, carrying water; and the unusual AQUAGE, a water course.

22. *BIZARRE*, bizarre (*bĭ-zăhr'*) *adj.* Odd, fanciful, fantastic,
   whimsical, grotesque, strange, queer, capricious.
BIZARRE, from the French *bizarre*, is accented in English as in
French on the last syllable. In Italian *bizarro* means original,

eccentric, spirited, much as in English. In Spanish *bizarro* means gallant, brave, valiant. In Basque *bizarra* is a beard; and in Spanish a man with a beard is a man of spirit. All of these ideas play parts in the meaning of BIZARRE today in English.

The mislead marked most often is USUAL, perhaps a misreading for UNUSUAL, a mistake which occurs in at least one other item. UNUSUAL would be correct.

23. *MELANCHOLY*, melancholy (*měl'-ăn-kŏ-lĭ*) *n.* Gloom, sadness, dejection, grief, unhappiness, hypochondria, an habitual state of mind.

MELANCHOLY comes from the Greek μέλας (*melas*), μελάνις (*melanis*), black and χολή (*chole*), bile.

Ephraim Chambers gives signs of MELANCHOLY as: 'A perpetual anxiety of mind, without any rational cause; a distaste and dislike to everything, even before it comes in sight, and often a weariness even of life itself. A frequent weeping for imaginary causes, or for no cause at all.

'Erratic MELANCHOLY is that species which seizes patients in the month of February.'

MELANCHOLY is thought by 24 per cent to mean GAIETY, an exact opposite.

24. *MARVEL*, marvel (*mahr'-věl*) *n.* An astonishing thing, miracle, prodigy, wonder, novelty, that which causes surprise.

MARVEL comes from the Latin *mirabilia*, wonderful things, from *mirari*, to wonder at, admire.

MARVEL is thought by 29 per cent to mean USUAL EVENT, an exact opposite, or perhaps it may be a misreading of USUAL for UNUSUAL.

25. *DETACHMENT*, detachment (*dē-tăch'-měnt*) *n.* Unconcern (v. b. 506), indifference, aloofness, sitting apart, lack of interest, impartiality, disinterest (v. b. 1955), freedom from prejudice (v. b. 518).

The noun DETACHMENT, and the verb to DETACH, were first used only in a military sense for a body of troops selected from the main army and assigned to some special task, or a number of ships taken from a fleet for separate service; and like so many military terms DETACHMENT and DETACH come directly from French.

From Thomas Babington Macaulay, whose History of England should be owned and easily available, comes: 'A strong DETACHMENT of Sarsfield's troops approached.'

Then DETACHMENT came to be used figuratively for lack of interest, sitting apart, as from Henry James: 'Her DETACHMENT, her air of having no fatuous illusions, and not being blinded by prejudice'.

DETACHMENT is thought by 24 per cent to mean INTEREST. ATTACHMENT (*ăt-tăch'-mĕnt*), from the same French source as DETACHMENT, is, figuratively, affection, regard, predilection, love, almost adoration, and this leads to underlining INTEREST as a meaning of DETACHMENT, an opposite of the correct meaning.

26. *SCUTTLE*, scuttle (*skŭt'-tl*) *v.* To hurry, scurry, scamper, rush, run with short steps.

SCUTTLE is the frequentative of SCOOT, SHOOT, and SCUD. To SCUD, which is Danish and Anglo-Saxon, is to run fast, much like SCOOT which seems to be a variant of SHOOT.

SCUTTLED is thought by 16 per cent to mean CRAWLED. To CRAWL is to CREEP SLOWLY, to drag one's self along the floor, an opposite in suggestion of SCUTTLE. CRAWL is slow; SCUTTLE is fast. CRAWL is lying on the ground; SCUTTLE is standing up, running.

27. *BALLERINA*, ballerina (*băl-lĕ-rē'-nă*) *n.* A girl ballet dancer, female coryphee.

The Greek βαλλίζειν (*ballizein*) is to dance, jump about. It comes from the verb βάλλειν (*ballein*), to throw, the source of BALLISTICS, the science of the motion of things thrown, study of projectiles. From the same source comes BALL, which, with the meaning dance, social assembly, first appeared in the 17th century.

Although the word BALL, meaning something round, spherical, globular, is Anglo-Saxon, the same word meaning a dance, social assembly, comes from the French *bal*, and partly from the Italian *ballare*, to dance, which in turn goes back to the Greek.

From the French and Italian come BALLAD, originally a dancing
song, and BALLET (*băl-lā'*), an elaborate, spectacular dance, with
a number of persons, performed for an audience. A BALLET is
danced to music, but the performers are silent.

The Italian *ballerino* is a man who performs in a BALLET;
ballerina is the feminine, now used as the English BALLERINA.

28. *HOG-TIED*, hog-tied (*hŏg'-tīd*) *adj*. Tied as a hog, all four
     feet together, bound, an obvious combination of two simple
words marked correctly by virtually everyone.

The dictionary defines a HOG as OMNIVOROUS and a NON-RUMI-
NANT. OMNIVOROUS (*ŏm-nĭv'-ō-rŭs*) comes from the Latin
omnis, all, and *vorare*, to devour. A HOG eats food of every sort.

Most cattle are RUMINANTS, that is, they chew their cud. The
hippopotamus and the swine, including the HOG, pig, sow, and
boar, are NON-RUMINANTS and do not chew their cud.

29. *PIOUS*, pious (*pī'-ŭs*) *adj*. Devout, religious, godly, holy
     (v. B. 79), righteous (v. B. 803), saintly, having reverence
for the Supreme Being.

PIOUS comes from the Latin *pius*, devout, affectionate, kind, and
through the Italian *pietà* (*pē-ä-tah'*), pity, mercy, from the
Latin *pietas*, *pietatis*, piety, come the nouns PIETY (*pī'-ĕ-tĭ*),
faith, reverence, godliness; PITY, compassion, sympathy, commiseration; and PITTANCE (*pĭt'-tăns*), originally an allowance of
food in a monastery, now any small portion, dole.

PIOUS is thought by 27 per cent to mean HARD-WORKING. ZEAL-
OUS (*zĕl'-ŭs*), which may mean HARD-WORKING, not only
sounds somewhat like PIOUS, but may at times be remarkably
close in meaning. ZEAL is passionate ardor, eagerness, intense
interest, devotion. ZEALOUS may mean devoted to a cause, and
so almost PIOUS. But ZEALOUS, from a Greek word meaning to
boil, implies energy, enthusiasm; while PIOUS is quietly devoted,
devout, and implies religious, an idea not contained in ZEALOUS.

30. *ALGAE*, algae (*ăl'-jē*) *n*. A seaweed, sometimes a shapeless
     jelly-like mass, sometimes with a long, trunk-like stem,
though its food, its nourishment, is never gained from roots but
always through the surface of the plant.

ALGAE is the plural of ALGA (*ăl'-gă*), the Latin word for SEAWEED. Although ALGAE is easy, marked correctly by almost everyone, with no concentration on any mislead, it is defined by one dictionary as a division of THALLOGENOUS (*thăl-lŏj'-ĕ-nŭs*), CHLOROPHYLLOUS (*klō-rō-fĭl'-lŭs*) CRYPTOGAMS. CRYPTOGAM (*krĭp'-tō-găm*) is the second greatest classification of Carolus (Karl von Linné) Linnaeus (*lĭ-nē'-ŭs*), the Swedish botanist, who lived from 1707 to 1778. The CRYPTOGAMS include all plants without flowers, among them: ALGAE, the LICHENS (use *lī'-kĕn*, though *lĭch'-ĕn* is also called correct), and the FUNGI (*fŭn'-jī*).

31. *METEORIC*, meteoric (*mē-tē-or'-ĭk*) *adj.* Swift, brilliant, flashing, flaring up, momentarily bright, bursting into sudden brilliance.

A METEOR, from the Greek μετέωρον (*meteoron*), a meteor, was originally any atmospheric disturbance, but has come to be more specifically a fiery body moving through the air, a shooting star which, because of air friction, burns up quickly and disappears. METEORIC is the adjective, with the suggestion of swift, brilliant, but not lasting, dying quickly. This last thought leads 17 per cent to select UNEVEN as the meaning of meteor.

32. *PAUSE*, pause (*pawz*) *n.* A stay, halt, intermission, temporary stop; in music, called a REST, in verse, a CESURA.

PAUSE comes through the Latin *pausa*, a halt, from the Greek παῦσις (*pausis*), a halt, stop, from the verb παύειν (*pauein*), to cause to stop.

PAUSE is thought by 18 per cent to mean SLUMBER. In music, a PAUSE is a REST between tones; and, in another sense, REST is SLUMBER. But, despite this connection, a PAUSE is a momentary stop. Another 13 per cent mark FINISH. The word FINISH has no suggestion of starting again, but seems final. A PAUSE is a halt, stop, but for the moment only, with the suggestion of starting soon again.

33. *HENCE*, hence (*hĕns*) *adv.* For this reason, for this cause, as a consequence, therefore, consequently.

THENCE, WHENCE, and even HENCE, have for years been a bit artificial. The ending -CE is not really Anglo-Saxon, but a misspelling of the original -ES. Especially do not say or write: 'FROM THENCE' or 'FROM WHENCE'. The one word THENCE means from that place, without another FROM in front of it; and WHENCE, best used in a question, as: 'WHENCE come you?' means from what place. All three go back to middle English, but not actually to Anglo-Saxon in their present state.

In one form of this vocabulary test, when the phrase read: 'HENCE, it is possible', where both so and THEREFORE were included among the choices, three quarters preferred THEREFORE and one quarter so. This may be accepted as the percentage of these ideas in the word HENCE. The choice so has been removed.

34. *ANTIPODES*, antipodes (*ăn-tĭp'-ō-dēz*) *pl. n.* Opposite points, opposed situations, diametrically adverse points of the globe, places on the surface of the earth directly opposite to each other.

ANTIPODES comes from the Greek αντί (*anti*), opposite, and πούς (*pous*), foot, with the plural πόδες (*podes*), feet, the source of TRIPOD, three footed, and the rare MONOPODE, one footed. In Greek, ANTIPODES meant having the feet opposite, and the original meaning in English designated those who dwell directly opposite to each other on the globe so that the soles of their feet were opposed.

ANTIPODES is thought by 11 per cent to mean SEASON CHANGES, and by another 10 per cent to mean TEMPERATE ZONE.

35. *DUBITATIVE*, dubitative (*dū'-bĭ-tā-tĭv*) *adj.* Doubting, uncertain, undecided, wavering, undetermined, hesitant, disputatious, tending to doubt.

To 4 per cent, DUBITATIVE means GROPING, a confusion of words used in the same situation and closely associated. To GROPE, directly from an Anglo-Saxon word meaning to grasp, was once to seize, but now means search out by the sense of touch, as in the dark, feel about with the hands as if blind, uncertain, DUBITATIVE.

DUBITATIVE comes from the Latin *dubitare*, to doubt, the the source also of the English DOUBT, to waver in opinion, be uncertain, hesitate, and connected with *dubius*, doubtful, the source of the English DUBIOUS, from *duo*, two.

DUBITATIVE is the kind of word used by George Meredith in The Egoist, where with long, rare, little known, and sometimes invented words, and such phrases as: 'Inordinate unvaried length, sheer longinquity, staggers the heart'; and: 'A conscientious transcription of all the visible, and a repetition of all the audible, is mainly accountable for our present branfulness'; and finally in the same Prelude: 'He hung DUBITATIVE', he sets the stage for one of the delightful stories of all time.

36. *AGAPE*, agape (*ă-gāp'*), *adv*. Yawning, gaping, or, figuratively, in wonder, admiringly, astonished.

Given a choice between YAWNING and HORRIFIED as the meaning of AGAPE, 78 per cent select HORRIFIED compared with only 16 per cent for YAWNING. To GAPE is to YAWN, open the mouth involuntarily as a result of sleepiness, weariness, dullness, or sometimes to stand with the mouth open in astonishment, wonder, or admiration.

In a comparison of STARE and GAPE the Century Dictionary says: 'To GAPE, in this sense, is to look with a bumpkin's idle curiosity or ignorant wonder'.

GAPE is an old word which goes back through Anglo-Saxon to the same Icelandic, Danish, and Swedish sources as GAP. The noun GAP (*găp*) has come to mean an opening in almost anything, as: 'A GAP in a fence'. But the noun and the verb GAPE (*gāp*) apply to the mouth. The initial A- stands for the Anglo-Saxon *of*, and, at the beginning of an Anglo-Saxon word, makes something equivalent to an adverb, as: ANEW, AFRESH.

Of AGAPE the Century says: 'An attitude of wonder'. In Paradise Lost Milton says: 'Dazzles the crowd and sets them all AGAPE', where the word means in wonder or expectation, and not really horror. GAPE should be used for YAWNING, and AGAPE for standing in wonder.

37. *BLEATING*, bleating (*blēt'-ĭng*) *n*. The crying of a lamb, sound of a sheep.

BRAY is the cry of a donkey, burro, or ass; BELLOW, that of a bull; ROAR, the voice of a lion; BARK, that of a dog. BLEATING, an Anglo-Saxon word, is the cry of a sheep, goat, or calf. To BLEAT is the verb, and BLEAT without the -ING may be the noun.

38. *INTERMINABLE*, interminable (*ĭn-tẽr'-mĭn-ă-bl*) *adj.*
Endless, without termination, unending, having no limits, limitless, illimitable, long drawn out.
INTERMINABLE starts with the Latin privative *in-*, and means not terminable. To TERMINATE comes from the Latin *terminatus*, the past participle of *terminare*, to limit, close, set bounds to, from the noun *terminus*, a limit, end. TERMINABLE is capable of being ended. To DETERMINE is to set limits to, fix the bounds of; while a TERMINAL is the end of an electric conductor.
INTERMINABLE is thought by 17 per cent to mean LIMITED, an exact opposite, for INTERMINABLE means UNLIMITED.

39. *HIRELING*, hireling (*hĩr'-lĭng*) *n.* One who is hired, a laborer (v. B. 102), unskilled worker, employee, servant, menial (v. B. 1165), servitor, factotum.
The Anglo-Saxon ending -LING is sometimes diminutive, as in DARLING, STRIPLING, DUCKLING and sometimes depreciative, demeaning, as in UNDERLING and HIRELING.
HIRELING is thought by 17 per cent to mean PEASANT. Both PEASANTS (*pĕz'-ănts*) and HIRELINGS are persons of inferior rank and condition. But a PEASANT may own his land, which he cultivates himself, whereas a HIRELING must be hired and so labor for someone else. Also a PEASANT lives in the country and works on the land while a HIRELING may live or work anywhere. A PEASANT although without education may be a delightful person; the word HIRELING is always unpleasant, contemptuous.

40. *APPENDAGE*, appendage (*ăp-pĕn'-dăj*) *n.* An annex, addition, adjunct, subordinate attached part, subsidiary portion superadded.
The ending -AGE, added to words from French, forms the noun, as: LANGUAGE, VOYAGE, BAGGAGE, SAVAGE.
The verb to APPEND comes from the Latin *appendere*, to weigh, consider, a combination of *ad*, to, and *pendere*, to hang, weigh, the source of PENDANT, DEPEND, EXPEND, IMPEND, SPEND, SUSPEND. To SUSPEND is to hang under, from *sub*, under. To DEPEND, to hang down, emphasizes the means of support. IMPEND is threatening, to hang over one's head, and about to fall. APPEND is to attach to, join, annex.

The only mislead chosen is WHOLE, in suggestion an opposite, for an APPENDAGE is a part of the WHOLE, or more correctly something added to the WHOLE.

41. *MULISHLY*, mulishly (*mū'-lĭsh-lĭ*) *adv.* Stubbornly, sullenly, obstinately, wilfully, perversely, obdurately, not submissively.

The Anglo-Saxon -LY at the end makes an adverb from an adjective. An adverb qualifies a verb, as: 'He acts MULISHLY', tells more exactly how he acts.

The Anglo-Saxon ending -ISH is added to all sorts of nouns to form the corresponding adjective as: PIGGISH, APISH, BOYISH, FOOLISH. MULISH is the adjective and this qualifies a noun as: 'A MULISH person', describing the person.

MULE is the noun to which these endings are added. The noun does not go back directly to Anglo-Saxon, but apparently to Old French, with however a closely related Anglo-Saxon word probably from the same original source.

The MULE is a cross between an ASS and a HORSE, usually between a JACKASS, a male ASS, and a MARE, a female HORSE; and is a valuable animal, able for its size to do more work than a horse under hard treatment and poor fare, serviceable as a pack animal, with the agility and sure-footedness of the ASS, and does not deserve the adjective MULISH.

DELIBERATELY, from the Latin *liberare*, to weigh, balance both sides, now means thoughtfully, carefully, with due consideration, but also implies slowly, not to be hurried, and this leads to its selection by the 6 per cent who choose it as a synonym of MULISHLY.

42. *ADORATION*, adoration (*ăd-ō-rā'-shŏn*) *n.* Worship, supreme reverence, homage, veneration (V. B. 1406), esteem, the highest degree of love; from Ephraim Chambers, 1728: 'The act of rendering divine honours; or of addressing God, or a being as supposing it a god'.

To ADORE (*ă-dōr'*), to worship, honor, pay supreme reverence to, comes from the Latin *adorare*, to speak to, address, beseech, pray to, a combination of *ad*, to, and *orare*, to speak, pray, beg, beseech, a verb of the first conjugation where the infinitive ends in -*are*. The Latin *orare*, the direct source of ORAL, ORATION, and ORATORY, is in turn from *os, oris*, the mouth.

ADORATION is thought by 11 per cent of examinees to be KIND-NESS, clemency, benevolence, another pleasant word; but one may be KIND to a beggar, KIND to an inferior, or even to an equal, while ADORATION and WORSHIP apply particularly to a deity, as: The ADORATION of the MAGI, the title of several paintings, one by Sandro Botticelli done in Rome in 1481, where the word MAGI (*mā'-jī*) is the plural of MAGUS (*mā'-gŭs*), originally a member of a learned and priestly caste in ancient Persia.

ADORE, WORSHIP, REVERENCE, VENERATE, and REVERE (*rē-vēr'*) are all strong words, as are the corresponding nouns ADORATION, WORSHIP, REVERENCE, and VENERATION.

43. *AGGRESSIVENESS*, aggressiveness (*ăg-grĕs'-sĭv-nĕs*) *n*. Tendency to encroach on the rights of others, push, offensiveness, picking a quarrel, contentiousness (v. B. 1666).

The noun AGGRESSIVENESS is the adjective AGGRESSIVE plus the ending -NESS so often added to form a noun. AGGRESSIVE comes from the Latin *aggressus*, the past participle of *aggredi*, to attack, assail, and more gently to approach, go to, a combination of *ad-*, to, and *gradī*, to walk, go, one of the DEPONENT verbs, with passive forms but active meanings, which has laid down its active form, for DEPONENT comes from the Latin *de-*, down, away, and *ponĕre*, to put, place, lay. Thus *gradī*, to walk, is the passive infinitive of a verb in the third conjugation where the final -*ere* of the active infinitive changes to *ī* in the passive. Directly from *gradī* comes GRADE, a step in a series; and from the past participle *gressus* come numerous words as: PROGRESS, DIGRESS, INGRESS, EGRESS, and others.

To 16 per cent AGGRESSIVENESS means ATTENTION, notice, heed, study, observance, directing the mind to a subject. ATTENTION comes from the Latin *ad-*, to, and *tendĕre*, to stretch. From the same source come CONTENTION and CONTENTIOUSNESS, a synonym of AGGRESSIVENESS.

44. *SPASM*, spasm (*spăzm*) *n*. A sudden muscular contraction, twitch, twinge, convulsion, involuntary movement. SPASM comes through the Latin *spasmus*, from the Greek

σπασμός (*spasmos*), a spasm, from σπᾶν (*span*), to pull, pluck, tear, rend. To SPAN in English, although directly from Anglo-Saxon, is to stretch across, reach over, as: 'To SPAN a river'.

The adjective SPASMODIC suggests starting and stopping, jerky, by fits and starts.

45. *ABORTIVE*, abortive (*ă-bor'-tĭv*) *adj*. Unsuccessful, useless, fruitless, coming to naught, failing of the intended effect, remaining rudimentary, not brought to completion.
ABORTIVE comes from a combination of the Latin *ab*, from, and *oriri*, to arise, grow, the source of ORIGIN, beginning, ORIGINATE, to start, arise, ORIGINAL, belonging to the beginning, and ORIENT, the east, direction of the rising sun.

The verb to ABORT means to miscarry, and so figuratively to bring to a premature termination. ABORTION is the corresponding noun, and ABORTIVE the adjective.

46. *PENDANT*, pendant (*pĕn'-dănt*) *n*. An ornament hanging from a necklace, locket.
Two Latin verbs *pendēre*, to hang, pronounced (*pĕn-dā'-rā*), of the second conjugation, and *pendĕre*, to weigh, pronounced (*pĕn'-dah-rā*), of the third conjugation, led to such English words as: IMPEND, APPEND, SUSPEND, DEPEND, EXPEND, and PENDULUM, as well as PENDANT.

PENDANT is thought by 16 per cent to mean SERVANT. A DEPENDANT (*dē-pĕn'-dănt*), from the same source as PENDANT and so literally one who hangs on another, is a retainer, servant; but a PENDANT is a hanging ornament, not a hanger-on.

Though most dictionaries give two spellings, H. W. Fowler in his English Usage feels strongly enough to say: 'PENDENT should not be used as a noun; PENDANT should not be an adjective'; or, stated positively, PENDANT is the noun, something hanging, while PENDENT is the adjective, hanging; DEPENDANT is the noun, the servant, while DEPENDENT is the adjective, hanging on.

47. *DAPPLED*, dappled (*dăp'-pld*) *adj*. Spotted, variegated, mottled, blotched, with dots of different colors.
DAPPLED is thought by 18 per cent to mean WRINKLED, crumpled, rumpled, jammed, with irregular folds.

The noun, a DAPPLE, meaning a spot, dot, goes back to Icelandic and the Scandinavian languages. The adjective DAPPLED,
a general word, goes back to the year 1400: 'The giraffe is a
fair beast well DAPPLED'. Today the word is used frequently of
horses, as: 'A DAPPLE-BAY' or 'DAPPLE-GREY'.

48. *ARDUOUS*, arduous (*ahr'-dū-ŭs*) *adj*. Laborious, attended
    with great labor, hard to accomplish, difficult, toilsome,
severe, requiring protracted effort.
Despite the similarity of the two words, ARDUOUS does not come
from the same direct source as ARDOR and ARDENT. ARDOR, the
noun, once meant intense heat, but has come to mean warmth
of affections, eagerness, fervor, intensity; while ARDENT, the
adjective, means intense, eager, fervid, keen, impassioned, glowing. Both come from the Latin *ardor*, heat, fire, burning; while
ARDUOUS comes from the Latin *arduus*, lofty, high, steep, and
from this difficult to climb, laborious, hard to reach. ARDUOUS
in English, as in Latin, once meant steep, and so hard to climb.
   In the test phrase: 'ARDUOUS search', the word is thought by
20 per cent to mean LONG. That which is ARDUOUS requires more
endurance, and is less within the reach of common powers than
is that which is HARD. ARDUOUS suggests severe and protracted
effort, and so LONG. ARDUOUS differs from HARD and DIFFICULT
by suggesting a long, hard task or a long, difficult task, but
LABORIOUS is a closer synonym as shown by the fact that everyone who scores high in the vocabulary test as a whole marks
LABORIOUS in preference to LONG.
   Crabb in his English Synonyms says: 'It is often DIFFICULT to
control our feelings; it is still HARDER to subdue our will; but it
is an ARDUOUS undertaking to control the contending will of
others'.

49. *VEXED*, vexed (*vĕkst*) *adj*. Annoyed, plagued, provoked,
    irritated, displeased, exasperated (v. b. 789), harassed (v. b.
1121).
VEXED is thought by 36 per cent to mean CONFUSED, bewildered, confounded, thrown into disorder. PERPLEXED means
CONFUSED. Also the verb to VEX comes from the Latin *vexare*,
the frequentative of *vehĕre*, to carry. Originally, in Latin, *vex-*

are meant to shake in carrying, to jolt, and so agitate, perhaps disturb, disquiet, almost CONFUSE. But today the verb to VEX is to fret, irritate, tease, annoy, plague, provoke.

50. *CONGLOMERATE*, conglomerate (*kŏn-glŏm'-ĕ-rāt*) *n.*
Anything composed of heterogeneous and incongruous materials. In geology, a rock made up of the debris of previously existing rocks.
CONGLOMERATE comes from the Latin *conglomeratus*, the past participle of *conglomerare*, to roll together, keep together, a combination of *com*, together, and *glomerare*, to gather into a ball, from *glomus*, *glomeris*, a ball. To CONGLOMERATE is to gather into a ball.
An AGGLOMERATE is a collection of all sorts of sizes, a pile, heap, gathered together. In a CONGLOMERATE the parts are more tightly held together so that a CONGLOMERATE is a single entity, made up of parts.

51. *OCCLUDE*, occlude (*ōk-klūd'*) *v.* To absorb, shut in, enclose, swallow, suck in, drink up.
From the Latin verb *claudere*, to close, shut, always spelt *-cludere* when used with a prefix, come a scramble of English words, many of them easy in both meaning and spelling. To CONCLUDE is to finish, end, stop, terminate, bring to a close, shut off further consideration. From the past participle *clausus*, or *clusus* when used with a prefix, come the noun CONCLUSION, ending, and the adjective CONCLUSIVE, final, definite. To EXCLUDE is to shut out, debar, prevent from entering; with the noun EXCLUSION, and the adjective EXCLUSIVE. To INCLUDE is to use as a part, comprehend, take in; with INCLUSION and INCLUSIVE. To SECLUDE is to shut off, set apart, withdraw; with SECLUSION and SECLUSIVE. To PRECLUDE is to shut off ahead of time and so prevent, anticipate.
These are already confused enough by experienced writers and dictionaries, so that OCCLUDE should be limited to its technical sense in physics and chemistry, the absorption of something, usually gas, by a solid, metal, shutting it in. To OCCLUDE is to hold within another substance in an almost imperceptible way. A gas is OCCLUDED within a metal, almost ABSORBED, a volume of gas occasionally several times as great as the metal which

OCCLUDES it. Thomas Edison had trouble holding a vacuum in his first electric light bulb, because of the OCCLUDED gases.

52. *RAVENOUS*, ravenous (*răv'-ĕn-ŭs*) *adj.* Hungry to the point of rage, voracious, rapacious, starved.

RAVENOUS comes through the Latin *rapina*, rapine, from the verb *rapere*, to seize. The English RAPINE (*răp'-ĭn*) is plundering, seizure of property. A RAVEN (*rā'-vĕn*), with a long A, is a bird; but another word, spelt the same but with a short A, RAVEN (*răv'-ĕn*), means plunder, robbery, furious violence.

RAVENOUS is thought by 31 per cent to mean OUTRAGED. To OUTRAGE is to assault brutally, attack. OUTRAGED means assaulted, attacked. RAVENOUS suggests driven to rage by hunger.

53. *MISAPPREHEND*, misapprehend (*mĭs-ăp-prē-hĕnd'*) *v.*
To misunderstand, misinterpret, err, apprehend incorrectly, mistake the meaning, take in a wrong sense.

The adjective PREHENSILE (*prē-hĕn'-sĭl*), from the Latin verb *prehendĕre*, to seize, means designed for grasping, seizing, taking hold of, like the hands and feet of monkeys. From Roman days, the verb APPREHEND, from the Latin *apprehendĕre*, to lay hold upon, seize, a combination of *ad*, to, and the same *prehendĕre*, to seize, has been applied both physically and mentally to mean seize, lay hold of, arrest a prisoner, take into custody, or grasp mentally, and so understand, comprehend. The prefix MIS- is Anglo-Saxon, used to mean wrong, bad, erroneous, as in: MISGUIDE, MISRULE, MISTAKE. To MISAPPREHEND is used only in the mental sense of failing to grasp mentally, never in the material sense of failing to lay hold of physically. In much the same way to TAKE something is physical; to MISTAKE, mental.

'He MISAPPREHENDED' is thought by 41 per cent to mean MISLED, an opposite in the sense of GIVE and TAKE. To MISLEAD (*mĭs-lēd'*), of Anglo-Saxon origin, with the past participle MISLED (*mĭs-lĕd'*), is to MISGUIDE, lead astray, delude, draw into error. To MISAPPREHEND, misunderstand, is the result of being MISLED. An ineffective teacher MISLEADS; a pupil MISAPPREHENDS.

From Archbishop Trench, who in 1851 wrote the Study of Words, followed in 1855 by English Past and Present, comes: 'We APPREHEND many truths which we do not COMPREHEND.

The great mystery of the Holy Trinity — we lay hold upon it; but we do not take it all in, we do not COMPREHEND it. It belongs to the idea of God, that he may be APPREHENDED though not COMPREHENDED; he has made them to know him, though not to know him all, to APPREHEND though not to COMPREHEND him'.

54. *REVERE*, revere (*rē-vēr'*) *v.* To regard with awe, reverence, worship, adore, venerate, respect, honor, look up to, hold in high esteem.

In the test phrase: 'They were REVERED', the word is thought by 22 per cent of high-school students to mean CHANGED. To REVERSE, from the Latin *vertere*, to turn, is to turn around, put in an opposite direction, change diametrically.

REVERE comes from the Latin *revereri*, a combination of *re*, back, again, and *vereri*, to fear, feel awe. From the same source come the adjectives REVERENT and REVEREND, and the noun REVERENCE. To REVERE suggests less solemnity, less awe, than REVERENCE, either noun or verb.

In the next revision of the vocabulary test containing this word, we might try DREAM, as a mislead, to suggest REVERY.

55. *CRESCENDO*, crescendo (*krĕ-shĕn'-dō*) *n.* A swelling, gradual increase (v. b. 94), a growing louder, becoming stronger.

CRESCENDO is thought by 19 per cent to mean NEW MOON, crescent moon, the growing moon before it reaches half full. Both CRESCENT, *crescent, crescentis*, the present participle, and CRESCENDO, come from the Latin *crescere*, to grow, increase. The NEW MOON, the CRESCENT moon is growing.

CRESCENDO, an Italian word used in music, means swelling, growing in sound, shown by the symbol $<$, the opposite of DIMINUENDO (*dē-mǐn-ū-ĕn'-dō*), another Italian word also from music, indicated by the symbol $>$.

56. *EJECTMENT*, ejectment (*ē-jĕkt'-mĕnt*) *n.* A throwing out, expelling, casting off, discarding, banishment (v. b. 134). From the Latin verb *jacĕre*, to throw, come INJECT, literally to throw in, cause to pass in, introduce, insert; PROJECT, throw ahead, shoot forward, cast in advance; DEJECT, to throw down,

and so depress; ABJECT, literally throw away, and now disheartened; as well as EJECT, throw out, expel.

This last plus the suffix -MENT, from the Latin *-mentum*,
added to a verb to form the corresponding noun, becomes
EJECTMENT, thought by 27 per cent to mean REFUSAL, declining.
To REJECT, originally to throw back, has come to mean decline,
spurn, refuse to receive; so that a REJECTMENT might be a
REFUSAL, though REJECTION is the form ordinarily used.

The REJECTION of an applicant to an organization is not allowing him to enter, refusing admittance. His EJECTMENT is throwing him out after his admission.

From The Education of Henry Adams, the first half of which
should be read by every statesman, politician, and boy serious in
selecting a life's work, comes: 'He was no worse off than the
Indians or the buffalo who had been EJECTED from their heritage'.

57. *BARTER*, barter (*bahr'-tĕr*) *v.* To bargain, trade, deal,
    traffic, truck, interchange, exchange one commodity for
another.

BARTER is an easy word for college graduates, the synonym
BARGAIN being chosen by almost everyone.

SELL, BUY, TRADE, are straightforward terms. BARTER is not to
sell for money, but to trade, exchange, swap, and still has in
it something of the old French word from which it comes,
which meant fraud, deception, cheating.

58. *ACME*, acme (*ăk'-mē*) *n.* The summit, top, peak, furthest
    point attained in height, utmost reach.

ACME is the Greek ἀκμή (*acme*), edge, peak, highest point,
written in Roman letters. Closely related words are the Latin
acus, needle, and *acer*, sharp. The English ACID comes from the
Latin *acidus*, sour, from *acere*, to be sour, related to *acer*, sharp.

ZENITH, NADIR (*nā-dēr*), and AZIMUTH (*ăz'-ĭ-mŭth*) are
astronomical terms, all three from Arabic. The ZENITH is the
point directly above the observer's head, and so figuratively the
highest point, summit, as opposed to NADIR, the lowest point,
under the observer, down through the earth and out the other
side, opposite the ZENITH. A confusion of opposites leads 8 per
cent to indicate LOWEST-POINT as the meaning of ACME.

Acme, zenith, and culmination, are all highest points. In astronomy, a culmination is the highest point which some heavenly body reaches during a day. Culmination suggests a high point for a moment only, and then descent. Zenith, the highest point in the heaven, is higher than culmination, but also has in it the idea of going down again. Acme is almost final perfection.

59. *BELLICOSE*, bellicose (*bĕl'-lĭ-kōs*) adj. Warlike, military, martial, belligerent, fighting, battling, combative (*kŏm'-bă-tĭv* or *kŏm-ba'-tĭv*), pugnacious, quarrelsome.

Bellicose, from the Latin adjective *bellicosus*, comes from the noun *bellum*, war, the source also of belligerent, originally in old Latin, *duellum*, a fight between two, from *duo*, the source of duel. There is a phrase: 'Bellum internecinum' (*bĕl'-lŭm ĭn-ter-nē-sĭ'-nŭm*), war to the death.

The mislead clamoring, noisy, a characteristic of war, is chosen by 4 per cent.

60. *INAUDIBLE*, inaudible (*ĭn-aw'-dĭ-bl*) adj. Incapable of being heard, not loud enough, imperceptible to the ear, silent.

Inaudible is thought by 17 per cent to mean continuous, unbroken, ceaseless, constant, uninterrupted. Incessant means continuous, going on without break.

Inaudible, a combination of the Latin privative *in-*, which means not, and *audibilis*, audible, comes from *audire*, to hear, a verb chosen by Latin grammars to illustrate the fourth conjugation ending in *-ire*. From *audire*, to hear, come audience, a group listening, hearing, and auditor, one who listens as contrasted with a spectator, one who watches.

Invisible means incapable of being seen with the eyes; inaudible, incapable of being heard with the ears.

61. *PRUDENTLY*, prudently (*prōō'-dĕnt-lĭ*) adv. With discretion, judiciously, thoughtfully, foresightedly, sagaciously (v. b. 756), sensibly, considerately, wisely, carefully, circumspectly (v. b. 1335), cautiously, warily (46).

Prudently is the adverb made by the addition of the Anglo-Saxon -ly to the adjective prudent. This in turn comes from the Latin *prudens*, *prudentis*, foreseeing, a contraction of *providens*, *providentis*, the direct source of the English PROVIDENT, the present participle of *providēre*, to foresee, a combination of *pro*, forward, and *vidēre*, to see. Though PRUDENT and PROVIDENT both imply looking forward, their association with the short-sighted PROVIDE and PROVISIONS, robs them of the distant view, of choosing the future, contained in, for example, WISDOM.

PRUDENTLY is thought by 21 per cent of high-school students in general, but by none of those who score high, to mean QUICKLY. PROMPTLY means quickly, readily, expeditiously, punctually, without delay; or the confusion may be an opposite, the last step in learning, for PRUDENTLY means cautiously, consideringly, carefully, which suggest SLOWLY, the opposite of QUICKLY.

62. *JARGON*, jargon (*jahr'-gŏn*) *n.* Confused talk, unintelligible language, gabble, gibberish, babble, argot (v. b. 1600); also the language of some profession, the cant of a peculiar science or art.

JARGON goes back to old French, Spanish, Portuguese, and Italian words for chattering. For a delightful discussion of JARGON, and its place among such words as: ARGOT, CANT, DIALECT, GIBBERISH, IDIOM, LINGO, PARLANCE, PATOIS, SHOP, SLANG, and VERNACULAR, read H. W. Fowler, English Usage, under JARGON.

JARGON is thought by 20 per cent to mean PRONUNCIATION, the spoken sound. PRONUNCIATION is not the selection of words, not the kind of words used, but the way they sound. DIALECT, any peculiar language spoken locally which differs from the ordinary, includes both the selection of the words used and the way they are spoken, their sound or PRONUNCIATION. JARGON does not include PRONUNCIATION but is the kind of words used, their selection by scientists, physicians, artists, educators, and others, which makes their utterances difficult to understand.

63. *BELEAGUERED*, beleaguered (*bē-lē'-gerd*) *adj.* Besieged (*bē-sējd'*), beset, assailed, invested, blockaded, hemmed in, surrounded by an enemy.

BELEAGUERED is thought by 28 per cent to mean JOINED, an answer chosen slightly more often by the population as a whole than ASSAILED, 24 per cent compared with 23 per cent, by 10 per cent of high-vocabulary students, and by three times as many low-vocabulary ones as ASSAILED.

A LEAGUE (*lēg*) is a group joined together, united; and the verb to LEAGUE is to form a LEAGUE, to join in friendship, combine. The word comes from the Latin *ligare*, to bind, tie, the source of LIGAMENT, a connecting tie, bond.

BELEAGUER, a combination of the Anglo-Saxon BE- and LEAGUER, could easily mean JOIN; but this LEAGUER (*lē'-ger*) ending in R comes not from Latin but directly from a Dutch word meaning to besiege, assail, beset. The difference of an R at the end makes the difference between HE and HER, between a BEE and BEER, and between the verb to LEAGUE, to join in friendship, combine for mutual interest, and the rare verb LEAGUER, meaning besiege, now written BELEAGUER.

64. *FLIPPANCY*, flippancy (*flĭp'-păn-sĭ*) *n*. Pertness, rude (v. b. 237) smartness of speech, trifling in conduct, lightness of manner, shallowness, glibness (v. b. 1264), volubility. Of the adjective FLIPPANT, Nathan Bailey, 1721, says: 'Nimble-tongued, jocund, brisk, airy'.

Although the endings -ANT and -CY give the impression of Latin, FLIPPANT and the noun FLIPPANCY come probably from an Icelandic word meaning babble, prattle, nonsensical talk.

FLIPPANCY is thought by 22 per cent to mean CHILDISH-IDEA, perhaps too close as a mislead, for FLIPPANCY is shallow, trifling, but the pert, rude smartness of an adult, not that of a child.

65. *UNMALLEABLE*, unmalleable (*ŭn-măl'-lē-ā-bl*) *adj*. Unyielding (v. b. 282), resistant, stiff (v. b. 602), brittle. Read MALLEABLE (v. b. 1589).

As compared with 23 per cent who mark the correct answer STIFF, 28 per cent believe that UNMALLEABLE means INCONCEIVABLE. CONCEIVABLE from the Latin *capere*, to take, means thinkable, supposable, capable of being taken in. UNIMAGINABLE, with something of the same sound as UNMALLEABLE, means INCONCEIVABLE, incredible, inexplicable.

MALLEABLE, from the Latin *malleare*, to beat with a hammer, from *malleus*, a heavy hammer, mall, the source also of MALLET, the diminutive of MALL, now more commonly spelt MAUL, means by derivation capable of being shaped by beating with a hammer. UNMALLEABLE, with the Anglo-Saxon prefix UN-, means not workable, incapable of being shaped with a hammer.

66. *CAVALCADE*, cavalcade (*kă-văl-kād'*) *n*. A procession of persons on horseback, parade, train of carriages.

CAVALCADE, directly from the French and this in turn from the Italian *cavalcata*, a troupe of horses, comes in turn from the Latin *caballus*, a horse, the source of CAVALRY, troops on horseback, and CHIVALRY (*shĭ'-văl-rĭ*), knighthood, originally horsemanship.

To 10 per cent CAVALCADE means SPECIMENS. This comes from the Latin *specimen*, sample, mark, token, that by which a thing is known, from the Latin *specere*, to see. From the same *specere*, to see, through the frequentative *spectare*, comes SPECTACLE, an exhibition, view, open display, public show, parade, pageant, and so almost a synonym of CAVALCADE.

'Onward came the CAVALCADE, illuminated by two hundred thick waxen torches in the hands of as many horsemen', comes from Sir Walter Scott.

67. *AMICABLE*, amicable (*ăm'-ĭ-kă-bl*) *adj*. Friendly, pleasant, harmonious, peaceable, kind, cordial, neighborly.

AMICABLE comes from the Latin *amicabilis*, friendly, through *amicus*, a friend, from *amare*, to love. AMIABLE, from the same *amare*, to love, but coming to English through French, means good-natured, not lovable or lovely, despite its derivation and its use in this sense by recognized writers.

FRIENDLY is strong, positive. AMICABLE is a negative way of saying: not disagreeable, not quarrelsome, NOT HOSTILE; and the only mislead marked by anyone, underlined by 5 per cent, is HOSTILE, the final step in learning the meaning of a word, the confusion with its exact opposite.

68. *CHINCHY*, chinchy (*chĭn'-chĭ*) *adj*. Cheap, mean, miserly, niggardly.

CHINCHY is not given in the big 8-volume Century Dictionary, and seems a strange word. But Chaucer uses CHINCHERY to mean niggardliness, and CHINCHE for miserly, mean; and these old words have an odd unexpected way of surviving in the modern mind. Of those who have taken this difficult form of the vocabulary tests, every person, thus far without exception, has chosen CHEAP as the meaning of CHINCHY, making CHINCHY statistically an easy word.

69. *ABHOR*, abhor (*ăb-hor'*) *v.* To shrink from, abominate, detest, loathe, hate, be horrified.

ABHOR comes from Latin *abhorrēre*, to shrink from, a combination of *ab*, from, and *horrēre*, to bristle with fear, the source of the adjective HORRID, dreadful, shocking, abominable, execrable, nefarious, frightful, fearful, awful, revolting, exciting HORROR, and the verb to HORRIFY, to cause loathing, in one sense an opposite of ABHOR, to feel loathing. One ABHORS something HORRID, something which HORRIFIES one.

ABHOR is thought by 19 per cent to mean SUSPECT, surmise, imagine, or, more strongly, mistrust, imagine guilty without evidence. SUSPECT (*sŭs-pĕkt'*) is vague, doubtful, uncertain, and after more proof may turn to ABHORRENCE. But to ABHOR is to react violently from that which is awful.

HATE, DETEST, and ABHOR, express strong dislikes. To HATE is general, permanent ill will. To DETEST is to condemn, bear witness against. To ABHOR is to shrink from with HORROR, have the better feelings aroused, as: 'To ABHOR cruelty'.

70. *PERAMBULATE*, perambulate (*per-ăm'-bū-lāt*) *v.* To walk about observing, wander around, go sightseeing.

The Latin *per-* sometimes means thorough, through to the end, as in PERUSE, to go through carefully, examine throughout; so that PERAMBULATE, a combination of *per-*, through, and *ambulare*, to go about, walk, travel, is more thorough, a more complete inspection, than AMBLE, wander, move easily and slowly, a word from the same source.

At the time of Nathan Bailey's Dictionary, 1726, a PERAMBULATOR was a wheel pushed ahead, with a counter, for measuring distances along a road. Today a PERAMBULATOR is a baby carriage; while in a medieval church the AMBULATORY (*ăm'-bū-lă-tō-rĭ*) is the walk around the east end, behind the sanctuary, a continuation of the aisles at each side of the nave.

To 22 per cent PERAMBULATING (*per-ăm'-bū-lā-tĭng*) means
WAITING, expecting, watching, stopping, one of the ideas in PER-
AMBULATING, separating it from WALKING, MOVING, ADVANCING,
which suggest continuing motion. To PERAMBULATE is to survey
starting and stopping, walking and waiting.

Under Love of the Long Word in Fowler, English Usage:
'It need hardly be said that shortness is a merit in words; extra
syllables reduce, not increase, vigour'. AMBLE seems pleasanter
than PERAMBULATE.

71. *DIAPHRAGM*, diaphragm (*dī'-ă-frăm*) *n.* Muscular partition, midriff.

Ephraim Chambers says: 'It was Plato, as Galen informs us, that
first called it DIAPHRAGM. It comes from the Greek διάφραγμα
(*diaphragma*), a partition, barrier, barricade, a combination of
διά (*dia*), between, and φράσσειν (*phrassein*), to fence, enclose.'

A DIAPHRAGM is a partition, something which separates. In
anatomy the DIAPHRAGM separates the thorax, above, from the
abdomen, below. DIAPHRAGM is thought by 35 per cent to mean
ABDOMEN. The ABDOMEN (*ăb-dō'-mĕn*) is below the DIAPHRAGM
and separated by it from the THORACIC CAVITY above.

Ephraim Chambers continues: 'By the contraction, or swelling of the fibres, the DIAPHRAGM becomes flat on each side; the
consequence of which is, that the cavity of the breast is enlarged, to give liberty for the lungs to receive the air in inspiration; in its relaxation, whereby it resumes its natural situation
(bulging up on the top, and concave underneath), the cavity of
the breast is diminished, and the lungs pressed for the expulsion
of the air in expiration'. The DIAPHRAGM is the chief muscle in
breathing.

72. *GAUNT*, gaunt (*gawnt*) *adj.* Thin, shrunken, emaciated,
lean, haggard, almost famished; according to E. Chambers:
'An old word for lean, or lank'.

SLENDER is pleasant. GAUNT is not only thin but HAGGARD,
wasted because of suffering. This leads 6 per cent to select
STOOPED, bent over, as the meaning of GAUNT, a confusion of
similar meanings, the third step in learning. HAGGARD, from an

earlier word meaning wild, untamed, and related to an old
French word for strange, contrary, unsociable, was used of a
hawk, and still has the suggestion of looking wild because of
long suffering, grim, grisly, careworn. EMACIATED, from a Latin
word for leanness, means literally made thin, wasted away, the
sense of gradually growing thin.

GAUNT goes back to Middle English, perhaps originally to
Scandinavian, to a Swedish word meaning a lean, starved horse.

73. *MARIONETTE*, marionette (*mă-rĭ-ō-nĕt'*) *n.* A puppet,
    little figure moved by strings on a small stage.

PUPPET, from the Latin *pupa*, a doll, is a little form moved by
the fingers or by cords or wires in a mock theater.

MARIONETTE, a French word for MARION, which in turn is a
diminutive of MARY, is the French word for PUPPET. One must
see a professional performance, such as those given at one time in
the Kungsholm Restaurant in Chicago, to realize how smoothly
and elegantly these tiny forms can be manipulated.

MARIONETTE is known to almost everyone, a few marking
VOCALIST and others SCREEN-ACTOR.

74. *NOVITIATE*, novitiate (*nō-vĭsh'-ĭ-āt*) *n.* Learning period,
    apprenticeship, initiation.

NOVITIATE comes from the Latin *novitius*, a novice, and the
source of the English NOVICE, a beginner, inexperienced person,
one who is new to the situation. The NOVITIATE is the period
during which one is a NOVICE.

NOVITIATE is thought by 23 per cent to mean ADMITTANCE.
The ADMITTANCE is the beginning, start, entrance. The NOVITIATE
is the learning period which starts with the ADMITTANCE.

75. *PONDEROUS*, ponderous (*pŏn'-der-ŭs*) *adj.* Very heavy,
    weighty, hard to lift; also clumsy, unwieldy, massive, bulky,
burly, because of weight rather than size.

To 14 per cent PONDEROUS means DEBATABLE, admitting of argument, disputable, questionable, controversial, probably because
of the word PONDERABLE.

PONDEROUS, from the Latin *ponderosus*, a great weight, from
pondus, weight, comes from *pendere*, to weigh. To PONDER, once

to weigh physically on a scale, has come to mean weigh in the mind, think about, consider carefully, contemplate, reflect upon, so that the corresponding adjective PONDEROUS might easily mean capable of being thought about. PONDERABLE may mean having weight, capable of being weighed, or worthy of consideration, and so DEBATABLE. But PONDEROUS means specifically weighty, heavy, and so massive, unwieldy because of weight.

76. *GROATS*, groats (*grōtz*) *n*. Always in the plural. Hulled grains of oats or wheat, grain without the husks.

Although the word GROATS is today rarely used, the answer HULLED-GRAIN is underlined by a surprisingly large percentage of individuals.

The only popular mislead, CULLS, inserted in a revision of the test in an effort to make this item harder, and now chosen by 20 per cent, is perhaps too close. The verb to CULL comes from the Latin *colligere*, to collect, select, the source of the English words COLLECT and COLLECTION. John Greenleaf Whittier says: 'To CULL of common things the beautiful'. The noun CULLS, like GROATS mostly in the plural, may be objects selected or rejected. GROATS are that part of the grain selected after the HUSKS have been rejected. GROATS and GRITS are difficult words, though both are Anglo-Saxon and mean hulled oats or wheat. GRITS are broken pieces. GROATS are ground up whole.

77. *SÉANCE*, séance (*sā-ŏns'*) *n*. A sitting, session at which spirits appear.

Among those who have tried this vocabulary worksample, 6 per cent select ADVENTURE. When a SÉANCE is held for the expressed purpose of communicating with the dead it can be an ADVENTURE, exciting experience, undertaking of uncertain outcome.

SÉANCE, a French word, comes from the Latin *sedens, sedentis*, the present participle of *sedere*, to sit. From this Latin verb *sedere* come a host of English words, among them: SEDENTARY, sitting; SEDIMENT, that which settles down and sits on the bottom; to PRESIDE, RESIDE, and many others.

A SESSION, from the same *sedere*, is a serious sitting together of a court, council, legislature. A SÉANCE, sometimes called a

SPIRITUALISTIC SÉANCE, is a gathering often in semi-darkness for the purpose of communicating with spirits.

78. *COPIOUS*, copious (*kō'-pē-ŭs*) *adj*. Plentiful, abundant, ample, large in quantity, plenteous, profuse, lavish, overflowing.

COPIOUS, from the Latin adjective *copiosus*, plentiful, comes from *copia*, the source of COPY, used originally to mean ample, plenty, abundant, and which appears unchanged in CORNUCOPIA (*kor-nŭ-kō'-pĭ-ah*), horn of plenty. The Latin may be a combination of *co-*, together, and *opes*, riches, the source of the adjective OPULENT, wealthy, rich, with plenty of money.

PLENTEOUS means a large amount in actual possession, as: 'A PLENTEOUS harvest'. AMPLE means enough for every need, sufficient, as: 'AMPLE resources'. COPIOUS implies an unfailing source, as: 'A COPIOUS supply'.

79. *MORPHEAN*, morphean (*mor'-fē-ăn*) *adj*. Dreamy, drowsy, sleepy, slumberous; lost in reverie.

The adjective MORPHEAN comes from the Latin MORPHEUS, the Roman god of dreams, from the Greek μορφή (*morphe*), form, the source of MORPHOLOGY, the science of form.

There is no common misunderstanding, those who do not know the answer scattering equally among the four misleads.

Ephraim Chambers, in his Cyclopedia of 1728, says: 'Morpheus – Ovid's name for the god of dreams, the son of sleep'.

Though the word MORPHEUS goes back to Chaucer, 1370, the Oxford Dictionary labels it: 'Not naturalized', and adds 'Popularly taken as the god of sleep'. SOMNIFEROUS means sleepy; MORPHEAN, dreamy.

80. *PATIENCE*, patience (*pā'-shĕns*) *n*. Calmness, endurance, forbearance, tolerance.

PATIENCE is thought by 65 per cent to mean CALMNESS, and by 32 per cent to mean UNDERSTANDING. Almost no one marks any other choice. UNDERSTANDING is the cause of PATIENCE.

From Ephraim Chambers comes: 'PATIENCE, in Ethics, is that virtue which preserves the mind firm and unbroken, under the evils of life; so that the spirits are kept from becoming tumultuous, and precipitating the sufferer into indecent or repining thoughts, words, or actions; and by which he is disposed to pay calm attention to the reasons of sacred philosophy, and to observe them'.

81. *CLAP*, clap (*klăp*) *v.* Slap, tap, pat, smack, hit, strike smartly; also applaud by striking the hands together. CLAP is heavier, harder, than PAT, but friendlier than HIT or STRIKE.
To 12 per cent 'CLAPPED his shoulder' means HELD. HELD, of Anglo-Saxon origin like CLAP, is the past of HOLD, to keep fast, grasp, retain, restrain. To CLAMP is to hold, and the past CLAMPED, HELD, sounds like CLAPPED. Also to CLASP is to catch and hold. Furthermore the phrase: 'To CLAP hold of' is to seize roughly; thus to CLAMP, CLASP, and CLAP may all mean hold; but the verb to CLAP alone is to pat, strike.
'"You've got it in you, my boy", put in the irrepressible Mr. Tomker, a big fellow with a paunch, a swollen face, and a humourous eye, CLAPPING Inigo on the shoulder'. Later in the same chapter of The Good Companions: 'Miss Georgia PATS him on the shoulder'.
'Now each man spat upon his hands, and, CLAPPING them upon his knees, squatted down, watching the other keenly, so as to take the advantage of him in the grip', from The Merry Adventures of Robin Hood, illustrated by Howard Pyle.

82. *CHARADE*, charade (*shă-rād'*) *n.* A popular social word-guessing game; acting out before an audience, syllable by syllable, a polysyllabic word the meaning of which must be guessed.
CHARADE, like MASQUERADE, is French. In a MASQUERADE everyone is in costume and wears a mask. In a CHARADE a small group, two, three, or four persons, plan the CHARADE and act it out and the group discusses and guesses the word portrayed.

83. *DERMATOID*, dermatoid (*děr'-mă-toid*) *adj.* Skinlike, resembling skin.
The termination -OID, from Greek, forms both adjectives and nouns. It means resembling, similar, almost like but not quite, as: ANTHROPOID, like man but not quite. Of the word PLANETOID, the

Century Dictionary says: 'The word PLANETOID, ending in OID, is incorrect because these small bodies are really small planets. Use ASTEROID because they are not stars and only resemble them.'

The Greek δέρμα (*derma*), skin, appears in numerous technical terms such as EPIDERMIS, the outer skin.

84. *ZUCCHINI*, zucchini (*zoo-kē'-nē*) *n*. An Italian squash, a variety of summer squash, shaped like a small cucumber, with a smooth dark green skin. ZUCCHINI is the Italian plural of *zucchino*.

Though the CUCUMBER is actually a different GENUS, of the same CLASS: MONOECIA (*mō-nē'-shah*), the ZUCCHINI, a kind of squash, looks like a small cucumber, though it may grow a foot or more in length.

From the book *Gourds*, by John Organ, published in 1959, in Newton, Massachusetts, comes: The ZUCCHINI 'are one of many excellent vegetable gourds, not so useful, however as some of the winter squashes which store well for long periods'.

GOURD is the popular name for the genus CUCURBITA (*kū-ker'-bĭ-tah*), which includes the winter squashes, summer squash, and the pumpkins, a species within the genus, GOURD. John Organ continues: 'Varieties of CUCURBITA were being developed by the use of X-rays. Visitors to Italy, who enjoy wonderful ZUCCHINI, are probably benefitting from early work carried out in Italy long before other countries were even considering utilizing such techniques.' ZUCCHINI are but one of the many excellent vegetables that we can grow.

ZUCCHINI is an Italian word spelt and pronounced Italian, and recently introduced into English.

85. *VYING*, vying (*vī'-ĭng*) *adj*. Competing with one another, contending, struggling, striving for superiority.

APHERESIS is losing the first letter of a word, or sometimes the first syllable. VIE may come from ENVY by APHERESIS, by the loss of EN- at the beginning of ENVY. ENVY comes from the Latin *invidia*, hatred, ill will, jealousy, envy, from the adjective *invictus*, having hatred, feeling ill will, envious, from the verb *invidere*, to hate. Even though this Latin verb is a simple combination of *in* and *videre*, to see, it came to mean look at with ill will. Despite this connection with ENVY, VIE is a pleasant word with no suggestion of hatred or ill will.

The corresponding French *envier* is used in card games to mean wager, increase a stake in gambling, and so challenge, from the Latin *invitare*, to invite.

DISHONEST is the only successful mislead, probably because of the word LYING. The verb to LIE is to speak falsely, tell an untruth, deceive, give a wrong impression. The present participle is LYING, just as the present participle of the verb to VIE is VYING, competing, contending, trying to win.

86. *IRREMISSIBLE*, irremissible (*ĭr-rē-mĭs'-sĭ-bl*) *adj.* Unpardonable, unforgivable, mortal, that cannot be remitted, not excusable.

From the Latin *mittere*, to send, comes TRANSMIT, to send across; and from the past participle *missus* come TRANSMISSION, as well as MISSION and MISSILE. From *remittere*, to send back, starting with *re-*, back, comes the English verb REMIT, to send back, put back in a previous position, replace, refer back for further consideration; and from *remissus*, the past participle of *remittere*, come the noun REMISSION, pardon, forgiveness, putting conditions back as they were before; and REMISSIBLE, capable of being put back as before, forgivable, excusable, pardonable, venial, also capable of being sent back for further consideration.

Despite the number of syllables and the length of this word almost everyone who has taken the vocabulary test in which this word appears underlines the correct synonym.

87. *KELP*, kelp (*kĕlp*) *n.* Great seaweeds, algae, tangle.

The word KELP may be used for the seaweed itself, or for the ash produced by burning the seaweed.

Great beds of KELP grow off the coasts of Ireland and Scotland, and in the Pacific Ocean off the west coast of the United States.

The ALGAE (*ăl'-jē*), the seaweeds, may be tiny, microscopic, and grow in fresh water, or heavy masses, in salt water, like the KELP.

From Pantologia a Cyclopedia of 1813, comes: 'KELP is thrown on the rocks and shores in great abundance, and in the

summer months is raked together and dried as hay, and afterwards burned to the ashes called KELP, for the glass makers.

'The progress by which a seaweed, formerly the slimy bed of
seals or dreary shelter of shellfish, is converted into a crystal
lustre for an assembly room, or a set of glasses for his majesty's
table, is a metamorphosis for an entertaining tale.'

88. *OGRE*, ogre (*ō'-gĕr*) *n*. A giant, hideous monster, demon,
   hobgoblin.

OGRE comes through the French, Spanish, and Italian, ultimately
from the Latin *orcus*, the abode of the dead, God of the lower
regions.

IMPS, SPRITES, and HOBGOBLINS are small and humorous. OGRES
are monsters, giants. Other monsters, with distinguishing
features, are: CENTAURS, half horse and half man, with the body
of a horse and a human head; SAGITTARY (*săj'-ĭt-tā-rĭ*), another
name for CENTAUR; SPHINX, a female monster with a lion's body
and human head; MANTICORES, like CENTAURS, with the body of
an animal and a human head; MINOTAUR, with a human body
and the head of a bull. OGRES are great, hideous, undescribed
giants. The synonym MONSTER is thus far marked correctly by
everyone who has taken the difficult vocabulary worksample in
which this word appears.

89. *CONTRADISTINCTION*, contradistinction (*kŏn-tră-
   dĭs-tĭngk'-shŏn*) *n*. Direct contrast, distinction by opposite
qualities.

CONTRA- comes directly from the Latin *contra*, meaning against,
opposite, in comparison with, in front of. DISTINCTION is the
noun corresponding to the verb DISTINGUISH, from the Latin *di*
and the Greek στίζειν (*stízein*), to prick. To DISTINGUISH is to
mark a difference.

The popularity of OPPOSITION as a synonym is probably a misunderstanding of this last word. OPPOSITION, and the short verb
OPPOSE, come from the Latin *ob*, against, before, and the Latin
ponere, to place, put. OPPOSITION refers to position.

CONTRADISTINCTION refers to ideas, a comparison of opposites,
and the word OPPOSITION cannot be used in this respect. CONTRA-
DISTINCTION differs little from any DISTINCTION but is stronger.

90. *MERIDIAN*, meridian (*mĕ-rĭd'-ĭ-ăn*) *adj.* Noon, midday,
   position of the sun at noon; also culmination, apex, summit.
MERIDIAN comes from the Latin *meridies*, midday, a combination of *medius*, middle, the source of the English MEDIUM,
middle, and MID; and *dies*, day. The Latin word seems originally
to have been spelt *medidies*, a clear combination of *medius* and
dies; and was changed to *meridies* probably for sound.
   MERIDIAN is thought by 17 per cent to mean EXACT, but almost
as many, 15 per cent, call it MIDNIGHT.

91. *DIVERT*, divert (*dĭ-vert'*) *v.* To turn toward a new goal
   and away from an old one, change direction, lead aside,
take off, advance in a new line.
DIVERT comes from the Latin *divertĕre*, to turn different ways,
separate, a combination of *di*, which stands for *dis-*, apart, and
vertĕre, to turn, the source of CONVERT (*kŏn-vert'*), to turn into
another form, change to another state, transmute, transform;
INVERT (*ĭn-vert'*), to turn upside down or end for end; AVERT
(*ă-vert'*), to turn away, avoid, ward off; and DIVERT, turn aside,
turn away, cause to move in a different direction.
   To 27 per cent of high-school students in general, and to
20 per cent of high-vocabulary ones, DIVERT means BAFFLE. To
BAFFLE is to check, balk, frustrate, thwart by placing obstacles
in the way, foil by interposing difficulties, and certainly suggests
DIVERTING in the original sense of turning one from a desired
objective. But DIVERTING is also used today with the suggestion
of amusing, entertaining, turning one away momentarily from
the daily routine.

92. *HYPERBOLE*, hyperbole (*hī-per'-bō-lē*) *n.* An obvious
   exaggeration, extravagant statement, overstatement not
likely to mislead, excessive enlargement of the truth.
HYPERBOLE is thought by 20 per cent to mean DESPAIR, despond-
ency, desperation, without hope, loss of confidence. HYPO-
CHONDRIA (*hī-pō-kŏn'-drĭ-ah*) is a morbid depression of spirits,
imagined ill health, anxiety, low spirits, and so DESPAIR.
   HYPERBOLE, from the same source as the mathematical term
HYPERBOLA, comes through the Latin *hyperbole*, from the
Greek ὑπερβολή (*hyperbole*), an overstrained phrase.

An EXAGGERATION (*ĕg-zăj-jĕ-rā'-shŏn*) is poor taste while, says the Century Dictionary, an HYPERBOLE is sanctioned by good taste as a means of lifting the sluggish mind of the hearer to the level of the truth.

93. *BALLET*, ballet (*băl'-lā*) *n*. A formal group dance on a stage in a theater watched by an audience.

The word BALLET, directly from the French *ballet* (*băl-lā'*) and often today accented on the last syllable, was first used in the 17th century. A BALLET is a spectacular dance, sometimes incidental to an operatic performance, elaborately designed with a number of performers often led by one important dancer. It is without vocal music, and frequently tells a story.

The suffix -ET is not the diminutive ending -ET, found in LOCKET, MALLET, JACKET, ISLET, but of Latin origin, another form of -ate and -ad as in SONNET, a doublet of SONATA, and SALLET, a doublet of SALADE. BALLET is a doublet of BALLAD.

94. *CHINO*, chino (*chē'-nō*) *n*. A tough twilled cotton cloth, used for uniforms, sports clothes, slacks, and trousers.

Despite the similarity of CHINO and CHINA, only 4 per cent select ORIENTAL as a synonym of CHINO, nearly everyone underlining COTTON-CLOTH. Yet in Spanish CHINO means Chinese, Oriental.

95. *TARPAULIN*, tarpaulin (*tahr-paw'-lĭn*) *n*. Canvas made waterproof with tar, often used on shipboard and in building construction.

The Encyclopaedia Britannica defines TARPAULIN as a 'Waterproof sheeting consisting of a stout canvas cloth impregnated and coated with tar'. From Ephraim Chambers' Cyclopaedia, or Universal Dictionary of Arts and Sciences, 1783 edition: 'TARPAULIN, or TARPAWLING, is a piece of canvas, well pitched and tarred over, to cover the hatchways of a ship at sea, in order to prevent the penetration of the rain or sea water'.

To 10 per cent a TARPAULIN is a TURTLE. A TERRAPIN (*tăr'-răpĭn*) is an edible TURTLE found on the Atlantic coast from New York to Texas, a delicacy used particularly in turtle soup.

From The Life and Strange Surprizing Adventures of Robinson Crusoe, written by Daniel Defoe and first published in 1719, comes: 'I made me a large tent, and covered the uppermost with a large TARPAULIN which I had saved among the sails'.

96. *STAPLES*, staples (*stā'-plz*) *pl. n.* Necessities in the nature of foodstuffs, everyday materials, provisions, viands (v. B. 1138), victuals, provender (v. B. 1318).
STAPLES are thought by 13 per cent to be BARNS. STABLES, from the Latin *stare*, to stand, are buildings equipped with stalls, racks, troughs, and bins for food, literally standing places for animals, mostly for horses and cows.

'STAPLE', says Ephraim Chambers, 1728, 'primarily signifies a public place or market whither merchants are obliged to bring their goods to be bought by the people. STAPLE also signifies a city or town where merchants jointly agree to carry certain commodities, as wool, cloth, lead, tin, in order to their being commodiously sold. By STAPLE goods are now generally meant any proper saleable commodities, not easily subject to perish.

'In the year 1248 a denomination was given to the first and most ancient commercial society of England, Merchants of the Staple, from their exporting the STAPLE wares of the kingdom, wool, skins, lead and tin, in their rough state for manufacture.'

Since Chambers, the word STAPLES has come gradually to signify the materials sold rather than the place, and now applies most frequently to ordinary foods in daily use.

97. *SKULK*, skulk (*skŭlk*) *v.* To lurk (v. B. 1303), sneak away from work, shrink from danger, slink off without sound, hide from shame, lie in concealment.
The verbs SKULK and SULK have much in common. Both suggest silence and separation from others. To SKULK, from Danish and Norwegian words with much the same meaning, is to sneak away, lurk, lie hidden from fear; while to SULK, with the present participal SULKING, is to be morose, glum, indulge in a SULLEN mood. The adjective SULKY is silently resentful, morose, splenetic, sullen, out of humor.

When given a choice between SNEAKING and MOVING SULLENLY as synonyms of SKULKING, 24 per cent of general readers select MOVING SULLENLY, compared with 31 per cent who mark SNEAKING. But among high-vocabulary readers 57 per cent select MOVING SULLENLY compared with only 43 per cent who select SNEAKING, the answer intended as correct. SULKING is not moving but a SULLEN, moody, morose, out-of-humor, withdrawal. SKULKING is more often moving in a SNEAKING, furtive manner but may also be withdrawing. The difference is that SULKING is moody, while SKULKING is slinking, hiding from detection, trying not to be seen.

98. *CLEFT*, cleft (*klĕft*) *n.* An opening, crevice, fissure, rift, furrow, chink.

The verb to CLEAVE is to split, sunder, separate. CLEAVAGE is a splitting; and a CLEFT is an opening made by a split. CLEAVE, CLEFT, and LEAVE, LEFT, all come from Anglo-Saxon.

CLEFT is thought by 12 per cent to mean STEEP ROCK. A CLIFF is a STEEP ROCK. A CLEFT is an open CRACK.

99. *LETHARGY*, lethargy (*lĕth'-ahr-jĭ*) *n.* Torpor, weariness, sluggishness, inertness, dullness, stupor, prolonged inactivity.

LETHARGY comes from the Greek λήθαργος (*lethargos*), forgetful, from λήθη (*lethe*), the river Lethe (*lē'-thē*) of hades, the river of forgetfulness, oblivion; its waters, according to poetic fiction, having the peculiar quality of making those who drank entirely forget everything that was past.

LETHAL (lē'-thăl), deadly, fatal, from the Latin *letalis*, deadly, from *letum*, death, now so similar in appearance, gained the H in the middle through some imagined connection with LETHE, forgetfulness.

To 6 per cent LETHARGY means POOR HEALTH, closely associated and perhaps correct, for in medicine LETHARGY is a disease involving profound drowsiness, deep sleep from which it is difficult to arouse the patient. To another 6 per cent LETHARGY means HATE, a strong Anglo-Saxon word for ill will, animosity, rancor, malignity, hatred, almost an opposite, for HATE is active, violent, while LETHARGY is a dull inactivity.

100. *PODIUM*, podium (*pō'-dĭ-ŭm*) *n.* A raised structure on which speakers stand in a hall or meeting place, platform, rostrum, pulpit, stage, scaffold; originally in Greece, a raised bench around an arena for the seating of important persons.

PODIUM, thought by 10 per cent to mean TABLE, comes from the Greek πόδιον (*podion*), a little foot, the diminutive of πούς (*pous*), ποδός (*podos*), a foot. Today a PODIUM is a slightly raised platform on which a speaker stands. The leader of an orchestra stands on a PODIUM, large enough for his music stand and for him to move about a bit.

ROSTRUM, from the Latin *rostrum*, the beak of a bird, and from this the prow of a ship, is another word for a raised platform, anciently in the Roman forum, heavier, permanent, and more elaborate than a PODIUM. STAGE is sometimes used in this way for an elevated place, larger than a PODIUM and raised higher. A PULPIT may be a flat platform with a railing around. SCAFFOLD has several meanings, but may also be a flat platform larger than a PODIUM and temporary, built for a special occasion.

101. *UPHEAVAL*, upheaval (*ŭp-hē'-văl*) *n.* Rising, lifting up, heaving up, raising aloft, eruption, disturbance.

The verb to HEAVE (*hēv*) goes directly back to Anglo-Saxon and means to raise, lift, hoist. From the same source comes HEAVY, weighty.

An ERUPTION, from the Latin *rumpere*, to break, is a breaking out, as: 'The ERUPTION of a volcano'. An UPHEAVAL is a lifting, perhaps of a part of the earth's surface. But UPHEAVAL is used also of a government or social order, and this leads 13 per cent to select DESTRUCTION as the meaning. DESTRUCTION is the result of an UPHEAVAL; but the UPHEAVAL is the uprising, which may result in DESTRUCTION.

102. *DETER*, deter (*dē-ter'*) *v.* To hinder, prevent, hold (v. B. 51) back, restrain, almost stop.

DETER seems a mild word to have a violent history, but it comes from the Latin *deterrēre*, to frighten away from, a combination of *de*, from, and *terrēre*, to frighten, the source of such English words as: TERRIFY, TERROR, and TERRIBLE.

'It DETERRED him' is thought by 29 per cent to mean BOTHERED. To BOTHER is to pester, annoy, worry, tease, disturb. This may be a confusion of words similar in sound, the first step in learning, for DISTURBED and DETERRED sound somewhat alike. Or it may be a confusion of words used in the same situation, the second step in learning. Anyone who is DETERRED, hindered, prevented, stopped, from doing what he wants, is BOTHERED, annoyed; but BOTHERED is a general term for being perturbed by anything which annoys one; whereas one may be DETERRED from taking a false step and in return be thankful.

103. *BAPTISM*, baptism (*băp'-tĭzm*) *n.* A ceremonial sprinkling with water on a believer, or sometimes complete immersion in water.

BAPTISM in some form of sprinkling, pouring, or immersion, has been a rite associated with nearly every church; and this leads 8 per cent to believe that BAPTISM means CHURCH.

Christian BAPTISM dates back to the time of Christ and is usually an initiation, the ceremony of joining the church, administered to children at a very early age. The BAPTISTS, a movement which started in England about 1600, and in the United States in Providence, Rhode Island, about 1635, believed however that BAPTISM should be administered to mature persons, old enough to be true believers.

BAPTISM, BAPTISTERY (*băp'-tĭs-ter-ĭ*), or BAPTISTRY (*băp'tĭs-trĭ*), and the verb to BAPTISE (*băp-tĭz'*), all come from the Greek βάπτειν (*baptein*), to dip in water, drench, soak, or, when the same Greek verb is applied to a ship, to sink. A BAPTISTERY, also called a BAPTISTRY, was often in early days a separate building near a church, in which the sacrament of BAPTISM was administered.

104. *BEHEMOTH*, behemoth (*bĕ-hē'-mŏth*) *n.* Any great animal, perhaps the hippopotamus.

Two great animals of the far distant past, long before the BEHEMOTH but probably within the period of man's existence, are the MAMMOTH and the MASTODON, both belonging to the elephant family. In 1799 the complete body of a MAMMOTH was found buried in ice in Siberia; and in 1845 the skeleton of a MASTODON was dug up in Orange County, New Jersey. Both animals are now extinct.

The BEHEMOTH is thought by some to be a term for any great animal, and by others to be what we now call the HIPPOPOTAMUS, from the Greek ἱπποπόταμος (*hippopotamos*), river-horse. The

BEHEMOTH is mentioned in the Book of Job: 'Behold now BEHE-MOTH, he eateth grass as an ox'.

The word BEHEMOTH, connected with an Egyptian word for water-ox, comes directly from a Hebrew word for great-beast. BEHEMOTH was used for some huge animal, still in existence and probably well-known.

105. *DISTRIBUTE*, distribute (*dĭs-trĭ'-bŭt*) *v.* To divide among several, apportion, allot, parcel out, assign, disburse, deal, portion out, partition, bestow (v. b. 342) in shares.

To DISTRIBUTE, starting with the Latin *dis*, apart, comes from the verb *tribuĕre*, to give, the source of TRIBUTE (*trĭ'-bŭt*), sometimes in history a sum paid by a conquered nation to the conqueror. From the same *tribuĕre* come: TRIBUTARY, a smaller river which gives its waters to a larger one; as well as the verb to ATTRIBUTE (*ăt-trĭ'-bŭt*), to ascribe, assign, impute, and the corresponding noun, an ATTRIBUTE (*ăt'-trĭ-bŭt*), accented on the first syllable, a quality given to one, trait, characteristic.

To CONTRIBUTE (*kŏn-trĭ'-bŭt*) and to DISTRIBUTE, thought by 13 per cent of high-school students to mean DONATE (*dō-nāt'*), should be differentiated. To DONATE, from the Latin *donatus*, the past participle of *donare*, to give, present, is to CONTRIBUTE, to give. To DISTRIBUTE is to divide among several.

106. *GRATING*, grating (*grā'-tĭng*) *n.* Latticework, cross-bars usually of iron, reja in front of a window, trellis, gridiron over an open hole in the ground.

By 16 per cent of high-school students, GRATING is thought to be PACKAGING. GRATE and CRATE (*krāt*) are doublets, two words originally the same but now different in form and meaning. CRATE is older and of more direct descent, from the Latin *cratis*, wicker work.

A CRATE was at first a basket of wicker work for packaging china and glass, but today a CRATE is more often a box made of wood slats. A GRATE is a framework of metal bars, sometimes the floor of a fire-box in a furnace.

CRATING is PACKAGING. GRATING, with something of the same construction, but usually of metal, is used in all sorts of ways but not for packaging.

107. *FLABBY*, flabby (*flăb'-bĭ*) *adj.* Hanging loose, lax, flaccid, limp, without firmness.

FLABBY is thought by 48 per cent to mean BADLY-DRESSED, compared with 44 per cent who want LAX. This may be a confusion of FLABBY with SHABBY, which originally meant scabby, mangy, but which has come to mean poorly dressed; or it may be just the suggestion of FLABBY clothes which hang loose.

FLABBY is a colloquial word, probably a variation of the verb to FLAP, which originally meant to strike a blow with something soft and flat, as to CLAP with the hands. CLAP, SLAP, FLAP, and so FLABBY, are said to be imitative, words made up to sound like the sound they name. Of these, the Oxford says: 'The voiced ending in FLAB- as compared with FLAP- gives to the syllable a feebler effect suited to the meaning'. Of these FLABBY is the only one which suggests hanging loose, with no sound, and no suggestion of hitting something else.

108. *WRITHE*, writhe (*rīTH*) *v.* To twist, turn, contort, wriggle, squirm, wiggle, wrench.

The TH in WRITHE is pronounced like the verb to CLOTHE (*klōTH*), and not like the noun CLOTH (*klŏth*).

As with most words which start with WR-, WRITHE is Anglo-Saxon, and so goes back to the years 500 to 1000, after the Romans were in England, and before the Norman conquest.

Unlike WIGGLE and WRIGGLE, WRITHE always has an unpleasant suggestion, as: 'To WRITHE with pain'.

109. *ENTERPRISING*, enterprising (*ĕn'-ter-prīz-ĭng*) *adj.*

Ready to undertake important projects, resolute, energetic, bold, vigorous in action. 'ENTERPRISING men often succeed beyond all human probability', says Noah Webster.

ENTERPRISING is thought by 32 per cent to mean ENGROSSING, absorbing. As an adjective, GROSS is big, large, bulky; as a noun GROSS is the chief part, the mass. To ENGROSS was once to make bigger, increase in bulk, enlarge by addition, a goal of the ENTERPRISING, vigorous person. Then ENGROSS came to be used figuratively to mean take over the attention as a whole, and so absorb, monopolize completely. That which ENTERTAINS, amuses, is ENGROSSING in this figurative sense.

From the Latin *prendĕre*, to take in hand, grasp, seize, lay hold of, a verb also spelt *prehendĕre*, come APPREHEND, to grasp knowledge, lay hold of information; COMPREHEND, to grasp in the sense of understand; COMPRISE, to hold, contain; and ENTER-PRISING, ready to take in hand additional responsibilities, ambitious, grasping, prompt to undertake.

The Century Dictionary compares ENTERPRISING, ADVEN-TUROUS, and RASH, though the last two seem of a different sort. RASH and ADVENTUROUS both suggest taking needless chances, RASH, without sufficient thought or consideration; ADVENTUROUS, for the love of danger. ENTERPRISING carries no implication of needless risk, but suggests an energetic, vigorous readiness to push ahead.

110. *BAMBOOZLE*, bamboozle (*băm-boo'-zl*) *v.* To hoax, deceive, trick, fool, cheat, abuse, cozen, impose upon.

To 5 per cent BAMBOOZLE means GET DRUNK. To BOOZE and to BAMBOOZLE are both on the edge of slang; but otherwise there seems no connection. To BOOZE is to drink alcoholic beverages, almost to GET DRUNK. To BAMBOOZLE is to cheat, trick.

In 1710, in one of his contributions to the Tatler, number 230, published first by Richard Steele, and then by Steele and Addison together, Jonathan Swift said: 'Certain words invented by some pretty fellows such as BANTER, BAMBOOZLE, and COUNTRY PUT, are now struggling for vogue'. PRETTY in this sense means clever, for it comes directly from an Anglo-Saxon word meaning wily, cunning, tricky. PUT as a noun, pronounced to rime with BUT, HUT, NUT, is a clown, rustic, simpleton, silly fellow, a word which has clearly not survived. BANTER, which once meant to BAMBOOZLE, cheat, a meaning now archaic, has survived and means to make fun of in a good-humored way.

Benjamin Franklin, in his Life, says: 'Americans are neither to be DRAGOONED nor BAMBOOZLED out of their liberty'. The word DRAGOON seems to have been introduced in the late 1500's, for a cavalry soldier; and the verb means set DRAGOONS upon, persecute, oppress, threaten, harass.

To DRAGOON is to force into submission. To BAMBOOZLE is to gain one's end by means of trickery, deception, craft, or artifice.

111. *RESIDUE*, residue (*rĕz'-ĭ-dū*) *n*. Remainder, rest, residuum, remnant, that which is left.

The doublets RESIDUUM (*rē-zĭd'-ū-ŭm*) and RESIDUE come from the same Latin *residuum*, the first directly, the second through French, from *resīdĕre*, to remain behind, reside, and so dwell permanently, a combination of *re-*, back, and *sedēre*, to sit, the source of PRESIDE, to sit in front.

A RESIDUE is thought by 16 per cent to be a WATER SUPPLY. RESERVOIR (*rĕz'-ĕr-vhawr*), the French *reservoir*, a storehouse, originally from the Latin *re-*, back, and *servare*, to keep, is an artificial pond or lake, a water supply for a community.

REST is the general term. BALANCE, though often heard, is not correct for REST or REMAINDER. REMAINDER and RESIDUE are small parts. REMAINDER is a part of little value. RESIDUE is that which is left over after much of the original has been used for some other purpose.

112. *TREACHEROUS*, treacherous (*trĕch'-er-ŭs*) *adj*. Betraying (v. B. 497) a trust, cheating, false, base, mean, deceitful, faithless, recreant, despicable, caitiff, treasonable, disloyal, traitorous, violating allegiance, perfidious (v. B. 1225). TREACHEROUS comes from the Latin *tricari*, the source of the English TRICK, originally to deceive, cheat, cozen.

To 15 per cent of those tested TREACHEROUS means FAR-FETCHED, literally brought from afar, and so irrelevant, strained, forced, remotely connected. A FAR-FETCHED scheme, it is said, could be TREACHEROUS, but the flavor of the two words differs.

TREACHERY and PERFIDY are kinds of faithlessness, disloyalty. The TREACHEROUS man betrays confidence reposed in him. The PERFIDIOUS man carries TREACHERY to the basest extreme, betraying an acknowledged obligation.

113. *UNMOLLIFIED*, unmollified (*ŭn-mŏl'-lĭ-fīd*) *adj*. Not pacified, stubborn, (v. B. 231), hard-hearted, unyielding (v. B. 282), obdurate (v. B. 805), not appeased (v. B. 866), implacable (v. B. 1265), inexorable (v. B. 1607), not softened. To 22 per cent UNMOLLIFIED means UNFITTED. MODIFIED, much like MOLLIFIED in sound, from the Latin *modus*, measure, and *facĕre*, to make, do, which in so many words becomes -FY,

means altered in measurement, changed a little, and so may suggest FITTED, adjusted, made suitable. UNMODIFIED is therefore not fitted, not adjusted, and so UNFITTED.

To MOLLIFY, from the Latin *mollis*, soft, and the same *facĕre*, is literally to make soft, and figuratively to calm, appease, soothe, pacify, quiet, mitigate. UNMOLLIFIED means obdurate, callous, inexorable, hardened, unyielding, stubborn, hard-hearted.

114. *DEBONAIR*, debonair (*dĕb-ŏn-ār'*) *adj.* Carefree, of
       gentle mien, courteous, affable, charming, attractive, gay, light-hearted, pleasant in manner.
DEBONAIR comes directly from the old French *de bon aire*, originally from the Latin *de*, of, *bonus*, good, and *aire*, mien, appearance. In about 1635, John Milton, in L'Allegro, wrote: 'So buxom, blithe, and DEBONAIR'.

Examinees divide between CAREFREE and CHARMING, both excellent synonyms of DEBONAIR, 52 per cent inclining toward CHARMING, and 20 per cent toward CAREFREE. The last should be removed from the test.

115. *SPARINGLY*, sparingly (*spär'-ĭng-lĭ*) *adv.* Meagerly (1),
       thriftily (v. B. 164), moderately, carefully, economically (v. B. 362), sparsely, reservedly, charily, grudgingly, frugally (v. B. 1122), with forbearance.
SPARINGLY, in small amount, is thought by 24 per cent to mean PLENTIFULLY, abundantly, amply, copiously, in large amount, an exact antonym of the correct meaning, a confusion of opposites, the final step in learning, similar to selecting FRAIL as the meaning of STALWART instead of STURDY, the correct answer.

The verb to SPARE, to refrain from using, as in the ancient proverb: 'SPARE the rod and spoil the child', goes directly back to an Anglo-Saxon word with the same meaning. From this comes the present participle and participial adjective SPARING, and from this, by the addition of -LY, the adverb SPARINGLY, which means using less than is actually available.

116. *PROXIMITY*, proximity (*prŏks-ĭm'-ĭ-tĭ*) *n.* Nearness,
       closeness, adjacency, neighborhood, vicinity, juxtaposition, being side by side.

PROXIMITY comes from the Latin *proximitas, proximitatis*, near-ness, vicinity, from the adjective *proximus*, nearest, the irregular superlative of *prope*, near. The comparative is *propior*, nearer.

To 23 per cent of high-school students and, which rarely hap-pens, to the same percentage of high-vocabulary ones, PROXIM-ITY means POSITION, place, situation, relation to others. PROXIM-ITY is POSITION, but the word emphasizes nearness in position, not remoteness, not distance. Also PROXIMITY may be used for nearness in time, or in relation, as in mathematics, an APPROX-IMATION is near to accuracy.

117. *LAUREATE*, laureate (*law'-rē-āt*) *n.* Distinguished (v. B. 156) poet, eminent individual, palmary man or woman, literally one crowned with laurel; sometimes defined as a court panegyrist (v. B. 1773) expected to praise the deeds of his country, to write encomiums for state occasions; Webster, first edition: 'Poet LAUREATE in Great Britain, an officer of the King's household, whose business is to compose an ode annually for the King's birthday, and for the new year'.

To 32 per cent LAUREATE means LASSO. A LARIAT (*lă'-rĭ-ăt*), from the Spanish *la*, the, and *reata*, rope, is a rope for tying horses while grazing. From: Our Wild Indians, by R. I. Dodge, as quoted in the Century Dictionary, comes: 'The LARIAT and the LASSO (*lăs'-sō*) are the same with a very great difference. The LASSO may be used for picketing a horse, but the rope with which a horse is ordinarily picketed would never be of use as a LASSO'.

LAUREATE comes from the Latin *laurus*, laurel, from *laureatus*, crowned with laurel, with a wreath made of leaves from the bay tree, a large evergreen shrub, a native of Italy and Greece. Years ago the verb to LAUREATE (*law'-rē-āt*) was to crown with such a wreath at graduation from a university. From this came BACCALAUREATE (*băk-kă-law'-rē-āt*), a made-up word for what used to be the lowest university degree. The word LAUREATE is used today mostly for the POET LAUREATE.

118. *SADIST*, sadist (*sahd'-ĭst*) *n.* One who practices sexual perversion marked by extreme cruelty. SADISTIC is the ad-jective, and SADISM the corresponding noun.

The Marquis de Sade, a French writer of obscene novels and plays, who lived from 1740 to 1814 and who was infamous for the licentiousness of his life and writings, is the source of the word SADISM. Condemned to death in 1772 for his vicious practices, he fled to Italy. Found guilty again five years later, he was committed to the Bastille, and finally to an insane asylum.

SADIST, a recent word marked correctly by almost everyone who has taken the difficult form of vocabulary test in which this word appears, is an eponym, a word made from a proper name, from the name of a person.

MONK, marked by 12 per cent, may possibly be suggested by the word SAD.

119. *PONTIFICAL*, pontifical (*pŏn-tĭf′-ĭ-kăl*) *adj.* Papal, popish, episcopal, pertaining to a prelate, befitting a high priest. PONTIFICAL is the adjective from PONTIFF, in almost every religion a high priest. In ancient Rome, the PONTIFEX (*pŏn′-tĭ-fĕks*) was equivalent to the modern PONTIFF.

The Latin seems to have been a combination of *pons, pontis*, bridge, and *facere*, to make, so that a PONTIFF was originally a bridge-builder.

PONTIFICAL is thought by 27 per cent to mean UNNATURAL. ARTIFICIAL (*ăhr-tĭ-fĭ′-shăl*), with many of the same letters as PONTIFICAL, is UNNATURAL, made by art.

120. *WARY*, wary (*wā′-rĭ*) *adj.* Careful, cautious, watchful, vigilant (v. B. 336), heedful, prudent (36), guarding against danger, alert against surprise.

To 26 per cent WARY means TIRED. The adjective WEARY (*wē′-rĭ*), also Anglo-Saxon but from a different source, means TIRED, exhausted, fatigued, jaded, worn out. The corresponding adverbs are WEARILY (*wē′-rĭ-lĭ*), in a tired, fatigued, exhausted manner, and WARILY (*wā′-rĭ-lĭ*), carefully, watchfully, wisely; while the nouns are WEARINESS (*wē′-rĭ-nĕs*), exhaustion, fatigue, and WARINESS (*wā′-rĭ-nĕs*), prudence, care, caution, heed.

There was a verb to WARE (*wār*), which now appears in BEWARE (*bē-wār′*), take care, take heed. Though now spelt WARY, this adjective is WARE plus -Y, an Anglo-Saxon ending added to form an adjective from a noun or occasionally from a verb.

121. *UNEQUIVOCAL,* unequivocal *(ŭn-ē-kwĭv'-ō-kăl) adj.*
Plain, clear, definite, unmistakable, obvious (v. b. 854), not ambiguous (v. b. 569). Read EQUIVOCAL (v. b. 1507).
To 51 per cent of those thus far tested but to only 3 per cent of that selected group who score generally high in vocabulary tests as a whole, UNEQUIVOCAL means UNCERTAIN. UNCERTAIN, starting with the Anglo-Saxon prefix UN-, not, means not certain, not definite, not sure, the opposite of CERTAIN, definite. EQUIVOCAL, without the initial UN-, a combination of the Latin *aequus,* equal, and *vox, vocis,* voice, sound, literally calling equally in different directions, means ambiguous, doubtful, questionable, the opposite of CERTAIN. Thus EQUIVOCAL means not CERTAIN, and so UNCERTAIN. UNEQUIVOCAL means not doubtful and so CERTAIN, definite.

122. *MANIFEST,* manifest *(măn'-ĭ-fĕst) adj.* Obvious, evident, plain, clear, apparent, patent *(pā'-tĕnt),* easily comprehended, readily perceived by the understanding.
MANIFEST comes from the Latin *manifestus,* evident, clear, plain, palpable, from *manus,* the hand, and *fendere,* to strike, and suggests just at hand, tangible.
To 9 per cent MANIFEST means EXPLAINED. To EXPLAIN, from *planus,* level, plain, is literally to flatten out, and so to make clear, and the verb to MANIFEST may have almost this sense, to show, and to prove.
Of the five words: CLEAR, PLAIN, OBVIOUS, EVIDENT, and MANIFEST, the first, CLEAR, means without dimness, sharp, distinct. PLAIN means seen at first glance. OBVIOUS means directly in the way. EVIDENT suggests a mental process. MANIFEST is stronger, involving intuition.

123. *GURU,* guru *(goo'-rŏo) n.* A Hindu spiritual teacher, learned head of a religious sect.
GURU is a Hindu word which goes directly back to the Sanskrit *guru,* which originally meant heavy, grave, dignified, and then important, and finally, worthy of honor. The word GURU dates back to 1500, and was originally limited to one person, the spiritual head of the SIKHS *(sēks),* another Hindu word which means disciple.

124. *FUSION*, fusion (*fū'-shŏn*) *n.* Combination, union, blending together, operation of melting.

Fusion comes from the Latin *fusio, fusionis,* pouring out, from
fusis, the past participle of *fundere,* to pour, melt, the source of
FUSE and FOUND. Fusion is the operation of melting, making
fluid by heat, the act of blending together through melting;
complete union of previously separate things.

There is an obsolete word *foison,* pronounced (*foi'-zŏn*),
which means abundance, plenty, and so EFFUSION, an outpouring, literal or figurative, a doublet of FUSION.

125. *RUSE*, ruse (*rūz*) *n.* A stratagem, artifice, trick, maneuver,
hoax, trap, snare, dodge, contrivance, deception.

A RUSE, a MANEUVER, and a STRATAGEM, are all endeavors to gain
an end by deceiving others, to catch an enemy at a disadvantage.
STRATEGY, from the Greek στρατηγία (*strategia*), the office of a
commander, generalship as a whole, is the grand plan, involving all aspects.

STRATAGEM, from στρατηγος (*strategos*), the commander
himself, leader of an army, general, is that part of STRATEGY
based on deceiving the enemy. Notice that in STRATEGY the
Greek ήτα (*ā'-tăh*) was long ago translated into a Roman A instead of the correct E, so that STRATEGY, the grand plan, is spelt
correctly with E, while STRATAGEM has A instead.

A MANEUVER involves motion, a carefully contrived movement with a definite purpose, moving an army, or a piece on a
chess board. It is a quiet and secret marshalling of one's forces.

RUSE acquired its military meaning in French, but comes
from the Latin *recusare,* to decline, refuse, and suggests refusing
combat. A RUSE was originally a way of escaping, of retreating,
and RUSE is still not a part of a big advance, but a trick played to
break away, a deception of some elaborateness to help one escape
from a predicament.

126. *ALABASTER*, alabaster (*ăl'-ă-băs-ter*) *n.* White marble,
soft stone like marble.

ALABASTER is thought by 20 per cent to mean BLACK STONE.
OBSIDIAN (*ŏb-sĭd'-ĭ-ăn*) is a volcanic glass, usually black in color,
the opposite of ALABASTER, which is soft and white.

The word ALABASTER comes through the Latin *alabaster*, a box for perfume, from the Greek ἀλάβαστρος (*alabastros*), a vase of ALABASTER.

The pure white variety of ALABASTER, which technically is not a marble, comes now from quarries near Florence, in Italy, though anciently another variety, a true marble, came from quarries in Egypt.

127. *FULCRUM*, fulcrum (*fŭl'-krŭm*), pl. FULCRA *n*. Support, prop, point of rest for a lever.

FULCRUM comes directly from the Latin *fulcrum*, specifically a bedpost, foot of a couch, or generally any support, prop.

To 14 per cent of those tested, FULCRUM means PLATFORM. A PODIUM (*pō'-dĭ-ŭm*), from the Greek πόδον (*podon*), a little foot, is a PLATFORM, another kind of support. Or the word FORUM, a market place, associated with the Latin *foris*, out of doors, and the same *foris*, a door, may add to the confusion. In the city of Rome, the FORUM was a public standing place where causes were judicially tried and orations delivered to the people.

Of the FULCRUM of a lever E. Chambers says: 'The point which sustains the pressure of a lever when employed either in raising or lowering bodies; frequently a roller set under a lever'.

128. *STALWART*, stalwart (*stawl'-wart*) *adj*. Stout, strong, sturdy (v. b. 207), brave, bold, vigorous, robust (v. b. 968).

STALWART seems to be the Scotch for STALWORTH, used of ships to mean serviceable, steadfast. STALWORTH goes directly back to two Anglo-Saxon words which meant foundation and firm, fast.

To 12 per cent STALWART means FRAIL, weak, delicate, fragile, not robust, an exact opposite of the correct meaning, a confusion of antonyms paralleling that of ECONOMICALLY and PLENTIFULLY as meanings of SPARINGLY; or ROOMY and CROWDED as meanings of COMMODIOUS.

From The Good Companions, by J. B. Priestley, a lovely story of musicians on the road, comes: 'Mr. Grundy is one of our old STALWARTS, a strong character and very deep-thinking man, entirely self-made and quite well-to-do'.

In The Merry Adventures of Robin Hood the great wrestling-match at Derby fair is called a STALWART game.

129. *FONDLE*, fondle (*fŏn'-dl*) *v.* To caress, treat with tenderness, dote on, cherish, pamper, show fondness toward.

To 28 per cent FONDLED means ADMIRED, looked at with wonder,
marveled at, esteemed, reverenced, too strong a synonym for
FONDLE. To ADMIRE, from the Latin *ad*, to, and *mire*, to wonder,
is to regard with wonder. To FONDLE, the frequentative of FOND,
dote, from Swedish and Icelandic words meaning foolish, simple,
silly, idiotic, is to caress, stroke, pat.

130. *DESPOILED*, despoiled (*dĕs-poild'*) *adj.* Plundered, pillaged, spoliated, robbed, sacked, stript of possessions.

DESPOILED, from the Latin *despoliare*, to plunder, is *de-*, which
here intensifies the meaning, and *spoliare*, to plunder, strip, the
source of SPOIL.

To SPOIL may mean to rob, pillage, plunder, but without the
initial DE- of DESPOIL, conveys a feebler sense of ruin, impair-
ment, injury to the beauty, reduction in value. This milder
meaning leads 8 per cent to believe that DESPOILED means LIT-
TERED. A LITTER was first a bed carried between shafts; then
loose straw spread on the floor as bedding for horses and cows;
and from this LITTER came to be scattered rubbish strewn about
carelessly, slovenly. LITTERED is cluttered with things in a slovenly manner, and so less pleasant, reduced in value, SPOILED. But
DESPOILED, with the initial DE-, is robbed, pillaged, sacked.

131. *APOTHECARY*, apothecary (*ă-pŏth'-ĕ-kā-rĭ*) *n.* Pharmacist, druggist, dispensing chemist, one licensed to compound drugs and medicines.

APOTHECARY comes from the Latin *apotheca*, a storehouse,
warehouse, from the Greek ἀποθήκη (*apothece*), storehouse, a
combination of ἀπό (*apo*), away, and τιθέναι (*tithenai*), to put.

While there is no popular mislead, DESERTER, marked by 5 per
cent, may be suggested by the difficult word APOSTATE, one who
deserts a religion or a cause.

DRUGGIST, PHARMACIST, and APOTHECARY are given as synonyms. A DRUGGIST is often the owner of a drug store, who
may sell almost anything, and even operate a lunch counter.
A PHARMACIST compounds and dispenses drugs, done formerly
by the physician himself. In the 18th century PHARMACY grad-

ually separated from medicine. The American Pharmaceutical Association was founded in 1851. Today in the United States a PHARMACIST must be licensed.

The words PHARMACIST and PHARMACEUTIST (*fahr-mă-sū'-tĭst*) are identical in meaning. The second comes to English through French and is used in the adjective PHARMACEUTICAL (*fahr-mă-sū'-tĭ-kal*); while the first, more usual as a noun, comes directly from the Greek.

In England and Ireland an APOTHECARY is licensed much as a PHARMACIST in the United States.

132. *INFIDEL*, infidel (*ĭn'-fĭ-dĕl*) *n*. One without faith, unbeliever, pagan, heretic, disbeliever, rejecting the doctrines of a particular religion.

A PAGAN is one who is not a Christian or a member of a Christian community; but the word recognizes the existence of another sort of faith, a believer perhaps in idols, images.

A HERETIC believes strongly in something very close to one's own religion. The danger of the HERETICS was their belief in freedom of choice, for the word comes from the Greek αἱρετικός (*haireticos*), able to choose, from αἱρεῖσθαι (*haireisthai*), to choose. A HERETIC is one who chooses his own philosophy or religion slightly at variance with the accepted standards of those in control at the moment.

INFIDEL was the word used in promoting the crusades. It comes from the Latin *infidelis*, unfaithful, unbelieving, a combination of the privative *in-* and *fidelis*, trustworthy, faithful. From this comes FIDELITY, good faith, exact observance of duty. The INFIDEL is not to be trusted.

BARBARIAN, a mislead selected by 8 per cent, is close to INFIDEL as that word was used when popular. A BARBARIAN was originally anyone who spoke a foreign language; and then came to mean more specifically anyone who does not believe in the Christian religion. Both conditions fit the INFIDEL.

133. *EQUABLE*, equable (*ĕk'-kwă-bl*) *adj*. Even, steady, uniform, regular, invariable, even-tempered.

EQUITY (*ĕ'-kwĭ-tĭ*), from the Latin *aequus*, equal, means equal justice to everyone, fairness, impartiality. From this comes

EQUITABLE (ĕ'-kwĭ-tă-bl), defined as fair and equal, which leads
16 per cent to select SIMILAR as the meaning of EQUABLE.

But EQUABLE, though from the same Latin source, through
aequabilis, that which can be made equal, consistent, uniform,
from *aequare*, to make equal, the source of the English EQUATE,
has come to have the specialized meaning of even, STEADY.

134. *BRAZEN*, brazen (brā'-zĕn) *adj.* Strong, impenetrable, or
    impudent, forward, impertinent, when applied to a person.
BRASS (brăs), an alloy of copper and zinc, is harder than copper,
and so suggests strength, hardness. To eat GRASS is to GRAZE, to
work with GLASS is to GLAZE, and so BRASS becomes BRAZEN. The
Anglo-Saxon suffix -en, added to the Anglo-Saxon noun GOLD,
forms the adjective GOLDEN, WOOD becomes WOODEN, and so the
noun BRASS becomes the adjective BRAZEN, which may mean
merely made of BRASS, or strong when applied to an object.
Used of a person the word is always unpleasant, shameless, too
pushing, and unfeeling.

135. *DISSOLUTION*, dissolution (dĭs-sō-lŭ'-shŏn) *n.* A sep-
    aration into parts, disruption, disintegration, resolution,
break-up, decomposition of a natural structure; also dissolving,
changing from a solid to a liquid.
To 10 per cent DISSOLUTION means DISAPPOINTMENT, defeat in a
realization of one's anticipations, failure of a desire, frustration,
miscarriage of plans, thwarting of a wish.

DISSOLUTION comes from the Latin *dissolvere*, with the past
participle *dissolutus*, to dissolve, a combination of *dis-*, apart,
and *solvere*, to loosen, the source of SOLUTION, a loosening, un-
raveling, disentangling of the parts of a problem; RESOLUTION,
intention, decision, determination; as well as ABSOLUTION, freeing from an obligation; and the corresponding verbs, to SOLVE,
RESOLVE, ABSOLVE, and DISSOLVE, to loosen.

136. *CENTUPLICATE*, centuplicate (sĕn-tū'-plĭ-kāt) *adj.*
    One-hundred-fold, one hundred times greater.
From the Latin *centum*, hundred, comes CENT, the hundredth
part of a dollar; CENTURY, a hundred years; CENTENARY (sĕn'-tĕ-
nā-rĭ), a hundred-year celebration; and CENTIPEDE, an animal

with literally a hundred legs. From *plicare*, to fold, come dozens of words, among them DUPLICATE, two-fold; and TRIPLICATE, three-fold; and CENTUPLICATE, one-hundred-fold.

137. *PERMEATE*, permeate (*pĕr'-mē-āt*) *v*. To penetrate, go through, pervade, also to saturate, diffuse through.

PERMEATE comes from the Latin *permeatus*, the past participle of *permeare*, a combination of *per-*, through, which also strengthens the meaning, and *meare*, to go.

The selection, by 15 per cent, of RUIN as a synonym of PERMEATE, may conceivably be a misreading of RUIN for RUN-IN, a perfect interpretation of PERMEATE. The verb to LEAK implies damage, destruction, RUIN. But the word PERMEATE has no such innuendo.

PENETRATE, PERMEATE, SATURATE are in order of spreading through a substance. To PENETRATE is to enter with difficulty. To SATURATE is to enter completely. To PERMEATE is between the two, more spreading than PENETRATE but far short of SATURATE.

138. *PROVISO*, proviso (*prō-vī'-zō*) *n*. Stipulation, clause in in a contract introducing a condition.

PROVISO is the Latin ablative neuter of *provisus*, the present participle of *providere*, a combination of *pro*, before, and *vidēre*, to see. A PROVISO is an attempt to look ahead to some possibility, and really means providing such and such a thing is true.

A WARRANTY, chosen by 16 per cent, the most frequently marked mislead, perhaps harder than PROVISO, is a promise, almost a guarantee, an assurance of some particular in connection with a contract.

A STIPULATION, the correct answer, is another difficult word, a final agreement, or, more often, the settlement of some particular part of a contract and in this sense is a synonym of PROVISO.

139. *JUVENESCENT*, juvenescent (*jū-vĕ-nĕs'-sĕnt*) *adj*. Growing young, becoming youthful.

To 5 per cent JUVENESCENT means TRITE. TRITE comes from the Latin *tritus*, the past participle of *terere*, to rub, the source of

DETRITUS, a mass of small rocks broken off by rubbing. TRITE means, worn-out, hackneyed, stereotyped, stale.

JUVENESCENT comes from the Latin *juvenis*, young, and is used incorrectly in English to mean young. JUVENILE (*jū'-vĕ-nīl*) means young, youthful. JUVENESCENT, from the Latin *juvenescens, juvenescentis*, the present participle, means becoming young, growing youthful. Similarly CONVALESCENT means growing well, recovering health; and RECRUDESCENT means breaking out again, coming into renewed activity.

140. *ALLURE*, allure (*ăl-lūr'*) *v.* To attract, entice, lure, decoy, invite, coax, fascinate, tempt, seduce.

The popular mislead, marked by 7 per cent, is MENTION. The verb to ALLUDE, differing from ALLURE by only a single letter, from the Latin *alludere*, to play with, from *ad*, to, and *ludere*, to play, is to refer to casually, and so may suggest MENTION.

To ALLURE and to LURE are to attract by bait, but the two differ slightly. To LURE has more the original sense of a physical bait or LURE. ALLURE is more figurative. To ALLURE and to ENTICE express the exercise of strong but subtle influence. ENTICE involves skill, sometimes flattery; ALLURE implies a more attractive, more beautiful bait.

141. *TRIBUTARY*, tributary (*trĭb'-ū-tā-rĭ*) *n.* A river which contributes to another, an affluent, something which flows in as contrasted with an effluent, which flows out. Reread the verb to DISTRIBUTE (105).

Originally a TRIBUTARY was a state paying TRIBUTE, sometimes to a conquering power.

The word comes from the Latin *tributum*, a tribute, originally from *tribus*, tribe; from the same source come ATTRIBUTE (*ăt'-trĭ-būt*), a given quality, characteristic, aptitude; CONTRIBUTION (*kŏn-trĭ-bū'-shŏn*), a gift usually of money; DISTRIBUTION, a division or sharing among several; the verb to DISTRIBUTE and the noun RETRIBUTION, a paying back often in revenge.

TRIBUTARIES, as applied to a river, are thought by 18 per cent to be INLETS, perhaps too close to use as a mislead, except that those who score otherwise high vocabulary mark SIDE-STREAMS in preference to INLETS.

An INLET, the opposite of an OUTLET, is an opening into an enclosed place, an entrance, a strip of water extending from a large body into the land, leaving a sea or lake but still forming a part of it, at its level.

In The Nile, Emil Ludwig writes: 'Many small TRIBUTARIES hurry to swell the stormy stream'; and of the great Blue Nile which joins the White: 'This is no TRIBUTARY which, like the other three, ends at its mouth'.

142. *PIVOT*, pivot (*pĭv'-ŏt*) *v.* To turn on a pin like a wheel, whirl about, hinge, swing on a turning point, revolve (V. B. 130) on an axle.

PIVOT is the French diminutive of an Italian word sometimes spelt *piva*, peg, and sometimes *pipa*, pipe.

To 11 per cent of examinees PIVOT means STAND-FAST, a choice almost justified, for in military language the soldier or officer who STANDS-FAST, and about whom a line of troops wheels, is called the PIVOT; but given a choice between STAND-FAST and HINGE, as meanings of PIVOT, no high-vocabulary person selects STAND-FAST.

From Ephraim Chambers, in his encyclopedic dictionary of 1728: 'PIVOT, a foot or shoe of iron, or other metal, usually conical, or terminating in a point; whereby a body intended to turn around, bears on another fixed at rest, and performs its convolution. Large gates usually turn on PIVOTS. The ancients tell us they have theatres in Rome that hold 80,000 people, which yet turned on a single PIVOT.'

143. *AGRARIAN*, agrarian (*ă-grā'-rĭ-ăn*) *adj.* Agricultural, relating to the land, especially public land, connected with cultivated land.

AGRARIAN comes from the Latin *ager*, field, country, land, from the same source as AGRICULTURE. The word AGRICULTURE comes from the Latin *agri*, the genetive of *ager*, and means the cultivation of land. The original AGRARIAN laws dealt with the division of public lands among free citizens.

The adjective AGRICULTURAL refers specifically to the cultivation of land, farming, tillage, husbandry. AGRARIAN refers to land in general.

144. *CORPULENT*, corpulent (*kor'-pū-lĕnt*) *adj*. Stout, fleshy, portly, fat, heavy, bulky, gross, big-bodied, the opposite of SLENDER.

To 7 per cent CORPULENT means DEAD. CORPSE, once the living body of a human being, has come to mean the DEAD BODY, so that DEAD CORPSE, once frequent, is now unnecessary, tautological, the word CORPSE alone meaning DEAD BODY.

From the Latin *corpus*, the body, come not only CORPSE and CORPULENT, from *corpulentus*, fat, large, fleshy, but also CORPS (*kōr*), the French *corps*, a number of persons acting together, as: 'A diplomatic CORPS', or in military language a unit of the army next above a division, usually two divisions.

E. Chamber says: 'CORPULENCY: the state of a person too much loaded with flesh and fat. CORPULENCY amounts to the same with OBESITY and popularly FATNESS.'

145. *GARLAND*, garland (*gahr'-lănd*) *n*. A festoon, daisy-chain, wreath, chaplet, string of flowers.

GARLAND goes back through Spanish, Italian, and Portuguese, perhaps to an Anglo-Saxon word for wire.

To 13 per cent GARLAND means FLOWER-BED. This is probably the result of confusion with the word GARDEN. A GARDEN is a FLOWER-BED, a lot of land for flowering plants. Bed is used in this sense to mean a plot of ground, often raised a little above the adjoining level.

According to E. Chambers: 'GARLANDS are ornaments of flowers, fruits, and leaves intermixed; anciently used at the gates of temples, triumphal arches, or any place where marks of public joy and gaiety were desired'.

146. *NOSEGAY*, nosegay (*nōz'-gā*) *n*. Small bouquet, posy, bunch of flowers.

NOSEGAY, used by Shakespeare (Winter's Tale), is a direct combination of NOSE and GAY. The noun GAY was originally an ornament, gaud, anything smartly or showily fine; and of NOSEGAY the Century Dictionary says: 'Literally a pretty thing to smell, used to regale the sense of smell'.

A NOSEGAY is almost always a GIFT, a present, token, attractive gesture, and this leads 8 per cent to select GIFT as a synonym.

147. *EMPOWER*, empower (*ĕm-pow'-er*) *v*. To authorize, license, warrant, qualify, commission, give power to.

In the verb EMPOWER, a combination of EM-, and POWER, the prefix *em-* which often makes a verb of a noun, is used before labials, such as p, in place of *en*. POWER is a noun; to EMPOWER is the verb, to give POWER to.

EMPOWERED is thought by 38 per cent to mean CONTROLLED. The verb to CONTROL, of Dutch, German, and Scandinavian origin and not apparently from Latin or Greek, is to rule, regulate, govern, direct, restrain, exert authority. The noun CONTROL is defined as the power to rule. To EMPOWER is to give this power to rule, bestow authority, grant permission to govern. Many of the troubles in the world, both past and present, are due to this confusion between CONTROLLING, exerting authority, using POWER, and having the right to CONTROL, being EMPOWERED to CONTROL. With no clear distinction between these words, it is impossible for many persons to recognize the distinction in life.

148. *FORMIDABLE*, formidable (*for'-mĭ-dă-bl*) *adj*. Difficult to overcome, hard to deal with, stupendous, appalling, redoubtable, exciting fear, inspiring dread, as from Macaulay: 'Frederick the Great, a FORMIDABLE enemy'.

FORMIDABLE comes through French, Spanish, and Italian words all spelt much like the English, from the Latin *formidare*, to fear, dread. FORMIDABLE means not only difficult to deal with, but also, especially in French and occasionally in English, having the power to overcome all obstacles, thus strong, forceful, almost IMPORTANT, a meaning of FORMIDABLE selected by 14 per cent, a correct interpretation of the French use of the word.

Of the five words: AWFUL, DREADFUL, FEARFUL, FRIGHTFUL, and FORMIDABLE, the first, when correctly used, means inspiring dread mingled with profound reverence, exciting a feeling of deep solemnity with a suggestion of fear. DREADFUL arouses an oppressive feeling of coming evil, without the reverence of AWFUL. FEARFUL is full of fear. FRIGHTFUL inspires sudden and paralyzing fear. FORMIDABLE challenges the strong, the powerful. The Century Dictionary gives: an AWFUL sight, a DREADFUL disaster, a FEARFUL leap, a FRIGHTFUL chasm. To this might be added a FORMIDABLE task.

149. *CHAOS*, chaos (kā'-ŏs) *n.* Originally an abyss, chasm,
       yawning hollow, vacant immeasurable space; then a form-
less elementary state, and finally disorder, confused mixture of ·
parts. The adjective is CHAOTIC (kā-ŏt'-ĭk).

The word CHAOS is known to almost everyone who has taken
the difficult form of vocabulary test in which this word appears. CLEFT, the only mislead thus far marked, is a CREVICE, the
open space left in a great crack, a chasm left by cleavage, and
so very close to the original meaning of CHAOS, chasm, abyss.

   CHAOS comes through the Latin *chaos*, from the Greek χάος
(*chaos*), empty space. In 1721 Nathan Bailey wrote of CHAOS:
'A Gap; also a dark or rude Mass of Matter, out of which the
World is supposed, by some, to be at first formed: A Confused
mixture of all sorts of particles together: a disorderly heap of
things'.

   One hundred years later, 1828, Noah Webster defined CHAOS
as: 'That confusion or confused mass in which matter is supposed to have existed before it was separated into its different
kinds and reduced to order, by the creating power of God. Confusion, disorder, a state in which the parts are undistinguished.'

150. *TOMB*, tomb (*toom*) *n.* A grave, excavation in the ground,
       dug to receive a coffin with a dead body, also a vault,
sepulcher of stone.

The meaning of TOMB, from the Greek τύμβος (*tumbos*), a
grave, barrow, tumulus, a sepulchral mound, is known to almost
every person who has taken this form of the vocabulary tests.

   Both a BARROW and a TUMULUS are ancient mounds of earth,
found in England, almost small hills of dirt piled on top of a
grave.

   Other more difficult words for different kinds of TOMBS are:
SEPULCHER (sĕp'-ŭl-kĕr), any TOMB; CATACOMB, an underground
room for burial vaults; MAUSOLEUM, a magnificent sepulcher,
stately edifice, splendid TOMB; CENOTAPH, an empty TOMB, where
no one is buried, erected to someone who is buried elsewhere.
A COLUMBARIUM, in Latin, a dove-cot, a pigeon house, is, in
Roman antiquity, a place for the ashes of the dead with recesses
for the cinerary urns; and SARCOPHAGUS, a stone coffin, ornamented with sculptures.

151. *SERRATED*, serrated (*sĕr'-rā-tĕd*) *adj*. Saw-like, notched
   on the edge, toothed, with sharp points, nicked, indented,
emarginate, dentate.
The adjective SERRATE comes from the Latin *serratus*, saw-like,
saw-shaped, from *serra*, a saw, perhaps from *secare*, to cut.
   Despite the rare occurrence of this word, its meaning is known
to a surprisingly large percentage, with no popular mislead.

152. *TRICE*, trice (*trīs*) *n*. A very short time, instant, moment.
   John Stevens, in a New Spanish and English Dictionary of
1706 quoted by the Century, says: 'A barbarous fram'd word
signifying nothing of itself, but as they make it, thus, *venir en un
tris*, to come in a TRICE, no less barbarous English'.
   TRICE, used only in the phrase: 'In a TRICE', in a jiffy, goes
back through Middle English, perhaps to Spanish, though this
is questioned.

153. *BOISTEROUS*, boisterous (*bŏĭ'-stĕr-ŭs*) *adj*. Rough,
   stormy, turbulent, noisy, clamorous.
BOISTEROUS goes back to Middle English but its origin is unknown. To 20 per cent BOISTEROUS means PLAYFUL, almost an
opposite. BOISTEROUS, applied to the weather, to the elements,
means rough and stormy, turbulent. When applied to people,
BOISTEROUS still means rough and noisy, clamorous, turbulent,
almost savage, not playful.
   The whole background of the word is rough, rude, massive,
full of fierce vigor, violent in action; but there is certainly a
tendency for its meaning to move toward good, natural exuberance of spirits, unbounded excess of energy, perhaps because
there is no other word. SPORTIVE, FROLICSOME, FRISKY are not
appropriate. CLAMOROUS is too noisy, and UPROARIOUS applies to
adults. Perhaps just plain NOISY is the word.

154. *THRESH*, thresh (*thrĕsh*) *v*. To separate grain from straw,
   to beat out the seed with a flail, or nowadays with a THRESH-
ING machine.
THRESH and THRASH are nearly the same word. Both go directly back through Middle English to the same Anglo-Saxon,
much as MESH and MASH. To THRASH is to hit, pound, beat,

strike, and is general and colloquial. To THRESH is technical, to separate grain from chaff and straw. To WINNOW, also technical, from an Anglo-Saxon word meaning fan, wind, is to blow chaff away from the grain.

To 14 per cent THRESHED means GATHERED, actions closely related. To GATHER is to collect, assemble, bring together. Wheat is GATHERED, harvested, reaped, and then THRESHED, beaten with a flail, or with a THRESHER, to separate the seed from the straw.

155. *ORACLE*, oracle (*or'-ă-kl*) *n.* The utterance of a priest, prophecy, divine announcement of a forthcoming event, inspired prediction of the future.

To 14 per cent ORACLE means SIGHT. INSIGHT is intellectual penetration, discernment, mental vision, almost the power of divining the future. But SIGHT, directly from Anglo-Saxon, is vision, the power of seeing. A SIGHT is also something seen, a show, spectacle. The word OCULAR, pertaining to SIGHT, from the Latin *oculus*, the eye, the source of OCULIST, one who treats the eyes, may add to the confusion.

ORACLE, with similar French, Spanish, Portuguese, and Italian words, comes from the Latin *oraculum*, a prophecy, revelation, through *orare*, to pray, from *os, oris*, the mouth, the source of ORATION, ORAL, and ORATORY, all dealing with speech.

According to E. Chambers: an ORACLE was an answer usually couched in very dark and ambiguous terms, supposed to be given by daemons of old; also the daemon who gave the answer. The SIBYLS (*sĭb'-ĭlz*) were female ORACLES, spread over the ancient world, believed to have the power of prophesying.

156. *SWIRL*, swirl (*swerl*) *v.* To turn about, twist around, eddy, whirl about, gyrate, curl.
SWIRL comes directly from Norwegian with similar words in Swedish and Danish.

To WHIRL, TWIRL, and SWIRL, are much alike and can often be used interchangeably.

157. *IGNOBLE*, ignoble (*ĭg-nō'-bl*) *adj.* Lowly, of low birth, unworthy, mean, vulgar, plebeian, contemptible, base.

IGNOMINY (*ĭg'-nō-mĭ-nĭ*) is public contempt; while IGNOMINIOUS (*ĭg-nō-mĭn'-ĭ-ŭs*) is disgraceful, discreditable, shameful.

To 3 per cent IGNOBLE means POOR, ideas too often and too closely associated. Even dictionaries give spiritless, cowardly, abject, mean, as synonyms of POOR, all synonyms also of IGNOBLE. St. Francis of Assisi was POOR, without money, but not IGNOBLE. One condition of joining the Franciscan order was disposing first of all property. Soon after St. Francis's death in 1226 dissensions arose between those who wished to continue carrying on the principles of St. Francis and those who preferred wealth. It is impossible to understand this sort of problem without knowing the distinction between the words POOR and IGNOBLE.

IGNOBLE comes from the Latin *ignobilis*, unknown, obscure, lowborn, from the privative *in-*, meaning not, and *gnobilis*, known, illustrious; and so by derivation not known, not illustrious. But as NOBLE has come to mean of exalted character; so IGNOBLE means the opposite, mean in spirit, unworthy, contemptible, base.

158. *GARB*, garb (*gahrb*) *n*. Dress, clothes, habit, costumes, accoutrements, apparel, raiment, garment, attire.

GARB and GARMENT, though much alike, come from different sources, with today different flavors. A GARMENT is a coat or gown, a piece of clothing. GARMENT and GARNISH are closely related and in this sense a GARMENT is a decoration, adornment. GARMENT and GARRISON are also related. A GARMENT is a protection, defense.

GARB, of Teutonic origin, with related words in French, Spanish, and Italian, is a more elegant expression. In Old French it meant comeliness, gracefulness, handsomeness, gentility, pleasing manners, and today still retains many of these delightful characteristics of grace and elegance. GARB, which goes back to 1600, includes mode of dress, demeanor, deportment, mien, fashion, stylishness, even manner of speech.

159. *STEEL*, steel (*stēl*) *v*. To harden, stiffen, make strong.

The metal IRON has given its name to objects made of metal as, in golf, an IRON is a metal club, and the verb to IRON is to use a FLAT-IRON for pressing clothing.

In both Latin and Greek there are words for gold and silver, *aurum* for gold, and *argentum* and ἄργυρος (*argyros*) for silver, but the words GOLD and SILVER themselves, as well as STEEL, have no roots in these languages. Both the noun STEEL, the metal, and the verb to STEEL, are from Anglo-Saxon. To STEEL is to render strong, to make as hard as STEEL.

The mislead COMPLETED, underlined by more than 10 per cent, the only mislead marked by anyone, is selected perhaps because of the verb to SEAL used figuratively to mean finish, complete. One STEELS one's purpose in order to COMPLETE an enterprise.

160. *SOPHOMORIC*, sophomoric (*sŏf-ō-mōr′-ik*) *adj.* Foolishly wise, in the United States an adjective characterizing a student in the second year of college.

SOPHOMORE is a made-up word combining the Greek σοφός (*sophos*), wise, with μωρός (*moros*), dull, silly, foolish. From σοφός (*sophos*), wise, skilled, learned, clever, comes SOPHIST, originally one versed in some special subject, and later a specialist who took pay for teaching.

From μωρός (*moros*) comes MORON, one who is backward mentally. A SOPHOMORE combines the two: a MORON in the eyes of the world; a SOPHIST in his own opinion.

The two misconceptions are LEARNED, an opposite, and SLEEP-PRODUCING, due obviously to the word SOPORIFIC.

161. *BLANCH*, blanch (*blănch*) *v.* To whiten, deprive of color, pale, bleach.

BLANK, which originally meant white, pale, but now empty, vacant, comes from the French masculine *blanc*; while BLANCH, which now means white, pale, comes from the femine *blanche*.

The past, BLANCHED, is thought by 25 per cent to mean LOOKED. To GLANCE, a word of Scandinavian origin, is to LOOK suddenly, snatch a hasty view, direct the vision momentarily. GLANCED is LOOKED; BLANCHED is WHITENED.

To WHITEN a wall is to add a white coating. Both to BLEACH and to BLANCH are to remove color previously present. BLEACHING is chemical, as to BLEACH linen. BLANCHING is a natural process. Celery is BLANCHED or ETIOLATED by excluding the light. Cheeks are BLANCHED by stopping the blood.

162. *GENESIS*, genesis (*jĕn'-ĕ-sĭs*) *n*. Source, production, creation, formation, origin, procreation.

GENESIS comes through the Latin *genesis*, from the Greek γένεσις (*genesis*), origin, source, beginning, nativity, creation. From the Latin comes GENIUS, originally used to mean the spirit of a person, his inborn nature; now more often an exceptional person, one born with rare gifts. From the Greek comes GENEALOGY, family tree, a record of one's ancestors, one's GENESIS.

GENESIS is thought by 20 per cent to mean UPBRINGING, training, education. This is the difference between NATURE and NURTURE. One of the unanswered questions is still how much of each human being is due to his UPBRINGING, his experiences, and how much to his origin, his GENESIS, how much can be taught, and how much should be accepted and used as assets.

163. *RAIMENT*, raiment (*rā'-mĕnt*) *n*. Clothing, vesture, garment, attire, garb, duds, costume, array, habiliments, that in which one is clad (v. B. 17).

RAIMENT, an abbreviation of ARRAYMENT, formerly spelt ARRAIMENT, starts with the verb to ARRAY, to dress, adorn, deck, ornament, decorate, clothe, invest, plus the ending -MENT, from the Latin *mentum*, added to a verb to make the corresponding noun, as: to POSTPONE and POSTPONEMENT; to MANAGE and MANAGEMENT; to ARRANGE and ARRANGEMENT.

RAIMENT is thought by 28 per cent to mean PREPARATION. The noun, an ARRAY, may mean PREPARATION, arrangement, and to ARRAY is to place in order. But RAIMENT, though from ARRAY, means specifically dress, attire, garb, costume, clothing.

164. *GARBLE*, garble (*gahr'-bl*) *v*. To give a false impression, mutilate, corrupt, misquote, misrepresent, falsify, pervert, sophisticate.

GARBLE goes back probably through Spanish to Arabic and Persian words meaning sieve, and originally meant sift, free from dirt and dross, cull out the good. In 1721 Nathan Bailey said: 'To cleanse from dross and dirt; commonly used of spices', and then adds: 'GARBLER of spices, an officer of great antiquity in the City of London, who might enter into any shop, warehouse, etc. to view drugs, spices, etc. and GARBLE them'.

Even a hundred years later Webster said of GARBLE: 'Properly to sift or bolt; to separate into the fine or valuable parts of a substance from the coarse and useless parts, or from dross or dirt'.

GARBLE has completely lost this early sense and came first to mean pick out the best for one's self. Such words as MISQUOTE, MISREPRESENT, and FALSIFY, all imply a dishonest purpose, an intention of doing harm. The background of GARBLE would put it with this group; but GARBLE has come to suggest stupidity, carelessness on the part of the GARBLER, rather than a dishonest intent. To GARBLE is often just to make a mess of.

165. *DEGRADATION*, degradation (dĕg-rǎ-dā'-shŏn) *n.*

Reducing in rank, lowering in grade, debasement, depriving of honor; or from Ephraim Chambers, 1728: 'In our law-books called DISGRADATION, and DEPOSITION, the act of depriving, or stripping a person forever of a dignity, or degree of honour; and taking away the title, badge, and privileges thereof'.

DEGRADATION is a combination of the Latin *de*, down, and *gradus*, a step, pace, also a step in a stair or ladder, from *gradi*, to go, walk, step. From *gressus*, the past participle, come PROGRESS, going ahead, advancement, CONGRESS, walking together, INGRESS, and EGRESS. From the verb *gradi* came INGREDIENT, that which goes in, part of a mixture. The derivation of DEGRADATION from *gradi* is clearer. A GRADE is a step in a stairs, a rung in a ladder. From the Latin *de-*, as in DESCEND, DECLINE, comes the verb to DEGRADE, to put down on a lower step, lower rung of a ladder, and with the Latin *-ation*, added to a verb to form a noun of action, it becomes DEGRADATION.

To 7 per cent DEGRADATION means SPEAKING. A DECLAMATION is a formal speech, oration, SPEAKING rhetorically. To DECLAIM is to speak, orate. To DEGRADE is to lower in rank.

Ephraim Chambers describes: 'In the time of Francis I, the DEGRADATION of Captain Fangel, who had in a cowardly manner given up Fontarabia whereof he was governor'. Fontarabia is a town in northern Spain, on the French frontier, taken and re-taken in wars between France and Spain.

'On this occasion, twenty or thirty cavaliers without blemish or reproach, were assembled; before whom the gentleman was accused of treason, and breach of faith. Two scaffolds were erected; the one for the judges, heralds, and pursuivants; and the other for the guilty cavalier, who was armed at all points. On one side assisted twelve priests, in surplices, who sung the vigils of the dead. At the close of each psalm they made a pause, during which the officers of arms stripped the condemned of some piece of armour, beginning with the helmet. Which done, they broke his shield in three pieces with a hammer.'

166. *ODE*, ode (*ōd*) *n.* A poem written to be sung to music, a lyric poem with the same measures preserved throughout, expressing exalted emotion, composed for an occasion.

Nathan Bailey says: 'A poem sung to the harp', while Webster, 1828, a hundred years after Bailey says: 'A short poem or song, poetical composition proper to be set to music or sung'.

ODE comes from the Greek ᾠδή (*ode*), song, poem, and this in turn from a contraction of ᾀδειν (*odein*), to sing. Originally an ODE was a poem intended to be sung. William Congreve, who wrote about 1700, called by Swinburne the greatest English comic dramatist, says: 'The ODES of Pindar are songs of triumph, victory, or success in the Grecian games'.

According to Ephraim Chambers: 'The distinguishing character of the ODE is sweetness; the poet soothes the minds of his readers by the variety of verse, and the delicacy of words; the beauty of numbers, and the description of things most delightful in themselves. Among the ancients, ODE signified no more than a song. The ancient ODES were generally in honour of their gods, as are many of those of Pindar and Horace. English ODES are generally composed in praise of heroes, and great exploits; as those of Dryden, Prior, etc.'

The Pantologia of John Mason Good says: 'Among modern ODES is Dryden's "On Saint Cecelia's Day".'

167. *SEMIDIURNAL*, semidiurnal (*sĕm-ĭ-dī-ĕr'-năl*) *adj.* Every half day, twelve hours.

DIURNAL comes from the Latin *diurnus*, daily, from *dies*, day, and means daily, pertaining to each day, or sometimes during daylight, an opposite of NOCTURNAL. The word JOURNAL comes from the same source but through the French where it acquired the initial J, and once meant daily; but a JOURNAL is now a day to day record, a DIARY, this last directly from the Latin *diarium*, which in turn comes from *dies*, day.

The only mislead, marked by 10 per cent, is MONTHLY, menstrual, this last from the Latin *mensis*, month. The words SEMI-MONTHLY, twice a month, every half month, and BIMONTHLY, every two months, are used frequently. But SEMIDIURNAL is almost never heard, and DIURNAL itself is more a technical term than literary English.

168. *INCOGITABLE*, incogitable (*ĭn-kŏj'-ĭ-tă-bl*) *adj.* Unthinkable, not to be solved by thought.

To COGITATE is to think earnestly, ponder deeply, consider seriously, reflect, meditate, ruminate, plan, contemplate studiously, from the Latin *cogitare*, a combination of *co-*, with, together, and *agitare*, to drive, move, arouse, excite, shake, the source of AGITATE, and the frequentative of *agere*, to drive, move, do. To COGITATE is to shake up all of one's thoughts together; while COGITABLE, the adjective, is capable of being thought out logically, possible of solution by mental processes. INCOGITABLE is the opposite.

UNTHINKABLE has come to mean unimaginable, impossible of attainment, out of reach as a goal too exalted. INCOGITABLE should not be used in this sense of UNTHINKABLE, unattainable. COGITABLE does not mean capable of being attained, within reach; but susceptible to being thought out logically, capable of being solved by mental processes. INCOGITABLE should be used only in this way, not susceptible to logical thinking.

169. *OBLIVESCENCE*, oblivescence (*ŏb-lĭ-vĕs'-sĕns*) *n.* The state of being forgotten, also the beginning of forgetfulness.

OBLIVESCENCE, from the same source as OBLIVION, state of being forgotten, forgetfulness, and OBLIVIOUS, forgetful, comes from the Latin *oblivius*, forgotten, a combination of *ob*, over, and *livere*, to grow dark, the source of LIVID, black and blue.

The ending -ESCENCE means beginning to be, dictionaries call it INCEPTIVE, beginning, starting, or INCHOATIVE, starting in a slightly different sense, rudimentary, not yet formed. Thus EFFERVESCENCE is starting to boil; DELIQUESCENCE, starting to melt, CONVALESCENCE, starting to get well.

OBLIVION should mean the state of having been forgotten. An author falls into a state of OBLIVION, is no longer remembered. The same word OBLIVION is sometimes used for the forgetfulness of a person, the tendency of an individual not to remember. In this case use FORGETFULNESS, not OBLIVION.

OBSOLESCENCE, going out of use, comes from the Latin *obsolescere*, to wear out, grow old, decay, and this may lead 15 per cent into selecting EXHAUSTION, fatigue, as the synonym of OBLIVESCENCE, beginning to be forgotten.

170. *POTPOURRI*, potpourri (*pō-pōr-rē'*) *n.* Medley, mixture, miscellaneous collection.

POTPOURRI, originally a stew of meat and vegetables cooked together, but now a miscellaneous collection.

POTPOURRI comes directly from the French *pot-pourri;* this last comes from the Latin *putrere*, to rot, the source of PUTRID.

171. *TENTATIVELY*, tentatively (*tĕn'-tă-tĭv-lĭ*) *adv.* Experimentally, probingly, by way of trial, almost cautiously.

At the end of this word, the Anglo-Saxon termination -LY makes an adjective into the corresponding adverb, something which modifies a verb, which tells how one acts. In the phrase: 'A TENTATIVE approach', the adjective TENTATIVE modifies the noun APPROACH. But in: 'He approached TENTATIVELY', the adverb TENTATIVELY modifies the verb APPROACH. The correct answer, PROVISIONALLY, is the adverb from PROVISION, from the Latin *pro*, forward, and *videre*, to see, which once meant foresight. But PROVISIONALLY has come to mean for the time being, for the moment only, with little suggestion of testing or trying.

TENTATIVELY, from the Latin *tentativus*, trying, testing, comes from *tentare*, to try, test, touch, feel, handle. This verb, *tentare*, to try, is the frequentative of *tentere*, to stretch, the source of TENT, a noun, a stretched cloth. TENTATIVELY suggests probingly, experimentally. The only mislead chosen is POLITELY.

172. *UNGUENT*, unguent (*ŭn'-gwĕnt*) *n.* Salve, any ointment of soft composition for lubrication.

An UNGUENT is thought by 15 per cent to be an URGENCY, ending in the Latin -CY, sometimes used with abstract nouns in place of the more common -CE. URGENT, the adjective, comes from the Latin *urgens, urgentis,* the present participle of *urgere,* to push, press, force, drive. To URGE is to push forward, force onward; while URGENT, much like UNGUENT in appearance, means pressing, demanding attention.

UNGUENT comes from the Latin *unguentum,* ointment, from the verb *ungere,* to smear, anoint, the source of UNCTION, rubbing with oil as a symbol of consecration to a holy office. From the same source, more indirectly, come ANOINT and OINTMENT. UNCTUOUS, originally the adjective, has come to be used of persons, to mean greasy, oily, too smooth, excessively suave, falsely devoted. To ANOINT is to pour oil on, a religious rite. An OINTMENT is an UNGUENT, salve.

173. *BALE,* bale (*bāl*) *n.* A heavy package, carton, large bundle held together with wires or metal hoops, generally soft and different from a box or crate.

A BALE is a large bundle made ready for shipment, and this leads 15 per cent into selecting SHIPMENT as the meaning of BALE. SHIPMENT, sending, transportation and safe delivery, is the purpose of a BALE.

A BUNDLE, from Dutch and German words meaning to bind, is a number of things tied together. A PACKAGE is tighter and more compact, things made into a pack. A CRATE, from the Latin *cratis,* wicker work, is today a packing case made of wooden slats, but was formerly a basket or wicker-work case. A BALE, which goes back through Old French to the same source as BALL, is big, heavy, soft, and held together by metal bindings.

174. *DIGIT,* digit (*dĭj'-ĭt*) *n.* Finger, toe, one of the first nine numbers.

DIGIT comes from the Latin *digitus,* a finger, a toe, also a finger's breadth. DIGIT is thought by 38 per cent to mean IMPLEMENT, from the Latin *implere,* to fill up, a combination of *in-,* and *plere,* to fill, the source of COMPLETE, to fill to the full, and DEPLETE, to un-fill, use up. An IMPLEMENT is a tool, utensil, piece of equipment. To DIG is to make a hole in the ground with a shovel, and this might conceivably suggest IMPLEMENT. The word DIGIT, to mean finger, should be recognized but rarely used.

175. *INHIBIT*, inhibit (ĭn-hĭb'-ĭt) v. To block, hold back, hinder, check, repress, slow down, stop for a moment.

HABIT, the noun, comes from the Latin, *habitus*, condition, appearance, dress, from *habere*, to have, hold, keep, the source of a long string of English words. From *habitare*, to live, dwell, the frequentative of *habere*, to have, comes INHABIT, to dwell, which misleads 25 per cent to believe that INHIBIT means LIVE IN, a justified translation of the Latin. But even in Latin *inhibere*, from the same *habere*, to have, hold, but spelt with I instead of A, meant to hold back, restrain. From the same general source come EXHIBIT, to hold out, offer, show, present, place on view; and PROHIBIT, to forbid, interdict, stop completely. To INHIBIT is to use influence against, block, make difficult, hinder, in one of its senses, for HINDER is used to mean both PROHIBIT and INHIBIT.

176. *AMALGAM*, amalgam (ă-măl'-găm) n. Technically, any alloy of mercury; loosely, any mixture (v. B. 35), combination of different things.

AMALGAM is thought by 32 per cent to mean ELEMENTS, a confusion of part with the whole. According to Nathan Bailey, 1721: 'ELEMENTS, among Natural Philosophers and Chymists are the simplest Bodies that can be, neither made of one another nor of anything else, but of which all things are made'. The element mercury unites with all other metals to form AMALGAMS.

AMALGAM, ALLOY, SOLUTION, and COMPOUND are technical terms unexpectedly difficult to define sharply. All are combinations of ELEMENTS. A COMPOUND is a combination in exact proportions, in which the combining ELEMENTS lose their own identity. AMALGAMS, ALLOYS, and SOLUTIONS are all mixtures in which the combining ELEMENTS may exist in gradually varying proportions and retain their own identities. A SOLUTION is ordinarily liquid. An ALLOY is much like a SOLUTION, but solid. An AMALGAM is an ALLOY in which one of the combining ELEMENTS is mercury.

177. *SEQUENTIAL*, sequential (sē-kwĕn'-shal), adj. Arranged in order, successive, coming one after another in line.

The adjective SEQUENTIAL, directly from the noun SEQUENCE, an orderly succession, one following another, as a chronological

SEQUENCE, based often on time, comes from the Latin *sequi*, to follow, and emphasizes not only orderly arrangement, but linear, one item after another in a row. SUBSEQUENT, starting with SUB-, which sometimes means after, stresses the position, coming after, following, succeeding, in contrast to PRECEDING, coming before.

From the same *sequi*, to follow, comes CONSEQUENTIAL, following as a result, from cause to effect. From the same *sequi* come such different words as EXECUTE and EXECUTIVE, PROSE-CUTE, SEQUESTER, OBSEQUIES, and ENSUE.

178. *METHODICAL*, methodical (*mĕ-thŏd'-ĭ-kăl*) *adj*. Systematic, orderly, neat, tidy, regulated, arranged.

ALPHABETICAL, selected by 7 per cent, is one manner of METHODICAL arrangement. The usual dictionary is in ALPHABETICAL order, starting with words beginning with A. This book arranges the same words in order of difficulty, starting with the easiest.

METHODICAL, from the Greek μέθοδος (*methodos*), a going after, pursuit, inquiring, comes from METHOD, a combination of μετά (*meta*), after, and οδός (*odos*), way, road. METHODICAL is placing things one after another, in order.

Bailey says: 'METHOD is an apt disposition of things, or a placing them in their natural order so as to be easiest understood or retained'. Webster, a hundred years later, says: 'Arranged in convenient order, disposed in a just and natural manner to facilitate practical operations.'

179. *PHANTOM*, phantom (*făn'-tŏm*) *n*. Ghost, apparition, ethereal being, specter, appearance, delusion, fancied vision, optical illusion.

PHANTOM comes through the Latin from the Greek φάντασμα (*phantasma*), appearance, vision, phantom.

FANCY and FANTASTIC, from the Greek φαντασία (*phantasia*), appearance, look, imagination, image, impression, both start with F, as in French, Spanish, and Italian. PHENOMENON, from a similar Greek source, starts with PH. PHANTOM was once spelt in English with F, fantom, but has been changed to PH.

According to Fowler who, in his Modern English Usage, quotes the Oxford English Dictionary, there are two separate words FANTASY and PHANTASY, identical in sound and ultimate etymology, but with different modern meanings. A FANTASY, starting with F, is a caprice, a fanciful notion. Of the three: PHANTASY, PHANTASM, and PHANTOM, the first is the least abnormal, perhaps because of its association with FANTASY. A PHANTASM (făn'-tăzm) is an unreal vision usually of a scene, of several objects. A PHANTOM is an unreal vision of a single object.

180. *BARNACLE*, barnacle (bahr'-nă-kl) n. A tiny crustacean, which hangs in clusters fouling the bottom of ships, a kind of shellfish which attach themselves to driftwood and to timber that lies in seawater. From this a BARNACLE is sometimes anything which holds on tenaciously.

To 12 per cent BARNACLES are ROCK PLANTS, an excellent description for, at low levels, plants and animals are nearly indistinguishable. Technically, in animals, the cell wall is nitrogenous; in plants, cellulose. But their fundamental characteristics are identical; and BARNACLES, as adults, are sedentary, attached, much like plants. According to Huxley, in his Anatomy of Invertebrates: 'A BARNACLE may be said to be a crustacean fixed by its head and kicking food into its mouth with its legs'. They do not move about, but in 1830 J. Vaughan Thompson demonstrated their development from free-swimming crustacean larvae; and in strict systems of classification BARNACLES are CRUSTACEANS, belonging to the same family as lobsters, crayfish, crabs, prawns, and shrimp.

The name BARNACLE, and similar words in French, Portuguese, Italian, and Danish, all come fabulously from the BERNICLE GOOSE, a bird which winters in Britain but nests in the Arctic. Before its origin was known the BERNICLE GOOSE was supposed to come miraculously from the fruit of a tree, which fell to the ground and turned into a goose. As this was always near the sea, BARNACLE came to mean shellfish.

181. *NARCOSE*, narcose (nahr'-kōs) adj. Benumbed, unconscious, stupefied, under the effects of drugs.

NARCOSIS and NARCOTIC, each letter by letter from the Greek, are real words, NARCOSIS (năhr-kō'-sĭs) coming from νάρκωσις (narcosis), a benumbing, stupefying; and the noun NARCOTIC, from ναρκωτικός (*narcoticos*), a making numb, rendering unconscious. NARCOSIS is the stupefying effect, the condition; NARCOTIC is that which produces the effect, renders one unconscious. The corresponding verb in Greek is ναρκοῦν (*narcoun*), to benumb, to render one unconscious; and in English to NARCOTIZE.

NARCOSE should be the adjective but seems a bit factitious, made up, artificial, starting with Greek and ending Latin, -OSE, an alternate form of the Latin *ous*.

To 12 per cent NARCOSE means DRUNKEN. The external effects are much the same. But DRUNKENNESS is limited ordinarily to the effects of alcohol; while NARCOTICS are more often drugs.

182. *DERELICT*, derelict (*dĕr'-ĕ-lĭkt*) *n*. Anything which is abandoned, goods thrown away, specifically a vessel abandoned at sea.

DERELICT comes from the Latin *derelictus*, the past participle of *derelinquere*, to foresake utterly, a combination of *de*, and *relinquere*, the source of RELINQUISH and RELICT, survivor, one who is left behind, as a widow.

LANDS, selected by 12 per cent, is actually correct, for the same word DERELICT is used of LAND left dry by a change in a water course.

183. *CANTANKEROUS*, cantankerous (*kăn-tănk'-ĕ-rŭs*) *adj*. Ill-tempered, contentious (v. B. 1666), ill-natured, waspish, mulish, ornery, difficult to get along with.

CANTANKEROUS goes back through Middle English perhaps to the same source as CONTENTIOUS, tending to fight, given to wrangling, combative (*kŏm'-bă-tĭv*), pugnacious.

CANTANKEROUS is thought by 19 per cent of high-school students to mean SPITEFUL, malicious, desiring harm, venomous, revengeful. Marked by 7 per cent of high-vocabulary examinees, SPITEFUL is perhaps too close for a mislead. But SPITE is deep-seated, always present, whereas the CANTANKEROUS person may be delightful at heart, but in a rebellious mood only for the moment.

From Oliver Goldsmith's She Stoops to Conquer, published in 1774, an amusing play which ought to be read by every high-school student both for background and enjoyment, comes:

'There's not a more bitter, CANTANKEROUS toad in all Christendom'. And from the same period from The Rivals, 1775, by Richard Brinsley Sheridan: 'I hope, Mr. Falkland, as there are three of us come on purpose for the game you won't be so CANTANKEROUS as to spoil the party by sitting out'.

184. *CONSTRAINT*, constraint (*kŏn-strănt'*) *n.* Violent compulsion, forceful pushing ahead, necessity, drive, coercion (V. B. 1267).

Both CONSTRAINT and RESTRAINT, with the corresponding verbs to CONSTRAIN, to oblige by force, and RESTRAIN, come from the Latin *stringĕre*, to tie, bind, close up. The modern spelling with -AI- started in France.

'All CONSTRAINT vanished' is thought by 29 per cent to mean INSPIRATION, awakening of thought, creation of purpose, intellectual exaltation, an opposite of RESTRAINT, hindrance to action of any kind, physical or mental, a forceful holding back, repression, restriction, limitation, checking, stopping.

CONSTRAINT is an irresistible force compelling action, a necessity, pushing ahead, driving on almost with violence, and so, often, an INSPIRATION.

185. *DEDUCE*, deduce (*dē-dūs'*) *v.* Conclude as a result, draw as a conclusion, infer (V. B. 1868) from what is known or assumed.

DEDUCE is thought by 36 per cent to mean TAKE AWAY, subtract, deduct. DEDUCE and DEDUCT come from the Latin *deducĕre*, to lead away, draw away, a combination of *de*, down, away, and *ducĕre*, to lead, the verb often selected in Latin grammars to illustrate the third conjugation, and so pronounced (*du'-kă-rā*). To CONDUCE (*kŏn-dūs'*) and to CONDUCT, both from the same *ducĕre*, have today different meanings. To CONDUCT is to lead, guide, direct someone. To CONDUCE is to lead in a more intangible way to a conclusion.

Originally DEDUCE and DEDUCT meant the same: to lead forth, CONDUCT; but this meaning is obsolete and with time DEDUCE and DEDUCT have parted. To DEDUCT now means take away mathematically, subtract; while DEDUCE means to draw a conclusion from what is already known.

186. *DOOM*, doom (*doom*) *n.* Judgment, fate, destiny, decision, decree, sentence, condemnation.

Doom goes directly back to an Anglo-Saxon word for judgment, sentence, decree. Destiny is often dependent upon a discernible cause. Fate is stronger. Doom is an unhappy destiny, more directly dependent on some personal action.

The popular mislead is warning, selected by 7 per cent. A warning comes in advance, with time to take action. Doom is final.

187. *HOMAGE*, homage (*hŏm'-ăj*) *n.* Adoration, reverence, obeisance, fealty, obedience, respect paid by external action. Of the pronunciation Thomas Sheridan, who was father of Richard Sheridan, in his dictionary of 1790, the first to include pronunciation, gives (*hŏm'-ĭdzh*); the Century Dictionary, a hundred years later, gives (*hŏm'-ăj* or *ŏm'-ăj*); but Phyfe in 18,000 Words Often Mispronounced says clearly: (*hŏm'-ăj*, not *ŏm'-ăj*).

The big mislead is gift, thought by 10 per cent to be a synonym of homage. There is much in common between the two words. Real homage is almost a gift.

Nathan Bailey says: 'Homage is the submission, promise, and oath of loyalty and service, which a tenant makes to his lord, when he is at first admitted to the land, which he holds of the lord in fee: Also that which is owing to the king or any superior'. He continues: 'Homage is where a man and his ancestors, have time out of mind held their land of the Lord and his ancestors by homage.'

188. *WINCE*, wince (*wĭns*) *v.* To shrink, flinch, jerk as in pain, start back involuntarily.

Make-faces is chosen by 20 per cent as the meaning of wince. To grimace (*grĭ-mās'*) applies to the face and may be an involuntary expression of pain, or a distortion of the countenance in disgust, a wry face. To flinch is to give way to fear, to shrink back partly unconsciously. Wince, which goes back to Old French, with similar words in German, rarely applies to the face but is more often a sudden jerk of the whole body and passes immediately.

189. *BACILLUS*, bacillus (*bă-sĭl'-lŭs*), *plural BACILLI* (*bă-sĭl'-lī*) *n*. Micro-organism.

BACTERIA, a general term for microscopic vegetable organisms, is the plural of BACTERIUM (*băk-tē'-rĭ-ŭm*). There are three forms: SPIRILLUM, spiral shaped; COCCUS (*kŏk'-kŭs*), from the Greek κόκκος (*coccos*), a berry, and so round; and BACILLUS, rod-shaped. BACILLUS comes from the Latin *bacillum*, a little rod, the diminutive of *baculum*, a stick, staff.

Despite the technical nature of the word BACILLUS, the meaning MICRO-ORGANISM is selected by almost everyone who has taken this difficult form of the vocabulary tests.

190. *DIGNITY*, dignity (*dĭg'-nĭ-tĭ*) *n*. Excellence (v. b. 64), nobleness (v. b. 232), worthiness, stateliness, majesty, eminence, loftiness, worth.

DIGNITY is thought by 19 per cent to mean COURAGE, fearlessness, fortitude, daring, hardihood, spirit, pluck, valor. Of these words, COURAGE is a spirit which enables one to face danger with full presence of mind and so is the nearest to NOBLENESS and to DIGNITY in its pleasantest sense.

DIGNITY and DAINTY are doublets, both coming from the Latin *dignus*, worthy, DAINTY indirectly from a Middle English word which meant honor, worth, and this in turn, through Old French, from the Latin *dignitas*, *dignitatis*, the direct source of the English word DIGNITY. DAINTY has lost all suggestion of this original honor, and now means delicate, fragile, pretty; while DIGNITY, although still meaning NOBLENESS, tends to suggest the outward appearance of NOBLENESS.

From Anthony Trollope: 'Dr. Thorne, though a graduated physician, though entitled beyond all dispute to call himself a doctor, made it known that his rate of pay was to be seven-and-sixpence a visit, and he would lug out half-a-crown from his breeches pocket in change, low, mean, unprofessional, and democratic. The man had no appreciation of the DIGNITY of a learned profession.'

191. *RENEGADE*, renegade (*rĕn'-ĕ-gād*) *n*. One who deserts a party, apostate, proselyte, convert, backslider, turncoat, deserter, traitor, one who abandons a religious faith.

RENEGADE, spelt with D, comes directly from Spanish. The earlier word, spelt with T, RENEGATE, is a combination of the Latin *re-*, and *negare*, to deny.

RENEGADE is thought by 42 per cent of those who have taken this vocabulary test to mean INDIAN WARRIOR, compared with only 39 per cent who prefer TRAITOR. Of those who score otherwise high vocabulary, 83 per cent select TRAITOR as the meaning, as opposed to only 17 per cent who want INDIAN WARRIOR.

RENEGADE and APOSTATE, the first Latin, the second Greek, both emphasize deserting a cause, leaving a faith. PROSELYTE may be used of the same person but stresses not so much leaving the old as joining the new.

192. *AMATORY*, amatory (*ăm'-ă-tō-rĭ*) *adj*. Loving, passionate, ardent, amorous, tender, enamored.

AMATORY, from *amatus*, loved, the past participle of *amare*, to love, is interpreted by 32 per cent of high-school students as IRREGULAR, compared with only 27 per cent who select the traditional meaning LOVING. An ANOMALY (*ă-nŏm'-ă-lĭ*) is an IRREGULARITY, something which departs from the ordinary, from the rule.

Despite the general acceptance by grammarians of the Latin verb *amo*, I love, to illustrate the first conjugation, because of its regularity, or a mistaken notion that it is easy, it would be wiser pedagogy to pick a verb from which comes a better known English word, and especially one not believed by a majority to mean IRREGULAR.

By another 23 per cent AMATORY is thought to mean INDIFFERENT, the final step in learning a new vocabulary word, the confusion of opposites.

193. *PREROGATIVE*, prerogative (*prē-rŏg'-ă-tĭv*) *n*. A peculiar privilege, special quality, characteristic right, exclusive privilege inherent in one's position.

The Latin *rogare* is to ask, and appears in the English verb INTERROGATE, to ask questions, examine, inquire. The verb *rogare* was not only to ask questions, but was to ask for the passage of a law, propose that it be enacted; and from this comes ABROGATE, to call back, annul, cancel, repeal a law.

The Latin *prorogare* was to prolong, extend, protract, continue, defer, put off; and so in English to PROROGUE is to put off meetings for a definite length of time.

PREROGATIVE, from the Latin *prae*, before, and *rogare*, to ask, originally meant asked to vote first, called upon to vote before others. Then PREROGATIVE came to mean having the right to vote first, hence any special right, special privilege.

Nathan Bailey says: 'A peculiar pre-eminence, or authority above the others or a special privilege'. The King's PREROGATIVES are those rights of Majesty which are peculiar to him and inseparable from his person.

194. *LAMENTATION*, lamentation (lăm-ĕn-tā'-shŏn) *n*. Expression of grief, sad complaint, bewailing, moaning, wailing, plaint, lament, repining, mourning, sounds of grief, sorrowful outcries.

LAMENTATION comes from the Latin *lamentari*, to weep, from *lamentum*, ordinarily in the plural *lamenta*, a wailing related to Greek and Russian words for snarl, scold, and bark, all noisy.

To 7 per cent LAMENTATION means BUILDING, suggested perhaps by LAMINATION, a term used in geology to mean built up of layers, of LAMINA, of thin sheets or plates.

GRIEF is deep quiet sorrow. MOURNING is quiet but apparent, seen by others but not heard. LAMENTATION is noisy.

195. *RACK*, rack (răk') *v*. To torture by violent stretching, strain on the rack or wheel, as to RACK a criminal or suspected person to extort a confession.

The noun RACK, a torturing engine, is used to force a confession from an offender.

RACKING goes back to an Anglo-Saxon word for stretch, and may be used not merely to mean torture, but stretch, pull, draw. One hears it today in the phrase: 'RACK one's brain'.

196. *GOADING*, goading (gō'-dĭng) *n*. Prodding, spurring, arousing, stirring up, stimulating (V. B. 458), driving, urging, instigating, rousing to action.

A STIMULUS, from Latin; a PROD, perhaps from Gaelic and Icelandic; and a GOAD, directly from Anglo-Saxon; are all sharp pointed sticks used in driving oxen. To STIMULATE, to PROD (*prŏd*), and to GOAD, are all to drive ahead by pricking.

GOADING is thought by 14 per cent to mean ASSISTANT, helper, attendant, one who aids. The verb to ASSIST comes from the Latin *ad-*, to, and *sistĕre*, to stand, from *stare*, to stand. An ASSISTANT, a helper, attendant, is one who stands ready to aid, not ordinarily one who drives, prods, GOADS.

By another 14 per cent, GOADING is thought to mean WAILING. Both GROANING and MOANING, similar in sound to GOADING, suggest WAILING, but GOADING is urging ahead.

197. *OMNISCIENT*, omniscient (*ŏm-nĭsh'-ĕnt*) *adj*. All-knowing, with infinite knowledge of all things, having universal information.

OMNISCIENT combines the Latin *omnis*, all, with *sciens, scientis*, knowing, the source of SCIENCE. OMNI- appears in OMNIVOROUS (*ŏm-nĭ'-vor-ūs*), eating everything, devouring food of all kinds; in OMNIPRESENT (*ŏm-nĭ-prĕs'-ĕnt*), seen everywhere; and in OMNIPOTENT (*ŏm-nĭ'-pō-tĕnt*), all powerful.

SCIENCE originally meant knowledge, comprehension of facts, understanding of principles, as in OMNISCIENT.

198. *AMPUTATE*, amputate (*ăm'-pū-tāt*) *v*. To cut off, lop off, prune, cut away.

AMPUTATE comes from the Latin *am*, which stands for *ambi*, around, and *putare*, which means to lop, prune, trim, from *putus*, pure, clean. The Latin word *amputare* was used especially of plants and meant to prune. AMPUTATE is used at present primarily in a medical sense, to cut off an arm or a leg, usually to prevent a disease from spreading to the rest of the body.

The correct meaning of AMPUTATE is known to everyone who has taken the easy vocabulary test in which this word appears. Thus far no one has marked a wrong answer. Why should AMPUTATE be so familiar? Perhaps because it has appeared with a clear-cut meaning in almost every dictionary for more than two hundred years. Perhaps because it goes back to agriculture, and so early civilization. Nathan Bailey, who published a Dictionary in 1721, says: 'AMPUTATE, to cut off, in gardening, to lop or prune', the original meaning of the word.

199. *RHETORIC*, rhetoric (*rĕt'-ō-rĭk*) *n.* The art of all literary uses of language in prose and verse; from Nathan Bailey, 1721: 'The art of speaking well and elegantly'; and according to the Pantologia of 1813: 'The art of speaking copiously with all the advantages of beauty and force'; and from Webster, 1828: 'The art of speaking with propriety, elegance, and force'. RHETORIC goes back to the Latin *rhetorica*, to the Greek ῥητορική (*rhetorice*), an adjective pertaining to a speaker, from ῥήτωρ (*rhetor*), a speaker, orator. RHETORIC, which includes both composition and delivery, is the art of discourse, using language so as to influence the mind, imagination, and emotion of others.

200. *CANKERED*, cankered (*kăn'-kĕrd*) *adj.* Ill-natured, cross, crabbed, malignant, uncivil, peevish, perverse, morose.
CANKER comes through the Anglo-Saxon *cancer*, from the Latin *cancer*, a crab, the direct source of CRABBED. CANCER (*kăn'-sĕr*), spelt with c, is sometimes another word for crab, with no unpleasant suggestion. CANCER is also one of the constellations, a sign of the zodiac, of the summer solstice. A CANCER, still spelt in the same way, may also be a malignant tumor. Spelt with k, CANKER, the word is always unpleasant, an ulcerous sore, an infection. Of CANKERED, Bailey says: 'Eaten with rust, or the canker. "A CANKERED fellow" a cross, ill-conditioned fellow.'
To 5 per cent CANKERED means AGREEABLE, a confusion of opposites, the final step in learning.

201. *PINIONED*, pinioned (*pĭn'-yŭnd*) *adj.* Held fast, bound, restrained, confined, shackled, fettered, manacled.
To 14 per cent PINIONED means ENSLAVED, the third step in learning, a confusion of words close in meaning but with different overtones. To ENSLAVE, literally to make a slave of, reduce to slavery, put under a yoke, is to subjugate to the will of the master and suggests a more or less permanent, perhaps mental condition. One may be PINIONED, held fast, by a fallen rock or heavy beam, without the restraint affecting one's will.
CHAINED, MANACLED, SHACKLED, FETTERED, and GYVED (*jīvd*), called archaic, used by Shakespeare and Ben Jonson and hardly since, are all CHAINED in various ways. A MANACLE is a HANDCUFF, an instrument for holding the hand or hands. To FETTER,

an Anglo-Saxon word, means to chain a person or an animal, usually to a post, in order to restrict movement.

A PINION, from the Latin *penna*, is a feather, wing, especially a flight feather. To PINION is literally to bind the wings of a bird, restrain, confine, and from this to bind the arms of a person.

202. *COVENANT*, covenant (*kŭv'-ĕn-ănt*) *n*. Mutual agreement, compact, contract, promise.

To CONVENE, from *con-*, together, and *venire*, to come, is in English to come together, assemble, customarily for some important purpose. A CONVENTION is the noun, a coming together. The Latin *convenire* meant not only to come together physically, in the sense of assemble, but also to come together mentally, and so agree. From this comes CONVENIENT, agreeable, and its doublet COVENANT, spelt years ago with an N, *convenant*, and then shortened by someone to COVENANT.

The mislead JUDGMENT, selected by 13 per cent, is intimately involved. Both a JUDGMENT and a COVENANT demand careful thought. Both are decisions. A JUDGMENT is the decision of one individual; a COVENANT is an agreement between two or more persons.

Of a COVENANT Bailey, 1721, says: 'An agreement or bargain, the mutual consent of two or more to one thing, to do or give somewhat'. In 1828 Webster says: 'A mutual consent, or agreement of two parties to do or to forbear some act or thing; a contract; stipulation. A COVENANT is created by deed in writing, sealed, and executed; or it may be implied in the contract. Literally a coming together; a meeting or agreement of mind.'

203. *HECTIC*, hectic (*hĕk'-tĭk*) *adj*. Feverish, febrile, consumptive, affected by fever.

QUESTIONING, interrogating, investigating, querying, asking, the only popular mislead, chosen by 11 per cent, is obviously the word to HECKLE. Although HECKLE means badger, annoy, torment, harass, keep at, the word is used so often of HECKLING a speaker, that it has come to be used for QUESTION annoyingly, severely, in an antagonistic manner.

HECTIC, from the Greek ἐκτικός (*hecticos*), habitual, from ἕξις (*hexis*), habit, from ἔχειν (*hechein*), to have, originally referred to something possessed, and meant habitual, customary, enduring. HECTIC has now lost all semblance of this original meaning, and means possessing an habitual flush due to fever, and so feverish. HECTIC is also used often to mean FEVERISH in a figurative sense: excited, confused, frenzied.

204. *INCURSION*, incursion (*ĭn-ker′-shŏn*) *n.* Hostile invasion, literally an inroad, running in, sudden attack, raid, intrusion, foray, hasty expedition into a region to plunder or destroy.

The Century Dictionary gives IRRUPTION as a synonym. An ERUPTION, from *rumpere*, to break, is the bursting out of a volcano; an IRRUPTION is a breaking in.

In one experiment, an INCURSION was thought by 22 per cent to be a REVERSAL. A REVERSAL, from the Latin *revertere*, to turn back, a combination of *re-*, back, and *vertere*, to turn, is a changing of position, in an alternate direction. An INVERSION, much like INCURSION in sound, and from the same *vertere*, to turn, is a turning upside down, or end for end, and so a REVERSAL.

INCURSION comes from the Latin *incurrere*, literally to run in, a combination of *in*, and *currere*, to run. From this same *currere*, to run, comes also EXCURSION, literally a running out, from the Latin *ex-*, out, and *currere*, to run, originally a destructive raid, sally in search of booty, but now a pleasure trip, jaunt, short journey, enjoyable expedition, day's outing.

205. *COMPEER*, compeer (*kŏm-pēr′*), *n.* An equal, especially a companion, associate, one who is the peer of another, of equal rank.

Though the word PEER has become the title of a nobleman, and in this sense is thought of as one higher up, a PEER, from the Latin *par*, equal, is in reality an equal, one of the same rank.

To 12 per cent, COMPEER means ASSISTANT, helper, usually one under another, lower down.

The word ASSOCIATE is general, implying an alliance of some permanence. A COLLEAGUE is an associate specifically for some particular purpose, or in some office. The word COMPEER emphasizes an equal, perhaps more than any of the other words, some one at the same level of understanding.

206. *CLIME*, clime (*klīm*) *n.* A tract of land, region, area, zone, belt of the earth's surface.

Both CLIME and CLIMATE come from the Latin *clima*, from the Greek κλίμα (*clima*), κλίματις (*climatis*), zone, area, belt of the earth, distinct portion of the earth's surface.

Today CLIMATE means so specifically temperature, and weather conditions in general, that it demands a mental effort to realize that originally CLIMATE meant region, zone, an area which changed with the growing knowledge of the earth's form. Once a CLIMATE was a zone measured by lines parallel to the equator. There were twenty-four between the equator and the pole. At another period the width of a CLIMATE depended on time; in traveling north or south the duration of daylight differed by half an hour from top to bottom of a zone.

To almost everyone CLIMATE now means hot, cold, rain, or shine; while the short form CLIME has retained the earlier suggestion of zone. REGION is selected by 72 per cent.

207. *SUBJUGATION*, subjugation (*sŭb-jū-gā'-shŏn*) *n.* Slavery, subjection, submission, subserviency, under bondage, captivity. See SUBJUGATE, *v.* (V. B. 671).

To 35 per cent of those tested SUBJUGATION means ISOLATION, solitude, loneliness, a word which comes through French from the Latin *insula*, island. SEGREGATION, from the Latin *grex*, *gregis*, flock, is separation from the flock, a setting apart, and so ISOLATION, living on an island. SUBJUGATION comes from the Latin *sub-*, under, and *jugum*, yoke, the source of CONJUGAL, pertaining to marriage, and CONJUGATION, an assemblage of verb forms. SUBJUGATION is by derivation putting under a yoke, conquering, vanquishing, subduing, compelling to submit.

This confusion of two words so much alike in sound must add alarmingly to the bitter resentment of those who are SEGREGATED, separated, and believe they are SUBJUGATED, enslaved.

208. *HOODWINK*, hoodwink (*hŏod'-wĭnk*) *v.* To blind by covering the eyes, blindfold, to blind mentally, deceive, beguile (V. B. 1506).

A HOOD, from various Anglo-Saxon words meaning HAT and HELMET, is more than a HAT, for it covers the back of the neck and at times even the shoulders, and, in falconry, the entire head; for a falcon or hawk is HOODED to blind it until the quarry is in position to be pursued when the HOOD is removed.

To WINK is to close and open the eyelids quickly, so as to be blind for a moment, as 'To WINK at' so as not to see something which is going on. To HOODWINK a person is both to BLIND him and to cause him to miss seeing what is going on.

HOODWINKED is thought by 20 per cent to mean CAGED, confined. HOODED might suggest CAGED or at least CONFINED but HOODWINKED is not merely blinded but deceived, duped, beguiled, cheated, fooled, cozened, gulled, deluded.

209. *ESSENCE*, essence (ĕs'-sĕns) *n*. Inward nature, true substance, essential (v. B. 152) element, the idea of a thing.
ESSENCE is thought by 34 per cent to mean GOAL, post set up to indicate the end of a race, or object in a game, and so final purpose in life, end, aim, termination.

ESSENCE, from the Latin *essentia*, being, made from the verb *esse*, to be, is the inner substance, conception, being, the idea.

Noah Webster in the first edition of An American Dictionary of the English Language, 1828, says of ESSENCE: 'That which constitutes the particular nature of a being or substance, or of a genus, and which distinguishes it from all others'.

210. *PALAVER*, palaver (pă-lah'-ver) *v*. To talk idly, discuss, confer, parley, prattle, speak plausibly.
To 9 per cent PALAVER means HUNT FOOD. To FORAGE is specifically to search for food, HUNT FOOD, to collect fodder from the territory of an enemy.

To PRATTLE is harmless, simple-minded. To PALAVER is to talk too long, unnecessarily, with intent to deceive by flattery.

The word PALAVER comes directly from the Portuguese *palvra*, talk, speech, word, and the Century Dictionary says: 'Seems to have been picked up by the English on the west coast of Africa where Portuguese was the chief language'.

211. *TABOO*, taboo (tă-boo') *adj*. Forbidden, interdicted, set apart, under ban, prohibited, excluded from use, not allowed. Also spelt TABU. Used by South Pacific Polynesians.

In the test phrase: 'Such things were TABOO', the word is marked correctly by 100 per cent of those who have thus far taken this form. For some time it has seemed that the difficulty of a word is not the difficulty of the word itself, perhaps its length, but depends on the difficulty of the idea which the word names. The word TABOO is not common, but the idea: 'Don't touch', 'Don't do that', is one of the first instilled in a child's mind.

The word TABOO was introduced into the language as an adjective, a noun, and a verb, in 1775 by Cook, Voyage to the Pacific. James Cook, born in 1728, in Yorkshire, England, entered the navy as an able seaman at the age of 27. Four years later he sailed for America where he surveyed the channel of the St. Lawrence River and the coast of Newfoundland and Labrador. At the age of 40 he commanded the Endeavor which carried a party of scientists to Tahiti to observe the transit of Venus. During this voyage, which lasted three years, he explored New Zealand and the east coast of Australia. On returning he was raised to the rank of Commander and set off again for another three years to explore the Pacific. On his return later to the Sandwich Islands he was murdered by the natives.

From Cook, Voyage to the Pacific at Tongalaboo: 'Not one of them would sit down or eat a bit of anything. On expressing my surprise at this, they were all TABOO, as they said; which word has a very comprehensive meaning; but, in general, signifies that a thing is forbidden. Why they were laid under such restraint at present, was not explained.'

Later, he said, when anything is forbidden to be eaten or made use of, they say that it is TABOO.

212. *CRAVAT*, cravat (*kră-văt'*) *n.* A necktie, neckcloth, a piece of silk or other material worn about the neck.
CRAVAT comes directly from the French *cravate*. According to Gilles Menage, in 1636, the name came from the Croats in the French military service.

213. *BARD*, bard (*băhrd*) *n.* Poet, singer, among the ancient Celts composer of music, strolling minstrel.
To 3 per cent BARD, a word of Celtic origin, means PROTECTOR, perhaps a confusion of BARD with GUARD, words much alike in

sound, the first step in learning. A GUARD is a PROTECTOR, one who shelters, shields another from danger, defends against harm.

From Bailey comes: 'The BARDS were ancient poets among the Gauls and Britons, who described and sung in verse the brave actions of the great men of their nation'. Chambers adds: 'With design to inculcate and recommend virtue, and even sometimes to put an end to the differences between armies at the point of engagement. The BARDS differed from the DRUIDS in that the latter were priests and teachers of the nation but the former only poets and writers.'

214. *SUNDRY*, sundry (*sŭn'-drĭ*) *adj*. Various, divers, several, more than one or two, miscellaneous.

SUNDRY comes directly from an Anglo-Saxon word for APART, separate, the source of SUNDER, to separate, divide, part, sever.

215. *MEANDERING*, meandering (*mē-ăn'-dĕr-ĭng*) *n*. Wandering, winding, proceeding by turning to and fro like a river.

MEANDER comes through Latin from the Greek μαίανδρος (*maiandros*), a winding, from the river MEANDER, which flows into the Aegean Sea near Miletus.

DREAMING, the only popular mislead, is almost correct, for the word to DREAM used figuratively means suppose indefinitely, think idly, MEANDER in one's thoughts.

216. *METTLE*, mettle (*mĕt'-tl*) *n*. Strength, courage, spirit, ardor, enthusiasm.

METTLE is a vernacular spelling of METAL, and pronounced like METAL. Both come from the Latin *metallum*, a mine, any mineral, from the Greek μέταλλον (*metallon*), a mine, pit, cave, quarry.

In the first form of this vocabulary test, examinees divided almost equally between STRENGTH and VALOR as synonyms, 40 per cent for the first and 24 for the second. METTLE is a combination of the two. It is both physical strength and valor.

217. *CONTEMPLATE*, contemplate (*kŏn'-tĕm-plāt*) *v*. Consider thoughtfully, weigh, muse upon, view, meditate upon, ponder, study, reflect on.

The Latin *contemplari* originally meant to mark out a *templum*, an open space for observing auguries. From this *contemplari* came to mean observe, view attentively. Because the *templum* was a sacred inclosure, consecrated place, the word came to mean a building erected for religious purposes.

The English CONTEMPLATE once meant to look, view, observe, and this may lead 24 per cent into selecting OVERLOOK, in the phrase: 'CONTEMPLATE the changes', though not one high-vocabulary person makes this selection. LOOK OVER would revert to the original meaning; but today OVERLOOK means ignore, forget, fail to consider, an opposite of CONTEMPLATE, consider thoughtfully.

218. *GLOOMY*, gloomy (*gloo'-mĭ*) *adj.* Melancholy, disheartened, also dark, dim, obscure, shadowy, somber, thickly shaded, as: 'A GLOOMY forest'.

The noun GLOOM is Anglo-Saxon and a variant of GLOAM, deep twilight, dusk, the fall of evening. The adjective GLOOMY is the noun GLOOM, plus the Anglo-Saxon ending -Y.

To many students, GLOOMY means WEARISOME, tiresome, fatiguing, tedious, irksome, a word with something of the same feeling, for GLOOMY, used of personality, means depressing, melancholy, doleful, morose, dispirited, despondent. Both have depressing in common. But WEARISOME means fatiguing as: 'A WEARISOME task'; GLOOMY means dark, as: 'A GLOOMY day'.

219. *LAMENT*, lament (*lă-mĕnt'*) *n.* Sorrow, expression of grief, jeremiad, bewailing, mournful outcry.

Of the three verbs: to GRIEVE, MOURN, and LAMENT, the first is silent and the deepest inner feelings of GRIEF. MOURN is external, as to wear MOURNING, but may still be silent. A LAMENT is always in sound, and so is the nearest of the three to SIGH, underlined by 8 per cent as the meaning of LAMENT.

A SIGH (*sī*), directly from Anglo-Saxon, is an audible indrawn breath and may express grief and so approach LAMENT in the sense of moaning; but a SIGH may also express relief, fatigue, or even pleasure.

A PETITION, selected by another 8 per cent, is an entreaty, prayer, solicitation, solemn supplication to a superior, formal written request. Both PETITIONS and LAMENTS are complaints; but the word PETITION has no suggestion of GRIEF as does LAMENT, which comes directly from the Latin *lamentum*, a wailing, moaning, weeping.

220. *HEINOUS*, heinous (*hā'-nŭs*) *adj.* Wicked, infamous, flagitious, atrocious, dreadful, horrible, reprehensible, odious, abominable, villainous.

HEINOUS and FLAGRANT usually characterize deeds; while WICKED, INFAMOUS, ATROCIOUS, and MONSTROUS apply as well to their perpetrators. WICKED is general and so often the weakest of these unpleasant words. INFAMOUS, the opposite of FAMOUS, is the justified loss of community standing. ATROCIOUS, from the Latin *atrox, atrocis*, fierce, cruel, savage, horrible, retains this meaning; while MONSTROUS is beyond the normal course of nature. FLAGRANT is literally flaming into notice.

HEINOUS, with -EI- pronounced as in VEIN (*vān*) and DEIGN (*dān*), goes back through French and German to Anglo-Saxon words for hate, and can be used in place of HATEFUL whenever one needs a stronger word.

To 14 per cent HEINOUS means OPPRESSIVE, unreasonably burdensome, heavy, overwhelming, unjustly severe, perhaps an association of ideas; for an OPPRESSIVE dictator, an OPPRESSIVE government, and OPPRESSIVE taxes, are easily regarded as atrocious, dreadful, perhaps even HEINOUS. One may speak of an INFAMOUS dictator, an ATROCIOUS government, MONSTROUS taxes; HEINOUS would fit all three.

221. *LARCENY*, larceny (*lahr'-sĕn-ĭ*) *n.* Theft, robbery, the wrongful taking of personal property, carrying away the goods of another.

LARCENY comes through the French from the Latin *latro*, robber, freebooter.

That LARCENY means theft is known to every person who has taken this worksample, except the lowest scoring, who believe it to mean GENEROSITY. Appropriation by an employee of something already in his possession is EMBEZZLEMENT. LARCENY is more serious. It is taking the goods of another and converting them to one's own use.

222. *DAUNT*, daunt (dănt) v. To discourage, frighten, sub-
    due, intimidate, put out of heart.
To 5 per cent DAUNT means CHALLENGE. CHALLENGE comes from
the Latin *calumnia*, a false accusation, the source of CALUMNY.
To DARE is to CHALLENGE, summon to fight, defy, provoke to
action, invite to single combat, call to a contest, summon to a
duel, call on a person to account for himself. A CHALLENGE
received may DAUNT, frighten, discourage; but in this case to
DAUNT, frighten, results from the CHALLENGE.
    The verb to TAUNT, differing from DAUNT by one letter, is to
tease insultingly, deride, mock, almost CHALLENGE.
    DAUNT goes back to the Latin *domitare*, to tame, the frequen-
tative of *domare*, to tame, then to conquer. DAUNT in English
once meant to tame, conquer, and then conquer the spirit, and
so intimidate, discourage, cause to quail, overcome with fear.

223. *REPOSE*, repose (rē-pōz') n. Rest, relaxation, a lying
    down, sleeping, quiet, peace, reclining.
To REST, SLEEP, and REPOSE, are much the same. The word REST
suggests a pause in LABOR, even stopping for a moment in standing position. REPOSE does not suggest previous work but does
imply quietness, and usually a reclining position. REPOSE, from
the Latin *re-*, again, and *pausare*, to pause, comes through a Latin
word meaning to quiet.
    From the same source come the verb to POSE, to arrange in a
fixed position; and COMPOSE, literally, to arrange together.

224. *INTEGRANT*, integrant (ĭn'-tĕ-grănt) n. Ingredient,
    constituent, element, component, factor.
The Latin *integer* means untouched, unchanged, unhurt, whole,
entire, sound, fresh, pure, honest. In English, an INTEGER, unchanged from Latin, is a whole number, 71 or 82, not a fraction,
not a part. INTEGRITY, from the same *integer*, untouched unimpaired, whole, means wholeness, completeness, soundness, freedom from corruption, honesty.
    The Latin *integer* is in turn a combination of *in-*, not, and
tangere, to touch, the source of a large family of English words.
    The verb to INTEGRATE is to bring together as a whole, and
INTEGRATION is the process of combining into a whole.

INTEGRANT is an awkward term, made up to sound scientific and exact. Use ELEMENT to mean a single distinct feature; or in cooking use INGREDIENT. SEASONING, the only attractive mislead, is an INGREDIENT, added to food to give flavor.

225. *ZANY*, zany (*ză'-nĭ*) *adj*. Comic, clownish, apish, boorish, loutish, gawky, awkward, clumsy, rude.

ZANY, originally a familiar form of Giovanni (John), comes through the French from the Italian. A ZANY was a comic performer on the Italian stage.

From the Edinburgh Review of 1869, quoted by the Century Dictionary, comes: 'The ZANY in Shakespeare's day was not so much a BUFFOON and MIME as the obsequious follower of a BUFFOON and the attenuated mime of a MIMIC. He was the vice, servant, or attendant of the professional clown or FOOL, who, dressed like his master, accompanied him on stage or in the ring, following his movements, imitating his tricks and adding to the general merriment by his ludicrous failures and comic imbecility. The professional CLOWN or FOOL might be clever and accomplished in his business, a skillful tumbler and mountebank, doing what he undertook to do thoroughly and well. But this was never the case with the ZANY. He was always slight and thin, well-meaning, but comparatively helpless, full of readiness, grimace, and alacrity, but also of incompetence, eagerly trying to imitate his superior, but ending in failure and absurdity.'

ZEST, according to the Imperial Dictionary of 1850 published in Glasgow, Scotland, is a piece of the outer rind of an orange or lemon used as a flavoring. ZEST adds flavor, piquancy, relish, and the ZANY adds ZEST to the performance of the clown. This leads 15 per cent to select ZESTY as the meaning of ZANY.

226. *TRAUMA*, trauma (*trăw'-măh*) *n*. The shock due to a wound, abnormal condition produced by any external violence.

TRAUMA is the Greek word τραῦμα (*trauma*), a wound, written in Roman letters. It comes from the verb τρώειν (*troein*), to pierce.

EMERGENCY, marked by 7 per cent, is the popular mislead. EMERGENCY comes from the Latin *emergere*, a combination of

e-, out, and *mergere*, to dip, dive, sink, bathe. To EMERGE is to
come forth, reappear, rise as from water. An EMERGENCY is a
sudden occasion for action, an urgent occurrence. The wound
or violence which produces TRAUMA is just such an EMERGENCY.

227. *MISSAL*, missal (*mĭs'-săl*) *n.* Mass-book, book containing
      the ceremonies of the Popish mass; Noah Webster says:
'The Romish mass-book, book containing the liturgy, originally
the Sacramentary used at the altar'.
MISSAL is thought by 26 per cent to mean ERROR. The verb to
MISS, unconnected with MISSAL, is to fail, come short of. From
this comes the noun a MISS, a failure to find, want of success, occasionally used to mean an ERROR, fault.
      The word MASS goes directly back to Anglo-Saxon, but comes
also from the Latin *missa*, the dismissal of the congregation after
MASS, from *missus*, the past participle of *mittere*, to send, the
source also of DISMISSAL, sending away. MASS was originally
the DISMISSAL of the congregation after the ceremony, but is
now the ceremony itself.
      The MASS-BOOK, MISSAL-BOOK, or just MISSAL, practically in
its present form, was issued by Pius V in 1570 and contained all
of the forms necessary for celebrating MASS throughout the
year. The original MISSAL, a word first used in the 8th century,
was smaller with only a part of what it now contains.

228. *INFEST*, infest (*ĭn-fĕst'*) *v.* Over-run, haunt, invade,
      molest, harass (*hăr'-ăs*) (v. B. 1121), attack, plague, vex.
INFESTED is thought by 21 per cent to mean ESTABLISHED. To
INVEST, from the Latin *vestire*, to clothe, may mean to put in
possession, as to INVEST a man with authority or to INVEST him
with rank, to appoint him, ordain him, and so ESTABLISH him.
To ESTABLISH, from the Latin *stabilire*, to make stable, from
stabilis, stable, may mean appoint, ordain, and so INVEST.
      To INFEST comes from the Latin *infestare*, to attack, molest,
from the adjective *infestus*, disturbed, molested, attacked, a
combination of *in-* and *fendere*, to strike, a word not found
alone but the source of FENDER, something which protects by
striking. To DEFEND is to guard against, protect, shield, shelter,
ward off a blow. To INFEST is the opposite, to attack, invade.

229. *FILTERED*, filtered (*fĭl'-terd*) *adj.* Sifted, purified, strained, percolated, separated from solid matter.

FILTERED, STRAINED, and the noun COLANDER, where there is no corresponding verb, name increasing degrees of coarseness. A COLANDER is usually metal with holes, perforations, to allow water to run off in washing vegetables. A STRAINER is finer, sometimes of woven wire. Of the three, FILTER is the only technical term; and this leads 15 per cent to believe that FILTERED means PROCESSED. In science the noun PROCESS, from the Latin *procedere*, to go forward, advance, proceed, is almost any proceeding, happening, action, operation, method of treatment, series of motions, way in which something is done. The less common verb, to PROCESS, with the participial adjective PROCESSED, means put through any series of operations.

Filtered, with related words in French, Spanish, and Italian, all meaning FELT, comes directly from Anglo-Saxon and the Latin *filtrum*, felt, an unwoven material dating far back in the history of Asia. To FILTER was originally to strain through felt; but is now more often to strain through FILTER-PAPER or some similar material, supported by a funnel, an inverted cone.

230. *POTENT*, potent (*pō'-tĕnt*) *adj.* Strong, powerful, effective, authoritative.

POTENT comes from the Latin *potens, potentis*, able, powerful, the present participle of *posse*, to be able. This in turn is a combination of *potis*, able, and *esse*, to be. From the same source comes POSSIBLE, that may happen.

231. *EBULLIENCE*, ebullience (*ē-bŭl'-lĭ-ĕns*) *n.* Enthusiasm, vitality, bubbling, boiling up, effervescence, intense activity, over-enthusiasm, bursting forth, overflowing, demonstrative, extravagance, like boiling water, literally a boiling over.

EBULLIENCE comes from the Latin *e-*, meaning out, and *bullire*, to boil. The Latin ending *-ence*, more commonly *ance*, is added to Latin verbs to form the corresponding noun.

It is hard to see why SWELLING is chosen more often than the correct ENTHUSIASM. PROTUBERANCE and PROMINENCE both mean SWELLING and a BULGE is also a SWELLING, but none sound enough like EBULLIENCE to be the cause.

232. *FLUNKY*, flunky (*flŭn'-kĭ*) *n.* Man servant, lackey, footman, doorman, servile follower, male attendant in livery.
The Century Dictionary says: 'FLUNKY is recent in literature
but probably much older in colloquial speech.' It is the Scotch
word FLUNKIE. FLUNKY, FAG, and FACTOTUM are three kinds of
servants. A FACTOTUM is a man of all work. A FAG works until
exhausted. A FLUNKY wears a gold-trimmed uniform.

To 7 per cent FLUNKY means TRASH COLLECTOR. Both TRASH
COLLECTORS and FLUNKIES score low in English vocabulary, but a
TRASH COLLECTOR does hard physical labor; while the principal
duty of a FLUNKY, as that word is used, is to wear an elaborate
outfit as a mark of consequence for his employer.

233. *IDEATE*, ideate (*ĭ-dē'-āt*) *v.* To form in thought, fancy,
think, apprehend, grasp mentally.
The English word IDEA is the Latin *idea*, from the Greek ἰδέα
(*idea*), the look of a thing as opposed to reality, its archetype,
mental image, picture. IDEATE is IDEA plus the ending -ATE, one
method of forming a verb.

To DEBATE, chosen by 15 per cent, was originally to fight, do
battle, from the Latin *de*, down, and *batuere*, to beat; and although the word is less violent, and may mean no more than
discuss, argue, even think, there should still remain the idea of
contention. To IDEATE is to think quietly, to form IDEAS in one's
mind. Ordinarily use the straightforward Anglo-Saxon THINK,
which the Century Dictionary defines as: to say to one's self
mentally.

234. *TIARA*, tiara (*tē-ah'-rah*) *n.* An ornamented head-dress,
diadem, miter, crown, turban, coronet.
TIARA is thought by 15 per cent of high-school students to mean
DIAMOND, the extremely hard and brilliant precious stone. A
DIAMOND may be the valuable part of a TIARA, but the TIARA is the
head-dress, not the precious stone set into it. Or the confusion
with DIAMOND may be the word DIADEM, much like DIAMOND in
appearance. A DIADEM (*dī'-ă-dĕm*) was originally a head-band
of silk, encircling the forehead, and later embroidered with
gold and often set with DIAMONDS. From this, DIADEM gradually
came to mean CROWN.

The MITER, also spelt MITRE, is a liturgical head-dress that is worn for public worship. In the Catholic Church the TIARA is the bulging bee-hive-shaped papal crown which signifies sovereign power, worn by Pope Paul VI, to emphasize his power, at the opening of the synod of bishops in October, 1967. TIARA comes from the Greek τιαρα (tiára), the head-dress of the Persian kings, a kind of turban. TIARA now means any rich ornament for the head, often one set with DIAMONDS.

235. *ABODE*, abode (ă-bōd') *n.* A home, residence, dwelling, habitation, domicile, house, lodging, quarters, homestead. The verb to ABIDE, to continue, tarry, stay, dwell, live in a place, comes directly from the Anglo-Saxon, with the past ABODE, as in the Anglo-Saxon RIDE, with the past RODE, DRIVE and DROVE. To BIDE and to ABIDE both mean to wait, remain steadfast, continue to stay, also dwell, reside, the initial *a-* contributing nothing except occasionally helping the rhythm. HOUSE, HOME, and DWELLING are also Anglo-Saxon.

The noun ABODE, with the suggestion of waiting, sometimes implies more briefness than for example RESIDENCE, which implies a permanent address.

236. *INCENTIVE*, incentive (ĭn-sĕn'-tĭv) *n.* A motive, inducement, incitement, motivation, prompting, stimulus, reason, whetting, spur, something which moves the mind to action. INCENTIVE comes from the Latin *incentivus*, that strikes up or sets the tune, from *incinere*, to sing, play, sound, with the past participle *incentus*, a combination of *in-* and *canere*, to sing, play.

One who designs a vocabulary test includes, as a wrong answer, a mislead close in meaning but not correct, not so near as the right answer. An INCENTIVE is an inner desire, not external pressure. A SPUR, goad, comes ordinarily from the outside; and SPUR was included to bring out this distinction. But the selection by 31 per cent of a presumably wrong answer demands a review both of the major test word and of the mislead. Though SPUR was used originally by horsemen, the word has come to be used figuratively, to suggest an inner SPUR, and so an INCENTIVE. In the next revision of the vocabulary test, SPUR will be removed and MOTIVE left as the correct answer.

237. *QUEUE*, queue (*kū*) *n.* A line of persons waiting in turn, row, column, file.

QUEUE is a French word from the Latin *coda* or *cauda*, a tail, the source of the English CAUDAL, tail-like.

To 9 per cent QUEUE means SURVEY. A SURVEY is a VIEW (*vū*), pronounced to rime with QUEUE, an inspection, beholding, seeing, an examination by the eye.

From Henry James in his International Episode comes: 'Several dozen men standing in a QUEUE at the ticket office'. Although the American College Dictionary calls QUEUE chiefly British, the word is familiar to some 80 per cent of American students.

238. *VERSUS*, versus (*ver'-sŭs*) *prep.* Against, toward.

VERSUS comes directly from the Latin *versus*, toward, against, the past participle of *vertere*, to turn. VERSUS appears in legal phraseology to denote the action of one party against another.

239. *ABJECT*, abject (*ăb-jĕkt'*) *adj.* Wretched, downcast, disheartened, hopeless, servile, groveling, mean, dependent, menial.

From the Latin *jacere*, to throw, cast, sling, hurl, come such modern technical terms as PROJECTILE, something thrown forward, as from a sling; to INJECT, literally to throw in; REJECT, to throw back, hurl back; TRAJECTORY, OBJECT, SUBJECT, ADJECTIVE, as well as JETTISON, EJACULATE, JET, and ABJECT, wretched, miserable.

To 5 per cent ABJECT means SUBORDINATE, below in rank, underneath, lower in position, a confusion of similar ideas, the third step in learning. A SUBORDINATE person takes orders from a superior; but nothing in the word suggests meanness, servility, ABJECTNESS.

Low applies to rank, position, condition; MEAN, to character, conduct, behavior; ABJECT, to spirit, mental state.

240. *GOSSAMER*, gossamer (*gŏs'-să-mer*) *adj.* Delicate, filmy, gauzy, flimsy, light and thin like a cobweb, transparent or nearly so; also, as a noun, the threads which float in the air spun by young spiders, said to carry them on long journeys.

GOSSAMER goes back to Middle English and is said to be a combination of *gos*, goose, and *somer*, summer, which does not really help for one must then explain SUMMER-GOOSE.

GOSSAMER, the noun, is a thin cobweb-like exhalation which flies abroad in hot summer-like weather, seen to float in the air, in clear days in autumn, and observable in stubble fields, and upon furze and other low bushes.

To 5 per cent GOSSAMER means HEAVY, an exact opposite, the fourth and final step in learning.

241. *PERIPHERY*, periphery (*pĕ-rĭf'-ĕ-rĭ*) *n*. External boundary, circumference, border, line forming the outside edge of a closed figure.

PERIPHERY comes from the Greek περιφέρεια (*periphereia*), a combination of περί (*peri-*), around, and φέρειν (*pherein*), to carry, from the same source as the Latin *ferre*, to carry. CIRCUMFERENCE, a combination of the Latin *circum*, around, and *ferre*, to carry, is an exact equivalent of the Greek PERIPHERY.

OUTLINE, marked by 25 per cent, and included in the vocabulary test as a mislead, is a line by which a figure is bounded, an accurate definition of PERIPHERY, too close to use as a mislead.

PERIMETER, from the same Greek root, meaning around, should mean the measurement around, while PERIPHERY means the outer edge; but they are too often used as synonyms.

242. *AGENDUM*, agendum (*ă-jĕn'-dŭm*) *n*. Program, items of business to be brought before a meeting, things to be put through.

The popular mislead is REPORT, selected by 20 per cent. REPORT comes from the Latin *reportare*, to carry back, bring back, a combination of *re-*, back, and *portare*, to carry. To REPORT is literally to bring back an answer. The noun, a REPORT, is a statement of fact in reply to a question, often the result of an investigation. REPORTS are made during a meeting.

The AGENDUM is the program made in advance of a meeting in which REPORTS are given. AGENDUM is the Latin neuter of *agendus*, the gerundive of *agere*, to do, the source of AGENT. The Latin *agendum* means something to be done, and is often used in the plural AGENDA.

243. *SCUFFLE*, scuffle (*skŭf'-fl*) *v.* To fight in a disorderly way, push, struggle confusedly. The noun, a SCUFFLE, is an affray, brawl, quarrel.

SCUFF, SCUFFLE, and SHUFFLE are closely related. SCUFFLE is the frequentative of SCUFF; and SHUFFLE perhaps no more than a variation. To SCUFF, from Swedish and Danish words meaning to push, shove, is now to walk without lifting the feet, drag along. Among its many meanings, the verb to SHUFFLE may mean move with a slow, clumsy motion, drag heavily along, and so suggest CRAWL, selected by 2 per cent as the meaning of SCUFFLE. Both SCUFF and SHUFFLE imply standing up. To CRAWL is to move on all fours. Of these similar words SCUFFLE has retained more of the meaning of the Scandinavian words of pushing, shoving, and is the only one which means fight, struggle, quarrel in a disorderly way without malice, as from Thackeray: 'SCUFFLING for the evening paper'.

244. *RAMPART*, rampart (*răm'-pahrt*) *n.* Parapet, bulwark, fortification, dirt wall, mound of earth around a place for protection, built usually of earth taken out of the ditch outside the RAMPART. Strictly a PARAPET is built on the RAMPART with a space on the RAMPART behind the PARAPET wide enough not only for soldiers to stand but also to pass one another.

RAMPARTS are thought by 14 per cent to be BANNERS, flags, pennants, standards, ensigns. RAMPARTS and BANNERS are closely associated. From Shakespeare's Macbeth comes: 'Hang out our BANNERS on the outward walls'. But BANNERS are flags; RAMPARTS, protecting walls of earth.

From the last page of Greenmantle by John Buchan, an adventure book every boy should read, comes: 'In the very front, now nearing the city RAMPARTS, was one man, riding like one possessed, the long looked-for revelation Greenmantle'.

245. *STIPEND*, stipend (*stĭ'-pĕnd*) *n.* Wages, pay, periodical allowance, fixed payment, salary, remuneration, once the income from an ecclesiastical living, a salary paid by an English or Scotch church; and the word has come to mean a small salary. STIPEND comes from the Latin *stipendium*, a tax, tribute, impost, assessment, and this may lead 10 per cent of those tested to be-

lieve that STIPEND means PENALTY, fine, for a TRIBUTE was often a PENALTY, and many think of the modern tax as little more. Even though tax, tribute, as a meaning of STIPEND disappeared from dictionaries long ago, these early meanings survive in the popular mind, unbelievably often, and long.

The Latin *stipendium* was in turn a combination of *stips*, a gift, donation, alms, and *pendere*, to weigh out, and this may lead another 12 per cent to believe that STIPEND means GIFT.

The word SALARY implies more or less permanent employment and payment for work done. A STIPEND is payment, but so carefully weighed out as to be little more than a GIFT in return for work done.

246. *MUNICIPAL*, municipal (*mū-nĭs'-ĭ-păl*) *adj*. Local, provincial, independent, free, pertaining to self-government.
MUNICIPAL comes from the Latin *municeps*, in ancient Rome, the citizen of a free or privileged town, having the right of citizenship, but governed by its own laws, from *munus*, a duty, and *capere*, to take. A MUNICIPALITY is a city, town, or community, with local self-government.

In the test phrase: 'The MUNICIPAL court', the word is thought by 4 per cent to mean HEAD. OCCIPITAL (*ŏk-sĭ'-pĭ-tăl*), somewhat like MUNICIPAL in sound, means pertaining to the back part of the head.

Today MUNICIPAL government is local self-government. MUNICIPAL records are local records.

BUREAUCRATIC and MUNICIPAL are opposites. BUREAUCRATIC is centralized. MUNICIPAL is local self-government.

247. *REMONSTRANCE*, remonstrance (*rē-mŏn'-străns*) *n*.
Rebuke, reproof, protest, objection, complaint, expostulation, statement against something, strong representation in opposition.
REMONSTRANCE comes from the Latin *re-*, again, and *monstrare*, to show, exhibit; and the verb to REMONSTRATE (*rē-mŏn'-strāt*) originally meant to exhibit, demonstrate in the sense of prove. A REMONSTRANCE was a showing, exhibit, and so DEMONSTRATION. DEMONSTRATION, like REMONSTRANCE, has numerous meanings, as: a showing, making plain, as: 'A DEMONSTRATION of

friendship'; also an exhibition in teaching, as well as a gathering
to make clear to the public a point of view. Although DEMON-
STRATION as a meaning of REMONSTRANCE is obsolete, SHOWING
could certainly be justified historically, and so perhaps SECOND
SHOWING, selected by 7 per cent.

From E. Chambers: 'A REMONSTRANCE is a complaint backed
with reason; an expostulation or humble supplication addressed
to a king or other superior to beseech him to reflect on the in-
conveniences, or ill-consequences, of some order, edict, or the
like.

'REMONSTRANCE is also used for an expostulary counsel or
advice; or a gentle and handsome reproof to apprise or correct
some fault.'

248. *ARABESQUE*, arabesque (*ă-ră-bĕsk'*) *adj*. Ornamental,
        Arabian, fanciful, intricately designed geometrical figures,
fruit, flowers, and foliage, but never animals.
ARABESQUE comes directly from the word ARAB, and -ESQUE, an
ending for French adjectives meaning having the style of, in the
manner of, as: GROTESQUE, and PICTURESQUE.

From Ephraim Chambers comes: 'ARABESQUE, something done
after the manner of the ARABIAN'.

ARABESQUE, GROTESQUE, and MORESQUE are terms applied to
such paintings or ornaments or friezes wherein there are no
human or animal figures but which consist wholly of imaginary
foliages, plants, stalks, etc. The Moors, Arabs, and other Mohammedans use these kinds of ornaments: their religion forbidding
them to make any images or figures of men, or other animals.

249. *SKIRMISH*, skirmish (*sker'-mish*) *n*. Irregular fight, en-
        gagement, contest, encounter, brush, rencontre, preliminary
trial of strength; Bailey: 'A small encounter of a few men, when
they fight in confusion without observing order'.
According to Ephraim Chambers, 1728: 'A SKIRMISH in war is a
disorderly kind of combat or encounter, in presence of two
armies, between small parties or persons, who advance from the
body for that purpose and introduce a general regular fight.
Many SKIRMISHES are performed by persons in ambuscade.'

This last idea leads to the selection of AMBUSH as the meaning of SKIRMISH. Also the word SKIRMISH goes back through French, Spanish, and Portuguese, to German words for shield, screen, shelter, guard. But today AMBUSH is the hiding place, or those in concealment. A SKIRMISH is the struggle of those who come out of concealment.

250. *CORTEGE*, cortege (*kŏr-tāj′*) *n*. A train of attendants, line of retainers, procession, parade.

CORTEGE comes through French from the Italian *corteggia*, from *corte*, court. A circus PARADES. A PARADE is gay. PROCESSION is the general word for any march in which one person precedes another. A CORTEGE is courtly, solemn, and made up of dignitaries.

The only popular mislead is FLORAL WREATH, selected by 20 per cent. The word CORTEGE is now used for a funeral procession, and this may suggest FLORAL WREATH. Also a CORSAGE is a small arrangement of flowers worn by women, and this may lead to the selection of FLORAL.

251. *CUMBROUS*, cumbrous (*kŭm′-brŭs*) *adj*. Burdensome, clogging, cumbersome, hindering, toilsome, obstructing, causing trouble.

Given a choice between TROUBLESOME and CLUMSY as a synonym of CUMBROUS 52 per cent prefer the second, compared with only 8 per cent for TROUBLESOME. Even when CLUMSY is removed and replaced by OAFISH which is obviously wrong, examinees still avoid TROUBLESOME. CLUMSY is apparently a more acceptable meaning of CUMBROUS.

CUMBERSOME is the noun CUMBER, a burden, hindrance, obstacle, plus the Anglo-Saxon ending -SOME, added to a noun to make an adjective which expresses a considerable amount. CUMBROUS is the same noun plus the Latin ending -OUS which makes an ordinary adjective. CUMBERSOME is a bit heavier, clumsier, than CUMBROUS.

To ENCUMBER, to clog, burden, overload, obstruct, oppress, weigh down, impede with a load, was probably the original word, of which CUMBER is a shortened form. The old French *combre* was a line of stakes in a river to catch fish. The verb to ACCUMULATE is to pile up in a heap, gather into a pile.

All of these come in some way from the Latin *cumulus*, a heap, pile, used of clouds which pile up in great white masses.

252. *DORY*, dory (*dō'-rĭ*) *n.* A small flat-bottomed rowboat, pointed front and back, with one pair of oars, used by fishermen.

There is also a fish called a JOHN DORY, often shortened to DORY, which Pantologia spells DORÉE and declares can be told from all other fishes by the black spot on each side, 'a circumstance from which superstition has made the DORÉE a rival of the haddock, for the honor of St. Peter's Touch, when he took the tribute money from its mouth'.

The DORY, the boat, is made so that one fits into another, as they are piled on the deck of a larger boat, available for fisher-mean at sea. DORIES are also seen on the Atlantic coast of New England. But the word is far from exact. From 1810 the Oxford quotes: 'The PIT-PAN being flat-bottomed, the DORY round'; and a few years later from Hawthorne: 'I launched my DORY, my little flat-bottomed skiff'. A PIT-PAN is a hollowed out log, and so apt to be round-bottomed. A DORY is flat-bottomed despite the quotation.

253. *ANXIETY*, anxiety (*ăng-zī'-ĕ-tĭ*) *n.* Apprehension (v. B. 625) of danger, concern, solicitude (v. B. 1271), uneasiness of mind, trouble, foreboding, disquiet, worry.

ANXIETY is thought by 17 per cent to mean DEVOTION, love, worship, dedication. ANXIETY comes from the Latin *anxietas, anxietatis*, from *anxius*, troubled, the source of the English ANXIOUS, from *angĕre*, to distress, to trouble, the source of ANGUISH, ANGER, and AGONY. ANXIETY implies both ANGUISH and AGONY, with neither thought contained in DEVOTION. This comes from the Latin verb *devovēre*, a combination of *de-* and *vovēre*, to vow, promise, pledge one's self.

Both DEVOTION and ANXIETY are strong emotions, feelings. DEVOTION is love, worship. ANXIETY is worry, fear of what will happen, as: ANXIETY to avoid an evil, ANXIETY as to the effect of frost on a garden.

Of the four words: CARE, CONCERN, SOLICITUDE, and ANXIETY, the last is the strongest.

254. *SCRIMP*, scrimp (*skrĭmp*) v. To skimp, stint, pinch, economize, go without, limit closely one's spending.
To 2 per cent SCRIMP means HOBBLED. This may be a confusion
with the word LIMP, ending in the same last three letters; for to
HOBBLE may mean to walk with a hitch, go on crutches, LIMP,
almost hop. HOBBLED also means with the feet tied together so
as to make normal walking impossible.

ECONOMIZING is a wise saving of money. SCRIMPING, which
goes directly back to an Anglo-Saxon SHRINK, is a niggardly,
miserly saving when one can afford to spend, almost like HOB-
BLING one's self.

255. *WISTFULNESS*, wistfulness (*wĭst'-fŭl-nĕs*) n. Pensive-
ness, musing silently, quiet attention, full of mute thoughts.
WISTFUL, the adjective, originally meant quiet, silent, hushed,
mute, and this is still the fundamental idea in the noun.

WISTFULNESS is thought by 21 per cent to mean AMBITION.
WISHFULNESS (*wĭsh'-fŭl-nĕs*), constantly confused by dictionaries with WISTFULNESS, is longing, covetous desire, but doing
nothing. AMBITION, from the Latin *ambitio, ambitionis*, a striving for favor, literally a going about as a candidate, soliciting
votes, from *ambire*, to go about, is more active than WISHFUL-
NESS, implying an effort to gain one's desire.

Of the verb to WIST, which the Century calls spurious, Nathan
Bailey says: 'To know, to think, to understand'. All three of
these ideas enter WISTFULNESS, together with silence.

256. *TAINTED*, tainted (*tān'-tĕd*), adj. Infected, contaminated, corrupted, stained, spoiled, bribed, attaint.
Bailey says: 'To ATTAINT is to stain the blood as high treason
does.' ATTAINT is apparently stronger than TAINT.

To 7 per cent of those tested, TAINTED means SEASONED. To
SEASON is to make pleasanter, render agreeable, bring to the best
state for use. Bailey says: 'To SEASON is to salt or give anything
a relish with salt, spice, etc.'

TAINT comes through an old French word meaning color,
hue, tincture, stain, dye, from the Latin *tinctus*, a dye.

E. Chambers says of TAINT: 'Used of a person convicted of a
felony, treason, etc.'

257. *TIDBIT*, tidbit (*tĭd'-bĭt*) *n.* A sweet morsel, small piece, choice bit, a delicacy, dainty fragment.

TIDBIT is thought by 3 per cent to mean GOSSIP. GOSSIP is idle talk, minutely confidential remarks about other people, tattle, scandal. GOSSIP is a TIDBIT of news.

Under TIDBIT the Century Dictionary says: 'Same as TITBIT'. A TIT is a BIT. A TIT was once a small horse, often a small child, and so a small piece, morsel, BIT. A TITBIT, occasionally written TIDBIT, is a BIT of a BIT.

258. *PREMEDITATE*, premeditate (*prē-mĕd'-ĭ-tāt*) *v.* To think ahead, meditate beforehand, consider in advance, deliberate, mull over. The past participle PREMEDITATED is the form seen most frequently.

The verb to MEDITATE comes from the Latin *meditatus,* the past participle of *meditare,* to think, reflect upon, design, purpose, intend, consider, related to the Greek μελετᾶν (*meletan*), to care for, attend to, study, practise, engage in mental contemplation, cogitate, ruminate. The noun is MEDITATION.

To PREMEDITATE is to contrive beforehand, revolve in the mind in advance; design previously, deliberate, form in the mind by prior meditation.

259. *ORBIT*, orbit (*ŏrb'-ĭt*) *n.* The elliptical track of a planet about the sun, the curved path described by a satellite about a celestial body, track, path.

ORBIT comes from the Latin *orbita,* a rut, track of a wheel, from *orbis,* wheel, circle, ring, the source of ORB, which is used sometimes to mean round, circular like a wheel, disk, but more often like a ball, globe, spherical. Nathan Bailey, in 1721, defines ORBIT as: 'The track or mark of a chariot or cartwheel'. Chambers says: 'In astronomy, the path of a planet or comet or the curve that it describes in its revolution around its central body'.

260. *FLAIR*, flair (*flār*) *n.* A talent, aptitude, bent, inclination, native gift, natural endowment, keen perception.

The big mislead, chosen by 17 per cent, is IMPERFECTION, which of course is FLAW. FLAW is Anglo-Saxon, a crack, break, defect, imperfection, fault, weak spot.

Through the French *flairer*, to smell, from the Latin *fragrare*, the source of FRAGRANT, comes FLAIR, originally an odor, smell, or in hunting, the scent. From its use in hunting, FLAIR came to mean the sense of smell and so keen perception, as: 'A FLAIR which always leads him right'. Today FLAIR is used more generally to mean not only keenness of smell, but a noticeable gift for any sort of activity.

261. *PESTIFEROUS*, pestiferous (*pĕs-tĭf'-ĕr-ŭs*) *adj*. Annoying, plaguing, mischievous, bothersome.
PESTIFEROUS comes through the French from the Latin *pestis*, plague, deadly epidemic, pestilence, destructive disease, and *ferre*, to carry. PESTIFEROUS is literally plague carrying, infectious, contagious. The word PESTILENTIAL is now used more often with this meaning and PESTIFEROUS is milder, mischievous, annoying.

PEST was originally directly from this Latin word and meant a plague, deadly epidemic, but has come to be applied to people who are merely annoying, mischievous, troublesome, bothersome, a nuisance.

262. *FIDELITY*, fidelity (*fĭ-dĕl'-ĭ-tĭ*) *n*. Good faith, exact observance of duty, faithful devotion, fealty (*fē'-ăl-tĭ*), allegiance, loyalty, integrity, trustiness, constancy, conscientiousness, trustworthiness, faithfulness, firmness.
From the Latin *fides*, faith, trust, loyalty, through the adjective *fidelis*, faithful, from *fidelitas*, *fidelitatis*, faithfulness, come FIDELITY, as well as the opposite PERFIDY, faithlessness, treachery. From the same source, but through the Old French where the spelling and pronunciation changed, comes FEALTY (*fē'-ăl-tĭ*), a doublet of FIDELITY.

To 2 per cent of high-vocabulary examinees FIDELITY means SKILL, but to another 1 per cent it means MISCHIEF, and to still another 1 per cent FALSEHOOD, an opposite, with no clear concentration on any single misunderstanding.

FIRMNESS is will, determination, which prevents one from yielding; CONSTANCY is a matter of the heart, holding one steadfast. FIDELITY is personal principle, loyalty, colder than FAITHFULNESS but unchanging.

263. *UNDULATING*, undulating (*ŭn'-dū-lā-tĭng*) *adj.* Moving in waves, fluctuating, rising and falling, rolling, wavy.
UNDULATING, from the Latin *undulatus*, appears as *unda*, a wave, in the center of REDUNDANT, overflowing, familiar as applied to writing in which too many words express an idea.

Of the verb to UNDULATE, N. Bailey, 1721, says: 'To roll as waves', and of the participial adjective UNDULATED: 'Made in the fashion of waves as watered silks and stuffs, and the grain of wainscot'. A few years later, 1728, E. Chambers added: 'UNDULATION, in physics, a kind of tremulous motion or vibration, observable in a liquid, whereby it alternately rises and falls like the waves of the sea'.

To 2 per cent UNDULATING signifies FLAT, even, level, smooth, broad, spreading, an opposite of UNDULATING, a confusion of antonyms, the last step in learning.

264. *NARCISSISM*, narcissism (*nahr'-sĭs-sĭzm*) *n.* Self-love, egoism, conceit, vanity, self-admiration.
The Greek suffix -ISM, from ἰσμός (*ismos*), the masculine, ἰσμα (*isma*), the feminine, denotes a condition, almost a state of mind. In Greek mythology, because NARCISSUS, a handsome youth, did not respond to the love of ECHO, a mountain nymph, NEMESIS, goddess of vengeance, made him fall in love with his own image reflected in a pool. Unable to grasp his image, he pined away and became the flower NARCISSUS, spelt in Greek letters νάρκισσος (*narcissos*), from νάρκη (*narce*), numbness, torpor, the source of NARCOTIC, the power of producing stupor, sleep, as OPIUM.

The mislead marked by 15 per cent is SELF-ABASEMENT, an exact opposite, perhaps a misunderstanding of ABASEMENT, for many persons know the story of NARCISSUS and should easily select the correct SELF-LOVE.

265. *GENIALITY*, geniality (*jē-nĭ-ăl'-ĭ-tĭ*) *n.* Cheerfulness, cordiality, warmth, friendliness, affability, heartiness.
GENIALITY, the adjective GENIAL plus -ITY, a frequent Latin ending of abstract nouns, comes from the Latin *genius*, the spirit of a person, inclination, inborn nature. GENIALITY is a tendency to MIX with others, which leads 11 per cent to select MIXING as the meaning of GENIALITY. One thinks of MIXING as stirring two

substances together; but it may also imply mingling with other people, MIXING in society, a characteristic of the GENIAL person.

266. *SUCCUMB*, succumb (*sŭk-kŭm'*) v. To yield, give up, give way under pressure, submit, surrender to power, acquiesce, comply, bow to the will of another.

SUCCUMB, from the Latin *succumbere*, to lie down, sink, submit, combines *sub*, under, and *cubare*, to lie down.

SUCCUMB is thought by 5 per cent to mean RECOVER, an opposite of the correct meaning. To SUCCUMB means not only yield, submit, be defeated, but also to die. To RECOVER in this last sense is to get well again.

267. *INEXPLICABLE*, inexplicable (*ĭn-ĕks'-plĭ-kă-bl*, not *ĭn-ĕks-plĭ'-kă-bl*) *adj*. Incapable of being explained, unaccountable, incomprehensible, inscrutable, mysterious, unintelligible, obscure, enigmatical.

INEXPLICABLE comes from the Latin privative *in-*, and *explicabilis*, that can be unfolded, a combination of *ex-*, out, and *plicare*, to fold.

To 10 per cent INEXPLICABLE means UNFORGIVABLE. In front of the Anglo-Saxon FORGIVE is the Anglo-Saxon prefix UN-; while in front of the Latin EXPLAIN is the Latin prefix IN-, not. Remove these, and -ABLE at the end, added almost indiscriminately to both Anglo-Saxon and Latin, and the real difference between these words is that between FORGIVE and EXPLAIN. Sometimes an EXPLANATION of why something happened is a step toward FORGIVENESS; but to FORGIVE was once to give up, forego, resign; then to give; and now to give pardon, cease to blame, restore to good will, give up all resentment, excuse, overlook.

To EXPLAIN is to unfold, make clear, interpret. That which is INEXPLICABLE cannot be explained.

268. *PANTHEISM*, pantheism (*păn'-thē-ĭzm*) *n*. The theory that God is the only substance. Webster: 'The doctrine that the universe *is* God, or the system of theology in which it is maintained that the universe is the supreme God'.

The modern dictionary lists ECONOMIZE, ECONOMIST, ECONOMY, ECONOMIZER, ECONOMICS, ECONOMICAL, and then advertises

350,000 words, or some figure which approaches half a million, in a dictionary which cannot be conveniently left in a desk drawer or beside one on a table. In 1828, Charles Richardson tried the experiment of grouping all of these and defining only ECONOMY. Though his dictionary, printed in two volumes, went through five editions, the idea did not survive, perhaps partly because of a rare error. He groups PANTHEISM and PANTHEON and defines them as one.

The Latin *pan-*, from παν- (*pan-*), which in Greek becomes παμ- (*pam-*) before a labial, as PAMPHAGOUS (*păm'-fă-gŭs*), omnivorous, eating everything, and παγ- (*pag-*) before a guttural, means all, universal. It is the combining form of the Greek πᾶς (*pas*), πάντις (*pantis*), all. Both PANTHEON and PANTHEISM come from PAN and θεός (*theos*), God; but a PANTHEON is a temple dedicated to all the gods and PANTHEISM is the belief that all is God.

The word PANTHEISM is said to have been first used in 1705 by the controversial John Toland, then applied to the philosophy of Benedictus de Spinoza, the Jewish Dutch philosopher, born in Amsterdam, who died in 1677.

Of a PANTHEIST, the person, Dr. Samuel Johnson, 1755, says: 'One who confounds God with the universe: a name given to the followers of Spinoza'; while from a Cyclopedia of 1813, entitled Pantologia, comes: 'A philosophical species of idolatry leading to atheism, in which the universe was considered the supreme god'. PANTHEISM is a belief in one universal vital force as contrasted with individual souls.

269. *CONSUMMATE*, consummate (*kŏn-sŭm'-māt*) *adj*. Supreme, complete, perfect, finished, carried to the utmost extent. The verb to CONSUMMATE (*kŏn'-sŭm-māt*), accented on the first syllable, is to achieve, perfect (*pĕr-fĕkt'*), bring to completion.

Each of the four wrong answers: WASTED, PRIMARY, MORE, LIMITED, attracts the same number of persons, a perfect item from the standpoint of test design.

The verb to FINISH, with the accompanying adjective FINISHED, from the Latin *finire*, to end, conclude, close, terminate, falls short of implying success. The verb to COMPLETE, with the adjective COMPLETE, from the Latin *plere*, to fill, suggests achievement.

The verb to CONSUMMATE, and the adjective CONSUMMATE, come from the Latin *consummatus*, summed up, finished, a combination of *com-*, together, and *summa*, the highest point, summit, top, the feminine of *summus*, highest, the superlative of *superus*, superior, higher, from *supex*, over. CONSUMMATE should be used only of superior achievement.

270. *PAGANISM*, paganism (*pā'-găn-ĭzm*) *n.* Irreligious idol-atry, heathenism, more exactly not Christian, Jewish, or Mohammedan, a sense which first appeared in A.D. 368.
At one time the Latin *paganus* meant a rustic, countryman, peasant, from *pagus*, the country, district. Quoting from Arch-bishop Trench, in his Study of Words: 'The Christian Church fixed itself first in the seats and centers of intelligence; in the towns and cities of the Roman Empire, and in them its first triumphs were won; while long after these had accepted the truth, heathen superstitions and idolatries lingered on in the obscure hamlets and villages of the country; so that PAGANS or villagers came to be applied to all the remaining votaries of the old and decaying superstitions'.

This history leads easily to the selection by 10 per cent of IGNORANCE as the meaning of PAGANISM. The word HEATHEN, applied to the wild dwellers on the heath, a synonym of PAGAN, has much the same background.

271. *ABSCOND*, abscond (*ăb-skŏnd'*) *v.* To run off, retire from public view, hide one's self, depart suddenly, escape, re-treat, flee, make off, take one's self off secretly in order to avoid a legal process.
To 4 per cent ABSCOND means OVERFLOW. To OVERFLOW, to spread over, flood, inundate, deluge, is to run over; to ABSCOND is to run off.

To ABSCOND, from the Latin *abscondere*, to hide, put away, a combination of *abs-*, and *condere*, to put, lay up, did not always imply dishonor, running away with money, as it does today, for in 1691 John Ray, the English naturalist, wrote in his Works of Creation: 'The marmot ABSCONDS in winter'.

272. *LAUDATORY*, laudatory (*law'-dă-tō-rĭ*) *adj*. Praise-
    worthy, speaking highly of, expressing praise in words,
applauding, extolling, commendatory, eulogizing.
To 2 per cent LAUDATORY means RELIGIOUS, but answers scatter
with no real concentration. LAUDATORY applies to that part of a
religious service which expresses praise.
   Of the four words: PRAISE, COMMEND, EXTOL, and LAUD, PRAISE
is the most generally applied and may be of any degree. COM-
MEND is mild, little more than to trust. To EXTOL (*ĕks-tōl'*), from
the Latin *ex-*, and *tollere*, to raise, is to give high praise, at length.
To LAUD, from the Latin *laudere*, to praise, is to give formally
still greater praise. LAUDATORY is the corresponding adjective.

273. *INJUNCTION*, injunction (*ĭn-jŭnk'-shŏn*) *n*. Admoni-
    tion (v. b. 1370), command, order, direction, requirement.
From the Latin *jugum*, yoke, and the related verb *jungĕre*, to
yoke, spring families of English words. Some, like SUBJUGATE,
suggest the unpleasantness of toiling under a burdensome yoke.
Others like JOIN, CONJOIN, to join together, combine, unite, and
CONJUNCTION, a union, combination, association, have a pleasanter feeling of YOKED together, associated. Still a third group
mean command, direct, order, as the verb ENJOIN, which Dr.
Johnson, 1755, says: 'Is more authoritative than DIRECT, and less
imperious than COMMAND', and the noun INJUNCTION.
   An INJUNCTION is thought by 21 per cent to be a SETTLEMENT.
A JUNCTION is a joining, union, meeting, and may suggest a meeting of minds and so a SETTLEMENT, agreement, establishment,
coming to terms. A JUNCTION may also be a meeting of roads or a
joining of railroads, frequently the location of a SETTLEMENT in
this sense, a small village, group of houses. But an INJUNCTION,
from the Latin *injunctus*, the past participle of *injungĕre*, to
command, is a command to act, or sometimes an order to
refrain from acting.

274. *ABET*, abet (*ă-bĕt'*) *v*. Encourage, incite, support, assist,
    help, further, aid, advocate.
ABET, to encourage usually in a bad sense, assist in a criminal
act, is a combination of the Latin *a*, meaning *ad*, to, and *betar*,
to bait, as to BAIT (*bāt*) horses, feed and give them water.

The past ABETTED is thought by 24 per cent to mean VETOED. To ABATE, literally to beat down, from the Latin *batuĕre*, to beat, is to stop, prevent, hinder, and so to VETO. VETO (*vē'-tō*) is Latin, meaning 'I forbid', the first person singular of the present indicative of the verb *vetare*, to forbid, prohibit, hinder, oppose. The right of VETO, of forbidding the passage of a bill of which they disapprove, belongs to certain high government executives. To ABET is the opposite, support, encourage.

From the Education of Henry Adams: 'Artists go on painting when no one buys their pictures; and society ABETS them and encourages their attitude of contempt'. And from Nero Wolfe, addressing Archie: 'Do you mean you are ABETTING it?'

CONNIVE, ABET, and PERPETRATE represent three degrees of taking part in a crime. To CONNIVE, literally to wink at, is to stand aside knowing a crime is going on but doing nothing about it. To PERPETRATE is to commit, execute, perform the deed directly. To ABET lies between the two, to encourage, even help, but not act alone.

275. *INGENIOUS*, ingenious (*ĭn-jē'-nyŭs*) *adj.* Possessed of
     genius, inventive, clever, skillful in contriving.
For the word INGENUOUS, which means FRANK, 64 per cent choose IMAGINATIVE, a synonym of INGENIOUS; but given the opposite opportunity, only 1 per cent choose FRANK as a meaning of INGENIOUS. One must know the far more difficult INGENUOUS to be misled by FRANK.

Of those tested, 6 per cent choose CRAFTY as the meaning of INGENIOUS. CRAFTY now implies skillful in devising evil schemes, cunning, artful, wily, sly, but originally meant possessing manual skill, displaying artistic gifts, and in this sense is too near INGENIOUS to remain as a mislead in the test.

276. *ARCHAIC*, archaic (*ahr-kā'-ĭk*) *adj.* Old, antiquated,
     primitive, ancient, obsolete, old-fashioned, borrowed from
older usage.
To 11 per cent ARCHAIC means STRUCTURAL. An ARCHITECT is skilled in the art of construction, building; and ARCHAIC might easily be an adjective made from ARCH and so mean STRUCTURAL. But the first five letters of ARCHITECT come from the Greek ἀρχι-

(*archi-*), first, chief, making the ARCHITECT the chief builder. The ARCH, as a form of construction, was unknown in early Greece, and the word ARCH meaning rounded top of a door or window is Latin, not Greek. ARCHAIC comes from the Greek ἀρχαῖος (*archaios*), old, antique, the source of ARCHAE-, which appears at the beginning of ARCHAEOLOGY, a study of the remote past.

ANTIQUATED implies out of date, old-fashioned, left behind, no longer of value. PRIMITIVE means crude, undeveloped. ARCHAIC falls between the two, more advanced and further developed than PRIMITIVE, but stronger and still of more value than old-fashioned, antiquated.

277. *LUSCIOUS*, luscious (*lŭsh'-ŭs*) *adj.* Highly pleasing to the taste, delicious, enjoyable, sweet, pleasant, delectable, succulent, savory.

Among 29 high-vocabulary adults 4 select INTOXICATING as a meaning of LUSCIOUS, the only misconception. INTOXICATING, inebriating, having qualities that produce drunkenness, comes from the Latin *in* and *toxicum*, poison, the source of the English TOXIC, poisonous. Figuratively INTOXICATING also means exciting enthusiasm, exaltation, elating, and this aspect of the word may lead to its selection as a synonym of LUSCIOUS, enjoyable.

LUSCIOUS, though of uncertain history, may come from LUSH, fresh, juicy, succulent, luxuriant; or it may be a decapitated form of DELICIOUS.

278. *ENGAGE*, engage (*ĕn-gāj'*) *v.* Hire, employ, obtain, secure, enlist, bind by contract.

ENGAGE is a combination of EN-, from the Latin *in*, conveying existence in a place as: ENCIRCLE, ENCOMPASS, ENLIGHTEN; and GAGE, to pledge, pawn, deposit as security.

To 26 per cent ENGAGED means CONSIDERED, looked at closely. To CONSIDER, from the Latin *considerare*, observe the stars for some prophetic sign, is to fix the mind upon, view carefully, study, ponder, reflect upon. In modern employment procedures, an applicant is CONSIDERED for a position, thought about, discussed before being hired, ENGAGED; but one quarter of those who are told they will be CONSIDERED believe they are ENGAGED.

279. *HAGGLE*, haggle (*hăg'-gl*) *v.* To bargain in a petty way,
    higgle, cavil, chaffer, balk at small points, dispute at
length.
To 2 per cent HAGGLE means EXHAUST, tire, fatigue, wear out.
HAGGARD, from a different parentage, once meant wild, untamed, but has come to mean looking wild from prolonged
suffering, and so careworn, wasted, lean, grim, EXHAUSTED. Also
EXHAUSTING an opponent with steady argument is one aspect of
HAGGLING.
    Of the three words: QUIBBLE, CHAFFER, and HAGGLE, the first
evades the point in question, plays upon words, prevaricates,
trifles in argument, also puns. To CHAFFER (*chăf'-fer*), to bargain, argue about a purchase, a combination of *cheap*, a bargain,
and *fare*, a going, is a legitimate bargaining.
    The word HAGGLE, like HACKLE, is probably a frequentative
of HACK, to cut at random, chop unevenly, notch irregularly.
HAGGLING is carrying bargaining too far, chopping at random
in every direction whether it is justified or not.

280. *TRANSITORY*, transitory (*trăn'-sĭ-tō-rĭ*) *adj.* Lasting a
    short time only, fleeting, vanishing, temporary, evanes-
cent, unstable, momentary, ephemeral, short lived, passing
quickly.
TRANSITORY comes from the Latin *transitus*, the past participle
of *transire*, to pass over, go across, a combination of *trans*, over,
and the irregular Latin verb *ire*, to go, with the parts *eo, ire,
itum.*
    To 5 per cent TRANSITORY means STABLE, durable, steady, fixed,
permanent, firm, established, sure, lasting, steadfast, an exact
opposite of TRANSITORY.
    TRANSIENT and TRANSITORY are nearly the same. TRANSIENT
means temporary, of short duration, not lasting, not durable,
not permanent. A TRANSIENT impression is momentary, a glance.
TRANSIENT and LASTING are opposites, for one may gain a LAST-
ING impression. FLEETING is still faster than TRANSIENT. TRANSI-
TORY, short lived, is more often an inherent characteristic of the
object to which it is affixed. TRANSITORY should be used in situations where the opposite, LASTING, could not fit, as: a TRANSI-
TORY life.

281. *BADGER*, badger (*băd'-jer*) *v*. To tease, pester, worry, bait, attack.

One dictionary says: 'A BADGER is a fossorial plantigrade, carnivorous mammal'. FOSSORIAL means digging, burrowing, excavating. The BADGER is a burrowing animal, digging into the earth for a retreat. The word comes probably from BADGE, because of the white stripes on the forehead.

TEASE, VEX, ANNOY, MOLEST, PESTER, BOTHER, WORRY, PLAGUE, TORMENT, all refer to repeated acts. TEASING is mild, may even be good-humored. VEX is stronger. BADGER-BAITING was a barbarous sport, where a BADGER was put into a barrel and two dogs set to get him out. The verb to BADGER comes from this practice.

282. *DIVAGATE*, divagate (*dī'-vā-gāt*) *v*. To stray from one subject to another, digress, wander about from place to place. Of the noun DIVAGATION (*di-vā-gā'-shŏn*) the Century Dictionary says: wandering, digression, deviation.

DIVAGATION, from the Latin *divagari*, to wander about, comes from *di-*, in different directions, and *vagari*, to wander, from *vagus*, wandering. From the same *vagari*, to wander, which contributes -VAGA- to many words, come EXTRAVAGANT, wandering beyond bounds, strained beyond reasonable limits, specifically spending more money than one should; and VAGABOND, one who wanders from place to place with no settled home, a rambler, rover.

To 7 per cent to DIVAGATE means to LIE. To LIE is specifically to stray from the truth. To DIVAGATE is to stray in general, wander about.

283. *ALIGN*, align (*ă-līn'*) *v*. Form in a line, adjust to a line.

According to the Century Dictionary, the correct spelling is the simpler ALINE.

This unusual ALIGN, from the French *aligner*, is a combination of the Latin *ad-*, to, and LINE, a word which goes back not only to Anglo-Saxon but also to the Latin *linea*, originally a linen thread, from *linum*, linen.

ALIGNED is thought by 18 per cent of high-school students, and by 10 per cent of high-vocabulary ones, to mean DIRECTED, too near the correct meaning to use as a mislead; for the verb to DIRECT comes from the Latin *dirigĕre*, to set in a straight line, straighten, an exact synonym of ALIGN.

The word ALIGN, spelt with the G, seems too rare to include in a high-school test, but in an article on the Rare Beauty in Common Rocks, in the National Geographic, Lorence G. Collins uses the corresponding noun twice: 'As I rotate a thin section in polarized light, the mineral ALIGNMENT continually changes'; and 'The color of a mineral depends on the ALIGNMENT with the plane of polarization'.

Or in the same magazine a few months later: 'Photons ALIGN in a pulse of laser light'. Perhaps this use by scientists of difficult English words is one of the reasons why, in a prominent institute of technology, we found classroom marks in physics checking more closely with a large and exact English vocabulary than with a knowledge of physics terms.

284. *ACOUSTICS*, acoustics (*ă-koos'-tĭks*) *n.* Hearing conditions, the science of sound, phenomena of hearing, study of vibrations which affect hearers.

Most words from Latin commence with ACC-, where the initial AC- stands for the Latin *ad*, to, which becomes *ac-* before another C. But ACOUSTICS, more directly from the Greek ἀκουστικός (*acousticos*), pertaining to hearing, from ἀκούειν (*acouein*), to hear, starts with only a single C.

The -ICS, at the end, is a Greek termination denoting a science or art. H. W. Fowler discusses in two columns the problem of treating these sciences ending in s as singulars or plurals, and concludes that it is almost, but not quite, personal fancy. ACOUSTICS, the science, IS singular; but the ACOUSTICS of a hall ARE good or bad.

285. *COVETABLE*, covetable (*kŭv'-ĕt-ă-bl*) *adj.* Endowed with desirable characteristics, attractive, arousing avarice, stirring up greed, greatly wished or longed for, fit to be coveted. COVETABLE goes back directly to the Latin, *cupere*, to desire, wish for, the source of CUPIDITY, immoderate craving, greed, hankering, grasping, covetousness, inordinate desire, lust for wealth, wish to possess something; and CUPID, the mythological Roman god of love.

OBTAINABLE, the only popular mislead, means within reach, capable of being possessed, almost an opposite of COVETABLE, which suggests a desire, never satisfied, for that which is out of reach.

COVETABLE, DESIRABLE, and ATTRACTIVE are synonymous but with different implications. The last two are pleasant. COVETABLE suggests arousing greed, avarice, and unlawful desire.

286. *PILLAGE*, pillage (*pĭl'-lăj*) *n.* Plundering, robbery, stealing, pilfering, preying, despoiling, rifling.

The verb to PILLAGE, from the Latin *pilare*, to plunder, is to strip of money or goods; to plunder, spoil.

PILLAGE differs from STEALING as it implies open violence, and from ROBBING, which may be committed by one individual on another. PILLAGING is usually the work of bands or numbers, against a country, group, or society. In The Heritage of Henry Adams, his brother Brooks Adams writes: 'The PILLAGE of the Public by the private man'.

287. *SERAPHIM*, seraphim (*săr'-ă-fĭm*) *pl. n.* Celestial beings with six wings, angels of the highest order.

CHERUBIM is the Hebrew plural of CHERUB, much as SERAPHIM is the plural of SERAPH. A CHERUB, a winged spirit, an order of angels under the SERAPHIM, is distinguished by knowledge as the SERAPH is by love. The adjective SERAPHIC (*sĕ-răf'-ĭk*) means celestial, angelic, pure, refined, superhuman, with no grossness.

The CELESTIAL HIERARCHY seems to have been named about 400 A.D., with nine orders, three sets of three each, with SERAPHIM at the top, and ANGELS at the bottom.

I. SERAPHIM	2. CHERUBIM	3. THRONES;
4. DOMINIONS	5. VIRTUES	6. POWERS;
7. PRINCIPALITIES	8. ARCHANGELS	9. ANGELS.

288. *BALK*, balk (*bawk*) *v.* To hinder, frustrate, disappoint, thwart, foil, baffle, outwit, circumvent, defeat.

The noun, a BALK, goes directly back to an Anglo-Saxon word for a ridge, mound of earth, sometimes a strip of land left unplowed between two pieces of property. The verb to BALK is to put a ridge in the way, and so to hinder, BALK, almost stop.

The only popular mislead is RIDICULE, which goes back to the Latin *ridiculum*, a jest, from the Latin verb *ridere*, to laugh. To RIDICULE is to mock, gibe, deride, jeer, sneer, make sport of, scoff at. To RIDICULE a suggestion, a plan, an idea, is one method of hindering, BALKING. But the word to RIDICULE is to make fun of with no purpose in mind.

289. *CHINK*, chink (*chĭnk*) *n.* Crack, cleft, rent, rift, crevice.
   A CHIP may be a bit broken off the edge, leaving an IRREG-ULARITY, selected by 28 per cent as the meaning of CHINK. A CHINK is a long open crack closed at both ends. One looks through a CHINK in a fence. A CRACK in a board or in a plate is seen as a line but is not open. One cannot look through a CRACK.
   A FISSURE is a long narrow CRACK in more or less level earth or rock, with sharp edges due to a break, an opening into which one looks down.
   The old Anglo-Saxon word CHINE once meant a crack, rift, chink, crevice, fissure; and then came to be a large fissure in a cliff and so a ravine. Somehow in Middle English a K was added to CHINE in place of the final E and the word CHINK came to mean an open crack in some sort of upright surface, as a fence, just wide enough to see through with one eye.

290. *NOCTURNAL*, nocturnal (*nŏk-ter'-năl*) *adj.* Belonging to the night, done at night, nightly, almost an opposite of DIURNAL (V. B. 1211).
To 4 per cent NOCTURNAL means FIENDISH (*fēn'-dĭsh*). A FIEND is an evil spirit, enemy of mankind, Satan, a demon, the devil, sometimes called Prince of Darkness. Such evil spirits are always associated with the night.
   NIGHTLY, from Anglo-Saxon, suggests occurring every night; while NOCTURNAL, from the Latin *nocturnus*, of the night, from *nox*, *noctis*, night, means belonging to the night, as NOCTURNAL birds like the owl.

291. *BELATED*, belated (*bē-lā'-tĕd*) *adj.* Coming late, behind time, delayed (v. b. 110), slow, behindhand, benighted, kept back, detained, tardy (v. b. 128).

BELATED, which starts with the Anglo-Saxon BE-, often used to form a verb, is literally to BE LATE. BENIGHTED, also with the Anglo-Saxon BE-, is to be overtaken by night.

BELATED is thought by 15 per cent of high-school students to mean RAGGED, torn, worn, tattered, hanging in shreds, shaggy. To BEDRAGGLE, with the same BE-, is to DRAGGLE, to drag in mud, soil, wet, dirty; and BEDRAGGLED is slovenly, soiled, almost RAGGED. BELATED can be used of anyone who is not on time.

Read The Education of Henry Adams who, on returning to the United States after seven years in London, calls himself: 'A BELATED reveller'.

292. *LIBEL*, libel (*lī'-bĕl*) *n.* Malicious (v. B. 777) publication, defamatory writing, slander (v. B. 456), untrue gossip, lampoon, injurious writing, aspersion. Read also LIBEL (v. B. 819). LIBEL comes from the Latin *libellus*, a little book, pamphlet, letter, the diminutive of *liber*, a book. A LIBEL was originally any small book, but is now a malicious publication, defamatory writing. In School for Scandal, by Richard Brinsley Sheridan, Maria says of her odious lover, Sir Benjamin Backbite: 'His whole conversation is a perpetual LIBEL upon all his acquaintance'.

Edmund Burke, a great name in political literature, who used the general ideas of the thinker to judge the particular problems of the statesman, gives five characteristics of a LIBEL: 1st the writing; 2nd the communication, publication; 3rd the application to persons and facts; 4th intent and tendency; and 5th the matter, diminution of fame.

Thomas McIntyre Cooley, professor of law at the University of Michigan in 1859, said: 'LIBEL is defamation published by means of writing, printing, pictures, images, or anything that is the object of the sense of sight'.

LIBEL is thought by 21 per cent to mean TRUTH, practically an opposite, for apparently if the published statement is TRUE, a statement of fact, the publication is not a legal LIBEL.

293. *CONCEIVE*, conceive (*kŏn-sēv'*) *v.* To imagine, get a notion, plan (v. B. 48), devise, formulate, design, form an image (v. B. 248).

'CONCEIVED the idea' is thought by 38 per cent to mean OBTAINED, received, acquired, got, procured. From the Latin verb *capĕre*, to take, seize, capture, hold, which appears with little spelling change in CAPACITY, CAPACIOUS, and CAPABLE, come a long list of English words ending in -CEIVE, a spelling which originated in Middle English. To PERCEIVE is to grasp with one's senses, notice, observe, come to know. To DECEIVE is to take from, cheat, dupe, cozen, beguile. To RECEIVE is to procure, get, OBTAIN, the popular misconception. CONCEIVE comes from the Latin *concipĕre*, which means to RECEIVE, take, OBTAIN; but despite this derivation, CONCEIVE today means form in the mind, imagine, devise.

294. *DISCONSOLATE*, disconsolate (*dĭs-kŏn'-sō-lāt*) *adj.*
    Hopeless, dejected, melancholy, sad, sorrowful, inconsolable (*ĭn-kŏn-sō'-lȧ-bl*), forlorn.
To 21 per cent DISCONSOLATE means IMPOLITE, rude, uncivil, discourteous. IMPOLITE, from the Latin *impolitus*, unpolished, rough, unrefined, is a combination of the privative *in-*, which becomes IM- before P, and *politus*, polished, from *polire*, to polish, make smooth. POLITE first meant smooth, polished, and then, of behavior, refined.
    DISCONSOLATE comes from the Latin privative *dis-*, not, and *consolatus*, the source of the English verb to CONSOLE, to encourage, cheer, and so lessen grief. The Latin in turn is a combination of *com*, together, and *solari*, to console, the source of the English SOLACE (*sŏl'-ȧs*). DISCONSOLATE is therefore *dis-* plus *con-*, which stands for *com-*, and so not with, without, SOLACE, comfort, soothing, cheer.

295. *MIGRANT*, migrant (*mī-grȧnt*) *n.* Traveller, wanderer, especially one who moves from one abode to settle in another.
MIGRANT comes from the Latin *migrare*, to migrate, to move from one place to another.
    An EMIGRANT is one who MIGRATES out of a country. An IMMIGRANT is one who moves into a country. These apply only to human beings. The noun MIGRANT is more general. Birds MIGRATE south in the fall, that is move south, and MIGRATE back toward the north in the spring. The verb to MIGRATE, the adjec-

tive MIGRATORY (*mĭ'-grᾰ-tō-rĭ*), the noun MIGRATION, the act of
MIGRATING, and MIGRANT, one who MIGRATES, are all used frequently of BIRDS; and this no doubt leads 5 per cent to believe
that MIGRANTS are BIRDS, and in zoology the word MIGRANT is
used of birds who MIGRATE.

296. *SATIATE*, satiate (*sᾱ'-shĭ-āt*) *v.* To satisfy, surfeit, glut,
     feed to the full, gorge, cloy, suffice, fill to repletion, be-
yond natural desire.

The verb to SATISFY was once two words, *satis*, enough, sufficient, and *facere*, to make, do, and meant to do enough, gratify,
make amends. To SATE, from the same *satis*, enough, is to fill full;
and so SATIATE, from the Latin *satiatus*, the past participle of
satiare, to fill, satiate.

    The noun, a SURFEIT (*ser'-fĭt*), with much the same implica-
tion, excess, repletion, plethora, comes through the French,
from the Latin *super*, above, and the same *facere*, to do, make;
and so the verb to SURFEIT.

    CONTENT, SATISFIED, and SATIATED, are three degrees of full-
ness. CONTENT is having just enough, so as not to find fault, not
to grumble. SATISFIED is that point at which one does not want
more. SATIATED is having more than one wants or can enjoy.

297. *DEPRECIATION*, depreciation (*dē-prē-shĭ-ᾱ'-shŏn*) *n.*
    A belittling, reduction, lessening, undervaluation, lowering
the purchase value of money.

DEPRECIATION comes from the Latin *depretiare*, to DEPRECIATE,
a combination of *de-*, down, and *pretium*, price. From *pretium*
come PRICE, PRECIOUS, PRAISE, APPRAISE, and similar words in
Spanish, Portuguese, and Italian.

    To APPRECIATE, from *ad-*, to, and *pretium*, price, is to price,
appraise, value justly, estimate the worth of. Because APPRE-
CIATE seems like an opposite of DEPRECIATE, it has come to mean,
not merely value justly, but also increase in value, as well as
sympathetic understanding. This makes DISAPPROVING, selected
by 15 per cent, very close to DEPRECIATION, perhaps too close to
use as a mislead.

    Of the verb to DEPRECIATE, Bailey said in 1721: 'To cry down
the price, to undervalue a thing'.

298. *MEDIEVAL*, medieval (*mē-dĭ-ē'-văl*) *adj.* Pertaining to
the middle ages, following Roman and just before the
Renaissance, from about 900 A.D. to 1250 or 1300.
The 17 per cent who chose PRE-CHRISTIAN are a thousand years
too early. The greatest Greek architecture, the Parthenon on
the Acropolis in Athens and the temples in Paestum in Italy
were all PRE-CHRISTIAN, five hundred years before Christ.

The term MEDIEVAL, from the Latin *medius*, middle, and
avum, age, period, is used primarily of European art and architecture to cover the period beginning nine hundred years after
Christ. In painting Giotto worked during this period; while in
architecture the Cathedral, the Baptistery, and the Leaning
Tower were built in Pisa.

299. *ANTHEM*, anthem (*ăn'-thĕm*) *n.* Church music, sacred
song for trained voices, hymn set to words from the Psalms.
An ANTHEM, for trained voices only, is a more elaborate composition than the usual hymn, sung by the congregation.
ANTHEMS, especially English, composed in the 16th, 17th, and
18th centuries, were sometimes for the full choir, sometimes
for solo voices only, or for both. One technical definition says:
'A hymn sung in alternate parts, with two choruses, answering
one another, or a chorus and soloists'. The word is Anglo-Saxon.

To nearly 10 per cent an ANTHEM is an OFFERING, a gift,
donation. In some church services an ANTHEM follows the third
COLLECT (*cŏl'-lĕkt*), and this may conceivably lead to the selection of OFFERING as the meaning of ANTHEM. But ecclesiastically
a COLLECT, as the word is used here, is a short prayer, perhaps a
a single sentence. An ANTHEM is a song.

300. *ACCEDE*, accede (*ăk-sēd'*) *v.* To attain, gain, reach, arrive
at, achieve, accomplish, obtain, as: 'To ACCEDE to the title'.
The verb to ACCEDE comes from the Latin *accedere*, to go to, a
combination of *ad-*, to, and *cēdere*, to go, move. From the same
cēdere, to go, move, walk, come PRECEDE, from *prae*, before,
to go before, in front of; RECEDE, to go back; SECEDE; and
CONCEDE; as well as others from the same *cēdere*, but which have
come to be spelt with EE, as: PROCEED, from *pro*, forth, EXCEED,
and SUCCEED.

To ASPIRE, selected by 16 per cent, is to hope, want. ASPIRE
is a first step toward gaining; to ACCEDE to is actually to obtain,
gain, get.

301. *MALFEASANCE*, malfeasance (*măl-fē'-zăns*) *n.* Evil-doing, wrongful conduct, misconduct, misbehavior, violation
of a public obligation.
To 22 per cent MALFEASANCE means DISORGANIZATION, a translation of the Latin *mal*, bad, and *facere*, to do; for ORGAN comes
from the Greek ἐργειν (*ergein*), to work. To ORGANIZE is to fit
together a group of ORGANS into a vital, living, working whole.
The privative DIS- has much the same effect as MAL-. DISORGAN-
IZATION is by derivation bad-working.
   But MALFEASANCE, directly from the French *malfaisance*,
evil-doing, wrong-doing, means not poor organization, but
wrong-doing in the legal sense, mis-conduct.
   NONFEASANCE (*nŏn-fē'-zăns*) is the omission of some act
which should have been performed. MISFEASANCE and MAL-
FEASANCE should strictly be distinguished. MISFEASANCE is the
misuse of power, wrongful application of lawful authority,
misbehavior in office. MALFEASANCE is an unlawful act, clearly
contrary to law.

302. *SALVO*, salvo (*săl'-vō*) *n.* A firing of guns in unison,
   fusillade, general discharge of artillery as a salute, concentrated fire in regular succession.
SALVO, from the Italian *salva*, comes from the Latin *salvus*, sound;
through the Latin exclamation *salve*, meaning hail.
   A FUSILLADE is a simultaneous discharge of firearms, usually in
preparation for an attack. A SALVO is more often a salute, and
this leads 14 per cent to select ADDRESS as the meaning of SALVO.
To SALUTE is defined as to address with expressions of good will,
and in this sense SALVO is close to ADDRESS.

303. *LINEAGE*, lineage (*lĭn'-ē-āj*) *n.* Race, stock, family, pedi-
   gree, genealogy, extraction, ancestry, progeny, parentage,
line of descent.
LINEAGE comes from the Latin *linea*, a line. A LINE is a thread,
string, cord, rope, as: fishing LINE, clothes LINE, BOWLINE.

LINEAGE was once spelt without the E: LINAGE (*lĭ'-nāj*), but changed gradually to agree with LINEAL, like a line, in a row. LINEAGE refers only to family descent.

LINEAGE is thought by 23 per cent to mean CONSCIENCE, but readers scatter uniformly enough among the four misleads of the test to suggest that the selection of CONSCIENCE is more luck than an actual misunderstanding.

304. *EXORCISE*, exorcise (*ĕks'-ōr-sīz*) *v.* To expel, dismiss, compel to leave, drive out by magical agencies, force out. To 23 per cent the participial adjective EXORCISED means TRAINED. EXERCISED, from the Latin *exercēre*, to exercise, practise, a combination of *ex-* and *arcēre*, to keep off, shut up, means practised, TRAINED. But EXORCISE, from the Greek ἐξ (*ex*) and ὅρκος (*orkos*), an oath, applies usually to evil spirits, malignant demons, and means driven out by conjuration, magical ceremonies.

To another 23 per cent EXORCISED means WELCOMED, a confusion of opposites, the last step in the learning process.

305. *INDENTURED*, indentured (*ĭn-dĕn'-tūrd*) *adj.* Bound under contract, covenanted, working by formal arrangement usually with a time limit. To INDENT is to make notches like teeth, cut jaggedly. Years ago, in law, to INDENT was to write an important agreement twice, on the same sheet of paper, one above the other, and then, after cutting them apart jaggedly, give each party his copy. A perfect fit of the two agreements along the ragged cut proved their authenticity. An INDENTURE then became any written agreement between two people.

In the more elegant language of Ephraim Chambers, 1728: 'INDENTURE, in law, a writing which comprises some contract between two, being INDENTED at top answerable to another part, which has the same contents'. The verb to INDENTURE applied frequently to an agreement between an apprentice who wanted to learn a trade and a master who agreed to teach. At the age of fourteen Michael Angelo was sent to the workshop of the painter Domenico Ghirlandaio to acquire the art of painting and INDENTURED, that is bound to continue to work for him for a period of three years.

INDENTURED is thought by 19 per cent to mean INDEPENDENT, at liberty, untrammeled, free to act, an exact opposite of the correct answer BOUND.

306. *INVIOLABLE*, inviolable (*ĭn-vī'-ō-lā-bl*) *adj*. Not breakable, permanent, lasting, sacred, free from outrage, not subject to injury (v. b. 16).

The adjective VIOLENT (*vī'-ō-lĕnt*) comes through the French from the Latin *violentus*, from the peculiar Latin noun *vis*, force, power, with the accusative *vim*, and the plural *vires*, strength. The verb to VIOLATE (*vī'-ō-lāt*), directly from the Latin *violatus*, the past participle of *violare*, is to treat with VIOLENCE. To VIOLATE an agreement, or an oath, is to break it. VIOLABLE refers to something which can be BROKEN; and despite the 26 per cent who believe that INVIOLABLE means BROKEN, the IN- is negative and INVIOLABLE means not breakable.

307. *MATTED*, matted (*măt'-tĕd*) *adj*. Entangled, twisted together, snarled, interwoven (v. b. 228), like a net.

The noun, a MAT, directly from Anglo-Saxon, is a small woven or plaited rug, and from this comes the verb to MAT, originally to weave together like a mat but now often to entangle.

MATTED is thought by 14 per cent to mean SPOTTED. MOTTLED is spotted, blotched, from MOTLEY, originally the suit worn by a jester, made of pieces of different colored cloth.

Another meaning of MATTED almost justifies ARRANGED, underlined by another 14 per cent, for to MAT a picture is to mount it, and so perhaps ARRANGE it. But given a choice between ARRANGED and ENTANGLED, as synonyms of MATTED, 97 per cent of high-vocabulary examinees select the latter.

308. *LEVERAGE*, leverage (*lē'-ver-āj* or *lĕv'-er-āj*) *n*. Mechanical advantage gained by using a lever, action of a lever, increased power of accomplishment.

Of the pronunciation, William Henry P. Phyfe says, in his *Words Often Mispronounced*: 'Oxford English Dictionary, Encyclopaedic Dictionary, Stormonth, and Worcester say (*lē'-ver*). Century Dictionary and Standard Dictionary prefer (*lĕv'-er*).' Phyfe himself gives (*lē'-ver*) first.

Although 60 per cent of high-vocabulary readers select AD-VANTAGE as the meaning of LEVERAGE, a surprisingly large number of this top group, 33 per cent, want EVENNESS. Of the total population, 43 per cent choose ADVANTAGE compared with 31 per cent for EVENNESS. A LEVEL (*lĕv'-ĕl*) is an instrument for determining lack of slope; while LEVELNESS is EVENNESS, smoothness parallel with the horizon, with everywhere the same elevation, words from the Latin *libella*, a balance, the diminutive of *libra*, a balance, a device with a FULCRUM much like a LEVER.

The word LEVER goes back through French to the Latin *levare*, to lift, raise, from *levis*, light, not heavy, the source of ELEVATE and ELEVATOR. According to the incomparable Ephraim Chambers a LEVER, or LEAVER, in mechanics, is an inflexible straight bar, supported, in a single point, on a fulcrum, a prop, and used for the raising of weights.

In LEVERS of the first kind the fulcrum or centre of motion is between the weight and the power, as with scissors (Chambers' spelling is scissars) and pincers. In LEVERS of the second kind the weight is between the fulcrum and the power as with oars, and doors which hinge. In LEVERS of the third kind the power acts between the weight and the fulcrum, as in lifting a ladder to raise it against a wall.

LEVERAGE (*lē'-ver-āj*) is the mechanical advantage gained, usually by LEVERS of the first kind.

309. *GAUCHO*, gaucho (*gow'-chō*) *n.* A South American race of mixed Spanish and Indian descent. Pronounce the first three letters to rime with COW, HOW, NOW.
Charles Darwin in the Voyage of the Beagle, a book which more boys should read, calls a GAUCHO a native of Spanish descent. He mentions their use of the BOLA. They are noted for their horsemanship, and ranching is their occupation. The GAUCHOS are a nomadic race, inhabiting the south of South America, Argentina and Uruguay. The word GAUCHO is said to come from Araucanian, an Indian language of Central Chile.

Edward Burnett Tylor, an English anthropologist, in his Primitive Culture of 1871, says: 'The GAUCHOS of the South American pampas, a mixed European and Indian race of equestrian herdsmen'.

310. *DIVINE*, divine (*dē-vĭn'*) *v.* To perceive, learn, penetrate,
    see through, use one's intuition, make out by observation;
according to Bailey: to foretell, guess, soothsay.

To CREATE, the popular mislead, is to bring into being, produce,
make, bring about, originally from a Sanscrit word meaning to
make, probably a confusion of DEVISE with DIVINE. To DEVISE is
to think out, invent, contrive, concoct, and so CREATE. A DEVICE
is something created, an invention, contrivance.

To DIVINE, from the Latin *divinare*, to foretell, foresee, presage (*prē-sāj'*), comes from *divinus*, divinely inspired.

311. *EPIC*, epic (*ĕp'-ĭk*) *n.* An heroic poem telling in metrical
    form a long series of achievements and adventures under
supernatural guidance, a narrative, rehearsing, epos (*ĕp'-ōs*), an
epopee (*ĕp-ō-pē'*). Nathan Bailey, 1721, who spells this word
EPICK, says: 'Consisting of heroick or hexameter verse whose
subject is always a prince or some great person'.
Epic comes from the Greek ἔπος (*epos*), word, speech, saying,
tale, a word which in English is a synonym of EPIC.

Ephraim Chambers, in his huge folios of 1728, writes: 'An
EPIC poem recites some signal transaction of a hero, such as the
Iliad and Odyssey of Homer, the Aeneid of Virgil, the Gier-
usalimme of Tasso, Paradise Lost of Milton, and the Henriade of
Voltaire'. To these add Beowulf in Anglo-Saxon, The Cid, in
Spanish, and the Nibelungenlied in German.

Chambers continues: 'An EPIC, written in honor of the
country and religion of the author is intended more for the
manners and habits than for the passions. These latter rise all
at once and their violence is of short duration; but the habits
are more calm and impressed or quitted more leisurely. Consequently, the EPIC action could not be included in the space of
a day, as that of the theatrical. The tragic violence requires a
more lively and animated representation. The poet never speaks
at all as he does in the EPIC'.

312. *BALLOT*, ballot (*băl'-lŏt*) *n.* Vote, decision, choice.
    BALLOT, first used in the 16th century, comes directly from
the Italian *ballota*, the diminutive of *balla*, ball. The original
BALLOT was a little ball used in voting. From this the word has

come to mean a printed paper for recording a vote, or sometimes a method of selecting by voting. Similar words appear in French and Spanish.

The word BALLET, pronounced (*băl'-lā*) without the T at the end, a spectacular dance, misleads many into selecting THEATRICAL PERFORMANCE as the meaning of BALLOT.

313. *ENCLAVE*, enclave (*ĕn-klāv'*) *v.* To enclose, surround completely by territories of other countries.

Among 29 high-vocabulary adults, 2 select VOTE FOR, and 2 others CONQUER as meanings of ENCLAVE. From the Latin *clavis*, key, come the verb ENCLAVE and the noun CONCLAVE (*kŏn'-klāv*). A CONCLAVE is specifically a meeting of the cardinals of the Roman Catholic Church to VOTE FOR a new Pope, a right of election vested in the cardinals in 1059.

To ENSLAVE (*ĕn-slāv'*) is to CONQUER; to ENCLAVE (*ĕn-klāv'*) is to surround a small nation by the lands of other countries.

314. *FLUME*, flume (*flūm*) *n.* A rapid mountainous stream flowing between steep restraining rocky sides, torrent in a deep narrow defile; or recently an artificial channel, trough for conducting water.

A FLOAT is a platform on wheels, drawn in a procession, and this may suggest the mislead BOX-CAR, chosen by 15 per cent. Also a FLAT is one name for a PLATFORM car, and this may contribute to the mislead, though a BOX-CAR is an enclosed covered freight car, not open.

There exist words specifically for artificial channels, as SLUICEWAY, often shortened to SLUICE, though strictly the SLUICE is the dam or gateway which holds the water back, when not in use, so that it is always available. There is no need of a second word for an artificial channel; and FLUME, from the Latin *flumen*, from *flumere*, to flow, should be reserved for a rapid stream flowing down a mountain gorge.

315. *SURROGATE*, surrogate (*sŭr'-rō-gāt*) *adj.* Appointed to act for another, substitute, deputy, alternate.

To INTERROGATE, from *inter*, between, among, and *rogare*, to ask, more specifically to ask for the passage of a law, is to question, examine by asking in detail. To ABROGATE, from *ab-*, from, and *rogare*, to ask, is to withdraw, rescind, repeal, abolish.

SURROGATE, now usually a legal term, comes from the Latin past participle of the verb *surrogare*, to substitute, put in another's place, a combination of *sub*, under, and *rogare*, to ask.

The noun, a SURROGATE, is one appointed to act in the place of another, an assistant, helper, deputy, originally to an ecclesiastical judge. The two ideas, law, and appointment, lead 20 per cent to choose COURT-APPOINTED as the synonym of SURROGATE, and there is much of the same flavor in both words.

316. *ARMOIRE*, armoire (*ahr'-mwäh*) *n*. A wardrobe, clothes closet, clothes-press.

Both ARMOIRE and AMBRY were probably originally for weapons, for armor, for both come from the Latin *arma*, arms, implements, and this leads 15 per cent to select WEAPON as the meaning of ARMOIRE.

A VESTRY, from the Latin *vestiarium*, a wardrobe, is a room or building, attached to a church, for holding the robes, the vestments of the clergy. An AMBRY is a closet, cupboard, locker, often for food, not necessarily for clothes. An ARMOIRE is now a wardrobe for clothes only, in which they hang full length.

An ARMOIRE can be a beautiful piece of furniture, which adds to the attractiveness of a room. ARMOIRES should be used more often instead of modern closets, which are expensive to build and contain much waste space in order to allow a person to enter.

317. *EXHILARATION*, exhilaration (*ĕks-ĭl-ă-rā'-shŭn*) *n*. Animation (V. B. 781), gaiety, joyousness, glee, hilarity (V. B. 601), elevation of spirits, cheerfulness, liveliness, merriment, elation (33).

The verb to EXHILARATE is a combination of the Latin *ex*, out, and *hilarare*, to gladden, cheer, from *hilaris*, glad, the source of HILARIOUS. 'HILARITY', says Noah Webster, 1828, 'differs from JOY; the latter, excited by good news or prosperity, is an affection of the mind; the former, by social pleasure, drinking, &c, which rouse the animal spirits'.

To 26 per cent EXHILARATION means PRIDE, from Anglo-Saxon, a word so often used to mean unreasonable self-esteem, exaggerated estimate of one's superiority, that one forgets that the same word may mean reasonable exultation as a result of one's real achievements. This sort of EXULTATION, from the Latin *exsulare*, to leap for joy, from *salire*, to leap, differs little if at all from EXHILARATION, joyousness, elation.

318. *ALMSHOUSE*, almshouse (*ahmz'-hows*) *n.* An abode for the needy supported by the public, poorhouse, beadshouse or bedeshouse, also HOSPITAL as used a century ago.
In The Warden, a short novel published in 1855, Anthony Trollope writes: 'John Hiram, who had made money in the town as a wool stapler, appointed in his will that an ALMSHOUSE should be built for the abode of twelve superannuated wool-carders, with a fitting residence for a warden'. Those who live in this ALMSHOUSE, Trollope calls BEDESMEN (*bēdz'-mĕn*), now more often spelt BEADSMEN. After The Warden, read Barchester Towers, then Phineas Finn, the aspirations of a young ambitious politician, and before you start Latin in school read The Life of Cicero, also by Anthony Trollope.
Trollope uses ALMSHOUSE and HOSPITAL interchangeably, for a HOSPITAL was once an institution caring for the needy, the indigent, an ASYLUM, originally, any sanctuary, inviolable shelter, place of refuge even for criminals; and today 18 per cent of readers believe that an ALMSHOUSE is an INSANE ASYLUM. But an INSANE ASYLUM is specifically for the housing of mental patients, while ALMS, from the Greek ἔλεος (*eleos*), pity, compassion, mercy, is money given to the poor and an ALMSHOUSE is for the poor of all kinds.
By another 17 per cent of high-school students, and even by the same percentage of high-vocabulary ones, ALMSHOUSE is thought to mean TEMPLE. Most ancient Grecian TEMPLES were temporary ASYLUMS for criminals, places of refuge, shelter, but an ALMSHOUSE is a permanent abode for the poor.

319. *STIFLED*, stifled (*stī'-fld*) *adj.* Choked, smothered, killed by covering the nose and mouth, throttled, suffocated, oppressed, strangled, gagged, muffled, muzzled.
The verb to STIFLE comes from Icelandic and Norwegian words meaning to choke, stop, dam up.

To 4 per cent STIFLED means DISCOURAGED. To DISCOURAGE is to dishearten, dispirit, deject, depress, hinder by opposition. STIFLE, used figuratively, means suppress, conceal, repress, and in this sense is somewhat similar in suggestion to DISCOURAGE.

320. *STANCHION*, stanchion (*stăn'-shŏn*) *n*. Post, pillar, prop (v. B. 365), staff, support. Specifically a STANCHION is one of the two uprights which form a yoke for securing cattle in a barn. It is used in ship-building for uprights to support a deck but rarely used in architecture.

A STANCHION, from the Latin *stans*, *stantis*, the present participle of *stare*, to stand, is thought by 30 per cent to mean DEPOT. STATION goes back through the Latin *statio*, *stationis*, a standing place, position, to the same verb *stare*, to stand. STATION and STANCHION have many similar meanings; but a STATION may be a stopping place for a railroad train and so a DEPOT, but STANCHION never means DEPOT.

321. *TEMPERANCE*, temperance (*těm'-per-ăns*) *n*. Moderation, sobriety, frugality, soberness, restraint of passions, abstinence from excess.

To 4 per cent TEMPERANCE means EXCESSIVE DRINKING, intemperance, excess in any action, indulgence, profligateness, which is an exact opposite of TEMPERANCE, restraint, drinking a little but not too much.

TEMPERANCE goes back to the Latin *temperantis*, moderation, sobriety, to the verb *temperare*, to moderate, temper, regulate, rule, divide correctly, mingle in due proportion, and finally to *tempus*, time, correct season. The TEMPERATE ZONES are moderate, mild, between the cold polar regions and the hot tropics. The verb to TEMPER is to modify, blend, combine in the correct proportions, and also, with a metal, to bring to the correct hardness. TEMPERANCE is the corresponding noun but is used almost entirely of moderation in drinking.

322. *GRACIOUS*, gracious (*grā'-shŭs*) *adj*. Showing good will, beneficent, benign (v. B. 1351), courteous, kind, friendly. To 27 per cent GRACIOUS means ARTFUL, a confusion of two pleasant words close in meaning. ARTFUL means skilful, clever,

cunning, literally full of ART, from the Latin *ars*, *artis*, skill, the source of ARTISAN, one skilled in some craft. Like other words of this sort ARTFUL has come to suggest too clever and so not to be fully trusted, cunning, in this exaggerated sense almost an opposite of GRACIOUS.

GRACIOUS goes back through French, Spanish, and Italian to the Latin *gratiosus*, enjoying favor, also showing favor, obliging, from *gratio*, favor, grace, the source of the English GRACE. GRACIOUS in English has come to mean showing kindness.

323. *BONANZA*, bonanza (*bō-năn'-zah*) *n*. Rich find, profitable thing, mine of wealth, rich mass of ore.
The BONANZA mines were the great silver ones on the Comstock lode, discovered in Nevada in 1859. The word was first used in English about 1866. Raymond in his Mining Glossary of 1881 says: 'BONANZA, in miners' phrase; Good luck', or a body of rich ore. A mine is in BONANZA when it is profitably producing ore. BONANZA is a Spanish word which means fair weather, prosperity. BONANZA, originally from the Latin *bonus*, good, is the opposite of the Spanish word *borrasca*, which means tempest, squall, storm or, in mining, barren rock.

324. *DELIRIUM*, delirium (*dē-lē'-rĭ-ŭm*) *n*. Unsoundness of mind, disordered state of madness, insanity, frenzy; Bailey, 1721, says: 'Light-headedness, dotage, raving'.
Of 27 high-vocabulary adults 4 select FORGETFULNESS as the synonym, failure to remember, loss of the power of recalling to consciousness, ceasing to take thought, known technically as AMNESIA, loss of memory.

DELIRIUM comes directly from the Latin *delirium*, madness, from *delirus*, mad, crazy, raving, literally to make balks in plowing, being out of the furrow, to err, wander, miss, a combination of *de*, away, and *lira*, furrow.

Noah Webster, in his first edition, 1828: 'A state in which the ideas of a person are wild, irregular, and unconnected, or do not correspond with truth or with external objects; a roving, or wandering of the mind; disorder of the intellect dependent on some other disease in distinction from idiopathic derangement or mania'.

325. *INCOMPREHENSIBLENESS*, incomprehensibleness
   (*ĭn-kŏm-prē-hĕn'-sĭ-bl-nĕs*) *n*. The quality of not being
grasped by the mind, not to be understood, not comprised
within limits, known as a fact but not understood.
The Anglo-Saxon suffix -*ness* makes from an adjective an abstract noun, as SWEETNESS, from SWEET, WHITENESS from WHITE.
Added to a Latin word this ending is sometimes unpleasant, un-
couth. Remove -NESS from INCOMPREHENSIBLENESS and the adjective INCOMPREHENSIBLE remains.

   The prefix IN- may mean NOT, or it may survive in words
where it once meant IN, but has lost most of this meaning, and
today adds little. In this case, IN- means NOT. COMPREHENSIBLE,
without IN- at the beginning, means UNDERSTANDABLE, capable
of being grasped by the mind. The Latin ending -BLE, when
added, transforms a verb into an adjective.

   At the heart of the word is the root HEND, to seize, grasp. To
COMPREHEND is to get hold of a number of ideas together, COM-;
beforehand, PRE-. INCOMPREHENSIBLENESS is an inability to
COMPREHEND.

326. *ELATED*, elated (*e-lā'-tĕd*) *adj*. Jubilant, overjoyed, exultant, exhilarated (34).
The verb to ELATE comes from the irregular Latin verb *ferre*,
to carry, with the past participle *latus*, the source of RELATE,
literally to bring back, but now more often tell, report, describe; COLLATE, to bring together and so compare; DILATE,
literally to carry apart, expand, enlarge, spread out; and a
dozen or more others. ELATED originally meant carried up,
lifted up, raised, and now lifted up in spirit.

   To 6 per cent the participial adjective ELATED means SAD.
DEFLATED, which suggests SAD, is an opposite of INFLATED, the
last sometimes included among the synonyms of ELATED; while
SAD itself is an exact opposite of ELATED, the final confusion in
the learning process.

327. *ELEMENTS*, elements (*ĕl'-ĕ-mĕnts*) *pl. n*. The weather,
   wind and rough water, thunder and lightning.
ELEMENTS are the ingredients of which things are made, the
factors, components, constituents, often the basic, smallest por-

tions. The ELEMENTS are the pieces of which the WHOLE, the entire, complete object is composed; and this relationship misleads 37 per cent into selecting WHOLE as the meaning of ELEMENTS, a confusion of the WHOLE with its parts.

The word ELEMENT comes through French from the Latin *elementum*, the first principle, rudiment, used ordinarily in the plural to mean first principles, as the ELEMENTS of geometry, the ELEMENTS of knowledge. One derivation suggests *el-em-en*, meaning the abc's of the subject, its lmn's.

In modern chemistry the ELEMENTS number over a hundred, as OXYGEN, HYDROGEN, NITROGEN; but in the days of alchemy, before about 1750, the ELEMENTS were: EARTH, FIRE, AIR, and WATER, and these survive today in the use of the plural ELEMENTS to mean weather as: 'The fury of the ELEMENTS'. WATER appears as rain, rivers, and oceans; FIRE as lightning and the sun; with EARTH and AIR added. The ELEMENTS in action make the weather.

328. *DISSERTATION*, dissertation (*dĭs-ser-tā'-shŏn*) *n*. A formal discourse, written essay, treatise, disquisition.

DISSERTATION comes from the Latin *dissertatus*, the past participle of *dissertare*, to discuss, argue, the frequentative of *disserere*, to discourse about, argue, discuss, literally to set apart in order, a combination of *dis-*, apart, and *serere*, to join, the source of SERIES. A DISSERTATION is an orderly presentation of an argument.

To 5 per cent a DISSERTATION is an HISTORICAL DOCUMENT. A DOCUMENT, from the Latin *docere*, to teach, is an authoritative statement, a written or printed paper, anything bearing a significant communication. History deals with past events. An HISTORICAL DOCUMENT is an accepted statement of facts. A DISSERTATION is an argument, discussion, presentation of a point of view.

329. *INDUBITABLE*, indubitable (*ĭn-dū'-bĭ-tā-bl*) *adj*. Too clear to admit of doubt, indisputable (v. B. 375), certain, sure, obvious (v. B. 854), not questionable, undeniable, incontrovertible (v. B. 702).

The verb to DOUBT is to question, be of two minds, be uncertain, not sure. The adjective DOUBTFUL, literally full of DOUBT, means uncertain, not sure, hesitant, questioning. DUBITABLE, directly from the Latin *dubitare*, to doubt, means doubtful, hesitant, uncertain, questionable, not sure, and so UNKNOWN. INDUBITABLE, the opposite, not UNKNOWN, not doubtful, and so certain, sure, is thought by 36 per cent of those tested to mean UNKNOWN, not known, compared with only 35 per cent who mark SURE.

Accepting this popular expression of opinion, DUBITABLE becomes KNOWN, and DOUBTFUL should mean CERTAIN, a meaning at which a clear majority rebel. Accepting usage, popular vote, is not the way to build a meaningful English language.

In this study of word meanings the bottom ten per cent often swing the vote away from the historical interpretation. Only by lifting the bottom ten per cent can public education swing the popular vote to the opinion now held by the high-vocabulary group; for among those generally high in vocabulary, in the top tenth, 87 per cent select SURE as the meaning of IN-DUBITABLE. DUBITABLE then becomes UNSURE, uncertain; and to DOUBT becomes to be uncertain. In building our vocabulary tests we follow the usage of high-vocabulary examinees, accepting their consensus of opinion. Should the United States become an oligarchy, allowing only the top to vote; or should we lift the controlling bottom to a higher-vocabulary level?

330. *ALLITERATION*, alliteration (ăl-lĭt-ĕr-ā'-shŏn) *n*. With the same consonant sound or sound group, initial rime, repetition, recurrence of some first letter.

To 11 per cent ALLITERATION means SLANDER. SLANDER is a false assertion, malicious declaration, calumniation, defamation published without legal excuse. An ALLEGATION (ăl-lĕ-gā'-shŏn) is an assertion, a formal declaration, not necessarily untrue.

ALLITERATION comes from the Latin *ad*, to, and *litera*, letter, the source also of LITERATE, able to read, and OBLITERATION. To OBLITERATE is to rub out, erase, blot out, render unreadable. The noun OBLITERATION is the act of rubbing out, making unreadable.

ALLITERATION is the repetition of the same letter at the beginning of two or more words immediately succeeding each other, or at short intervals, a repeating and playing upon the same letter, as F and G in the following line:

'Fields ever fresh; and groves ever green', or
'Many men, many minds', or
'Apt alliteration's artful aid'.

331. *SPECTER*, specter (*spĕk'-ter*) *n*. Ghostly apparition, dis-
embodied spirit, vision, image, appearance, manifestation.
To 8 per cent of those tested a SPECTER is a WAND. A SCEPTER
(*sĕp'-ter*), staff of office, an emblem of authority, symbol, baton,
is a WAND. SCEPTER comes through the Latin *sceptrum*, from the
Greek σκῆπτρον (*sceptron*), a staff to lean on.

E. Chambers says of SCEPTER: A royal staff, or baton, borne
on solemn occasions by kings as a badge of their command and
authority. The SCEPTER is an ENSIGN of royalty of greater antiquity than the crown. Neptune's SCEPTER is his trident. With
the early French kings the SCEPTER was a golden rod, almost
always the same height as the king who bore it, and crooked at
one end like a CROZIER.

SPECTER, from the Latin *spectrum*, a vision, apparition, image,
appearance, comes from *specere*, to see, the source of SPECIES,
ASPECT, INSPECT, and PROSPECT, as well as SPECTACLE, an exhibition, showing, display, sight, from *spectare*, to behold, the frequentative of *specere*. A SPECTER is something seen.

332. *IMPROMPTU*, impromptu (*ĭm-prŏmp'-tū*) *adj*. Impro-
vised, offhand, extempore, hastily arranged, without preparation, unprepared, not expected, suddenly made, composed
on the spur of the moment, for the occasion only.
From the Latin verb *emere*, to take, acquire, or more specifically
to buy, comes the English verb, to PREEMPT, to buy before
others, or obtain the right to buy, usually applied to land. From
the Latin *promere*, to take out, bring forth, produce, comes the
Latin *promptus*, visible, apparent, at hand, ready, and so the
English PROMPT, and then the Latin phrase: *in promptu*, in
readiness, and so the English IMPROMPTU.

Of EXTEMPORE, (*ĕks-tĕm'-pŏ-rē*), a synonym of IMPROMPTU,
Fowler in his English Usage comments: 'EXTEMPORANEOUS and
EXTEMPORARY are cumbersome words; EXTEMPORE is seldom
unequal to the need'. Of the pronunciation, Phyfe adds: (*ĕks-
tĕm'-pŏ-rē*; not *ĕks-tĕm'-pŏr*).

Though nothing in the derivation justifies the distinction, EXTEMPORE seems to suggest that the performance, act, or speech, would have been better if more time had been spent in preparation, while IMPROMPTU applies to situations of less consequence: an EXTEMPORE speech; an IMPROMPTU suggestion.

The only misconception, selected by 8 per cent, is EXPECTED, an opposite, for IMPROMPTU implies an UNEXPECTED situation.

333. *PATRONAGE*, patronage (*păt'-rŏn-āj*) *n.* Support, favor, protection, defence; Webster, first edition: 'Special countenance or support; favor or aid afforded to second the views of a person or to promote a design'.

PATRONAGE comes from the Latin *patronus*, a patron, protector, defender, from *pater, patris*, father, the source of PATERNAL.

DEPENDENCE is occasionally marked as a meaning of PATRONAGE. A DEPENDENT is one who receives, obtains. A PATRON is one who gives, helps.

Of PATRON (*pā'-trŏn*) Bailey says: 'A powerful friend, protector, advocate'; while one of the oft quoted definitions of the misanthropic Dr. Johnson was: 'Commonly a wretch who supports with insolence and is paid with flattery'.

334. *STANCHLESS*, stanchless (*stănch'-lĕs*) *adj.* That cannot be stopped, incessant, unquenchable, insatiable, perpetual. See the discussion of the verb to STANCH (v. B. 236).

To 15 per cent STANCHLESS means SLUGGISH, inactive, slow, with little energy, indisposed to exertion, an opposite in suggestion. To STANCH is to check, appease, allay, assuage, stop the flow of and so to make more SLUGGISH. But STANCHLESS is the opposite, flowing actively.

335. *PLAIT*, plait (*plāt*) *v.* To braid, interweave, also fold, as a plaited gown folded in small folds.

PLAIT goes back through French, Portuguese, Spanish, and Italian to the Latin *plicare*, to fold. Under PLEAT (*plēt*), the Century Dictionary says: 'See PLAIT'. A PLAIT is a fold in cloth, also a BRAID.

For the pronunciation, Fowler, who is English, says merely: (*plăt*). Phyfe gives (*plāt*); and then quotes Webster: 'Now perhaps more often (*plēt*); also, especially in British use and for sense of BRAID, (*plăt*). The pronunciation with ă is perhaps due to the influence of Old French *pleier*, to fold, bend; PLEAT, with ē, being the form to be expected.'

From the Latin *plicare*, to fold, some directly and others by more roundabout ways, come PLIABLE, capable of being folded, easy to bend; DUPLICATE, by derivation folded twice; COMPLEX, folded together; the simple PLY, a fold; and PLAIT, though this last comes more directly from a closely related Latin verb which meant more specifically to weave, rather than merely fold.

336. *SPELUNKER*, spelunker (*spē-lŭnk'-ĕr*) *n*. One who explores caves, caveman, troglodyte.

A SPELUNC (*spē-lungk'*) is a cave, cavern, vault, from the Latin *spelunca*, from the Greek σπῆλυγξ (*spelugx*), σπηλυγγις (*speluggis*), from σπέος (*speos*), cave. TROGLODYTE, from the Greek τρωγλη (*trogle*), hole, cave, and δίειν (*diein*), to enter, may be a noun, one who lives in a cave, and so a synonym of SPELUNKER, or an adjective pertaining to a cave, cavernous, forming a cave, and so a synonym of SPELUNCOUS, or SPELEAN. The Oxford gives quotations dating from 1300 to 1563, which include the word SPELUNC, but nothing more recent. Ephraim Chambers, who does not mention SPELUNC, says of the TROGLODYTES: 'A people of Ethiopia, said to have lived in caves under ground', who 'did not so properly speak as shriek'. Why this unusual word should be answered correctly by so many still seems a mystery, even though it appears in a difficult vocabulary test taken only by high-vocabulary persons. HIKE, marked by 10 per cent, is the only attractive mislead.

337. *ARCHIVES*, archives (*ahr'-kīvz*) *pl. n.* Now only in the plural. When used in a word directly from Greek, ARCH- is usually pronounced with a hard K. It may be this prefix which leads 3 per cent to believe that ARCHIVES are GODS. Files of public records, place for historical documents, record office, registry for storing chronicles, annals, muniments.

ARCHIVES comes through the French, from the Latin *archivum*, a place where records are kept, from the Greek ἀρχεῖον (*archeion*), a public building, from ἀρχειν (*archein*), to rule, literally to be first. The prefix ARCH-, which goes back both to Anglo-Saxon and to the Greek ἀρχι- (*archi*-), means first, principal, chief, and appears in ARCHITECT.

From E. Chambers, 1728: 'ARCHIVES, a chamber or apartment wherein the records, charters, and other papers and evidences of a state, house, or community, are preserved to be consulted occasionally, as the ARCHIVES of a college. The ARCHIVES of ancient Rome were in the temple of Saturn.'

338. *EQUITABLE*, equitable (*ĕ'-kwĭt-ā-bl*) *adj*. Fair, just, right, upright, honest, evenhanded, due, lawful, proper, correct, deserved, condign.

The corresponding noun, EQUITY, comes through the French from the Latin *aequitas, aequitatis*, equality, justice, fairness, from *aeque*, equal, just, the source of the English EQUAL. EQUITY, honesty, uprightness, justice, right, rectitude, fairness, impartial justice, is the application of the dictates of good conscience to the settlement of controversies, that which is equally right for all concerned. This may suggest POPULAR, from the Latin *popularis*, of the people, belonging to the people, from *populus*, the people, as a synonym of EQUITABLE, selected by 4 per cent of high-vocabulary examinees.

339. *BIER*, bier (*bēr*) *n*. A framework on which rests a coffin before burial, catafalque.

Until recently spelt *beer*, the word BIER, a structure for supporting a coffin, goes directly back to an Anglo-Saxon word for bear, hold up, sustain, support.

A PIER, now a quay (*kē*), wharf, mole, or jetty, comes from the Latin *petra*, a mass of rock, then a castle of stone, and this may help lead 30 per cent into believing that BIER means MONUMENT. Also from Ephraim Chambers, 1728, comes: 'BIER is more peculiarly used for that whereon the bodies of saints are placed in the church to rest, and exposed to the veneration of the devout'.

A MONUMENT, from the Latin *monēre*, to remind, is almost anything built to remind people of someone or some event. Both MONUMENTS and BIERS are structures, but a BIER is specifically a support for a coffin.

340. *JETTY*, jetty (*jĕt'-tĭ*) *n.* Wharf, pier, landing, a projection built as a place for landing from boats; also mole, quay.
The second step in learning is the confusion of words with
different meanings but used in the same situation. A SAIL is a
large piece of cloth spread to catch the wind, and 7 per cent
select SAIL as the meaning of JETTY. A SAIL drives a boat through
the water; a JETTY is the place at which the boat lands.

A MOLE, from the Latin *moles*, is a great mass, structure of
stone built to enclose a harbor or protect an anchorage. A QUAY
(*kē*) is specifically a landing-place, along the shore line and not
jutting out. A PIER (*pēr*), from the French *pierre*, a stone, with
similar words in Spanish and Italian also meaning stone, rock,
comes through the Latin *petra*, a mass of rock, from the Greek
πέτρα (*petra*), a rock, crag, ridge, ledge. A PIER may be either
an embankment to protect ships from the open sea and so part of
a harbor; or a quay, wharf, landing place.

The verb to JUT, a variation of JET, is to project forward, extend beyond some fixed line. A JETTY JUTS out and was once
called a JUTTY. Ephraim Chambers says: 'In the royal dock-
yards, a JETTY is that part of a WHARF which projects beyond the
rest; but more particularly the front of a wharf, whose side
forms one of the cheeks of a wet or dry dock'.

341. *PROMONTORY*, promontory (*prŏm'-ŏn-tō-rĭ*) *n.* Rocky
ledge, high point of land, headland, rocky projection into
the sea.
PROMONTORY is the Latin *pro-*, forth, and *mons, montis*, mountain; the source also of the adjective PROMINENT (*prŏm'-ĭn-ĕnt*),
standing out from others, projecting, jutting out.

To 10 per cent PROMONTORY means BOULEVARD, a confusion of
PROMONTORY with PROMENADE (*prŏm-ĕn-ahd'*). Both BOULEVARD
and PROMENADE are French words. A BOULEVARD, originally the
bulwark around the city, became a public walk when no longer
needed as a fortification. A PROMENADE is likewise a place for
walking, a public walk.

According to E. Chambers, a PROMONTORY: 'In geography is
a high point of land or rock projecting out into the sea, the
extremity of which to the sea-ward is usually called a CAPE or
HEADLAND'.

342. *AFFLUENCE*, affluence (*ăf'-floo-ĕns*) *n*. Wealth, store
     of material goods, profusion of riches, abundance, opu-
lence, prosperity, fortune, ample means, great plenty, supply of
worldly things; also rarely abundance of thoughts, exuberance.
AFFLUENCE comes from the Latin *affluere*, a combination of *ad*,
to, and *fluere*, to flow, the source of FLUENT, literally flowing,
voluble, ready in the use of words, and INFLUENCE. This last
leads 25 per cent of high-vocabulary adults to underline POWER
as the meaning of AFFLUENCE. INFLUENCE, by derivation a flowing in of energy and so a power of producing, means authority,
power, ascendency over others. But AFFLUENCE is wealth.

   OPULENCE is the dignified possession and enjoyment of property. AFFLUENCE suggests a flowing in of wealth and its free
expenditure.

343. *SECRETARY*, secretary (*sĕk'-rē-tā-rĭ*) *n*. A piece of fur-
     niture with a cabinet above and drawers below; a writing
desk.
From 1833 comes a description of a SECRETAIRE (*sĕk-rē-târ'*), a
piece of furniture, usually cabinet shaped in which private
papers can be kept, with a shelf for writing and drawers and
pigeonholes; a bureau; a writing desk. SECRETARY, from the
Latin *secretus*, private, secret, is the English spelling and pronunciation of the same word.

   An ESCRITOIRE (*ās-krē-twahr'*), the French *écritoire*, is also for
writing, often with an opening top, or falling front panel on
which to write. It has places for pens, stationery, and ink, but
no high cupboard built up at the back, as does a SECRETARY.

   From 1763 comes the phrase: The mahogany SECRETARY-desk.
A SECRETARY is usually of mahogany, lined with green baize or
leather, with a lot of little drawers, a shelf for writing, pigeonholes, and a high cabinet.

344. *OVERTURE*, overture (*ō'-vĕr-tŭr*) *n*. Proposal, offer,
     opening, proposition, introduction, prelude, something
offered to open the way, submission of a judicatory.
OVERTURE is the French *ouverture*, a proposal, opening, from the
verb *ouvrir*, to open. From the same come the English OVERT,
apparent, manifest, open, clearly seen, the opposite of COVERT.

In music, an OVERTURE is a prelude, the beginning, introduction to an opera or oratorio, or sometimes a separate orchestral composition of similar character. In a book, the words FOREWORD and PREFACE, or INTRODUCTION, are used instead of OVERTURE, though the last is sometimes used in poetry. In business, OVERTURE is a tentative opening of a negotiation, a first informal proposal.

To 20 per cent OVERTURE means SUMMARY, an opposite, for a SUMMARY comes at the end, an OVERTURE at the beginning.

An INTRODUCTION, from the Latin *intro*, within, and *ducere*, to lead, is something which leads one in to what will follow, a more or less elementary beginning. A FOREWORD is a few words said beforehand. INTRODUCTION, PREFACE, and FOREWORD are all used of books. OVERTURE is the only one used in music. OVERTURE and PROPOSAL are used in business.

345. *ASSESSMENT*, assessment (*ăs-sĕs'-mĕnt*) *n.* The amount of taxation to be paid, official valuation of property for tax purposes, appraisement, sum charged for community expenses; also the act of determining this figure.

To 5 per cent ASSESSMENT means FUNDS. FUNDS are accumulated money, resources, supplies, stock, wealth available for some purpose, almost CAPITAL. ASSETS, from the same source as SATISFY, are FUNDS enough to pay one's debts.

To ASSESS, a combination of the Latin *ad-*, to, and *sedere*, to sit, is to set a value, appraise, fix a charge, estimate an amount.

346. *BIVOUAC*, bivouac (*bĭv'-oo-ăk*) *n.* An encampment of soldiers in the open air without tents; originally a patrol of citizens added in time of emergency to the regular town watch.

To 4 per cent BIVOUAC, which comes directly from the French *bivouac*, perhaps from German and Swiss dialect, means MARSHLAND, and to another 4 per cent PUBLIC PARK, suggesting that the word is wholly unknown to this group.

BILLETS, CAMPS, and BIVOUACS are three degrees of protection from the weather. BILLETS are lodgings assigned to soldiers in relatively comfortable houses. John Buchan, who uses an interesting word on every page, says of a German retreat: 'Level-

ling buildings which might give BILLETS to the allies'. CAMPS
are set up in the open, but with the protection of tents or temporary structures. BIVOUACS are in the open with no protection
against the weather except that which is carried by each man.

347. *APPARITION*, apparition (*ăp-pă-rĭ'-shŏn*) *n.* Coming
    into sight, appearance, becoming visible, specter, phantom,
ghost, manifestation.

APPARITION, through the French *apparition*, from the same
Latin source as the verb to APPEAR, is thought by 24 per cent
to mean PARTING, separation. Three Latin verbs: *parare*, of the
first conjugation, to provide, arrange; *parēre*, of the second
conjugation, to come into sight, appear; and *pa'rĕre*, of the
third, to produce; differ in one letter only. Each leads to a
group of English words. From *parare*, to provide, come the
verb to SEPARATE (*sĕ'-pahr-āt*), literally not to provide, and so
to part, and SEPARATION, parting. From *pa'rĕre*, to produce,
comes PARENT. While from *apparēre*, a combination of the
Latin *ad*, to, and *parēre*, to come into sight, come APPEAR, AP-
PEARANCE, and APPARITION.

From the great Encyclopaedia of Ephraim Chambers, published in 1728, almost thirty years before Dr. Johnson's Dictionary in 1755, and later translated into French as the basis for
the Encyclopédie of Diderot, comes: 'APPARITION is used to
denote a spectre, a praeternatural appearance of some spirit
or the like.

'Many of the APPARITIONS, we are told of by writers, are
doubtless mere delusions of the sense; many others were seen
but in dreams or deliriums; many others are fiction contrived
merely to amuse'.

Chambers continues: 'APPARITION, in astronomy, denotes a
star's or luminary's becoming visible, which before was hid'.

348. *GARNISHED*, garnished (*gahr'-nĭshd*) *adj.* Ornamented,
    adorned, decorated, set off, embellished, decked, beauti-
fied, invested, arrayed.

The verb to GARNISH, with similar words in French, Spanish,
Portuguese, Italian, German, and the Scandinavian languages,
all spelt much like the English, goes back to Anglo-Saxon.

Though answers to the meaning of GARNISHED scatter, showing that to those who have taken the test the word is almost unknown, and the selection of a synonym almost a guess, 4 per cent pick TASTY, a colloquial word which means done with good taste, a confusion of words from the same situation, an early step in learning, the second. Attractive GARNISHING depends on TASTE. One without TASTE rarely takes the trouble to GARNISH.

From E. Chambers: 'GARNISHING is popularly used for the furniture, assemblage, or sortment necessary for the adornment of anything. The GARNISHING of a dish consists of certain things which accompany it either as a part or ingredient thereof; in which sense pickles, mushrooms, oysters, etc. are GARNISHINGS; or as a circumstance or ornaments; as when leaves, flowers, roots, etc. are laid about a service to amuse the eye. The same word is used for the finer herbs, fruits, etc. GARNISHINGS are lemons, pistachios, pomegranates, yokes of hard eggs, artichoke bottoms, capers, truffles, sweetbread, etc.'

349. *DIFFRACTED*, diffracted (*dĭf-frăk'-tĕd*) *adj*. Bent, deflected, broken, spread.

DIFFUSED comes from the Latin *diffundere*, to pour in different directions, a combination of *dis-*, away, and *fundere*, to pour, which means scattered, dispersed, and so when applied to rays of light, not sharp, blurred, and so suggests CLOUDED, chosen by II per cent. DIFFUSED is literary; DIFFRACTED is a more exact scientific term for the bending of light on passing through certain substances as the glass of a prism.

DIFFRACTED comes from the Latin *diffractus*, the past participle of the verb *diffringere*, to break into pieces. E. Chambers says DIFFRACTION was first used by Grimaldi, a Jesuit, to denote that property of the rays of light which others called INFLECTION, the discovery of which some attribute to Grimaldi and others to Dr. Hook.

350. *RASH*, rash (*răsh*) *adj*. Reckless, headstrong, impetuous, venturesome, precipitate, foolhardy, headlong, heedless, careless, inconsiderate, hasty in council.

To 3 per cent RASH means BOLD, a confusion of words used often in the same situation but differing fundamentally. BOLD, stout, undaunted, is facing a risk with knowledge of the consequences and the goal to be gained, but ready to take a greater chance than would the really COURAGEOUS person. Neither RASH nor RECK-LESS is complimentary. To RECK is to take care, heed, watch out, mind, as in the phrase: 'Mind your step'. RECKLESS is careless, without heed, unmindful. RASH, which goes back to Middle English, comes from and is related to similar words in Dutch, German, and the Scandinavian languages, all meaning quick, speedy, hasty; and RASH means overhasty, too quick, precipitous.

351. *SUBSIDY*, subsidy (*sŭb'-sĭ-dĭ*) *n.* Gift, an aid in money, subvention, grant.

SUBSIDY comes from the Latin *subsidium*, troops stationed in reserve for help in battle and so from this, help, aid, relief, from *subsidere*, to sit in wait, remain at hand. To SUBSIDE is to settle to the bottom, sink in a liquid.

E. Chambers says of SUBSIDY: 'Originally any aid, tax, or tribute granted to the king on pressing occasions of the State. Duties and impositions are divers kinds of SUBSIDY.'

352. *BLUSTER*, bluster (*blŭs'-tĕr*) *n.* The loud noise of a storm, tumultuous gust, boisterous blast, perhaps an imitative word made up to sound like a blast of wind.

The popular mislead, selected by 19 per cent, is FIGHT, a word which goes directly back to Anglo-Saxon. A BRUSH, somewhat like BLUSTER in sound, is an encounter, skirmish, and may contribute to the misinterpretation of BLUSTER. Also a FLUSTER is a mental confusion, momentary embarrassment. BLUSTER is primarily sound.

A FIGHT is a confused struggle. Both FIGHT and BLUSTER are noisy. But a FIGHT is a conflict, combat, encounter, fray. A BLUSTER is noise, the sound of the wind.

353. *TARRY*, tarry (*tăr'-rĭ*) *v.* To delay, stop by the way, stay, continue in a place, linger, loiter, put off going or coming.

TARRY goes back to Middle English and its first meaning is to continue in a place, remain, stay, abide. Another meaning is delay, linger, loiter, and in this sense WASTE TIME, marked by 26 per cent, is too near the inherent meaning to use as a mislead.

354. *DANDY*, dandy (*dăn'-dĭ*) *n*. A man who attracts attention
    by the fastidiousness of his dress, fop, popinjay, coxcomb,
prig, an exquisite, a man of excessive neatness in fine attire.
DANDY, spelt with a capital, is a variation of ANDY, a familiar
form of the popular name ANDREW. The word dates from the
early 1800's.

To 16 per cent the plural DANDIES means FASHIONS. FASHION is
the mode of the moment, customary style in dress, personal
adornment prevalent at the time, any form, shape, or appearance
subject to variations of taste. DANDIES are men of FASHION.

A COXCOMB displays vanity as regards his own achievement.
A FOP displays vanity more particularly in dress, and pertness in
conversation. An EXQUISITE prides himself on his superfine taste,
in dress, manners, and language. A DANDY dresses elegantly but
affectedly. BEAU is an old word for one who has too much understanding to be a mere DANDY, but still overdoes his dress.

355. *USURY*, usury (*ū'-zū-rĭ*) *n*. An unreasonable amount of
    interest demanded for borrowing money.
USURY, from the Italian *usura*, comes from the Latin *usura*, use,
employment, interest, from *uti*, to use, the source of the adjectives UTILE, USABLE, USUAL, as well as USAGE, USURP, UTENSIL,
and ABUSE.

To 16 per cent USURY means UNDERHANDEDNESS. In 1179,
USURERS were warned by the Third Lateran Council that they
would not receive a Christian burial. Gilbert S. Rosenthal says:
'Religious taboos and laws were quite explicit in forbidding the
taking of interest, USURY, or any kind of increase of money', for
in the 12th century INTEREST and USURY were synonymous.
Both were condemned.

In the 13th century, the new economy began, exemplified by
the Buonsignori family of Siena. In the 14th century the Floren-
tines rose, and with the call for new buildings, churches, monasteries, and wars, the great bankers flourished in the 15th century, with Jacques Coeur in France about 1450, and the Medici
in Florence at the same time. Simultaneously USURY took on its
new meaning of too high interest. As early as 1241 interest was
fixed at 20 per cent, while Alfonso X set it at 33½ per cent,
with the stipulation that it could not exceed the principal.

356. *EFFETE*, effete (*ĕf-fēt'*) *adj*. Exhausted, unproductive because of age, worn-out, barren of results, unfruitful, spent.
EFFETE comes from the Latin *ex*, out, and *fetus*, a word used
unchanged in English for the young of an animal in the womb.

The popular mislead, chosen by 14 per cent, is AGGRESSIVE,
energetic, vigorous, an opposite certainly in suggestion.

357. *RUE*, rue (*rū*) *v*. To regret, repent, feel remorse, mourn,
grieve, lament, be sorrowful, suffer in expiation (v. B.
1511). See RUEFUL (v. B. 1322), doleful lugubrious, regretful.
To 20 per cent RUE means WRECK, ruin, demolish, undo, spoil,
destroy. To RECK (*rĕk*), pronounced like WRECK but spelt
without the w-, is to think, heed, mind, regard, consider, take
care, in something of the same area as RUE, but with none of that
word's regret, sorrow, remorse. To WRECK, starting with a w-,
is to destroy, far from RUE in meaning. To RUE, which goes back
through Middle English to Anglo-Saxon, is to regret.

358. *HUSK*, husk (*hŭsk*) *n*. The outer covering of corn, glume,
epicarp, rind, hull, shell. Ephraim Chambers says: 'The coat
of corn, grain, seed, etc.'
HULL, a word related to HOLD and HOLLOW, is the outer covering
of a nut or of a ship. HUSK, related to Scandinavian words, goes
back probably to Anglo-Saxon.

HUSKS are thought by 32 per cent to be CORN-COBS. The COB
or CORN-COB is the hard, woody, central part of an ear of CORN
or maize. The HUSKS are the outer covering stripped off to get
at the CORN. The Century Dictionary groups SKIN, HIDE, RIND,
HUSK, and HULL, as similar words.

359. *IRREVOCABLY*, irrevocably (*ĭr-rĕv'-ō-kă-blĭ*, W. H. P.
Phyfe says: not *ĭr-rē-vō'-kă-blĭ*) *adv*. That cannot be re-
pealed, beyond recall, not capable of being annulled, not revo-
cably, and so lastingly, enduringly, perpetually (v. B. 442).
IRREVOCABLY is thought by 38 per cent to mean UNWILLINGLY
compared with only 29 per cent who mark the correct answer
FOREVER, perhaps only because of the Anglo-Saxon negative UN-
at the beginning of UNWILLINGLY, equivalent to the Latin IN-
which becomes IR- before another R as in IRREVOCABLY.

From the verb to WILL, of Anglo-Saxon origin, comes the present participle WILLING used as an adjective to mean ready, favorably disposed, inclined, desirous, minded, as: 'WILLING to learn'. UNWILLING is then disinclined, indisposed, loath, reluctant, averse. With the addition of -LY, WILLING becomes WILLINGLY, voluntarily, readily, of one's own choice, without pressure; while UNWILLINGLY is against one's wishes, reluctantly, involuntarily.

From the Latin *vocare*, to call, come VOCAL, pertaining to the voice, to speech, VOCABLE (*vō'-kă-bl*), a word, name, term, VOCABULARY, a list of words, and VOCATION, one's calling. To REVOKE, where c before e changes to k in order to keep the pronunciation (*rē-vōk'*), from the Latin *re-*, back, and *vocare*, to call, is to call back, take back, withdraw, and so cancel, annul.

The adjective REVOCABLE (*rěv'-ō-kă-bl*, not *rē-vō'-kă-bl*), spelt with c before a, is capable of being recalled, subject to withdrawal; and IRREVOCABLE is the opposite.

360. *PESTILENCE*, pestilence (*pěs'-tĭ-lěns*) *n.* A disease called the PLAGUE, pest; E. Chambers calls it: 'An epidemical malignant and contagious disease usually mortal; popularly known under the name PLAGUE'.

To 5 per cent PESTILENCE means IMPATIENCE. The noun IMPATIENCE, and the corresponding adjective IMPATIENT, starting with the Latin privative *in-*, come from *patiens, patientis*, enduring, suffering. IMPATIENCE is intolerance, uneasiness, restlessness, unquiet, not enduring with composure. To PESTER is to annoy, bother, tease, plague by repeated acts, until the one PESTERED loses PATIENCE, becomes IMPATIENT. A PEST is one who PESTERS, a troublesome, annoying person. The verb to PLAGUE is used in much the same way, in a mild sense to mean vex, annoy, tease, trouble, worry.

But PESTILENCE, from the Latin *pestilentis*, plague, from the adjective *pestilens, pestilentis*, infected, noxious, unwholesome, malignant, is a widespread, sweeping, deadly illness carried by rats and their fleas. In the 6th century A.D. it spread over the Roman world and then extended through Egypt to the north of Africa.

361. *REDUNDANT*, redundant (*rē-dŭn'-dănt*) *adj.* Too
    many, exceeding what is necessary, superabundant, super-
fluous, or specifically using too many words, verbose, pleonastic,
tautological.

REDUNDANT, from the Latin *redundare,* to overflow, joins *red-*,
again, to *undare,* to inundate, surge, flow, from *unda,* a wave,
undulating.

    E. Chambers: REDUNDANCY or REDUNDANCE, a fault in dis-
course consisting in the use of a superfluity of words. Words
perfectly synonymous are REDUNDANT and ought to be re-
trenched. REDUNDANCY makes the style weak and languid.

    PLEONASTIC and REDUNDANT styles both use extra words. A
PLEONASM may use these words justifiably for emphasis. REDUN-
DANT is using too many words to no avail.

362. *GLAMOUR*, glamour (*glăm'-ôr*) *n.* Charm, enchantment,
    witchery, spell, allurement, magic, a word revived by Sir
Walter Scott.

In the test phrase: 'Full of GLAMOUR', the popular mislead, chosen by 10 per cent of those tested, is RENOWN, fame, repute.

363. *IMBUE*, imbue (*ĭm-bū'*) *v.* To saturate, impregnate by
    soaking, dye by steeping.

IMBUE, from the Latin *imbuere,* to wet, soak, moisten, combines
an unimportant *in-* with *bibere,* to drink, the source of IMBIBE,
to drink.

    To 7 per cent IMBUED means DECORATED, adorned, ornamented,
embellished, beautified, decked out. To INDUE, from the Latin
induere, is to put on as a garment, furnish, supply, and so ENDOW;
and this may lead to the selection of DECORATED.

    Bailey makes a nice distinction between IMBUE and IMBRUE.
To IMBRUE is to moisten or wet or steep. To IMBUE is to season
the mind with good principles, virtues, learning.

364. *INNATELY*, innately (*ĭn-nāt'-lĭ*) *adv.* Naturally, by birth,
    inborn, inherited, instinctively, inherently, not acquired.

INNATELY comes from the Latin *innatus,* inborn, the past participle of *innasci,* to be born, from *nasci,* to be born, the source of
NATIVE, and NATAL.

To 5 per cent INNATELY means STUPIDLY. STUPID, originally from the Latin *stupere*, to be amazed, struck dumb, may mean dull, heavy, or muddle-brained, slow-witted, lethargic, foolish, crass.

Bailey says of INNATE: inbred, natural. INNATE principles are stamped upon the soul or mind at its first make and which it brings into the world with it.

365. *CHAMOIS*, chamois (*shăm'-ĭ*) *n.* An agile, goat-like animal of high mountains in Europe.

A CHAMOIS leaps precariously from rock to rock in the high mountains and this suggests ACROBAT to 20 per cent as a synonym of CHAMOIS. But an ACROBAT is a human being who does rope dancing, trapeze performing, and tumbling. A CHAMOIS is an animal, a kind of antelope.

Under the heading ANTELOPE, Pantologia lists the CHAMOIS, the GNU, the GAZELLE, as well as various types of ANTELOPES. The CHAMOIS it describes as: 'Horns erect, round, smooth, tips hooked back. Inhabits the Alps in troops; feeds on shrubs, herbs, and roots; size — that of a goat; flesh good.'

Of ANTELOPES in general Pantologia continues: 'Inhabitants of all the continents but America, in which none have hitherto been discovered. They are chiefly found in hilly country, climb up rocks, are very gregarious, active, timid, and swift.'

366. *CERULEAN*, cerulean (*sē-rū'-lē-ăn*) *adj.* Sky-colored, clear light blue.

CERULEAN comes from the Latin *caeruleus*, perhaps from *caelum*, the sky.

To 15 per cent CERULEAN means GOLDEN YELLOW. CERULEAN always has a pleasant suggestion, such as that contained in GOLDEN YELLOW; but CERULEAN is blue, sky-colored, not YELLOW.

367. *BALDERDASH*, balderdash (*băhl'-dĕr-dăsh*) *n.* Noisy nonsense, trashy talk, senseless chatter, nonsensical prattle, unmeaningful writing.

BALDERDASH, perhaps one of the amusing combinations of words popular at the time of Queen Elizabeth I, is thought by 15 per cent to be a game, obviously suggested by BATTLEDORE and

SHUTTLECOCK. The BATTLEDORE is a racket used in batting back and forth across a high net, the SHUTTLECOCK, a piece of cork with feathers stuck into it at one end.

BALDERDASH, originally a jumble of liquors, came to mean a jumble of talk. RIGAMAROLE, a ragman's role, is talk which has the form of sense but is really nonsensical. TWADDLE is silliness in talk. GIBBERISH is mere sound strung together. BALDERDASH is noisy talk without thought.

368. *REJOIN*, rejoin (*rē-join'*) *v.* To answer a reply, respond
     further, advert, retort, rebut (V. B. 1317).
The corresponding noun REJOINDER, with the D pronounced, parallels REMAIN and REMAINDER. In both instances, the original Latin lacks D, the nouns, with D, being French infinitives used as nouns.

REJOIN comes from the Latin *jungĕre*, to join, a verb of the third conjugation, with short *-ĕre*, and so accented (*jūn'-gā-rā*), the source of numerous English words such as ADJOIN, CONJOIN, DISJOIN, SUBJOIN, most of which mean JOIN in various ways. Only ENJOIN and REJOIN indicate speaking. To ENJOIN is to direct, almost command, urge, give an order. To REJOIN is not merely to answer, reply, but strictly to answer an answer, to reply further. In law, a REPLICATION is an answer, a reply, and to REJOIN is to answer a REPLICATION.

REJOINED is thought by 15 per cent to mean QUESTIONED, asked, inquired, an opposite, as QUESTION and ANSWER are opposites. The teacher QUESTIONS, the student ANSWERS.

369. *SUPPLENESS*, suppleness (*sŭp'-pl-nĕs*) *n.* Quality of be-
     ing easily bent, flexibility (V. B. 58), pliableness (V. B. 328),
limberness, malleability (V. B. 1589). See SUPPLE (V. B. 637).
SUPPLENESS, from the same source as SUPPLICATE, to bend down, kneel down, and beg, is thought by 26 per cent to mean CUNNING. Originally CUNNING meant knowledge, learning, and then skill, dexterity, and then too great knowledge, magical understanding, craftiness. Following the same route, SUBTLE-NESS (*sŭt'-l-nĕs*), from the Latin *subtilis*, fine, thin, delicate, nice, originally finely woven, came to mean skill, dexterity, and too great cleverness, craftiness. CUNNING and SUBTLENESS are

nearly identical; but SUBTLENESS, cunning, both praiseworthy and questionable, and SUPPLENESS, despite their likeness in sound, differ in meaning. SUPPLENESS comes from the Latin *sub*, under, and *plicare*, to bend, fold, and means capable of being bent.

370. *IMPUDENT*, impudent (*ĭm'-pū-dĕnt*) *adj.* Shameless, saucy, insolent, brazen, disrespectful, bold, presumptuous, pert, rude (v. B. 237), offensively forward in behavior.

Among high-vocabulary students 80 per cent believe that IMPUDENT means SAUCY; but in the population as a whole 43 per cent select THOUGHTLESS, as opposed to only 32 per cent who mark SAUCY. IMPUDENT and IMPRUDENT (*ĭm-proo'-dĕnt*) differ by only a single letter, but so do CAB and CRAB, TACK and TRACK. To retain English as an exact language IMPUDENT and IMPRUDENT should be differentiated despite contrary popular vote.

IMPRUDENT (*ĭm-proo'-dĕnt*), accented on the second syllable, is a combination of the Latin privative *in-*, not, and *prudens*, *prudentis*, an adjective of the third declension meaning foresighted. IMPRUDENT means not foresighted, not careful of consequences, heedless, THOUGHTLESS.

IMPUDENT, without the R, a combination of *in-*, and *pudens*, *pudentis*, ashamed, means not ashamed, shameless. RUDENESS may be lack of culture; but IMPUDENCE is conscious impertinence.

371. *CAUSTIC*, caustic (*kaw'-stĭk*) *adj.* Corroding (v. B. 1098), burning, cutting, stinging; and figuratively sarcastic, acrid (v. B. 1143), pungent (v. B. 1446), severely critical, escharotic. CAUSTIC, directly from the Greek καυστικός (*causticos*), caustic, corrosive, capable of burning, from καίειν (*caiein*), to burn, when used figuratively, is thought by 17 per cent to mean ANGRY, and by the same percentage, 17, of high-vocabulary readers. ANGRY means wrathful, incensed, irate, furious, passionate, resentful, indignant, inflamed, choleric, stormy, causing trouble, showing resentment, and is apparently too close to CAUSTIC to use as a mislead in a vocabulary test.

372. *ABEYANCE*, abeyance (*ă-bā'-ăns*) *n.* Suspended action, temporary inactivity, contemplation, waiting, suspension of existence.

Guesses as to the meaning of ABEYANCE divide almost evenly among the four misleads, with 4 per cent concentrating on IGNORANCE, lack of knowledge, uneducated, without information, from the Latin *ignorantia*, want of knowledge, lack of information, from *ignore*, to have no knowledge, take no notice, ignore, a combination of the Latin privative *in-* and *gnarus*, knowing, from the Greek γνωριζειν (*gnorizein*), to make known.

ABEYANCE, from *a-*, which stands for the Latin *ad*, to, and old French *beance*, expectation, desire, from *beer*, to gape, gaze at, expect anxiously, suggests holding everything as it is, almost breathlessly, in anticipation. SUSPENSION has the same suggestion of interrupting, stopping for a time, as from the American historian William Hickling Prescott, born in Salem, Massachusetts, in 1796, in his History of the Reign of Ferdinand and Isabella, published in 1838: 'A SUSPENSION of hostilities'.

According to Nathan Bailey 1726: 'ABEYANCE signifies a thing to be in posse only, and not in actu; lands, tenements, goods, etc. are said to be in ABEYANCE, when they are only in expectation or understanding and not in actual possession'.

373. *CAREEN*, careen (*kă-rēn′*) v. To lean on one side, lurch, slant, tip; also to tip a ship on one side to examine, calk, repair, cleanse, or in technical language, BREAM, heat the bottom of the boat to soften the pitch enough to free shells and seaweed sticking to it so that they can be brushed off.
To 18 per cent CAREEN, which goes back through French, with similar words in Spanish, Portuguese, and Italian, to the Latin *carina*, the keel of the ship, is thought to mean PLAY. The unusual verb to CAREER is to run rapidly as children CAREER about, and this may suggest PLAY.

E. Chambers, 1728, says: 'CAREENING, a term in the sea-language, used for the laying of a vessel on one side, to caulk her seams, or mend any fault she has under water, stop up leaks, and refit and trim the other side'.

374. *EMANCIPATION*, emancipation (*ē-măn-sĭ-pā′-shŭn*) n. Liberation, freedom, release, discharge, setting free from bondage, freeing from any sort of burden on a large scale.

The word comes from *e-*, out, and *mancipare*, to give, a combination of *manus*, hand, and *capere*, to take.

To LIBERATE is the general word meaning to free in any way; with LIBERTY, the noun, meaning freedom. To MANUMIT is technical, the act of an individual in freeing a slave. To EMANCIPATE is broader. EMANCIPATION is a general setting free from bondage.

375. *PRECONCERTED*, preconcerted (*prē-kŏn-ser'-tĕd*) *adj.*
    Agreed-upon, arranged beforehand, constituted in advance.
PRECONCERTED comes from the Latin *pre*, before, and CONCERT. To CONCERT (*kŏn-sert'*), from the Latin *com*, with, and *certare*, to contend, has come to mean debate matters, contrive, lay a design, in order to bring an affair to pass. The past, CONCERTED, means agreed upon, connected by a plan. PRECONCERTED is agreed upon in advance, ahead of time.

376. *DECK*, deck (*dĕk*) *v.* To adorn, array, embellish, invest,
    clothe in splendor, cover with ornaments.
The verb to DECK first meant to cover, and the noun a DECK, used for a ship, is the covering from side to side, the floor.

To 5 per cent the verb to DECK means to CUT OFF. To DOCK, which goes back to Middle English, and probably to Icelandic, is to CUT OFF, clip, curtail, shorten, originally to cut-short the tail of a horse, but now used figuratively as: 'To DOCK his pay'. To DECK, which goes back through Dutch and German to similar words in Anglo-Saxon and the Scandinavian languages, is to cover with finery, adorn, set off.

The Anglo-Saxon BE- means around, about, all over, so that BEDECK is a bit more splendid, more all over than DECK alone.

377. *MACABRE*, macabre (*mă-kah'-brĕ*) *adj.* Gruesome, hor-
    rible, terrible, repulsive, depressing, dismal, causing one
to shudder.
According to the simplest theory, MACABER, an old German poet of whom little is known, wrote dialogues of death on which is based The Dance of Death, involving a skeleton or a figure representing death, a favorite subject in the literature and art of Europe in the Middle Ages, beginning in the 14th century, found in paintings, stained glass, and decorated manuscripts.

MACABRE, as an adjective, seems recent, for it does not appear in the Century Dictionary of 1914.

Those who do not know the meaning of MACABRE divide almost equally among the four misleads, with no concentration on any one.

378. *DOSSIER*, dossier (*dŏs'-sĭ-ā*) *n.* A bundle of writings, documents concerning one subject, detailed information about some person, enclosed in a wrapper with a list of the papers on the band.

DOSSIER comes from the French *dos*, back, because a heavy package of papers resembles the back of a heavily stuffed chair. The word DOSSIER first appeared in 1894, when Captain Alfred Dreyfus was on trial for treason, when certain documents are said to have been shown to the jury secretly.

There is no concentration on any one mislead.

379. *AGNOSTIC*, agnostic (*ăg-nŏs'-tĭk*) *adj.* Unbelieving, non-Christian.

According to Edward Gibbon in his Decline and Fall of the Roman Empire, 1782: 'The Gnostics were distinguished as the most polite, the most learned, and the most wealthy of the Christian name, a general appellation which expressed a superiority of knowledge'.

From this AGNOSTIC, starting with the Greek privative *ả*, meaning not, seems a small step; but the word appears to have been first suggested by Professor Huxley in 1869, for one who disclaims any knowledge of God, who believes human knowledge limited to experience.

380. *HINT*, hint (*hĭnt*) *n.* Suggestion (v. B. 81), implication (v. B. 624), intimation, insinuation (v. B. 862), allusion (v. B. 1765).

HINT, which goes back through Middle English to Anglo-Saxon, is thought by 33 per cent to be a WARNING. In the phrase: 'A HINT of danger', the word is close to a WARNING, almost too close for a mislead in a vocabulary test, except that among high-vocabulary students 87 per cent choose SUGGESTION when given a choice between this and WARNING as meanings of HINT.

A WARNING is notice given of approaching danger, advice beforehand of consequences to come. A WARNING may be a yell, loud, clear, and direct. A HINT is indirect, not straightforward. A SUGGESTION is also open. One SUGGESTS a plan. A HINT is letting one's thoughts be known in a somewhat roundabout manner.

381. *INDIGNANT*, indignant (*ĭn-dĭg'-nănt*) *adj*. Stirred by a combination of scorn and anger, provoked by an injustice, incensed, exasperated, excited by a feeling of contempt and displeasure.

A DIGNITARY is one who holds a high office, exalted position. To DIGNIFY a position, a combination of *dignus*, worthy, and *facere*, to make, is to exalt it, honor it, fill it in such a way as to lift it to a new level. DIGNIFIED means noble, eminent, stately, serious, grave, considerate.

INDIGNANT, from the Latin privative *in-* and *dignari*, to consider worthy, is the reaction of the world toward one who is not filling his position with DIGNITY.

To 6 per cent INDIGNANT means UNCONCERNED. CONCERNED is interested, affected, touched, disturbed, disquieted, uneasy, anxious, troubled. An INDIGNANT person is worried, disturbed, CONCERNED. UNCONCERNED means indifferent, an exact opposite of INDIGNANT, emotionally stirred up.

382. *CURTLY*, curtly (*kert'-lĭ*) *adv*. Abruptly, tartly (v. b. 429), brusquely (v. b. 2055), sharply, concisely, summarily, in a short and dry manner.

CURTLY is thought by 13 per cent to mean NOBLY, honorably, grandly, magnanimously, an opposite in feeling, for CURTLY is almost impolitely. Although COURTEOUSLY (*ker'-tē-ŭs-lĭ*) and CURTLY start with the same sound, the two come from different sources. COURTEOUSLY, politely, elegantly, NOBLY, comes from the same source as COURT (*kōrt*) and COURTLY (*kōrt'-lĭ*), the Latin *cortis*, first a courtyard, farm, villa, and later a palace and retinue; while CURT and CURTLY go back to the Latin *curtus*, clipped, shortened, docked. CURTLY first meant briefly, shortly, concisely, and then, as applied to manners, came to mean abruptly, brusquely, almost sharply, tartly.

383. *BUNKER*, bunker (*bŭng'-ker*) *n.* Bin, chest, box, storage place in a ship.

BUNKER is thought by 25 per cent to mean BED. A BUNK, of Scandinavian origin from similar words in Icelandic, Swedish, Norwegian, and Danish, all relating to ships, is a sleeping berth, a BED enclosed by three walls. From BUNK comes BUNKER, a large bin on a ship, as a COAL-BUNKER, the hold of a ship.

By another 13 per cent BUNKER is thought to mean METAL GUARD. A BUMPER is a METAL GUARD; a BUNKER, a storage bin.

Among several illustrations, the Oxford gives one from 1851: 'BUNKERS to hold 890 tons of coal', and another from 1864: 'Her BUNKERS filled with upwards of 200 tons of coal'.

384. *VERGE*, verge (*verj*) *n.* Grass edging of a flower bed, margin, brink, side, edge of anything. A VERGE-BOARD is the board edging the gable of a roof, barge-board.

With surprising historical justification, 24 per cent believe that VERGE means DESIRE. An URGE is a DESIRE, impulse to do something. Nathan Bailey in 1721, and Samuel Johnson, 1755, intermingle the letters U and V, starting URGE with U-, and VERGE with V-, but arranging both under V so that VERGE comes before URGE. Noah Webster, 1828, separated, perhaps for the first time, these two letters.

URGE goes back to the Latin *urgēre*, to press, push, drive, force, perhaps originally to *vergĕre*, the source of VERGE, border.

Today URGE means desire, impulse; while VERGE may be either the rod, staff of office, of a VERGER, or a border, edge, margin.

385. *VALIDITY*, validity (*vă-lĭd'-ĭ-tĭ*) *n.* Soundness, strength, justness, efficacy.

The corresponding adjective VALID, from the Latin *validus*, strong, powerful, effective, means well-grounded, supported by fact, as a VALID reason, a VALID objection. The Latin ending -*ity*, more commonly -*ty*, transforms an adjective of Latin origin into the corresponding noun as: CIVIL and CIVILITY, ACTIVE and ACTIVITY, where the final E of the adjective disappears.

In psychology RELIABILITY is the accuracy of the measuring instrument, its reproducibility. VALIDITY is reserved for the accuracy with which the score checks with some activity in life.

VALIDITY is thought by some to mean PERMANENCY. VALID-
ITY suggests permanent lasting value, but the two words differ.
PERMANENCY implies lasting, while VALIDITY is worth, value.

386. *CHALICE*, chalice (*chăl'-ĭs*) *n.* A drinking cup, goblet,
     cup in which wine is administered in the celebration of the
Eucharist. It is like a goblet in shape with a wide heavy base to
prevent any chance of its spilling.
There seem to have been two Latin words, both meaning cup.
From one spelt *calix* comes CHALICE; and from the other *calyx*,
comes the cup of a flower spelt CALYX, with Y instead of I. A
CHALICE, made of silver or gold, may be of silver with gilt inside.

387. *SWARTHINESS*, swarthiness (*swar'-thē-nĕs*) *n.* Dark-
     ness, tawniness, moderately black, especially of the skin.
SWARTHINESS is thought by 5 per cent to mean FREEBOOTING,
robbery, pillage, plundering, piracy, a word from Swedish,
Danish, German, and Dutch. BUCCANEERS and FREEBOOTERS,
marauders, robbers, plunderers, pillagers, really pirates, are
often described as SWARTHY, though nothing in these words
suggests skin color.

388. *BENIGN*, benign (*bē-nīn'*) *adj.* Kindly, gracious, benig-
     nant, gentle, courteous, good-natured, of a kind disposi-
tion. The corresponding noun BENIGNITY (*bē-nĭg'-nĭ-tĭ*) is
goodness, tenderness, courtesy, sweetness of disposition.
BENIGN comes from the Latin *bonus*, good, and *-genus*, born,
from *gignere*, to beget. From the same source, and in much the
same manner, comes MALIGN, starting with the Latin *mal*, bad.
To 15 per cent BENIGN means SILENT, quiet, still, free from
noise; also not speaking, using few words. BENIGN, applied to
weather, means mild, gentle, favorable, serene, and so free from
disturbance, calm, tranquil, quiet, a synonym of SILENT, though
the word SILENT itself is seldom used of weather.

389. *OOZE*, ooze (*ooz*) *v.* To pass through, percolate, leak,
     drip.
The verb to OOZE, and the noun, go directly back to an Anglo-
Saxon word which began with a w, which has since been lost.

The noun OOZE is slime, wet mud, earth soft enough to flow. To OOZE, the verb, is to flow slowly like OOZE.

The only mislead marked thus far by anyone is OVERFLOW, chosen by 27 per cent. Both OVERFLOW and OOZE describe liquid leaving a container, the first by flowing over the edge or brim of something which is too full, the second by flowing through the porous material of which the container is made. To OVERFLOW is to flow over; to OOZE is to flow through. The noun, an OVER-FLOW ($\bar{o}'$-$v\breve{e}r$-$fl\bar{o}$), may be an inundation, flood. OOZING by comparison is slow, gradual, gentle.

390. *FLANK*, flank (*flănk*) *n.* Side, right or left, wing (v. B. 255), a lateral (v. B. 838) part.

To 25 per cent of those tested FLANK means REAR, partly from the Latin *retro*, back, from *re*, back. REAR means back, behind, hinder, posterior. FLANK, from Dutch, Danish, Swedish, is neither front nor back, but at the side, at the right or left.

The word FLANK, to mean the side of an animal, goes back to before 1200. Not until nearly 1600 was FLANK used for the side of an army, one of the common applications of the word today.

391. *DEFT*, deft (*dĕft*) *adj.* Clever with the hands, apt, skilful, nimble, adroit, neat (v. B. 155) in performance, dexterous (v. B. 1097). DEFTLY (*dĕft'-lĭ*), skilfully, aptly, with the Anglo-Saxon -LY, is the adverb; and DEFTNESS (*dĕft'-nĕs*), dexterity, neatness of action, the corresponding noun.

To 35 per cent DEFT, which goes directly back to Anglo-Saxon, means HARD-OF-HEARING, compared with only 32 per cent who mark the traditional NIMBLE. When spoken DEAF (*dĕf*) and DEFT (*dĕft*) sound alike; but the vocabulary test is printed. DEAF, hard-of-hearing, is learned probably from conversation, and the unfamiliar DEFT could easily be accepted as the spelling of DEAF. Following popular opinion, DEAF and DEFT would be identical and the language would soon lose DEFT. But English is too important a language to allow changes without careful consideration.

DEFT originally meant simple, meek, a variant of DAFT, silly, simple, foolish, stupid, weak-minded, and it is not easy to see how DEFT came to mean dexterous, clever, nimble, skilful.

392. *COAGULATE*, coagulate (*kō-ăg'-ū-lāt*) *v.* To thicken, congeal, clot, curdle, concrete, change from a fluid to a thick viscous mass.

Coagulate comes from the Latin *coagulatus*, the past participle of *coagulare*, to curdle, a combination of *co-*, together, and *agere*, to drive, lead, and so literally to bring together, collect, gather.

To 9 per cent COAGULATING means GROUPING, a perfect description of what takes place, for COAGULATING is sometimes defined as the coalescence of separate particles.

E. Chambers says: 'COAGULATING is the condensing or thickening of fluid matter; an operation in which fluid bodies become solid', and he continues: 'CONCRETION includes COAGULATION, CONDENSATION, and HARDENING'. To CONCRETE, from the Latin *concrescere*, to grow together, is to unite in a mass, coalesce in a solid body, form concretions. A COAGULATION is not so hard as CONCRETE, but of a jellied consistency, like cheese or butter, as from Sir Walter Raleigh, History of the World: 'The cheesewife knoweth that sour rennet doth COAGULATE her milk into a curd'; or from Boyle: 'Did there COAGULATE into a whitish body, almost like butter'.

393. *DANK*, dank (*dănk*) *adj.* Disagreeably cold and moist, damp, humid (v. b. 521), unpleasantly wet, watery and chilling.

Dank, related to Swedish and Icelandic words, is thought by 19 per cent to mean SMELLY, having an offensive odor, as in the line from the Water Babies by Charles Kingsley, an English clergyman, who lived from 1819 to 1875, and who from his thirtieth year to his death published a book almost annually: 'Nasty, dirty, frowzy, grubby, smelly, old monks'. RANK, directly from Anglo-Saxon with similar words in Swedish and Icelandic, means offensive to the senses, rancid and so SMELLY. DANK air is unpleasantly moist and suggests SMELLY; but DANK means damp, moist, cold.

Of the four words: MOIST, DAMP, HUMID, DANK, the first is never unpleasant, while DANK, at the other extreme, is chilly, disagreeable, unwholesome, and of the four the only one which suggests SMELLY.

394. *CORPORATE*, corporate (kŏr'-pōr-āt) *adj*. United in
the legal sense, legally organized, collected, common,
combined.

CORPORATE comes from the Latin *corporare*, to make into a
body, a verb of the first conjugation, from the noun *corpus*,
corporis, body, often used in Latin grammars to illustrate the
third declension, where the stem *corpor-*, which shows in the
genitive *corporis*, ends in a consonant. From *corpus*, *corporis*,
come CORPSE, body; CORPULENT, fat, stout, portly; CORPOREAL
(kor-pō'-rē-ăl), physical, material; and others.

CORPORATE is thought by 28 per cent to mean BUSINESS, now
an occupation, trade, vocation, way of earning a living, a combination of BUSY and -NESS, originally being busy. The words
CORPORATE and BUSINESS are closely connected. A CORPORATION,
or CORPORATE body, is an artificial person set up legally to do
BUSINESS. But a man who goes into BUSINESS does not become
automatically a CORPORATE body.

The adjective BUSINESS, as: 'A BUSINESS enterprise', means
money-making, or at least an attempt to make money. 'A COR-
PORATE enterprise' is a group enterprise.

395. *FIESTA*, fiesta (fĭ-ĕs'-tă) *n*. Feast, festival, festivity, holiday. FIESTA, given in English dictionaries as an English
word, is the Spanish word for feast.

FIESTA is thought by 15 per cent to mean AFTERNOON NAP, the
only mislead marked by anyone thus far. SIESTA and FIESTA are
both Spanish words. A SIESTA is an AFTERNOON NAP. A FIESTA is
a FESTIVAL.

396. *CATARACT*, cataract (kăt'-ă-răkt) *n*. Waterfall, furious
downpour, rush of water, series of cascades, descent of
water over a steeply sloping but not perpendicular surface.

CATARACT may come from the Greek καταρράκτης (*catarractes*),
a waterfall; or perhaps from a combination of κατά (*cata*),
down, and αράσσειν (*arassein*), to dash to pieces.

Of CATARACT Bailey says: 'A steep place in a river, made by
rocks stopping the course of its stream, and so causing water
to fall with great force and noise'. According to E. Chambers:
'A fall or precipice, in the channel or bed of a river; caused by

rocks, or other obstacles stopping the course of the stream; whence the water falls with a noise and impetuosity, as the CATARACT of the Nile, the Danube, Rhine, etc.'

A WATERFALL is a single perpendicular drop. A CATARACT is a series of CASCADES, where a large body of water rushes over and between rocks.

Those who fail to recognize the meaning of CATARACT divide almost evenly between TOMB, confusing it with CATACOMB; DISASTER, confusing it with CATASTROPHE; and HAZE, mist, an idea from the same situation.

397. *TRANSFUSE*, transfuse (*trăns-fūz'*) *v.* To pour out of one vessel into another, transfer.

To FUSE (*fūs*) is primarily to pour, for FUSE comes from *fusus*, the past participle of *fundere*, to pour, shed, spread. FUSING a metal renders it capable of being poured, and so FUSE has come to mean MELT, liquefy, soften by heat, reduce from a solid to a liquid state. FUSE has also come to mean mix; so that today FUSE means either MELT or MIX.

To TRANSFUSE is not to melt together, the easy translation, but to pour from one container to another. To TRANSMIT, from *mittente*, a sender, is to send from one place to another. To TRANSFER, from *ferre*, to carry, is to carry from one place to another, with emphasis on the places; and thus differs from TRANSPORT, from *portare*, to carry, which stresses the act of carrying, with no interest in the places. TRANSFUSE, and especially the noun TRANSFUSION, is the pouring operation.

398. *SUBSEQUENT*, subsequent (*sŭb'-sē-kwĕnt*) *adj.* Following in time, succeeding, next after, happening later, occurring afterward.

From the Latin verb *sequi*, to follow, come SEQUEL (*sē'-kwĕl*), that part of a story or article which follows an earlier part already published, conclusion; and SEQUENTIAL (*sē-kwĕn'-shăl*), succeeding in order, following in succession; as well as SUBSEQUENT.

To 5 per cent SUBSEQUENT means PREVIOUS, from the Latin *prae*, before, and *via*, way, road, and so occurring before, happening earlier, preceding, prior, antecedent, an opposite of

SUBSEQUENT, happening afterward. Although the Century Dictionary gives PRIOR as the correct opposite of SUBSEQUENT, ANTECEDENT, before in time, place, rank, or order, is another equally satisfactory opposite. Other pairs of opposites are: FORMER and LATTER; ANTERIOR and POSTERIOR; PRECEDING and FOLLOWING.

The adjective CONSEQUENT means following as a result, ensuing, caused by something which has already taken place. The noun CONSEQUENCE is a conclusion, inference, result, orderly following. SUBSEQUENT means merely coming after, following in time, and does not imply cause and effect as does CONSEQUENT.

399. *CULMINATING*, culminating (*kŭl'-mĭn-ā-tĭng*) *adj*. At the highest point, acme, summit, top, crowning, pinnacle, apex, elevated in quality, rank, or power; as from John Ruskin: 'The CULMINATING power of Gothic art in the 13th century'. The verb to CULMINATE, and the present participle CULMINATING, come from the Latin *culmen, culminis*, the highest point.

To 6 per cent CULMINATING means STARTING. The START is the beginning; then later comes the summit, peak, CULMINATION of one's efforts; followed by a decline, deterioration, sinking.

400. *OBLIQUELY*, obliquely (*ŏb-lēk'-lĭ*) *adv*. Slantingly, crookedly (v. B. 70), slopingly, aslant, askew (v. B. 724), awry, askance, technically at an angle less than 90°, also not straight ahead. See OBLIQUITY (V. B. 1530).

OBLIQUELY, from the Latin *obliquus*, slanting, awry, sidelong, bent, acute, neither perpendicular nor parallel, is thought by 20 per cent of high-school students, and by 23 per cent of high-vocabulary ones, to mean UNSEEINGLY, blindly.

Several words beginning with O-, OB-, and even OBLI-, mean dark, shady, and so suggest UNSEEINGLY. OPAQUE (*ō-pāk'*), from the Latin *opacus*, shady, dark, means not transparent, not letting light through, impenetrable to sight, and may suggest UNSEEINGLY. OBSCURE, from the Latin *obscurus*, with the same meaning dark, shady, means not clearly seen.

OBLIVIOUS comes from the Latin *oblivius*, forgotten. OBLIVION (*ŏb-lĭv'-ĭ-ŏn*) is forgetfulness, from the Latin *ob-*, over, and *livēre*, to grow dark, the source of LIVID, black and blue. OBLIVIOUSLY may suggest UNSEEINGLY, though the word means FORGETFULLY, disposed to forget. OBSERVINGLY means seeingly, and opposites are confused. But none of these seems near enough to OBLIQUELY to mislead 23 per cent of the high-vocabulary students into marking UNSEEINGLY as its meaning. OBLIQUELY ordinarily means slantingly, at an angle, askew.

401. *JUBILATION*, jubilation (*jū-bĭ-lā'-shŏn*) *n*. A rejoicing, exultation, festive celebration.

EXULTATION, selected by 55 per cent, and EXCITEMENT by 45 per cent, are both close synonyms of JUBILATION, as confirmed by the nearly equal number of persons choosing each.

EXCITEMENT, which characterizes a JUBILATION, comes from *ex-*, out, and *ciere*, to call. To EXCITE is to call into action, stimulate.

JUBILATION comes from a Hebrew word for ram's horn, used as a trumpet blown to announce the JUBILEE which, among ancient Hebrews, occurred every 50th year.

To EXULT is to rejoice; and EXULTATION, rejoicing, is a close synonym of JUBILATION.

402. *DOGMA*, dogma (*dŏg'-măh*) *n*. A system of tenets, prescribed doctrine, settled belief, principle, maxim, established opinion.

DOGMA comes from the Latin *dogma*, from the Greek δόγμα (*dogma*), δόγματις (*dogmatis*), an opinion, view, edict, decree, from the Greek δοκεῖν (*docein*), to think, seem, appear. In 1828 Webster said of DOGMA: 'A doctrinal notion particularly in matters of faith and philosophy'.

An ASSUMPTION, selected by 25 per cent as a synonym of DOGMA, is something supposed, assumed proposition, postulate, from the Latin *assumere*, to take to one's self, adopt. ASSUMPTION and DOGMA differ primarily in the areas where the two circulate. An ASSUMPTION is made in science with the idea of testing it. A DOGMA is a settled religious belief adopted with the conviction that it will never change.

403. *SYNOD*, synod (*sĭ'-nŏd*) *n*. Assemblage of ecclesiastics, meeting, council, convention, convocation, presbytery, session, gemot.

SYNOD comes from the Greek σύν (*syn*), together, and ὁδός (*odos*), way, road; the source of EXODUS, a pouring out of multitudes, and METHOD, from μετά (*meta*), after, and ὁδός (*odos*), road, way, an arrangement of objects one after another, in order.

From Nathan Bailey, 1721: 'A meeting (or assembly) of ecclesiastical persons to consult concerning religion and church affairs'. The SYNOD is often the highest judicatory body. Under the SYNOD, in some church organizations, comes the PRESBYTERY, and under this the SESSION. Elsewhere SYNODS are of five types as discussed under ECUMENICAL.

404. *DAMASK*, damask (*dăm'-ăsk*) *n.* A fabric woven in an
        elaborate pattern of heavy silk thread, linen, wool, or
cotton.

DAMASK comes from the city of Damascus, where the fabric was originally made. The word goes back through the Latin *Damascus*, and the Greek Δαμασκός (*Damascos*), to the Hebrew and Arabic *Damascus*.

DAMASK is thought by 25 per cent to be a BRANDY GLASS, perhaps remotely suggested by FLASK, ending in the same last three letters. A FLASK, directly from Anglo-Saxon, is a bottle, often used for whiskey.

405. *VOCIFEROUS*, vociferous (*vō-sĭf'-ĕ-rŭs*) *adj.* Noisy,
        clamorous, making an outcry, bellowing, roaring, shouting,
brawling.

VOCIFEROUS comes from the Latin *vociferatus*, the past participle of *vociferari*, to cry out, scream, a combination of *vox, vocis,* voice, and *ferre*, to carry. From this same *ferre* come ODORIFEROUS, fragrant, producing an odor; SOPORIFEROUS, producing sleep; and numerous other little known words: LUCIFEROUS, producing light; NUCIFEROUS, producing nuts; MELLIFEROUS, producing honey; and FRUGIFEROUS, fruit.

To 8 per cent VOCIFEROUS means SUBDUED, an exact opposite.

406. *ACETOUS*, acetous (*ăs'-ē-tŭs*, or *ă-sē'-tŭs*) *adj.* Having a
        sour taste, vinegary.

From the Latin *acetum*, vinegar, comes easily the adjective ACETOUS, like vinegar, and so sour. From the Latin verb *acere*, to be sour, and the related *acer*, sharp, sour, comes the Latin *acidus*, and from this the English ACID, for all acids were originally defined as sour in taste.

To 20 per cent ACETOUS means dry, parched, without water, compared with 70 per cent who prefer SOUR, and this is about the amount of DRYNESS in the word. A DRY remark is often caustic, sharp, biting, like ACID: but ACETOUS means SOUR, not DRY.

407. *BANAL*, banal (*băh-năl'*) *adj*. Commonplace, hackneyed, trite, stale, trivial, insipid, jejune, flat, vapid, bromidic, platitudinous.

BANAL, still with its French accent on the last syllable, the French *banal*, with a similar word in Provençal, all applied originally to public wells, communal ovens and mills, used by the lower classes. All come from the word BAN, a proclamation, because such wells were proclaimed, declared, as being for common use.

The popular mislead, selected by 20 per cent, is RUDE, on the edge of correct, for RUDE may mean humble, of low position and so very close to BANAL in its original sense. BANALITY is the corresponding noun.

408. *PARADIGM*, paradigm (*pă'-ră-dĭm*) *n*. Example, model, pattern, exemplar, idea, archetype (*ahr'-kĭ-tīp*).

PARADIGM, which goes back in English to 1500, comes from the Greek παρά (*para*), beside, and δεικνύναι (*deiknunai*), to show. From παρά comes PARALLEL, beside another, from ἄλλος (*allos*), another.

A PROTOTYPE is the original pattern, model from which others are formed. A PARAGON (*pă'-ră-gŏn*) is superb, a model of perfection, excellence. A PARADIGM is an example of something done, an instance of something said, as: 'A PARADIGM of a nation's literary existence', an illustration, example.

409. *GAFF*, gaff (*găf*) *n*. A strong hook with a handle but without a barb, used for landing large fish such as pike and salmon.

To 5 per cent GAFF means CRUTCH, probably suggested by the word STAFF which ends in the same last three letters as GAFF.

Although a CRUTCH, directly from Anglo-Saxon, is a support for the lame, the word is related to CROOK and CROZIER and close to STAFF, at first a stick, pole, directly from Anglo-Saxon, then a stick used in walking, now also a FLAG-STAFF.

To another 4 per cent GAFF means WINE BOTTLE. A CARAFE (kă-răf´) is a water bottle, decanter, or WINE BOTTLE.

GRAPNEL, GRAPPLE, and GAFF are three kinds of hooks. A GRAPNEL is a cluster of perhaps six hooks used for grasping, often dragged under water. A GRAPPLE, an older word, is a single large hook used to hold one ship to another, or a ship to a pier. A GAFF, of Celtic origin, from an Irish word meaning hook and a Welsh one for GRAPPLE, has no barb and is used only for landing large fish.

410. *SYNDICATE*, syndicate (sĭn´-dĭ-kāt) *n*. A council, body of syndics, association of persons, combination of corporations.

SYNDICATE comes from the Greek σύνδικος (*sindikos*), an advocate in a court of justice, a combination of σύν (*sin*), together, and δίκη (*dice*), justice, law.

TRUSTS, POOLS, COMBINES, and SYNDICATES are groups of corporations, or of various sorts, working together. A TRUST may be a combination of corporations. A POOL is a more informal working together. The word COMBINE suggests an underhanded goal.

A SYNDICATE is an association of corporations to promote some enterprise or discharge some trust. SYNDICATES were once combinations of newspaper publishers to purchase and publish simultaneously in different parts of the country stories and articles by popular writers. 'SYNDICATED articles' still appear.

411. *ANCHOVY*, anchovy (ăn-chō´-vĭ) *n*. A tiny fish like a sardine, eaten as an appetizer, caught in vast numbers in the Mediterranean.

From the astonishingly up-to-date Encyclopaedia of Ephraim Chambers, 1728, comes: 'ANCHOVY, in matters of commerce, a little sea-fish, much used by way of sauce or seasoning.

'Scaliger describes the ANCHOVY as of the herring kind, about the length of a finger having the pointed snout, a wide mouth and no teeth, but gums as rough as a saw. Others make it a sort of sardine, or pilchard; but others hold it a peculiar species very different from either.

'The ANCHOVY is caught in the month of May, June, and July, on the coasts of Catalonia, Provence, etc., at which season it repairs up the Straits of Gibraltar into the Mediterranean.

'The fishing for them is chiefly in the night-time; when a light being put on the stern of their little fishing-vessel, the ANCHOVIES flock round and are caught in the nets. But then it is asserted to have been found by experience that ANCHOVIES taken thus by fire, are neither so good, so firm, nor so proper for keeping as those taken without fire.

'The common way of eating ANCHOVIES is with oil, vinegar, &c. In order to do which they are first boned, and the tails, fins, &c slipped off. Some also pickle ANCHOVIES in small Delft, or earthern pots, made on purpose, of two or three pounds weight, which they cover with plaster, to keep them the better. ANCHOVIES should be chosen small, fresh pickled, white on the outside, and red within. They must have a round back; for those which are flat or large are often nothing but sardines.'

CAVIAR (*kah-vĭ-ahr'*), the preserved eggs, roe, of certain large fish, principally the BELUGA, is another appetizer. Both words CAVIAR and ANCHOVY are Italian. CAVIAR goes back to an earlier Turkish word, while ANCHOVY may come from a Greek word which meant either ANCHOVY or SARDINE.

ANCHOVY is thought by 33 per cent to be a VEGETABLE. An ARTICHOKE, another Italian word, is a VEGETABLE; ANCHOVY is fish.

412. *NULLITY*, nullity (*nŭl'-lĭ-tĭ*) *n*. Nothingness, invalidity, something of no legal value.

The adjective NULL, void, worthless, of no value, comes from the Latin *nullus*, not any, none. The verb to ANNUL, spelt with only a single L, is to render NULL and void, annihilate, abolish, abrogate, do away with. To NULLIFY, a combination of NULL and *facere*, to make, is much the same, to make void, invalidate, annul. NULLITY, ending in the Latin -*ity*, added to an adjective to form the corresponding noun, is the state of being void. Nathan Bailey, 1721, says: 'The being NULL, void, or of no effect'.

413. *PREOCCUPATION*, preoccupation (*prē-ŏk-ū-pā'-shŏn*)
  n. Engrossment, absorption, engaged in reverie, complete
concern, abstraction.

From the Latin verb *capere*, to take, seize, grasp, come many
English words, including the adjective CAPABLE, able to seize,
grasp, take hold of. From the same *capere*, through the Latin
occupare, to take possession of, starting with the almost mean-
ingless *oc*, to, come OCCUPY, to seize, take; and OCCUPATION,
that which seizes one, takes up one's time, occupies one's attention. An OCCUPATION ought to absorb one completely.

A PREOCCUPATION is then the state of being wholly engrossed
in something before something else attempts to gain one's attention, a taking possession before another, prepossession.

414. *LUMINARY*, luminary (*lū'-min-ă-rĭ*) *n.* Any person who
  enlightens mankind, dignitary, celebrity, star.
Given a choice between RESEARCHER and CELEBRITY, neither of
which is really correct, 25 per cent select the first. A RESEACHER,
if successful, may enlighten the world, but many hard workers
spend a life searching only to find nothing.

The word CELEBRITY comes from the Latin *celeber*, famous,
renowned, from the same source as the verb to CELEBRATE, to
observe, commemorate with appropriate rites. A CELEBRITY is
renowned, famous, talked about, publicly known for any reason, but not necessarily for enlightening the world.

Today a DIGNITARY, from the Latin *dignus*, worthy, is a church
official with an exalted title. But even in Latin, *dignitas* came to
mean of rank, public standing, rather than inherent worthiness.

In the church, DIGNITARY is the word; in the theater, STAR. A
LUMINARY, from the Latin *lumen*, light, the source of LUMINOUS
and ILLUME, is by derivation anything which gives light. Of
these various words, LUMINARY is the only one which has retained its original meaning. A LUMINARY is one who lights the
way for humanity.

415. *INCOMPACT*, incompact (*ĭn-kŏm-păkt'*) *adj.* Diffused,
  scattered, spread out, loosely knit.
The Latin verb *pingere* means to strike, hit, push, drive. From
this comes *impingere*, to push in, strike, and the English word

IMPINGE (*ĭm-pĭnj'*), to push in, collide, hit, dash against. Robert Burton, who died in 1640, writes of a ship IMPINGING on a rock, correct etymologically, but IMPINGE seems now a gentler word. One IMPINGES on the privacy, on the rights of another, breaks in on them.

From the past participle *impactus*, of the same Latin verb, comes the noun IMPACT (*ĭm'-păkt*), a blow, collision, striking against, a word which has kept its original force. From *compactus*, pushed together, comes COMPACT, tightly pushed together, closely united, dense, solid, spissate. INCOMPACT is clearly the opposite. But these negative terms are unpleasant. Avoid them if you can find a more direct, positive approach.

416. *LEMMING*, lemming (*lĕm'-mĭng*) *n.* A rodent, kind of rat; Ephraim Chambers says: 'Of the bigness of a squirrel, their skin is streaked with brown and black, a fine deep color'. LEMMING is a Norwegian word for a small mouse-like animal, one of the rodents, a gnawer.

BIRD attracts 25 per cent as a synonym of LEMMING. STARLING is a BIRD; a LEMMING is one of the rat family.

In their march, they usually keep a direct line from northeast to southwest and always travel in thousands. They march only from the time of twilight to the morning, lying still all day. If they meet with anything in their way that might deter another animal, it never stops them; though it be fire, a deep well, or a bog, they without hesitation venture through, and by that means many thousands are destroyed. They commonly visit a country once or twice in twenty years. After ravaging the country, destroying the grass, they at length perish either through want of food or in some great water or the sea.

417. *BACCALAUREATE*, baccalaureate (*băk-kă-law'-rē-āt*) *n.* University degree of bachelor. One who has attained the lowest degree in a university.

BACHELOR, formerly a person in the first step toward knighthood, is now one who has taken the first degree at a university, who is not yet a MASTER of the arts.

Skeat, in his Etymological Dictionary, does not mention BACCALAUREATE; but the Oxford calls it Latinized as *baccalarius*, with some imaginary reference to laurel berry, *bacca*, berry, and *laurus*, laurel. Although the Oxford gives no illustration of the word prior to 1625, it may have come into existence, in its Latinized form, in the 13th century, at the time of the great universities, when it is said that the University of Bologna in Italy may have had twenty thousand students.

REUNION, the only frequently marked mislead, is often the anniversary of receiving a degree.

418. *SIESTA*, siesta (*sē-ĕs'-tah*) *n*. A rest at noon, nap in the hottest part of the day.

SIESTA, a Spanish word, comes from the Latin *sexta*, the sixth hour after sunrise, noon, the feminine of *sextus*, from *sex*, six.

A FIESTA is a holiday, festival. A SIESTA is a nap, rest in the middle of the day.

419. *HARBINGER*, harbinger (*hahr'-bĭn-jer*) *n*. A forerunner, herald, precursor, one who gives notice of something to come.

The familiar phrase: 'HARBINGER of spring', leads 6 per cent into selecting WARMTH, and another 5 per cent LAST-SNOW, as meanings of HARBINGER, each an association of ideas, the second step in learning.

Skeat, in his Etymological Dictionary, calls the N in HAR-BINGER, EXCRESCENT, an abnormal growth, like the N in PAS-SENGER and MESSENGER, which come from PASSAGE and MESSAGE, with no N's. In a more roundabout way SCAVENGER comes from SCAVAGE, the official who years ago collected toll from mer-chants, who later took over the direction of street cleaning. Here the verb to SCAVENGE has the N, for it comes from the noun SCAVENGER and not the original official SCAVAGE.

Even more indirectly PORRINGER, with the EXCRESCENT N, comes from POTAGE; and in something of the same way HAR-BINGER comes from HARBOR, originally a place of shelter, lodg-ing, inn, accommodation.

According to Ephraim Chambers: 'The HARBINGER was an officer of the King's household, having four yeomen under him, who rode a day's journey before the court, when it traveled, to provide lodging'.

420. *BASTION*, bastion (*băs'-tĭ-ŏn*) *n.* A pile of earth faced
    with sods, brick, or stone, standing out from a rampart.
To 3 per cent BASTION means MOAT. A MOAT (*mōt*), fosse, is a
deep trench filled with water, dug around the rampart of a
castle. MOAT once meant a mound, hill, and all of the words
from which it comes, Spanish, Portuguese, and Provençal, mean
embankment. But MOAT has come to mean ditch, not mound.
    RAMPART, a French word meaning fortify, defend, built
around a town, is a mound of earth, ordinarily built of the
material taken out of the surrounding ditch or MOAT.
    Of BASTION E. Chambers, 1728, says: 'A hugh mass of earth
usually faced with sods, sometimes with brick, rarely with
stone, standing out from a rampart, of which it is a principal
part. They were well known after the year 1500.'

421. *DILEMMA*, dilemma (*dĭ-lĕm'-mă*) *n.* Two equally un-
    desirable alternatives, often termed the HORNS of the DI-
LEMMA, a difficulty, doubtful choice.
DILEMMA comes from the Greek δίλημμα (*dilemma*), a conclusion from two premises, a combination of δι- (*di-*), two,
and λῆμμα (*lemma*), a proposition, assumption. From The
Arte of Logike, 1599, by Thomas Blunderville, who wrote
on astronomy, maps, geography, and other technical subjects,
comes: 'An argument of two members, repugnant to one another, whereof whichsoever thou grantest, thou art by and by
taken'.
    To 16 per cent, DILEMMA means EMERGENCY. An EMERGENCY
is an unexpected happening, unforeseen occurrence, sudden condition, perplexing contingency, complication of circumstances,
crisis, strait, exigency calling for action. Of these various meanings of EMERGENCY, both a perplexing contingency and a complication of circumstances approach DILEMMA; but an EMER-
GENCY calls for immediate action, while a DILEMMA demands
thought, an intellectual decision.

422. *CONFRÈRE*, confrère (*kŏn-frãr'*) *n.* Fellow member of a
    learned profession, colleague, brother, associate.
CONFRÈRE, a French word, from the Latin *con*, with, and *frater*,
brother, was used in the 15th and 16th centuries pronounced

(*kŏn'-frār*), with a spoken accent on the first syllable, and spelt without a written accent. Then it dropped out of existence. But about 1750 it began to be used again, this time almost as a French word, spelt with a French accent, CONFRÈRE, and stressed on the last syllable.

423. *DISSENSION*, dissension (*dĭs-sĕn'-shŏn*) *n.* Disagreement, contention, discord, dispute, differing, variance. DISSENSION comes from the present participle *dissensus* of the Latin *dissentire*, a combination of *dis-*, apart, and *sentire*, to feel, think, the source of the English words: SENSE, SENSIBLE, SENSITIVE, and SENTIMENT.

To 28 per cent DISSENSION means SINKING. To DESCEND is to SINK, to go down. The corresponding noun is ordinarily DESCENT (*dē-sĕnt'*), a going down, sinking, also a downward slope. But there is also a rarely heard noun DESCENSION, a SINKING, going down, differing in spelling from DISSENSION, disagreement, but almost identical in sound. DESCEND, DESCENT, and DESCENSION all start with the Latin *de-*, down, and come from *scandere*, to climb. DISSENT and DISSENSION start with *dis-*, apart.

The verb to CONSENT (*kŏn-sĕnt'*), still from the same *sentire*, is to agree in sentiment, be at one, of the same mind. To CONSENT is to agree with that which one has the power and disposition to prevent. One CONSENTS to a son's going. Both the verb and the noun are identical. ASSENT (*ăs-sĕnt'*) is an act of understanding. One ASSENTS to an argument.

To DISSENT (*dĭs-sĕnt'*) is to disagree, hold fast to a contrary opinion. Of DISSENSION Webster, in his first edition 1828, says: 'Usually a disagreement in opinion which is violent producing a warm debate or angry words, contention in words, strife, discord; quarrel; breach of friendship and union.

'We see DISSENSION in Church and State, in town parishes, and families, and the word is sometimes applied to differences which produce war.'

424. *MEAD*, mead (*mēd*) *n.* A strong liquor, not inferior to good wine, drink, beverage, fermented honey and water enriched with spices; according to Ephraim Chambers: 'A wholesome agreeable liquor prepared of honey and water'.

MEAD comes directly from Anglo-Saxon, dating back to a Sanscrit word for honey and sugar.

Continuing from Ephraim Chambers, 1728: 'One of the best methods of preparing MEAD is as follows: Into twelve gallons of water slip the whites of six eggs; mixing these well together, and to the mixture adding twenty pounds of honey. Let the liquor boil an hour, and when boiled, add cinnamon, ginger, cloves, mace, and a little rosemary. As soon as it is cold put a spoonful of yeast to it, and tun it up keeping the vessel filled as it works; when it has done working stop it up close; and, when fine, bottle it off for use'.

425. *OMNIPOTENT*, omnipotent (*ŏm-nĭp'-ō-tĕnt*) *adj.* Al-
    mighty, all-powerful, with absolute authority, infinite in power, strictly said of God.

OMNIPOTENT comes from the Latin *omnis*, all, and *potens*, *potentis*, able, powerful, much as OMNISCIENT (*ŏm-nĭsh'-ĕnt*) comes from the same Latin *omnis*, all, and *sciens*, *scientis*, know-ing, the source of SCIENCE.

OMNIBUS, used as an adjective, means including all, where despite the fact that the French *omnibus* refers primarily to a vehicle for all, the ending is not the English BUS, but the Latin dative plural ending of *omnis*, all, every.

POTENT in English means strong, powerful; so that OMNIP-OTENT is literally all-powerful.

426. *WHET*, whet (*hwĕt*) *v.* To sharpen by rubbing on a
    grindstone, to produce a keen edge by friction, figuratively to stimulate, excite, make eager.

To 4 per cent WHET means BUILD-UP. To WHET one's appetite is to stimulate it, sharpen it, and so figuratively to build it up.

WHET, which goes back to the year 900, comes directly from an Anglo-Saxon word meaning sharp, with many similar words in the Scandinavian languages. A WHETSTONE is a STONE for WHETTING or sharpening knives.

Is the order of difficulty in this book, and in the two pre-ceding volumes I and II, a difficulty of words themselves, or of the ideas which the words express? The fact that a hundred hard words at the end of Volume II have practically the same number

of letters per word as easy words at the beginning of volume I
suggests that the words themselves are not the problem.

We must now discover how often similar ideas, expressed in
different languages, are of the same order of difficulty. The
noun a WHET, used figuratively, and an INCENTIVE (236) are
similar ideas, the first from Anglo-Saxon and the second from
Latin.

Of the pronunciation, Phyfe stresses in a score of instances
the difference between w- and wh- (*hw*). WET (*wĕt*) means
damp, soaked, not dry. WHET (*hwĕt*) means to sharpen, grind
on a WHETSTONE (*hwĕt'-stōn*).

427. *INVOCATION*, invocation (*ĭn-vō-kā'-shŏn*) *n*. The act
of summoning aid, prayer, asking the blessing of God for
some undertaking; from E. Chambers: 'In theology, an act
whereby we adore God, and call on him for His assistance'.
INVOCATION, from the Latin *invocare*, to call upon, is a combination of *in-*, on, and *vocare*, to call, the source not only of
VOCATION, one's CALLING, occupation, profession, work, as: medicine, law, engineering, business, but also of PROVOCATION, REVO-
CATION, CONVOCATION, and countless others. Of these the verb
to EVOKE, to call forth, summon out, and the little used corresponding noun EVOCATION, have kept close to the literal Latin to
call out. To REVOKE, where REVOCATION is the noun, which originally meant call back, summon back, has come to mean cancel,
repeal, annul, recant, abjure, make void. To PROVOKE, where
PROVOCATION is the noun, which originally meant call forth,
summon, has come to mean irritate, offend, exasperate, excite
to anger.

A CONVOCATION is literally a calling together, assembly, meeting, gathering, convention, congress, council, synod, diet; and
this no doubt leads 16 per cent to select LECTURE as the meaning
of INVOCATION. A CONVOCATION is a meeting at which an address,
LECTURE, is given. An INVOCATION is the act of calling in prayer.

428. *HEPTARCHY*, heptarchy (*hĕp'-tahr-kĭ*) *n*. Government
of seven persons, rule of seven.
HEPTARCHY goes back to the Greek ἑπτά (*hepta*), seven, and
ἄρχειν (*archein*), to lead, govern, rule. ANARCHY, starting with

the Greek privative ἀν (*an*), is without rule, without a government. An OLIGARCHY, from the Greek ὀλίγος (*oligos*), few, is government by a few; but strangely the choice FEW, in the vocabulary test, which one might expect to be attractive, has been marked by no one.

A MONARCHY, from the Greek μόνος (*monos*), alone, is government by one alone; and this leads to KINGDOM as the popular mislead, selected by 10 per cent.

Of HEPTARCHY Webster says in the first edition of his Dictionary, 1828: 'A government of seven persons, or the country governed by seven persons. But the word is usually applied to England when under the government of seven kings and divided into seven kingdoms; as the Saxon HEPTARCHY, which comprehended the whole of England, when subject to seven independent princes. The petty kingdoms were those of Kent, the South Saxon (Sussex), West Saxon, East Saxon (Essex), the East Angles, Mercia, and Northumberland'.

429. *EMBELLISHMENT*, embellishment (ĕm-bĕl'-lĭsh-mĕnt) *n.* Beautification, ornamentation, decoration, adornment, enrichment, anything which adds beauty and elegance.
EMBELLISHMENT is the verb to EMBELLISH plus -MENT. To EMBELLISH, from the Latin *in-* and *bellus*, beautiful, fair, is to make attractive, pleasing, beautiful.

Bailey said of EMBELLISHMENT: an ornament, or setting off. To EMBELLISH: to adorn, beautify or set out to the eye.

430. *IMPROPRIETY*, impropriety (ĭm-prō-prī'-ĕ-tĭ) *n.* Unfitness, unsuitableness, indelicacy, boorishness, barbarism. IMPROPRIETY comes directly through the French, from the Latin *improprietas, improprietatis*, impropriety, from *improprius*, improper. From the Latin *proprius*, special, proper, one's own, personal, come PROPER, PROPERTY, APPROPRIATE, and PROPRIETY. PROPERTY and PROPRIETY are doublets. PROPRIETY once meant possession, ownership, exclusive right to hold; but the two words have exchanged meanings. PROPERTY has come to mean that which is owned, goods, chattels, effects; while PROPRIETY has come to mean suitableness, fitness, correctness, appropriateness, seemliness.

DEVELOPMENT is the only attractive mislead selected by 15 per cent. A DEVELOPMENT may be an IMPROVEMENT, a word which starts with the same five letters as IMPROPRIETY, and this may suggest DEVELOPMENT as a mislead.

IMPROPRIETY may apply to character, time, place, circumstance, or technically to writing. According to G. Campbell, in his Philosophy of Rhetoric, 'A BARBARISM is the use of a word which is not English, a violation in the form of words; a SOLECISM is the construction of a sentence which is not good English, a violation in construction'. IMPROPRIETY is the use of words with other than their precise meanings.

431. *TIRADE*, tirade (*tĭ'-rād*) *n*. A long uninterrupted speech, on a single subject, bombast, rant, fustian, hyperbole, boisterous declamation.

TIRADE has come in English to mean a long, violent speech, harangue, vituperation, vehement outburst; and this leads 4 per cent to select HARSHNESS, roughness, severeness, austerity, ill-naturedness, as a meaning of TIRADE. HARSHNESS may be a characteristic of a TIRADE; but a TIRADE is long and uninterrupted.

A RANT is noisy, violent language, without sense, lacking dignity. BOMBAST, originally soft, loose, cotton used for padding, is a speech full of high-sounding words, extravagant language, too big for the occasion. A TIRADE, from the Italian *tirare*, to prolong, protract, drag out, and connected with the word TIRE, to fatigue, weary, is long, fatiguing, tiring, a speech often harsh and always too long.

432. *HEWN*, hewn (*hūn*) *adj*. Chopped, cut (v. B. 26) with an axe, hatchet, or adze, with a swinging blow.

HEWED is past, as: 'He HEWED yesterday'. HEWING is the present participle, as: 'He is HEWING now'. HEWN is the past participle, used also as an adjective as: 'A HEWN beam'. From the same Anglo-Saxon source comes HOE, the garden tool used with two hands but with the same chopping motion. Other Anglo-Saxon words, with the same sort of past participle, are BLOW and BLOWN, as: 'BLOWN leaves'; GROW and GROWN, as: 'A GROWN boy'. With SEW (*sō*) the historically correct past participle is SEWED not SEWN.

HEWN trees are thought by 17 per cent to be SPREAD OUT. To STREW (*strū*), with the same Anglo-Saxon past, STREWN (*strūn*), is to scatter, spread out loosely.

By another 17 per cent HEWN trees are thought to be FALLEN trees. To HEW down is to cut down, fell, but to HEW alone is to cut with a swinging motion as implied in the following quotation from the colorfully illustrated Tutankhamen, the Life and Death of a Pharaoh by Christiana Desroches-Noble-court: 'After the remains of the XXth Dynasty workmen's dwellings below the entrance to the Syrix (*sĭr'-ingks*) had been thoroughly removed, Carter saw what looked like the beginning of a step HEWN in the rock'.

433. *VERNACULAR*, vernacular (*ver-năk'-ū-lahr*) *adj.* Belonging to one country, native, indigenous, natural, domestic, colloquial, pertaining to the ordinary idiom; according to Nathan Bailey: 'Proper and peculiar to the house or country one lives or was born in'.

VERNACULAR comes from the Latin *vernaculus*, native, domestic, specifically pertaining to home-born slaves, from *verna*, literally a dweller, one born in his master's house.

To 12 per cent VERNACULAR means MODERN, present, recent, now, not past. Webster gives as a second meaning of MODERN: common, mean, vulgar. Though the word VULGAR has come to mean rude, boorish, unrefined, offensive, coarse, it derives from the Latin *vulgaris*, pertaining to the multitude, the common people, from *vulgus*, the multitude, throng, crowd, masses. VULGATE, which as an adjective means common, popular, as a noun is sometimes the popular tongue, the VERNACULAR.

Despite the overlappings MODERN today means at present, not ancient, not of the past; while the VERNACULAR, according to H. W. Fowler, in his English Usage: 'Describes the words that have been familiar to us as long as we can remember, the homely part of the language, in contrast with the terms that we have consciously acquired'.

ENGLISH is the generic term for the language as a whole. VERNACULAR is ENGLISH as correctly spoken and written excluding technical terms. COLLOQUIAL is that part of the VERNACULAR which is spoken but not written.

434. *PASTY*, pasty (*pās'-tĭ*) *adj*. Colorless, of the color of paste, suggesting unhealthy, sallow, lacking the reddish tone of health, pale, wan, pallid.

PASTE is a mixture of flour or starch and water, dough, creamy white in color.

Both SALLOW and PASTY suggest an unhealthy color. Of the two SALLOW is yellowish or brownish, while PASTY is more whitish, the opposite of RUDDY, reddish.

435. *BALM*, balm (*bahm*) *n*. Healing ointment, oily exudation from trees, balsam, aromatic resin; Bailey says: 'BALM, the juice of a tree growing in Palestine and Egypt; also a sweet-smelling herb'.

From the Greek βάλσαμον (*balsamon*), balsam, comes the Latin *balsamum*, and from this come similar words in Anglo-Saxon, Spanish, Portuguese, and Italian, all spelt with L, as well as a shorter form of the same word in French with no L. From this comes BALM, where the L has been reinstalled recently.

To 7 per cent BALM means STILLNESS. CALM is STILLNESS, quiet, tranquillity, serenity, peace; originally the hot part of the day, from the Greek καῦμα (*cauma*), great heat. Here the L, not in the original Greek, has been inserted to make the word agree in appearance with BALM and PALM.

BALM of Gilead (*gĭl'-ē-ăd*) came from Gilead, an old section of Palestine, as well as from Mecca and Syria.

MYRRH (*mĕr*) is another aromatic, resinous exudation used for perfumes and in incense; while BALM is an ointment noted especially for healing, soothing.

436. *PRECLUDE*, preclude (*prē-klūd'*) *v*. Shut out, prevent, prohibit, bar, impede, debar, stop, hinder by excluding. From the Latin *cludere*, to shut, close, come EXCLUDE, to shut out; INCLUDE, literally to shut in; and CONCLUDE, by derivation to close with. This last leads 8 per cent to select SUM UP as the meaning of PRECLUDE. To CONCLUDE is to make an end, finish, draw consequences upon something said before, and so SUM UP.

PRECLUDE, from the Latin *prae*, before, and the same *cludere*, to shut, close, is to close beforehand, shut off in advance, and so prevent.

437. *BANTAM*, bantam (*băn'-tăm*) *adj.* Very small, minute (*mĭ-nūt'*), diminutive, tiny, puny.

The popular mislead is TWIN, chosen by 10 per cent, originally an adjective, as: 'TWIN children'. TWIN, which goes directly back to the Anglo-Saxon prefix meaning two, *twi-*, as in twice, may be chosen as a synonym of BANTAM because of the word TANDEM, from the Latin *tandem*, at length, from *tam*, so much. A TANDEM is a pair of horses harnessed one in front of the other; or a bicycle on which two can ride, again one in front of the other. From this comes the adverb TANDEM, as to drive TANDEM, one behind the other.

A BANTAM is a small hen, diminutive fowl, developed in Java. Many varieties are small editions of full-sized breeds, sometimes absurdly combative. BANTAM, applied to a professional boxer, means up to 118 pounds in weight, lighter than a featherweight.

438. *ECHELON*, echelon (*ĕsh'-ĕ-lŏn*) *n.* A steplike arrangement of troops so that each column from front to back is a little behind the one to its left or, in another arrangement, the one to its right, so that the front line is not straight across but stepped back from right to left, or left to right.

Directly from the French *échelon*, a step, rung of a ladder, originally Latin *scala*, a ladder, the source of the English SCALE, ECHELONS are thought by 29 per cent to be STRAGGLERS. To STRAGGLE is to stray, wander, ramble; and STRAGGLERS move slowly, scattered about, with no fixed course, almost an opposite of ECHELON, a rigid formation.

439. *SALINE*, saline (*sā'-līn*) *adj.* Salty, tasting like salt.

The Century Dictionary prefers (*sā-līn'*), with the accent on the second syllable; but W. H. P. Phyfe, in his Words Often Mispronounced, gives (*sā'-līn*) first, with a note from John Walker: 'As this word is derived from the Latin *salinus*, by dropping a syllable, the accent ought, according to the general rule of formation, to remove to the first syllable'. John Walker, best known for his Rhyming Dictionary of 1775, published in 1791 a Critical Pronouncing Dictionary, a decade after the Dictionary of Thomas Sheridan, of 1780, the first to indicate pronunciation.

To 5 per cent SALINE means CLEANSING. Difficult words for
CLEANSING are PURGATIVE, PURGATORY, EXPIATORY, and CATHARTIC.

The word SALT goes back through Anglo-Saxon to the Latin
sal, salt. SALINE comes more directly from the Latin *salinum*,
a salt-cellar, and *salinae*, salt-pits, both from *sal*, salt, known
today as the chemical compound NaCl.

From the Latin *sal* come not only SALTPETER, SALMAGUNDI,
but also SALARY, originally SALT-MONEY, a stipend given to
soldiers for SALT. From this comes the familiar phrase: 'Not
worth his SALT'. Every third year students at Eton in England
used to go to a hill near the Bath road and collect SALT-MONEY
from every passer-by to help pay the expenses of the Senior
Scholar. It is said that the SALT-MONEY thus collected sometimes
approached five thousand dollars.

440. *ANTIPATHY*, antipathy (*ăn-tĭp'-ă-thĭ*) *n.* Repugnance,
disgust (V. B. 77), dislike, distaste, aversion (V. B. 1514).
ANTIPATHY, from the Greek ἀντί (*anti-*), against, and πάθος
(*pathos*), feeling, is thought by 32 per cent to mean PITY, compared with nearly the same number, 34 per cent, who mark the
dictionary answer DISLIKE. SYMPATHY, a combination of the
Greek σύν (*syn*), with, an opposite of *anti-*, against, and the
same Greek πάθος (*pathos*), feeling, is a feeling with, and so
PITY, compassion, commiseration.

Of AVERSION, ANTIPATHY, and HATRED, in order of violence,
AVERSION is the mildest, a tendency to turn away from that one
dislikes; HATRED, from Anglo-Saxon, is much the strongest; with
ANTIPATHY between the two.

441. *REMUNERATION*, remuneration (*rē-mū-nĕr-ā'-shŏn*)
n. Payment, compensation, salary, wages, pay, reward for
service, repayment for loss, recompense, requital, indemnifi-
cation.

The original meaning, now obsolete, was the act of repaying
for some loss, making good, which probably justifies RESTORA-
TION as a synonym, selected by 11 per cent.

In the test phrase: Important REMUNERATIONS, no one marks
BRANCHING, put in to suggest RAMIFICATIONS. It has been replaced by COUNTING, to suggest RENUMERATION. The verb to

RENUMERATE is to count over again, number once more; and the corresponding noun, though rare, should be RENUMERATION, with the same letters as REMUNERATION, but with two transposed.

REMUNERATION comes from the Latin *re-*, again, *munerari*, to give, from *munus, muneris*, a service, duty, gift, present, function, office.

REMUNERATIONS are thought by 30 per cent to be RECOLLECTIONS. REMEMBRANCES and REMINISCENCES are both RECOLLECTIONS, the act of recalling to mind, remembering.

442. *MONOLITHIC*, monolithic (*mŏn-ō-lĭth'-ĭk*) adj. One-stone, formed of a single stone, as an OBELISK or shaft of a column, menhir (*mĕn'-hĭr*).

To 15 per cent MONOLITHIC means ANCIENT, words used often in the same situation, for most MONOLITHIC remains are ANCIENT, many of them prehistoric. But ANCIENT means old.

MONOLITHIC comes from the Greek μόνος (*monos*), one, single, from the same source as a MONOGRAM, literally a single letter; MONOLOGUE, a talk by one person; and MONOCHROME, a painting in one color. The second half -LITHIC comes from λίθος (*lithos*), stone, so that MONOLITHIC is literally of one stone. But the word is used of ANCIENT groups of massive stone blocks.

A MENHIR, a Cornish word from the southwest of England, is a single crude stone, set up on end, usually uncut, one of several found together, but not forming an obvious structure.

A DOLMEN is a structure with walls of crude upright stones and a single huge stone laid horizontally on top.

The adjective MEGALITHIC emphasizes the size of each stone used in a structure; MONOLITHIC emphasizes the singleness of each stone standing alone.

443. *SUSTAIN*, sustain (*sŭs-tān'*) v. To uphold, support, prop up, strengthen, maintain, nourish, bear up, keep from falling.

To CONTAIN, to hold as a box; to RETAIN, to continue to hold; to OBTAIN, to get hold of; to PERTAIN; MAINTAIN; and SUSTAIN; all come from the Latin *tenere*, to hold; but according to Skeat, an authority on derivations, ATTAIN, to get or compass a thing, come to, despite the similarity, comes not from *tenere*, to hold, but from *tangere*, to touch. Either ATTAIN, to reach by effort, achieve, gain, literally to come near enough to touch, or OBTAIN, to get hold of, gain, succeed in the pursuit of a thing, lead 11 per cent to believe that SUSTAINED means COMPLETED, perfected, filled. To COMPLETE is to finish, accomplish. To SUSTAIN is to support from underneath, hold up.

444. *POSTERITY*, posterity (*pŏs-tĕr'-ĭ-tĭ*) *n.* Future generations, descendants, issue, offspring, progeny.
To 9 per cent POSTERITY means SUCCESS. PROSPERITY, so much like POSTERITY in sound, is SUCCESS, good fortune, weal, welfare, thriving. PROSPERITY comes from the Latin *prosper, prosperus*, favorable, fortunate, the source of the word PROSPEROUS, liter-ally according to one's hopes, from *pro*, for, according to, and *spes*, hope.

To another 10 per cent POSTERITY means HISTORY. HISTORY is a record of the past, of PRIOR times, a story of PROGENITORS, for while PROGENY, which once meant ancestors of the past, has come to mean offspring of the future, PROGENITOR has kept the original meaning of ancestors, forefathers.

POSTERITY comes from the Latin *posterus*, coming after, following, next in order; related to *posterior*, the comparative of *post*, after, the opposite of *pro-*, before. OFFSPRING are definite children. POSTERITY is the race, the whole indefinite future.

445. *ODIOUS*, odious (*ō'-dĭ-ŭs*) *adj.* Hateful, offensive, disgusting, repugnant, disagreeable, repulsive, heinous.
ODIOUS comes from the Latin *odiosus*, hateful, odious, and *odium*, hatred, ill will, offense, from *odi*, hate, hatred, dislike.

To 12 per cent ODIOUS means SMELLY. An ODOR is a smell, from the Latin *odor*, smell, scent, odor, perfume, from the verb *odere*, to smell. As near synonyms, the Century Dictionary gives SMELL, SCENT, ODOR, SAVOUR, PERFUME, FRAGRANCE, AROMA, STENCH, STINK, the last two always unpleasant.

Although ODOROUS and ODIOUS are so alike in sound, ODOROUS means fragrant, balmy, sweet-scented, aromatic, while ODIOUS means hateful, disgusting.

446. *VISAGE*, visage (vĭz'-āj) *n.* The face, countenance, look
   of a person, appearance, aspect.

VISION, from the Latin verb *videre*, to see, with the past participle *visus*, is SIGHT, the ability to see. From *videre* come not
only such words as VISIBLE, capable of being seen; VISUAL, pertaining to sight; but also VISIT, SUPERVISE, PROVIDENCE, and
INVIDIOUS. From the same *videre*, to see, through *visus*, a look,
vision, comes VISAGE, that which one sees of a person.

   FACE is the combination of eyes, nose, and mouth, the features.
COUNTENANCE, which used to mean estate, is the character of
one's FACE. VISAGE is that which is seen.

447. *GRAPNEL*, grapnel (grăp'-nĕl) *n.* A contrivance usually
   with several hooks for catching hold of something, used
also for a small anchor with several claws.

GRAPNEL comes from an old French word *grape*, the source of
the word GRAPPLE, to seize, hold, clinch, fasten. GRAPPLING IRONS
are used to seize and hold vessels fast. From the same source
comes GRAPE, the fruit, named from the arrangement of GRAPES
in bunches.

448. *CONJURER*, conjurer (kŏn'-jūr-ĕr) *n.* One bound by
   oath, one who calls upon the devil, magician.

The word comes from the Latin *conjurare*, a combination of
con-, with, and *jurare*, to swear, and now means to swear
together. To 23 per cent CONJURER means THINKER. To CON-
JECTURE, from the Latin *com-*, together, and *jacere*, to throw,
is almost to THINK. It is to throw together various bits of facts,
and has come to mean conclude from insufficient evidence, almost guess, surmise, form an opinion without enough grounds.

   There are two pronunciations of the word CONJURE. One is
(kŏn-jūr'), with the accent on the second syllable, and the other
(kŏn'-jūr), with the accent on the first syllable. The first is to
constrain by oath, appeal to solemnly, implore, entreat. The
second, with the accent on the first syllable, is to call upon the
devil, or command a spirit by some spell. In this sense, a CON-
JURER is one who calls upon spirits to perform miracles and so a
MAGICIAN. From this the word came to be used also for JUGGLER,
and one who practices legerdemain.

449. *INNUENDO*, innuendo (*ĭn-nū-ĕn'-dō*) *n*. An unpleasant
    hint, indirect intimation, oblique derogatory statement,
injurious insinuation.

INNUENDO comes from the Latin *innuere*, to give a nod, a combination of *in-*, and *nuere*, to nod, and so to INTIMATE.

GOSSIP, marked by 25 per cent, is idle talk, prattle, spreading
reports about others, but suggests destructive tattle, harmful
intent. Richard Brinsley Sheridan, in his School for Scandal,
describes: 'A set of malicious, prating, prudent GOSSIPS who
murder characters to kill time'. Both GOSSIP and INNUENDO imply
a malicious desire to destroy others, for in law INNUENDO is used
in libel suits to explain in parentheses the words involved.

A LIBEL is a direct false statement with intent to harm. Such
a statement may occur in the course of GOSSIP; but GOSSIP is
largely idle talk, continuous prattle, indulged in by those who
score low in vocabulary. INNUENDO is subtle, clever, a sly hint,
which may be libelous but is too indirectly stated to be cause
for legal action. Fundamentally GOSSIP is idle waste of time; an
INNUENDO is a hint.

450. *PRUDENTIAL*, prudential (*prū-dĕn'-shăl*) *adj*. Careful,
    cautious, foresighted.
To 20 per cent PRUDENTIAL means MODEST. PUDENCY, with no
R, is MODESTY; and the adjective PUDENT, MODEST, is a word easily
confused with PRUDENT.

Both PRUDENTIAL and PRUDENT come from the Latin *prudens,
prudentis*, foreseeing, a contraction of *providens, providentis*,
from *pro*, before, and *videre*, to see.

PRUDENT and PRUDENTIAL differ primarily in usage. The adjective PRUDENT means thoughtful, sensible, careful, circumspect,
sagacious, cautious; and one speaks of a PRUDENT man, a PRUDENT
person. PRUDENTIAL applies to acts which demand PRUDENCE.
One speaks of PRUDENTIAL motives, PRUDENTIAL plans.

451. *PATENTLY*, patently (*păt'-ĕnt-lĭ*) *adv*. Openly, expand-
    edly, publicly, obviously, open to the approval of all,
evidently, conspicuously, overtly.
Phyfe says: 'The first syllable is generally pronounced (*păt*) in
the United States and (*pā*) in Great Britain'.

To 16 per cent PATENTLY, openly, means PRECISELY, exactly, accurately, definitely, justly.

From the phrase: LETTERS PATENT, an official document granting a privilege, comes PATENT, used as a noun, a grant by a government to an author or inventor, for the exclusive right to some new principle or idea.

Opposites of PATENTLY, the adverb, are: SECRETLY, COVERTLY, PRIVILY, PRIVATELY, CONFIDENTIALLY.

452. *REQUITE*, requite (*rē-kwīt'*) *v.* To repay, return, reward, retaliate, remunerate, indemnify, recompense, pay back. REQUITAL is the corresponding noun.

To 22 per cent REQUITE means ABSOLVE, forgive, free from the consequences of some action. This may be a confusion of REQUITE with ACQUIT. To ACQUIT is to find not guilty, free from punishment, and so ABSOLVE. To REQUITE is to repay. To RECOMPENSE is to return good in payment for some action. To RETALIATE is to return bad, almost get even. To REQUITE can mean return either good or bad.

453. *AMULET*, amulet (*ăm'-ū-lĕt*) *n.* Any object worn as a protection against bad luck, accident, disease, or witchcraft; a talisman (v. b. 1401), phylactery, often a pendant, pectoral, scapular.

To 20 per cent AMULET means DREAM. Both a DREAM and an AMULET have supernatural implications. A DREAM is a series of unreal images seen during sleep. An AMULET wards off bad luck.

Both an AMULET and a TALISMAN are charms. A TALISMAN produces good luck; an AMULET wards off bad.

From the Encyclopaedia of Ephraim Chambers, which goes back to 1728 and from which so often come excellent descriptions: 'AMULET. A kind of external medicament to be worn about the neck to prevent disease. The ancients made great use of gems for AMULETS. The whole East wore a kind of jasper for this purpose.

'Charms, words, scrolls, magic figures, and numbers make a large class of AMULETS to which the Turks are greatly devoted. Their AMULETS are little bits of paper of two or three inches breadth, rolled up in pieces of silk, containing short prayers or sentences. They hung these about their necks or placed them under their arm-pits, or in their bosom, near their hearts, and especially when they go to war, as a preservative against the dangers of it.'

454. *SAUTÉ*, sauté (*sō-tā′*) *v.* To fry lightly.

From Way of Cooking comes merely: 'To cook in a small amount of fat'. From Fannie Farmer's Boston Cooking-School Cook Book, which in 1937 had sold 1,700,000 copies, comes a more complete description: 'To SAUTÉ is to cook in a small quantity of fat in a pan over direct heat. To prevent too great an absorption of fat, keep the food moving. French cooks shake the pan constantly — *sauter* being the French word for jump.'

455. *CRANNY*, cranny (*krăn′-nĭ*) *n.* Any small narrow opening, crack, crevice, fissure, chink, groove, notch, clove, chasm, crevasse (*krĕ-văs′*).

CRANNY goes back to old French, with similar words in German, perhaps to the Latin *crena*, a notch. To 6 per cent CRANNIES are DUNES. A DUNE (*dūn*), a mound of loose sand often blown by the wind, grain by grain, to some new location, a hill, ridge, is perhaps the same word as DOWN. A DOWN, directly from an Anglo-Saxon word meaning hill, and related to several words in the Teutonic languages for sand-bank, sand-hill, shifting ridge of sand, is the opposite of a VALLEY, VALE, DALE.

A CRACK is a narrow fracture, partial separation, often without an opening, as a CRACK in a dish. A CHINK, directly from Anglo-Saxon, is an open crack, gap, as a CHINK in a board fence wide enough to squint through with one eye. A CRANNY is wider, often used as an opening, wide enough to squeeze through. Also, CRANNY has the suggestion of being hidden, not the right way to get in if one does squeeze through.

456. *LICHEN*, lichen (*lī′-kĕn*) *n.* A rock-plant, a gray dry-looking plant which grows on rocks, tree stumps, and old wood.

To 13 per cent LICHEN means BLOODSUCKER. A LEECH is a blood-sucking worm, used as early as the year 900 for sucking blood, a parasite living usually in fresh-water ponds.

The word LICHEN comes through the Latin *lichen*, from the Greek λιχήν (*lichen*), a tree moss, and the LICHEN today looks like a dry moss. LICHENS, mostly a soft gray, range in color from an occasional almost white through yellow and browns to nearly black They grow commonly on rock, but also on tree trunks in nearly all parts of the world, surviving the severest droughts. Botanically they are now believed to be a symbiosis, a living together of an alga, a seaweed, and a fungus.

457. *SWATHE*, swathe (*swāth*) *n.* Bandage, binding, wrapping of fabric.

There are two pronunciations of -TH, as: BATH (*băth*), the noun, and BATHE (*bāTH*), the verb; CLOTH (*klŏth*), the noun, and CLOTHE (*klōTH*), the verb; also two nouns which differ, LATH (*lăth*), a narrow strip of wood, and LATHE (*lāth*), a machine. A SWATH (*swawth*), pronounced to rime with CLOTH, is a path cut through grass, Bailey, 1721, says: 'Grass or corn as it is laid in rows by the mower from the scythe'; while a SWATHE (*swāth*), pronounced to rime with BATHE and LATHE, is a bandage, winding of linen, binding cloth, wrapping of fabric.

The verb, to wrap with a bandage, should certainly be SWATHE, like the verb to BATHE; but several of the older dictionaries in the late 1700's pronounced both the path through grass and the bandage the same and, despite modern dictionaries, it might be well to spell and pronounce the noun SWATH, and the verb SWATHE.

458. *GRIMACE*, grimace (*grĭ-mās'*) *n.* Wry face, twisted expression, facial contortion indicating displeasure, disgust, pain, or the like.

GRIMACE is thought by 21 per cent to mean SEVERE LOOK. According to the Century Dictionary a GRIMACE may be a distortion of the face to express disapproval and in this sense SEVERE LOOK might be correct. But in the high-vocabulary group as a whole every person marks FACIAL CONTORTION. A GRIMACE is a distortion of the countenance indicating an unpleasant reaction of any kind. GRIMACE comes from an Old German word meaning GRIM, but the word has come to mean a spontaneous expression of almost any unpleasant sensation.

459. *DOGGEDLY*, doggedly (*dŏg'-gĕd-lĭ*) *adv.* Steadfastly, with pertinacity, unyieldingly, persistently, stubbornly, obstinately, with determination.

DOGGEDLY is the Anglo-Saxon DOG, plus the Anglo-Saxon suffix -ED making the adjective DOGGED, plus the Anglo-Saxon -LY, to make the adverb.

Customarily, the ending -ISH added to the name of an animal makes the adjective, as BULLISH, used of the stock market, to mean tending to advance; BEARISH, heavy, tending to go down; MULISH, stubborn; and SHEEPISH, bashful, timid. Partly because the ending -ED, in this context, is rare, the adjective DOGGED has a clear meaning, persistent, persevering, with DOGGEDLY the corresponding adverb.

460. *EXHORTATION*, exhortation (*ĕks-or-tā'-shŏn*) *n.* Advice, incitement, admonition, argument, appeal, encouragement.

The adjective EXORBITANT, from the Latin *ex-*, out, and *orbita*, track, orbit, means going beyond proper limits, beyond the bounds of reason, unreasonable, inordinate, unconscionable, transgressing normal restrictions. An EXORBITANT charge is an OVERCHARGE, the popular misconception of EXHORTATION.

The verb to EXHORT, from the Latin verb *exhortari*, a combination of *ex*, out, and *hortari*, to urge, is to encourage, stimulate, incite, enjoin, adjure, beg. EXHORTATION, from the past participle *exhortatus*, is the corresponding noun.

According to E. Chambers: EXHORTATION differs only from SUASION, in that the latter principally endeavors to convince the understanding, and the former, EXHORTATION, to work on the affections.

461. *WALLABY*, wallaby (*wawl'-lă-bē*) *n.* The small brush kangaroo of Australia, one of the marsupials.

The KANGAROO was described by Captain James Cook, who sailed from England in 1772 on a three-year voyage of discovery, and who saw the KANGAROO in Australia. The fur of the KANGAROO is soft; the hind legs large and strong for hopping, and the front legs short by comparison. The young live for some time after birth in a pouch, which leads to the name MARSUPIAL, from the Latin *marsupium*, pouch, bag. WALLABY is the name by which most of the smaller forms are known. There are also thicket-loving rock WALLABIES. The great, gray, robust, KANGAROOS of the grassy plains are called WALLAROOS.

To 10 per cent, WALLABY means PENGUIN; to another 10 per cent, PARROT; and to still a third 10 per cent DEER. Despite these misconceptions, the unusual word WALLABY, which hardly belongs to an English vocabulary test, is surprisingly well known, of the same level of difficulty as QUAHOG, more familiar than JUNCO, and marked correctly by twice as many persons as RECRUDESCENCE, PROSCENIUM, GASCONADE, and PLANGENT.

462. *PINCE-NEZ*, pince-nez (*păns′-nā*) *n.* Eyeglasses kept in
     place on the bridge of the nose by a spring, and without
bows over the ears.
SPECTACLES was once the general term for a pair of lenses, held by a BRIDGE which rests on the nose, and with BOWS back to the ears. A LORGNETTE (*lŏr-nyĕt′*), from the French *lorgner*, to spy, is a pair of lenses, with no bows, but with a handle. A LORGNETTE is not worn, but is held in front of the eyes for a moment or two, to read small type. A MONOCLE is a single EYE-GLASS, with no bridge over the nose, and no handle.

SPECTACLES without BOWS, held in place by a spring which pinches the nose, are EYEGLASSES or in French PINCE-NEZ, from the French *pincer*, to pinch, and *nez*, nose.

463. *SPECTRAL*, spectral (*spĕk′-trăl*) *adj.* Ghostly, ghostlike,
     like a specter.
SPECTRAL, from the Latin *spectrum*, a vision, apparition, image, appearance, comes from *specere*, to see, the source of SPECTACLE, SPECIAL, and SPECIES. The Latin word SPECTRUM is used today in science for the breaking up of light into the rainbow colors, caused by sunlight passing through a prism.

To 10 per cent SPECTRAL means SPECIAL, perhaps because of the similarity of the two words. SPECIAL is the adjective which means belonging to a SPECIES, to a kind, sort, form, from the same *specere*, to see. The English SPECIES (*spē′-shēz*) is the Latin *species*, literally a seeing, sight, look, and so appearance, form, a group with some common characteristic.

SPECTRAL is the adjective for SPECTER, a ghostlike apparition which appears at night, leading 57 per cent to mark NIGHT as the meaning of SPECTRAL.

464. *VESPER*, vesper (*vĕs'-pĕr*) *adj.* Evening, eventide, also the evening star.

MATINS (*măt'-ĭnz*) are early morning religious services, much as VESPERS are the evening services.

VESPER is the Latin *vesper*, evening, eventide, used also for the evening star, and poetically for the west; and equivalent to Hesper, the Greek Ἑσπερος (*Hesperos*), also the evening star, the planet Venus when east of the sun, when it sets after the sun.

The only misconceptions are DAWN, an opposite, and ANTIQUE.

465. *AGGRANDIZE*, aggrandize (*ăg-grăn'-dīz*) *v.* To make greater, honor, elevate, dignify, advance, exalt, give luster to.

AGGRANDIZE, the French *aggrandise*, defined by Randle Cotgrave in his French-English Dictionary of 1611, as to greaten, augment, enlarge, comes from the Latin *ad*, to, and *grandire*, to increase, from *grandis*, large, great, the source of GRAND. The English GRAND means more than just big, large, great. It suggests old, as in GRANDFATHER, GRANDMOTHER, GRANDAM; and magnificent, majestic, imposing, as in the French GRANDEUR (*grăn'-dūr*); and noble, as in the Spanish GRANDEE.

Given a choice between ENLARGE and DEVELOP, 15 per cent select the last. To AGGRANDIZE is more than ENLARGE, increase. It should be reserved for make grand with all of its implications.

466. *DIATRIBE*, diatribe (*dī'-ă-trīb*) *n.* Violent denunciation, continued rant, bitter accusation, originally a disputation, controversy, debate.

DIATRIBE comes from the Greek διατριβή (*diatribe*), a wearing away, spending time, pastime, waste of time, and from this a discussion, from the verb διατρίβειν (*diatribein*), to rub away, spend time, discuss, a combination of διά (*dia*), through, and τρίβειν (*tribein*), to rub. A DIATRIBE was originally a prolonged discussion, dragged out debate, now more often a bitter criticism, violent invective.

467. *EDIFICE*, edifice (*ĕd'-ĭ-fĭs*) *n*. Building, structure, often a large public building, an architectural fabric.

To 22 per cent EDIFICE means TEACHING, instructing, educating, imparting knowledge. EDIFICE, from the Latin *aedificium*, a building of any kind, and the verb to EDIFY, both come from *aedificāre*, to build, erect, construct, a combination of *aedis*, a building, temple, dwelling, hearth, and the familiar *facĕre*, to build, make, do. To EDIFY once meant to build a house, but now means to build knowledge, instruct, particularly in morals and the principles of religion. The noun EDIFICATION means both building and teaching, and EDIFICE might mean education but has always been an architectural structure, large building.

468. *CONSORT*, consort (*kŏn'-sort*) *n*. Specifically a wife or husband, spouse; also a partner, companion, associate, intimate, fellow.

The verb to CONSORT (*kŏn-sort'*), accented on the second syllable, is to associate, keep company, join, unite in friendship, but does not imply marriage as does the noun.

To 4 per cent the noun CONSORT means CASTLE, and to another 3 per cent CLOWN, with no concentration on any one misinterpretation.

CONSORT, from the Latin *consors, consortis*, a partner, comes from *con-*, together, and *sors, sortis*, lot, destiny, fate, future, and denotes casting one's lot together. From the same Latin *sors, sortis*, comes SORCERER, one who casts lots, a conjurer, wizard, one who predicts the future.

The PRINCE CONSORT, the husband of a queen, has no royal authority himself. A QUEEN CONSORT, the wife of a king, is distinguished from QUEEN REGNANT (*rĕg'-nănt*), reigning, who rules in person.

469. *RENT*, rent (*rĕnt*) *n*. A tear (*tār*), rip, crack, break, rift (v. B. 539), breach (v. B. 698), rupture, crevice, fissure, separation, schism (v. B. 1393); in geology: fault, split.

The verb to REND, with the past RENT, which corresponds to the noun RENT, is to tear asunder, split, rift, rive, cleave. Such verbs as SEND, the present tense, and SENT, the past, BEND and BENT, LEND and LENT, REND and RENT are Anglo-Saxon, though the

change of -D to -T in the past, called PRETERIT, and in the past
participle, first appeared in Middle English.

RENT is thought by 17 per cent of high-school seniors to mean
RAVING, a confusion of RENT with RANT, which sound alike, the
first step in the learning process. To RAVE is to talk like a mad-
man, speak deliriously. To RANT is to rave, talk violently, declaim with little sense. The corresponding noun RANT is bombast, boisterous language without substance or meaning. A RENT
is a tear.

By another 19 per cent RENT is thought to mean PATCH, a piece
of cloth sewed over a tear. This is like the confusion of THRESHED
with GATHERED, words used in the same situation, the second
step in learning. One GATHERS grain, collects it before THRESHING
it, beating it to free the seeds from the stalks. One must tear
cloth, REND it, before PATCHING, repairing, the RENT.

470. *INTIMATION*, intimation (*ĭn-tĭ-mā'-shŏn*) *n.* Sugges-
    tion (V. B. 81), hint, insinuation (V. B. 862), information
covertly imparted.
The corresponding verb is INTIMATE (*ĭn'-tĭ-māt*), to suggest,
hint, insinuate, indicate, point out indirectly. Of the two verbs
HINT and INTIMATE, the first is more hesitant, less direct, the
lightest possible suggestion. The second, INTIMATE, is a bit
plainer, clearer, but still far from direct.

The noun INTIMATION is thought by 23 per cent to mean
THOUGHTS, a confusion of ideas closely related. A THOUGHT is
a mental act, intellectual activity. An INTUITION is almost a
THOUGHT. An INTIMATION is an indication of one's THOUGHTS,
originally a formal publication, open announcement of one's
THOUGHTS; but INTIMATION comes from the Latin *intimus*, inmost, a superlative, and the idea of innermost is now in INTIMA-
TION, which is no longer a public announcement but a hint of
one's inner THOUGHTS.

471. *COMMISERATION*, commiseration (*kŏm-mĭz-ĕ-rā'-
    shŏn*) *n.* Sympathetic suffering for the afflictions of others,
pity, compassion, tenderness, concern, fellow feeling.
The verb to COMMISERATE comes from the Latin *commiseratus*,
the past participle of *commiserari*, to pity, from *com-*, which

intensifies the meaning, and *miserari*, to pity, from *miser*, wretched, the source of MISERABLE and MISER.

To 10 per cent COMMISERATION means EXPRESSION. CONDOLENCE (*kŏn-dō'-lĕns*), Phyfe says: not (*kŏn'-dō-lĕns*), for which there is no dictionary authority, is more often the EXPRESSION of pity. PITY implies a tinge of contempt, for both PITY and COMPASSION come from a superior. SYMPATHY comes from an equal. CONDOLENCE is sharing another's grief; while COMMISERATION is sharing another's misery. The Century Dictionary says: 'It galls one to be PITIED; it is irksome to need COMPASSION. It gives strength to receive SYMPATHY. It gives comfort to receive CONDOLENCE or COMMISERATION.'

472. *NATAL*, natal (*nā'-tăl*) adj. Birth, pertaining to one's birth, connected with one's origin.

In the test phrase: 'His NATAL night', WEDDING, the popular mislead, is marked by 15 per cent, probably because of the word NUPTIAL, pertaining to marriage, used of a WEDDING ceremony, matrimonial.

NATAL comes through French, from the Latin adjective *natalis* and the past participle *natus* of the verb *nasci*, to be born, the source of many English words: NASCENT, beginning to exist, coming into being; NATIVE, pertaining to one by birth; NATURE; and NATURAL. NATAL is limited to the event of one's birth.

473. *TRIM*, trim (*trĭm*) adj. Neat, tidy, in good order, spruce, smart, properly kept.

In the test phrase: 'Trim sails', the word is thought by 21 per cent to mean ROLLED, a confusion of closely associated ideas, the second step in learning a word. A ROLLED sail is TRIM, neat; but among those who score high in this vocabulary test as a whole, above 110 correct out of 150 items, no one marks ROLLED. TRIM, of Anglo-Saxon origin, means well-prepared, suitable, good, excellent, a vague term of approval.

474. *CREVASSE*, crevasse (*krĕ-văs'*) n. Fissure, deep cleft in the ice of a glacier, cavern usually of great depth, narrow canyon, cleft in the landscape, rent, used by English writers in describing glaciers.

CREVASSE is the French for CREVICE. A CREVASSE in ice may be only a few inches in width or it may be many feet. CREVICE (*krĕ'-vĭs*) is the usual word for a crack, fissure, rent, narrow opening of some length. CREVASSE is the more technical term for a crack in a glacier.

The popular mislead is CLIFF. A CLIFF is a precipice, high rocky face, steep headland. A CLEFT is a crack, fissure, opening made by splitting. A CLIFF stands alone. A CREVASSE may be thought of as two CLIFFS facing each other, but the CREVASSE is really the crack between. One falls off a CLIFF, but into a CREVASSE.

475. *BLAND*, bland (*blănd*) *adj*. Mild, soft, gentle, balmy, agreeable.

BLAND, directly from the Latin *blandus*, caressing, agreeable, flattering, mild, and soft, can be used for weather, food, and medicine.

To 17 per cent BLAND means IMPASSIVE, words with much the same implications, the third step in learning. IMPASSIVE is unmoved, showing no emotion, apathetic, without sign of feeling, never a complimentary word; while the Century Dictionary considers BLAND to be always pleasant, suggesting warm breezes.

476. *INDOMITABLE*, indomitable (*ĭn-dŏm'-ĭ-tă-bl*) *adj*. Unyielding, unconquerable, determined not to be overcome, not to be tamed.

INDOMITABLE derives from the *Latin in-*, not, and *domitare*, the frequentative of *domare*, to tame.

RELENTLESS, chosen by 20 per cent, has in some of its senses much the same idea. But to RELENT now often means to become less harsh, not so cruel, to yield, comply, give way; and RELENTLESS, unmoved by pity, insensible to the distress of others. RELENT comes from the Latin *re-*, back, and *lentus*, slow, slack, and at one time meant to slacken, stay, slow down; and in this sense RELENTLESS is not slowing down, characterizing one who continues to push. Even in this sense RELENTLESS is active, more like the verb to DOMINATE, from a different source, *dominus*, master, lord. INDOMITABLE is quiet, applying to one who holds his ground.

477. *TENACIOUS*, tenacious (*těn-ā'-shŭs*) *adj*. Holding (v. b. 51) fast, retaining possession; figuratively stubborn (v. b. 231), obstinate.

From two Latin verbs, *tenēre*, to hold, of the second conjugation, and *tendĕre*, to stretch, of the third, come lists of English words. From *tendĕre* come TENSION, a stretching, TENDON, and TENT. From *tenēre*, to hold, come TENANT, literally one who holds property, TENABLE, capable of being held, maintained, TENACITY and TENACIOUS, through *tenax*, *tenacis*, holding fast.

TENACIOUS is thought by 28 per cent to mean FALSE, not true. FALLACIOUS, from the Latin *fallax*, deceptive, deceitful, from *fallĕre*, to deceive, means delusive, deceptive, misleading, and so FALSE; and MENDACIOUS, starting with M in place of T, and with D added, but otherwise identical in spelling, means lying, dishonest, FALSE. Learn MENDACIOUS, FALLACIOUS, and TENACIOUS. TENACIOUS means holding fast.

478. *BUBONIC*, bubonic (*bū-bŏn'-ĭk*) *adj*. Pertaining to the bubo, the black death, one of the causes of the destructive plagues of the past.

BUBO (*bū'-bō*), a medical term from the beginning, goes back to the Greek βουβών (*boubon*), a tumor, swelling, inflammation of the lymphatic gland.

To 9 per cent BUBONIC, the corresponding adjective, means RURAL (*rōō'-răl*), from the Latin *ruralis*, pertaining to the country as opposed to the city. BUCOLIC, starting and ending with the same two letters as BUBONIC, but with no other connection, means pastoral, rustic, rural, pertaining to the country specifically connected with a shepherd's life, from the Greek βουκόλος (*boucolos*), a cowherd, herdsman, goatherd, from βοῦς (*bous*), an ox.

In the 14th century the BLACK DEATH, a combination of the BUBONIC, the SEPTICEMIC, a severe BUBONIC, and the PNEUMONIC PLAGUES wiped out twenty-five million people, one quarter of the total population of Europe.

479. *ADROITLY*, adroitly (*ă-droit'-lĭ*) *adv*. Dexterously, skilfully, readily, handily, cleverly, ingeniously, with nice manipulation.

To 17 per cent ADROITLY means EFFECTIVELY, with much the same suggestion. EFFECTIVELY is the general term for producing the intended purpose, gaining the result desired. EFFICIENT is producing actual results; while EFFECTIVE implies the power to produce, even when that power is not used, and so is close to ADROIT. But ADROIT comes directly from the French *adroit*, dexterous, literally *á droit*, toward the right, and so applies specifically to the hand, the opposite of MALADROIT (*măl-ă-droit'*), clumsy, awkward, bungling, unhandy, inexpert, wanting skill. ADROITNESS is a part of EFFECTIVENESS, the finger dexterity part.

ADROIT, DEXTEROUS, EXPERT, and SKILFUL, express various degrees in the combination of manual facility with knowledge. In SKILFUL, knowledge is the principal element, implying more use of knowledge than EXPERT, which emphasizes experience, practice. DEXTEROUS suggests sustained agility; while ADROIT involves more quickness, suddenness.

480. *FAGOT*, fagot (*făg'-ŏt*) *n.* Bailey and the Oxford use two G's, FAGGOT; the Century only one: FAGOT. A bundle of sticks used for fuel, fascine (*făs-sēn'*), from the Latin *fascin*, a bundle.

To 8 per cent FAGOT means SWORD. A FOIL is a blunt-pointed fencing SWORD used in practice in friendly bouts. FAGOT, which goes back to Old French and Italian to an uncertain origin, is a bundle of wood three feet long and two feet around.

481. *FLACCIDITY*, flaccidity (*flăk-sĭd'-ĭ-tĭ*) *n.* Flabbiness, limberness, laxity, want of firmness, with no elasticity. One opposite is RIGIDITY.

FLACCIDITY, and the adjective FLACCID (*flăk'-sĭd*), flagging, withering, are the only English words from the Latin *flaccidus*, flabby, pendulous, from *flaccus*, flabby. INERT, LISTLESS, LANGUID, and FLACCID, all suggest a more or less permanent element of character. INERT is motionless. LISTLESS is lack of interest, with no desire; while to LANGUISH is to become spiritless, sad, to pine, wither. FLACCID is flabby, drooping of its own weight.

To 10 per cent, FLACCIDITY means ANEMIA. ANEMIA is lack of blood in a living body, which leads to weakness. ANEMIA is the cause of FLACCIDITY, drooping.

482. *GAMBOL*, gambol (*găm'-bŏl*) *v.* To caper, leap, jump, romp, frolic, skip about.

MOVE, a choice selected by 15 per cent, can certainly be justified and should probably not be used as a mislead; but MOVE is too general. FROLIC, as a meaning, is closer.

To FROLIC is gay, joyous, and comes from Dutch and German. FRISK is lively, brisk. To GAMBOL, from the Italian *gambe*, leg, is to kick, leap, spring about. GAMB in English means leg, shank.

483. *COALITION*, coalition (*kō-ă-lĭsh'-ŏn*) *n.* A growing together, alliance, league, confederacy, voluntary union of individuals.

COALITION comes from the Latin *coalitus*, the past participle of the verb *coalescere*, the source of the English verb COALESCE (*kō-ă-lĕs'*), to grow together, unite by growth, combine, join, a combination of *co-*, together, and *alescere*, to grow up, from *alere*, to nourish. From this last comes ALIMENT (*ăl'-ĭ-mĕnt*), food, nourishment, sustenance. COALITION is correctly a uniting by growing up together.

484. *COUNTENANCE*, countenance (*kown'-tĕn-ăns*) *n.* Feature, visage, facial aspect, face.

COUNTENANCE, from Latin *continentia*, moderation, continence, demeanor, gesture, is thought by 42 per cent to mean SECURITY, freedom from care, confidence, safety, compared with only 25 per cent who underline FACE. In old law, before 1600, some 400 years ago COUNTENANCE meant credit, wealth, one's estate; and so implied SECURITY, an interpretation unknown today, another unusual instance of an early meaning surviving in the popular mind long after its disappearance from ordinary usage.

Strictly, FACE is the unchanging combination of physical features; COUNTENANCE is the FACE enlivened by thought, experience, and feelings. William H. Prescott, in his Conquest of Mexico, speaks of a friend of Montezuma with: 'Yellow hair and sunny COUNTENANCE'.

485. *CONTRITION*, contrition (*kŏn-trĭsh'-ŭn*) *n.* Deep sorrow for sin, sincere penitence, repentance, pious compunction, conscience-stricken by a sense of guilt; or, from E.

Chambers: 'In theology expresses a real sorrow, resulting from the thought of having offended God, without any regard to the punishment the sin is entitled to'.

CONTRITION comes from the Latin *contritus*, the past participle of *conterere*, to bruise, rub, wear out, a combination of *con-*, together, and *terere*, with the past participle *tritus*. From the same source comes ATTRITION, the rubbing of one thing against another, abrasion, wearing away by friction.

To 10 per cent of those tested CONTRITION means ANXIETY, from the Latin *angere*, to trouble, distress, the source of ANGUISH, and so worry, fear, foreboding, solicitude, apprehension, concern because of danger.

CONTRITION, PENITENCE, REPENTANCE, and REGRET, all express the sorrowful feeling of a wrong-doer. REGRET is the feeblest. REPENTANCE expresses a real resolve of turning from sin to righteousness. PENITENCE involves deeper feeling and applies to an offense against God. CONTRITION, literally a breaking or bruising, is deep, quiet, and continued sorrow for specific acts, a brokenness of spirit, with perhaps a bit of ANXIETY for having given offense.

486. *COTILLION*, cotillion (*kō-tĭl'-lĭoṅ*) *n*. A lively French dance, elaborate series of figures, the German, with giving of favors, a kind of quadrille which became fashionable about 1800.

COTILLION comes directly from the French *cotillon*, literally a petticoat, the diminutive of the French *cotte*, a coat.

To 11 per cent COTILLION means EXHIBITION, from the Latin *ex-*, out, and *habere*, to hold, have, a showing, presenting to view, act of displaying for inspection, public display of personal performances. This aspect of an EXHIBITION might lead to its selection as the meaning of COTILLION.

Also the word GERMAN is used not only for the dance, but also for an entertainment at which the so-called GERMAN is danced. Still further a PAVILION, somewhat like COTILLION in sound, is a large tent, a type that is occasionally used for an EXHIBITION.

According to E. Chambers, 1728: 'COTILLION is the name of a well-known brisk-dance, in which eight persons are employed'.

487. *REGICIDE*, regicide (*rĕj'-ĭ-sīd*) *n*. King-killer. The same word can be used either for the person who does the killing, or for the act of killing.

The word REGICIDE is thought by 18 per cent of persons to mean OFFICIAL RECORDER, probably a confusion of REGICIDE with REGISTRAR, one who keeps an OFFICIAL RECORD.

REGICIDE comes from the Latin *rex, regis*, a king, and *caedere*, to kill, which in English becomes -*cide*, the ending of several English words such as HOMICIDE, the general term for the killing of a human being by another human being.

        PATRICIDE — murder of a father
        MATRICIDE — murder of a mother
        FRATRICIDE — murder of a brother
        SUICIDE — self-murder, killing one's self
        INSECTICIDE — a substance which kills insects
        INFANTICIDE — murder of an infant
        TYRANNICIDE — murder of a tyrant
        GENOCIDE — murder of a race, ethnic group

Specifically in English history, the word REGICIDE was a member of the high court of justice constituted by Parliament for the trial of Charles I, by which he was found guilty of treason and sentenced to death in 1649. The REGICIDES themselves were later brought to trial in the Old Bailey.

488. *IMPINGING*, impinging (*ĭm-pĭnj'-ĭng*) *adj*. Hitting, colliding, striking, conflicting, interfering.

This present participle, IMPINGING, comes from the verb to IMPINGE, to fall against, collide, strike, conflict, interfere, dash against, from the Latin -*in*, on, and *pangere*, to strike, fix. From the past participle, *impactus*, comes the noun IMPACT, the act of IMPINGING.

Of 27 high-vocabulary adults, 9 select CLOSE (*klōs*) as the meaning of IMPINGING. Of the twenty-one meanings of the adjective CLOSE given by Webster, 1828, number 8 is: 'Near; within a very small distance'; and number 11: 'Very near in place or time; adjoining or nearly so'; but between these, number 9: 'Joined; in contact or nearly so, crowded'. Despite this definition, the suggestion of CLOSE, as an adjective, is near, but not actually IMPINGING, hitting, striking.

489. *USURPER*, usurper (*ū-zĕr'-pĕr*) *n*. Of the pronunciation, Phyfe goes out of his way to say: not (*ū-sĕr'-pĕr*). One who takes the place of another, tyrant, one who seizes power without right, holds by force, appropriates illegally, assumes wrongfully.

USURPER comes from the Latin *usurpare*, to make use of, take possession of, perhaps originally from *rapare*, to seize.

An AUTOCRAT is one who rules without restrictions, with absolute power concentrated within himself. The word TYRANT emphasizes unlimited powers, suggests oppression, cruelty, irresponsibility. The verb to USURP, and the corresponding noun USURPER, specify how the power was gained, it was seized, grabbed, taken usually by force.

490. *CARDINAL*, cardinal (*kahr'-dĭ-năl*) *adj*. Basic (v. B. 516), fundamental (v. B. 732), important, principal, chief.

From The Warden, by Anthony Trollope, comes: 'The clean and sombre apparel of our great church dignities exacts from us faith and submission, and the CARDINAL virtues seem to hover round their sacred hats'. This kind of quotation misleads 43 per cent of students into concluding that CARDINAL means RELIGIOUS, compared with only 31 per cent who mark BASIC.

In the Roman Catholic Church a CARDINAL is a member of the Sacred College, the governing group responsible to the Pope. But the word CARDINAL comes from the Latin *cardinalis*, pertaining to a hinge, from *cardo*, hinge, the pivot, around which things swing, and on which they depend. From this CARDINAL used figuratively has come to mean important, preeminent, chief, fundamental, principal.

The CARDINAL virtues are: justice, prudence, temperance, and fortitude, and in this phrase, CARDINAL might mean RELIGIOUS; but the CARDINAL POINTS are: north, south, east, and west, clearly not RELIGIOUS, and the CARDINAL NUMBERS are: one, two, three, four, etc., as opposed to the ORDINAL numbers: first, second, third, fourth, etc.

To read with understanding, one must interpret the adjective CARDINAL as meaning BASIC, fundamental. Even today, more students select RELIGIOUS in preference to the historical BASIC. Despite such opinion, CARDINAL should mean BASIC, fundamental.

491. *WRYLY*, wryly (*rī'-lĭ*) *adv.* Awkwardly (v. b. 75), dis-
    tortedly (v. b. 978), obliquely (v. b. 1530), slantingly,
slopingly.
WRYLY is thought by 14 per cent to mean ELOQUENTLY, fluently,
expressively, speaking stirringly. ELOQUENTLY comes from the
Latin *eloquens, eloquentis*, speaking out, the present participle
of *eloqui*, a combination of *e*, out, and the deponent verb *loqui*,
to speak.
    When the four misleads of a vocabulary test attract the
same number of persons or nearly the same, the choice of one
in lieu of another is largely luck and, as here, there is no obvious
explanation.
    Most words starting with WR-, such as WRECK; WRITE, to use
a pencil; WRONG, the opposite of RIGHT with no W-; and WRY;
go directly back to Anglo-Saxon; and then back through Ger-
manic to that theoretical Indo-European language, of which so
little is known.
    The adjective WRY, directly from an Anglo-Saxon verb to
bend, turn, means abnormally bent, twisted, distorted, askew,
crooked, turned, as: 'A WRY face'. WRYLY is the adverb.

492. *NAP*, nap (*năp*) *n.* Wooly substance on the surface of
    cloth, the short pile of velvet, according to Bailey, 1726,
the hairy or shaggy part of woolen cloth.
NAP is thought by 32 per cent of high-school students in general, and by 30 per cent of high-vocabulary ones, to mean TOP.
Another word NAP comes from an Icelandic word meaning
protuberance, knob, top of a hill; and KNAP, a knob, protuberance, top of a hill, is sometimes spelt NAP, so that TOP is an unusual but correct answer and should not be used as a mislead
in a vocabulary test.
    NAP, meaning the wooly substance on cloth, goes back
through Middle English, perhaps to Anglo-Saxon, and seems
related to Dutch and Danish words. Though NAP and PILE
appear indifferently, PILE, from the Latin *pilus*, hair, is always
produced during weaving, by leaving threads standing upright,
packed tightly like growing hair. NAP, a downy, furry surface,
can be produced after weaving, and should probably be limited
to this application.

493. *CAUCUS*, caucus (*kaw'-kŭs*) *n.* A private meeting of
     local members of a political party to nominate a candidate,
preliminary meeting of members of the same party, meeting
within a party in advance of voting.
The word arose in New England, and is said to have been used
in Boston before 1724. An entertaining story, though probably
not true, is that CAUCUS is a corruption of calkers' meeting, a
term applied by the Tories to meetings of citizens, calkers and
rope-makers. The word appears in John Adams' Diary of 1763:
'The Caucus Club meets'. Even in those days CAUCUS meant a
private meeting for political purposes.

494. *ENCUMBER*, encumber (*ĕn-kŭm'-bĕr*) *v.* To weigh
     down, impede with a load, clog, hinder, overload, obstruct,
embarrass, burden, handicap, oppress. An ENCUMBRANCE is a
burden, dead weight, hindrance.
CUMBER comes from the Latin *cumulus*, a heap, pile, used of
summer clouds which pile up in white snowy mounds, the
source of CUMULATE and ACCUMULATE. ENCUMBER, starting
with the almost useless EN-, was probably the original word.
   Bailey, 1721, gives INCUMBER and ENCUMBER as separate
words: INCUMBER meaning to crowd, to stop, to clog, to hinder;
and ENCUMBER to embarrass, perplex, trouble. A hundred years
later for INCUMBER Webster gives: 'To burden with a load; to
embarrass', confounding the clear distinction of Bailey; and under ENCUMBER gives also both meanings.
   Among 27 high-vocabulary adults 3 select CONFINE as a synonym of ENCUMBER. To CONFINE is to restrain within limits,
bind, imprison, enclose, shut up, immure, restrain from escape
by insurmountable obstacles.
   Again Bailey includes both INCLOSE and ENCLOSE: INCLOSE
meaning to shut in, fence about; and ENCLOSE meaning include.
Today the choice between EN- and IN- is largely personal, neither
being clearly right or wrong; but a return to Nathan Bailey's
sharp distinction would improve the language.

495. *FOIST*, foist (*foist*) *v.* To work in wrongfully by a trick,
     thrust in surreptitiously, palm off as genuine, pass as
worthy, deceive intentionally, forge without warrant.

Foist comes from a Dutch word meaning take in the hand. The popular mislead is LIFT, selected by 22 per cent. To HOIST (*hoist*), which rimes with FOIST, is to lift, raise, elevate, usually by a machine.

A FORGERY is made to imitate something of value, and sold or used in place of the original. To FORGE, which may mean make, construct of metal, acquired long ago a second meaning, to make a FORGERY. A FORGERY is one way of FOISTING on the public something worthless.

496. *MANIC*, manic (*măn'-ĭk*) *adj.* Frenzied, violent, insane, crazy, abnormally high strung.

The noun MANIA (*mā'-nē-ăh*) is the Latin *mania*, madness, from the Greek μανία (*mania*), madness, frenzy, almost any kind of madness with an exaltation of spirit. In the Century Dictionary the adjective is MANIAC (*mā'-nē-ăk*) or MANIACAL (*mă-nī'-ă-kl*), mad, in an insane state, crazy. Only later did the word MANIC appear.

The mislead INSECURE, selected by 20 per cent, means liable to give way, uncertain, unstable, not free from fear, and so fearful. Both UNSTABLE and FEARFUL might be synonymous with MANIC, and INSECURE is on the borderline of being correct, for INSECURITY of various sorts may be a cause of MANIA.

497. *REPAST*, repast (*rē-păst'*) *n.* A meal, supper, refection, eating, collation, feast, act of taking food.

REPAST and REPOSE look much alike, and Spenser, in the Fairie Queen, used one word for the other, partly because he needed a rime. To REPOSE, from the Latin *pausare*, to pause, is to rest; and this may lead to the selection, by 22 per cent, of SIESTA as a synonym of REPAST. SIESTA is a Spanish word for a MIDDAY REST, NAP, taken in the hottest part of the day.

REPAST comes from *re*, again, and *pastus*, food, the source of PASTURE. PASTURE originally meant food, nourishment, and then grass as food for cattle, and now more commonly ground covered with grass for the grazing of cattle.

A REPAST is a meal, simpler than a FEAST, but more than a COLLATION, this last a modest meal for monks after reading the collected lives of the Saints.

498. *MARAUDER*, marauder (*mă-raw'-der*) *n.* Plunderer, freebooter, robber.

To MARAUD is to rove in quest of plunder. The French *marauder* is to play the rogue, go about begging. The French *maraud* is a rogue, knave, scoundrel. A ROBBER takes openly; a THIEF takes stealthily; a MARAUDER roves about robbing and plundering.

Ephraim Chambers says: MARAUDING, from the French, *maraude*, in military language, is a term applied to a party of soldiers who, without any order, go into the neighboring houses or villages, when the army is either in camp or garrison, to plunder and destroy.

499. *EXHUMATION*, exhumation (*ĕks-hū-mā'-shŏn*) *n.* Dis-interring, digging up, digging out of the earth something which has been buried.

To 34 per cent, EXHUMATION means DEGRADING, compared with only 24 per cent who mark the dictionary answer: DIGGING-UP. HUMILIATION (*hū-mĭl-ĭ-ā'-shŏn*), a synonym of DEGRADING, debasing, mortifying, and EXHUMATION both come from the same Latin *humus*, ground, earth, the direct source of the English HUMUS (*hū'-mŭs*), dirt, vegetable mold. HUMILIATION and the verb to HUMILIATE come through the Latin *humilis*, lowly, humble; while EXHUMATION comes from the past participle *exhumatus* of the verb *exhumare*, a combination of *ex-*, out, and *humus*, ground, earth. EXHUMATION is literally a digging out of the ground again after burial, often for the purpose of gaining additional evidence for some legal procedure.

500. *ATTEST*, attest (*ăt-tĕst'*) *v.* To certify (v. b. 330), affirm (v. b. 644), corroborate (v. b. 846), authenticate, confirm, vouch for, bear witness, declare true. Read ATTEST (v. b. 1062). The verb to ATTEST comes from the Latin *ad-*, to, and the deponent verb *testari*, to bear witness, corroborate, confirm, from *testis*, a witness, the source of TESTIFY.

From History of the Anglo-Saxons by Francis Palgrave, a man with a remarkable knowledge of his period, comes: 'The name of Edmond, transmitted from generation to generation in Norfolk and Suffolk, ATTESTS the respect rendered in East Anglia to the martyred Sovereign'.

The participial adjective ATTESTED, used in the phrase: 'The ATTESTED record', where it means the true record, sworn to, is thought by 34 per cent to mean DISPUTED, argued about, fought over. To DETEST (*dē-tĕst'*) is to hate, execrate, dislike violently, almost denounce. One PROTESTS, declares, asserts, affirms one's own innocence; one ATTESTS, swears to, the innocence of some one else. To CONTEST (*kŏn-tĕst'*), from *con-*, together, and the same *testari*, to bear witness, was originally call to witness, bring an action, and then argue, contend, DISPUTE, so that: 'The CONTESTED record' is DISPUTED, challenged, questioned, opposed, an opposite of ATTESTED, confirmed, vouched for, authenticated, corroborated, guaranteed.

501. *RUMMAGE*, rummage (*rŭm'-māj*) v. To look for by moving things about, ransack, hunt through, explore; Webster, first edition: 'To search narrowly by looking into every corner and tumbling over things'.
RUMMAGE, probably at first another pronunciation of ROOMAGE, originally meant space, capacity, particularly in the hold of a ship. From this, the verb to RUMMAGE came to mean arrange and stow the cargo of a ship in the hold, and so move things about. From this it came to mean move things about in search of something.
A RUMMAGE SALE was originally a sale at the docks of unclaimed goods brought in by ships; also later a sale of articles left in a warehouse, articles ready to be scrapped. The phrase RUMMAGE SALE leads 24 per cent to believe that RUMMAGED means SOLD, and another 23 per cent to believe that it means SCRAPPED, discarded, thrown away. A RUMMAGE SALE involves both, SELLING things which have been SCRAPPED. But to RUMMAGE as a word by itself is to move things about looking for something.
Though published at the incredibly early date of 1719, The Life and Strange Surprizing Adventures of Robinson Crusoe by Daniel Defoe still belongs in every boy's list of good books. 'At low water', says Robinson Crusoe, 'I went on board; and, though I thought I had RUMMAGED the cabin so effectively as that nothing more could be found, yet I discovered a locker with drawers in it'.

502. *COMMODIOUS*, commodious (*kŏm-mō'-dē-ŭs*) *adj.*
Comfortable because of size, convenient and roomy, suitable, fit and spacious (v. b. 369), proper, useful.
The verb to ACCOMMODATE is to make suitable, proper, render fit; while an ACCOMMODATION is the corresponding noun.

COMMODIOUS, from the Latin *commodum*, something useful, convenient, a combination of *com*, with, and *modus*, measure, means, like COMELY and CONVENIENT, fit, suitable, becoming, useful, comfortable, proper, and also because of its derivation, from *modus*, measure, adds to these, roomy, spacious, large.

To 33 per cent COMMODIOUS means CROWDED, crammed, squeezed, pushed together, jammed, pressed, INCOMMODIOUS, an exact opposite of COMMODIOUS.

503. *LITTER*, litter (*lĭt'-ter*) *n.* Bed suspended between shafts, stretcher for carrying a wounded person.
LITTER comes through the French from the Latin *lectus*, bed. The same word LITTER means straw, hay, used as bedding for animals and from this has come to mean rubbish scattered about, disorder, untidiness. This no doubt leads 7 per cent to marking NEWSPAPERS, easily scattered about to make LITTER.

The same word LITTER may be applied to the number of young brought forth at birth by such animals as the sow, bitch, cat, and rabbit, which regularly give birth to more than one; and LITTER is thought by 23 per cent to mean PUPPY. A LITTER is never a single PUPPY, but must be more than one.

504. *SHIRE*, shire (*shīr*) *n.* An English county, district, subdivision, diocese, large area; Ephraim Chambers, 1728, says: 'A part or portion of the land, called also a county'; to which Nathan Bailey adds: 'There are forty in England and twelve in Wales and twenty-four in Scotland, besides stewarties, baileries, and constableries'.
Of 28 high-vocabulary adults 3 select TOWN as the meaning of SHIRE. VILLAGES, TOWNS, and CITIES are groups of houses, collections of people. A TOWN, directly from an Anglo-Saxon word meaning fence, hedge, inclosure, originally a collection of houses surrounded by a wall for safety, is larger than a VILLAGE, usually with a market, but smaller than a CITY.

SHIRES, RIDINGS, and HUNDREDS, all English terms, are divisions of land. SHIRE, an Anglo-Saxon word for office, business, administration, was an administrative area, governed by an earl or alderman. YORKSHIRE, pronounced (*shēr*, not *shīr*), in the north of England, was at one time divided into three TRITHINGS, which by an easy corruption came to be denominated RIDINGS; while in the center and south SHIRES were divided into HUNDREDS.

505. *AGATE*, agate (*ăg'-āt*) *n.* A kind of quartz banded in two
    or more different colors built up by slow deposits; a semi-precious stone or sometimes called the least valuable of the precious stones.
AGATE, a stone in layers, is a variety of quartz. Other forms of quartz are CARNELIAN, CHALCEDONY, ONYX, and SARD.

There are two equally popular misleads: CASTING and JADE; each selected by 15 per cent. An INGOT, a word which goes directly back to the Anglo-Saxon and sounds somewhat like AGATE, is a mass of metal cast in a mold. JADE is extensively used as another semi-precious gem, but is uniform in color, usually green or creamy white, not banded.

506. *DEBACLE*, debacle (*dā-băhk'-l*) *n.* Specifically the break-
    ing up of ice in a river; a confused riot, uncontrolled rush.
DEBACLE is the French *débâcle*, a breaking up, overthrow, from the verb *débâcler*, to break up, literally unbar, a combination of the privative *de-*, which comes from the Latin *dis-*, apart, and *bacler*, to stop, shut, bar. This last comes from the Latin *baculus*, a stick, staff, bar, recognizable through its diminutive, BACILLUS, a microscopic stick-like vegetable organism.

The mislead LIBERATION, underlined by 20 per cent, is a literal translation of DEBACLE, an unbarring, and so LIBERATION of a great mass of water which has been held back. One of the early uses of DEBACLE was in geology to describe an uncontrollable rush of water caused by the sudden breaking up of an ice block. But DEBACLE today includes the confusion and destruction left behind. The great flood in Florence, Italy, in 1967 was a DEBACLE.

507. *VERMILION*, vermilion (*ver-mĭl'-yŏn*) *adj.* A brilliant
    red (v. B. 68), Chinese red, cinnabar, sulphide of mercury.

Of those who score generally high in vocabulary tests, 70 per cent underline RED as the meaning of VERMILION, while in the bottom 10 per cent no one marks this choice. In the population as a whole 33 per cent concentrate on BALLROOM. A COTILLION (*kō-tĭl'-lyon*), originally a petticoat, the diminutive of the French *cotte*, coat, is now a dance for four or eight persons who, with changing partners, form elaborate figures.

VERMILION comes from the Latin *vermiculus*, a little worm, the diminutive of *vermis*, worm, the source of the English VERMIN. CARMINE, CRIMSON, and VERMILION, were all at one time made from the kermes insect, called also COCHINEAL (*kōch'-ĭ-nēl*). VERMILION, spelt with one L, is red with yellow, not blue as in CARMINE and CRIMSON.

508. *LANGUID*, languid (*lăng'-gwĭd*) *adj*. Drooping from
       weakness, faint, weary, exhausted, spiritless, flagging, indisposed, sluggish, lacking energy.
To 10 per cent LANGUID means WET, moist, covered with water, soaked in liquid. This may be the adjective LIQUID, somewhat similar in sound to LANGUID, and ending in the same last three letters. LIQUID, the opposite of SOLID, from the Latin *liquidus*, fluid, moist, from the verb *liquere*, to be fluid, characterizes a substance which flows.

LANGUID, and the accompanying verb to LANGUISH, come from the Latin *languere*, to be faint, weak. LIMP, an adjective from Anglo-Saxon, means weak in fibre, lacking firmness, flaccid. From this comes the pleasanter LIMBER, LIMP plus -ER, yielding, lithe.

Of the noun LANGUOR, E. Chambers says: 'In medicine, signifies a faintness, or relaxation arising from want or decay of spirit'.

509. *RECONNOITER*, reconnoiter (*rē-kŏn-noi'-ter*) *v*. Explore, investigate, examine with the eye, survey the whole situation, inspect before taking action.
Both the English verb to RECOGNIZE, literally to know again, and the French verb *reconnaître*, with the same meaning, to recognize, the source of RECONNOITER, go back to the Latin *re-*, again, and *cognoscere*, to know, the source of the English COGNITION.

Despite this derivation RECONNOITER now has the specialized meaning of investigating in advance as a basis for planning future action.

To 18 per cent RECONNOITER means RETRACE. To TRACE, with no RE- at the beginning, is to draw, mark out, delineate, sketch; also to follow a track by observing signs, very near RECONNOITER. To RETRACE, starting with RE-, is to go over again in the reverse direction, TRACE back; or sometimes merely to TRACE again, renew the lines.

According to E. Chambers: 'RECONNOITER in war is to view and examine the state of things in order to make a report thereof. A body of horse was sent to RECONNOITER their camp, the ground, the condition of the road, rivers, etc. A general ought to go to RECONNOITER in person the place to be besieged, in order to learn its situation, and avenues, its strengths and weaknesses.'

510. *BANSHEE*, banshee (*băn'-shē*) *n.* In Ireland and Scotland, a female spirit, a hideous old woman, who attaches herself to a family or house. As VAMPIRE is Slavic, BANSHEE is Irish.

To 19 per cent of those tested BANSHEE means DEATH-CHANT, mournful song, solemn melody. The BANSHEE sang a DEATH-CHANT under windows in a sad, supernatural voice to warn the family of an approaching death. But BANSHEE, which goes directly back to Gaelic and Irish words for woman, refers not to the song, but to the female spirit, phantom, apparition.

511. *PATRICIAN*, patrician (*pă-trĭ'-shăn*) *adj.* Aristocratic, belonging to the nobility, originally to the class of senators, noble, of high rank.

PATRICIAN comes from the Latin *patres*, senators, literally fathers, the plural of *pater*, father.

In the test phrase: 'The PATRICIAN class', MIDDLE is the only mislead marked. This is probably due to the word PLEBEIAN which comes from the Latin *plebs*, the common people. The *plebs* were free citizens but not among the founders of Rome.

The word PROLETARIAN (*prō-lĕ-tă'-rĭ-ăn*) is more recent and means specifically the working class. A PROLETARIAN is possessed of labor-force, and of nothing else. The PROLETARIAN class is the lowest, poorest, dependent on daily employment for support. In ancient Rome the PLEBEIAN class were the common people, free citizens, not descended from the original PATRICIAN families.

512. *GLEEMAN*, gleeman (*glē'-măn*) *n.* A singer, strolling minstrel, musician, troubador, jester, player.

GLEE, an Anglo-Saxon word, originally meant laughter, joy, mirth, gaiety, merriment; and then music, specifically a composition for three or more solo voices without accompaniment.

Of 28 high-vocabulary adults 6 select SURVEYOR as a synonym of GLEEMAN. In surveying, a CHAINMAN carries the chain, 66 feet in length, with 100 links each 7.92 inches called a gunter's CHAIN, or occasionally in the United States, a CHAIN fitted with 100 links but each a foot long.

From Marco Polo: 'At the court of the Great Khan there was a great number of GLEEMEN and jugglers'.

Joseph Strutt, an English engraver and author of many books, such as: The Dress and Habits of the People of England published in 1796, writes in his Sports and Pastimes of the People of England, 1801: 'The GLEEMEN added mimicry and other means of promoting mirth to their profession, as well as dancing and tumbling, with sleights of hand, and variety of deceptions to amuse the spectators'.

513. *DESIST*, desist (*dē-sĭst'*, sometimes pronounced *dē-zĭst'*) *v.* To leave off from action, stop, cease, forbear, pause, discontinue, break off, give over.

The verb to DESIST comes from the Latin, *desistere*, to leave off, a combination of *de*, down, and *sistere*, to place, set, plant, the causal form of *stare*, to stand, and so to cause to stand, make stand. From the same *sistere* come ASSIST, EXIST, INSIST, PERSIST, CONSIST, as well as RESIST. This last leads 2 persons in a group of 28 high-vocabulary adults to mark OBJECT as meaning DESIST.

514. *CANONIZE*, canonize (*kăn'-ŏn-īz*) *v.* To enroll, declare to be a saint.

The word CANON goes back through the Latin *canon*, to the Greek κανών (*canon*), both with the meaning rule, in the sense of law, regulation, also sometimes a catalogue of sacred writings.

From this comes the modern use of CANON to mean a list of saints. The same word CANON may be a list of members of a chapter of a cathedral or a collegiate church.

The big mislead is BOMBARD, selected by 15 per cent. BOMBARD (*bŏm'-băhrd*) was the name given in Europe to the earliest cannon; and the verb to BOMBARD (*bŏm-băhrd'*), accented on the second syllable, was to fire BOMBARDS (*bŏm'-băhrdz*) or CANNONS. A CANNON, spelt with two N's, is a large gun, and a CANNONADE is a continued discharge.

The selection of BOMBARD as a synonym of CANONIZE is spelling more than vocabulary, the difference between the two N's in CANNON, the gun, and one N in CANON, the list of saints.

Rock, in his Church of Our Fathers, defines BEATIFICATION as making a holy person a saint. BEATIFICATION, from the Latin *beatus*, happy, blessed, cannot take place until fifty years after death, and is more often a step toward CANONIZATION, placing a name in the official list of saints.

515. *DISCONCERTED*, disconcerted (*dĭs-kŏn-ser'-tĕd*) *adj.*
     Ruffled, disturbed, confused, unsettled, discomposed.
The verb to DISCONCERT, to throw into disorder, disarrange, obstruct, ruffle, discompose, confuse, embarrass, irritate, starts with the privative *dis-* before *concertare*, to contend, dispute, debate. The verb to CONCERT is to arrange, adjust, contrive mutually. The Century Dictionary says: 'The sense of arrange, bring to agreement arises naturally from that of debate'.

The two popular misleads are AMUSED and ASTONISHED. One of the original meanings of the verb to AMUSE was bewilder, puzzle; one who concentrates on a puzzle is both AMUSED and BEWILDERED, perplexed, and so perhaps DISCONCERTED. But the flavor of the two words differs. One is AMUSED so long as one feels that the solution is within one's capabilities. One is DISCONCERTED when one begins to realize that the solution is beyond one's abilities.

516. *PHILANTHROPIC*, philanthropic (*fĭl-ăn-thrŏp'-ĭk*) *adj.*
     Loving mankind, generous, charitable, kind, humane, beneficent, helpful in reducing suffering, generally benevolent toward the human species.

The adjective PHILANTHROPIC, and the corresponding noun PHIL-
ANTHROPY (fĭ-lăn'-thrō-pĭ), come from the Greek φιλανθρωπία
(philanthropia), generosity, benevolence. Break this into its
parts: φιλεῖν (philein), to love, the source of PHILANDER, to
love indiscriminately; and ἄνθρωπος (anthropos), man, the
source of ANTHROPOLOGY, the study of man. PHILANTHROPY is
literally the love of mankind.

To 6 per cent of those tested PHILANTHROPIC means WISE.
PHILOSOPHY, from the same φιλεῖν (philein), to love, and
σοφός (sophos), wise, is a love of wisdom; PHILANTHROPY, a
love of mankind.

Once CHARITY and PHILANTHROPY were the same. But CHARITY
now applies to a specific act, to giving money to another person,
or to some organization, with no deep feeling; PHILANTHROPY
is helping human welfare, giving for the good of large numbers
and the future.

517. *ENIGMATICAL*, enigmatical (ē-nĭg-măt'-ĭ-kăl) adj.
    Puzzling, ambiguous (v. B. 569), obscure, mysterious,
recondite (v. B. 1975), inexplicable, difficult to understand,
relating to an ENIGMA (v. B. 1396).
ENIGMATICAL comes from the Greek αἴνιγμα (ainigma), αἴνιγ-
ματις (ainigmatis), a riddle, conundrum. An ENIGMA was a
dark saying which concealed a thought under obscure words,
a question containing a hidden meaning or even a design or
representation.
    ENIGMATICAL is thought by 27 per cent to mean PROFOUND,
from the Latin *profundus*, deep, vast, from *pro*, forward, and
fundus, bottom, a word much too close to use as a mislead in a
vocabulary test, for though PROFOUND means deep, penetrating
below the surface, not superficial, it may also mean hidden, obscure, abstruse, all synonyms of ENIGMATICAL.

518. *SILO*, silo (sĭ'-lō) n. A fodder pit, vat, circular tank for
    packing away fodder to convert it to silage. Silage is fod-
der for winter preserved by its own fermentation.
The process of preserving green crops in a succulent, juicy
condition, in a silo, is called ENSILAGE (ĕn'-sĭ-lāj), and the fodder
produced is SILAGE (sĭ'-lāj). The method goes far back as shown

by the derivation of SILO, which comes through the Latin *sirus*, a pit, from the Greek σιρός (*siros*), a pit for storing grain.

But the modern commercial SILO, with an understanding of the chemical reactions which take place, is recent, within the past hundred years, dating from about 1877. A SILO is a round tower, really a tank, twelve to twenty feet across, and thirty to forty feet high, built of wood, metal, or concrete.

519. *PARITY*, parity (*pă'-rĭ-tĭ*) *n.* Equality, equivalence, similarity, agreement, likeness, evenness, close correspondence, like state.
PARITY is the French *parité*, from the Latin *par*, equal. In English, 'on a PAR with' means equal to, at the same level as. In business, 'at PAR' means at its face value, neither above nor below. In golf, PAR is a theoretically perfect score, depending on distance, plus two putts.

The word DISPARITY seems somehow easier to grasp. A DISPARITY is an inequality, unlikeness. In much the same sense, a PARITY is a sameness, equalness, similarity.

520. *INAUSPICIOUS*, inauspicious (*ĭn-ŏs-pĭ'-shŭs*) *adj.* Ill-omened, unlucky, not propitious, unfavorable, unpromising, untoward, not auspicious.
Pantologia, a Cyclopaedia of 1813, says: 'When men considered the wonderful migration of birds, how they disappeared at once, and appeared again at stated times, and could give no guess where they went, it was almost natural to suppose that they retired somewhere out of the sphere of the earth, and perhaps approached the ethereal region, where they might converse with the gods, and thence be able to predict events'.

The Latin *avis* means bird. From this comes *auspes*, a diviner, one who foretells the future from the flight of birds, a combination of *avis*, and *specere*, to view. From this comes the adjective AUSPICIOUS, which has come to mean favorable, fortunate, kind, propitious, promising success.

To 13 per cent INAUSPICIOUS means QUESTIONABLE. SUSPICIOUS, from the Latin *suspicere*, to suspect, is a combination of *sub*, under, and the same *specere*, to look at. INAUSPICIOUS, starting with IN, not, means not promising success.

521. *MOLLIFY*, mollify (*mŏl'-lĭ-fī*) *v.* To soften, soothe, mitigate, appease, pacify, calm, quiet, ease.

Mollify, from the Latin, *mollis*, soft, and *facere*, to make, means
literally to soften, make soft, make tender. From the same
source, through the verb *mollire*, to soften, comes the unusual
EMOLLIENT (*ē-mŏl'-lyĕnt*), used both as an adjective, softening,
and as a noun.

To 20 per cent MOLLIFIED means CHANGED. To MODIFY is to
CHANGE, implying the continued existence of the subject matter
CHANGED. MODIFY, from the Latin *modus*, measure, originally
meant to reduce in extent, so that to MODERATE, from the same
Latin *modus*, measure, again literally to reduce in amount, is a
synonym of MODIFY. But MODERATE, used figuratively, has also
come to mean pacify, calm, quiet. MODIFY means change, alter;
while MOLLIFY, used figuratively, means soothe, calm, pacify.

522. *TRAVAIL*, travail (*tră'-vāl*) *n.* Labor, toil, work, effort,
trouble.

TRAVAIL, originally from a Latin word *trabs*, which meant a
beam across a building, is the oldest form of the modern word
TRAVEL. Of TRAVAIL and TRAVEL Fowler says: 'Distinguished in
pronunciation, but rather slightly, as (*tră'-vĭl*) and (*tră'-vĕl*)'.
W. H. P. Phyfe says: 'TRAVAIL (*trăv'-āl*); TRAVEL (*trăv'-l*)'.

The mislead PURSUIT (*per-sūt'*), following after, is suggested
probably by TRAVEL, which now means journeying, often for
pleasure, moving from one place to another. TRAVAIL is an old-
fashioned word, and when used means labor, effort, toil.

523. *INIQUITOUS*, iniquitous (*ĭn-ĭk'-wĭ-tŭs*) *adj.* Wicked,
criminal, illegal, nefarious, unprincipled, unrighteous, unfair, unjust.

EQUITY is equal justice to all, from the Latin *aequus*, which
really means equal, but came to mean equal rights, and so fairness, justice. INIQUITOUS, starting with the Latin privative *in*,
should mean unequal, at most unjust, but is today much stronger,
meaning WICKED.

The only attractive mislead is NERVOUS, selected by 8 per
cent. INQUIETUDE (*ĭn-kwī'-ē-tūd*) is restlessness, uneasiness, and
so apprehension, nervousness. The rare adjective is INQUIET.

NEFARIOUS means unspeakably wicked; EXECRABLE, worthy of being cursed. INIQUITOUS is not so strong, but should always have the suggestion of grossly unjust, wicked in relation to the rights of others.

524. *APPENDANT*, appendant (*ăp-pĕn'-dănt*) *adj.* Annexed, attached, concomitant, connected, adjoined.

HANGING, the only popular mislead, marked by 22 per cent, is technically correct, for APPENDANT, DEPENDENT, PENDANT, and SUSPENDED, all come from the Latin *pendere*, to hang; but each has developed its own implications. SUSPENDED means simply HANGING. DEPENDENT means HANGING, but suggests the need of support, a subordinate HANGING on to someone or something stronger. An INDEPENDENT person needs no such support.

APPENDANT has come to be largely a legal term, applied to a document attached to another: 'An APPENDANT paper', supplementary, adjoined. An APPENDAGE is something APPENDED.

525. *COVEY*, covey (*kŭv'-ĭ*) *n.* A flock, brood, pack, bevy, band, company of many sorts.

COVEY, which goes back through French probably to Anglo-Saxon, is thought by 17 per cent to mean THICKET. The adjective COVERT (*kŭv'-ert*) means hidden, secret, concealed, covered, sheltered; and from this the noun, a COVERT, is a shelter, and so a THICKET, shady place, cover for game.

FLOCK applies to wild ducks and geese; GAGGLE more especially to geese. Among birds PACK is used of grouse; GANG of wild turkey; BEVY of quail; WISP of snipe; and COVEY of partridges.

526. *DISQUIETED*, disquieted (*dĭs-kwī'-ĕ-tĕd*) *adj.* Disturbed, uneasy, restless, unsettled, vexed, alarmed, harassed, robbed of tranquillity.

DISQUIETED unites the Latin privative *dis-*, and QUIET, plus the Anglo-Saxon -ED, added customarily to weak verbs to form the past tense.

To 7 per cent DISQUIETED means STILLED. The Anglo-Saxon adjective STILL means remaining at rest, in repose, motionless, calm, peaceful, undisturbed, tranquil, QUIET. STILLED is lulled, pacified, QUIETED, and so an exact opposite of DISQUIETED.

527. *AWE*, awe (*aw*) *v*. To strike with fear mingled with ad-
     miration, cause dread, terrify, inspire with reverence.
The adjective AWFUL, literally filled with AWE, means dreadful,
fearful, frightful, arousing a feeling of deep solemnity and reverence with a mixture of fear.

To 18 per cent AWED means PLEASED. The verb to PLEASE is
to satisfy, suit, content, delight, humor, make seem good, allow
agreeable sensations. The corresponding noun is PLEASURE, and
the adjective PLEASANT.

REVERENCE expresses something less than VENERATION, but
both lack the feeling of dread, fear, terror, aroused by AWE, a
word which goes back to Icelandic, Danish, and Anglo-Saxon
words all meaning fear.

528. *QUARRY*, quarry (*kwor'-rĭ*) *v*. To dig, excavate, obtain
     from the ground such materials as marble and granite.
The noun, a QUARRY, is a pit, excavation, usually open, from
which are dug marble, slate, lime, cement, and building stone.

To 10 per cent, the verb to QUARRY means to ASK. To QUERY
(*kwē'-rĭ*), to ask, question, inquire, interrogate, comes from
the Latin *quaere*, the imperative of the verb *quaerere*, to ask,
inquire, seek, search for, the source of QUEST, a search, seeking,
pursuit, and QUESTION. QUARRY comes from the Latin *quadratus*,
square, the source of QUADRANGLE, a square court.

Of QUARRY, the noun, E. Chambers says: 'A place under
ground out of which are dug marble, free-stone, etc'. A MINE
is generally covered, a deep cavern, the source of coal and
various metals. To QUARRY is to dig from an open pit.

529. *SOBRIETY*, sobriety (*sō-brī'-ĕ-tĭ*) *n*. Moderation, temper-
     ance, avoidance of excess, soberness, abstemiousness.
SOBRIETY is thought by 26 per cent to mean INTEMPERANCE,
probably a confusion of TEMPERANCE, sobriety, moderation,
with INTEMPERANCE; or it may be a misinterpretation of SOBRI-
ETY with the opposite of its correct meaning.

530. *PRESCRIPTION*, prescription (*prē-skrĭp'-shŏn*) *n*. Direc-
     tion for medical treatment, prescript, statement, order,
command, dictation.

The Latin verb *scribere* is primarily to write, but also means to order, command, dictate, ordain, appoint, lay down beforehand in writing. From the Latin *scribere* come the Italian *scrivere*, and the Spanish *escribir*, as well as almost countless English words, including the obvious SCRIBE, one who writes.

Through the past participle *scriptus* come SCRIPT and INSCRIPTION, an important writing done in stone or some permanent material; DESCRIPTION, a picture in written words; CONSCRIPTION, registering men for military service; TRANSCRIPTION, a copy, writing over again something already written; ASCRIPTION, referring a writing to a particular writer; and finally PRESCRIPTION, usually a medical direction, recipe, established by rules. The popular misconception is SUGGESTION, chosen by about 10 per cent. COMMAND, PRESCRIPTION, and SUGGESTION are in order of authority. A COMMAND is absolute, arbitrary, cannot be questioned. A SUGGESTION is a hint, with no pretence of authority back of it. A PRESCRIPTION is half way between. It is clear, sharp, direct, from one in authority in the sense of knowledge and skill, but not from one in control.

531. *DISSENTIENT*, dissentient (*dĭs-sĕn'-shĭ-ĕnt*, almost *dĭs-sĕn'-shĕnt*) *adj.* Dissenting from the opinion of the majority, non-conforming, heretical, differing from others.

DISSENTIENT comes from *dissentiens, dissentientis*, the present participle of *dissentire*, a combination of *dis-*, apart, and *sentire*, to feel. SENTIENT (*sĕn'-shĭ-ĕnt*) is from the Latin *sentiens*, the present participle of *sentire*, to perceive, feel, the source of SENTIMENT, SENSIBLE, and SENSITIVE.

SENTIENT alone means having the power of perception by the senses, sensing the outside world through one's five physical senses: sight, hearing, feeling, tasting, and smelling. DISSENTIENT is not the opposite, does not mean blind or deaf, not seeing, not hearing, but holding beliefs contrary to those held by the majority or by the governing group.

To DISSENT is to feel against, think apart from the group. To CONTROVERT, from *contro*, against, and *vertere*, to turn, is by derivation, to turn against, contend against in discussion, oppose, very close to DISSENT. But CONTROVERT has come to mean dispute, argue a point, deny. One DISSENTS quietly, CONTROVERTS noisily.

To CONFORM applies to act rather than to thought. One may CONFORM to the customs of a community; and yet DISSENT mentally. Given a choice between NONCONFORMING and CONTROVERSIAL as synonyms for DISSENTIENT, 50 per cent select the first and 40 per cent the second. CONTROVERSIAL emphasizes arguing, debating, disputation, often taking sides for the sake of argument. DISSENSION expresses a quiet, not disputatious, difference of opinion.

532. *MEGACEPHALY*, megacephaly (*mĕg-ă-sĕf'-ă-lĭ*) *n.*
Large-headedness; a head larger than normal in proportion to height. Sir Richard Quain, in his Dictionary of Medicine, 1882, says: 'Applied to skulls whose cranial capacity exceeds 1450 cubic centimeters'.
MEGACEPHALY, like many other medical terms, comes directly from the Greek μέγας (*megas*), large, as in MEGAPHONE, and MEGALITH, a great stone used in ancient construction. The second part, CEPHALIC (*sē-făl'-ĭk*), comes from the Greek κεφαλή (*cephale*), head. MICROCEPHALIC, small-headed, is the opposite.
The CEPHALIC index, used in classifying ancient skulls, is the ratio of the breadth of the head to its length from front to back. DOLICHOCEPHALIC means long-headed. BRACHYCEPHALIC (*brăk'-ĭ-sĕ-făl-ĭk*) is literally short-headed from front to back, or broadheaded from side to side, having a breadth at least 4/6th the length.
LARGE-HEADEDNESS, the correct answer, is chosen by 65 per cent; while SEIZURES and ITCHING each attract 15 per cent.

533. *AVIDLY*, avidly (*ăv'-ĭd-lĭ*) *adv.* Greedily, graspingly, avariciously, with intense eagerness.
AVID, from the Latin *avidus*, from the verb *avere*, to long for, crave, wish, means extremely eager, ardently desirous, greedy.
AVIDLY is thought by 17 per cent to mean CAREFULLY. According to the Century Dictionary CAREFUL, long ago, meant eager, vehement, almost AVID. But today CAREFUL means CAUTIOUS, watchful, attentive, wary; while AVID means greedy, grasping.
AVARICE, an inordinate desire of acquiring wealth, cupidity, greediness of gain, is perhaps better known.

534. *RAJ*, raj (*răhj*) *n.* Rule, dominion, authority, control, direction, management.

RAJ goes back through Hindu to a Sanskrit word for rule, dominion. RAJ is the rule, the authority of a RAJA, also spelt RAJAH, the ruler, chief, dignitary.

To 15 per cent RAJ means SUBJUGATION. The boundary between SUBJUGATION and RULE is far from sharp. SUBJUGATE, and the corresponding noun SUBJUGATION, come from the Latin *sub*, under, and *jugum*, yoke. To SUBJUGATE is to put under a yoke, subdue, conquer, vanquish. None of these are included in RAJ, rule, dominion, authority. But SUBJUGATION also includes: compelled to submit to the control of another. This is a part also of authority. SUBJUGATION takes over when force is used or needed.

535. *LEITMOTIF*, leitmotif (*līt'-mō-tēf*) *n.* A leading theme, guiding motive, a musical theme associated throughout with a particular idea.

LEITMOTIF, a German word, is a combination of *leiten*, to lead, and *motiv*, motive, theme, in French *motif*, used frequently in music. According to Grove's Dictionary of Music: 'The term was invented by Hans von Wolzogen who analysed Wagner in the second half of the 19th century'.

FUNERAL-DIRGE attracts 40 per cent as a synonym of LEITMOTIF. The word DIRGE was originally *dirige*, the first word of the Latin hymn beginning: '*Dirige, Domine, Deus meus, in conspectu tuo viam meam*'. (Direct, Lord, my God, in thy sight my way.) LEITMOTIVE are appropriate to descriptive instrumental music, called programme music, and to opera.

In dramatic music, a LEITMOTIF is a theme of a few notes, a short figure of marked character by which a person or object, situation, emotion, or thought, is indicated, and which recurs whenever the idea appears. The principle was recognized in the 1700's but Richard Wagner gave the LEITMOTIF general currency in Der Ring des Nibelungen, constructed on the most elaborate network of leading themes.

536. *MYTHIC*, mythic (*mĭth'-ĭk*) *adj.* Imaginary, invented, created, fictitious, legendary, made up; the usual adjective is MYTHICAL, shortened occasionally to MYTHIC.

The noun MYTH, which goes directly back to the Greek μῦθος (mithos), tale, speech, legend, was an imaginary history, invented story of some super-human being, so ancient that no one knows who created it.

Two nearly equally attractive choices are IMAGINARY, selected by 55 per cent, and SPIRITUAL, by 45 per cent. IMAGINARY means existing in the mind only, fancied, visionary; and MYTHS, though perhaps based originally on some actual exploit, are not history, for the name and identity of the hero have long since disappeared and his feats have been exaggerated and multiplied by imagination. MYTHS are today largely IMAGINARY.

SPIRITUAL, from the Latin spirare, to breathe, is nearly impossible to define sharply; but every MYTH perpetuates something more than mere imaginary adventure. It exemplifies courage, spirit; and the percentages obtained in this vocabulary test give a fair picture of the elements IMAGINATION and SPIRIT which make up a MYTH.

537. *INCIVILITY*, incivility (*ĭn-sĭ-vĭl'-ĭ-tĭ*) *n.* Disrespect, impoliteness, unmannerliness, almost impudence, ill-mannered discourtesy, uncomplaisance, rudeness (v. B. 237) of behavior. CIVILITY (*sĭ-vĭl'-ĭ-tĭ*) comes from the Latin civilitas, civilitatis, the art of government, from civilis, civil, belonging to a citizen. urbane, courteous. This comes in turn from civis, a citizen.

Although high-vocabulary students select INSOLENCE as the meaning of INCIVILITY; of the big middle-vocabulary group 23 per cent choose DISHONESTY, compared with 22 per cent who prefer INSOLENCE; while among low-vocabulary students 47 per cent select DISHONESTY compared with only 13 per cent who mark INSOLENCE.

Originally CIVILITY meant citizenship and implied the characteristics which should go with such an honor, including perhaps HONESTY; but CIVILITY has come to mean politeness, good breeding, courtesy, kind attention; and INCIVILITY is the opposite, poor breeding, impoliteness, discourtesy.

When the Human Engineering Laboratory tests delinquent boys, in conflict with the law, their common trait is a small, inexact English vocabulary in the bottom 5 per cent of their age. In native aptitudes, inherent abilities, which must be expressed, they score above normal and cannot sit and do nothing. But they lack such words as CIVILITY and HONESTY, and have no conception of the ideas which these words convey.

538. *PRODIGIOUS*, prodigious (*prō-dĭj'-ŭs*) *adj.* Wonderfully large, immense, huge, enormous, monstrous, extraordinary, amazing, marvellous, astounding, excessive (v. B. 763), preternatural (133), contrary to the course of nature.
PRODIGIOUS is thought by 20 per cent to mean EXTRAVAGANT. Although the Latin word *prodigus*, wasteful, lavish, prodigal, might easily be pronounced PRODIGIOUS, it comes from *prodigĕre*, to consume, squander, a combination of *pro*, forward, before, and *agĕre*, to drive. From it comes PRODIGAL, lavish, wasteful, given to extravagance, and the noun PRODIGALITY, but not PRODIGIOUS.
PRODIGIOUS comes from the Latin *prodigiosus*, unnatural, strange, marvellous, from *prodigium*, a portent, an omen, sign, token, a combination of *pro*, before, and *dicĕre*, to say. From this comes PRODIGY, originally something extraordinary from which an omen was drawn, a sign, miracle, wonder, now a person so unusual as to excite wonder.
From John Milton in the poem Paradise Lost comes: 'All monstrous, all PRODIGIOUS things'.

539. *INVOLUNTARILY*, involuntarily (*ĭn-vŏl-ŭn-tā'-rĭ-lĭ*) *adv.* Spontaneously, unintentionally, without conscious mental effort, independent of volition, with no consenting action of the mind. Read VOLUNTARY (v. B. 201).
INVOLUNTARILY is thought by 20 per cent to mean ROUNDABOUT, indirect. INVOLVED, starting with the same first five letters, from the Latin *volvĕre*, to roll, means entangled, complicated, intricate, and so ROUNDABOUT.
When given a choice, 73 per cent of high-vocabulary readers select SPONTANEOUSLY as the meaning of INVOLUNTARILY compared with only 7 per cent who want DELIBERATELY; while of readers in general 47 per cent select SPONTANEOUSLY compared with only 15 per cent who choose DELIBERATELY. Despite this clear choice the Century Dictionary gives NOT SPONTANEOUSLY as a meaning of INVOLUNTARILY, an exact opposite.

The difficulty is the word SPONTANEOUSLY, from the Latin *spons, spontis*, will, one's own accord, which the Century Dictionary defines as occurring without the intervention of external forces, not controlled, proceeding from conscious, or unconscious internal forces, springing from one's own desire or volition, and so VOLUNTARILY. The Century adds: 'The employment of SPONTANEOUS in the sense of irreflective is creeping in from the French, an objectionable use'. SPONTANEOUSLY should not be used in a vocabulary test as a synonym of INVOLUNTARILY.

VOLUNTARY comes from the Latin *voluntarius*, willing, of free will, from *voluntas, voluntatis*, will, choice, from *velle*, to will, the infinitive of *volō*, wish, want, will, determine. VOLUNTARY means done by choice, of one's own free will, of one's own accord, without pressure from the outside.

INVOLUNTARY ought perhaps to mean against one's will, contrary to one's choice, and the word has been used in this way; but its more frequent use seems to be without conscious choice, without making a counter decision, without exercising one's own will, without thought.

540. *LANYARD*, lanyard (*lăn'-yahrd*) *n*. Short rope, small cord used for all kinds of purposes on shipboard.

To 8 per cent LANYARD means SAIL, the second step in learning, a confusion of words used frequently in the same situation, in this instance both associated with sailboats.

Of LANYARD, the Complete Boating Encyclopedia says only: 'Any of various short ropes or cords used for lashing, tying, or holding jobs afloat'.

From Piloting, Seamanship, and Small Boat Handling, by Charles F. Chapman, comes: 'Ropes, rove through deadeyes for setting up rigging. Also a rope made fast to anything to secure it'. To REEVE is to pass the end of a line through a hole in a block. ROVE is the past, and past participle. A DEADEYE is a circular block of wood, with holes through it, for the LANYARD or rigging to REEVE through.

A SHROUD is wire rope from the upper part of a sailboat's mast to the deck. The bottom end is fastened in one hole of a DEADEYE. A LANYARD, through the other hole in the DEADEYE, attaches this to the deck. Tightening the LANYARD tightens the SHROUD.

From Chapman: 'SHROUDS, ropes on each side of a vessel, reaching from mast-heads to the vessel's sides to support the masts'.

Under LANYARD E. Chambers says: See LANIARD: 'A small rope in a ship, reeved into the dead-men's-eyes of all the shrouds and chains. Their use is to slacken or set taught the shrouds. The term is generally applied to any short piece of cord or line, fastened to several machines in a ship, and serving to secure them in a particular place, or manage them more conveniently.'

541. *ADAMANTINE*, adamantine (ăd-ă-măn'-tēn) *adj*. Hard, impenetrable, of surpassing hardness, impregnable.

PRAYING, the popular mislead, is suggested, no doubt, by MANTIS, from the Greek μάντις (*mantis*), a prophet, seer, diviner, familiar in the name of the insect, PRAYING MANTIS.

The noun ADAMANT (ăd'-ă-mănt) was used of various metals and specifically of the diamond, also of the MAGNET. It comes from the Greek privative ά and δαμᾶν (*daman*), to conquer. ADAMANT was literally unconquerable. Of ADAMANTINE, Bailey says: 'Hard, inflexible', and of ADAMANT: 'A diamond, the most glittering, hardest, and most valuable of all other stones'.

542. *MAHOUT*, mahout (măh-hŏut') *n*. An elephant driver, keeper and driver of an elephant.

MOHAMMED (mō-hăhm'-mĕd), who lived from 570 to 632, was founder of the Moslem religion. The name is spelt and pronounced variously, sometimes MAHOUN, and this may lead 25 per cent to select HINDU-PRIEST as the meaning of MAHOUT, compared with 45 per cent who select ELEPHANT-DRIVER, a surprisingly large number for so unusual a word.

543. *PRONUNCIAMENTO*, pronunciamento (prō-nŭn-sē-ăh-mĕn'-tō) *n*. Proclamation, declaration, manifesto, formal announcement.

To 15 per cent PRONUNCIAMENTO means CORRECT SPEECH. The surprise is not that some mark this, but that many more do not. PRONUNCIAMENTO, a Spanish word, and PRONUNCIATION, CORRECT SPEECH, both come from the Latin *pronunciatio, pronunciationis*, a proclamation, publication, from the verb *pronun-*

ciare, to announce, proclaim. The verb to PRONOUNCE originally meant declare, announce, proclaim, but has come to mean articulate correctly, utter the right sounds. The corresponding noun, PRONUNCIATION, is CORRECT SPEECH. The unusual word PRONUNCIAMENTO has retained the original meaning of announcement, proclamation.

544. *KOHLRABI,* kohlrabi (*kōl-răh'-bǐ*) *n.* A variety of cabbage with a longer stem than usual, which swells out into a sort of turnip, resembling the Swedish variety of RUTABAGA (*rŏo-ta-bā'-gah*), a kind of turnip.
KOHLRABI is a German word, a combination of the German *kohl,* from the Latin *caulis,* cabbage, and *rube,* from the Latin *rapum,* turnip.

545. *TARDIGRADE,* tardigrade (*tahr'-dĭ-grād*) *adj.* Slowing down, going deliberately, slow paced, moving sluggishly, slothful, phlegmatic, slack. The term is used of the SLOTH family. From the same verb *gradi,* to walk, go, and formed in much the same manner, come RETROGRADE, moving backward, having a backward motion, retreating, starting with the Latin *retro,* backward; GRAVIGRADE, heavy-footed; and PLANTIGRADE, walking on the whole sole of the foot, as men and bears, from the Latin *planta,* sole, opposed to DIGITIGRADE (*dij'-ĭ-tĭ-grād*), walking on the toes, as do cats and dogs, from the Latin *digitus,* finger. GRADIENT (*grā'-dĭ-ĕnt*), moving by steps, is the present participle of the verb *gradi.*
    Despite the unfamiliarity of this word, a surprisingly large number of the high-vocabulary group select SLOW as the meaning of TARDIGRADE, from the Latin *tardus,* slow.

546. *DULCET,* dulcet (*dŭl'-sĕt*) *adj.* Sweet, luscious, exquisite, melodious, harmonious.
In the first form of this vocabulary worksample, where both SWEET and HARMONIOUS appeared in this item, 60 per cent selected the first, and only 12 per cent HARMONIOUS. Today the word DULCET, from the Latin *dulcis,* sweet, applies most frequently to tones, sounds; but originally DULCET meant sweet to the taste, and SWEET is the modern interpretation.

547. *ENDOGENOUS*, endogenous (*ĕn-dŏj'-ĕ-nŭs*) *adj.* Growing from within, originating inside.

ENDOGENOUS is thought by 16 per cent to mean SKIN, the outer covering.

An EXOGEN (*ĕk'-sō-jĕn*) is a plant whose stem grows by layers added on the outside. Each ring of a tree trunk is a new year's growth, added on the outside, without changing the inside. This is EXOGENOUS (*ĕk-sŏj'-ĕ-nŭs*), from the Greek 'ἔξω (*exo*), outside, and γενής (*genes*), producing, literally producing outside.

ENDOGENOUS is growing from the center, from inside, and pushing out. The ENDOGENS (*ĕn'-dō-jĕns*) were thought at one time to be an important subdivision, but members of the same family may be both EXOGENOUS and ENDOGENOUS.

548. *RACQUET*, racquet (*răk'-kĕt*) *n.* Light bat, battledore, a catgut network stretched tightly in a more or less oval frame with a handle.

Etienne Pasquier, 1529 to 1615, a French lawyer, man of letters, and author of Recherches sur la France, observed that anciently players at tennis used no rackets but played instead with the palm of the hand, adding that rackets were not introduced until a little before his time.

RACKET, also spelt RACQUET with the QU of the French, and similar words in Spanish, Italian, and the Scandinavian languages, all go back to an Arabic word meaning the palm of the hand. To 6 per cent RACQUET means SHELF-SUPPORT. A SHELF-SUPPORT is a BRACKET, from Spanish and Portuguese, an ornamental projection from a wall to hold up a shelf.

Of RACKET E. Chambers says: 'A kind of bat for striking the ball at tennis, consisting usually of a lattice, or net-work of cat gut, strained very tight over a circle of wood with a handle or shaft of moderate length'. And he adds: 'RACKET is also a machine which the savages of Canada bind to their feet to enable them to walk more commodiously over the snow, made much in the manner of the tennis RACQUET'.

549. *FRESHET*, freshet (*frĕsh'-ĕt*) *n.* A small flood, moderate inundation, sudden overflowing of a river because of melting snow.

To 14 per cent FRESHET means WELL. FRESHET comes from an old French word which meant fresh and was applied to water from a spring, a use suggesting the modern selection of WELL as the meaning of FRESHET.

Of FRESHET, FLOOD, INUNDATION, and CATACLYSM, the last is the most serious partly because of the similarity to CATASTRO-PHE. An INUNDATION suggests something covered with water and so damaged. FLOOD is general. A FRESHET is sudden, small, temporary, and nothing in the word suggests destruction.

550. *FATUITY*, fatuity (*fă-tū'-ĭ-tĭ*) *n.* Foolishness, uncon-
     scious stupidity, weakness of mind, self-conceited silliness.
To 8 per cent FATUITY means DONATION. A GRATUITY, ending in the same last six letters as FATUITY, is a free gift, donation, present, from the Latin *gratuitus*, given without demand, from the Latin *gratia*, favor, and *gratus*.

SENILITY, something like FATUITY in sound, is the weakness of old age, and this may lead another 8 per cent to select OLDNESS as a synonym of FATUITY. Although FATUITY, directly from the Latin *fatuitas*, *fatuitatis*, foolishness, from *fatuus*, foolish, silly, simple, is foolishness, almost at times idiocy, imbecility, there is nothing in the word FATUITY to suggest age, almost the op-posite, for the word comes from the same source as FATUOUS, self-conceited, self-esteemed.

551. *FETE*, fete (*fāt*) *v.* To entertain with a feast, honor with
     festive entertainment.
FETE is French, from Old French *feste*, the source of the English FEAST. The noun, a FETE, is a feast, festival, holiday, celebration and is the French for FEAST. FEAST itself comes from the Latin *festum*, a festival, feast. The corresponding Spanish is FIESTA.

In the test phrase: 'The king was FETED' the most popular mis-lead is DECORATED. To DECORATE may be to honor with a medal, a badge, a ribbon. To FETE is to honor with a feast.

552. *INVECTIVE*, invective (*ĭn-věk'-tĭv*) *n.* Vehement de-
     nunciation, sharp words, violent utterance of censure, sarcasm, abuse, reproach, vituperation, railing, virulent accusa-tion, objurgation, diatribe, philippic, abusive tirade.

INVECTIVE comes from *invectus*, the past participle of the Latin *invehere*, to carry, bear, bring in, but also to attack with words, scold. Directly from the verb comes the English verb INVEIGH (*ĭn-vā'*), to attack verbally, rail against. An INVECTIVE is a denunciation, a railing against, unless we accept popular interpretation.

INVECTIVE is thought by 43 per cent of those who have taken this vocabulary form, nearly twice as many as mark the established answer, to mean STIMULUS. An INCENTIVE, somewhat like INVECTIVE in sound, is a STIMULUS, a spur, goad, impulse, incitement, which excites, rouses, spurs, encourages, provides a motive. To INCITE is the verb. To INVEIGH is to make a verbal attack, rail against, utter a vehement denunciation.

LAMPOONS, PASQUINADES (*păs-kwĭ-nād'*), INVECTIVES, and SATIRES are all attacks. A LAMPOON is malicious, aimed to insult. A PASQUINADE is shorter and lighter than a LAMPOON. An INVECTIVE is a scolding, more intense than a SATIRE, and lacks any attempt at reform.

INVECTIVE differs from REPROOF, as the latter proceeds from a friend and is intended for the good of the person REPROOVED; whereas INVECTIVE is the work of an enemy and entirely designed to vex and give uneasiness to the person against whom it is directed.

553. *DROLL*, droll (*drōl*) *adj*. Comical, funny, waggish, mirthful, facetious, laughable, ludicrous, amusing, whimsical, farcical, ridiculous.

DROLL goes back to a Dutch word meaning humorous fellow, merry-andrew; also a short thick person. DROLLERY is a merry or facetious way of writing, full of waggish wit.

To 19 per cent DROLL means UNINTERESTING, perhaps a confusion of DROLL with DULL; for the UNINTERESTING person is DULL, wearisome, tedious, tiresome, without interest; or perhaps because the DROLL person is not a clown, does not pretend to be funny, may even try to seem UNINTERESTING.

554. *INEXTRICABLY*, inextricably (*ĭn-ĕks'-trĭk-ă-blĭ*) *adj*.
Permanently, so as not to be freed, beyond disentanglement, inseparably, incapable of being disengaged.

INEXTRICABLY, ending in the Anglo-Saxon -LY which converts
the adjective into an adverb, is a combination of the Latin
privative *in-*, not, and the adjective EXTRICABLE, pronounced
(*ĕks'-trĭk-ă-bl*), Phyfe adds: not (*ĕks-trĭk'-ă-bl*). This comes
in turn from the Latin *extricare*, to extricate, a combination of
ex-, out, from, and *tricae*, trifles, toys, a word used also for
hindrances, impediments. To EXTRICATE is to free from hindrances, disentangle, relieve, disengage, set free, untangle that which
is INTRICATE, complicated, a word from the same *tricae*, trifle
or impediment.

To 11 per cent INEXTRICABLY means UNACCOUNTABLY, without
explanation. INEXPLICABLY (*ĭn-ĕks'-plĭk-ă-blĭ*, not *ĭn-ĕks-plĭk'-
ă-blĭ*), differing from INEXTRICABLY in only two of the twelve
letters, comes from the adjective EXPLICABLE (*ĕks'-plĭk-ă-bl*),
where Phyfe again adds: not (*ĕks-plĭk'-ă-bl*).

EXPLICABLE, from the Latin *explicare*, to unfold, spread out,
set in order, a combination of *ex-*, out, and *plicare*, to fold, the
source of APPLICABLE, PLAIT, and PLEAT, but not of EXPLAIN,
which comes from *planare*, to flatten, make level, from *planus*,
level, plain.

EXTRICATE, DISENTANGLE, RELEASE, and DISENGAGE, are in order
of involvement. DISENGAGE suggests one has been caught for a
moment only and is easily freed; RELEASE, that one has been
caught and held.

DISENTANGLE suggests that one is TANGLED, caught or snarled
up in something from which one can be set free only with
time and patience; while EXTRICATE suggests a pitfall or quagmire from which one must be pulled out.

555. *SEAMED*, seamed (*sēmd*) *adj.* Sewed together, stitched
        together, joined with a seam.
A SEAM, which goes directly back to an Anglo-Saxon word for
SEW, is a ridge formed by the sewing together of two pieces of
cloth. From this comes the figurative use of the word to mean
lined.

E. Chambers says: 'SEAMS of a ship are placed where her
planks meet and join together; they are always filled with a
quantity of OAKUM, and covered with hot pitch to prevent the
entrance of the water'.

556. *AFFRAY*, affray (*ăf-frā'*) *v.* To agitate, frighten, terrify, arouse, disturb, terrorize.

The verb to AFFRAY, which goes back through French with related words in Provençal, is to frighten, terrify, and more gently, to arouse, disturb, disquiet. The noun an AFFRAY is now a broil, scuffle, tumult, disturbance, brawl, public fight, noisy quarrel, a fight in a public place which terrorizes others. An AFFRAY differs from QUARREL in that it is always in a public place. BRAWL emphasizes noisiness and unbecoming character.

To 17 per cent of those tested the verb to AFFRAY means to SOOTHE. To SOOTHE, of Anglo-Saxon origin, is to prove true, confirm, verify, but has come to mean compose, tranquilize, pacify, ease, alleviate, an exact opposite of AFFRAY, frighten.

From E. Chambers: 'An AFFRAY differs from ASSAULT: An ASSAULT is of a private nature. An AFFRAY is a wrong to the public. In an AFFRAY a stroke must be given or offered or a weapon drawn.'

557. *SARDONIC*, sardonic (*sahr-dŏn'-ĭk*) *adj.* Bitterly ironic, derisive, sneering; a milder meaning is a forced smile not really coming from gaiety.

SARDONIC may come from the Greek σαρδάνιος (*sardanios*), bitter, scornful, used in a Greek phrase meaning bitter laughter; SARDONIC retains this conflict of bitterness and forced laughter.

SARDONIC is thought by 19 per cent to mean wicked, which is much too strong; and by another 17 per cent to mean SLY. SLY means crafty, meanly artful, insidious, cunning.

CUNNING, ARTFUL, SLY, SHREWD, TRICKY, WILY, and CRAFTY, all suggest underhand, deceptive. SARDONIC has no underhand implication but suggests sneering, a superior looking down.

558. *OPEROSE*, operose (*ō'-per-ōs*) *adj.* Laborious, tedious, troublesome, toilsome; Webster: attended with labor.

OPEROSE comes from the Latin *operosus*, giving much labor, costing much work, from *opera*, work, the feminine form of *opus*, *operis*, work. Among 29 high-vocabulary adults, 7 mark MUSICAL, perhaps because of the word OPERA, and the frequent use of OPUS in music, to mean a work in the sense of a musical composition, numbered in order for easy reference.

An OPERA is a musical drama enriched by magnificent scenery. Some say that it started with the Venetians. The unusual adjective OPEROSE comes from the same source, but means laborious, or according to Nathan Bailey: 'Costing much pain and trouble'.

559. CAMPANILE, campanile (kăm-pă-nē'-lā) n. An Italian bell-tower, belfry, steeple.

CAMPANILE, an Italian word pronounced with the Italian long Ā at the end, comes from the Latin *campana*, bell, from which comes CAMPANULA (kăm-păn'-ū-lah), the bell-flower, the diminutive of *campana*, bell.

STEEPLE, BELFRY, BELL TURRET, and CAMPANILE are all BELL-TOWERS. A STEEPLE, an Anglo-Saxon word, is always part of a building, and usually sharp pointed at the top. The word BELFRY goes back through Middle English to Old French, with related words in Dutch and German. A BELFRY was originally a wooden movable tower used in attacking a fortress, but is today almost any kind of tower which holds a bell. In medieval architecture the lower part of a BELL TURRET is often used as a staircase; and this leads 20 per cent to believe that CAMPANILE means STAIRCASE.

A MINARET corresponds to the CAMPANILE of a Christian Church, a slender tower rising in several stages with a balcony at each, from which criers summon worshippers to prayer.

CAMPANILE should be reserved for a free-standing Italian BELL-TOWER, near a church, but not part of it. The Leaning Tower of Pisa in Italy is a CAMPANILE.

560. JUDICATURE, judicature (jū'-dĭ-kā-tŭr) n. The power of administering justice, judicial authority, determination by trial.

JUDGE, the noun, comes from the Latin *judex, judicis*, one who declares the law, from *jus*, right, law, plus *dicere*, to say, declare. To JUDGE, the verb, comes from *judicare*, to decide, declare the law. JUDICATURE comes from the same Latin *judicare*.

JUDICATURE is a vague, general term. It may mean judicial authority, as used in this test item: 'Civil JUDICATURE', where the correct answer is AUTHORITY. Or it may mean the administration of justice; the extent of the authority of a judge; or even a body of judges.

561. *CIRCUIT*, circuit (*ser'-kĭt*) *n*. Boundary, circumference,
     outline, compass, contour, periphery, progress around.

To 9 per cent CIRCUIT means AREA, the space inclosed within a
circle, or inside other limits. Correctly used the CIRCUIT is the
boundary line, distance around any space, not the AREA; for
CIRCUIT comes from the Latin *circuitus*, a going around, the
past participle of *circuire*, a combination of *circum*, around,
and *ire*, to go, from the Greek ἰέναι (*ienai*), a going around,
circular journey.

E. Chambers says: 'CIRCUIT, of which there are six in England, is the journey or progress the judges take twice every
year through the several counties of England and Wales'.

562. *DATED*, dated (*dā'tĕd*) *adj*. Old-fashioned, out of date,
     past, obsolete, bygone, no longer in vogue.

From the Latin verb *dare*, to give, through *datum*, the neuter
of *datus*, the past participle, come both DATA and DATE. DATA,
the plural of DATUM, comes directly from the Latin *datum*, a
gift, present. Today a DATUM is a fact given, position of reference by which other positions are determined. As most experi-
ments need more than a single DATUM, the plural DATA is generally used.

Originally the DATE included both place and time, the DATA
needed, but now the DATE is more often the day, month, and
year only.

In numerous circumstances, as with rare paintings, old wines,
and first editions, a recorded DATE helps prove authenticity.
Thus PROVEN, selected by 3 per cent, is frequently a correct
interpretation; but DATED has come to mean not up to date,
but not old enough to be valuable.

563. *INTRACTABLE*, intractable (*ĭn-trăk'-tă-bl*) *adj*. Un-
     manageable, stubborn, refractory, obstinate, ungovernable,
unruly, wilful, uncontrollable.

INTRACTABLE comes from the Latin *tractus*, the past participle
of *trahere*, to draw, carry off, also to draw out, and so protract,
delay, the source of large groups of English words such as:
ATTRACT, CONTRACT, DETRACT, RETRACT, as well as TRACTOR, and
TRACTION.

To 14 per cent INTRACTABLE means UNBROKEN. INTACT, which means UNBROKEN, unimpaired, in good condition, comes from the Latin *intactus*, untouched, uninjured, a combination of *in-*, not, and the past participle *tactus* of *tangere*, to touch. This differs by only one letter from *tractus*, the source of INTRAC- TABLE, a combination of the Latin privative *in-*, not, and the adjective TRACTABLE, docile, pliant, easily led. This in turn comes from *tractabilis*, manageable, from the Latin *tractare*, to take in hand, and so manage, handle, the frequentative of *trahere*, to draw. But *tactus* is the past participle of *tangere*, to touch, so that INTACT means untouched; while *tractus* is the past participle of *trahere*, to lead, so that INTRACTABLE means not easily led.

On the other hand, another meaning of the verb to BREAK is to tame, train to obedience, make TRACTABLE, as: 'To BREAK a horse'. In this restricted sense UNBROKEN is a correct answer and must be removed in the next revision of the vocabulary test.

564. *CURATOR*, curator (*kū'-rā-tor*) *n.* Director; now spe-
    cifically one who has the care and superintendence of a
public museum or fine arts collection.
To the CURATOR of a University belonged at one time, accord- ing to E. Chambers, its direction, the administration of its revenue, and inspection of its professors.

CURATOR comes directly from the Latin *curator*, a guardian, trustee, manager, from *curare*, to take care of, the source of the verb to CURE, fundamentally to care for. Among the Romans, a CURATOR was an officer who regulates the price of all kinds of merchandise and vendible commodities. In Roman law, minors had TUTORS until the age of fourteen; and then between the age of fourteen and twenty-four they had CURATORS assigned them.

To 11 per cent CURATOR means ASSISTANT RECTOR, suggested by the word CURATE. A RECTOR, from the Latin *regere*, to rule, is one who governs, often an ecclesiastic at the head of a college. A CURATE (*kū'-rāt*) is properly a parson, or vicar of a parish, who has the charge or CURE of the parishioners' souls.

To another 11 per cent CURATOR means JANITOR. A JANITOR, porter, from the Latin *janitor*, a doorkeeper, from *janua*, a door, cares for buildings, keeping them clean and in order, much of the work of a museum CURATOR but at a lower vocabulary level.

565. *PLAINTIVE*, plaintive (*plān'-tĭv*) *adj.* Sad, mournful, melancholy, sorrowful, querulous, rueful, woeful.

To 20 per cent PLAINTIVE means INNOCENT. INNOCENT (*ĭn'-nō-sĕnt*), guiltless, sinless, faultless, unblamable, also harmless in effect, innocuous, comes from the Latin *innocens, innocentis,* harmless, blameless, upright, a combination of the Latin privative *in-*, not, and *nocens, nocentis,* the present participle of *nocere,* to hurt, harm. Though INNOCENT and PLAINTIVE differ in meaning, they have much the same intangible suggestion.

PLAINTIVE comes from the French *plaintif,* ending in F, which survives in the noun a PLAINTIFF, one who complains, one who begins a law suit, as opposed to the DEFENDANT. PLAINTIVE originally meant lamenting, complaining, repining, but has come to suggest a mournful expression of melancholy.

PLAINTIVE and QUERULOUS (*kwer'-ŏŏ-lŭs,* Phyfe says: not *kwer'-ū-lŭs*) agree in expressing weakness. The QUERULOUS person finds fault over trivial things in a weak, captious, tired way. PLAINTIVE involves regret, lamentation, A PLAINT, from the Latin *plangere,* to lament, beat the breast, is a lamentation, expression of sorrow, complaint.

566. *QUAFF*, quaff (*kwăf*) *v.* To drink, swallow in large drafts, also drink greedily.

By 27 per cent, more than a quarter, to QUAFF is thought to mean SMELL, perhaps a confusion of QUAFF with WHIFF.

QUAFF goes back to Early England but the exact derivation is unknown.

567. *CHANTRY*, chantry (*chăn'-trĭ*) *n.* A chapel attached to a church, originally a chapel endowed with a revenue for the maintenance of prayers.

CHANTRY, from the Latin *cantare,* to sing, the C of the Latin becoming CH when a word comes to English through French, at first meant singing, chanting the Mass, and then came to mean a gift to maintain daily singing for the soul of the donor. From this CHANTRY came to mean the chapel or part of a church endowed for this kind of singing. CHANTRIES of this sort were added to churches, or enclosed by screens within them for the erection of altars.

568. *TENABLE*, tenable (*tĕn'-ă-bl*) *adj*. Capable of being held,
     defensible, defendable, having a position which can be
maintained against an assailant, used of a theoretical stand justified in an argument.

From the familiar Latin verb *tenere*, to hold, keep, come TEN-
ACIOUS (*tĕn-ā'-shŭs*), holding fast, hanging on, persistent; a
TENANT, one who holds something, land, property, often under
a superior owner; LIEUTENANT, one who holds in LIEU of another, instead of another, in the place of another; and finally
the adjective TENABLE, as: 'A TENABLE position', one which can
be held.

569. *JURISPRUDENCE*, jurisprudence (*jū-rĭs-prū'-dĕns*) *n*.
     Knowledge of legal procedures, literally the science of
law, practice of law.

Of 28 high-vocabulary adults 3 select DECISIONS as the meaning
of JURISPRUDENCE, a confusion of words often associated in life,
used in the same situation, step two in the learning process.
A DECISION is the stated determination of a question, answer to
a doubt, final judgment, legal opinion in a case which has been
under discussion as: the decision of a court based on JURISPRU-
DENCE, a knowledge of law.

JURISPRUDENCE is a combination of the Latin *juris*, the genitive of *jus*, law, and *prudentia*, knowledge, skill, and so knowledge of law. Webster says: 'A knowledge of the laws, customs,
and rights of man in a state or community necessary for the due
administration of justice'; and he adds in his first edition, 1828:
'The study of JURISPRUDENCE next to that of theology is the
most important and useful to men'.

570. *MOGUL*, mogul (*mō-gŭl'*) *n*. One of the Mongol con-
     querers of India; one of their descendants down to 1857.
The name MOGUL was given to a follower of Baber (*bah'-ber*),
conqueror of Hindustan in the 16th century. The GREAT
MOGUL was the sovereign of the MOGUL empire of India from
1526 to 1857. During this period the Taj Mahal was built, in
the 17th century.

To 13 per cent of those who have tried this vocabulary test,
MOGUL means FARM-WORKER, and to another 13 per cent CHAIR-

COVERING. This last is probably the word MOHAIR ($m\bar{o}'$-$h\bar{a}r$), a cloth made from the hair of the Angora goat.

MOGUL, used in English and the European languages, is the Arabic and Persian form of MONGOL.

571. *FOREBODE*, forebode ($f\bar{o}r$-$b\bar{o}d'$) v. To announce beforehand, predict, presage, foretell, prophesy, augur, portend, prognosticate, foreshadow, betoken.

While PREDICT has no sense of good or bad, to FOREBODE is ominous, threatening, usually to PREDICT something evil to come, as from Matthew Arnold: 'My heart FOREBODES danger'.

To 13 per cent FOREBODES means BELIES. The verb to BELIE, which goes directly back to the Anglo-Saxon *be*-, about, by, and *leogan*, to lie, is to spread false reports, tell lies, calumniate. FOREBODE goes directly back to the Anglo-Saxon combination of *fore*, before, and BODE. To BODE, directly from the Anglo-Saxon *bodian*, to announce, tell, from an earlier *boda*, a messenger, once meant to announce, proclaim, preach, and although it has come to mean predict, augur, portend, FOREBODE should still suggest announcing ahead of time, and not merely knowing, foreseeing.

572. *NODE*, node ($n\bar{o}d$) n. A bump, projection, knot, swelling, knob.

To 12 per cent, NODE means DEPRESSION. A DEPRESSION is a hollow, sinking, from the verb to DEPRESS, a combination of the Latin *de*-, down, and *premere*, to press. A NODE, from the Latin *nodus*, knot, is a bump, knot, knob, protuberance.

The same word NODE, wandering from its original meaning, is used for the stationary point in a vibrating cord; and in astronomy for the point of intersection of two orbits.

573. *MANTLE*, mantle ($m\breve{a}n'$-tl) n. A cloak, loose sleeveless garment falling in straight lines from the shoulders.

Strictly a CAPE is circular and sometimes attached to a CLOAK. A MANTLE is long, almost to the ground, brought together and fastened at the neck, a single piece of cloth covering the arms.

To 25 per cent, one quarter of those tested, MANTLE means FIREPLACE; for MANTLE has two distinct meanings. In architecture, a MANTEL, ending according to modern usage in -EL, the older spelling of both words, is the lower part of the breast or front of a chimney, the decorative facing around the fireplace, including the MANTEL shelf when present, but strictly not the FIREPLACE itself.

MANTLE, by custom ending in -LE, and similar words in Spanish where *mantel* means a table-cloth, in French where *manteau* means a cloak, in Portuguese, and in Italian, all come from the Latin *mantellum*, a cloak, perhaps originally a combination of *manus*, hand, and *tela*, cloth, web, texture. A MANTLE in this sense was once a military habit worn by ancient cavaliers over their armor to preserve it from rust.

574. *MONSTROSITY*, monstrosity (*mŏn-strŏs'-ĭ-tĭ*) *n.* Deformity, not natural (v. b. 56) production, abnormality (v. b. 575), anything formed out of the common order of nature. The noun MONSTROSITY, ending in -ITY from a Latin termination added to an adjective to make the corresponding abstract noun, comes from the adjective MONSTROUS, and this in turn from the Latin *monstrum*, a portent, sign, marvel, from the verb *monēre*, to warn, foretell, advise. A MONSTER was originally anything extraordinary which could be interpreted as a divine omen of misfortune.

MONSTROSITY is thought by 19 per cent to mean WRETCHEDNESS. A WRETCH, from Anglo-Saxon, originally a banished person, outcast, exile, is a miserable person exposed to unavoidable suffering. WRETCHED, the adjective, means miserable, unhappy, forlorn; while WRETCHEDNESS is the quality, affliction. But the word WRETCHEDNESS was once used for that which was WRETCHED, for the thing. This meaning is obsolete, but WRETCHEDNESS is too near MONSTROSITY to use as a mislead in a vocabulary test. Strictly a MONSTROSITY is anything unusual, unnatural, out of the ordinary, but the word has come to suggest an unpleasant deformation, shocking production of nature.

575. *EXPIATION*, expiation (*ĕks-pĭ-ā'-shŏn*) *n.* Atonement, reparation, appeasement, making satisfaction.
Among 27 high-vocabulary adults 3 select EXPULSION as the meaning of EXPIATION. EXPATRIATION (*ĕks-pă-trĭ-ā'-shŏn*), from

the Latin ex-, out of, and *patria*, one's native country, father-land, is banishment and so EXPULSION, from the same ex-, out, and *pellere*, to drive.

REPARATION, literally a REPAIRING, from *parare*, to prepare, is a material making right. Both ATONEMENT and EXPIATION suggest a previous crime, fault, or guilt. ATONEMENT, AT-ONE-MENT, implies a reconciliation, a getting together as one, after a separation. EXPIATION, from the Latin *expiare*, to expiate, a combination of *ex*, out, and *piare*, to appease, from *pius*, pious, devout, the source also of PIETY and PITY, conveys a religious, moral feeling, implying a reconciliation with one's own conscience.

576. *EXTOL*, extol (*ĕks-tōl'*) *v.* To appreciate good qualities, praise strongly in words, applaud, laud, eulogize, celebrate, glorify, cry up, commend greatly, exalt in commendation.
EXTOL comes from the Latin *extollere*, to raise up, lift up, elevate, a combination of *ex*, out, and *tollere*, to raise.

Of 29 high-vocabulary adults, 2 select INFLAME as the meaning of EXTOL. To INFLAME is violent, to kindle, excite, aggravate, provoke. To EXHORT is to incite by words, stimulate, encourage. EXTOLLING may encourage by praise; but the meaning of EXTOL is to praise to excess.

577. *MAGUS*, magus (*mā'-gŭs*) *n.* with the plural MAGI (*mā'-jī*). A wise man, learned member of the priestly caste in ancient Persia.
MAGUS, spelt with a capital, is a Latin word, from the Greek μάγος (*magos*), spelt with a small letter, which means magician, wizard, enchanter. From this come MAGIC and MAGICIAN.

An ORACLE, marked by 16 per cent as the meaning of MAGUS, may be the utterance, often the prediction of some future event, or the person who utters the prediction. From this ORACLE has come to mean a wise person of great authority whose opinions are accepted, an exact synonym of MAGUS.

In Christian history the MAGI, sometimes called kings, came from the East to Jerusalem. In the Adoration of the MAGI, painted by Andrea Mantegna and now in the Uffizi, two of the MAGI are older men with beards, while one, the youngest, is dark, a Moor from northern Africa.

578. *BILK*, bilk (*bĭlk*) *v.* To defraud, cheat, swindle, deceive, cozen, sponge.

BILK is apparently slang, although its exact origin is unknown. To 20 per cent the verb to BILK means to REPLENISH, from the Latin *re*, again, and *plenus*, full, the source of PLENTY and PLENARY, full, complete, entire. To REPLENISH is literally to fill again, and so by suggestion an opposite of BILK, cheat, defraud.

To COZEN is to cheat by claiming falsely to be a cousin or relation of some sort. To SPONGE is to live meanly at the expense of others, to soak up what one can from others. SYCOPHANT, PARASITE, FAWNER, TOADY, TOAD-EATER, and FLUNKY, are various words for one who SPONGES. To BILK is to cheat, defraud, swindle.

579. *PUGILISTIC*, pugilistic (*pū-jĭ-lĭs'-tĭk*) *adj.* Fighting with the fists, boxing.

By 6 per cent of those tested, PUGILISTIC means VICIOUS. VICIOUS, from the Latin *vitium*, a fault, vice, imperfection, now means wicked, depraved, evil, bad, pernicious, addicted to vice; and in most parts of the world a PRIZE-FIGHT, a PUGILISTIC encounter, is illegal.

PUGILIST comes from the Latin *pugil*, a boxer, from *pugnus*, the fist, the source of PUGNACIOUS, contentious, quarrelsome, combative, disposed to fight. A PUGILIST is one trained, skilled in fighting with the fists as a type of sport.

580. *CATALEPTIC*, cataleptic (*kăt-ă-lĕp'-tĭk*) *n.* A person inflicted with attacks of abnormal muscular rigidity (v. B. 635), suffering from seizures connected with hysteria.

CATALEPTIC, the person, comes from CATALEPSY (*kăt'-ă-lĕp-sĭ*) the disease, a noun directly from the Greek κατάληψις (*catalepsis*), cataleptic, a grasping, seizing, a combination of κατά (*cata*), down, and λαμβάνειν (*lambanein*), to take.

CATALEPTIC is thought by 18 per cent to mean ACROBAT, a rope dancer, one who practises feats of agility, as tumbling, vaulting. ACROBAT comes from the Greek ἀκρόβατος (*acrobatos*), walking on tiptoe, a combination of ἄκρον (*acron*), the highest point, top, summit, and βατός (*batos*), going. ATHLETIC, somewhat like CATALEPTIC in sound, means strong, robust, vigorous, almost an opposite of CATALEPTIC.

581. *COLONNADE*, colonnade (*kŏl-ŏn-nād'*) *n*. A row of
    columns, peristyle, range of columns, any series of pillars
    placed at intervals from one another.
In a COLONNADE, from the Latin *columna*, a column, the columns
support a level beam running horizontally at the top. In an
ARCADE, a series of columns or piers support arches. A COLON-
NADE, or usually an ARCADE, often surrounds an open inner
COURT, and this leads 12 per cent to believe that COLONNADE
means COURTYARD; and the definition of COLONNADE from Nathan
Bailey, 1721, adds to this misconception: 'A range of pillars
running quite round a building and standing within the walls
of it'. A COURTYARD is an open area sometimes surrounded by
a building. A COLONNADE, row of columns, may extend across
one or more sides of such a COURTYARD, or may have no connection with a COURTYARD.
    E. Chambers' description ignores the possibility of a straight
COLONNADE or one within a building: 'A PERISTYLE of a circular
figure, a series of columns disposed in a circle, such as the COL-
ONNADE on the palace of Saint Peter at Rome, which consists of
284 columns of the Doric order, each about 4 feet and a half
in diameter'.

582. *ACCOLADE*, accolade (*ăk'-kō-lād*) *n*. Award, honor,
    embrace, commendation, prize, reward.
ACCOLADE, directly from the French *accolade*, an embrace, kiss,
from the Latin *ad*, to, and *collum*, neck, the source of the English
COLLAR, was originally an embrace.
    A CITATION is a reference to an author, title, and even page,
without however giving the exact words. A QUOTATION is an
actual repetition of something which has been said or written.
Thus a CITATION is almost a QUOTATION. Also in military circles
a CITATION has come to be a mention of outstanding bravery,
almost an ACCOLADE. This roundabout association, through the
word CITATION, may lead 15 per cent to select QUOTATION as
the meaning of ACCOLADE.
    Ephraim Chambers says of ACCOLADE: 'A ceremony anciently
used in conferring knighthood, literally denotes embrace or
hugging. At one time a blow with the flat of a sword on the
shoulder of a knight'.

583. DEXTER, dexter (*dĕks'-ter*) *adj.* Right, opposite of left, opposite of sinister.

DEXTER, the adjective, with the addition of the Latin ending -ITY, becomes the more common noun DEXTERITY, as the adjective VALID becomes the noun VALIDITY.

DEXTER, directly from the Latin *dexter*, on the right side, also handy, dexterous, comes in turn from the Greek δεξιτερός (*dexiteros*), right, also fortunate. From the same source comes DEXTEROUS, possessing manual skills, adroit, precise in action.

Were the idea the only important factor in determining the difficulty of a word then DEXTER should be as easy as the word RIGHT. But Latin words in general are less known than Anglo-Saxon. RIGHT is Anglo-Saxon, DEXTER of Latin origin.

DEXTER is thought by one quarter, 25 per cent of those who have been tested, to mean REVERSE. OBVERSE and REVERSE are the two sides of a coin; the OBVERSE side, the important side with the head, the REVERSE side, the other side. The front and back of a human being are known technically as VENTRAL and DORSAL. But in another sense the two sides of a human being, the RIGHT and LEFT, are DEXTER, right, and SINISTER, left.

584. COLLOQUIAL, colloquial (*kŏl-lō'-kwĭ-ăl*) *adj.* Characteristic of ordinary speech, vulgar, appropriate to familiar conversation; Webster (1828) says: pertaining to mutual discourse.

COLLOQUIAL comes from the Latin *colloquium*, conversation, a combination of *com*, together, which becomes COL- before another L, and *loqui*, to speak, the source of the English COLLOQUY (*kŏl'-lō-kwĭ*), a conversation, discussion, conference, dialogue, mutual discourse of two or more; LOQUACIOUS, talkative, garrulous; and a dozen other words.

Among 27 high-vocabulary adults, 6 select NEIGHBORLY as a synonym, a word with much the same connotation. The language spoken by neighbors is usually COLLOQUIAL; but a NEIGHBOR may be a recent arrival of foreign birth, who lives near but speaks no English. 'In large towns, a NEIGHBOR is one who lives within a few doors. In the country, a NEIGHBOR may live at a greater distance; and in new settlements, where the people are thinly scattered, a NEIGHBOR may be distant several miles'; according to Webster, in his first edition, 1828: 'Such is the use of the word in the United States'.

The distinction of words close in meaning but fundamentally different is the third step in learning. A NEIGHBOR lives near and may be one with whom one talks COLLOQUIALLY. But COLLOQUIAL means informal, appropriate to everyday conversation.

585. *ANTERIOR*, anterior (ăn-tē'-rĭ-ōr) adj. Going before in position, in front, fore, toward the beginning, earlier, preceding, placed ahead, prior, antecedent; according to Nathan Bailey, 1721: 'That is before the former'.

ANTERIOR is a Latin comparative adjective, from *ante*, before, as in ANTEROOM, a small room leading into another, and so before another, also ANTEDATE, to come earlier, before, prior to.

To 25 per cent of high-vocabulary adults ANTERIOR means OUTSIDE, the popular misconception. EXTERIOR, OUTSIDE, external, outward, comes from the Latin *exterior*, outer, outward, the comparative of *exter*, a combination of *ex*, out, and *ter*, another comparative suffix.

In the test phrase: 'The ANTERIOR position', a popular mislead is of course BACK, the opposite of the correct answer. POSTERIOR, situated behind, hinder, back, is the antonym of ANTERIOR.

Familiar pairs are EXTERIOR, outer surface, opposed to INTERIOR; SUPERIOR, and its opposite INFERIOR; ANTERIOR, in front, and POSTERIOR, behind. When used of time, ANTERIOR means happening before, not after. Used of location in space, it means in front.

586. *AGGRIEVE*, aggrieve (ăg-grēv') v. To oppress, injure, vex, harass, distress, afflict, bear hard upon.

To GRIEVE (grēv), through the French from the Latin *gravare*, to weigh down, oppress, from *gravis*, heavy, was originally to oppress, injure, cause grief. But this verb to GRIEVE has come to mean feel grief, mourn, sorrow, rather than to cause it. AGGRIEVE, from the same source, has retained the original strong meaning of oppress, injure, wrong, but is now commonly used in the passive, as: 'To feel AGGRIEVED', to feel injured or oppressed. AGGRAVATE, more directly from the Latin *gravare*, not through French, has taken on the active meanings.

NEGLECTED is selected by 22 per cent as the meaning of AGGRIEVED. To NEGLECT is to pay no attention to, disregard, ignore, fail to perform a duty. One who NEGLECTS parents or friends may injure their feelings, so that NEGLECT and AGGRIEVE are closely associated. But NEGLECT is the cause; to feel AGGRIEVED, as a result, is the outcome.

587. *GLOWER*, glower (*glow'-er*) *v.* To stare threateningly, frown, look angrily, scowl, glare severely, wrinkle the brows as in displeasure.

To 11 per cent GLOWERED means STARED, much too close to use as a mislead in a vocabulary test. To STARE, directly from Anglo-Saxon, is to gaze steadily with the eyes wide open, fasten a continued look on some object.

To GLARE, from the same Middle English as GLOWER, and related historically to Anglo-Saxon words for AMBER and GLASS, may mean to shine brightly, intensely; or to GLOWER, STARE.

Of the three verbs: to FROWN, to SCOWL, and to GLOWER, and the corresponding nouns all spelt in the same way, FROWN is the only one which can be used of intellectual perplexity, puzzlement, deep thinking. GLOWER is the fiercest, but with no real anger, threat, or sincerity back of the GLOWER.

588. *EXPEDIENT*, expedient (*ĕks-pē'-dĭ-ĕnt*) *adj.* Advisable, suitable for the purpose, proper under the circumstances, desirable, wise, useful, convenient, necessary, advantageous, profitable, conducive to self-interest for the time being.

The Latin *expedire* meant to bring forward, dispatch, be serviceable, profitable, advantageous, literally to free the foot from a snare, made up of *ex-*, out, and *pes, pedis*, foot, the opposite of IMPEDE (*ĭm-pēd'*), to hinder, delay, put obstacles in the way. From the present participle *expediens, expedientis*, comes EXPEDIENT; while from the past participle *expeditus*, comes EXPEDITE, to free the foot, remove obstacles and so push, quicken, accelerate, speed up, put forward, hasten, press, advance, drive, dispatch. This may lead 7 per cent to select FIRST as the meaning of EXPEDIENT. FIRST, from Anglo-Saxon, means initial, foremost, preceding, earlier, primary, as well as higher, chief. To EXPEDITE is to push forward, and so suggests placing FIRST.

The noun an EXPEDIENT, contrivance, device, way, means, indicates an artificial way of escaping a difficulty. When resources begin to fail, one has recourse to EXPEDIENTS, temporary measures.

589. *COMELY*, comely (*kŏm'-lĭ*) *adj.* Proper, suitable, fit, meet, appropriate (v. B. 265), becoming, convenient, seemly, decent.

COMELY, from an Anglo-Saxon word fit, comely, suitable, sometimes means pleasing in appearance, attractive, handsome, but more often becoming, and so seemly, proper, the meaning selected by 80 per cent of high-vocabulary students, but by only 33 per cent of students in general, including the top, as compared with 42 per cent who select EVERYDAY, ordinary, commonplace, daily. COMMONLY (*kŏm'-mŏn-lĭ*), much like COMELY in appearance, means generally, usually, ordinarily, and so EVERYDAY.

Despite popular vote against the historical meaning, COMMONLY means EVERYDAY, and COMELY should be taught as meaning beautiful, fine, or seemly, proper, and in a perfect language should be limited to the last, fit, suitable, the meaning of the Anglo-Saxon word from which it comes.

590. *CAPITAL*, capital (*kăp'-ĭ-tăl*) *n.* That part of the produce of industry available for further production; accumulation of past labor capable of being used in the support of present or future labors; all forms of wealth employed in future production; that part of wealth devoted to acquiring an income; money employed in carrying on a particular trade, manufacture, business, or undertaking; financial resources.

CAPITAL, with similar words in the Scandinavian languages, comes from the Latin *capitalis*, principal, chief, from *caput*, *capitis*, head. From the same source come CHATTEL, something one owns and so a form of CAPITAL, and CATTLE, one of the earliest forms of CAPITAL.

To 12 per cent CAPITAL means PROFIT. PROFIT is the excess of the selling price over the original cost, income, emolument, revenue returned, the gain resulting to the owner of CAPITAL from its employment in any enterprise.

E. Chambers says: 'CAPITAL in commerce is the fund or stock of a trading company or corporation. The sum of money put out to INTEREST. The same with PRINCIPAL, opposed to INTEREST.'

In terms of money, the difference between cost and selling price is PROFIT. If one puts part of this PROFIT aside to buy or build something else to sell, or to cover some future loss, that amount becomes CAPITAL. Grasping this sort of distinction is one of the reasons why top executives score higher English vocabulary than any other group tested.

591. *NUANCE*, nuance (*nū-ŏns'*) *n.* A shade of meaning, variation of a color, expression, feeling, shading, trace, trifle, delicate degree of difference.
NUANCE is a French word for shade, shading; and is used in English much like the word SHADE, in the phrase: 'A SHADE of difference'. The French NUANCE comes from *nuer*, shade, from *nue*, a cloud, and this in turn from the Latin *nubes*, cloud. A NUANCE is a delicate difference perceived by any of the senses.

H. W. Fowler, in his Modern English Usage, lists NUANCE among his French words and notes: 'To say a French word in the middle of an English sentence demands an acrobat's mouth'.

592. *ABERRATION*, aberration (*ăb-ĕr-rā'-shŏn*) *n.* An actual wandering, straying, roving, swerving, rambling, divergence, deviation, going out of the way, or lapsing from a sound mental state, derangement, departure from normal.
A SHORTENING, selected by 11 per cent, is an ABBREVIATION (*ăb-brē-vi-ā'-shŏn*), much like ABERRATION in sound. An ABBREVIATION is a contracting, curtailing, abridgement, condensation, reduction, compressing, epitomizing, from the Latin *brevis*, short. An ABERRATION is a wandering.

To another 16 per cent ABERRATION means UNCONSCIOUSNESS, near ABERRATION as applied to the mind. UNCONSCIOUSNESS is without feeling, without thought. ABERRATION is a wandering of thought.

ABERRATION comes from the Latin verb *errare*, to stray, the source of ERROR, a mistake, a straying from the truth; the verb to ERR, pronounced to rime with HER; and ERRANT, familiar in the phrase: 'Knight ERRANT', a wandering knight. Starting with the letters AB-, from, come the adjective ABERRANT ($\breve{a}$-$b\breve{e}r'$-$r\breve{a}nt$), wandering, straying from the course, differing from the group, and finally, ABERRATION.

The Encyclopedic Dictionary, volume I, 1888, says: 'SPHERICAL ABERRATION in optics is that wandering of the rays of light from the normal path which takes place when they are made to pass through curved lenses or are reflected from curved mirrors'.

593. *DESHABILLE*, deshabille ($d\breve{a}$-$sh\breve{a}$-$b\bar{e}l'$) *n.* Negligee, undress, careless attire, loose morning gown, half-clad.

DESHABILLE comes from the French *des-*, not, much the same as *un-*, not, in English, and *habiller*, to dress, the source of the English word HABILIMENT. DESHABILLE means not dressed.

To 30 per cent DESHABILLE means CONFUSION. This may be the word DISHEVELLED ($d\breve{i}$-$sh\breve{e}v'$-$\breve{e}ld$), which means literally with disordered hair, from the Latin *dis-*, apart, and *capillus*, hair; or it may be because the French word DESHABILLE has in it the implication of CONFUSION.

NEGLIGEE ($n\breve{a}$-$gl\bar{e}$-$zh\bar{a}'$) is a carefully arranged loose garment. DESHABILLE adds to NEGLIGEE a sense of confusion, disorder.

DESHABILLE is French, ánd if used at all should retain its French flavor. Some dictionaries are anglicizing the word, spelling it DISHABILLE and pronouncing it ($d\breve{i}s$-$\breve{a}$-$b\bar{e}l'$). LOOSE is Anglo-Saxon, and GOWN goes well back in English, though its origin seems uncertain. Use LOOSE GOWN or HALF DRESSED. Even with the authority of a recognized dictionary anglicizing the pronunciation of DESHABILLE gives an impression of ignorance.

594. *HYMENEAL*, hymeneal ($h\bar{\imath}$-$m\breve{e}$-$n\bar{e}'$-$\breve{a}l$) *n.* Marriage song.

As an adjective, the same word means pertaining to marriage, nuptial; connubial, matrimonial, conjugal.

The adjective MATRIMONIAL, and the noun MATRIMONY, from the Latin *mater*, mother, suggests married life. CONNUBIAL, from the Latin *nubere*, to marry, has something of the same suggestion. But NUPTIAL ($n\breve{u}p'$-$sh\breve{a}l$), directly from *nupta*, bride, with the past participle *nuptus*, of *nubere*, to marry, and HYMENEAL, both suggest the marriage ceremony, rather than married life later.

HYMEN (*hī'-mĕn*) comes from the Greek 'Υμήν (*Hymen*), the Greek god of marriage, in some legends the son of Bacchus and Aphrodite (Venus). HYMENEAL, as a noun, means specifically marriage song.

595. *QUAHOG*, quahog (*kwă'-hŏg*) *n*. The hard clam, as opposed to the soft clam.

To 14 per cent QUAHOG means PIGLET, a clear guess because of the -HOG at the end of the word.

The hard clam, the QUAHOG, which grows on the Atlantic coast of North America, is used as food and, by fishermen, as bait. Young clams, young QUAHOGS, are the LITTLE NECKS of New York. The hard shells of the QUAHOG were the WAMPUMS, shell beads, of the American Indians.

596. *SIMOON*, simoon (*sĭ-moon'*) *n*. A hot, suffocating, sand-laden wind of the desert, occurring in the deserts of Arabia, Syria, and northern Africa.

A TYPHOON, from an Arabic word meaning tempest, hurricane, is a violent STORM: and this leads 20 per cent to select STORM as the meaning of SIMOON.

The MONSOON, from a Portuguese word, which in turn comes from an Arabic word meaning time, season, is a seasonal wind of the Indian Ocean, blowing in one direction half of the year and in an opposite direction the other half. The SIROCCO (*sĭ-rŏk'-kō*) is an Italian wind much like the SIMOON, hot and dust-laden, blowing from Africa to Malta, Sicily, and Naples.

597. *TWADDLE*, twaddle (*twŏd'-dl*) *v*. To prattle, babble, gabble, tattle, prate idly, chatter foolishly, talk unmeaningly.

To 40 per cent TWADDLE means SWAY. To WOBBLE is to SWAY, totter, move from side to side.

PRATTLE is harmless, even if not pleasant. PRATING suggests boasting, talking above one's knowledge. CHAT is light conversation. CHATTER is incessant. BABBLE is foolish. TATTLE is gossip, blab, carrying tales, and breeds scandal. GABBLE is a contemptuous word, uttering the sound of a goose. TWADDLE, a variation of TWATTLE, which goes back to Icelandic and the Scandinavian languages, is silliness in talk.

598. *HURST*, hurst (*hĕrst*) *n.* A grove, thicket, coppice, woods.

Hurst goes directly back to the Anglo-Saxon *hyrst*, a grove, thicket, a spelling still seen on occasion in English today.

Hurst is thought by 20 per cent to be a MEETING. A TRYST is a MEETING, a Scotch variation of TRUST, usually pronounced (*trĭst*) today although the Century gives only (*trīst*). Phyfe gives (*trĭst*) first, and says that (*trīst*) is Scotch.

Some of these old words now rarely heard separately make current compound words more interesting when recognized as in ELMHURST or PINEHURST.

599. *SIBLING*, sibling (*sĭb'-lĭng*) *n.* A brother or sister, member of the family born to the same parents, a word invented by Karl Pearson by adding to SIB the diminutive -LING, as in DARLING, STRIPLING.

To 6 per cent a SIBLING is a PET. A PET is a tamed animal, a fondling, also a favorite child. A SIB, which goes directly back to an Anglo-Saxon word for relationship, is a relative, kinsman, kindred, person related by blood, a brother or sister.

CHILD, HEIR, OFFSPRING, stress the parent-child connection, the relationship between generations. SIBLINGS are of the same generation: two or more brothers, two sisters, or a brother and sister.

600. *ABROGATE*, abrogate (*ăb'-rō-gāt*) *v.* To abolish summarily, annul by an authoritative act, rescind, repeal, cancel, invalidate, disannul, dissolve, countermand, take away, make void a law, often as the act of a ruler, but sometimes of a representative body.

ABROGATE comes from the Latin *abrogare*, to annul, repeal, a combination of *ab-*, from, and *rogare*, to ask, also to propose a law, the source of ROGATION, the proposing of a law to be passed by the people; as well as INTERROGATION, a questioning, asking.

Among those tested, 10 per cent select TRANSFER, from the Latin *transferre*, to carry from one place to another; another 9 per cent GRANT; and 8 per cent EXTEND as meanings of ABROGATE, with no clear concentration on any one, indicating that these are guesses with little knowledge of its meaning.

From E. Chambers, 1728, comes as so often happens a nice distinction of related words. In Roman law, ROGATION was a demand by the consuls for a law to be passed by the people. REPEALING and REVOCATION, calling back, are opposites of ROGATION, and distinguished from DEROGATION (dĕ-rō-gā'-shŏn), which is taking away only some part of a law. SUBROGATION is adding a clause. DISPENSATION is setting a law aside in a particular instance. ANTIQUATION is refusing to pass a law; while ABROGATION is abolishing a law by the authority of its maker.

601. *CONSIGNEE*, consignee (kŏn-sĭ-nē') n. The person to whom goods are addressed, receiver, one to whom something is sent by carrier, a factor, one who has the care of goods received upon consignment.

The verb to CONSIGN comes from the Latin *consignare*, to sign, seal, attest, record, register, a combination of *com-*, together, and *signare*, to sign, to add one's SIGNATURE, the source also of RESIGN, to withdraw.

To CONSIGN was once to impress, seal with a stamp, but now means to make over to another, transfer, deliver into the possession of another.

To 19 per cent CONSIGNEE means SENDER. The ending -EE, of French origin, denotes the person to whom something is done, as opposed to -ER, the person who does something. An EMPLOYER, ending in -ER, hires; an EMPLOYEE is the person hired, who works for the EMPLOYER. The SENDER is the one who SENDS, mails, gives to a messenger; the CONSIGNEE is the one to whom something is addressed, sent, the receiver, as opposed to the SENDER.

602. *CORNICE*, cornice (kŏr'-nĭs) n. The top molding, ornamental molding running around the walls of a room just below the ceiling.

One kind of joint is the line at which the walls of a room meet the ceiling. The fact that a molding or CORNICE at the top of a room sometimes covers this JOINT between the wall and the ceiling, leads 13 per cent to select JOINT as the meaning of CORNICE.

CORNICE comes from the Greek κορωνίς (*coronis*), a wreath, garland, and so crown. The CORNICE is the crowning member. Of CORNICE E. Chambers says: 'In architecture, the uppermost member of the entablature of a column, that which crowns'. In classical architecture, the ENTABLATURE consists of three parts, called MEMBERS: the ARCHITRAVE, the FRIEZE, and at the top the CORNICE.

603. *TENOR*, tenor (*tĕn'-or*) *n.* Prevailing direction, usual course, tendency, drift, general purport, substance, uninterrupted sense; from Bailey: 'The substance of true intent or meaning of a writing'.

TENOR, from the Latin *tenor*, a holding on, from *tenere*, to hold, is that thought to which one holds throughout a conversation.

Of 28 high-vocabulary adults, 6 mark PERSONALITY as the meaning of TENOR, very close to correct. PERSONALITY is the essential character of a person, his qualities, endowments, individuality. Perhaps the difference is largely application. PERSONALITY is the essential quality of a living being; TENOR is the essential thought in a discourse.

604. *NEOLOGISM*, neologism (*nē-ŏl'-ō-jĭzm*) *n.* A new word, an original phrase, introduction of new words, use of new senses of old words.

The ending -ISM, the Greek ισμός (*ismos*), when added to a noun, suggests the teaching of the subject, its practice, theory, system, principle, doctrine. NEOLOGISM should be the practice of using new words, not the new word itself, but is used in both senses.

NEO-, the Latin *neo-*, from the Greek νέος (*neos*), new, appears in the chemical element NEON (*nē'-ŏn*), and in numerous compounds such as NEOCLASSIC.

The -LOG-, in the middle of NEOLOGISM, comes from λογια (*-logia*), from the verb λέγειν (*legein*), to speak, as in DIALOGUE, the talking of two persons; MONOLOGUE, the talking of one person; and PROLOGUE, something said in advance.

Among 29 high-vocabulary adults 3 select PICTURE-WRITING as the meaning of NEOLOGISM. A HIEROGLYPHIC (*hī-ĕ-rō-glĭf'-ĭk*), from the Greek ἱερός (*hieros*), sacred, and γλυφή (*glyphe*), a carving, is a picture of an animal, weapon, tree, or other familiar object, and so HIEROGLYPHICS is PICTURE-WRITING. NEOLOGY (*nē-ŏ'-lō-gĭ*) is the construction of new words, as in chemistry where the names of many elements are NEOLOGISMS.

605. *OPUSCULE*, opuscule (*ō-pŭs'-kūl*) *n.* A small literary
     work, sometimes of minor importance; also a musical
composition.

OPUSCULE, from the Latin *opusculum*, a little work, comes from *opus*, work, used without change in music to mean a composition, a work, and appears in music abbreviated Op. 22 (or some other number). The plural *opera*, a closely related word, appears in OPERATOR, one who works, in the verb to OPERATE, to work, and the noun OPERATION.

The Latin diminutive, -CULE, from *culus*, appears also in RETICULE, originally a net-work bag, the diminutive of the Latin *rete*, net; and, in the Latin form -*culum*, in CURRICULUM, a planned course of study in a college or university. From the same *currere*, to run, comes CURRICLE, a carriage with two wheels drawn by two horses. The diminutive ending -CULE, shortened to -CLE, forms the ending for ARTICLE, PARTICLE, CANTICLE and VENTRICLE.

Of 29 high-vocabulary adults, 3 mark BOIL as the meaning of OPUSCULE. A BOIL is a kind of sore, pimple, which contains PUS, thick matter which issues from wounds and sores. PUSTULOUS, full of blisters, is the corresponding adjective. But answers to the meaning of OPUSCULE scatter enough to suggest that they are largely guesses, rather than misunderstandings.

606. *PALTRY*, paltry (*păl'-trĭ*) *adj.* Trivial, mean, worthless,
     despicable, of little value, petty, insignificant, wretched.

To PALTER is to BABBLE, to talk in a trifling manner. PALTRY and PITIFUL apply to insignificant things, hardly deserving of consideration.

The mislead is RAGGED and, as so often happens, this is the meaning of the Scandinavian word from which PALTRY comes, rag, tattered, fragment, piece. A related German word means RAG; an old German word PALTRIC meant RAGGED; and a Danish word related to PALTRY means RAG.

607. *TAUNT*, taunt (*tawnt*) *n*. A bitter reproach, mocking
    words, invective, upbraiding, chaffing, deriding, ridicule.
To 10 per cent TAUNT means TENSION. TENSION is a bending
under pressure, against resistance, or a stretching out. TAUT,
without the N, is tight, TENSE, stretched, not loose, not limp.

The verb to TAUNT was once to tease, rally, but soon became
stronger and meant to tease spitefully, reproach with insulting
words. Bailey says of taunt: Reproachful abuses or biting jest.
To TAUNT: to joke sharply upon, revile, rail at.

Charles John Smith, an English clergyman, in his Synonyms
Discriminated of 1879, says: 'DERISION is ill-humored and scornful; it is anger wearing the mask of ridicule'. To MOCK, in its
strongest sense, expresses the next degree beyond DERISION, but
with less pretense of mirth. To FLOUT, to mock with energy or
abruptness, is the most intense of these vigorous words. To
DERIDE is hard and contemptuous. To TAUNT is to press facts and
accusations of a reproachful nature unsparingly with the aim
of shaming, and glorifying in the effect.

608. *CONTOUR*, contour (*kŏn'-toŏr*) *n*. Outline, periphery,
    profile, circuit, circumference.
From Ephraim Chambers, 1728: 'CONTOUR, outline; that which
terminates and defines a figure. A great part of the skill of a
painter consists in managing the CONTOURS. The CONTOUR of a
figure makes what we call the draught or design. The CONTOUR
of the face, the Italian painters ordinarily call the LINEAMENTS.'

CONTOUR is thought by 20 per cent to mean VOYAGE, trip,
cruise, tour. A VOYAGE was once any journey either by land
or sea, now an excursion by water only.

CONTOUR goes back through French to the Latin *com-* which
usually means with, but here merely intensifies the meaning,
and *tonare*, to turn. From this come the English noun, a TURN,
a short walk, promenade, and TOUR, a journey, usually to several
different places, and so a VOYAGE. A CONTOUR is not a TOUR,
journey, but a line.

By the top vocabulary group CONTOUR is thought to mean
SURFACE. A CONTOUR-LINE joins points of equal elevation, of
the same height above the sea and so defines a SURFACE; but a
SURFACE is an area. A CONTOUR is a line.

609. *TAWNY*, tawny (*taw'-nĭ*) *adj*. Tan, swarthy, fawn-colored, buff, ochre, dull yellowish in color; from Nathan Bailey, 1721: 'Of a TANNED, yellowish, dusky color'.

To 18 per cent TAWNY means STRONG, probably a confusion of TAWNY with BRAWNY, ending in the same last four letters. BRAWNY, which goes back to German, Dutch, and Anglo-Saxon words for roast meat, joint of meat, flesh for roasting, boar's meat, means muscular, bulky, firm, heavy, and so STRONG.

To another 17 per cent TAWNY means LEAN, thin. This may be the word SCRAWNY, wasted, meager, raw-boned, LEAN.

TAWNY goes back through French to the word TAN, the bark of various trees, as the oak and larch, used by TANNERS in the TANNING of hides to make leather. The same word TAN, brown, TAWNY, is the color of skin after days in the hot sun.

610. *INCULCATE*, inculcate (*ĭn-kŭl'-kāt*) *v*. To instruct, teach, inspire, instil; or according to Bailey, 1721: 'To repeat and insist upon a thing often, as it were to beat it into one's head'; or from Webster: 'To impress by frequent repetitions; to urge on the mind'.

Of 28 high-vocabulary adults 4 select ACQUIRE as the meaning of INCULCATE. To ACQUIRE, from the Latin *acquirere*, to get, obtain, from *quaerere*, to seek, the source of INQUIRE, REQUIRE, and QUERY, is to get, obtain permanently, an opposite of INCULCATE, in the sense of TEACH and LEARN. A teacher INCULCATES, drives home a lesson; a pupil ACQUIRES, learns.

INCULCATE comes from the Latin *inculcare*, to tread down, force upon, a combination of *in*, on, and *calcare*, to tread, from *calx*, heel, the source of RECALCITRANT, kicking against, refractory. To INCULCATE is by derivation to kick knowledge into another's head.

611. *BENEFICE*, benefice (*bĕn'-ĕ-fĭs*) *n*. A gift, grant of land, revenue from an ecclesiastical living; from Bailey, 1721: 'Originally signified funds given to soldiers as a reward for services; but it passed afterward into the Church, where funds were given for the subsistence of the clergy'.

BENEFICE comes from the Latin *beneficium*, a favor, kindness, from *beneficus*, kind, liberal, a combination of *bene*, well, and *facere,* to make, which so often becomes -FY at the end of a word, but occasionally -FICE, as in SACRIFICE, EDIFICE, and BENEFICE.

Of 27 high-vocabulary adults, 5 mark PATRIMONY as the meaning, the second step in the learning process, a confusion of words used in the same situation. Of PATRIMONY Bailey says: 'An inheritance or estate left by a father to his son'. A PATRIMONY is personal, individual, private.

Of BENEFICE, Webster, 1828, says: 'Literally a BENEFIT, advantage, or kindness. But in present usage an ecclesiastical living, a church endowed with a revenue for the maintenance of divine service, or the revenue itself.'

Ephraim Chambers is more technical: 'All Church preferments are called BENEFICES, except BISHOPRICS, which are called DIGNITARIES. But ordinarily the term DIGNITY is applied to BISHOPRICS, DEANERIES, ARCH-DEACONRIES, and PREBENDARIES; and BENEFICE to PARSONAGES, VICARAGES, and DONATIVES.'

612. *INTERNECINE,* internecine (*ĭn-tĕr-nē'-sĭn*) *adj*. Slaughtering, murderous, deadly, massacring, destructive; also mutually destructive.

CIVIL, underlined by 30 per cent, is chosen because of the INTER- at the beginning which actually adds little to the word. A CIVIL war is mutually destructive, INTERNECINE; but the word CIVIL means done by citizens, pertaining to the state, from the Latin *civis,* citizen. The phrase CIVIL WAR has come to mean a war between parties within their own country.

INTERNECINE comes from the Latin *inter-,* between, and *necare,* to kill, and ought to mean killing between states, between parties, between cities, but means merely destructive, deadly.

613. *ITINERANT,* itinerant (*ĭ-tĭn'-ĕr-ănt*) *adj*. Traveling, wandering, journeying, strolling, not settled, not rooted.

ITINERANT, from the Latin *iter,* a going, journey, also way, road, still used occasionally in English to mean a regular circuit, route traveled repeatedly, comes from the verb *ire,* to go. The Latin *iter* appears clearly in the English EXIT, a way out, or a going out; and in TRANSIT, familiar in the phrase RAPID TRANSIT, going quickly through a city. A CIRCUIT is a going around.

ITINERANT can be either noun or adjective. The word is not used of traveling for pleasure, or of an isolated trip, but exclusively of one who moves from place to place as a part of life or work, as: an ITINERANT judge, ITINERANT preacher, ITINERANT beggar.

To 10 per cent ITINERANT means PLANNING, suggested perhaps by the verb to ITEMIZE, to list ITEM by ITEM, not from *ire*, to go, but from the Latin *item*, likewise, also taken into English without change. To another 10 per cent ITINERANT means ROOTED, fixed, an opposite.

614. *PALE*, pale (*pāl*) *n.* An inclosure, court, corral (*kor-răl'*),
    stockade, cloister (v. b. 1926), courtyard, inclosed place, region within determined bounds.

To 30 per cent PALE means CASK, a water-tight container like a barrel, closed at both ends and made of wooden staves held together by metal hoops. A PAIL, a bucket for carrying water, pronounced like PALE but spelt with I, although now usually of metal, was originally made of wooden staves, much like a CASK in construction, but open at the top, and with a handle.

The word PALE, spelt with no I, comes from a different Latin source, from *pālus*, a stake, stay, prop, from the same original source as POLE (*pōl*). A PALE, in English, was first a stake, picket, pointed piece of wood driven into the ground. From this, PALE came to mean a fence or PALING made of PALES, of stakes close together; and then from this the area inclosed by a fence, PALE, or PALING.

615. *THANE*, thane (*thān*) *n.* A nobleman in Anglo-Saxon
    England, characterized by ownership of land; the meaning is nearly the same as that which KNIGHTHOOD developed after the Norman conquest.

Among the first 27 high-vocabulary examinees, 8 concentrate on PEASANT. A PEASANT may own land, but he is of a lower social class than a THANE. He is a countryman whose business is rural labor, one of a class of people of little education whose lives are devoted to cultivating the land.

THANE is the Anglo-Saxon word THEGN meaning nobleman. From J. R. Green: The Making of England comes: 'The king's THEGNS were his body-guards, the one force ever ready to carry out his will. They were his nearest and most constant counsellors. As the gathering of petty tribes into larger kingdoms swelled the number of earls in each realm, and in a corresponding degree diminished their social importance, it raised in equal measure the rank of the king's THEGNS. A post among them was soon coveted and won by the greatest and noblest.'

According to Webster, 1828, the THANES of England were formerly of some dignity; of these there were two orders, the king's THANES, who attended the Saxon and Danish kings in their courts and held lands immediately of them; and the ordinary THANES, who were lords of manors, and who had a particular jurisdiction within their limits. After the Conquest (1066), this title was disused, and BARON took its place.

616. *DECLAMATORY*, declamatory (dē-klăm'-ă-tō-rĭ) adj.
    Rhetorical, oratorical, stilted, ranting.

Of DECLAMATORY, Bailey says: 'Belonging to a DECLAMATION, a declaring, setting forth or shewing'.

Among 27 high-vocabulary adults 5 select DESCRIPTIVE, representing, depicting, delineating, from the Latin *describere*, to copy off, paint, sketch in writing, a combination of *de*, off, and *scribere*, to write. The Century Dictionary groups: DESCRIBE, NARRATE, PORTRAY, and EXPLAIN, all unemotional, factual.

The verb to DECLARE, the noun DECLARATION, and the unusual adjective DECLARATORY (dē-klăr'-ă-tō-rĭ), all come from the Latin *declarare*, to make clear, show, from *clarus*, clear. DECLARATORY and DESCRIPTIVE are practically synonymous.

But DECLAMATORY, with an M in place of R, comes from the Latin *declamare*, to DECLAIM, a combination of the Latin *de-*, used here to intensify the meaning, and *clamare*, to cry, shout, clamor. Of DECLAMATORY Webster says: 'Declaiming, declamation treated in the manner of a rhetorician, appealing to the passions, noisy, rhetorical without solid sense or argument'.

The difference between DESCRIPTIVE, from *scribere*, to write, and DECLAMATORY, from *clamare*, to yell, comes out clearly in the fourth precept of Robert of Sorbonne, founder of The Sorbonne: 'Write a résumé, for words which are not confided to writing fly as does dust before the wind'.

617. *DISPASSIONATE*, dispassionate (*dĭs-păsh'-shŏn-āt*) *adj.*
Free from passion, calm, impartial, unbiased, devoid of any personal feeling.
The popular mislead, selected by 25 per cent, is LISTLESS. To LIST, from Anglo-Saxon, is to listen, heed, pay attention. LIST-LESS means not heeding, not listening, not paying attention, without feeling, lacking desire for anything, apathetic, indifferent, without interests, somewhat the same in effect as DIS-PASSIONATE, except that LISTLESS is undesirable, a lack, weakness, indifference, while DISPASSIONATE is positive, resulting in fairness in a decision. The difference parallels that between UNINTER-ESTED and DISINTERESTED, often confounded even by contemporary dictionaries. An UNINTERESTED judge pays no attention, is bored, LISTLESS, not listening, and sacrifices his right to judge. A DISINTERESTED judge is not personally involved, not taking sides, impartial, DISPASSIONATE.

EMOTIONAL, selected by 15 per cent, not so intense as PASSION-ATE, is a closer opposite of DISPASSIONATE than PASSIONATE itself.

618. *CULL*, cull (*kŭl*) *v.* To gather, pick, collect, separate,
    select, single out, choose, opt, prefer, elect.
CULL comes from the Latin *colligere*, from *com-*, together, and *legere*, to gather, the source of COLLECT, and a doublet of COIL, originally to pick and choose, and so a synonym of CULL. But COIL, pronounced to rime with OIL, has come to mean gather a rope together into rings.
To 9 per cent CULL means SHELL. The noun HULL, meaning SHELL, husk, skin, covering, case, sheath, like CULL except for the first letter, goes directly back to Anglo-Saxon. From this comes the verb to HULL, to SHELL.
To another 19 per cent the verb to CULL means to CONSIDER. To CONSIDER, a combination of *con-*, and *sidus*, star, constellation, is to regard, contemplate, look attentively, view with care. To CULL is to pick and choose after CONSIDERATION. CON-SIDERING comes first, looking at, regarding. Then comes CULLING, actual selecting, gathering together.

619. *PARBOILED*, parboiled (*pahr'-boild*) *adj.* Boiled slightly,
    partially boiled, cooked to a moderate degree, half boiled.

To 20 per cent PARBOILED means DOUBLE-BOILED, the initial meaning, for the verb to PARBOIL comes from the Latin *per*, completely, thoroughly, utterly, as in PERFECT and PERVADE, and to
PARBOIL once meant to boil thoroughly, an opposite of the
modern BOIL SLIGHTLY.

The most common misconception of many words today is
their exact opposite; and this helps to explain why a word such
as PARBOIL has shifted in the past to an opposite of its first
meaning.

620. *RIFE*, rife (*rīf*) *adj.* Great in quantity, abundant, plentiful,
    rich, replete, filled, well supplied, prevalent, widespread,
numerous.

To 10 per cent RIFE, from Anglo-Saxon and Icelandic, means
WILD. WILD, from Dutch and German, may mean unrestrained,
not cultivated, and so suggest abundant; but WILD means uncontrolled, unbridled. RIFE means full, plentiful. An opposite
of WILD is CULTIVATED; an opposite of RIFE is SCARCE.

Among a dozen illustrations of RIFE from literature, each one
is poetry.

621. *RESPITE*, respite (*rĕs'-pĭt*) *n.* Pause, interval of rest, stop,
    stay, cessation, adjournment, recess, temporary intermis-
sion of labor.

To 38 per cent RESPITE means ILL WILL, malevolence, rancor,
grudge, animosity, enmity, a disposition to thwart the wishes
of another. DESPITE (*dĕs-pīt'*), from the Latin *de-*, down, and
specere, to look, which originally meant looking down upon,
scorn, contempt, malignity, extreme malice, has lost its initial
DE- by a process called APHERESIS, and is now SPITE, ILL WILL.

RESPITE, from the Latin *respectus*, consideration, respect, is a
combination of *re*, back, and the same *specere*, to look at, see.
RESPITE once meant respect, regard, attention, an exact opposite
of DESPITE. But RESPITE has lost its first meaning, and is now a
pause from work, short rest in labor.

622. *DESCANT*, descant (*dĕs-kănt'*) *v.* To comment, expound,
    continue discourse, make remarks about, conduct a dis-
quisition on a series of subjects.

DESCANT is thought by 18 per cent to mean PONDER, think, consider, contemplate, from *pendere*, to weigh, the source of PENDENT. To COMMENT, from the same origin as the word MIND, is to talk thoughtfully on a subject in a few words. To EXPOUND, from *ponere*, to put, place, is to lay out elaborately, put forth at length, COMMENT in detail, still with the idea of talking thoughtfully. DESCANT comes from the Latin *dis-*, away, apart, and *cantare*, to sing, the source also of INCANTATION, a magical combination of words, and the verb to ENCHANT, which comes to English through French where the Latin C changed to CH. To DESCANT is to talk at length, without much thought, using numerous words and phrases for the same idea.

623. *COMPOSITE*, composite (*kŏm-pŏz'-ĭt*) *adj.* Made up of distinct parts, put together, united, compounded of elements so combined as to manifest diversity of origin.

COMPOSITE, from the Latin *compositus*, the past participle of *componere*, to put together, is a combination of *com-*, together, and *ponere*, to put, place, the source of OPPOSITE, and APPOSITE. Starting with the Latin *ob-*, before, against, OPPOSITE means set in front, face to face, across from. APPOSITE means suitable, fit, appropriate, pertinent, applicable, well adapted, as: 'APPOSITE to the circumstances'; and this may lead 7 per cent to believe that COMPOSITE means WELL-DESIGNED. Also the noun, a COMPOSITION (*kŏm-pō-zĭ'-shŏn*), originally something put together, and the verb to COMPOSE, fundamentally to put together, are used to imply well put together, and so WELL-DESIGNED. But the adjective COMPOSITE means merely put together, with no judgment expressed as to the outcome.

624. *FEINT*, feint (*fānt*, with the same long Ā as in VEIL, VEIN, and DEIGN) *n.* In fencing, a false attack, pretense, simulation, motion made to deceive an adversary, apparently aiming at one point when another is the real goal. In the corresponding verb, to FEIGN (*fān*), the G is a recent insertion.

The Latin *fingere*, to finger, handle, touch, came to mean to shape, form, mold, and so to form in the mind, imagine, conceive, devise. From this the verb, to FEIGN, came to mean invent, and then to invent falsely, deceitfully, pretend, profess.

To 27 per cent FEINT means SIDE-STEP, stepping aside, the reaction to a real thrust which follows the FEINT.

From E. Chambers: 'A FEINT is a show of making a stroke or push, with design to bring the enemy to guard that part, and leave some other part unguarded where the stroke is really intended'.

625. *EWER*, ewer ($\bar{u}'$-$\breve{e}r$) *n.* Pitcher, beaker, large water pitcher with a wide spout, used with a basin.

EWER goes back through Middle English to Anglo-French. The word is little known in the United States. With the four misleads: BOWL, closely associated with EWER; PLATE; ALE; and STEEL-PIN, because of SKEWER; each attracts 11 per cent.

626. *RUNE*, rune (rōon) *n.* One of the twenty-four letters of an early Scandinavian alphabet; also mystic sentence, obscure saying, early rime.

The RUNIC language and letters of the ancient Goths, Danes, and other northern nations, which date back to the third century, were first cut as furrows or channels in wood or stone. Some RUNES, or letters of this alphabet, seem related to Greek, others to Latin. Whatever its origin, the RUNES were an alphabet used in Denmark, Norway, and Sweden, from the third century to 800 A.D., or later in remote spots.

Of 28 high-vocabulary adults, 5 select STEPS as the meaning of RUNE. The noun a RUN (rŭn), pronounced to rime with FUN and GUN, may mean a trip, journey from some specific place to another, and this may suggest a step in a larger enterprise. Here the plural is RUNS. RUNE, meaning a letter, is spelt with an E at the end, pronounced to rime with MOON and NOON.

627. *SEQUEL*, sequel (sē'-kwĕl) *n.* That which follows, continuation, succeeding part.

A large family of English words, including SEQUEL, come directly from the Latin *sequi*, to follow, such as the adjective SUBSEQUENT, following after; CONSEQUENCE, following as a result; and SEQUENCE, following in order.

To 11 per cent a SEQUEL is a DUPLICATE. A DUPLICATE, from *plicare*, to fold, is a copy, a double, repetition of the first, one of a pair. The DUPLICATE of a book is a SECOND book like the first. The SEQUEL to a book is its continuation, different from the first.

628. *ENNUI*, ennui (*ŏn-wē'*) *n.* A weariness of mind due to lack of interest, boredom, tedium, lassitude, exhaustion, life languor.

Of the pronunciation Phyfe says: 'Although ENNUI has long been used in English it has not been naturalized in pronunciation'. Pronounce the first two letters as in: ENCORE, and accent the final syllable.

FATIGUE results from hard honest labor and vanishes with rest. WEARINESS comes with lack of sleep and with age, and leads 11 per cent to select WEAKNESS as the meaning of ENNUI. WEAKNESS is negative, the antithesis of STRENGTH. 'The dreadful disease of ENNUI, of life weariness, attacks all who have no aims, no permanent purpose', writes James Freeman Clarke, born in 1810, of whom the Encyclopaedia Britannica comments: 'Few Americans have done more to give breadth to the published discussion of religious philosophy'.

For a delightful intellectual discussion against the use of most French words read the pages: French Words, in his book Modern English Usage by H. W. Fowler. ENNUI, which goes back to an old French word, the source of the English ANNOY, expresses a kind of languor found among those who use French words at random.

629. *PHILOLOGY*, philology (*fĭ-lŏl'-ō-jĭ*) *n.* Love of learning, study of literature, according to Bailey: 'The study of humanity, or skill in the liberal arts and sciences'.

PHILOLOGY comes from the Greek φιλόλογος (*philologos*), fond of words; from φιλεῖν (*philein*), to love, and λόγος (*logos*), word, speech, discourse.

Of 28 high-vocabulary adults, 22 select LEARNING as the meaning of PHILOLOGY; but 3 choose SCIENCE and 2 others POETRY, both of which Ephraim Chambers includes in his discussion of PHILOLOGY: 'PHILOLOGY, a science, or rather assemblage of several sciences, consisting of grammar, rhetoric, poetry, antiquities, history, and criticism.

'PHILOLOGY is a kind of universal literature, conversant about all sciences, their rise, progress, authors who have cultivated them, etc.

'In the university it is also called the HUMANITIES'. This appeared in Ephraim Chambers' Dictionary of 1728.

630. *CADENCE*, cadence (*kā'-dĕns*) *n*. General modulation of tones, fall of the voice in reading, concluding part of a melody; Bailey, 1721, says: 'A just fall of the tone or voice in a sentence; a kind of conclusion of the tune made of all the parts together, in divers places of any key'. Webster, 1828, says; 'A fall of the voice in reading or speaking or at the end of a sentence; also the falling of the voice in the general modulation of tone in reciting. The ordinary CADENCE is a fall of the last syllable of a sentence.'

CADENCE and CHANCE are doublets, both coming from the Latin *cadens, cadentis*, the present participle of *cadere*, to fall, CHANCE coming through French where it gained the CH- at the beginning, and CADENCE coming more directly from Latin. CHANCE was once the fall of dice, and so risk, hazard, uncertainty.

CADENCE and DECADENCE (*dĕk'-ă-dĕns*) are both a falling off, DECADENCE a deterioration, decay, often of a civilization or of some human effort, perhaps in art. (Of the pronunciation W. H. P. Phyfe says: *dē-kā'-dĕns*, not *dĕk'-ă-dĕns;* but H. W. Fowler says: *dĕk'-ă-dĕns*.) CADENCE is used most often in a pleasant sense for the fall of the voice in reading or of a sequence of chords expressing a conclusion occurring at the end of a phrase or period.

Among high-vocabulary adults, 21 per cent choose MONOTONY as the meaning of CADENCE, the popular misconception. MONOTONY comes from the Greek μόνος (*monos*), single, and τόνος (*tonos*), tone, sameness of tone, want of modulation, the confusion of a word with its opposite, the final step in learning, for the Century Dictionary defines MONOTONY as lack of CADENCE.

631. *AQUAGE*, aquage (*ā'-kwāj*) *n*. Any natural water course, gentle brook, quiet river, mill-stream before the pond. AQUAGE comes from the Latin *aqua*, water, as do all English words beginning with AQU-, and not with ACQU-, the more

frequent start. The -AGE comes from the Latin verb *agere*, to do, make, manage, lead, the source of AGENT, one who does. An AQUEDUCT is a more formal water course, built artificially for conducting water.

MEADOW, the popular mislead selected by 16 per cent, and directly from Anglo-Saxon, is any piece of grassland, pasture, low level tract, with much the same pleasant sunny suggestion as AQUAGE, a stream running perhaps through a MEADOW.

632. *BLOWZY*, blowzy (*blow'-zĭ*) *adj*. Unkempt, disheveled, sloppy in appearance; also high-colored, fat and red faced in an unattractive way, ruddy, ruddy-faced.

To 32 per cent BLOWZY means LOOSE-FITTING, suggested perhaps by the word BLOUSE, which is always loose fitting, a word which seems to have no connection with BLOWZY, despite the similarity in sound. Also LOOSE-FITTING has something of the same suggestion as DISHEVELED, unkempt.

UNKEMPT means literally uncombed; for KEMPT, combed, is the past participle of an obsolete verb to KEMB, to comb.

DISHEVELED, through French from Latin, applies by derivation to neglected hair. BLOWZY is more complete and unpleasant, generally sloppy in appearance.

A BLOWZE was originally a beggar's wench, and then became any fat-faced woman. Today the adjective BLOWZY suggests fat, red-faced, and disheveled.

633. *ALLEGORICAL*, allegorical (*ăl-lē-gŏr'-ĭ-kl*) *adj*. Figurative, symbolic, veiled, suggested by analogy, described by resemblance, pertaining to an allegory.

An ALLEGORY is a sentence, discourse, or narrative, relating to material things but intended as an exposition of spiritual thoughts, though not expressly mentioned.

ALLEGORICAL, from the Latin *allegoricus*, comes from the Greek ἀλληγορία (*allegoria*), a description of one thing under the image of another, a combination of ἄλλος (*allos*), other, and ἀγορεύειν (*agoreuein*), to speak, from ἀγορά (*agora*), the market place, public square for popular assembly and discussion.

To 7 per cent ALLEGORICAL means RECORDED. Today the verb to RECORD (*rē-kord'*) means to write down, note, inscribe in a book, preserve in writing; but once meant to remember, recall, bear in mind.

E. Chambers says: 'Divines find divers senses in Scripture as literal, mystical, and ALLEGORICAL. ALLEGORY, a figure in rhetoric, whereby we make use of terms which, in their proper signification, mean something else than what they are brought to describe; or it is a figure whereby we say one thing, expecting that it shall be understood of another, to which it alludes. Horace uses the word SHIP to stand for the REPUBLIC; WAVES for CIVIL WAR; PORT for PEACE; OARS for SOLDIERS; and MARINERS for MAGISTRATES.'

634. *TACTFUL*, tactful (*tăkt'-fŭl*) *adj.* Courteous, perceptive, discerning, considerate, discreet, intuitive, adroit, clever, avoiding giving offense.

To 19 per cent of those tested TACTFUL means GRACEFUL. GRACEFUL, elegant, applies particularly to motion, looks, whole appearance. GRACE, from the Latin *gratia*, favor, esteem, from *gratus*, beloved, dear, is that quality of form, manner, movement, carriage, deportment, language, which renders it elegant and beautiful. GRACE is inherent. TACT is more superficial.

TACT comes from the Latin *tactus*, sense of touch, nice feeling, the past participle of *tangere*, to touch. Nathan Bailey gives: INTACT, untouched, uninjured; TACTILE, that may be touched; CONTACT, the touch or touching. TACT was once an actual touching but has come to mean mental perception, intuitive sense of what is proper, fineness of discernment, adroitness, address, cleverness. TACT is the noun. TACT plus the Anglo-Saxon -FUL, added to a noun to form the corresponding adjective to mean full of, becomes TACTFUL.

635. *PORTENT*, portent (*por'-tĕnt*) *n.* Indication, omen, sign, symptom, prognostication, prediction, token, suggestion, hint, precursor, harbinger.

REASON, the popular mislead, may be the cause of something happening, and may at the same time be an indication in advance that it will happen. But PORTENT, omen, sign, stresses the indication in advance and need not be the cause of the happening, its REASON. Every scientist and every clear thinker must distinguish that which happens before some occurrence from that which causes it. Darkness may be the PORTENT of a coming storm, but darkness does not cause the storm, is not the REASON.

636. *SUBSIST*, subsist (*sŭb-sĭst'*) *v.* To remain, continue to live, retain the present existing state of life, exist.

The Latin verb *sistere*, to place, set, is the causal form of *stare*, to stand, and means to make stand, cause to stand. To RESIST is to stand against. To DESIST is to stop, cease from some action. To EXIST is to stand forth, live, have being. To SUBSIST is to continue to exist, retain the present state. SUBSISTENCE refers to food only, to bare living, enough to keep one alive; and the verb SUBSIST has this suggestion.

The Rev. Thomas R. Malthus in his Essay on Population, first published in 1798, uses the noun SUBSISTENCE repeatedly to mean just enough to keep life going: 'Population limited by the means of SUBSISTENCE', 'Scanty means of SUBSISTENCE', 'Absolutely necessary for the annual SUBSISTENCE of the tribe', 'A scarcity of SUBSISTENCE'.

637. *DECLIVITY*, declivity (*dē-klĭv'-ĭ-tĭ*) *n.* Slope, descent, downward inclination, steepness, that part of a mountain on one side or the other of a crest.

DECLIVITY goes back to the Latin *de-*, down, and *clivus*, a hill, slope, the source of ACCLIVITY and PROCLIVITY. An ACCLIVITY is an upward slope, ascent, and in this sense an opposite of DECLIVITY, a downward slope.

To 14 per cent DECLIVITY means TENDENCY. From the Latin *pro-*, forward, and *clivus*, and so literally a slope forward, PROCLIVITY has come to mean an inclination, bias, bent, predisposition, aptitude, TENDENCY. DECLIVITY, though from the same source, is never used in this way. DECLIVITY, which corresponds to the verb DECLINE, should be used only of a physical downward slope.

638. *DILATORY*, dilatory (*dĭl'-ă-tō-rĭ*) *adj.* Slow, tardy, delaying, deferring, lagging, lingering, loitering, sluggish, dawdling, inactive, not prompt, given to procrastination.

DILATORY comes from the Latin *dilatus*, easy to think of as a combination of *di-*, which represents the negative *dis*, not, and *latus*, the past participle of the irregular verb *ferre*, to carry. Thus *dilatus* is not carried; and DILATORY is delaying, lagging.

To 14 per cent DILATORY means INDUSTRIOUS, a confusion of opposites, the fourth and last step in learning; for INDUSTRIOUS, from the Latin *industrius*, diligent, active, means working with diligence, busy, occupied, active, attentive, productive, sedulous, hard working.

To another 11 per cent DILATORY means PROMPT, another opposite. Both DELAY, from the same *latus*, and DEFER, from the same *ferre*, mean more specifically put off, postpone; while DILATORY combines the ideas of not working and delaying, not being INDUSTRIOUS, and not being PROMPT.

639. *MACROGRAPHY*, macrography (*mă-krŏg'-răf-ĭ*)   *n.*
Abnormally large handwriting, forming unusually large letters.

MACRO-, from the Greek μακρός (*macros*), means large, great, long. From this word comes MACRON (*măk'-rŏn*), the horizontal line written over a vowel to indicate a long sound: Ā, Ē, in pronunciation.

The ending -GRAPHY, from the Greek γραφία (*graphia*), from γράφειν (*graphein*), to write, draw, mark, appears at the end of many words as: GEOGRAPHY, drawing, writing, study of the earth; BIOGRAPHY; TOPOGRAPHY; and others.

MACROGRAPHY is a medical psychiatric term. MACROGRAPHY, this strangely large handwriting, is believed to indicate an abnormal personality.

The mislead BLOW-UP, which attracts 30 per cent, may result from the great nuclear explosions.

640. *INCULPATORY*, inculpatory (*ĭn-kŭl'-pă-tō-rĭ*)   *adj.*
Incriminating, censurable, imputing blame, reprehensory, culpatory, blameworthy.

The Latin *culpa* is a fault, and *culpare* is to blame, censure. From these come the English CULPABLE, faulty, deserving blame, blameworthy; CULPRIT, a guilty person, offender; and the verb to INCULPATE (*ĭn-kŭl'-păt*), to charge with a fault, accuse, blame. INCULPATORY, from the Latin *inculpare*, is the adjective.

The popular mislead, marked by 20 per cent, is FLIMSY, fragile, unsubstantial, trivial, not solid, almost IMPALPABLE, perhaps the word in the minds of those who mark FLIMSY as the meaning of INCULPATORY.

641. *LADRONE*, ladrone (*lă-drōn'*) *n.* A robber, freebooter, highwayman, brigand, mercenary, bandit, corsair.

LADRONE comes through the Spanish *ladron,* from the Latin *latro, latronis,* bandit, robber, mercenary. A LADRONE was at first a hired servant, then a mercenary soldier; and from this came to mean bandit, highwayman. From the same Latin *latro,* robber, came LARCENY, taking money or the personal property of another and using it for one's own benefit.

Of the misleads, LABORER attracts 15 per cent. A DRONE, of Anglo-Saxon origin, connected with LADRONE, is the stingless male of the honey bee, one who does nothing, and so an indolent person, idler, sluggard, the opposite of a LABORER. A DRUDGE is a hard worker at a wearisome task.

A PICARO (*pē'-kă-rō*) is a horse-thief; a PICAROON (*pē-kă-rōon'*) is one who lives by his wits; a LADRONE is simply a brigand, bandit, robber.

642. *QUATERNION*, quaternion (*kwă-tĕr'-nĭ-ŏn*) *n.* A set of four.

QUATERNION comes from the Latin *quaternio, quaternionis,* the number 4 or a group of four, from the Latin *quattuor,* four, the source of the English words QUART, the fourth of a gallon, and QUIRE. A QUATERNION is any set of 4, a group of four things, a body of four persons. In mathematics a QUATERNION is an expression containing four unknowns.

A QUIRE was originally a set of 4 sheets of parchment folded so as to make eight leaves but the word has come to be used for twenty-four sheets of paper.

QUATERNION is thought by 16 per cent to mean COURTYARD. A QUADRANGLE is an oblong court surrounded by buildings; from the Latin *quadrus,* square, and *angulus,* an angle, corner, the source of the English word ANGLE. A QUADRANGLE was originally a four-cornered figure. The word QUADRILATERAL is now more common and QUADRANGLE is used for a COURTYARD.

643. *VOLUBILITY*, volubility (*vŏl-ū-bĭl'-ĭ-tĭ*) *n.* Excessive
fluency, glibness, loquacity, quickness of speech, readiness
of utterance, unchecked flow of talk; according to Nathan
Bailey: 'A round delivery, easy pronunciation'.
VOLUBILITY, through the Latin *volubilis*, whirling, turning
around, comes from *volvere*, to turn around, from *volve*, which
appears in REVOLVE, to turn.

One of the obsolete meanings of VOLUBLE is changeable,
mutable, and this leads 7 per cent to select FICKLENESS as the
meaning of VOLUBILITY. FICKLE, originally deceitful, false,
treacherous, from an Anglo-Saxon word meaning deceitful,
now means unstable, inconstant, variable, changeable, easily
persuaded to alter one's mind, another instance of an obsolete
meaning surviving in everyday language.

644. *OFFICIOUS*, officious (*of-fĭsh'-ŭs*) *adj.* Meddlesome, ob-
truding uninvited in the affairs of others, over-zealous in
interfering, over-attentive.
To 23 per cent OFFICIOUS means WORKING, laboring. The verb
to OFFICIATE, from the Latin *officium*, duty, office, is to perform
OFFICIAL duties, formal acts, render useful help, and so WORK.
But OFFICIOUS, although from the Latin *officiosus*, dutiful, obliging, originally courteous, attentive, friendly, has come to mean
interfering in the affairs of others, meddling, too eager to give
unwanted help.

IMPERTINENT is pushing forward, often with intruding curiosity. OFFICIOUS is the same kind of pushing forward to offer
help, but stresses the fact that such assistance is neither wanted
nor needed.

645. *CANNILY*, cannily (*kăn'-nĭ-lē*) *adv.* Cleverly, knowingly,
   warily, cautiously, prudently, cunningly, craftily, watchfully.
To 15 per cent CANNILY means INSTINCTIVELY, much too close
to call wrong, except that INSTINCTIVELY means naturally, while
CANNILY suggests experience. INSTINCT is a gift for gaining a
result apparently without reason or knowledge. CANNILY suggests knowledge, skill, experience, and in this sense is almost
opposed to INSTINCTIVELY.

CRAFTILY, CUNNINGLY, and even CLEVERLY may all suggest skilful, and so a bit dishonest. CANNILY, a Scotch word of which little is known, is always in commendation.

646. *WOOF*, woof (*wŏof*) *n.* Cross threads, weft, carried by the shuttle back and forth across the warp.

WOOF comes directly from an Anglo-Saxon word meaning to weave. The WOOF is the thread that weaves its way in and out, above and below the fixed stretched WARP threads.

To 10 per cent WOOF means VERTICAL LINES. When a loom stands up and down, as do some of the smaller hand looms, the vertical up and down lines are the WARP. WARP comes directly from an Anglo-Saxon word meaning to throw, pass, and by derivation the WARP should be the thread thrown across, but through some confusion of the past, similar to modern confusions, WARP has come to be the upright threads, while WOOF is the thread thrown across.

647. *DALLIANCE*, dalliance (*dăl'-lĭ-ăns*) *n.* Idle talk, chat, gossip, a trifling away of time, idle loitering.

DALLIANCE goes back to Old English *dalien*, to dally, plus -ANCE, a Latin ending, added usually to an adjective to form a noun, but sometimes as here added to a verb. To DALLY is to linger, loiter, delay, procrastinate, to play with a subject which one does not intend to take seriously.

The colloquial verb to DAWDLE (*dăw'-dl*) is to idle, loiter, linger, saunter, trifle, waste time, an exact synonym of DALLY. To DELAY may mean to linger, loiter, be dilatory, and so to DALLY. By mistake, both DAWDLING and DELAY appeared in the first version of this vocabulary worksample, and the two were selected equally often as synonyms of DALLIANCE. A DAWDLER is a person who DAWDLES. DALLIANCE is the act, the process of DALLYING.

PRESSURE, an opposite certainly in suggestion, is selected by 15 per cent.

648. *APOSTOLIC*, apostolic (*ă-pŏs-tol'-ĭk*) *adj.* Pertaining to an apostle, especially to one of the twelve apostles, also now to the Pope, papal.

UNANIMOUS, chosen by 20 per cent as the meaning of APOSTOLIC, comes from the Latin *unus*, one, and *animus*, mind, and means of one mind, agreeing, consistent.

A DISCIPLE, from the Latin *discere*, to learn, is a learner, scholar, one who receives instruction. APOSTOLIC is the adjective from the noun APOSTLE, which comes from both Anglo-Saxon and the Greek ἀπόστολος (*apostolos*), a messenger, envoy, ambassador, from ἀπό, (*apo*), off, away, and στέλλειν (*stellein*), to send. An APOSTLE is any person sent to perform an important duty. The word was used by Christ for his twelve disciples sent forth to preach.

An ENVOY, from the French *envoyer*, to send, is often a diplomatic agent, not religious. A LEGATE, from the Latin *legere*, to send, appoint, from *lex, legis*, law, is specifically an ecclesiastic sent by the pope as his representative. Because of its derivation, the word suggests the legal duties of a representative, rather than religious or teaching responsibilities.

APOSTLE, from the Greek, has none of the subtle diplomatic innuendoes of the French, nor the brittle harshness of Roman laws. An APOSTLE is one who has learned from a master, who has been his disciple, and who now goes out into the world to teach.

649. *ALACRITY*, alacrity (ă-lăk'-rĭ-tĭ) *n.* Liveliness, sprightliness, briskness, readiness, quickness.

ALACRITY comes from the Latin *alacritas, alacritatis*, liveliness, briskness, from *alacer*, lively, brisk, quick, eager, active, cheerful, the source of the Italian *allegro* (ahl-lā'-grō), sprightly, cheerful, brisk, good-humored, lively, rapid.

To 14 per cent ALACRITY means OPTIMISM, remarkably close in suggestion. QUICKNESS, SWIFTNESS, NIMBLENESS, describe physical speed. ALACRITY adds to these the idea of cheerfulness, and so OPTIMISM.

650. *COGNOMEN*, cognomen (kŏg-nō'-mĕn) *n.* A surname, appellation, designation, denomination, family name, distinguishing word by which a person is known.

To 28 per cent COGNOMEN means TITLE, a word used in so many ways that one can almost accept it as a synonym of COGNOMEN.

The TITLE of a book is its name. The TITLE of a person may show his rank, office, or profession: General, President, or Professor.

In Rome the COGNOMEN was the last of three names, indicating the family or house to which a person belonged, directly from the Latin *cognomen*, a combination of *co-*, together, and *gnomen*, an old form of *nomen*, name, the source of NOMINATE, literally to name.

The unusual AGNOMEN (*ăg-nō'-mĕn*) is any nickname; also, more exactly, a fourth name added in commemoration of some great achievement, as: P. Cornelius Scipio Africanus, for his invasion of Africa and his command in the second Punic war which ended about 201 B.C.

651. *AMNESTY*, amnesty (*ăm'-nĕs-tĭ*) *n*. A forgetting, over-
      looking, a general pardon, absolution, act of oblivion.
From E. Chambers, 1728, comes: 'A kind of general pardon which a prince grants to his subjects by a treaty or edict, wherein he declares that he forgets and annuls all that is past, and promises not make any further enquiries into the same'. AMNES-TIES are usually reconciliations of the sovereign power with the people after rebellion or some general defection.

AMNESTY is thought by 15 per cent to mean FRIENDSHIP. AMITY, from the Latin *amicus*, friend, means friendship, kindness, affection, especially political friendship. From the same source comes AMIABLE, friendly, kindly, from *amare*, to love.

AMNESTY comes through the Latin *amnestia*, from the Greek ἀμνηστία (*amnestia*), forgetfulness, a combination of the privative ἀ- and μνᾶσθαι (*mnasthai*), to remember. From the same source comes AMNESIA (*ăm-nē'-shah*), loss of memory, inability to recall a word.

PARDON, REMISSION, ABSOLUTION, AMNESTY, all are complete, so that the offense becomes as if not committed. PARDON is the general word. REMISSION applies to a fine, penalty, or part of a prison term. ABSOLUTION is strictly ecclesiastic; while AM-NESTY is political, a pardon of persons who have committed offenses against the state.

From Theodore Dwight Woolsey, Introduction to International Law, published in 1860: 'All peace implies AMNESTY, or oblivion of past subjects of dispute'.

652. *MATRICULATING*, matriculating (*mă-trĭk'-ū-lā-tĭng*)
n. Registering, enrolling, signing the register; also admission to membership. The noun is more often MATRICULATION (*mă-trĭ-kū-lā'-shŏn*).

To 11 per cent of those tested MATRICULATING means RESIGNING. The verb to RESIGN, a combination of the Latin *re-*, back, and *signare*, literally to sign back, abandon, abdicate, give back, surrender, relinquish, renounce, is an exact opposite of the verb MATRICULATE, to enroll, register, sign.

To another 10 per cent MATRICULATING means MOTHER-KILLING. MATRICIDE, from *mater*, mother, and starting with the same first six letters as MATRICULATE, is the killing of one's mother.

MATRICULATE comes from the Latin *matricula*, a published register, roll, list, the diminutive of *matrix*, a published register. The verb to MATRICULATE is to enroll, register, enter one's name in the records. Of the noun MATRICULA, E. Chambers says: 'A register kept of the admission of the officers, or persons entered into any body or society where a list is made. Hence those who are admitted into our universities, are said to be MATRICULATED'.

653. *CABALISTIC*, cabalistic (*kăb-ăl-ĭs'-tĭk*) adj. Mystic, secret, occult, symbolic, esoteric, having a hidden meaning.
CABALA (*kăb'-ă-lah*) is the mystic philosophy of the Hebrew religion which gave hidden meaning to sacred Hebrew writings, and grew up at the beginning of the 10th century. The word CABALA is sometimes shortened to CABAL (*kă-băl'*) with its original meaning. This same word was used for the unpopular ministry of Charles II, because the initials of the five members happened to spell CABAL.

A CABALIST was one versed in the study of the CABALA, one engaged in the mystic theology of the Jews. From this comes the adjective CABALISTIC, mystic, hidden.

654. *RILL*, rill (*rĭl*) n. Small brook, shallow stream, rivulet, streamlet, purl, narrow channel of water.
A PURL is a murmuring brook, rippling stream of water, or more correctly the sound which a shallow stream makes in running over small stones.

To 15 per cent RILL, which goes back to Dutch, German, and Scandinavian words for channel and also small furrow, means RUFFLE. A FRILL is a RUFFLE, RUFF, narrow flounce. The verb to RUFFLE is to draw into gathers, folds, plaits, to pucker.

A RILL is a tiny brook, a RIVULET. E. Chambers, who did much for precision in English, says: RIVULETS have their rise, sometimes, from great rains, or great quantities of thawed snow; especially in mountainous places. But the generality of RIVULETS arise from springs. Rivers themselves all arise either from the confluence of several RIVULETS or from lakes.

655. *ARRAIGNMENT*, arraignment (*ăr-rān'-mĕnt*) *n.* An accusation, prosecution, indictment, impeachment, the act of putting a prisoner before the court to answer a charge.
The verb to ARRAIGN, to accuse, charge, indict, goes back through the French, and an obsolete verb AREASON, to question, call to account, a doublet of ARRAIGN, to the Latin *ad-*, to, and *rationare*, to reason, discourse.

The legal verb to CHARGE someone with doing wrong is general. To ACCUSE is more serious and more formal than CHARGE. The verb to INDICT is technical and limited to the decision of a grand jury to make a formal complaint in order that the offender may be brought to trial. ARRAIGN is much the same as INDICT, but is not so technical, and is often used in literature.

656. *INTIMIDATE*, intimidate (*ĭn-tĭm'-ĭ-dāt*) *v.* Overawe, scare, frighten, daunt, cow, abash, dishearten, affright, inspire with fear, stop by threat.
To 7 per cent INTIMIDATED means HINTED, undoubtedly a confusion of INTIMIDATED with INTIMATED (*ĭn'-tĭ-mā-tĕd*), HINTED, suggested. The verb to INTIMATE (*ĭn'-tĭ-māt*) comes from the Latin *intimatus*, the past participle of *intimare*, to announce, publish, make known, from *intimus*, inmost, intimate, a superlative from *in*, and so innermost. Although INTIMATED, like the verb *intimare*, originally meant announce publicly, it has come, perhaps because of the word *intimus*, to mean make known indirectly, indicate covertly, hint at, suggest, insinuate.

INTIMIDATE, from the Latin *in-*, and *timidus*, afraid, timid, frightened, is to scare, daunt, cow, make timid.

657. *BRUSQUELY*, brusquely (*brōōsk'-lĭ*) *adv*. Abruptly in
manner, roughly, rudely (v. b. 237), hurriedly, bluntly,
hastily, curtly, shortly, summarily (v. b. 2055).
This word may be spelt either BRUSKLY, given first in the Century Dictionary, or BRUSQUELY, the spelling of the French word from which it comes. The French comes in turn from the Italian, *brus'co*, rude, sharp, sour.

In the second book of the Chronicles of Barsetshire, 1858, following The Warden and Barchester Towers, Anthony Trollope uses the adjective BRUSQUE numerous times in describing his hero Dr. Thorne: 'There was not much in his individual manner to recommend him to the ladies. He was BRUSQUE, authoritative, and given to contradiction'; and further along: 'To trifling ailments he was too often BRUSQUE'.

The adverb BRUSQUELY is thought by 17 per cent to mean HEAVILY. HEAVY and HEAVILY are used in so many ways that it is difficult to know which is in the mind of those who mark this mislead. A HEAVY manner is sluggish, slow, the opposite of BRUSQUE, hurried, curt. But HEAVY may also mean serious, somber, an attitude which leads easily to BRUSQUENESS, bluntness, abruptness.

658. *CONTEND*, contend (*kŏn-tĕnd'*) *v*. To struggle in opposition, strive, endeavor, wrangle, contest, dispute, quarrel.
From the Latin verb *tendere*, to stretch, come not only CONTEND, starting with *con-*, together, but also EXTEND, to stretch out, lengthen; ATTEND; and INTEND, from the Latin *intendere*, literally to stretch out toward, and so to aim at, direct toward, fix the mind on something to be done. This leads 10 per cent to believe that CONTEND means PLAN. To INTEND is to PLAN; to CONTEND is to struggle, strive, endeavor.

659. *EFFACE*, efface (*ĕf-fās'*) *v*. To remove, rub out, erase, obliterate, destroy, render illegible.
Although ERASE, from the Latin *ex*, out, and *radere*, means to scratch out, rub off, remove, it has come to be used in schools for wiping off writing from the blackboard and so by implication cleaning the blackboard.

According to Bailey, EFFACE is to deface, raze out, destroy. DEFACE emphasizes injuring, marring, spoiling, disfiguring. To EFFACE, a combination of the Latin *ex*, out, and FACE, is to remove completely.

660. *ADJUDICATE*, adjudicate (*ād-jū'-dĭ-kăt*) *v.* To settle, pronounce judgment, decide, declare, adjudge, award judicially. Of the noun ADJUDICATION Nathan Bailey says: 'A judging, settling by sentence, judgment or decree'.

To 16 per cent ADJUDICATE means to PONDER, a confusion of words closely associated in the same situation. To PONDER, from the Latin *pendere*, to weigh carefully in the mind, is to think about, consider, deliberate, reflect upon. To ADJUDICATE, from the Latin *ad*, to, and *judicare*, to judge, when correctly used, is to make a decision after careful thought. PONDERING is a necessary step toward ADJUDICATION.

661. *FLURRIED*, flurried (*flŭr'-rēd*) *adj.* Confused by excitement, disturbed, agitated, alarmed, perturbed, disordered, excited, fluttered, fussed.

To 12 per cent FLURRIED means INDISTINCT. INDISTINCT comes from the Latin privative *in-*, not, and *distinctus*, the past participle of *distinguere*, the source of DISTINGUISH, from *di-*, which stands for *dis-*, apart, and *stinguere*, which appears again in EXTINGUISH. INDISTINCT means obscure, undefined, vague, dim, BLURRED; and this may lead to the selection of INDISTINCT, for BLURRED looks somewhat like FLURRIED. To BLUR is to smudge, smear, blemish, bedim, make INDISTINCT.

To FLUTTER, directly from Anglo-Saxon words meaning float about, fly around, as the FLUTTERING of a bird, suggests petty energy, anxious activity, but accomplishing nothing.

FUSSED and FLURRIED are much alike. FUSSED, colloquial and dialect, is needlessly confused by trifling matters, unnecessarily disturbed by petty annoyances. FLURRIED, related to Scandinavian words for disordered in various ways, but with an unknown early history, is the pleasantest word of the group. Thus one speaks of a FLURRY to mean a gust of wind, or a FLURRY of snow flakes. FLURRIED means disturbed for the moment only and not seriously.

662. *RENCONTRE*, rencontre (*rĕn-kŏn'-ter*) *n.* Sudden
    meeting, hostile collision, skirmish, brush, antagonistic
encounter.

From Fowler, English Usage: 'The display of knowledge is a
greater vulgarity than the display of wealth'. RENCONTRE is a
French word, not yet naturalized, directly from the French
rencontrer, a combination of *re-*, again, and *encontrer*, to meet.
Do not use it, but know its meaning. Use ENCOUNTER instead.

To 16 per cent RENCONTRE means CHECK. Originally CHECK
was the Persian word for KING in the game of chess. From this,
CHECK came to mean an attack, hostile move, and is still so used
in chess. Both CHECK and RENCONTRE suggest meeting an enemy.

According to E. Chambers: 'RENCOUNTER, from the French
rencontre, meeting, the encounter of two little bodies or parties
of forces. RENCOUNTER in single combat is used by way of contradistinction to DUEL. When two persons fall out and fight on
the spot, without having premeditated the combat it is called
a RENCOUNTER'.

663. *LIBATION*, libation (*lī-bā'-shŏn*) *n.* A pouring out, a
    pouring of wine often on a victim in sacrifice, in honor
of a divinity, drink-offering.

Both LIBATIONS and SACRIFICES are religious observances. A
SACRIFICE, from the Latin *sacer*, sacred, and *facere*, to make,
is literally a making sacred, and might involve a LIBATION. But
a LIBATION, from the Latin *libatus*, the past participle of *libare*,
to pour out, from the Greek λείβειν (*leibein*), is to pour out
in honor of a divinity.

Bailey says of LIBATION: A ceremony used in the pagan sacrifices wherein the priest poured down wine, milk, and other
liquids in honour of the deity, to whom he sacrifices, after he
had first tasted a little of it.

E. Chambers says of LIBATION: A ceremony in the heathen
sacrifices wherein the priest spilt some wine, milk, or other
liquor, in honor of the deity, to whom the sacrifice was offered.

664. *LURID*, lurid (*lū'-rĭd*) *adj.* Pale, wan, ghostly, dull,
    gloomy.

LURID, from the Latin *luridus*, pale yellow, originally from χλωρός (*chloros*), greenish yellow, comes from the same Greek source as CHLORINE, a greenish yellow chemical element.

LUMINOUS, from *lumen, luminis*, light, from *lucere*, to shine, is slightly more popular than other misleads. LURID presupposes light to be seen; but LUMINOUS means bright, radiant, shining; while LURID is gloomy, dull, wan.

665. *IMPARITY*, imparity (*ĭm-păr'-ĭ-tĭ*) *n*. Inequality, imbalance, non-equivalence.

PARITY, DISPARITY, and IMPARITY, all come from the Latin *par*, equal. PARITY means equality, equivalence, correspondence, equal standing. DISPARITY, starting with the Latin privative, *dis-*, means inequality, dissimilarity, want of PARITY. According to the Century Dictionary, DISPARITY applies to a difference in rank or age. IMPARITY is perhaps more general but with much the same meaning.

666. *DISPARATE*, disparate (*dĭs'-păr-āt*) *adj*. Distinct in kind, separate, unlike, dissimilar, essentially different.

DISPARATE comes from the Latin *dis-*, apart, and *parare*, to make ready, and suggests made separately, differently. From *parare* come SEPARATE, a synonym of DISPARATE, the verb to PREPARE, to make ready beforehand, and the short word to PARE (*pār*), to cut off the outer layer and so make ready. From the same *parare*, to make ready, come APPARATUS, PARRY, PARADE, and PARURE, a set of ornaments, jewelry put on to make ready for a party, but not COMPARE or DISPARITY, both of which seem to come more directly from *par*, equal, and not through *parare*.

To 35 per cent DISPARATE means CONFLICTING. CONFLICT comes from the Latin *conflictus*, the past participle of *confligere*, to strike together, from *fligere*, to strike, come into collision, clash, fight, battle. CONFLICTING suggests violence; while DISPARATE means not alike, having nothing in common.

667. *GLENGARRY*, glengarry (*glĕn-găr'-rĭ*) *n*. A Scotch cap with upstanding sides, narrowing at the top with a crease between.

The GLENGARRY is named for a valley in the north of Scotland. The DERBY (*dĕr'-bĭ*; Fowler says pronounce *dar'-*), named for

Derby, England, is a stiff, almost hard, round felt hat with a spherical top. A TAM-O'-SHANTER, named for the hero of a poem by Robert Burns, is of soft, floppy, flat material, wider all around the band that fits the head. A BERET (bă-rā') is a soft woolen French cap with a broad flat crown much like the English TAM-O'-SHANTER.

The word BIRETTA, the source also of BERET, a stiff square hat worn by Roman Catholic ecclesiastics, comes from the Latin *birrus*, cloak, and this association of cloak with hat leads 20 per cent of those taking the vocabulary test to select SPORT-COAT as the meaning of GLENGARRY.

668. *STERLET*, sterlet (stĕr'-lĕt) *n.* A variety of sturgeon, great fish living in the sea.

Almost no one need know the word STERLET. The fun of chasing it down is the knowledge gathered about all kinds of other subjects, things one knows all about until one suddenly approaches them from a new angle.

A STERLET is not a young STURGEON, but a variety of STURGEON, which is in fact small. The STURGEONS are fish 8 to 10 or more feet in length, associated with southern Russia. They live mostly in the sea, but in the spring ascend large rivers to deposit their spawn.

To 25 per cent STERLET means SALMON. The classification of fish seems to be a new science. The PTERYGIUM (tĕ-rĭj'-ĭ-ŭm), from the diminutive of the Greek πτερόν (*pteron*), little wing, small feather, and so fin, are the fish in general. The NEOPTERYGIL are the new fish, and to this group belong the SALMON. The PALEOPTERYGIL are the old fish, such as the STURGEON.

BELUGA is the Russian word for white; and so the name of the great white STURGEON twelve to fifteen feet long, and sometimes weighing two thousand pounds or more, with as much as eight hundred pounds of BELUGA CAVIAR, the eggs or roe of the STURGEON.

In addition to the CAVIAR, the air bladder of the STURGEON, its rudimentary lung, called its SOUND, is made into ISINGLASS, a pure, translucent type of gelatin, used in glues and jellies.

The STERLET, although much smaller, also produces both CAVIAR and ISINGLASS.

669. *CELEBRATE*, celebrate (*sĕl'-ĕ-brāt*) *v.* To observe with
gaiety, mark with joy, remember with festivity.

The verb to CELEBRATE comes from the Latin *celebratus*, the
past participle of *celebrare*, to go in great numbers, frequent
(*frē-kwĕnt'*), honor, praise, from *celeber*, popular, frequented.
From this comes the English CELEBRITY (*sĕ-lĕb'-rĭ-tĭ*), a person
known to the multitude. One CELEBRATES with others, with a
group, never alone.

CELEBRATE is thought by 24 per cent to mean BLESS. To BLESS
is to make holy, sanctify, pronounce holy, set apart as sacred.
To CELEBRATE may mean to perform solemnly with rites and
ceremony, as: 'To CELEBRATE mass'. In this sense synonyms are
keep, commemorate, solemnize, observe in a reverent way, in
suggestion not far from BLESS, except that when given a choice
between OBSERVE and BLESS as synonyms of CELEBRATE, high-
vocabulary persons choose OBSERVE.

Pick up the book Great Symphonies and add it to your library. In it Sigmund Spaeth says that on the title-page of the
third symphony, the Eroica, Beethoven wrote in Italian: 'Composed to CELEBRATE the memory of a great man'. The great
man was Napoleon Bonaparte.

670. *CONSEQUENTLY*,   consequently   (*kŏn'-sē-kwĕnt-lĭ*)
adv. By consequence, therefore, accordingly, wherefore,
by the connection of cause and effect.

From the Latin past participle *secutus*, followed, come PER-
SECUTE, PROSECUTE, and EXECUTE, all meaning follow up, as well
as the noun EXECUTIVE, one who follows through to completion,
and the adjective CONSECUTIVE, following in order or succession.

CONSEQUENTLY, from the Latin *consequens, consequentis*, following, is thought by 22 per cent to mean AFTERWARD. Both
CONSEQUENTLY and SUBSEQUENTLY come from the present participle *sequens, sequentis* of the deponent verb *sequi*, to follow,
the source also of SEQUENCE, and both could today mean following afterward. But SUBSEQUENTLY has come to be used for
that which follows in time, comes afterward; while CONSE-
QUENTLY applies to that which follows as a result of some previous cause. SUBSEQUENTLY is the relation of before and after;
CONSEQUENTLY, the relation of cause and effect.

671. *MODULATION*, modulation (*mŏd-ū-lā́-shŏn*) *n*. Variations, adjusting, regulating, adapting, modifying.

MODULATION is from the Latin *modulus*, measure, the diminutive of *modus*, measure, the source of MODULE (*mŏd́-ŭl*), a standard of measurement, and MODE. Nathan Bailey, in his dictionary of 1721, is of little help in defining this illusive word, for he says: MODULATION, tuning, warbling, agreeable harmony.

Ephraim Chambers, a few years later, in his Cyclopaedia, is more explicit: MODULATION, in music, is the art of keeping in, and, on occasion, changing the mode or key; and returning to it again; without offense to the ear. Under this term is comprehended the regular progression of the several parts through the sounds that are in the harmony of any particular key, as well as the proceeding naturally and regularly from one key to another.

672. *PENULTIMATE*, penultimate (*pē-nŭĺ-tĭ-māt*) *adj*. Next before the last, the last but one, preceding the last.

To 22 per cent, PENULTIMATE means CONFINED. A PEN, from Anglo-Saxon, is a small inclosure built to CONFINE, as a STY for pigs, a COOP for chickens, or a FOLD for sheep. Or the confusion of PENULTIMATE may be the word PENITENTIARY, once a person who repented, now a prison in which convicts are confined.

PENULTIMATE comes from the Latin *paene*, almost, and *ultimus*, last. The same PEN- occurs at the beginning of PENUMBRA (*pē-nŭḿ-brah*), the edge of a deep shadow, between the dark and the light, almost in shadow.

The adjective ULTIMATE from the Latin *ultimus*, last, final, means last, farthermost, end; PENULTIMATE is almost the last. The PENULTIMA is the last syllable of a word save one, the foot immediately before the last. The ANTEPENULTIMATE is just before the PENULTIMATE, or the last but two.

673. *LARGO*, largo (*lăhŕ-gō*) *adj*. Slow, dignified, stately, august, majestic.

To 15 per cent LARGO means OVER-LONG. The word LONG, and the corresponding noun LENGTH, come directly from Anglo-Saxon. LARGO comes from Latin, from *largus*, large, abundant, plentiful, liberal, the source of LARGESSE, generous gifts.

LARGO, like most musical terms, is Italian and means slow, the opposite of ALLEGRO, another Italian word, which means rapid, brisk, from the Latin *alacer*, lively.

674. *QUAGGY*, quaggy (*kwăg'-gĭ*) *adj.* Boggy, spongy, poachy, yielding to the feet.

QUAGGY comes from QUAG, an abbreviation of QUAGMIRE, and this in turn is a variation of QUAKEMIRE, something that shakes. MIRE goes back to the Icelandic word for deep mud. The verb to MIRE means to stick in the mud.

A QUAGMIRE is soft, wet, boggy, land that trembles under foot, a marsh, bog, fen, slough (*slow*), pronounced to rime with HOW and COW. A MARSH is covered with water like salt marshes at the border of the ocean. A FEN is a marsh with coarse vegetation. A SLOUGH is deep mud with no vegetation. A BOG is characterized by decaying vegetation. A QUAGMIRE is the worst kind of bog. QUAGGY is the adjective.

To 25 per cent QUAGGY means RUGGED. CRAGGY (*krăg'-gĭ*) is RUGGED, mountainous, precipitous, rocky. QUAGGY (*kwăg'-gĭ*) is boggy, wet, marshy.

675. *UMPIRAGE*, umpirage (*ŭm'-pĭr-āj*) *n.* The position of one who arbitrates, the post of an umpire, arbitrement. The ending -AGE is French, originally Latin, used to form a noun, sometimes in designating a collection, as BAGGAGE, a group of BAGS. At other times -AGE indicates the condition, the office, the rank, the service. As PEERAGE is the rank or state of a PEER; UMPIRAGE is the office of an UMPIRE.

An UMPIRE is the man, a judge, referee, arbitrator. The word goes back through the French *nompair*, not equal, to the Latin combination of *non*, not, and *per*, equal. The modern UMPIRE is said to be a wrong division of *a numpere* into *an umpere*. An UMPIRE is one who makes an instant decision between almost equal situations.

The terms ARBITRATOR, JUDGE, REFEREE, and UMPIRE, are much alike in function. Although JUDGE is used loosely for one who makes a considered judgment, the term is primarily technical and legal. An ARBITRATOR is a person agreed upon by both sides to settle a dispute without taking it to court. A REFEREE is a person to whom some one particular decision is referred. But the word is also used instead of UMPIRE in some sports. UMPIRE is used mostly in athletics to designate a person to whom has been assigned authority to make instant and final decisions.

To 25 per cent UMPIRAGE means ROYAL-DECREE, which at least in suggestion is perhaps closer than ARBITREMENT, called correct. An ARBITRATOR almost always makes some sort of compromise. An UMPIRE makes his own decision, which is binding, a 'ROYAL-DECREE'.

676. *RIPOSTE*, riposte (*rĭ-pŏst'*) *n.* A quick, short thrust in fencing, also a smart reply, repartee, ready retort, sharp answer.

In fencing, RIPOSTE is a quick, short thrust, to catch an opponent unprotected after parrying his lunge.

RIPOSTE is a French word, spelt as in French, meaning repartee, quick reply. This in turn comes from the Latin *respondere*, to answer, a combination of *re*, again, back, and *spondere*, to promise.

From *spondere*, to promise, comes SPONSOR (*spŏn'-sĕr*), one who promises to answer for another, to be responsible for another's defaults. From *respondere* comes the verb to RESPOND, to reply, answer. In Italian *respondere* changes to *rispondere*, and so to RIPOSTE, a sharp reply.

The marking of the misleads scatter, with no concentration on any single misinterpretation of the word RIPOSTE.

RETORT, REPARTEE, and RIPOSTE are three types of quick answers. A RETORT may be blunt, without wit, even unpleasant, a keen prompt answer, a serious turning back of derision in a sharp, short expression. A REPARTEE (*rĕp-ahr-tē'*) is a witty and good-humored answer, always pleasant, and suggesting give and take. A RIPOSTE centers between the two, not so sharp and blunt as a RETORT, nor so good-natured as a REPARTEE, without the wit of a REPARTEE, but more subtle than a RETORT, with more finesse.

677. *LACTEAL*, lacteal (*lăk'-tēl*) *adj.* Milky, resembling milk; as a noun: one of many tiny tubes picking up and carrying a white fluid to the alimentary food-bearing canal.

To 16 per cent LACTEAL means DIRTY; to another 12 per cent WEEPING. This last is the word LACHRYMOSE, WEEPING, from the Latin *lacryma*, a tear, and so the English adjective LACHRYMAL.

From the Greek γάλα (*gala*), milk, comes Galaxy, the Milky Way. From this comes the adjective GALACTIC, and so the closely related Latin *lac, lactis*, milk, and finally LACTEAL.

678. *COSSET*, cosset (*kŏs'-sĕt*) v. To fondle, pamper, make a pet of.

The noun COSSET was a pet lamb, a lamb brought up by hand, from an Anglo-Saxon word meaning house-dweller.

The popular mislead, LEFT ALONE, is an opposite, certainly in suggestion.

679. *SUMP*, sump (*sŭmp*) n. A pit, pool of dirty water; in mining, the bottom of a shaft where water collects.

SUMP goes back to Dutch and German words, perhaps originally to the same beginnings as SWAMP.

To 30 per cent SUMP means REFUSE-HEAP. A DUMP is a place where REFUSE, something refused, discarded, is piled up, heaped up. REFUSE is dross, dregs, trash, rubbish, useless matter.

A SUMP is a pit in which waste water collects so that it can be pumped out, by a SUMP-PUMP. Both a REFUSE-HEAP and a SUMP are collections of waste. One is a pile of solid waste above ground; while a SUMP is a hole, pit, below the level, to collect liquid, water.

680. *EPONYM*, eponym (*ĕp'-ō-nĭm*) n. The name of a place derived from the name of a person, also anything named for an individual.

WASHINGTON, the city, is an EPONYM, a place named for George Washington. DELAWARE, the state, was named for Lord Delawarr, who sailed into the bay of Delaware in 1610.

An EPIC is a long poem, the adventures and achievements of a hero; and this leads 25 per cent into selecting HEROIC POEM as the meaning of EPONYM. Epic, occasionally called also by the unusual term EPOPEE (*ĕp-ō-pē'*), comes from the Greek ἔπος (*epos*), which meant word, but came to mean a saying, and then a story, tale, narrative, such as the Iliad or Odyssey.

EPONYM comes from the Greek ἐπώνυμος (*eponymos*), from ἐπί (*epi*), upon, and ὄνομα (*onoma*), name, the source of ANTONYM, the opposite of a name, and SYNONYM.

Many electrical units of measurement are EPONYMS, as: WATT, from James WATT, the Scottish engineer, 1736 to 1819; VOLT, from Alessandro VOLTA, 1745 to 1827; AMPERE, from Andre Marie AMPERE, 1775 to 1836; OHM, from G. S. OHM; and JOULE, from J. P. JOULE, 1819 to 1889.

Also more recently the DIESEL engine is named for Rudolf DIESEL, a German engineer who lived from 1858 to 1913; and of course the verb to PASTEURIZE and the noun PASTEURIZATION are EPONYMS from the proper name Louis PASTEUR, 1822 to 1895.

681. *DEPREDATION*, depredation (*dĕ-prĕ-dā'-shŏn*) *n.* A plundering, robbing, pillaging, despoiling, laying waste, devastating, rapine, seizing, spoiling, marauding.

DEPREDATION comes from the Latin *de-* and *praedari*, to rob, plunder, from *praeda*, to prey upon. From the same source comes the adjective PREDATORY (*prĕd'-ă-tō-rĭ*), pillaging, plundering.

DEPREDATION is thought by 30 per cent to mean UNDERMINING. To UNDERMINE is to destroy by removing the foundation secretly, injure by invisible means, literally to dig under with the purpose of destroying.

Both UNDERMINING and DEPREDATION have the purpose of destroying, the first secretly, the second by an open raid.

682. *AUTISTIC*, autistic (*aw-tĭs'-tĭk*) *adj.* Self-centered, sufficient unto one's self, introspective, dominated by subjective trends of thought, observing what happens in one's own consciousness.

In a letter from David Ransom: 'AUTISTIC was coined as a technical term in psychiatry to describe a very withdrawn, extremely subjective person who daydreams and thinks in self-centered patterns and fails to relate to other people. It shows up in a 1934 Webster.

'Eugen Bleuler, a Swiss psychiatrist, who originated the word, lived from 1857 to 1939.'

The word comes of course from the Greek αὐτο- (*auto*), self, from αὐτός (*autos*), myself, himself, which appears in AUTOGRAPH, one's own signature, and in AUTOMOBILE, a machine which moves by itself, and which becomes AUT- before most vowels.

To 24 per cent AUTISTIC means UNRULY, sometimes a characteristic of the introspective, self-centered child.

From Black's Medical Dictionary: AUTISM, a form of mental disturbance in children, a severance from reality, with relative preponderance of the inner life, cut off from human relationships and contact. This is an excellent description of what the Laboratory calls SUBJECTIVITY, possessed normally by one quarter of persons, and opposed to OBJECTIVITY, possessed by three quarters, abnormal only because displayed by a minority.

683. *EXTRUSION*, extrusion (*ĕks-trū'-shŏn*) *n.* Thrusting forth, expulsion, expelling, forcing out, pressing out.

To 24 per cent EXTRUSION means FORGING, perhaps a confusion of FORGING with FORCING. To FORGE is to shape by hammering, beat into shape, and sometimes more generally to fabricate, manufacture, frame. Certain types of objects are formed today by EXTRUSION, forcing through a die. But FORGING is more specifically hammering, pounding, not pushing.

EXTRUSION comes from the Latin *extrudere*, from *ex*, out, and *trudere*, to push, thrust, urge, crowd, with the past participle *extrusus*. An INTRUSION is forcing one's way in. An OBTRUSION, a combination of *ob*, before, and the same *trusus*, is forcing one's way forward into undue prominence. One OBTRUDES one's opinions. One INTRUDES one's self. A PROTRUSION is almost the opposite of EXTRUSION. That which is EXTRUDED, pushed out, PROTRUDES on the other side, juts out.

684. *PROFFER*, proffer (*prŏf'-fer*) *v.* To tender, propose, volunteer, offer, hold out.

To 22 per cent 'He PROFFERS' means GAINS. To PROFIT, from the Latin *proficere*, to go forward, advance, the source of PROFICIENT, is to GAIN.

OFFER is Anglo-Saxon; PROFFER with much the same meaning is Latin from *proferre*, to bring forth, a combination of *pro*, forth, and *ferre*, to bring. From the same *ferre* come: CONFER, literally to bring together with the additional suggestion today of discussing; REFER, to bring back, carry back; DEFER, to carry off, put off, delay; and INFER, believe because of something observed; all relatives of PROFFER, but unconnected with the simple Anglo-Saxon OFFER.

685. *AMPHORA*, amphora (*ăm'-fō-rah*) *n.* A Greek vase, usually tall and slender with two handles, one on each side of a narrow neck, with a pointed bottom for pushing into the ground, made of hard baked clay, unglazed. Wrong answers as to the meaning of the plural AMPHORAE (*ăm'-fō-rē*) divide evenly between MEDICINES, MICROBES, and COLANDERS, with no connection on any one popular mislead.

686. *BARED*, bared (*bārd*) *adj.* Uncovered, naked, disclosed, without clothes, exposed to view.

BARED, which goes back through Middle English to Anglo-Saxon, with related words in the Scandinavian languages, is thought by 47 per cent to mean KEPT OUT, obviously a confusion of spelling and not vocabulary and should not be used in the vocabulary test.

To BAR (*bahr*), pronounced like FAR, is to hinder, prohibit, obstruct, prevent, restrain, KEEP OUT. Here the past is spelt with two R'S, BARRED, and pronounced (*bahrd*). To BARE (*bār*) is to uncover, divest of clothes, disclose. Here the past is spelt with one R, BARED, and pronounced (*bārd*). CAR, an automobile, and CARE, help, which in the past becomes CARED (*kārd*), differ in the same way as BAR and BARE. BARRED, pronounced to rime with CARD and HARD, is kept out; BARED, riming with CARED and DARED, is uncovered.

687. *PECCADILLO*, peccadillo (*pĕk-kă-dĭl'-lō*) *n.* Slight offense, small crime, minor fault, petty trespass, trivial vice, venial sin, one which is forgivable, pardonable.

The Spanish PECCADILLO, spelt with one C in Spanish, and *pecado*, a real sin, come from the Latin *peccatum*, a sin, from *peccare*, to sin, transgress, offend, the source of the adjective PECCANT, sinful.

To 19 per cent PECCADILLOS are SPANISH HORSEMEN. The Spanish word for horseman is *caballero*, with the same CA and double L and O at the end. The GAUCHOS, also Spanish, are natives of the South American pampas, of Spanish descent and noted for their daring horsemanship. PECCADILLOS, sometimes spelt PECCADILLOES, are small faults, minor crimes, pardonable sins.

ARMADILLO (*ahr-mah-dĭl'-lō*), a small animal with a hard shell, is the Spanish diminutive of ARMADA, an armed fleet, while the VIOLONCELLO is the Italian diminutive of VIOLONE (*vĭ-ō-lō'-nā*), the largest of these stringed instruments.

688. *IMPALPABLE*, impalpable (*ĭm-păl'-pā-bl*) *adj.* Intangible, unsubstantial, imperceptible, not felt, incapable of being perceived by touch.

IMPALPABLE, a combination of IM-, and PALPABLE, with similar words in French, Spanish, Portuguese, and Italian, all come from the Latin *palpare*, to touch, feel, stroke.

To 19 per cent IMPALPABLE means OFFENSIVE. OFFENSIVE may mean aggressive, invading, attacking, opposed to DEFENSIVE; or it may mean disagreeable, unpleasant. In Roget's Thesaurus, one of the first synonyms of OFFENSIVE in this sense is UNPALATABLE, much like IMPALPABLE in sound. PALPABLE means touchable, responding to the sense of touch, capable of being grasped, that may be easily felt or perceived, unmistakable, obvious, manifest, plain, evident. PALATABLE means pleasant to the sense of taste. UNPALATABLE is disagreeable, OFFENSIVE to the taste.

Of IMPALPABLE E. Chambers says: 'That whose parts are so extremely minute that they cannot be distinguished by the senses, particularly by that of feeling'.

689. *ORDAIN*, ordain (*ŏr-dān'*) *v.* To appoint, select, establish, set apart for an office, order, exact, destine, prescribe.

In making laws ORDAIN, directly from the Latin *ordinare*, to order, is the most solemn word in use. The noun ORDER was originally a row, line, rank. To ORDER was to put in order, arrange in a line. People divide almost equally between CONFIRM and APPOINT as the meaning of ORDAIN. To CONFIRM comes from the Latin *confirmare*, make firm, establish, a combination of *com*, together, and *firmare*, to make firm.

To CONFIRM may mean to make certain, sanction, ratify, corroborate, substantiate. The second meaning of ORDAIN is precisely this, and for that reason, CONFIRM will be removed as a mislead in the revision of this vocabulary test, and APPOINT left as the correct answer.

690. *SONIFEROUS,* soniferous (*sō-nĭf'-ĕr-ŭs*) *adj.* Sound-producing, resonant, echoing, resounding.

Many words from the Latin verb *ferre,* to carry, end in -FER, as: TRANSFER, to carry across; REFER, to carry back; CONFER, to bring together, INFER, to form an opinion from evidence brought in; and DEFER, to delay, postpone, put off.

Others come from *latus,* the past participle of *ferre,* as: RELATE, assert a connection with, ascribe to an origin, also tell, narrate, recite; COLLATE, gather together, assemble; TRANSLATE, originally to carry from one place to another, now more often to transfer from one language to another.

Fewer words, ending in -FEROUS, come from *ferre,* in the sense of bear, bring forth, produce, as: GRANIFEROUS, grain producing, seed carrying; ODORIFEROUS, smell producing, SOMNIFEROUS, sleep producing; and SONIFEROUS, sound producing.

From *sonare,* to sound, come the noun *sonus,* sound, and so in English not only the word SOUND itself, but the adjective SONOROUS (*sō-nō'-rŭs*), giving out sound when struck, full volumed; RESONANT, resounding, sounding again; and SONIFEROUS, sound producing. The popularity of the misleads scatters, with no clear concentration on any one.

691. *TORPOR,* torpor (*tor'-por*) *n.* Numbness, stupor (V. B. 112), sluggishness, insensibility, apathy (V. B. 1809), dullness, dormancy, inactivity, quiescence (V. B. 1339) of mind.

To 20 per cent of those tested TORPOR means HAT. A man's tall silk hat, top-hat, is colloquially known as a TOPPER (*tŏp'-per*).

With more reason 15 per cent choose DIZZINESS. DIZZINESS, vertigo, giddiness, a whirling in the head with the sense of about to fall, comes directly from an Anglo-Saxon word which meant foolish, stupid, almost STUPOR; and DIZZY in English once had this meaning, another instance of modern youth returning to a meaning which has long since gone out of use.

TORPOR, from the Latin *torpor*, numbness, from the verb *torpēre*, to be numb, stiff, is today inactivity of mind, apathy. TORPOR is natural and lasting, as the TORPOR of a hibernating animal. STUPOR is unnatural, almost a sudden daze, of short duration.

692. *CARMINE*, carmine (*kahr'-mĭn*) *n.* Crimson, scarlet, lake, a bright red color. CARMINE is the finest of the red lakes. CARMINE is the essential coloring principle of cochineal (*kŏch'-ĭ-nēl*), a dye obtained from the dried body of an insect which lives on the cactus plant. The pure coloring matter of cochineal has the formula $C_{17}H_{18}O_{10}$ and is said to form a purple mass.

The differences between MADDER, LAKE, and CARMINE, three kinds of red, are not so much differences in color as in the chemical properties of the three.

CARMINE is thought by 15 per cent of those who have been tested to mean DEEP ORANGE; and by another 14 per cent to mean WHITE FUR, this last an obvious confusion of CARMINE, crimson, with ERMINE.

693. *DENOMINATE*, denominate (*dē-nŏm'-ĭ-nāt*) *v.* To name, call, entitle, designate, dub, style, give an epithet to. To 19 per cent DENOMINATE means COUNT. To NUMERATE, from the Latin *numerare*, to count, and *numerus*, a number, is to count, reckon. Also the more frequent ENUMERATE is to count, as well as to mention in detail, recount. From the same *numerus* comes NUMBER, the B having been added long ago by the French.

To NOMINATE, from the Latin *nominare*, to name, and *nomen*, a name, is to name, appoint, designate by name. To NOMINATE a candidate is to name him. To DENOMINATE is to give a name to.

The word NAME goes directly back to Anglo-Saxon but seems closely related to the Greek word for KNOW. A NAME is that by which one KNOWS a thing; and perhaps conversely, to KNOW a thing one must name it. To DENOMINATE is to NAME.

694. *FAUNA*, fauna (*faw'-nă*) *n.* Animal life in general, living in some given area; the animals of a region or period. FAUNA is thought by 44 per cent to be PLANT-LIFE, and by only 37 per cent to be ANIMAL-LIFE. FAUNA and FLORA, much alike in sound, are ANIMAL LIFE and PLANT LIFE. Of the two, FLORA

is probably the easier to remember, for it starts with the same first three letters as FLOWER and FLORIST, and is the noun from which comes the adjective FLORAL, pertaining to flowers. Also, in line with the discovery that old words are easier than recent ones, FAUNA is recent, used by Linnaeus in 1746; while FLORA, though used also by Linnaeus, goes much further back. FLORA, the name of the Roman goddess of flowers, comes from the Latin *flos, floris*, flower, and is today the plant life of a region. FAUNA, which corresponds to the Latin *Faunus*, in Roman mythology the protecting deity of shepherds, from the same source as FAUN, the figure of a man with the ears, horns, and tail of a goat, is then the opposite, the animal life. Were the majority to rule, were popular opinion to be followed, these two words would cease to have different meanings.

695. *JAPANNED*, japanned (*jă-pănd'*) *adj.* Lacquered, varnished, shellacked, with a smooth glossy surface.
LACQUER, JAPAN, SHELLAC, and VARNISH are all much alike. The substance JAPAN was named for JAPAN, the country, and for a while the verb to JAPAN started with a capital letter, but is now spelt with a small letter. LACQUER is also used principally in JAPAN. All four leave a smooth surface, which leads 15 per cent to select SMOOTH as the meaning of JAPANNED.

JAPANNED means coated with a partly transparent substance almost colorless which leaves a smooth, often glossy surface.

696. *CHAFFER*, chaffer (*chăf'-fĕr*) *v.* To buy, sell, trade, bargain, haggle, deal in merchandise.
Several times in this vocabulary study, a word with a double consonant, as FF in this case, is confused with another, nearly identical, where the consonant is single. The vowel before a doubled F is short, CHAFF (*chăf*) and CHAFFER (*chăf'-fĕr*); before a single F, it is long: CHAFE (*chāf*); and this confusion leads 50 per cent to select IRRITATE as the meaning of CHAFFER. To CHAFE (*chāf*), with long A, is to wear out by rubbing, irritate, annoy, fret.

There is also another word CHAFF (*chăf*) with several meanings. The verb to CHAFF means to make fun of, ridicule, tease. The noun CHAFF is the husks of grain, wheat, or oats.

CHAFFER is a different word. It goes back to Anglo-Saxon, a word meaning TRADE, a combination of CHAF-, which stands for CHEAP, bargain, trade, and -FER from *fare*, a doing, going, business.

HAGGLE is unpleasant. CHAFFER is not. It is to buy and sell, to bargain with a steady flow of words.

697. *BADINAGE*, badinage (*băd'-ĭ-năhj*) *n*. Frivolous raillery, playful jesting, light banter.

BADINAGE is a French word, going perhaps back to Portuguese. It is always pleasant, playful, frivolous, jesting, never sarcastic.

The popular mislead SYMPATHY is marked as often as the correct answer JESTING.

698. *TRIPTYCH*, triptych (*trĭp'-tĭk*) *n*. A three panelled painting; picture in three upright parts, side by side, the center section usually complete in itself, with the two side paintings sometimes jointed to the central portion by hinges.

TRIPTYCH, from the Greek τρίπτυχον (*triptychon*), three-fold, comes from τρεῖς (*treis*), three, which becomes τρι- (*tri*), as in TRIANGLE, three-angled, and TRICYCLE, three-wheeled; and πτυχή (*ptyche*), a fold.

To 13 per cent TRIPTYCH means ALTAR, the second step in learning, a confusion of words used frequently in the same situation. ALTAR, from the Latin *altare*, literally a high place, from *altus*, high, was originally a large flat-topped stone block. Today many TRIPTYCHS are ALTARPIECES, hung above and behind the ALTAR.

699. *BROODING*, brooding (*brŏod'-ĭng*) *adj*. Thoughtful, pondering, meditating, thinking deeply, dwelling mentally upon a subject.

BROODING goes back to a Middle English word meaning BREED, and from there to an Anglo-Saxon word meaning to keep warm, cherish, nourish. The verb to BREED is to produce offspring; and the noun BROOD is the family produced, those hatched at one time. The verb to BREED and the noun BROOD are related much as are the verb to FEED and the noun FOOD, also from Anglo-Saxon. Then the verb to BROOD came to mean sit on eggs, as a fowl, to hatch them. Finally to BROOD came to mean figuratively sit on one's thoughts, to develop them as a bird sits on her nest, remain a long time in solicitous thought, meditate anxiously.

To 36 per cent BROODING means SAD, two thoughts close to one another, so that their separation is next to the last step in learning. SAD means unhappy, mournful, depressed, and BROODING suggests SADNESS. But BROODING is thinking deeply, not necessarily sad thoughts.

700. *CAPITALISTIC*, capitalistic (*kăp-ĭ-tăl-ĭs'-tĭk*) *adj*. Pertaining to that part of income available for further production, to materials used to produce.

Of the noun CAPITALIST, Webster says, in his first edition, 1828: 'A man who has capital or stock in trade, in manufactures, or in any business requiring the expenditure of money with a view to profit, usually denoting a man of large property which is or may be employed in business'. CAPITALISTIC is the corresponding adjective.

Of 29 high-vocabulary adults 18 mark MONEYED as the meaning in the phrase: 'CAPITALISTIC society', and 9 mark INDIVIDUALISTIC. The words: CATTLE, CHATTEL, and CAPITAL all come from the same original Latin source and the three as a group suggest individual ownership rather than MONEY. To stress ownership the choice MONEYED, despite its popularity, has been removed in the revised form of the vocabulary test and INDIVIDUALISTIC retained.

701. *LUGUBRIOUS*, lugubrious (*lū-gū'-brĭ-ŭs*) *adj*. Mournful, doleful, dismal, dejected, funereal, melancholy, plaintive, woeful, sorrowful, sad, wretched.

MELANCHOLY comes from the Greek μελαγχολία (*melagcholia*), the condition of having black bile, jaundice, madness, a combination of μέλας (*melas*), μέλανις (*melanis*), black, and χολή (*chole*), bile, the source of CHOLIC. MELANCHOLY, which originally meant insanity of any kind, should be used only of a permanent, gloomy state of mind, depressed spirit of long duration.

LUGUBRIOUS, which goes back in English to the year 1600, comes through the French *lugubre*, from the Latin *lugubris*,

mournful, from *lugere*, to mourn. The only mislead selected is
HAPPY, an exact opposite.

702. *CLAMBER*, clamber (*klăm'-ber*) *v.* To climb with diffi-
     culty, mount slowly with effort, scale, ascend using both
hands and feet.
To 18 per cent the verb to CLAMBER means to CRY-OUT. To
CLAMOR is to CRY-OUT. The noun CLAMOR, from the Latin
clamare, to cry out, is a tumultuous outcry, exclamation made
in a loud voice, vociferation by a multitude, great noise, hub-
bub, uproar, din, ado.
    CLAMBER comes probably from various Scandinavian words
meaning climb, grasp firmly, and may be the frequentative of
CLIMB.
    To CRAWL, to SCRAMBLE, and to CLAMBER, all use both hands
and feet in moving. To CRAWL is to push forward on the floor
with both hands and feet like an infant. To SCRAMBLE is to crawl
up a slight incline with difficulty. To CLAMBER is used of adults
who crawl up a steep mountain with both hands and feet.

703. *BENISON*, benison (*běn'-ĭ-sŏn;* Phyfe prefers: *běn'-ĭz-n*)
     n. A blessing, benediction, act of invoking happiness upon
another.
BENISON is a shortened form of BENEDICTION, from *benedicere*,
to bless, usually written in Latin as two words: *bene*, good,
from *bonus*, good, and *dicere*, to say, speak. A BENEDICTION is
speaking good, declaring well. A MALEDICTION (*măl-ĕ-dĭk'-
shŏn*), from *malus*, evil, bad, wicked, and *dicere*, to speak, the
source of DICTION, is a curse, imprecation, execration, literally
a speaking bad, declaring evil. Here the short form is MALISON
(*măl'-ĭ-sŏn*).
    BENEVOLENCE (*bĕ-nĕv'-ō-lĕns*), from the Latin *bonus*, good,
and *volens, volentis*, wishing, the present participle of *velle*, to
wish, will, is wishing well; while MALEVOLENCE (*mă-lĕv'-ō-
lĕns*) is wishing ill, enmity, hatred, ill will. The adjectives are
BENEVOLENT (*bĕ-nĕv'-ō-lĕnt*) and MALEVOLENT (*mă-lĕv'-ō-lĕnt*).
    A BENEFACTOR (*běn'-ĕ-făk-tor*), from *bene, bonus*, good, and
facere, to do, is one who does good; while a MALEFACTOR, from
malus, bad, and *facere*, to do, is one who does evil.

BENIGN (*bē-nīn'*), from *bonus*, good, and -*genus*, born, of good disposition, gracious, kind, is literally born good; while MALIGN (*mă-līn'*), from *malus*, bad, evil, and -*genus*, born, means born bad.

THOUGHTFULNESS, as the meaning of BENISON, is the big mislead. THOUGHTFULNESS may mean full of thought, serious consideration, meditation; or it may suggest considerateness, thoughtfulness of others, almost kindness, and in this sense has something in common with BENISON, well wishing. A BENISON is a formal invocation of divine blessing, sometimes by a private individual, sometimes by a church official, pronounced at the close of a divine service. BENISON is sometimes used in poetry for BENEDICTION.

704. *TRACTATE*, tractate (*trăk'-tāt*) *n.* A treatise, tract, homily, discourse, dissertation, essay, disquisition, paper, discursive composition.

TRACTATE comes from the Latin *tractatus*, a treatise, homily, treatment, from *tractare*, to handle, treat, the frequentative of *trahere*, to draw.

Among 28 high-vocabulary adults, 3 select PLAY as a synonym of TRACTATE. Both a TRACTATE and a PLAY are written. But a PLAY, a tragedy or comedy, is written to be acted and heard from a stage. A TRACTATE is an essay or treatise written to be read.

Both ESSAYS and TREATISES are written compositions explaining and discussing the principles of a particular subject. Of the two, an ESSAY is shorter; a TREATISE, more formal, more methodical. A TRACT and a TRACTATE are between the two. Thus Ephraim Chambers says: 'TRACT or TRACTATE does also signify a small TREATISE, or written discourse, upon any subject'. But a TRACT has also the suggestion of a HOMILY, a sermon, applying a precept rather than explaining it. TRACTATE has no such religious implication.

705. *ASPERSION*, aspersion (*ăs-pĕr'-shŏn*) *n.* Originally, a sprinkling with water; today: criticism, charge, censure, defamation, calumny, damaging imputation, derogatory assertion, calumnious report.

By far the most popular mislead is IDEALS, chosen by almost as many as the correct answer, a confusion of ASPERSION with ASPIRATION. ASPIRATION comes from the Latin *ad*, to, and *spirare*, to breathe, from the same source as INSPIRATION and INSPIRE. ASPIRATION was originally breathing but has come to mean a lofty desire, ambition. Both IDEALS and ASPIRATIONS exist only in the imagination, in the mind. Both are elevated hopes, ardent desires. An IDEAL is a standard of desire, ultimate aim, mental conception of a goal; while an ASPIRATION is an ardent desire to attain such a goal.

ASPERSION, and the verb to ASPERGE, come from the Latin verb *aspergere*, to sprinkle, a combination of *ad*, to, and *spergere*, to sprinkle, scatter, the direct source of SPARSE, thinly scattered, dispersed around. The English verb to ASPERSE, to sprinkle, came to mean bespatter, and so figuratively to assail with insinuations, cast reproach upon by foul report. ASPERSION, originally a sprinkling, is now figuratively a damaging imputation, defamation, calumny, derogatory criticism.

706. *CONGLUTINATE*, conglutinate (*kŏn-glū'-tĭn-āt*) *adj.*
    Joined with glue, fastened, stuck together.
A CONGLOMERATE is a rock made of various kinds of rock. CON-GLOMERATE comes from the Latin *con*, with, together, and *glomerare*, to gather into a ball, from *glomus*, a ball. A CON-GLOMERATE today is a mixture of all sorts of things gathered together; and this leads 20 per cent to select MIXED as the meaning of CONGLUTINATE.

CONGLUTINATE comes from the Latin *con*, with, together, and *glutinare*, to glue, from *gluten*, glue. CONGLOMERATE is scientific and seems justified; and the world is accustomed to it. But CONGLUTINATE is still awkward. Use instead the Anglo-Saxon STUCK TOGETHER.

707. *TRUNDLE*, trundle (*trŭn'-dl*) *v.* To roll, wheel, turn, twist, twirl, push along on a wheel.
TRUNDLE comes from an Anglo-Saxon word meaning ring, circle, disc. A TRUNDLE, the noun, is always a small wheel, small in diameter but wide like a caster to support weight. A TRUNDLE BED is low on casters, and wheels under another bed. A TRUNDLE

may even be so wide as to be called a ROLLER. The wheel of a wheelbarrow is a TRUNDLE, a small single wheel designed to carry a load. A PINION is another small wheel but with teeth.

The verb to TRUNDLE is to cause to rotate, twirl, roll a hoop, or push along on a wheel, as to TRUNDLE a wheelbarrow.

The misleads WALK and DANCE are occasionally chosen as synonyms of TRUNDLE, but neither often enough to be called popular.

708. *BASAL*, basal (*bā'-săl*) *adj.* Basic, fundamental, forming
    a base.

BASAL is an adjective constructed by adding the ending -AL to the noun BASE, the bottom of anything, foundation, ground-work, that on which something rests. BASE comes through the Latin *basis*, from the Greek βασις (*basis*), base.

The endings -AL and -IC are both Latin, though -IC goes further back to Greek. Both are added to Latin nouns to form adjectives, as MANUAL, done by hand, and ORAL, pertaining to the mouth, or PUBLIC and METALLIC. Few words occur with both endings as BASAL and BASIC, with really identical meanings.

To translate BASAL as BASIC, fundamental, in a vocabulary test, especially where BASAL appears among difficult words, seems too easy and many persons, doubtful of the exact meaning of BASAL, avoid the obvious BASIC and, misled by BASALT, turn to VOLCANIC. BASALT (*bă-săwlt'*, preferred by the Century Dictionary, or *băs'-ăwlt* as usually heard) is a VOLCANIC rock, sometimes dark lava. Here the adjective is BASALTIC, pertaining to igneous, volcanic rock. BASAL means fundamental, as in BASAL metabolism.

709. *JUDICIOUS*, judicious (*jū-dĭsh'-ŭs*) *adj.* Exercising sound
    judgment, careful, wise, prudent, rational, discerning, saga-
cious, discreet, intelligent, sound.

To 18 per cent JUDICIOUS means OFFICIAL. JUDICIOUS has been used to mean relating to the court and the OFFICIAL administration of justice; but JUDICIAL and JUDICIOUS should be separated. JUDICIAL, from the Latin *judicialis*, belonging to a court of justice, from *judex*, *judicis*, judge, is the word for OFFICIAL justice. JUDICIOUS is the general adjective for a fair judgment.

710. *RUMINATE*, ruminate (*rū'-mĭn-āt*) *v.* To meditate, pon-
    der, muse, consider, reflect upon, contemplate, deliberate,
cogitate, turn over in the mind, think about.
RUMINATE comes from the Latin *ruminatus*, the past participle
of *ruminare*, to chew the cud. Among the RUMINANTS are the
GIRAFFE and CAMEL. To RUMINATE is to think about over and
over as a cow chews the cud.

711. *THREAD*, thread (*thrĕd*) *v.* To wind, weave, pass through
    with the precision of one who is THREADING a needle.
To 19 per cent 'He THREADED his way' means BLAZED. One
meaning of the word to BLAZE is to notch tree trunks to indicate
a path through a forest so that others can follow. To THREAD
one's way is to wind around obstacles, perhaps again among
tree trunks.
    To WEAVE and to THREAD in this sense are both figurative.
To WEAVE is to pass a thread, called the WOOF, from side to side,
under and over the thick threads called the WARP. To THREAD
a needle is to put the THREAD through the eye.

712. *BACCHANALIA*, bacchanalia (*băk-kă-nā'-lĭ-ă*) *n.* A
    festival, feast, banquet, sumptuous entertainment in honor
of BACCHUS; nowadays a drunken orgy, riotous revelry.
An ORGY, directly from the Greek ὄργια (*orgia*), was also a
celebration in honor of BACCHUS or Dionysus, a revel, wild
carouse, BACCHANALIA.
    Those who do not know the correct meaning of BACCHANALIA
often select the mislead CARD GAME. BACCARAT (*băk'-kă-răt*, or
with the French pronunciation without the T, *băk-kă-răh'*) is a
gambling CARD GAME played with three persons or more, one of
them the banker, and with three packs of cards.
    BACCHUS, from the Greek βάκχος (*bacchos*), is an alternate
name for the Greek god of wine, DIONYSUS. The word BACCHUS
has survived and BACCHANALIA is the festival in his honor.

713. *PURVEYOR*, purveyor (*pĕr-vā'-ŏr*) *n.* A supplier, pro-
    vider, caterer, especially one who furnishes food.
A PURVEYOR is thought by 20 per cent to be a CARRIER, a confusion of PURVEYOR with CONVEYOR, from quite unlike sources

though so similar in sound and appearance. CONVEYOR, which
the Century Dictionary spells CONVEYER, and the verb to CON-
VEY, to carry, transport, bear, come from the Latin *com-*, with,
and *via*, way, road. A CONVEYOR is a mechanical contrivance,
often an endless belt, designed to transport material a short
distance, sometimes in a factory from one location to another.

The verbs to PURVEY and to PROVIDE are doublets, both coming
from the Latin *providere*, a combination of *pro*, before, forward, and *videre*, to see, the second directly from Latin, the
first through French where the spelling changed. To PURVEY
originally meant to foresee, an exact translation of the Latin,
but has come to mean furnish provisions, supply necessities
usually for a number of persons.

E. Chambers says: 'POURVEYOR or PURVEYOR, an officer of the
household who provides corn, victuals, fuel, and other necessities for the King's house. POURVEYOR became a term so odious
in times past that the heinous name was changed to that of
ACHATOR (*ă-kā'-ter*), or buyer', today a CATERER.

714. *ENCYCLICAL*, encyclical (*ĕn-sĭk'-lĭ-kăl*) *n.* A general
    communication to all members of a group, circular letter
to a council; now in the Roman Catholic Church written instructions from the Pope to his bishops, circular to his whole
jurisdiction.
ENCYCLICAL comes from the Greek ἐνκύκλιος (*encyclios*),
circular, round, a combination of ἐν (*en-*), *in*, and κύκλος
(*cyclos*), a circle, the source also of ENCYCLOPEDIA, a circle of
sciences.

To 15 per cent an ENCYCLICAL means REPORT. A REPORT, from
the Latin *re-*, back, and *portare*, to carry, is literally to carry
back. A REPORT is an account brought back, communication,
description, recital, narrative, statement. An ENCYCLICAL is a
directive, almost a command, announcement of a policy, and
in this sense comes very close to REPORT, for an ENCYCLICAL
may be a REPORT of a decision reached.

In building a vocabulary test there is always an effort to select
misleads close in meaning to the test word but not correct.
In this instance REPORT may be too close to ENCYCLICAL to score
as wrong.

715. *COMPLEMENT*, complement (*kŏm'-plē-mĕnt*) *n.* Full
    amount, complete allowance, perfect state, that which
completes, quantity that fills, the amount needed to bring
something to its full.

The difference between COMPLIMENT and COMPLEMENT, one
with I and the other with E, is spelling and not vocabulary, but
should be recognized. Both come from the Latin *complemen-
tum*, that which completes, from *complere*, to fill up, complete,
a combination of *com*, which in this case intensifies the meaning,
and *plere*, to fill up, as: 'The ship had its COMPLEMENT of
storms', or 'The company had its COMPLEMENT of men'. COM-
PLIMENT with an I comes through Italian, where the original E
changed to I, and now means flattery, commendation, tribute,
encomium, formal expression of polite praise.

From the same *plere*, to fill up, but starting with the privative
de- comes the verb to DEPLETE, to empty, exhaust, reduce. Still
from *plere* come the adjective REPLETE, completely full, filled
to the brim, satiated; as well as the noun PLENTY, profusion,
abundance; and finally the verb to COMPLETE, perfect, make
whole. A COMPLEMENT is that which is needed to COMPLETE,
or sometimes the whole when COMPLETE.

To 24 per cent COMPLEMENT means MIXTURE. Both COM-
POUNDS and COMBINATIONS are MIXTURES, and both start with
the same COM- as COMPLEMENT, but it is hard to see why MIX-
TURE should attract so many as a synonym of COMPLEMENT.

716. *AGRONOMY*, agronomy (*ă-grŏn'-ō-mĭ*) *n.* The science
    of farm management, a branch of agriculture, husbandry;
in a special use to feed and graze cattle, art of cultivating the
ground.

AGRICULTURE comes from the Latin *agri*, the genitive of *ager*,
land, field. AGRONOMY comes from the Greek ἀγρονόμος (*ag-
ronomos*), an overseer of public lands, from ἀγρός (*agros*),
field, and νέμειν (*nemein*), to deal with, administer.

717. *SECULAR*, secular (*sĕk'-ū-lahr*) *adj.* Worldly, temporal,
    mundane, profane.

SECULAR, from the Latin *seculare*, belonging to a particular
period, comes from *seculum*, a generation, age. SECULAR once

meant occurring once in a generation and so dependent on time. From this SECULAR came to designate things which changed with time, and so worldly, temporal, as opposed to spiritual, religious, sacred. The word SECULAR stands almost alone in English with no obvious relations.

To 17 per cent SECULAR means PUBLIC, a word used in many of the same situations. PUBLIC education is open to everyone; whereas SECULAR suggests limited in the sense of not religious, not ecclesiastic. SECULAR and TEMPORAL are more nearly alike. TEMPORAL suggests a connection with time; while SECULAR means not connected with the church.

Of SECULAR Ephraim Chambers says: Something that is temporal in which sense the word stands opposed to ecclesiastical.

SECULAR is more particularly used for a person who lives at liberty in the world; not shut up in a monastery, not bound by vows nor subject to the rules of any religious community.

718. *TURPITUDE*, turpitude *(ter'-pĭ-tūd)* *n.* Depravity, inherent baseness, shameful wickedness, vileness, badness.
TURPITUDE, from the Latin *turpitudo*, baseness, from *turpos*, base, must be learned almost in isolation, for it has no near relations in English. Perhaps its opposite RECTITUDE, uprightness, honesty, integrity, from the Latin *rectus*, straight, is the easiest association, for it leads 17 per cent to select UPRIGHTNESS as the meaning of TURPITUDE.

719. *TETTERED*, tettered *(tĕt'-tĕrd)* *adj.* Affected by eczema, scabby, reddened, inflamed.
Either FETTERED or TETHERED may lead to the misconception RESTRAINED, marked by 25 per cent as the meaning of TETTERED. A TETHER is a rope, chain, halter used to confine an animal within given limits. The verb to TETHER, related to Danish and Icelandic, is to restrain a grazing animal to a limited range.

FETTER, directly from Anglo-Saxon like TETHER, is a chain frequently used to tie the front legs of an animal loosely so that he moves with difficulty and cannot run away. SHACKLE and FETTER are close in meaning, to confine, restrain, bind.

TETTERED goes directly back to Anglo-Saxon and is today a name for several skin diseases such as eczema.

720. *MAJUSCULE*, majuscule (*mă-jūs'-kūl*) *adj.* Large as
applied to printed or hand-written letters of the alphabet.
MAJUSCULE, MINUSCULE (*mĭ-nŭs'-kūl*), and UNCIAL (*ŭn'-shĭal*),
though technical terms in the development of writing, appear in
the vocabularies of many high-scoring persons. Early letters of
inscriptions, carved in stone, were both large and angular,
called MAJUSCULE, from the Latin *majuscula*, the diminutive of
major, larger, greater, and were all of one size, all capitals. Then,
in monastic scripts of the 4th century and thereafter, some
letters, though still large, began to be rounded in a style called
UNCIAL, from the Latin *uncia*, a twelfth part, sometimes translated as an inch. Then in the 8th and 9th centuries small letters
appeared, MINUSCULE, from the Latin *minusculus*, rather small,
the diminutive of *minor*, *minus*, small, of reduced form.

Much modern writing is CURSIVE, in which the letters are
joined and written without lifting the pen, from the Latin
cursus, to run, the source of CURRENT.

721. *DRAMA*, drama (*drah'-mă*) *n.* Story put into action, play,
either comedy or tragedy, theatrical entertainment. COME-
DIES, TRAGEDIES, and even FARCES, are kinds of DRAMA.
DRAMA, from the Greek δρᾶμα (*drama*), δρᾱματις (*dramatis*),
an action represented on the stage, deed, act, especially a tragedy, is thought by 29 per cent of high-school students in
general, and by 30 per cent of high-vocabulary ones, to mean
EXCITEMENT. To EXCITE, from the Latin *ex*, out, and *cĭēre*, to call,
is to call out for action, stir up, stimulate, set in motion, animate,
arouse. A DRAMA, a story of human life leading often to a catastrophe, acted on the stage, should be EXCITING, arousing, stirring;
and the adjective DRAMATIC has come to mean just this. But
despite the connection, a DRAMA is still a play acted on the stage
or written to be acted, a bit of human life put into action.

722. *DECIDUOUS*, deciduous (*dē-sĭd'-ū-ŭs*) *adj.* Falling off,
transitory, fleeting, perishing, losing foliage every year,
shedding leaves at the end of the season, not perennial, not
permanent.
DECIDUOUS comes from the Latin *decidere*, to fall down, fall off,
perish, from *de*, down, and *cadere*, to fall. From this comes

CADENCE, the fall of the voice at the end of a sentence, the easier DECAY, and DECADENCE (*dĕ-kă'-dĕns*).

To 15 per cent DECIDUOUS means DEEP ROOTED. This may be a confusion of DECIDUOUS with ASSIDUOUS, working hard, constant in application, unremitting, persevering, laborious, unceasing. DEEP can mean absorbed, engrossed, immersed, as: 'Deep in thought', ROOTED, firmly fixed.

From E. Chambers: 'In some plants the leaves are DECIDUOUS or fall off in autumn; in others, they remain all winter. In some plants the CALYX is DECIDUOUS with the flower, that is, falls off the plant with it; in others, not.'

FUGACIOUS (*fū-gā'-shŭs*), from the Latin *fugare*, to flee, means fleeting or, in botany, falling early, soon after appearance. DECIDUOUS means falling in the autumn. EVERGREEN means shedding leaves in the spring, after the new foliage is formed.

723. *SINUOUS,* sinuous (*sĭn'-ū-ŭs*) *adj.* Twisting, full of curves, abounding in turnings, winding, tortuous, wavy, devious, serpentine.

To 20 per cent SINUOUS means MUSCULAR, assuredly a confusion of SINUOUS with SINEWY, different words from different sources despite their similarity. SINEWY comes directly from Anglo-Saxon, while SINUOUS comes from the Latin *sinuosus*, full of folds, from *sinus*, a bend, fold, hollow, bay, a Latin word taken over unchanged by the medical profession. From the Latin *insinuatus*, the past participle of *insinuare*, to bring in by winding, creep in, steal in, a combination of *in*, and the same *sinus*, a winding, comes INSINUATE, originally to work one's way in by twisting and turning, now to suggest indirectly, intimate, hint obliquely.

In the phrase: 'In SINUOUS fashion', the popular misconception is EVIL, due probably to the word SIN, and the adjective SINFUL, wicked. SINUOUS means full of bends, and so CROOKED. Much as CROOKED has come to mean not honest, so SINUOUS is sometimes used to mean morally crooked, deviating from the right, and in this sense EVIL is a correct answer.

Of the noun SINUOSITY E. Chambers says: 'A series of bends or turns in arches or other irregular figures; sometimes jutting out and sometimes falling in, such as described by the motions of a serpent. It is the SINUOSITY of the sea-coasts that forms bays, ports, capes, etc. The course of the river MEANDER, creeping in a thousand agreeable SINUOSITIES, served Daedalus as a model for his labyrinth.'

724. *LENITIVE*, lenitive (*lĕn'-ĭ-tĭv*) *adj.* Assuaging pain, softening, soothing, mitigating, palliative, tranquilizing, alleviating, moderating, abating.

LENITIVE comes from the Latin *lenitus*, the past participle of *lenire*, to soften, from *lenis*, soft, mild, the source of LENIENT, merciful, tolerant, clement, gentle, mild in judgment.

The two misleads are REGRETFUL and PROVISIONING. But the choices scatter, suggesting that LENITIVE is unknown to many.

LENIENT, referring to decisions by authorities of any kind, is a general English literary word. The noun, a LENITIVE, is medical; and the adjective LENITIVE is not only unusual, but has a distinct medical suggestion.

725. *CHARTACEOUS*, chartaceous (*kahr-tā'-shŭs*) *adj.* Paper-like, made of paper, resembling writing-paper.

CHARTACEOUS comes through the Latin *charta*, paper, thin sheet, also writing, from the Greek χάρτης (*chartes*), a leaf of paper, thin sheet, the source of the English word CHART, a map, and CARD. From the same Greek comes CHARTER (*chahr'-tĕr*), an agreement on paper; and this idea of a legal contract may in some remote way lead 30 per cent to believe that CHARTACEOUS means EXPENSIVE. The verb to EXPEND comes from *ex-*, out, and *pendere*, to weigh, and means to pay out.

The ending -ACEOUS appears almost exclusively in botany and zoology, as: HERBACEOUS, GALLINACEOUS, pertaining to poultry; CRUSTACEOUS (*krŭs-tā'-shŭs*), with crusts, shells; CRETACEOUS (*krē-tā'-shŭs*), chalky. CHARTACEOUS should be used only as a technical term in botany or some allied science.

726. *CELERITY*, celerity (*sĕ-lār'-ĭ-tĭ*) *n.* Speed, swiftness, rapidity, quickness.

To 40 per cent CELERITY means SOPHISTICATION. In one sense something SOPHISTICATED is highly technical, complicated, up-to-date, perhaps implying speed, quickness.

SOPHISTICATION comes from the SOPHISTS, Greek wise men noted for specious logic, clever but fallacious reasoning. Although SOPHISTICATED now often means worldly, complex, not simple, in the original sense, a SOPHISTICATED design is one made with the intent of deceiving the public; it is fallacious, tricky, sound in appearance only.

CELERITY comes from *celeritas*, from *celer*, swift, quick, rapid, a Latin word associated with the Greek κέλης (*celes*), a racer. From the same *celer*, quick, comes the verb to ACCELERATE, to make quicker, and the noun ACCELERATION, going faster, both through the Latin verb *celerare*, to hasten. CELERITY is quickness, speed.

727. *NICTITATE*, nictitate (*nĭk'-tĭ-tāt*) *v.* To wink, lower the eyelid. The common form is NICTATE.

To 30 per cent the verb NICTITATE means to SMOKE, misled by the word NICOTINE, a poisonous chemical substance, $C_{10}H_{14}N_2$, found in tobacco.

NICTITATE comes from the Latin *nictitare*, the frequentative of *nictare*, to wink. The NICTITATING MEMBRANE is a third thin eyelid, possessed by birds and some animals, but not by man, which can be drawn across the eyeball, independent of the usual heavier lid.

728. *SORDID*, sordid (*sŏr'-dĭd*) *adj.* Foul, gross, vile, mean, base, dirty, filthy, ignoble, mercenary, low, degraded.
SORDID comes from the Latin *sordidus*, dirty, filthy, foul, vile, mean, base, from the verb *sordere*, to be dirty.

To 38 per cent SORDID means AGONIZING, the popular mislead. SORE, directly from Anglo-Saxon, and much like SORDID in appearance, means painful, aching, distressing, AGONIZING; and SORE has from time to time in the past been used to mean vile, base, mean, SORDID. But today, SORE means painful, distressing; while SORDID means dirty.

729. *TITULAR*, titular (*tĭt'-ū-lahr*) *adj.* Having a title, nominal, pertaining to a title, not actual, bearing a title.
TITULAR, from the Latin *titulus*, is the adjective, pertaining to TITLE, having a title, much as ANGULAR is the adjective for ANGLE.

TITULAR is thought by 20 per cent to mean SUPREME. A TITLE suggests SUPREMACY; but the adjective TITULAR suggests having a TITLE but without authority to go with it, and so at most INEFFECTUAL, the second most popular mislead.

730. *APPRISE*, apprise (*ăp-prīz'*) *v.* To inform, advise, give notice, acquaint, tell, warn, notify, mention to.

APPRISE comes through the French from the Latin *apprendere*, to teach, inform.

To 38 per cent APPRISE means JUDGE. To APPRAISE (*ăp-prāz'*) is to set a price on, estimate the value of, and so to JUDGE the worth of. But APPRAISE has in the past been spelt APPRISE and, though some may be confusing the modern APPRAISE, to judge, and APPRISE, to tell, inform, they are justified historically.

731. *TIPPLE*, tipple (*tĭp'-pl*) *n.* A strong, intoxicating drink, liquor, alcoholic beverage.

Both TIPPLE and GROG are general terms for alcoholic drinks. GROG is a strong drink of any sort, served out to sailors. TIPPLE is more elegant, and drunk in small quantities, almost sipped. To TIPPLE is to drink any strong drink, stimulant, in quantity, to excess.

A TIPPLER, a TOPER, and a DRUNKARD are in increasing order of seriousness. A DRUNKARD is so affected by alcoholic liquors as to be unable to live normally. A TOPER drinks habitually, but is less affected, though recognized by the community as a drinker. A TIPPLER drinks in small amounts, sips his drinks.

732. *CONCOURSE*, concourse (*kŏn'-kŏrs*) *n.* An open space, area in which crowds gather; also a driveway in a park, popular promenade, specifically an open place in a railway station through which passengers throng.

CONCOURSE, from the Latin *concursus*, the past participle of *concurrere*, to run together, derives from *con*, together, and *currere*, to run; from the same source as CONCURRENT, used of events running along together, happening at the same time. Nathan Bailey uses CONCOURSE for the actual running or resorting of people to a place; a multitude of people assembling together upon some particular occasion.

To 15 per cent CONCOURSE means HARMONY. CONCURRENCE (*kŏn-ker'-rĕns*) is agreement, cooperation, and so HARMONY, and comes from the same Latin *con*, together, and *currere*, to run; and the verb to CONCUR (*kŏn-ker'*) is literally to run together, and so coincide, agree, be in HARMONY. CONCURRENCE and CONCOURSE may both be used to mean a running together; but the two have come to convey quite different secondary meanings. CONCURRENCE is agreement, HARMONY; while a CONCOURSE is an area in which people gather.

733. *MULCT*, mulct (*mŭlkt*) *v.* To punish by forfeiture, fine, penalize, deprive of some possession as a penalty, demand payment in money for some misdemeanor.
Of 28 high-vocabulary adults 16 mark TAX as the meaning of MULCT. The verb to TAX, from the Latin *taxare*, may mean make demands upon, lay a burden on, task, put to a certain strain, as: 'To TAX one's memory'; also to take to task, censure, blame; but as the word is ordinarily used TAX is the general term for an amount demanded by the government, for its own purposes, from those under its authority. TAXES include DUTIES, CUSTOMS, TOLLS, ASSESSMENTS, but not FINES imposed as a punishment for wrong-doing. To MULCT, from the Latin *mulctare*, is to fine, punish, penalize.

MULCTS include the AMERCIAMENT (*ă-mĕr'-sĭ-ă-mĕnt*), a pecuniary punishment imposed on offenders at the mercy of the court. This differs from a FINE, a punishment certain and determined by some statute.

734. *CAVIL*, cavil (*kăv'-ĭl*) *v.* To find fault without reason, carp, object frivolously, mock captiously.
Ephraim Chambers says: 'CAVIL is defined by some as a fallacious kind of reason, carrying some resemblance of truth, which a person knowing its falsehood, advances in dispute for the sake of victory'.

CAVIL comes directly from the Latin *cavillari*, to mock, jeer, scoff, quibble, from *cavilla*, a jeering, scoffing.

The popular mislead is CRINGE. To CRINGE (*krĭnj*) is to cower, stoop in fear, crouch in servility. One may CRINGE as the result of a CAVILING comment. CAVIL is the cause; CRINGE is the result.

CAPTIOUS describes a tendency to catch at minute faults and exaggerate them into real defects. CARPING, a stronger word, is faultfinding, which is both unreasonable and unceasing. CARPING is criticism of conduct; CAVILING, put forward by a hypocritical, pettish, petulant opponent, is criticism of argument.

735. *LISSOME*, lissome (*lĭs'-sŭm*) *adj.* Limber, flexible, lithe, nimble, active, willowy, agile, light, supple.

LISSOME is a shortened form of LITHESOME, much as BLISS is short for BLITHESOME. The Anglo-Saxon LITHE, pronounced with the TH as in THE, THEN, THERE, and CLOTHE, not CLOTH, originally meant soft, tender, agreeable, but has come to mean willowy.

The -TH is an old Anglo-Saxon ending added years ago to make abstract nouns from adjectives and verbs, as: GROWTH from GROW, TRUTH from TRUE, HEALTH from HEAL, STEALTH from STEAL, and so LITHE from a much earlier LISS, which meant gentleness, mildness, ease, softness.

The Anglo-Saxon -SOME, at the end of LITHESOME, makes adjectives from nouns, as: TROUBLESOME, QUARRELSOME, LONESOME.

Although LISSOME is thoroughly Anglo-Saxon in every aspect, AGILE, from the Latin *agere,* to do, move, is usually preferable.

736. *PRETERNATURALLY,* preternaturally (*prē-ter-nă'-tūr-ăl-lĭ*) *adv.* Beyond the normal, extraordinarily, remarkably, specially, uncommonly, prodigiously, uniquely (v. B. 780), eminently, egregiously (v. B. 2064).

PRETERNATURALLY is a combination of the Latin *praeter,* beyond, over, more than; NATURAL; and finally the Anglo-Saxon -LY, added to an adjective to form the corresponding adverb.

The adjective NATURAL, through the Latin *naturalis,* by birth, according to nature, comes from *natura,* birth, nature, from the past participle *natus,* of the verb *nasci,* to be born, the source of NASCENT, beginning to exist, coming into being, incipient.

PRETERNATURALLY is thought by 14 per cent to mean MYSTERIOUSLY, actually a correct answer, certainly too close to be a mislead in a vocabulary test. SUPERNATURAL, starting with the Latin *super,* above, is above nature, applied to acts in a realm

higher than man and so miraculous. PRETERNATURAL is outside
nature and so MYSTERIOUS, cabalistic, inexplicable, mystic, obscure, incomprehensible.

737. *KEEN*, keen (*kēn*) *v.* To wail over any loss, lament loudly,
mourn, weep.
The verb to KEEN, and the present participle KEENING, come
from an old Irish word meaning to lament, weep. A banshee
KEENS to warn an aristocratic family of an approaching death.
To 20 per cent of those who have tried this vocabulary test,
KEENING means REJOICING, an exact opposite.

738. *CROTCHET*, crotchet (*krŏt'-chĕt*) *n.* Whimsical fancy,
odd notion, eccentric conceit, singular opinion, fantastic
idea, perverse whim, peculiar turn of the mind, sometimes the
ill-tempered idea of an elderly person.
CROTCHET, from Old French, is a diminutive of the French
croche, a hook, the source of CROCHET (*krō-shā'*), the diminutive
of *croc*, hook, the source of CROOK.
Among 29 high-vocabulary adults guesses as to the meaning of
CROTCHET divide almost equally among BROKEN BOWL, CRIPPLE,
and WHEEL. A CROCK is a pot, jar, receptacle of coarse earthenware; also a fragment of earthenware, a potsherd, the Century
says: 'Such as is used to cover the hole in the bottom of a
flower pot'.
A RATCHET, ending in the same five letters as CROTCHET, is a
detent, designed to fit into the notches of a RATCHET-WHEEL,
part of a stopping and starting mechanism.
Both QUIPS and GIBES are taunting, sharp, cutting, sarcastic,
made at the expense of another. A CROTCHET is purely personal,
the expression of an idiosyncrasy, never with others in mind.

739. *BAIZE*, baize (*bāz*) *n.* A coarse woolen cloth, heavy stuff.
The color BAY is a brownish red, chestnut, rufous. From
this, the plural BAYS came to mean a light woolen bay-colored
fabric. Today BAIZE is singular, not plural.
BAIZE, at first a fine thin material used for clothing, was manufactured in England in 1561 by refugees from the Netherlands
who settled in Sandwich. BAIZE is now coarser, heavier.

The mislead is FURNITURE, closely associated, for BAIZE, sometimes in plain red, more often in green, is used for billiard tables, desk tops, and card tables.

740. *INUSITATE*, inusitate (*ĭn-ū'-sĭ-tāt*) *adj.* Unused, neglected, unusual, disused, fallen into desuetude.

INUSITATE, directly from the Latin *inusitatus*, unused, combines the privative IN-, and *usitatus*. This in turn is the past participle of *usitari*, to use often, the frequentative of *uti*, to use. Immediately from *uti*, to use, come UTENSIL, anything used, now more often something used in the kitchen; UTILITY, usefulness, state of being serviceable, beneficial; and the unusual INUTILE (*ĭn-ū'-tĭl*), useless, worthless, unprofitable.

To 23 per cent INUSITATE means UNCONQUERABLE. To USURP, from the Latin *usurpare*, make use of, perhaps from *usus*, the past participle of *uti*, to use, is to seize and hold; and this leads easily to UNCONQUERABLE. In place of INUSITATE, an awkward word, use NEGLECTED.

741. *SATELLITE*, satellite (*să'-tĕl-līt*) *n.* An attendant, follower, guard, subordinate; or from Bailey: 'Small secondary planets, which are, as it were, rolled about or waiting upon other planets'.

Of 29 high-vocabulary adults, 11 select STAR as the meaning of SATELLITE. In 1721 Bailey used STAR and SATELLITE interchangeably, as: 'SATELLITES of Jupiter, little wandering STARS or MOONS which move about the body of Jupiter, first discovered by Galileus, by the help of a telescope'; or in the succeeding paragraph: 'SATELLITES of Saturn, 5 small stars that roll about Saturn in the like manner, discovered by G. D. Cassini in 1684'.

Historically STAR is correct; but, as science penetrates the unknown, words become more precise. A STAR is a hot sun, giving off light of its own, like our sun, but far distant. A SATELLITE, from the Latin *satelles*, *satellitis*, attendant, revolves around a larger body, as the moon, a SATELLITE of the earth, revolves around the earth approximately once every month. The earth in turn is a SATELLITE of the sun, an attendant on the sun, revolving around the sun once a year. The earth is commonly called a PLANET, one of nine orbiting the sun.

742. *BANTLING*, bantling (*bănt'-lĭng*) *n.* A young child, infant, connoting a shade of contempt.

The diminutive suffix -LING appears in FOUNDLING, FONDLING, and NURSELING. A FOUNDLING is a child without a parent; BANTLING is a contemptuous or sneering word for small child.

The popular mislead is LIGHT TIMBER, suggested perhaps by the word SCANTLING, a small beam less than 5 inches square.

MONEY-CHANGER, marked by 24 per cent, may be suggested by BANKING, something like BANTLING in sound and looks.

743. *YEARLING*, yearling (*yēr'-lĭng*) *n.* Any year-old animal, in its second year.

The only mislead marked is SIBLING, due probably to the difficulty of this word. Two boys may be brothers; two girls, sisters; but until recently there has been no word for the relationship of a boy and girl born of the same parents. Karl Pearson defined SIBLING as including this connection as well as brothers and sisters; and E. L. Thorndike used it in 1905.

WHELP is an old native Anglo-Saxon word for the young of many sorts. CUB is recent. BULLOCK is a young bull; HEIFER (*hĕf'-er*), a young cow. A COLT is a young male horse; FILLY, a young female horse. For some animals there is a special term for those more than 5 years old. A thoroughbred COLT becomes a HORSE when 5 years old. A male deer becomes a STAG at the same age. In his fourth year he is a STAGGARD. YEARLING is a general term which applies to any animal in his second year. To be exact one may speak of a YEARLING HEIFER.

744. *TRIREME*, trireme (*trī'-rēm*) *n.* An ancient Greek warship with three banks of oars, later copied by the Romans, a long narrow, swift vessel with 170 rowers, 3 tiers on each side. TRIREME, from the Latin *tres, tris*, three, and *remus*, oar, is thought by 22 per cent to mean SAIL-BOAT. A TRIREME often had masts and sails, which were hoisted when the winds were favorable. But the TRIREME was fundamentally handled by rowers, not by sails.

The earliest Greek merchant ships were the TRIACONTERS (*trī'-ă-kŏn-ter*), from the Greek τριάκοντα (*triaconta*), thirty, with thirty oars, one man at each, and the PENTECONTERS, with

fifty oars, all at the same level. Warships had two levels, with
several men at each oar, as the BIREME; three levels, or banks,
as the TRIREME; or occasionally four, as in the QUADRIREME.

745. *PILLORIED*, pilloried (*pĭl'-lōr-ēd*) *adj.* Punished, ridi-
      culed, abused, exposed in a PILLORY, according to Bailey,
a wooden frame or engine on which cheats and other offenders
stand to be examples of public shame.
Of 28 high-vocabulary adults, 4 select INVADED as a synonym of
PILLORIED. To INVADE is to penetrate enemy country with hostile
intent. PILLAGED, starting with the same four letters, means
PLUNDERED, robbed, taken by open force, usually in war, and
so is close to INVADED.

PILLORIED, from the Latin *pila*, a pillar, is individual punishment. From Ephraim Chambers: 'PILLORY was anciently a post
erected in a cross road by the lord, as a mark of his seigniory
with his arms on it, and sometimes with a collar to tie criminals
to.

'PILLORY, at present (1728), is a wooden machine, whereon
certain criminals, as perjurers, are fastened, and exposed to the
public derision. It was peculiarly intended for the punishment
of bakers who should be caught faulty in the weight or fineness
of their bread.

'With us it is in the form of a frame erected on a pillar, and
made with holes and folding boards, through which the heads
and hands of criminals are put.'

746. *SEPAL*, sepal (*sē'păl*) *n.* In botany, one of the leaves that
      make up the outer circle of a flower, a calyx-leaf, one of
the individual leaves which make up the CALYX, sometimes called
the cup of the flower.
In his Philosophy of the Inductive Sciences, 1840, William
Whewell (*hū'-ĕl*) says: 'The term SEPAL was devised by Necker
to express each of the divisions of the CALYX'. It comes from the
Latin *separ*, the source of separate, different, and was later accepted by A. P. de Candolle.

The SEPALS are the bright, colored leaves which often give
the beauty to a flower, seemingly held together or growing out
of a cuplike formation, the CALYX.

747. *FORENSIC*, forensic (fŏr-ĕn'-sĭk) *adj.* Belonging to courts of law, pertaining to legal proceeding.

FORENSIC comes from the Latin *forensis*, belonging to the FORUM. The FORUM, from *foris*, out of doors, was originally the market place, and so a gathering place; then the official center of the corporate life of the city where justice was administered. From this comes the adjective FORENSIC, pertaining to the market place; then to public discussion; and finally to legal argument. Because of this derivation, FORENSIC suggests argument, the presentation of a court case as opposed to the JUDICIAL aspects of law.

Of 28 high-vocabulary adults, 6 underline ESTABLISHED as the meaning of FORENSIC. The verb to ESTABLISH comes from the Latin *stabilire*, to make stable, from *stabilis*, stable, firm, fixed, planted. To ESTABLISH is to make firm, to settle, fix. This may be a recognition of the relationship of law and order to a firm basis, an efficient state.

748. *FLANNELLY*, flannelly (flan'-nĕl-lĭ) *adj.* Flannel-like, pertaining to a warm, soft, woolen fabric, loosely woven.

FLANNEL may be a noun, the cloth, or an adjective, as FLANNEL clothing. FLANNELLY as an adjective is awkward and unnecessary.

The use of FLANNELLY to mean BLURRED is figurative and should not appear in a dictionary or in a vocabulary test. If an author wants to suggest that a style is loosely woven, that is the author's privilege, but FLANNELLY does not mean BLURRED.

749. *FALCATE*, falcate (fahl'-kāt) *adj.* Curved like a sickle, hooked, crooked, crescent, shaped like a scythe.

FALCATE comes from the Latin *falx, falcis*, sickle, the source of FALCON, a kind of female hawk used in hunting, named for its hooked talons, its claws.

The big mislead is FAULTY, selected by 35 per cent, compared with only 30 per cent who select CROOKED. A FAULT, from the Latin *fallere*, to deceive, disappoint, is a defect, flaw, failing, error, mistake, FALLACY. FALLACIOUS is the adjective which goes with FAULT. STRAIGHT, the opposite of FALCATE, is also popular as a mislead.

750. *ECTOMORPHIC*, ectomorphic (*ĕk-tō-mŏr'-fĭk*) *adj.* A recently devised word, a combination of ECTO, from the Greek ἐκτός (*ectos*), outside, and μορφή (*morphe*), form. Thin-bodied, slim, bony.

ECTOMORPHIC is thought by 23 per cent to mean MUSCULAR, and by another 15 per cent to mean OVER-WEIGHT. Sheldon, in his book on Body Types, divides men into three groups: ENDOMORPHIC, those with heavy bodies, which leads to the selection of OVER-WEIGHT; MESOMORPHIC, the muscular, sturdy type, which leads to the selection of MUSCULAR; and finally ECTOMORPHIC, or thin-bodied.

ENDOMORPHS, with a tendency to put on fat easily, become roly-poly. The MESOMORPHS tend toward massive strength and muscular development, and continue through life in the general proportions of athletic shapeliness, expanding within their established mold. ECTOMORPHS, tending to be thin, sacrifice bodily mass in favor of the sensory organ system, of increased surface area with consequently greater sensory exposure to the outside world.

751. *ANDROCENTRIC*, androcentric (*ăn-drō-sĕn'-trĭk*) *adj.* Male dominated, centered around man.

The Greek prefix ANDRO-, from ἀνήρ (*aner*), ἀνδρός (*andros*), means man, male. The second part, -CENTRIC, and the word CIRCLE, both come through Latin *centrum*, center, from the Greek κέντρον (*centron*), originally a sharp point, goad, prod, and so the point of a compass, and from this, a CIRCLE, the round shape drawn by a compass.

CONCENTRIC (*kŏn-sĕn'-trĭk*) means having the same center. Two circles may be CONCENTRIC, with the same center. ECCENTRIC (*ĕk-sĕn'-trĭk*), a combination of *ex-*, from, and -CENTRIC, may mean not having the same center, but has come to be used figuratively with reference to unusual conduct, unexpected, deviating from the ordinary. GEOCENTRIC means with the earth at the center; EGOCENTRIC (*ē-gō-sĕn'-trĭk*), with one's self at the center. The unusual ANDROCENTRIC, with man at the center, should rarely be used.

PLEASURE-SEEKING, selected by 30 per cent, is the attractive mislead.

752. *FETISH*, fetish (*fĕt'-ĭsh*) *n.* An idol, image, effigy, anything regarded as the habitation of a deity, material object
looked upon with awe.

Similar words in various languages mean sorcery, charms,
witchcraft, wizard, bewitchment, and artificial. FETISH was
first applied by Portuguese traders, on the west coast of Africa,
to charms and talismans worshipped by the natives. FETISH
comes to English through many sources, perhaps most directly
from the French, but appears in German, Portuguese, and
Swedish, perhaps originally from the Latin *facere*, to make.
FACTITIOUS (*făk-tĭsh'-ŭs*), made artificially, produced by art,
and FEAT, something done, an accomplishment, are both doublets
of FETISH, that is, come from the same source.

To 32 per cent a FETISH is a CREED. Both a CREED and a FETISH
may be regarded with awe; both may be objects of blind
reverence, both represent systems of religious belief. A CREED
is a formal statement in words; while a FETISH is a material
object, and should continue with this meaning, though the
word has come to be used loosely for any false standard.

753. *PERIPHRASIS*, periphrasis (*pĕ-rĭf'-ră-sĭs*) *n.* A roundabout way of speaking, circumlocution, pleonasm, wordi-
ness, verbosity, prolixity, verbiage, abundance of words, using
more words than necessary; Bailey, 1721: 'Expressing a thing
in many words when a few would have served'.

PERIPHRASIS comes from the Greek περί (*peri*), around, about,
and φράζειν (*phrazein*), to declare, point out, show, speak,
tell. A PHRASE is a brief expression; while the verb to PHRASE
is to put into words. The Greek περί (*peri*), around, appears
in PERISCOPE (*păr'-ĭ-skōp*), an instrument for looking around;
and PERIMETER (*pĕ-rĭm'-ē-ter*), the measurement around a
figure, circumference.

Of 28 high-vocabulary adults, 3 select DICTION as the meaning
of PERIPHRASIS. DICTION is a choice of words, manner of expressing one's self, one meaning of the Greek φράσις (*phrasis*).
PERIPHRASIS is a special kind of DICTION; but answers scatter
suggesting that PERIPHRASIS is difficult, almost unknown.

Distinguish PARAPHRASE (*păr'-ă-frāz*) from the verb PERI-
PHRASE (*per'-ĭ-frāz*). To PARAPHRASE is to restate for clearness,

express the sense in other words, repeat in a different way, with the purpose of clarification. To PERIPHRASE is to employ too many words, resort to circumlocution. PERIPHRASIS is the noun.

754. *BAIT*, bait (*bāt*) *v.* To torment, tease, provoke, harass, set dogs on, annoy, nag, badger, worry.

BAIT comes directly from an Icelandic word meaning to feed; also to hunt with hounds or with hawks; supposed to be related to an Anglo-Saxon word meaning to bite.

To BAIT is primarily to cause to bite, specifically to set dogs on another animal, to cause them to bite, as: 'To BAIT a bear'. The same word then came to mean put food on a hook and so cause fish to bite. From this it was a short step for the noun BAIT to mean an enticement, allurement, temptation, and for the verb to BAIT to mean entice, allure, a meaning more popular today than the original, as shown by the fact that 67 per cent select INVITE as the meaning compared with only 33 per cent who underline TORMENT.

755. *LUCULENT*, luculent (*lū'-cū-lĕnt*) *adj.* Clear, evident, unmistakable.

LIGHT is Anglo-Saxon, as are most words with this kind of -GH- in the middle, as: BRIGHT, MIGHT, NIGHT, RIGHT, SIGHT, TIGHT. To ENLIGHTEN is to make clear, explain.

LUCENT (*lū'-sĕnt*), bright, shining, lustrous, resplendent, is Latin, from *lucens, lucentis*, the present participle of *lucere*, to shine. LUCID means clear to the understanding; while ELUCIDATE is to make clear, explain.

LEUCOUS (*lū'-kŭs*), light-colored, white, from λευκός (*leukos*), light, bright, white, appears today mostly as a part of some highly technical term, to mean white, light-colored.

LUCULENT is Latin, but rarely seen. Originally it meant bright, luminous, transparent; but has come to mean clear, evident, unmistakable.

756. *UMBRAGE*, umbrage (*ŭm'-brāj*) *n.* The feeling of being overshadowed, annoyance, injured self-respect, offense at being slighted, displeasure, irritation, wounded pride, vexation, almost anger.

To 18 per cent UMBRAGE means COERCION, almost compulsion, constraint, forcing another to act. COERCION may be selected only because it is itself a difficult word unknown to 31 per cent.

UMBRAGE originally meant shade, shadow, obscurity, through the French *ombrage*, shade, shadow, and the Latin adjective *umbraticus*, pertaining to shade, from *umbra*, shade, shadow. From this comes the feeling of being overshadowed, and so resentment, annoyance, irritation, pique, wounded vanity. Neither PIQUE nor UMBRAGE suggest a desire to retaliate. PIQUE is quick, momentary, soon gone. UMBRAGE, offense at being slighted, is stronger and more lasting than PIQUE.

757. *FIDUCIARY*, fiduciary (*fĭ-dū'-shē-ā-rĭ*) *adj.* Of the nature of a trust, pertaining to a financial trust.

FIDUCIARY, from the Latin *fiduciarius*, relating to something held in trust, comes from *fiducia*, trust, anything held in trust, and this from *fides*, faith, and *fidere*, to trust. From this last verb come such widely different words as: FIDELITY, INFIDEL, AFFIDAVIT, PERFIDY.

'FIDUCIARY agreement' is thought by 44 per cent to mean TRUST, but by another 26 per cent to mean FISCAL, and this is about the proportion of these two ideas in the word FIDUCIARY. FISCAL, from the Latin *fiscus*, the state treasury, once meant pertaining to the public treasury, relating to taxes, pertaining to the financial operation of the government, but has come to refer to financial matters in general. FIDUCIARY means trust, but is almost always applied to financial trust.

758. *PHANTASMAGORIC*, phantasmagoric (*făn-tăz-mă-gō'-rĭk*) *adj.* Illusive, fantastic, spectral, strange, wild, freaky, of an illusion.

To 44 per cent PHANTASMAGORIC means DECEPTIVE, illusive, false, deceiving by illusion. PHANTASMAGORIC comes from the Greek φάντασμα (*phantasma*), a phantasm (*făn'-tăzm*), specter, vision, apparition, illusion, hallucination, and ἀγορά (*agora*), assembly, market-place. A PHANTASMAGORIA is an assemblage of specters, a fantastic series of apparitions, a collection of terrifying figures; and PHANTASMAGORIC is the adjective.

But to another 34 per cent PHANTASMAGORIC means WHIMSI-CAL, full of whims, freaky, capricious, singular, odd, grotesque. The same noun PHANTASMAGORIA was used years ago for an exhibition of pictures, shown by two magic lanterns or stereopticons arranged so that one view merged into the next. Today PHANTASMAGORIC may mean either DECEPTIVE, illusive, spectral, or WHIMSICAL, capricious; or a bit of both.

759. *PRINK*, prink (*prĭnk*) *v.* To adorn, prim, prune, preen, trim, deck out ostentatiously, dress for show, decorate one's self.

PRINK, and the original verb PRANK, are related much as CLINK, a light sharp sound, and CLANK, a deeper one. PRANK survives as a noun, a whim, playful trick.

PRINK is thought by 18 per cent to mean DAUB, smear, cover over with something soft. In provincial England the verb PRINK means look, gaze, and today implies fussing over one's appearance, especially before a looking glass. This leads another 14 per cent to select ADMIRE as the meaning, close in suggestion but not so close as dress, ADORN.

760. *HENCHMAN*, henchman (*hĕnch'-măn*) *n.* A follower, adherent, groom, footman, hireling, mercenary, venal attendant.

To 34 per cent, a third of those tested, HENCHMAN means EX-ECUTIONER. A HENCHMAN is a HANGER-ON, parasite, dependent, one who clings to another when he is unwanted, but HANGMAN, executioner, though so similar in appearance to HANGER-ON, is never used in this way.

HENCHMAN goes back through Middle English, where it meant a groom, page, attendant, horseman, to a much earlier Anglo-Saxon word for horse.

A FACTOTUM does all kinds of work but is not subservient to the will of another. A FAG is learning to be a HENCHMAN, an attendant with no will of his own and without the colorful uniform of many doormen.

'A HENCHMAN is a necessity in the machine of politics, in the present mode of getting and keeping high office', said a quotation three-quarters of a century ago.

761. *REPINE*, repine (*rē-pīn'*) *v.* To fret, complain, murmur, grieve, be unhappy, indulge in discontent.

Of 28 high-vocabulary adults, 6 select DIE as the meaning of REPINE. To PINE, directly from an Anglo-Saxon word for pain, torment, misery, torture, is to be consumed with real grief, grow thin, flag, wither, droop, actually to waste away with pain, ending sometimes in death. To REPINE, which goes back through the French to the same Anglo-Saxon, suggests complaining too much, fretting needlessly, indulging in grief.

762. *CHURL*, churl (*chĕrl*) *n.* A peasant, rustic, rude boor, surly person.

CHURL is a more difficult word than one would expect. It is Anglo-Saxon; and Anglo-Saxon words average easier than Latin. CHURN leads 15 per cent to select BUTTER-MAKER as the meaning of CHURL. WHIRL leads even more to select SPIRAL; and HUT is equally popular.

Coming from an Anglo-Saxon word meaning a freeman of the lowest rank in early England, called also a free-tenant-at-will, a CHURL may today mean a peasant, rustic, countryman, laborer. Or the same word has come to mean a rude fellow, surly person, ill-bred man. In his dictionary of 1721 Nathan Bailey says: 'A covetous hunks'; and of HUNKS he says: 'A miser, covetous, niggardly wretch'.

763. *FOOLSCAP*, foolscap (*fools'-kăp*) *n.* Writing paper about 13½ by 16½ inches in size.

FOOLSCAP is a size of writing paper, so named because of its water-mark, a fool's cap and bells, dating back to just before the year 1500.

A twelve-volume Cyclopedia of 1813, in its article on paper manufacture, says: 'The principal labor consists in assorting the paper according to its quality and faults'.

Water-marks, seen by holding the paper to the light, are not printed, but are made during manufacture, by pressure against the soft pulp. Water-marks today indicate the name of the manufacturer, the quality of the paper, and sometimes, especially in England, the size, as: POST, ELEPHANT, CROWN, and POT, 12½ by 15½, an inch smaller each way than FOOLSCAP.

764. *VERNAL*, vernal (*ver'-năl*) *adj.* Pertaining to spring, spring-like.

By 15 per cent WINTER is selected as the meaning of VERNAL. VERNAL, ESTIVAL (*ĕs'-tĭ-vahl*), AUTUMNAL, and HIBERNAL or HIEMAL (*hī'-ĕ-mahl*), are adjectives for the four seasons.

VERDURE, greenness, the fresh green of early vegetation, and VERDANT, green, despite the similarity of both to VERNAL, come from the Latin *virere*, to be green, fresh, vigorous, and do not come from *ver*, the Latin for spring, the source of VERNAL.

765. *VISCERA*, viscera (*vĭs'-ĕr-ă*) *n.* Internal organs.

VISCERA, plural of VISCUS, comes from the Latin *viscus*, with the plural *viscera*, any one of the inner organs of the body. The four great cavities of the body are the HEAD, THORAX, ABDOMEN, and PELVIS; and these contain the brain, heart, lungs, liver, intestine, kidney, bladder, womb, etc. VISCERA are especially abdominal, the intestine.

766. *ACHROMIC*, achromic (*ă-krōm'-ĭk*) *adj.* Without coloring matter, colorless.

The metal, the chemical element CHROMIUM (*krō'-mĭ-ŭm*) was so named because of the brilliant colors of its compounds, as CHROME-YELLOW. From this comes the adjective CHROMIC (*krō'-mĭk*), which should be reserved ordinarily for chemistry. CHROMATIC (*krō-mă'-tĭk*) should be used of lenses, in physics rather than chemistry.

ACHROMATIC, starting with the Greek privative *à*, is usually applied to light and means without color. ACHROMIC should mean without CHROMIUM, but is used occasionally by chemists to mean without coloring matter.

The only mislead so far selected by anyone is SPARKLING, underlined by 30 per cent, another instance of the confusion of a word with its opposite.

767. *AFICIONADO*, aficionado (*ă-fē-sē-ō-nah'-dō*) *n.* An ardent devotee, zealot, enthusiast, votary, one zealously devoted to any cause.

To 25 per cent AFICIONADO means PARTICIPANT, one who actually takes part, shares in the activity, partakes of the action.

One meaning of the Spanish verb *aficionar* (*ah-fē-sē-ō-nahr'*) is to inspire affection; and the same dictionary defines *aficionado* as an AMATEUR, originally a French word for the Latin *amator*, a lover, from *amare*, to love. AFICIONADO is a Spanish word which does not appear in the Century Dictionary, but is answered correctly, as DEVOTEE, by a surprisingly large number.

768. *ABSCIND*, abscind (*ăb-sĭnd'*) *v*. To cut off, sever, separate
    one part from another.
The verb to RESCIND, like ABSCIND, is to cut off, cut short; but RESCIND is used more frequently to mean repeal, revoke, annul, cancel, as: 'To RESCIND a law'. ABSCIND, though rare, retains more of the original meaning, cut off.

To ABSCIND is thought by 20 per cent to mean STRIP, with something of the same suggestion. To STRIP is to take away, remove, dispossess, deprive, divest, the opposite of supply, furnish. To SEVER, a synonym of ABSCIND, is to separate, break, cut, cleave, the opposite of UNITE.

ABSCIND comes from the Latin *abscindere*, to cut off, a combination of *ab*, off, and the Latin verb *scindere*, to cut, the direct source of SCHISM, a split, division in a religious or political party, and SCISSION, a cleavage, the act of cutting, dividing, splitting. From this same source, by a roundabout route, comes SCISSORS. To ABSCIND is literally to cut off.

769. *BOVINE*, bovine (*bō'-vēn*) *adj*. Relating to oxen; figur-
    atively: stolid, inert, ox-like, boviform.
BOVINE comes from the Latin *bos, bovis*, ox, oxen. Sheep, goats, and antelope all belong to the BOVIDAE family, the hollow-horned ruminants. From the Latin CAPER, goat, comes CAPRICIOUS, leaping about mentally like a goat, whimsical.

To 15 per cent BOVINE means SHEEPLIKE. SHEEP is Anglo-Saxon, with no corresponding adjectives inspired by Latin.

770. *TRITURATE*, triturate (*trĭt'-ŭ-rāt*) *v*. To grind to a
    powder, rub, pulverize, bruise, bray, crush with a mortar
and pestle.
TRITURATE comes from the Latin *tritura*, a rubbing, threshing, from the past participle *tritus* of the verb *terere*, to rub, grind,

thresh, the source of TRITE, worn-out, frayed, rubbed, and so commonplace, stale, hackneyed. From the same past participle *tritus* come ATTRITION, a gradual rubbing and so wearing away; DETRITUS, accumulated particles of rock which have been worn away by rubbing; and finally CONTRITE, broken in spirit by a sense of guilt, penitent, conscience-stricken.

771. *AESTHESIA*, aesthesia (*ĕs-thē'-zĭ-ah*) *n.* Perception, feeling, sensation, sensibility, the opposite of ANAESTHESIA. Two Greek words: αἴσθησις (*aisthesis*) and αἰσθητός (*aisthetos*) mean, respectively, perception by the senses, and perceptible. From the latter word comes AESTHETICS, the science of the sense of beauty, study of taste, theory of the fine arts; and this leads 40 per cent to believe that AESTHESIA means BEAUTY, AESTHETICS. AESTHESIA is used in the original Greek sense of perception by the senses, feeling; so that ANAESTHESIA (*ăn-ĕs-thē'-zĭ-ah*) is loss of the sense of touch, state of insensibility produced by chloroform or ether. An ANAESTHETIC is the agent, something which produces temporary loss of sensation.

Should these words start with AE- or with E- alone? The Century Dictionary prefers AESTHESIA, but ESTHETICS for the sense of beauty. In his English Usage, Fowler inclines toward shortening AE- to E-. Either can be argued for or against. Too much has been done at the moment, and too rapidly, to cheapen the language. This book will use AE- for AESTHETICS, AESTHESIA, and ANAESTHESIA, perhaps just because it seems more AESTHETIC, to use that word as Fowler says it should never be used, to mean merely beautiful.

772. *PRECURSORY*, precursory (*prē-kĕr'-sō-rĭ*) *adj.* Introductory, forerunning, prefatory, preliminary, preparatory, preceding, going before.
PRECURSORY, from the Latin *praecursor*, a forerunner, from *praecurrere*, to run before, adds *prae*, before, to *currere*, to run.

An EXCURSION is a running out; and INCURSION, from *in*, and *currere*, to run, is a running in, an inroad, invasion, raid. INCURSIVE is the adjective. To RECUR, still from the same *currere*, to run, is to run again; OCCUR, to run, to meet, and so meet, appear, happen; while a CURRENT is a running.

PRECURSORY is thought by 40 per cent to mean EXPLORATORY, a word with much the same feeling. To EXPLORE is the Latin *ex-*, out, and *plorare*, to cry out, wail, weep; the source of DEPLORE, wail for, weep for. EXPLORE has left almost completely its original meaning, its meaning by derivation, and now means look for, search for, examine, scrutinize, investigate.

PRECURSORY suggests coming beforehand, as a herald, in preparation for something to follow.

773. *PALIMPSEST*, palimpsest (*păl'-ĭmp-sĕst*) *n*. Any writing material from which old writing has been removed and new writing made, stone rubbed smooth for a new inscription. PALIMPSEST comes from the Greek πάλιν (*palin*), again, once more, back to a former condition, and ψάειν (*psaein*), to rub. Of 29 high-vocabulary adults, 4 select LAID-PAPER and 3 others MONUMENT as meanings of PALIMPSEST. LAID-PAPER, when held to the light, shows delicate parallel lines, once made by wires on which the paper rested in the process of manufacture. Those who select LAID-PAPER know that a PALIMPSEST is material on which to write.

A PALIMPSEST was once a stone slab rubbed or scraped smooth for a new inscription and this may suggest MONUMENT. An OBELISK, somewhat like PALIMPSEST in sound, is a tall pointed pillar; but answers to the meaning of PALIMPSEST scatter enough to suggest that the word is almost unknown.

In the 9th century writing materials were costly and hard to obtain, so that leaves from Euclid's Elements of Geometry were erased in order that the papyrus might be used again. A PALIMPSEST is now any material, often parchment, from which earlier writing has been removed to make a surface for new.

774. *APOSTROPHE*, apostrophe (*ă-pŏs'-trō-fē*) *n*. Digression, interruption.
APOSTROPHE comes through the Latin from the Greek ἀποστροφή (*apostrophe*), a turning away, a combination of ἀπό (*apo*), away, and στρέφειν (*strephein*), to turn, the source of STROPHE. In writing, an APOSTROPHE is an interruption.

In grammar the sign which is used for the omission of a letter, also the sign which indicates possession, is called an APOSTROPHE.

Although spelt and pronounced today like APOSTROPHE, an interruption, the word APOSTROPHE as a grammatical sign may have come originally from a different source.

775. *COMPATIBLE*, compatible (*kŏm-păt'-ĭ-bl*) *adj*. Consistent, sympathetic, existing together, reconcilable, concurrable, congruous, harmonious, appropriate, accordant; Nathan Bailey, 1721: 'That agrees or suits, or subsists with; suitable; not incongruous; agreeable'.

Of 27 high-vocabulary examinees 9 select FRIENDLY, in place of SYMPATHETIC, as a synonym, very close, for COMPATIBLE comes from the Latin *com*, together, and *pati*, to suffer, endure, the source of COMPASSION and PATIENCE, enduring.

Of FRIENDLY, Webster, in his dictionary of 1828, says: 'Kindly, favorable, disposed to promote the good of another, amicable, not hostile'; and of the noun: 'A FRIEND is attached to another by affection; entertains for another sentiments of esteem, respect, and affection which lead him to desire his company and to seek to promote his happiness and prosperity; opposed to foe or enemy'.

776. *URBANE*, urbane (*er-bān'*) *adj*. Refined, polished, cultured, cultivated, experienced, citified, sophisticated, suave, courteous, well-bred, civil, worldly, elegant.

URBANE comes from the Latin *urbanus*, pertaining to city life and so refined, polished, from *urban*, originally from *urbs*, *urbis*, city, the source also of SUBURB, literally under the city, in the plains beneath the hills of Rome, and the adjective SUBURBAN.

URBAN (*er'-băn*), with no E at the end, means belonging to a city, as: 'An URBAN population'. URBANE, spelt with an E and accented on the last syllable, means having the personal characteristics of one who lives in a city. In much the same way HUMAN (*hū'-măn*) means pertaining to man, a living animal. HUMANE (*hū-mān'*) means kindly, merciful, literally having the disposition of a man.

URBANE is thought by 22 per cent to mean TOLERANT, forbearing, enduring, consenting, brooking, allowing, suffering, bearing with. Perhaps a city person is more TOLERANT, puts up with things with which he is not necessarily in sympathy.

777. *SOLIPSISM*, solipsism (*sŏl'-ĭp-sĭzm*) *n.* The theory that nothing but the self exists, one's self is the only object for verifiable knowledge, that everything is taking place only in one's mind.

SOLIPSISM comes from the Latin *solus*, alone, and *ipse*, self, a Latin word seen in the familiar *ipso facto*, in the fact itself.

Among 29 high-vocabulary adults, 14 concentrate on GRAMMATICAL-ERROR as the meaning of SOLIPSISM. A SOLECISM is a gross GRAMMATICAL-ERROR, an impropriety in language, or a deviation from the rules of syntax; the remarkable fact here is that the word SOLECISM is well enough known to be so popular a mislead.

SOLIPSISM is the belief that everything one sees and hears takes place in one's own mind only, an idea impossible to disprove by any experiment ever devised.

778. *RECRUDESCENCE*, recrudescence (*rē-krū-dĕs'-sĕns*) *n.*
A revival, reappearance, renewed activity, breaking out afresh, coming again into active existence. The verb to RECRUDESCE is to break out again, erupt anew.

DECLINE, from the Latin *de-*, down, and *clinare*, to bend, an exact opposite, is selected as a synonym by 40 per cent, a few more than mark REVIVAL, the correct answer.

RECRUDESCENCE comes from the Latin *re-*, again, and *crudescere*, literally to grow raw, from *crudes*, raw, the source of the English CRUDE. RECRUDESCENCE was originally the breaking out again of an old sore, and correctly should be used for the reappearance of something undesirable.

The French word RENAISSANCE (*rĕn-ă-sāwns'*), or even RENASCENCE (*rĕ-năs'-sĕns*), which means rebirth, and so renewal, both a combination of the Latin *re-*, again, and *nasci*, to be born, should be used for the reappearance of anything desirable.

779. *LONGANIMITY*, longanimity (*lŏng-gă-nĭm'-ĭ-tĭ*) *n.*
Long suffering, patience, forbearance, moral strength, fortitude, endurance.

LONGEVITY (*lŏng-jĕ'-vĭ-tĭ*) comes from the Latin *longus*, long, and *aevum*, age. From this same *aevum*, age, and *medius*, middle, comes MEDIEVAL which really means middle age. LONGEVITY is

literally long life; and this leads 30 per cent to believe that
LONGANIMITY means GREAT AGE, almost a translation of the
Latin, for LONGANIMITY comes from the same *longus*, long, plus
animus, mind, feeling, will. ANIMUS, in English, is spirit, temper,
but has come to mean hostile spirit, ANIMOSITY, which is in turn
ill will, enmity. Despite these connections LONGANIMITY means
patience, forbearance, fortitude.

This last word, FORTITUDE, from *fortis*, strong, is moral
strength, endurance, an exact synonym of LONGANIMITY.

780. *PAREGORIC*, paregoric (*păr-ĕ-gor'-ĭk*) *adj.* Soothing,
      consoling, assuaging, relieving pain. PAREGORIC may also
be a noun, an anodyne.

PAREGORIC comes from the Greek παρήγορος (*paregoros*),
soothing, consoling, from παρά (*para*), beside, and ἀγορεύειν
(*agoreuein*), to speak in an assembly, from ἀγορά (*agora*),
assembly, marketplace, for public discussion.

CLEANSING is the popular mislead, selected by 25 per cent.
CATHARTIC means cleansing; PAREGORIC means soothing.

781. *POGROM*, pogrom (*pō'-grŏm*) *n.* An organized massacre,
      slaughter; originally a mass killing of Jews in Russia.

MASSACRE is a French word for the indiscriminate killing of
groups of people. SLAUGHTER goes back through Middle English
to the same Anglo-Saxon and Scandinavian sources as SLAY.
POGROM comes from a Russian word meaning destruction.

The SLAUGHTER of the Innocents was the murder of the children of Bethlehem by King Herod. The MASSACRE of the
Huguenots in Paris occurred on Saint Bartholomew's Day,
August 24, 1572. The MASSACRE of Glencoe was the killing of
the Macdonalds of Glencoe, Scotland, by the Campbells in
1692.

Given a choice between SLAUGHTER and TORTURE, 55 per cent
select the first and 30 per cent the second; about the percentage
of the two ideas in a POGROM.

782. *UNGUIS*, unguis (*ŭng'-gwĭs*) *n.* The plural is UNGUES
      (*ŭng'-gwēz*). Hoof, the heavy protected end of a horse's
leg, of the same material as a human finger nail.

To 15 per cent UNGUIS means OINTMENT. An UNGUENT (*ŭng'-gwĕnt*), is an OINTMENT, from the Latin *unguentum*, ointment, from *unguere*, to smear, anoint, rub. The adjective is UNGUINOUS (*ŭng'-gwĭ-nŭs*), oily, unctuous, resembling fat.

UNGUIS comes directly from the Latin *unguis*, nail, claw, talon, hoof. The UNGULATA are hoofed animals, the horse, cow, etc.; not including the elephant.

783. *REDACTION*, redaction (*rē-dăk'-shŏn*) *n.* Revising, editing, preparing a literary work for publication.

The verb to REDACT (*rē-dăkt'*) comes from the Latin *redactus*, the past participle of *redigere*, a combination of *red-*, which stands for *re-*, back, and *actus*, a doing, from *agere*, to drive, do, act; and this derivation leads 25 per cent to select CUT-BACK as the meaning of REDACTION.

The EDITING of a magazine or newspaper may involve management, the entire process of publication; but the verb to REDACT, and the noun REDACTION have come to mean literary revision, not including management.

784. *BANDY*, bandy (*băn'-dĭ*) *v.* To toss back and forth, give and take, throw from side to side, hit to and fro, pass from one to another.

The word BANDY first appeared about 1600, in John Florio's World of Words, in Elizabethan times, as the English meaning of the Italian *bandare*.

The mislead WAVE is marked by 27 per cent, perhaps because of the verb to BRANDISH. This comes through the French BRAND, sword, from the Anglo-Saxon word for sword. To BRANDISH is by derivation to WAVE a sword in the air, but the Century Dictionary gives TOSS as an obsolete meaning, so that BRANDISH might be a synonym of BANDY. But to WAVE is to flourish in the air while continuing to hold. To BANDY is to throw, toss, let go of. BANDY differs from both throw and toss in suggesting not merely a single act, but throwing back and forth from one to another.

To HURL is to throw with force. To PITCH is to throw with skill. To BANDY is to throw back and forth from one to another several times.

785. QUASI, quasi (*kwā'-sī*) *adj.* Seeming, apparent, as it were, expressing some resemblance.

The Latin *quasi*, as if, as it were, just as, from *quam*, as, how, and *si*, if, means literally as if.

QUASI and PSEUDO (*sū'-dō*) are nearly identical, the first from Latin, the second from the Greek ψευδο (*pseudo*), spelt in Roman letters, from the noun ψεῦδος (*pseudos*), a falsehood, lie. PSEUDO implies and perhaps means false, sham, spurious, counterfeit. In science, PSEUDO means that on the surface something looks like something else, but is not really like it.

Given a choice between RESEMBLING and FALSE as meanings of QUASI, five times as many select the first as the second; but the suggestion FALSE is nevertheless present and strong. QUASI scientific means as if it were scientific but suggests that it is not. Of QUASI the Century Dictionary says: 'Expressing some resemblance but generally implying that what it qualifies is in some degree fictitious and unreal'.

786. ACATALEPSY, acatalepsy (*ă-kăt'-ă-lĕp-sĭ*) *n.* Incomprehensibility, doctrine of the skeptics, unknowableness with certainty, insistence on the impossibility of complete discovery, impossibility of being comprehended.

To 18 per cent ACATALEPSY means DISEASE. Occasional words, used positively, apply materially to bodily acts, and mentally when used negatively. To TAKE is to grab physically, with the hand; to MISTAKE is to fail to TAKE mentally. To APPREHEND is to arrest physically; to MISAPPREHEND is to misunderstand mentally.

CATALEPSY, from the Greek κατάληψις (*catalepsis*), a seizure, is a DISEASE, the sudden suppression of motion, a kind of APOPLEXY in which the patient is speechless, senseless, and fixed in one position, with the eyes open, without seeing or understanding. ACATALEPSY, starting with the privative A, is the impossibility of seizing mentally, incapability of grasping with the mind.

787. SUFFUSE, suffuse (*sŭf-fūz'*) *v.* To overspread, cover with fluid, literally to pour under.

SUFFUSE comes from the Latin *suffusus*, the past participle of *suffundere*, to pour underneath, from *sub*, under, and *fundere*, to pour. The verbs to CONFUSE (*kŏn-fūz'*), DIFFUSE (*dĭf-fūz'*), EFFUSE (*ĕf-fūz'*), TRANSFUSE (*trăns-fūz'*), and the adjective PRO-FUSE (*prō-fūs'*), all come from the same *fundere*, to pour. To CONFUSE is to pour together and so mix. To AFFUSE, though rare, is merely to pour. To INFUSE is obviously to pour in, and some-times to steep. To EFFUSE, starting with the Latin *ex*, forth, is to pour out.

In the first form of this vocabulary worksample both SPRINKLED and FLUSHED appeared as possible synonyms of SUF-FUSED, the first marked by 32 per cent and the second by 42 per cent. SPRINKLED comes from outside, on the surface. SUF-FUSED has the suggestion of flowing under, similar to a FLUSH, redness caused by a sudden flow of blood to the face.

788. *TAMBOUR*, tambour (*tăm'-boŏr*) *n.* Specifically a brass drum, with a single head.

TAMBOUR is the French *tambour*, drum, which goes back through Spanish and Portuguese words to Arabic.

A TAMBOURINE, the diminutive of TAMBOUR, is a hoop of wood or ring of metal, with a single head of stretched parch-ment, played by shaking or by hitting. Though of Oriental origin, it is common in Spain, where it is called a TAMBOUR de Basque.

A TYMPANUM is a large metal bowl, with a rounded bottom, and also a single head. A GONG was at first much like the TYM-PANUM, struck with a stick with a leather end. Then the same word GONG came to be applied to a bell, held in a fixed position, not swinging, but struck. The TOM-TOM is an Indian drum, with two heads far apart, and a long barrel connecting them.

The word TAMBOUR seems to have had many meanings, for Nathan Bailey says: 'A bell, a loud-sounding instrument or vessel. A musical warlike instrument'.

789. *PAUCITY*, paucity (*paw'-sĭ-tē*) *n.* Scantiness, fewness, scarcity, rarity, dearth, smallness of quantity, insufficiency of amount, not many.

PAUCITY comes through French and Italian from the Latin *paucus*, few, little, from the same original source as PAUPER, a person with little money, and perhaps as POOR.

DEARTH implies dear, expensive because of scarcity. RARITY has the same suggestion of valuable. PAUCITY has neither of these suggestions, but, like PAUPER, means merely lacking in quantity. Opposites are PLURALITY and ABUNDANCE.

790. *SYMPOSIAC*, symposiac (*sĭm-pō'-zē-ăk*) *adj.* Pertaining to a gathering of persons for discussion, convivial; Noah Webster, 1828, says: 'Pertaining to compotations and merry-making; happening where company is drinking together'.

Webster's synonym COMPOTATION comes from the Latin *con*, together, and *potare*, to drink, the source of POTABLE, drinkable, good to drink; POTION, a draught, amount drunk; and POTATION, both a drink and a drinking party. COMPOTATION is said to be Cicero's Latin translation of the Greek συμπόσιον (*sympos-ion*), from σύν (*syn*), together, and πίνειν (*pinein*), to drink. A SYMPOSIUM is an intellectual conversation with wine after dinner. SYMPOSIAC is the adjective.

Among 29 high-vocabulary adults, 7 concentrate on DIAGNOSTIC as a synonym of SYMPOSIAC, clearly a confusion of SYMPTOMATIC, an adjective from SYMPTOM, with SYMPOSIAC, from SYMPOSIUM. Of SYMPTOM Webster says: 'Properly something which happens in concurrence with another thing as an attendant. In medicine any affection which accompanies disease. Particular SYMPTOMS which uniformly accompany a morbid state are called DIAGNOSTIC symptoms'.

Ephraim Chambers, in his Cyclopedia of 1728, which still gives some of the clearest definitions ever written, says of SYMPOSIUM: 'A conference or conversation of philosophers at a banquet'; and he adds: 'Plutarch has nine books which he calls: Disputations at Table'.

791. *ADYTUM*, adytum (*ăd'-ĭ-tŭm*) *n.* A secret shrine, sanctuary, sacred place open only to priests; according to Bailey, a retirement in the pagan temples, into which none but priests were admitted, where oracles were given.

ADYTUM is the Greek ἄδυτον (*adyton*), spelt in English letters, a combination of the Greek privative ἀ- and δυτός (*dytos*), from δίειν (*diein*), to enter. An ADYTUM was a place not to be entered.

To 23 per cent ADYTUM means MARKET-PLACE. In ancient Athens the AGORA (*ă-gō'-răh*), often pronounced (*ă'-gŏr-ăh*), was the MARKET-PLACE, which has only recently been uncovered. A MARKET-PLACE is public and so an opposite of ADYTUM.

792. *JUNCO*, junco (*jŭn'-kō*) *n*. A small slate-colored bird with two white tail feathers, a part of the large family of finches.

The word JUNCO comes directly from the Spanish *junco*, which means rush. The RUSHES are plants, tall green stems without leaves, growing in water. They include the HORSETAIL. The name of the genus is the Latin JUNCUS, a rush or reed.

To 30 per cent JUNCO means BUSH. A BUSH or a SHRUB is smaller than a tree, usually with no main trunk, but several small branches springing directly from the ground. If instead of BUSH examinees marked RUSH the answer would be justified, but a BUSH, a SHRUB, and the JUNCO, the bird, differ widely.

Does a word like JUNCO belong in a vocabulary test? Just what are the characteristics of a technical term? Where does a general literary vocabulary stop, and a specialized one begin? We are finding evidence that a high-vocabulary individual knows many technical terms in almost every direction, a narrowly defined technical vocabulary and general knowledge differing less than we had expected.

793. *BRUIT*, bruit (*broŏt*) *v*. To report, communicate, advertise, publish, spread a rumor, gossip about, make known.

To BRUIT, directly from the French *bruit*, from the verb *bruire*, to make a noise, is to noise abroad, spread the fame of. BRUIT, the noun, originally meant noise, din; and the verb to BRUIT means publicize in a loud noisy way.

To PUBLISH, marked by 15 per cent, is much too close to use as a mislead, and must be removed in the next revision of the test.

794. *MACULATE*, maculate (*măk'-ū-lăt*) *v*. To spot, stain, stipple, dot, speckle, mark with blotches.

MACULATE, from the Latin *macular*, a spot, means spotted, stained. The better known word, IMMACULATE, starting with the Latin IN-, which becomes IM- before another M, means not spotted, not stained, and so spotless. This leads 40 per cent to underline WASH as the meaning of MACULATE, twice as many as select the opposite, STAIN, the correct answer.

795. *BARKANTINE*, barkantine (*bahr'-kăn-tēn*) *n.* A three-masted sailing ship with the foremast square rigged and the other two fore and aft.
A BARK, another three-masted vessel, has the two forward masts both square rigged and only the stern mast, called the MIZZEN-MAST, fore and aft.

BARK comes from the French *barque,* with similar words in Spanish, Portuguese, Italian, Dutch, German, Danish, and Icelandic.

A BRIGANTINE, from the word BRIGAND, a pirate, is a two-masted vessel, the foremast square rigged.

The popular misleads are WHARF and SHIPYARD, both connected with boats, the second step in learning, using a word in the correct situation, but with the wrong meaning.

796. *INEFFICACIOUS*, inefficacious (*ĭn-ĕf-fĭ-kā'-shŭs*) *adj.*
Not effective, inadequate, without force, ineffectual (v. b. 329), inefficient (v. b. 448). Read EFFICACY (v. b. 1650).
For INEFFICACIOUS the four misleads are almost equally marked, INSULTING by 23 per cent, HARMFUL by 22 per cent, etc., suggesting that the word is so far beyond those who have tried the test that the answers are largely guesses.

The verb to EFFECT (*ĕf-fĕkt'*), from the Latin *facĕre,* to do, make, build, is to achieve, produce a result, bring about, accomplish, realize.

EFFECTIVE and EFFICACIOUS are two corresponding adjectives with nearly identical meanings, though by custom applied in different situations. Thus one speaks of an EFFECTIVE person, but an EFFICACIOUS remedy. Of the two, EFFICACIOUS is the stronger. When strictly used EFFECTIVE applies to that in operation, actually underway, as an EFFECTIVE blockade. EFFICACIOUS applies to that which would be EFFECTIVE if used. An EFFECTIVE treatment is underway, being used; an EFFICACIOUS treatment would be EFFECTIVE if it were used.

797. *PERFERVID*, perfervid (*per-fer'-vĭd*) *adj.* Ardent, zealous, animated, eager, vehement, impassioned, very hot.

FERVENT, from the present participle *fervens, ferventis,* and FERVID from the verb *fervere,* to boil, glow, both mean glowing, burning, fiery, vehement.

In the adjective PERFIDIOUS, a combination of PER- and the Latin *fides,* faith, the prefix means from. The PERFIDIOUS person is faithless, not to be trusted. In PERDITION, from *dare,* to give, the initial PER- gives the same negative sense. This leads 15 per cent to believe that PERFERVID means UNRESPONSIVE, an exact opposite, for in this case the prefix PER- intensifies the meaning, almost in the sense of thoroughly, through to the end. PERFERVID means very eager, extremely ardent, overly impassioned or animated.

798. *ECUMENICAL*, ecumenical (*ĕk-ū-mĕn'-ĭ-kăl*) *adj.* General, universal, whole; also, in a more limited sense, belonging to the entire Christian Church, where ECUMENICAL means entire.

ECUMENICAL comes directly from the Greek οἰκουμενικός (*oicoumenicos*), general, universal, strictly pertaining to the whole inhabited world, from οἶκος (*oicos*), house, the source of ECONOMY, household management.

The phrase ECUMENICAL COUNCIL, an assemblage of church dignitaries called by the Pope, leads naturally to the misconception RELIGIOUS, selected by 40 per cent, compared with 45 per cent who mark the right answer UNIVERSAL.

There are five kinds of SYNODS, religious assemblies, councils, meetings, from the Greek σύν (*syn*), together, and ὁδός (*odos*), way road: ECUMENICAL, GENERAL, NATIONAL, PROVINCIAL, and DIOCESAN (*dī-ŏs'-ē-săn*). A DIOCESAN council, with a bishop at its head, is a meeting of the ecclesiastics of a DIOCESE, a division of a country, vague in extent, but in a religious sense an area under a bishop. A PROVINCIAL council is a meeting of the churchmen under several bishops with an archbishop at its head. A NATIONAL or PLENARY council is a meeting of all bishops or archbishops of a nation. A GENERAL council is one to which the church as a whole is invited but which is not actually attended by all representatives.

The Lateran council, held in Rome in the Lateran basilica in 649, and others beginning in 1123, were councils of the Western Church, though one held in 1215 was regarded by Roman Catholics as ECUMENICAL, general, universal. An ECUMENICAL council must actually be attended by representatives of all parties from all parts of the inhabited world.

799. *LODGMENT*, lodgment (*lŏdj'-mĕnt*) *n*. A room, dwell-
       ing, quarters, lodging, house, habitation, usually lived in
temporarily.
The ending -MENT comes from the Latin -*mentum*, frequently added to a verb to form the corresponding noun, the result of the verb. To LODGE, which goes directly back to the French *lodge*, a hut, cot, and is related to the Italian *loggia* (*lōj'-jah*), gallery, balcony, may mean to live, dwell, or sometimes to furnish a temporary habitation, harbor, quarter, provide an abode.

To 22 per cent, nearly a quarter of those tested, LODGMENT means DECISION, probably a confusion of LODGMENT and JUDG-MENT, differing only in the first two letters. JUDGMENT, according to one definition, is the intellectual power of perceiving relations between ideas, understanding, sagacity, good sense, the process of arriving at a conclusion; but in law JUDGMENT is JUDICIAL DECISION. According to the Century Dictionary: 'DECISION is the quality of being able to make up one's mind promptly, clearly, and firmly, as to what should be done and the way to do it'. JUDGMENT, involved in every DECISION, and LODGMENT may both be spelt without an E, or as a second choice with an E, as JUDGEMENT and LODGEMENT.

800. *PALL*, pall (*pawl*, pronounced to rime with FALL, TALL,
       CALL) *n*. A covering, specifically a cloth over a coffin, a
cloth of velvet that covers a coffin at a funeral; also a long robe or mantle worn upon solemn occasions by the Knights of the Garter, but originally an elegant cloak or mantle worn by men upon solemn occasions.
To 25 per cent, PALL means COLD, suggested perhaps by the figurative use of PALL to mean a covering of cloud: 'By this dark PALL thrown o'er the silent world'; 'The sky was over-

spread with a PALL of darkness'; and 'Too cold to melt its PALL of snow'; all citations in the big Oxford Dictionary.

The word PALL, in the general sense of fine cloth, rich material, goes back before the year 1000, to an Old English word for purple robe belonging to a person of high rank, costly cloak usually of purple; and so back to an Anglo-Saxon word for outer garment, cloak, mantle.

From this, PALL came to be a coverlet, canopy, elegant cloth spread over something of value, as an altar-cloth; and so in the 15th century a cloth to cover a coffin. From this comes PALL-BEARER, one of those who supported the corners and edges of the PALL when the coffin was carried on wheels or on an open vehicle.

801. *CRUSTY*, crusty (*krŭs'-tĭ*) *adj*. Crabbed, peevish, surly, curt in manner, harsh in speech, literally like crust.

CRUSTY, the noun CRUST plus Y, comes from the Latin *crusta*, the hard outside surface of any body, outer coating, shell, rind.

To 22 per cent CRUSTY means AGED, the second step in learning, a confusion of words often used together. AGED means old, elderly, ancient, along in years, having reached an advanced period of life, and, though the two are frequently associated, nothing in the word AGED suggests CRABBED or CRUSTY.

PEEVISH is disturbing others with minor complaints, and is more youthful than SURLY which implies a sour disposition, as: 'A SURLY fellow', and applies to those old enough to have turned sour, but not to be AGED. Of the three, CRUSTY is the only one used of age and never of youth. Also of the three it is the only one which suggests the possibility of a really pleasant disposition under a hard surface.

802. *GASCONADE*, gasconade (*găs-kŏn-ād'*) *n*. Bragging, vaunting, blustering, bravado, rodomontade, boastful talk.

OSTENTATION, HAUGHTINESS, PRIDE, are all silent; BRAGGING, BOASTING, and GASCONADE, are noisy. From the same source as BLARE and BRAY, BRAGGING is empty, devoid of substantiation, originally the sound of a trumpet. BOASTING is talking over much about something one has done or owned. Both BRAGGING and BOASTING are dull.

GASCONY was a region in the southwest of France, in the same general area from which came the Troubadours. The GASCONS, named for GASCONY, were noted for their boasting. A GASCONADE is always an interesting exaggeration based on some real deed. In an obituary, written on January 2, 1710, to Sir Hannibal, a gambler, and published in the Tatler, Number 115, Richard Steele defines GASCONADE: 'His great volubility and inimitable manner of speaking, as well as the great courage he showed on those occasions, did sometimes betray him into that figure of speech which is commonly distinguished by the name GASCONADE'.

803. *VISCOUS*, viscous (*vĭs'-kŭs*) *adj*. Jelly-like, glutinous, sticky, clammy, adhesive.

The popular mislead, WICKED, selected by 45 per cent, more than underlined JELLY-LIKE, is obviously the word VICIOUS (*vĭsh'-ŭs*), wicked, depraved, characterized by vice. The confusion may be spelling. Ordinarily c before e or i is pronounced soft, SH, as in VICIOUS; while the same c before A, O, or U, is hard, with a K sound, as in VISCOUS.

VISCOUS comes from the Latin *viscus*, bird-lime, also a name for mistletoe, a parasitic plant. VISCOSITY (*vĭs-kŏs'-ĭ-tĭ*), the noun, is the quality of flowing slowly as pitch, molasses, honey, and the syrups. Such liquids are often sticky, but this is not essential to VISCOSITY, an opposite of MOBILITY. Thus syrups, as opposed to alcohol, are VISCOUS.

804. *RAFFISH*, raffish (*răf'-fĭsh*) *adj*. Worthless, useless, rowdy, disreputable, scampish.

In some dictionaries and in the vocabulary worksample, VULGAR is the synonym. But VULGAR has two quite distinct meanings. One immediately thinks of VULGAR as indecent, offensive, coarse, bawdy, obscene. This is not the meaning of RAFFISH. The noun VULGAR originally meant the common people; and the adjective meant belonging to the common people, and, in this sense, is not far from RAFFISH.

CARELESS, selected by 32 per cent as a meaning of RAFFISH, means negligent, inattentive, heedless, perhaps a characteristic which goes with RAFFISH, but not its meaning.

The noun RAFF is the rabble, scum, worthless persons, sweepings of society. RIFFRAFF goes back to the French-English Dictionary of Randle Cotgrave, 1611, as two words, RIFF and RAFF, scraps, refuse, trash, rubbish; and RAFFISH, when correctly used, has this sense of trashy, worthless.

805. *CATACLYSMAL*, cataclysmal (*kă-tă-klĭz'-măl*) *adj.*
Violent, overwhelming, sweeping, destructive, of the nature of a CATACLYSM; E. Chambers says: 'CATACLYSMUS, a Greek name for a deluge or inundation of waters'.
A CATACLYSM (*kă'-tă-klĭ-zm*) is a deluge, flood, inundation, overflowing of waters, as the Noachian (*nō-ā'-kĭ-ăn*) flood in the time of Noah.
To 22 per cent CATACLYSMAL means REACTION-INDUCING. A CATALYST (*kă'-tă-lĭst*), with no C in the middle, is a substance which accelerates a chemical reaction while remaining unchanged itself, something the presence of which causes a change which would not occur spontaneously, and so REACTION-INDUCING.
MISCHANCE, MISHAP, MISFORTUNE, DISASTER, CALAMITY, CATASTROPHE, are in ascending order of violence. CATASTROPHE, through the Latin *catastropha*, from the Greek καταστροφή (*catastrophe*), an overthrowing, sudden turn, from κατά (*cata*), down, and στρέφειν (*strephein*), to turn, is the general word for a serious disaster, calamity, great misfortune.
CATACLYSM (*kă'-tă-klĭ-zm*), through the Latin *cataclysmos*, from the Greek κατακλυσμός (*cataclysmos*), a flood, deluge, from κατά (*cata*), down, and κλυζειν (*cluzein*), to wash like waves, is specifically a flood, deluge, great rush of waters.

806. *CAVEAT*, caveat (*kă'-vē-ăt*) *n.* Warning, admonition, hint, intimation of caution, legally a notice preventing some action without warning, and so a warning in general.
In Latin CAVEAT means: Let him beware, the third person singular of the present subjective of *cavere*, to beware, take heed, the source also of the English word CAUTION. For those who have taken this vocabulary form, CAVEAT is difficult enough so that the selection of a synonym seems largely luck, with no concentration on any one of the misleads.

From John Ayliffe (*ā'-lĭf*), 1726, an English jurist, a graduate of Oxford, New College, but later deprived of his degree because he criticised the University: 'A CAVEAT in law is an intimation given to some ordinary or ecclesiastical judge, notifying him that he ought to beware how he acts in such and such an affair'.

According to Nathan Bailey, 1727: 'A CAVEAT is a caution, warning, admonition, or legally a bill entered in the ecclesiastical court, to stop the proceedings of one who would prove a will or obtain letters of administration to the prejudice of another'.

In his Commentaries on the Laws of England, 1765-1768, Sir William Blackstone accepted this definition almost verbatim.

807. *CUNEAL*, cuneal (*kū'-nē-ăl*) *adj.* Wedge-shaped, triangular, cuneiform, arrow-headed, tapering to a point.

CUNEAL, and the more usual CUNEIFORM (*kū-nē'-ĭ-form*), come from the Latin *cuneus*, a wedge. CUNEIFORM started perhaps as early as 3000 B. C., and lasted to the time of NEBUCHADNEZZAR (*nĕb-ū-kăd-nĕz'-zahr*), about 600 B. C. Each letter was a design of wedges, tapering to a point usually at the base except for those placed horizontally under other wedges.

POINTED, the most frequently selected choice, though not quite so exact as WEDGELIKE, is another way of describing CUNEIFORM writing, and this mislead must be removed.

The ROSETTA STONE was cut in three sets of characters: ancient Egyptian hieroglyphics; DEMOTIC, a more recent and popular language; and Greek. DEMOTIC was used in Egypt about 600 B.C., about the time of CUNEAL in Assyria, Mesopotamia, and Persia.

808. *OBTUND*, obtund (*ŏb-tŭnd'*) *v.* To blunt, dull, deaden, quell.

OBTUND comes from the Latin *obtundere*, to strike upon, beat, blunt, a combination of *ob-*, upon, and *tundere*, to strike. A CONTUSION (*kŏn-tū'-shŏn*) is the result of a blow from a blunt instrument.

To OBTUND is thought by 20 per cent to mean INCREASE, suggested perhaps by OBTAIN.

An OBTUSE angle, from *obtusus*, the past participle of *obtundere*, is a blunt angle, dull, pounded upon at the point, technically greater than 90 degrees, more than a right angle. An OBTUSE person is dull, not sharp, not acute.

809. *RESTIVE*, restive (*rĕs'-tĭv*) *adj.* Restless, uneasy, hasty, impetuous, unquiet, unsettled, continually moving, refusing to stand still, impatient under restraint.

The noun REST goes directly back to Anglo-Saxon and from there to Sanskrit, and means quiet, repose, absence from labor, and at one time in the past a stage in a journey, and so a stop. RESTIVE originally meant stopping, and then more strangely, obstinate, stubborn, unwilling to move, the exact opposite of the present, refusing to rest. The Century Dictionary explains this as a confusion of RESTIVE, the original meaning, with RESTLESS, without REST. It is probably also in part a confusion of the word with its opposite, a common error, the last step in the learning process.

IMPATIENT, a mislead in the original vocabulary test, selected by 24 per cent, is one of the meanings of RESTIVE, assumed in its change from unwilling to move, to the present meaning, refusing to rest. Whatever the explanation, RESTIVE now means RESTLESS, unable to relax, unwilling to REST.

810. *PLICATION*, plication (*plĭ-kā'-shŏn*) *n.* The act of folding, putting into folds.

To 40 per cent of high vocabulary adults PLICATIONS are CONCILIATIONS. To PLACATE (*plā'-kāt*), with the third letter A, is to appease, pacify, conciliate, from the Latin *placatus*, the past participle of *placare*, to appease. The unusual corresponding noun is PLACATION (*plā-kā'-shŏn*), propitiation, the act of PLACATING, appeasing, pacifying, conciliating.

To PLICATE, from the Latin *plicatus*, the past participle of *plicare*, is to fold, bend, double up. The word is technical, used in zoology, entomology, anatomy, and botany, where it often means PLAITED, folded like a fan. Here the corresponding noun is PLICATION. This is familiar in MULTIPLICATION, from the Latin *multus*, many, literally folding over and over many times. To DUPLICATE is to repeat, copy, do again; where DUPLICATION is the corresponding noun. The same combination of letters is familiar in COMPLICATION; but PLICATION above, a folding, plaiting, is seldom met, and so easily confused with PLACATION.

811. *PLUMBEOUS*, plumbeous (*plŭm'-bē-ŭs*) *adj*. Leaden, heavy, metallic, grey and weighty.

The Latin *plumbare* was to solder with lead, from *plumbum*, lead; and a PLUMBER was originally one skilled in handling lead pipes, and in lead soldering. Lead pipes have disappeared, at least as they were formerly used, but the word PLUMBER survives.

To PLUMP, to fall heavily, like a lump of lead, may come from the same source; and perhaps even PLUNGE.

A PLUMB is a heavy lead weight tied to the bottom end of a string, used to PLUMB a wall, to build it upright, without leaning. The same sort of PLUMB, called also PLUMMET, the French diminutive of *plomb*, is used in measuring the depth of water; and this leads 30 per cent to select PROBING as the meaning of PLUMBEOUS, perhaps too close to be used as a mislead in a vocabulary test. But PLUMBEOUS has come to be used more or less specifically to mean simultaneously both heavy and lead-colored.

812. *SANHEDRIN*, sanhedrin (*săn'-hē-drĭn*) *n*. Supreme council of the Jewish nation, judicial tribunal of 70 members. Moses appointed seventy elders to assist him as magistrates.

The word SANHEDRIN comes directly from the Greek συνέδριον (*sunedrion*), a combination of σύν (*syn*), together, and ἕδρα (*hedra*), a seat. The Greek word ἕδρα appears in the architectural term EXEDRA, sometimes spelt EXHEDRA, a raised platform with a long bench and steps leading up to it, in the open air by the roadside. The SANHEDRIN became extinct in 425.

813. *CAESURA*, caesura (*sĕ-zū'-rah*) *n*. In the scanning of a verse in ancient poetry, the division of a word so that one part seems cut off, and goes to a different foot from the rest. To 16 per cent CAESURA means POEM, the second step in learning, placing the word in its correct environment, with no idea yet of its meaning.

Ephraim Chambers seems clearer in his great Cyclopaedia of 1728, translated into French by Denis Diderot, who, as so often happens, receives more credit than the originator: 'CAESURA more properly denotes a certain and agreeable division of the words, between the feet of a verse; whereby the last syllable of a word becomes the first of a foot'.

Although the word comes from the Latin *caesura*, literally a cutting, from *caedere*, to cut, CAESURA has come to mean the pause which results, rather than the cutting. Thus Chambers continues: 'In modern poetry, a CAESURA is a rest or pause toward the middle of a long verse'; a breathing place in the midst of the verse.

814. *CHIMERA*, chimera (*kĭ-mē'-răh*) *n.* Fabled monster, fire-
    breathing animal with a head and forelegs of a lion and the hind legs and tail of a dragon, sometimes said to have three heads.

Of the adjective CHIMERICAL (*kĭ-mē'-rĭ-kăl*), Nathan Bailey says: 'Imaginary, whimsical, that never was nor will be'. This idea of unreality may lead 39 per cent to select REFLECTION as a meaning of CHIMERA. A REFLECTION, from the Latin *re*, back, and *flectere*, to turn, bend, is a turning back of the rays of light from a reflecting surface such as a mirror. The image given back is unreal.

The GORGON, another unreality, was a woman with writhing serpents on her head in place of hair. The SPHINX in Greek mythology was a female monster with wings, the body of a lion, and the head of a woman. The CHIMERA, through the Latin *chimera*, from the Greek χίμαιρα (*chimaira*), was, according to Bailey: 'A monster, feign'd by the poets to have the head and breast of a lion, the belly of a goat, and the tail of a dragon that belches out fire; a strange fancy, a castle in the air, an idle conceit'.

815. *ADJURE*, adjure (*ăd-jŭr'*) *v.* To entreat, command, im-
    plore, pray, beg, beseech, supplicate, request earnestly.

To ADJURE, to beg, implore, and ABJURE, to abandon, disavow, renounce, differing by only one letter, and much alike in sound, both come from the Latin *jurare*, to swear, from *jus*, *juris*, law, right. To ABJURE is to renounce upon oath, forswear, abandon, disavow, withdraw from formally, and this may suggest DISMISS, thought by 17 per cent to be a synonym of ADJURE. To DISMISS is to send away, let go, give permission to depart. To ADJOURN (*ăd-jĕrn'*), connected with the French *jour*, day, and so literally to put off to another day, from the same source as JOURNAL, a daily record, and much like ADJURE in sound, is to postpone, defer, and so in a sense, DISMISS.

According to Ephraim Chambers, in his Cyclopaedia of 1728: 'ADJURATION is a part of exorcism, wherein the devil is commanded in the name of God to depart out of the body of the possessed'.

To ADJURE is to charge in God's name, strictly and earnestly; to put one to his oath; to command an evil spirit by the force of enchantment; today to beg, implore, beseech.

816. *CREDENDA*, credenda (*krē-dĕn'-dă*) *n.* Articles of faith, belief, that which is to be believed. CREDENDUM is the singular.

CREDENDUM is the Latin neuter from the verb *credere*, to believe, the source of the English word CREED, which in turn comes directly from Anglo-Saxon, and also from the Latin *credo*, I believe.

A CREDENTIAL, usually in the plural, is anything that gives CREDIT or title to confidence, and this leads to the most popular mislead, RECOMMENDATION. Letters of CREDENCE, TESTIMONIALS, are letters of RECOMMENDATION, from the Latin *credens, credentis*, believing, the present participle of the same *credere*, to believe, the source of the English word CREDIT.

AGENDUM, another popular mislead, from the Latin verb *agere*, to do, the neuter of *agendus*, means items of business to be brought up before a group as things to be done. It has also a second meaning, matters of practice, and in this sense AGENDA is an opposite of CREDENDA, matters of belief.

817. *DISTEND*, distend (*dĭs-tĕnd'*) *v.* To stretch apart, expand, dilate, swell, enlarge.

DISTEND comes from the Latin *distendere*, a combination of *dis*, apart, and *tendere*, to stretch. To EXTEND is to reach out, as:

'To EXTEND the hand'. To INTEND originally meant to stretch out, but has come to mean fix one's mind on some distant purpose.

To 24 per cent DISTEND means DECREASE, an opposite, and so the last step in learning, or a possible translation of the Latin, for the prefix *dis-* has two distinct meanings, one is privative, negative, as: DISSIMILAR, not similar, DISFAVOR, DISLIKE. In the other, *dis-* means apart, asunder, in different directions, as in DISTEND, to stretch apart, asunder.

818. *DIALECTIC*, dialectic (*dī-ă-lĕk'-tĭk*) *n.* A branch of logic, art of critical examination, the logic of probable reasoning, discussion based on probabilities. Cicero meant by DIALECTIC the art of discussing in general.

To 42 per cent DIALECTIC means ORATION. An ORATION is an eloquent address. Roger Bacon states: 'ORATIONS are pleadings, speeches of counsel, laudatives, invectives, apologies, reprehensions'. The DIALECTIC of Socrates and Plato was a conversational discussion. A DIALECTIC is a logical argument.

819. *VORTEX*, vortex (*vōr'-tĕks*) *n.* A whirl, eddy, whirlpool, swirl.

To 28 per cent VORTEX means OUTER PART. VERTEX is used today for the top, summit, crown, apex, highest point. In mathematics VERTEX is sometimes used for that point of a figure most distant from the center and in this sense OUTER PART is almost correct, for the Latin *vortex*, the immediate source of the English VORTEX, and VERTEX were different spellings of the same word. Today VERTEX is the top, summit; while VORTEX is specifically a whirlpool.

820. *OBSIDIAN*, obsidian (*ŏb-sĭd'-ĭ-ăn*) *n.* Volcanic glass, black stone with brilliant lustre, homogeneous, nearly opaque, often used for Indian arrowheads, and sometimes as cut gemstones.

To 28 per cent OBSIDIAN means AUXILIARIES, compared with 40 per cent who select GLASS. An AUXILIARY is a helper, assistant, SUBSIDIARY, a word with the same middle six letters as OBSIDIAN. SUBSIDIARY comes from the Latin *subsidium*, troops stationed in reserve, auxiliary forces, help, relief, aid, and so an AUXILIARY.

According to Pliny, the Roman naturalist who lived from 23 to 79 A.D., in his Natural History, in 37 books, an inexhaustible storehouse of information, the word OBSIDIAN comes from Obsius, the name of the man who first called attention to this volcanic glass.

821. *PHARISAICAL*, pharisaical (*fă-rĭ-sā'-ĭ-kăl*) *adj*. Observance of external forms without genuine piety, ceremonious, insincere, hypocritical.

PHARISAICAL is thought by 24 per cent to mean SOPHISTICATED. The Sophists and the Pharisees, though some three hundred years apart, had remarkably parallel histories. Both groups started with high ideals, the Sophists as teachers intent on general background, in education, for citizenship; the Pharisees with the goal of improving the Jewish faith. In ancient Greece, in the 5th century before Christ, the Sophists were wise and distinguished for learning. They engaged in the pursuit and communication of general knowledge as opposed to specialized, technical training.

According to Ephraim Chambers: In 125 B.C. the Pharisees were a celebrated sect among the ancient Jews; so called, say some, because separated from the rest by the austerity of their life, and by their professing a greater degree of holiness, and a more religious observation of the law.

The characteristics of both groups were then exaggerated, and both words are used slightingly today. SOPHISTRY implies too clever, brilliant on the surface but false at heart. The popular term SOPHISTICATED, applied to intricate technical designs, means complicated on the surface, but undependable. In similar manner, PHARISAICAL suggests a superficial observance of strict rules, without inner faith or true devotion.

822. *COTERIE*, coterie (*kō'-ter-ĭ*) *n*. A circle of persons, literary set, social clique, intimate group, company of scholars.

COTERIE, a French word meaning circle, set, comes from the Scotch COTTER, cottager, one who lives in a COT or COTTAGE, dependent upon a farm.

To 40 per cent COTERIE means ASSEMBLAGE, and to another 36 per cent ASSOCIATION. A COTERIE is half-way between.

An ASSOCIATION, in this sense, has usually some sort of formal organization, perhaps with elected officers, sometimes with dues. A COTERIE is wholly informal, no more than a group of persons with similar interests, who enjoy one another.

An ASSEMBLAGE is a group meeting together, and a COTERIE meets for conversation and discussion. But again an ASSEMBLAGE gathers usually with a formal purpose; a COTERIE meets informally. Furthermore a COTERIE may be fewer than a dozen persons and one would rarely apply the word ASSEMBLAGE to so small a number.

823. *DEFY*, defy (*dē-fī'*) *v.* To challenge, brave (v. B. 483),
take a stand against, dare (v. B. 380) to meet in combat; originally to reject, denounce, repudiate (v. B. 1112).
'He DEFIED them' is thought by 28 per cent of high-school students, and, surprisingly, by 27 per cent of high-vocabulary ones, to mean FOUGHT, the past of the verb to FIGHT (*fīt*), to engage in battle, contend, struggle in combat, from Anglo-Saxon, as are most words with this sort of past tense.

PUGNACIOUS (*pŭg-nā'-shŭs*), from the Latin *pugnus*, fist, means longing for a fight, disposed to attack, quarrelsome, contentious, combative, antagonistic. BELLIGERENT (*bĕl-lĭj'-ē-rĕnt*), from the Latin *bellum*, war, is warlike, eager to fight on a grander scale.

The verb to DEFY, from the Latin *diffidĕre*, to distrust, a combination of *dis*, away, and *fides*, faith, once meant to denounce as lacking good faith, reject, repudiate, and still has the suggestion of challenging a distrusted person. To DEFY is to brave to battle, challenge to combat. DEFY is an attitude leading up to a fight but is not the actual struggle, for a challenge does not always lead to the requested FIGHT.

824. *IMPRECATION*, imprecation (*ĭm-prē-kā'-shŏn*) *n.* Cursing, malediction, execration, the act of invoking evil, a prayer that a curse may fall on someone.
IMPRECATION, from the Latin *imprecatio, imprecationis*, an invoking of evil, is a combination of *in*, upon, and *precari*, to pray. To PRAY is to ask earnestly, entreat, urge, implore, beseech, and so BEG; and this derivation leads 24 per cent into selecting

BEGGING as the meaning of IMPRECATION. To BEG is to ask for alms, supplicate, beseech, entreat, request, pray for. A SUPPLICATION, somewhat like IMPRECATION in sound, is also a begging, imploring. An IMPRECATION is begging that bad luck befall someone else.

E. Chambers says: An IMPRECATION is a curse or wish that some evil may befall anyone. Bailey says of IMPRECATION: A curse or calling down mischief upon another.

825. *BANTER*, banter (*băn'-tĕr*) *n.* Teasing, good-humored raillery, mischievous chaff, light conversation, joking, jesting, quizzing.

To one third of those tested BANTER means DEBATE, and to the same number, JESTING. Both BANTER and DEBATE are today good-natured; but both come from words which originally meant beat down, to conquer. To BATTER, to beat, as on a door, differs from BANTER by only a single letter, and comes from the Latin *batuere*, to beat, the source of DEBATE, literally to beat down, which originally meant to fight, do battle seriously, but which has come to be applied mentally rather than physically, and means argue, take sides in a discussion.

BANTER is the frequentative of an old word which meant to beat down; but BANTER is today a pleasant joking, frivolous conversation.

The second popular mislead, EXCHANGE, selected by 23 per cent, is obviously the word BARTER, which goes back to Old French, with a parallel word in Italian. To BARTER is to bargain, buy and sell, and so EXCHANGE.

TEASING is persistent, to gain a purpose and usually childish. RIDICULE, although from *ridere*, to laugh, is unpleasant, sarcastic, at the expense of the one ridiculed. BANTER is harmless with little more purpose than spending time.

826. *GONFALON*, gonfalon (*gŏn'-făl-ŏn*) *n.* A pennant, banderole, little banner of the middle ages, ensign, standard, with three points, streamers, or tails, small pennon attached to a lance.

A GONFALON is a flag, banner, a fact unknown to nearly half of those who have tried this vocabulary test.

To those who know this first step, the next is to learn the additional word GONFALONIER (*gŏn-fă-lō-nēr'*), for the shape, form, design of the GONFALON was not so important as the honor conferred on its bearer, or more precisely on one who had the right of having the GONFALON carried before him in battle or on formal state occasions.

In the middle ages, in the year 1300, the chief magistrate of Florence had the title GONFALONIER. Subsequently other Italian Republics, such as Siena and Lucca, adopted the same title for their chief magistrates.

The King of France had a GONFALON borne before him. This became the GONFALON of St. Denis; and finally the ORIFLAMME (*or'-ĭ-flahm*), said to have been a plain red GONFALON.

GONFALON goes back through French, Portuguese, Spanish, and Italian, perhaps to Anglo-Saxon or to two German words meaning war and flag, originally indicating a rallying point in battle. The word is now of historical interest.

827. *MALINGER*, malinger (*măl-ĭng'-ger*) *v.* To pretend ill-
    ness, feign indisposition, sham sickness to avoid duty,
counterfeit disease, shirk work.

The present participle MALINGERING, directly from French slang, but found in the French-English Dictionary of Randle Cotgrave as early as 1611, is thought by 31 per cent to mean DELAYING, correct in suggestion, but not accurate, for MALINGERING is specifically pretending illness.

828. *GLEBE*, glebe (*glēb*) *n.* Cultivable land belonging to a
    parish church, portion of land going with an ecclesiastical
benefice, land for use by a religious person as part of his income.
GLEBE comes from an Old French word meaning land belonging to a parsonage. This in turn comes from the Latin *gleba*, a lump of earth, clod, mass, soil, land.

The mislead MANOR, marked by 20 per cent, is more properly the house, mansion, dwelling; but has come to be used for a large estate including the building, a tract of land owned by a lord or baron, over which he has authority often to collect rents. GLEBE is more correctly religious, not including a house, and cultivated as part of an income.

829. *ALTRUISM*, altruism (*ăl'-trū-ĭzm*) *n.* Generosity, un-
    selfishness, benevolence, consideration, beneficence, regard
for the interest of others.
The term ALTRUISM was introduced by the French philosopher
Comte to denote benevolent instincts. The word comes from the
Latin *alter*, other, the source of the verb to ALTER, to change,
make different, vary in some degree, convert into another form;
and the noun an ALTERNATE, one to take the place of another.

To 17 per cent of those tested ALTRUISM means SELFISHNESS,
an exact opposite. SELFISHNESS is exclusive regard for one's own
interests, disregard for the rights and feelings of others. EGOISM,
a word from the Latin *ego*, I, self, is the habit of evaluating
everything in reference to one's personal interests, pure SELF-
ISHNESS, opposed to ALTRUISM.

From Herbert Spencer, Data of Ethics, comes: 'We define
ALTRUISM as being all action which, in the normal course of
things, benefits others instead of benefitting self'.

830. *PALING*, paling (*pāl'-ĭng*) *n.* A fence of vertical stakes,
    picket fence.
To 17 per cent PALING means SKIN, a confusion of PALING with
PEELING. A PEELING as: 'A potato PEELING', or 'Apple PEELING',
from the Latin *pellis*, skin, the direct source of another English
word PELL, skin, hide, is the outside, rind, coating, covering.
A PALING is a fence.

Strictly a PALISADE is a defense, the initial purpose of all FENCES,
for FENCE, spelt with a c instead of an s, is an abbreviation of
DEFENSE. A PALISADE is made of heavy upright stakes set solidly
in the ground. A PICKET is thinner, lighter, and pointed. A
PICKET-FENCE is made of narrow upright boards spaced a little
apart and pointed at the top. A PALING is lighter than a PALISADE
and built of stakes called PALES, from the Latin *palus*, pole.
These are not set in the ground and not pointed at the top, but
held together like a PICKET-FENCE by horizontal rails, and used
to inclose an area as a garden or orchard.

831. *CONSTRAIN*, constrain (*kŏn-strān'*) *v.* To compel, drive,
    oblige, necessitate, exert force, urge to action. The cor-
responding noun CONSTRAINT is force, compulsion, violence.

To 44 per cent the verb to CONSTRAIN means to CRIPPLE, compared with only 41 per cent who select COMPEL. To CRIPPLE is often to injure a leg or a foot, so that walking is difficult; but CRIPPLE is also used more generally for disable in part, maim, weaken. To STRAIN may mean to injure by stretching, harm by too great exertion, and so CRIPPLE. STRAIN, RESTRAIN, and CONSTRAIN, all come from the Latin *stringere*, to bind, constrict, draw together, fetter. To RESTRAIN is to draw back, hold back. To CONSTRAIN is to oblige by force.

832. *NECROPOLIS*, necropolis (*nĕ-krŏp'-ō-lĭs*) *n.* A cemetery, burial ground.

To 20 per cent NECROPOLIS means HILL, and to another 30 per cent CITY. The Greek πόλις (*polis*) means city, or sometimes state. From this comes the word POLICE, which originally meant public order, the right of a district to maintain order, the power to suppress whatever is injurious to the peace, health, morality, safety, or comfort of a community.

From the same Greek *polis* comes also METROPOLIS (*mĕ-trŏp'-ō-lĭs*), from μήτηρ (*meter*), equivalent to the English word MOTHER. A METROPOLIS is the mother-city, not an isolated center, no matter how large, but one from which other cities spring, with which they keep in touch.

The ACROPOLIS is the HILL in Athens on which stands the PARTHENON. The word comes from the Greek ἄκρος (*acros*), highest, upper, top, summit, a word which appears in ACROBAT, a person who performs high in the air. NECROPOLIS, from νεκρός (*nekros*), a dead body, is the city of dead bodies, a cemetery.

833. *BLANDISHMENTS*, blandishments (*blăn'-dĭsh-mĕnts*) *n.* Flattering attention, cajolery, endearments, compliments, insincere commendations, actions expressive of devotion, each tending to win the heart.

BLAND, from the Latin adjective *blandus*, gentle, agreeable, soft, caressing, is a pleasant word suggesting gentle breezes, and means mild, balmy, soothing, kindly, affable. But the Latin verb *blandari*, from the adjective *blandus*, and the English verb BLANDISH, both mean to FLATTER; and FLATTERY is usually undeserved praise, offered to gain favor for the FLATTERER.

Blandishments, usually in the plural because they are cheap to give, are obvious compliments. Praise is real, and deserved when received. A compliment may or may not be honest; one can never be quite sure. Blandishments are almost always false, given with the hope of gaining some sort of favor in return.

The popular mislead salesmanship, preferred by 15 per cent, expresses the point of view of those tested. The goal of both salesmanship and blandishments is gaining a profit.

834. *COUNTERPANE*, counterpane (*kŏwn'-tĕr-pān*) *n*. Bedspread, coverlet, quilt, puff, comforter.

Counterpane is a corruption of counterpoint, originally in French a quilt, literally a stitched quilt, sometimes made of squares stitched together called a crazy-quilt, made of crazy-work, a patchwork of odd-shaped pieces of different colors.

835. *BALLAST*, ballast (*băl'-lăst*) *n*. Heavy material loaded in
   a ship to keep it upright, to hold it in equilibrium, weights formerly carried by an airplane to make it steady, bags of sand in a balloon for the same purpose.

Despite the similarity of balance and ballast, in both sound and meaning, they come from different sources. Balance, with one l, starts with the Latin *bi*, two, and means two scales. A counterpoise is a weight to balance another weight. Ballast, spelt with two l's comes from a Scandinavian *bar*, near, bare, mere, and *last*, load, directly from Anglo-Saxon, and designates mere weight, a bare load carried for weight only and not for pay.

To 50 per cent ballast means steadiness, compared with only 41 per cent who select load. Steadiness is the result of ballast, the purpose, the goal. But ballast means weight, load, and is never used for the result, steadiness.

836. *IRREFRANGIBLE*, irrefrangible (*ĭr-rē-frăn'-jĭ-bl*) *adj*.
   Not to be broken, unbreakable.

The verb in Latin is *frangere*, to break, with the past participle *fractus*, broken. From this come the English fragile, easily broken, the French *fragile*, the Italian *fragile*, and the Spanish *fragil* with no e at the end; also the English fraction, a piece broken off. To REFRACT, from the past participle *fractus*, is to break back, as a ray of light in going from air to water, which makes a stick look broken at the surface. The science term REFRACTABLE means capable of being broken in this technical sense; for FRAGILE and FRANGIBLE are general words.

Though FRANGIBLE is literary, REFRANGIBLE is again from physics, capable of being bent in going from one medium to another. IRREFRANGIBLE, not REFRANGIBLE, seldom if ever appears in physics, but applies occasionally to rules, laws which cannot be broken.

To 20 per cent IRREFRANGIBLE means UNENFORCIBLE, a confusion due to prefixes. FORCE and FRAGILE are easily distinguished. But as one adds prefixes the two words become increasingly confused, until it requires almost a mathematical process to separate UNENFORCIBLE from IRREFRANGIBLE.

837. *MONOCHROME,* monochrome (*mŏn'-ō-krōm*) *n.* A painting in one color with light and dark shades; in the arts, a painting in a single color, varied only in shade, as distinguished from a POLYCHROME (*pŏl'-ĭ-krōm*).

MONOCHROME comes from the Greek μόνος (*monos*), single, one, which appears in MONOGRAPH, a short essay on one subject, in MONOLITH, a single great stone, as well as in MONOTONY; and χρῶμα (*chroma*), color. The word is so little known that guesses as to its meaning seem pure chance, 13 per cent selecting SPECKLED SURFACE, spotted, flecked, piebald; 11 per cent SIGN; another 11 per cent TREATISE, suggested by MONOGRAPH; and still another 11 per cent INSTRUMENT.

GRISAILLE (*grĭ-zāy'*), from the French *gris*, gray, is a kind of MONOCHROME, a painting in grays of various shades obtained by mixing black and white. CAMAIEU (*kăm'-ĭ-ū*), another MONOCHROME, is a painting in any single color.

838. *PAEAN,* paean (*pē'-ăn*) *n.* A war song, victory hymn to Apollo asking for aid in war, song of triumph in general. PAEAN comes from the Greek Παιάν (*Paian*), a name for Apollo used by Homer.

To 30 per cent PAEAN means LAMENT. An ELEGY, a DIRGE, and a REQUIEM are all LAMENTS. An ELEGY is a mournful poem. A

DIRGE is a service for the dead, lamentation at a funeral. A REQUIEM is a mass for the repose of the soul of the deceased. A PAEAN is a hymn in honor of Apollo chiefly used on occasions of victory and triumph.

Bailey says of PAEAN: A hymn or song of praise made to Apollo, at such time as any plague or pestilence raged.

839. *AVER*, aver (ă-vĕr′) *v*. To assert the truth of, affirm with confidence, declare, allege, maintain, insist, attest, corroborate, substantiate, authenticate, verify.

AVER, from the Latin *ad*, to, and *verus*, true, means to assert the truth of. From the same *verus* comes VERITY, from *veritas, veritatis*, truth, truthfulness.

To 19 per cent AVER means DENY, the exact opposite. To DENY, from *de*, and *negare*, to deny, say no, the source of NEGATION, is declare to be untrue, reject as false, disclaim, renounce, abjure, a confusion of opposites, the last step in learning the meaning of a word.

840. *KIRK*, kirk (kĕrk) *n*. A church, religious building, place of worship.

KIRK goes back, through Middle English, straight to Anglo-Saxon, and is a survival of the Middle English pronunciation of the modern word CHURCH. KIRK is still used in Scotland and the north of England for CHURCH.

KIRK seems an easy word, but those tested divide equally among BRIDGE, FORTIFICATION, CHURCH, and WALL, as meanings of KIRK, one quarter of the population selecting each of the four as the correct answer.

841. *EFFULGENT*, effulgent (ĕf-fŭl′-jĕnt) *adj*. Radiant, splendid, luminous, shining forth brilliantly, gleaming, glittering, lustrous, dazzling.

To 35 per cent EFFULGENT means RADIANT, the correct answer; but to almost as many, 30 per cent, it means DEMONSTRATIVE (dē-mŏn′-stră-tĭv), energetically expressive, exhibiting strong feeling. EFFUSIVE (ĕf-fū′-sĭv) comes from the Latin *ex-*, out, and *fundere*, to pour, and refers to an outpouring of feelings, extravagant expression of emotion.

EFFULGENT comes from the Latin *effulgere,* a combination of the same *ex-* and *fulgere,* to shine, flash, gleam, glitter, the source of FULGENT, shining, dazzling; REFULGENT, reflecting a bright light; and EFFULGENT, giving out a direct radiance.

842. *LITIGIOUS,* litigious (*lĭ-tĭj'-ŭs*) *adj.* Fond of litigation, contentious, disputatious, argumentative, querulous, eager to go to court, always ready for a law-suit.

To 40 per cent LITIGIOUS means PIOUS, due no doubt to the word LITURGY. Originally in ancient Athens a LITURGY, from the Greek λειτουργία (*leitourgia*), public servant, was a personal service to the state required of all citizens possessing property. It might be financing the presentation of a dramatic performance, or of a musical, or of a poetic contest. From this, LITURGY came to mean the method of conducting public worship, the words and acts used in Christian ceremonies. Then LITURGY was the book in which were recorded the forms of all services.

LITIGIOUS comes directly from the Latin adjective *litigiosus,* from the verb *litigare,* to dispute, a combination of *lis, litis,* strife, dispute, and *agere,* to drive, carry on. LITIGATION is the noun, the carrying on of a law-suit.

843. *BORASCA,* borasca (*bō-răs'-kă*) *n.* A violent squall of wind, accompanied by thunder and lightning.

To nearly half of those who have tried this vocabulary test, BORASCA means DRY-SEASON, an opposite certainly in suggestion, for a BORASCA is a storm.

The word comes from the Italian BORA, one of the special winds of the Mediterranean, familiar to meteorologists as the MISTRAL, the SIROCCO, and the BORA. The SIROCCO of Sicily is a hot and dry wind from the south and southeast which blows in the early months of the year. The SIROCCO of the Adriatic is equally hot but humid, again from the south. The MISTRAL (*mĭs'-trăl*) comes from the north, a dry wind belonging to the south of France, to the Mediterranean coast, strongest over the estuary of the river Rhone. The BORA is a cold, dry wind in the territories of Istria and Dalmatia, on the Adriatic Coast, the cold air of the mountains sliding down to the sea, a wind strong enough to destroy fruit trees and to be a danger to fishing.

The word comes from the Latin *Boreas*, god of the north wind, familiar in the phrase AURORA BOREALIS, the northern lights, from AURORA, goddess of the dawn, and BOREAS, the north.

The BORASCA is the BORA with thunder and lightning and storm.

844. *AERUGINOUS*, aeruginous (*ē-rū'-jĭ-nŭs*) *adj*. Like ver-
      digris, bluish green in color, like copper rust.
VERDIGRIS (*vĕr'-dĭ-grēs*) is a pigment, a coloring matter made from copper, an acetate of copper, varying from green to bluish green in color.

AERUGINOUS, another word for this same color, comes from the Latin *aeruginosis*, from *aerugo*, a Latin word for VERDIGRIS; and this comes in turn from *aes*. The Latin *aes*, pronounced (*ēz*), really meant ore in general, but was used largely for copper or for bronze, an alloy consisting mostly of copper, about four fifths, with some tin.

STIPPLED, made up of tiny dots, small points, is the only popular mislead, selected as often as the right answer, BLUISH GREEN.

845. *OUTRAGE*, outrage (*owt'-rāj*) *n*. Violent assault, griev-
      ous affront, injury, infamous wrong, atrocious ill-treat-
ment, wanton mischief. The corresponding adjective is OUT-
RAGEOUS, cruel, fierce, violent, highly injurious.
To 40 per cent OUTRAGE means ANGER. RAGE is ANGER, ire, wrath, a word which goes directly back to Icelandic. ANGER is sudden, violent, in retaliation for any injury received. RAGE is ANGER exhibited with no self-control. RAGE, which originally meant madness, insanity, but which has come to mean ANGER, indigna-
tion, fury, frenzy, goes back through Middle English to the Latin *rabere*, to be mad, to rage, the source of RABID.

OUTRAGE, the French *outrage*, does not come from RAGE, but from the Latin *ultra*, beyond, moreover, on the further side, occasionally used as an adjective in English, ULTRA, to mean extreme, extravagant, fanatical. An OUTRAGE is beyond reason.

846. *ADVENTITIOUS*, adventitious (*ăd-vĕn-tĭ'-shŭs*) *adj*.
      Accidental, foreign, extraneous, extrinsic, entering by chance, coming from without.

ADVENTITIOUS comes from the Latin *advenire*, a combination of *ad-*, to, and *venire*, to come. The ADVENTITIOUS enters from the outside. It does not properly belong to the subject at hand but cannot be ignored.

Given a choice of synonyms for ADVENTITIOUS, 50 per cent select ACCIDENTAL and 30 per cent EXTRINSIC. ADVENTITIOUS is neither ACCIDENTAL nor EXTRINSIC, three words which should be in the vocabulary of every artist, writer, and scientist.

That which is ACCIDENTAL, from the Latin *ad-*, to, and *cadere*, to fall, just happened, and should be forgotten, or avoided by greater care. It is casual, unintentional, by chance, not essential, nothing at the moment can be done about it. But take advantage of it. If you are an artist, perhaps it is just that combination of colors you have been seeking. But the ACCIDENTAL is momentary, it will not occur again in just that way.

EXTRINSIC comes from the Latin *extrinsecus*, outer, from *exter*, the opposite of INTRINSIC. The EXTRINSIC is outside, not a part of the problem under discussion. Ignore it.

But the ADVENTITIOUS is something real. It has come from the outside. It is no longer EXTRINSIC. It must be considered.

The scientist must ignore the EXTRINSIC, or he will waste time. He must be more careful and avoid the ACCIDENTAL. But the ADVENTITIOUS he must follow to its source and understand.

847. *BAILIWICK*, bailiwick (*bā'-lǐ-wǐk*) *n.* A region, area, precinct, district, hundred.

BAILIWICK is a combination of the Scottish word BAILIE and WICK, the region in which a sheriff exercises his office, the precincts in which a BAILIFF has jurisdiction, a hundred, a liberty, or a forest. A BAILIFF is a minor officer. A SHERIFF is a king's BAILIFF with jurisdiction over a BAILIWICK.

WICK goes directly back to the Anglo-Saxon word *wic*, a town, village, camp, sometimes a street, more recently a district, thus BAILIWICK, often becoming WICH in the names of places, as GREENWICH, SANDWICH. A HUNDRED was at one time an administrative district in southern England, a division of a country. The word HUNDRED was carried over to the colonies of Pennsylvania, Virginia, Maryland, and Delaware. A LIBERTY is another word for a district in which certain privileges are granted.

848. *CHORISTER*, chorister (*kŏr'-ĭs-ter*) *n.* A singer in a
      choir, male member of a church choir; also occasionally,
in some churches, a choir leader, a precentor, one who leads
the singing of a choir or a congregation.

To 21 per cent CHORISTER means LEADER, a correct answer which
should not have been a mislead in the vocabulary test.

Of the words CHANTER (*chăn'-ter*), CANTOR, and CHORUS, the
first comes from the Latin *cantator*, one who chants, a singer,
songster, minstrel. A CANTOR (*kăn'-tor*), another Latin word
for singer, is an officer who leads the singing in a parish church,
a precentor. A CHORUS, the Latin *chorus*, from the Greek χορός
(*choros*), was originally a dance accompanied by song. From
this CHORUS has come to mean any organized group of singers.
A CHORISTER, from the same Greek source, is a chanter or singer
in a chorus or choir.

849. *SUPINE*, supine (*sū'-pīn*) *adj.* Lying on the back, face
      upward, the opposite of PRONE, which is face downward.
PROSTRATE comes from the Latin *pro*, before, and *sternere*, to
spread, strew, the source of STRATUM (*strā'-tŭm*), once in
Latin a bedspread, quilt, something spread over a bed. PROS-
TRATE means spread out on the ground either face up or face
down.

PRONE, from the Latin *pronus*, comes from *pro*, forward, and
suggests falling forward, and so face down.

SUPINE, from the Latin *supinus*, thrown backward, means
lying on the back, face up.

850. *HOLOGRAM*, hologram (*hŏ'-lō-grăm*) *n.* A letter, deed,
      will, testament, written wholly by the hand of the author,
manuscript, anything in the handwriting of the person who
signs it.

SACRED WRITING, a popular misinterpretation, is an interpretation of HOLY and -GRAM. But HOLO-, at the beginning of HOLO-
GRAM, comes not from HOLY, but from the Greek ὅλος (*holos*),
whole, entire, complete, which appears also at the beginning
of HOLOCAUST, a fire which consumes everything completely.

HOLOGRAPH, directly from the Greek ὁλόγραφος (*holo-
graphos*), with the same meaning as the English, written wholly

by the hand of the author, is the original word but, with the introduction of the word TELEGRAM in 1852, came the word HOLOGRAM.

851. *HACKLES*, hackles (*hăk'-kĕls*) *n.* The neck feathers of the domestic cock, the long slender feathers in the neck of the peacock or pigeon.

To 24 per cent HACKLES means SHACKLES. A SHACKLE was first a bent bar, a link in a chain, also something securing two ankle rings, but has come to mean anything which hinders motion.

The Oxford Dictionary gives a two-column discussion of numerous meanings of HACKLE, out of all proportion to what seems so unimportant a word. But HACKLE goes far back in history, before the year 1500. It occurs in the Compleat Angler of Izaac Walton in 1653, in building an artificial fly: 'Take the HACKLE of a cock or capon's neck'. The word also appears in the phrase: 'With the HACKLES up', because the HACKLES of a cock stand on end when he is angry.

852. *AGAMIST*, agamist (*ăg'-ă-mĭst*) *n.* One who is not married, who choses not to be married, non-marrier.

AGAMIST is thought by 40 per cent to mean UNBELIEVER. An AGNOSTIC (*ăg-nŏs'-tĭk*) is an UNBELIEVER, a word suggested by Thomas Henry Huxley in 1869 to mean one who disclaims any knowledge of God. AGNOSTIC comes from the Greek ἄγνωστος (*agnostos*), unknowing, also unknowable, a combination of the privative ἀ-, and γνωστός (*gnostos*), known.

AGAMIST comes from the same Greek privative ἀ- and γάμος (*gamos*), married, the source of the modern biological term GAMETE. A BIGAMIST is a man with two or more wives, from the Latin *bigamus*, a combination of *bi-*, twice, two, and the same Greek γάμος (*gamos*), married. An AGAMIST is one who is not married.

853. *WAGGISH*, waggish (*wăg'-gĭsh*) *adj.* Like a wag, given to buffoonery, jocular, abounding in antics, jocose, humorous, droll, facetious, joking, jesting, sportive, frolicsome.

HUMOR is kind, goes deeply into the nature of thought; though the adjective HUMOROUS loses some of this pleasant feeling.

WIT is more intellectual, depending upon passing circum-stances, catching surprising and delightful far-fetched resem-blances between really dissimilar ideas.

Of WAG, Richard Steele, in The Tatler, number 184, writes: 'A WAG is the last order even of pretenders to wit and good humor. He has generally his mind prepared to receive some occasion of merriment, but is of himself too empty to draw out any of his own set of thoughts; and therefore laughs at the next thing he meets not because it is ridiculous but because he is under a necessity of laughing'.

854. *MAUL*, maul (*mawl*) *n.* A heavy hammer, wooden mallet used by carpenters, beetle, sledge, mall.

To 16 per cent of those tested MAUL means COAT, an outer gar-ment worn by men. A SHAWL, which rimes with MAUL, is a cov-ering for the shoulders worn mostly by women, sometimes square, sometimes rectangular, much like a MANTLE but lighter. Also a COAT OF MAIL, the last word differing from MAUL by only one letter, is a garment made of small rings of metal.

To another 13 per cent MAUL means HATCHET. A HATCHET is much like a MAUL, but used with one hand and designed like an axe for cutting; while a MAUL is for pounding, hammering.

A BEETLE, directly from an Anglo-Saxon word to beat, is usually for swinging, to drive wedges, but also at times for ramming dirt underfoot, with a wooden handle attached at the end of the head instead of at right angles. In this form a BEETLE is lifted and not swung, and may be heavy enough for two or more men to lift, using a bar across the handle.

A MALLET, a small wooden hammer used by stone cutters for driving another tool, is swung by one hand only, while a MAUL requires both hands. MAUL, a recent spelling of the earlier MALL, pronounced like MAUL, goes back to the Latin, *malleus*, a hammer.

855. *VERMICULAR*, vermicular (*ver-mĭk'-ū-lahr*)   adj.
          Wormlike, having the wiggly outline of a worm, charac-terized by tortuous lines, sinuous, wavy.

VERMICULAR comes from the Latin *vermiculus*, the diminutive of *vermis*, worm, the source of the more familiar VERMIN, animals of any objectionable kind. According to E. Jenks, in his Government of Victoria, 1891, VERMIN includes kangaroos, wallabies, dingos, stray dogs, foxes, and rabbits. A VERMICULE (*ver'-mĭ-kūl*) is a small worm or worm-like creature, with little of the unpleasantness of VERMIN. VERMICULAR, directly from VERMICULE, has no unpleasant suggestions but means twisting.

856. *CLERICAL*, clerical (*klĕr'-ĭ-kl*) *adj*. Priestly, religious, sacerdotal, ecclesiastical, pertaining to the clergy.

The noun CLERK, a title given to a clergyman or minister of the church, goes back almost to the year 1000 and then directly back to Anglo-Saxon. Perhaps because an adjectve modifying a noun is often more difficult than the noun itself, CLERICAL in English did not appear for another five hundred years. A CLERK was originally the member of a religious community, one in holy orders, a clergyman, priest, cleric, ecclesiastic; and CLERICAL meant pertaining to the clergy, of the church. Because, during the Middle Ages, only this group was learned, the word CLERK came to mean scholar, and then in a more limited sense, one who wrote for others, a notary or secretary; or according to Nathan Bailey, 1721: 'Such as lived or exercised any function by the pen in any court or elsewhere'.

Today a CLERK is an office worker, a person employed to keep records; and this leads 12 per cent to select EXACT as the meaning of CLERICAL. EXACT means correct, precise, accurate, and to one who does not know PRIESTLY as the meaning of CLERICAL is perhaps the nearest to office worker. But the first meaning, PRIESTLY, ecclesiastic, still survives in good use.

857. *SCUDDING*, scudding (*skŭd'-dĭng*) *v*. Hurrying, running swiftly, flying along, moving with haste, traveling before a gale of wind.

To 32 per cent SCUDDING means DRIFTING, almost an opposite in suggestion. To DRIFT is to float along with the current, carried at random.

The verb to SCUD comes from Danish with related words in Swedish, Icelandic, and other Scandinavian languages. To SCUD is to run swiftly, fly along with haste, also to run before a gale of wind.

To scoot, called colloquial, is to dart, run, fly; and scud has much this same feeling of speed with the added suggestion of wind and sea.

E. Chambers says of scudding: 'In sea language, denotes the movement by which a ship is carried precipitately before a tempest. A ship scuds with a sail extended on her foremast.'

858. *NOISOME*, noisome (*noi'-sŏm*) *adj*. Ill-smelling, disgusting, loathsome, pernicious, noxious, pestiferous, poisonous, corrupting, offensive to smell.

To 54 per cent noisome means loud, compared with only 36 per cent who prefer offensive. Despite the similarity in sound, noisome has no connection with noisy, loud, but is a combination of noy and some. The obsolete noy, by apheresis from annoy, is to trouble, vex, hurt, afflict. The suffix -some not only forms adjectives, as: troublesome, quarrelsome, wholesome, loathsome, but multiplies the meaning. Noisome is extremely disgusting.

Noxious means energetically harmful; pernicious is destructive; noisome is now primarily ill-smelling.

859. *ROTUNDA*, rotunda (*rō-tŭn'-dă*) *n*. A building round both outside and inside; also a circular hall in a large building, generally surmounted by a dome.

Rotunda comes from the Latin *rotunda*, the feminine of *rotundus*, round, the source of rotund (*rō-tŭnd'*), rounded, fat.

To 42 per cent rotunda means dome, two words closely associated. The rotunda is the round building, or high round hall inside a larger building. The dome is the rounded hemispherical roof of the rotunda. Strictly the dome is the roof; the rotunda is the building below, the walls, which support the dome.

Cupola (*kŭ'-pō-lă*), the diminutive of *cupa*, tub, cask, is the Italian word for dome; but in English the word cupola is used for both walls and dome, usually of a small ornamental tower built on top of a large roof.

860. *MISFEASANCE*, misfeasance (*mĭs-fē'-zăns*) *n*. Originally any wrong-doing, trespass; now specifically the misuse of power, misbehavior in office, wrongful exercise of authority.

To 38 per cent MISFEASANCE means MISMANAGEMENT, while only 24 per cent select CORRUPTION. MISFEASANCE is not CORRUPTION as a whole, but specifically CORRUPTION in MANAGEMENT. MISMANAGEMENT may be merely poor handling due to INCOMPETENCE, a word selected by another 30 per cent as the meaning of MISFEASANCE. Or MISMANAGEMENT may imply improper handling and so be a synonym of MISFEASANCE.

As discussed under MALFEASANCE, two words should be separated. MALFEASANCE is doing something positively unlawful. MISFEASANCE is using authority in a wrong way.

861. *CENOTAPH*, cenotaph (*sĕn′-ō-tăf*) *n.* An empty tomb built in honor of someone buried elsewhere, sepulchral monument.

To 38 per cent CENOTAPH, from the Greek κενός (*cenos*), empty, and τάφος (*taphos*), tomb, means MONUMENT; and to another 36 per cent INSCRIPTION, from the Latin *inscriptio, inscriptionis*, and *inscriptus*, the past participle of *inscribere*. The Latin *scribere* is to write, and an INSCRIPTION, though cut in stone, is primarily a writing.

The confusion is perhaps the word EPITAPH, from the Greek ἐπί (*epi*), over, and the same τάφος (*taphos*), TOMB. From the Arte of English People, edited by Puttenham, comes: 'An EPITAPH is an INSCRIPTION such as a man may commodiously write or engrave upon a tombe in few verses, pithie, quicke and sententious, for the passer by to peruse and indulge upon without any long tariance'.

A CENOTAPH is a building, MONUMENT, technically an empty tomb.

862. *COXCOMB*, coxcomb (*kŏks′-kōm*) *n.* Dandy, vain showy fellow, fop, conceited dunce, pretentious beau, prig, popinjay, jackanapes, an exquisite.

By 22 per cent COXCOMB is thought to be a ROOSTER. A COCK is a ROOSTER, the male of the domestic fowl, and a COCK'S COMB, also written as one word COCKSCOMB, is the comb of the cock, called CARUNCLE (*kahr′-ŭng-kl*), a fleshy growth on the head of a bird. COXCOMB is another spelling, ordinarily used when this word means a dandy, fop, conceited fool, silly fellow.

MONK'S-HOOD is another frequent misconception. Both COCKS-COMB and MONK'S-HOOD are also the names of flowers and the latter may be marked because of this association. A COXCOMB was originally a cap resembling a COCK'S COMB worn by professional fools, and this may suggest hood.

A CURRYCOMB is a comb for rubbing, currying horses, and so a HORSE-BRUSH, another frequently marked mislead.

A DANDY is elegant, expensively dressed. A FOP is vain in dress and impertinent in manner. A COXCOMB is vain, conceited.

863. *PHYSIOGNOMY*, physiognomy (*fĭz-ĭ-ŏg′-nō-mĭ*)   *n.*
Face, countenance, appearance, expression, aspect, cast. In an early study, more persons selected LIFE-SCIENCE as the meaning of PHYSIOGNOMY than the correct answer FACE. PHYSIOLOGY (*fĭz-ĭ-ŏl′-ō-jĭ*) was originally science as a whole, from the Greek φυσιολογία (*physiologia*), a combination of φύσις (*physis*), nature, and λογία (*logia*), science, study, learning. Thus by derivation PHYSIOLOGY is the study of nature. But the word is now limited more narrowly to the study of living things, the science of life, as opposed to physics, which has become the study of materials, non-living matter.

PHYSIOGNOMY comes from the Greek φυσιογνωμονία (*physiognomonia*), the art of judging a man by his features, a combination of the same φύσις (*physis*), nature, the source of the word PHYSICS, and γνώμων (*gnomon*), a judge, interpreter, literally one who knows, the source of the English word GNOMON, the pointer of a sun-dial, a combination of letters which appears in the unusual word AGNOMICAL, starting with the Greek privative *a-*, without a pointer, with no purpose in life. PHYSIOGNOMY is the face as an indication of one's mind, the countenance as an expression of one's disposition.

864. *NIGRITUDE*, nigritude (*nĭg′-rĭ-tŭd*) *n.* Blackness, darkness, duskiness.

To 20 per cent NIGRITUDE means SUFFERING. MEGRIM (*mē′-grĭm*), also MIGRAINE (*mĭ-grān′*), is a kind of headache, and this may suggest SUFFERING.

NIGRESCENT (*nĭ-grĕs′-sĕnt*), blackish, somewhat dark, dusky, fuscous, comes from the Latin *nigrescens, nigrescentis*, the present participle of *nigrescere*, to become black, grow dark, the inceptive of *nigrere*, to be black, from *niger*, black. The rare NIGRITUDE, through the Latin *nigritudo*, blackness, comes from the same *niger*.

865. *MOTTLINGS*, mottlings (mŏt'-tlĭngz) *pl. n.* Irregular spots, variegations, blotches mingling.

MOTTLINGS, a verbal noun formed from the verb to MOTTLE, to blotch, spot, comes from MOTLEY, which goes back to Middle English and can with certainty be traced no further. The noun, a MOTLEY, is the suit made of glaringly different colored pieces of cloth, worn by clowns and court jesters.

To 23 per cent, practically a quarter of those tested, MOTTLINGS are DIRTY STREAKS. A STREAK, from Anglo-Saxon, is a line, band, stripe, not a round dot, SPOT. SPOT goes back to Flemish, Dutch, Danish, and Swedish words for speck, spot, dot. A SPOT may be a stain, speck, and often has the suggestion of blemish, fault, something not wanted. A BLOTCH, a large irregular SPOT, is again derogatory. MOTTLING has not this destructive, harmful suggestion; and MOTTLINGS are not DIRTY. Instead the word implies something thoughtfully designed.

866. *ENSCONCE*, ensconce (ĕn-skŏns') *v.* To cover, hide, protect (as with a fort); to shelter, fit securely.

ENSCONCE is from EN-, in, and SCONCE, a word with many diverse meanings; in this context SCONCE comes from the German and means a fort, bulwark, defense work.

ENSCONCE contains both the aspect of protection, and now more generally, the feeling of security and snugness which such protection gives. "We make trifles of terrors, ENSCONCING ourselves in seeming knowledge", from Shakespeare's All's Well That Ends Well, illustrates both these aspects.

867. *GENIUS*, genius (jē'-nyŭs) *n.* The ruling spirit of a person, power, personality, principle that determines character.

The usual meaning of GENIUS today, a remarkably gifted person, one who has gained distinction by the expression of born ability, first appeared in the 18th century. The original meaning was the spirit of a person.

To 32 per cent GENIUS means ORIGIN, a confusion of GENIUS with GENESIS, the first stage in learning. GENESIS (jĕn'-ē-sĭs) comes from the Greek γένεσις (genesis), origin, source, beginning, creation. GENIUS comes directly from the Latin genius, guardian spirit of a person, inborn nature, inclination.

Of GENIUS Nathan Bailey says: 'A good or evil angel or spirit, supposed to attend upon every person; also a man's nature, fancy, or inclination'. A few years later Ephraim Chambers supplements: 'It seems to be nothing else but the particular bent and temper of each person; and everyone's own temper is in a great measure the cause of his happiness or misery'.

868. *EDIFICATION*, edification (ĕd-ĭ-fĭ-kā'-shŏn) n. Enlightenment, instruction, teaching, schooling, improvement of the mind.

EDIFICATION, from the Latin aedificare, to build, erect, establish, from aedes, a building for habitation, dwelling house, originally meant the act of building, constructing. An EDIFICE is today a building, structure, architectural fabric. But the verb to EDIFY, and the noun EDIFICATION, which once referred to physical structures, have come to apply to the mind and not to material.

Given a choice between SCHOOLING and MORAL UPLIFT, as synonyms of EDIFICATION, nearly half of those who have taken this vocabulary test prefer the second. Perhaps this fraction of the public no longer think of SCHOOLING as EDIFYING. Or perhaps the term EDIFICATION includes MORAL UPLIFT. Of EDIFICATION the Century Dictionary says: 'Frequently with reference to morals'.

869. *WEAL*, weal (wēl) n. Wealth, riches, prosperity, success, well-being, good fortune, the opposite of WOE in the phrase: 'WEAL and WOE'.

To 28 per cent WEAL, which comes directly from an Anglo-Saxon word for wealth, prosperity, means PROVISIONS, perhaps a confusion of PROPERTY, PROSPERITY, and PROVISIONS. PROVISIONS, from videre, to see beforehand, are ordinarily food stuffs gathered in advance, provender, victuals; but the word is sometimes used loosely for the accumulation of materials in general, and thus close to WEAL, wealth. PROPERTY is often land, but may be anything owned. PROSPERITY, from *pro-* and *spes*, hope, is well-being, success, good fortune, WEAL, coming up to one's hopes, the condition of life when one achieves one's expectations.

870. *SURCHARGE*, surcharge (*sĕr'-charj*) *n.* An overload, burden, weight too heavy to carry.

The French prefix *sur-* is the Latin *super-*, over, above; while CHARGE, in its original sense, means weight, load, burden, cargo.

Both the noun and the verb SURCHARGE are related to Spanish, Portuguese, and Italian words all of which mean overload. A SURCHARGE is a load too great to bear. To SURCHARGE is to pile on an animal more than he can carry.

Given a choice between INCOME TAX and BURDEN as the meaning of SURCHARGE, 50 per cent select INCOME TAX and only 16 per cent BURDEN. In current income tax forms the term SURCHARGE means a charge over and above the tax itself, a percentage of the tax added to the tax. But in general a SURCHARGE is an additional load, burden, too great to carry.

871. *OVINE*, ovine (*ō'-vĭn*) *adj.* Sheeplike, oviform.

BOVINE (*bō'-vĭn*), from the Latin *bos, bovis*, ox, means ox-like, and so figuratively stolid, dull, inert. PORCINE (*por'-sĭn*) means piglike; VULPINE, fox-like, and so cunning. OVINE comes through the Latin *ovis*, sheep, from the Greek οις (*ois*), sheep.

With numerous words ending in -INE, why, in a vocabulary test, should FISH-LIKE be underlined as the meaning of OVINE nearly as often as the correct answer, SHEEPLIKE?

872. *RAPACIOUS*, rapacious (*ră-pā'-shŭs*) *adj.* Greedy for plunder, predatory, raptorial, plundering, pillaging, predaceous, grasping in nature, living by rapine.

Naturalists divide birds into RAPACIOUS, from the Latin *rapere*, to seize, CARNIVOROUS, and FRUGIVOROUS; and E. Chambers adds: 'RAPACIOUS animals are such as live upon prey'.

The Century Dictionary compares RAPACIOUS with RAVENOUS and VORACIOUS; but the last two apply specifically to food, whereas RAPACIOUS is seizing in general, plundering by disposition without the excuse of hunger; and this may lead 29 per cent to select FIERCE as the meaning of RAPACIOUS. Also FIERCE comes from the Latin *ferus*, savage, wild, untamed, cruel, ferocious, and the Century Dictionary adds: with a RAPACIOUS disposition, which indicates that FIERCE may be too close to use as a mislead.

873. *BANE*, bane (*bān*) *n*. Originally a murderer, now something which destroys life, causes death, a deadly poison, scourge, pest, curse.
BANE goes directly back to an Anglo-Saxon word for murderer, slayer, killer. From this it has come to mean destruction, ruin.

874. *MERCURIAL*, mercurial (*mĕr-kū'-rĭ-ăl*) *adj*. Pertaining to the god Mercury, volatile, flighty, fickle, quick, active, sprightly.
WITTY attracts 35 per cent, compared with only 20 per cent who prefer VOLATILE. WIT, directly from Anglo-Saxon, originally meant knowledge, wisdom, sagacity, intelligence. WIT is a mature characteristic, demanding knowledge. MERCURY was young, a messenger of the gods, probably not WITTY.

POLISHED draws another 25 per cent, perhaps because the metal MERCURY is shiny, with a POLISHED appearance. But the adjective MERCURIAL refers ordinarily to the characteristics conferred by the planet MERCURY, and not to the metal.

875. *ELDRITCH*, eldritch (*ĕl'-drĭtch*) *adj*. Weird, uncanny, unearthly, wild, hideous, ghastly, preternatural.
To 35 per cent, the same number who mark the correct answer, ELDRITCH means BIRD-LIKE. An OSTRICH is a bird, and the word sounds something like ELDRITCH, which may lead to the selection of BIRD-LIKE.

The origin of this strange word is unknown; it might be a shortened form of ELDER WITCH, but that is pure imagination.

876. *OPPILATED*, oppilated (*ŏp'-pĭ-lā-tĕd*) *adj*. Stopped-up, obstructed, choked, plugged, filled up with matter.
OPENED-UP, an exact opposite of STOPPED-UP, is selected by 30 per cent, compared with 10 per cent who select OBSTRUCTED.

WELL LIGHTED is also more popular than OBSTRUCTED, suggested perhaps by ILLUMINATED, somewhat like OPPILATED in sound.

OPPILATED comes from the Latin *oppilatus,* the past participle of *oppilare,* a combination of *ob-,* against, and *pilare,* to ram down. STOPPED-UP is Anglo-Saxon; OPPILATED is Latin for precisely the same idea. In this case use the Anglo-Saxon. But there are literally hundreds, perhaps thousands of other Latin words, which give fine shadings of meaning which help in clear thinking, for which we have inherited no equivalent from Anglo-Saxon.

877. *DENDRITIC,* dendritic *(děn-drĭt'-ĭk) adj.* Branching, arborescent, marked like a dendrite.

DENDRITE, like many science terms, comes directly from the Greek δενδρίτης *(dendrites),* the branches of a tree, from δένδρον *(dendron),* a tree. A DENDRITE is a design resembling a tree which forms in certain minerals due to the presence of a foreign substance in the process of crystallization. In anatomy, it is the branch-shaped part of a neuron which conducts impulses toward the cell.

The mislead TOOTHLIKE selected by 25 per cent is of course suggested by one of the many words from the Latin *dens, dentis,* tooth.

ARBORESCENT, branching like a tree, comes from the Latin word for tree, *arbor,* much as DENDRITIC comes from the Greek.

878. *APOTHEGM,* apothegm *(ă'-pō-thĕm) n.* A short pithy instructive saying, terse remark, maxim, axiom, sententious precept.

APOTHEGM comes directly from the Greek ἀπόφθεγμα *(apophthegma),* a terse, pointed saying, and is sometimes correctly spelt in English with both -PH- and -TH- in the middle: APOPHTHEGM.

Nearly half of those who have taken this worksample concentrate on DRUG as the meaning of APOTHEGM, more than select the correct answer: MAXIM. An APOTHECARY, starting with the same six letters, is someone skilled in the preparation of DRUGS. APOTHECARY comes from the Greek ἀποθήκη *(apothece),* a warehouse, storehouse, a combination of ἀπό *(apo),* away, and τιθέναι *(tithenai),* to put, with originally no suggestion of DRUGS.

Even though Macaulay says of Sir Richard Blackmore: 'He confounded an APHORISM with an APOPHTHEGM', the two are nearly indistinguishable. An APHORISM is supposed to be at a higher level, a philosophical truth pointedly set down, a speculative principle; while an APOTHEGM is more practical. Thus:
'Life is short, and art is long'
is an APHORISM from Hippocrates; while:
'He who fights and runs away may live to fight another day', good practical advice from Oliver Goldsmith, is called an APOTHEGM.

879. *COCHLEATE*, cochleate (*kŏk'-lē-āt*) *adj*. Having the form of a snail's shell, screwed, spiral, coiled, winding around a fixed center, helical, helicoidal.
In the first version of the vocabulary test, where SPIRAL and SHELL appeared as choices, 40 per cent preferred the first and 20 per cent the second. In the revised form SHELL was changed to CLAM-SHELL with the result that both groups, or a total of 60 per cent, now underline SPIRAL.
COCHLEATE comes from the Latin *cochleatus*, spiral, from *cochlea*, a snail's shell, and this in turn from the Greek κοχλίας (*cochlias*), a snail, as well as something spiral. From the same Greek comes COCHLEA (*kŏk'-lē-ăh*), a division of the inner ear, spiral in form.

880. *SMIRKING*, smirking (*smer'-kĭng*) *adj*. Smiling affectedly, grimacing (*grĭm-ā'-sĭng*) in a conceited manner, offensively familiar (v. B. 535).
In 1721 Nathan Bailey defined both SMIRK and SIMPER as smiling pleasantly, and of SIMPER said: 'Putting on a holiday look'. SMILE retains today this agreeable impression; but SMIRK and SIMPER are both unpleasant.
Two separate studies, each based on four hundred different persons, give MASKING as the popular misconception chosen by 21 per cent of the first group and by 37 per cent of the second, a concentration on one mislead too great for luck, and not yet understood. Both SMIRKING and SIMPERING are unreal, affected, and so may suggest disguising, MASKING one's inner feelings. SIMPERING is silly, simple; SMIRKING is conceited, offensive.

881. *HETERODOX*, heterodox (*hĕt'-er-ō-dŏks*) *adj.* Contrary, heretical, holding opinions at variance with those accepted, opposed to those believed right.

To 51 per cent HETERODOX means MIXED, a confusion of HETERODOX with HETEROGENEOUS, both starting with the Greek ἕτερος (*heteros*), different, other. HETEROGENEOUS (*hĕt-er-ō-jē'-nē-ŭs*) ends with γένος (*genos*), sort, genus, and so different in kind, consisting of parts of dissimilar sorts. Of HOMOGENEITY and its opposite HETEROGENEITY Ephraim Chambers quotes Quincy as saying: 'In effect they are two terms which serve frequently as a refuge for ignorance; otherwise the common terms of LIKE and UNLIKE serve every whit as well'.

HETERODOX ends in the Greek δόξα (*doxa*), opinion. HETERODOX is differing in sentiments from the generality of mankind; contrary to the faith or doctrine established in the true church. The word stands in opposition to ORTHODOX.

882. *IMPUGN*, impugn (*ĭm-pūn'*) *v.* To attack in words, gainsay, contradict, malign, call in question.

IMPUGN comes from the Latin *impugnare*, to attack, assail, a combination of *in*, against, and *pugnare*, to fight, the source of PUGNACIOUS, quarrelsome, inclined to fight, from *pugnus*, fist, the source of PUGILIST, one who fights with his fists.

To 30 per cent IMPUGN means CONSIDER, and to another 25 per cent REVIEW. To IMPUGN is to CONSIDER, REVIEW, and then to attack in words.

883. *ARGENTAL*, argental (*ăhr-jĕn'-tăl*) *adj.* Pertaining to silver, silvery, silvern.

The Anglo-Saxon word SILVER, the Spanish word *plata*, and the Latin *argentum*, are closely associated. The chemical symbol for SILVER is Ag, standing for *argentum*. PLATARESQUE means like SILVER-WORK, ornamental, used in architecture, and this may suggest CARVED, chosen by 35 per cent. The name ARGENTINA comes from the Latin *argentum;* while Rio de la Plata, a river in ARGENTINA, is Spanish.

From the Latin *argentum* come also the English ARGENT (*ahr'-jĕnt*), a word once used for money, and the adjective ARGENTAL, made of SILVER, like silver, consisting of silver.

884. *APHOTIC*, aphotic (*ă-fō'-tĭk*) *adj*. Dark, without light.

APHOTIC is a combination of the Greek privative ἀ-, not, and φῶς (*phos*), light, and means without light.

To 25 per cent APHOTIC means DEEP, compared with 30 per cent who prefer DARK. The word is a combination of both, though by derivation it means DARK. According to the Century Dictionary, it was first used by Wilhelm Philipp Schimper in his Plant Geology, in reference to the deepest parts of the oceans where there is no light.

885. *BICKER*, bicker (*bĭk'-ĕr*) *v*. To quarrel, contend, wrangle, engage in petulant altercation.

BICKER goes back to Middle English but the origin is unknown. Isaac Barrow, an English divine and mathematician who died in 1677, groups CARP and BICKER together, and the dictionary uses PETULANT in both definitions. To CARP is to find fault without reason, PETULANT is peevish; except that PEEVISH is longer lasting, almost a part of the person. PETULANT is unexpected, quick, impatient, momentary. Both CARP and BICKER suggest shortlived and without reason. To BICKER is to quarrel, wrangle, argue.

To 50 per cent BICKER means DIFFER, compared with only 30 per cent who prefer WRANGLE. CARPING, from Icelandic, Swedish, and Norwegian words meaning brag, boast, is DIFFERING unpleasantly, finding fault. BICKERING is outright quarreling, WRANGLING, and once meant even exchanging blows.

886. *BRINDLED*, brindled (*brĭn'-dld*) *adj*. With bands of different colors, correctly gray with streaks of darker gray or black, sometimes reddish brown with lines or spots of dark brown.

BRINDLED, perhaps a diminutive of BRINDED, goes back to various Scotch words; it is closely related to BRANDED, and applies almost exclusively to animals, originally in Scotland to cows, but is used by William Cullen Bryant of the CATAMOUNT, another name for the wildcat, lynx, or cougar.

To 30 per cent BRINDLED means WILD; to 20 per cent PURE BRED; and to only 15 per cent STREAKED. BRINDLED, streaked, is virtually unknown.

887. *STULTIFYING*, stultifying (*stŭl'-tĭ-fī-ĭng*) *adj*. To cause
to look foolish, silly, reduce to absurdity.

STULTIFYING comes from the Latin *stultus*, foolish, silly, and
facere, to make, and so, by derivation, to make seem stupid,
reduce to absurdity.

The Imperial Dictionary, which first appeared in 1850 in
Glasgow, Scotland, in two volumes, with a third volume of
illustrations, based on Webster's Dictionary of 1828, published
in New Haven, Connecticut, defines STULTILOQUENT as given to
STULTILOQUENCE, foolish talk. More than a century earlier, in
his first General English Dictionary of 1721, Nathan Bailey had
given STULTILOQUENCE as senseless babble, stupid talk.

To 25 per cent STULTIFYING means FUTILE, a closer synonym
than DISCOURAGING, selected by 30 per cent. FUTILE comes from
the Latin *fundere*, to pour, from the same source as *futtile*, with
two t's, a sort of pitcher, large at the top, small at the bottom.
By derivation, FUTILE means too easily poured out and so glib,
loquacious, and from this, ineffective, useless, unavailing, of no
value, very close to silly, foolish, the correct meaning of
STULTIFYING.

FRUSTRATE and STULTIFY have something of the same suggestion. To FRUSTRATE is to bring to naught by fraud, deception,
trick. To STULTIFY is to force to appear foolish.

888. *MEGRIM*, megrim (*mē'-grĭm*) *n*. 'Blues', lowness of
spirits in the plural; in the singular the word means a form
of headache confined to one side of the head.

MEGRIM goes back through the French, Spanish, and the Italian
emigrania to the Latin *hemicranium*, half the head, to the Greek
ἡμι- (*hemi-*), half, and κρανίον (*cranion*), head, cranium.

889. *PHOENIX*, phoenix (*fē'-nĭks*) *n*. A wonderful bird of
great beauty, the only one of its kind. The size of an
eagle; its head finely crested, with a beautiful plumage; its neck
covered with feathers of a gold colour, and the rest of its body
purple; only the tail white, intermixed with carnation, and its
eyes sparkling like stars. After living five or six hundred years
in the Arabian wilderness, the PHOENIX built itself a funeral
pyre and arose young again from the ashes.

The Phoenicians gave the name PHOENIX to the date palm tree because, when burnt down to the very root, it normally rises again fairer than ever.

A PARAGON, used as a synonym in one form of the vocabulary test, comes from the Spanish phrase *para con*, in comparison with. A PARAGON is a model to be followed, a pattern of excellence.

PHOENIX comes directly from the Anglo-Saxon *fenix*, from the Latin *phoenix*, and the Greek φοῖνιξ (*phoinix*), a fabulous bird.

The word has come to be used figuratively to mean a person of distinction, also one of great beauty; but the word PHOENIX has a unique meaning of beauty, great age, and the renewal of youth, and PHOENIX should be reserved for the situation where all three are wanted.

890. *HUMECTANT*, humectant (*hū-mĕk'-tănt*) *adj.* Moistening, dilutant, watery, wet, damp.

HUMECTANT comes from the Latin *humectare*, to moisten, wet, from *humere*, to be moist, the source of HUMID, watery, wet, damp, dank. A HUMIDOR is a box or container in which cigars are kept moist and so prevented from drying. MOISTURE and MOIST are pleasant. HUMID is apt to carry with it a feeling of STICKINESS, and this leads 20 per cent to select STICKY as a synonym of HUMECTANT, another word for HUMID, called obsolete by the dictionaries.

891. *RABID*, rabid (*răb'-ĭd*) *adj.* Furious, raging, mad, frenzied, raving; also intense, rampant.

RABID comes from the Latin *rabidus*, mad, furious, from *rabere*, to be mad, to rage; also from the Latin *rabies*, a fatal, infectious disease. From the same Latin source also come RAGE, ENRAGE, and RAVE.

Among the five choices in the first version of the vocabulary test were EXTREME, preferred by 52 per cent, and PRESSURE-DRIVEN, marked by 40 per cent. RABID is used figuratively, as: 'A RABID socialist', 'A RABID democrat', to mean INTENSE, rampant, and so perhaps EXTREME, though this is far removed from the original sense.

RABIES (*rā'-bǐ-ēz*), madness, rage, may be thought of as an external manifestation, giving vent to some sort of internal pressure; so that PRESSURE-DRIVEN is a vivid description of RAGE.

RAGE may be the extreme anger, fury, of a usually normal person; RAVE is abnormal, the result of madness even if temporary. RABIES is a fatal disease; and the adjective RABID, when used, should have something of this suggestion.

892. *DECOLLATION*, decollation (*dē-kō-lā'-shǒn*) *n.* The act of beheading, decapitation.

DECOLLATION comes from the Latin *decollare*, to behead, a combination of *de*, from, and *collum*, neck, the source of COLLAR. The French *décolleté* (*dā-kǒl-tā'*) is almost the same word in which the *de* means down, low-necked.

893. *ADDLED*, addled (*ǎd'-dld*) *adj.* Rotten, putrid, filthy, applied particularly to eggs.

To 60 per cent, more than half, a clear majority, ADDLED means COMBINED, united, put together, no doubt because of ADDED. To ADD, from the Latin *ad*, to, and *dare*, to give, is to sum up, join, unite, attach, affix, as: 'To ADD to one's knowledge', to increase it.

The noun ADDLE goes directly back to an Anglo-Saxon word for MUD, and means liquid filth, drainage from dung, mire. From this comes the verb to ADDLE, to spoil, and so the participle adjective ADDLED, spoiled, rotten.

Of 'An ADLE egge' Mincheu, 1600, says: 'An idle egg because it is good for nothing'. From this, ADDLED has come to mean empty, idle, vain, barren, muddled, as well as rotten.

894. *APPELLATE*, appellate (*ǎp-pěl'-lāt*) *adj.* Pertaining to appeals.

APPELLATE comes from the Latin *appellatus*, the past participle of *appellare*, to appeal, sue.

APPELLATE is the adjective which corresponds to the verb APPEAL, to refer to a higher judge.

APPELLATE means with the power to review and affirm, reverse, or modify the judgment of a lower tribunal; and this leads 27 per cent to select LOWER as the meaning of APPELLATE.

According to John Caldwell Calhoun, elected vice president of the United States in 1824, APPELLATE stands in contradistinction to original jurisdiction. APPELLATE implies that the case must commence in an inferior court, not having final jurisdiction.

895. *PILEOUS*, pileous (*pī'-lē-ŭs*) *adj.* Hairy, covered with hair, especially fine soft hair.

PILE, hair, from the Latin *pilus*, hair, is the nap of a rug, short threads, standing straight up, close together to form a solid surface. From the same *pilus*, hair, through French, come PLUSH, a heavy velvet cloth with the same PILE surface; and, after numerous alterations, PERUKE, a wig.

To 12 per cent PILEOUS means WRETCHED, and to another 12 per cent HOWLING. There is a word BILIOUS (*bĭl'-yŭs*), pronounced differently but, except for two letters, spelt the same as PILEOUS, which may suggest WRETCHED, even perhaps HOWLING.

Three adjectives: PILOUS (*pī'-lŭs*), PILOSE (*pī'-lōs*), and PILEOUS (*pī'-lē-ŭs*), all mean covered with hair, furry, hairy, especially covered with fine soft hair.

896. *ASTRINGENT*, astringent (*ăs-trĭn'-jĕnt*) *adj.* Contracting tissues, binding, constrictive, styptic, tightening, drawing together.

TANNIC ACID has a most ASTRINGENT taste; it is one of the important ASTRINGENTS.

ASTRINGENT comes from the Latin *astringere*, to draw together, from *ad*, to, and *stringere*, to bind fast, draw tight, the source of the English word STRINGENT. STRINGENT, without the initial A, means exacting, rigid, tight, as STRINGENT regulations. ASTRINGENT should not be used in this way, but reserved for drawn together, contracted, in the literal, physical sense. STRICT, from the past participle *strictus*, of the same verb *stringere*, to draw tight, has come to mean severe, rigid, exacting, rigorous, as a STRICT teacher.

To 31 per cent ASTRINGENT means acid. The American College Dictionary groups ACID and ASTRINGENT as nearly the same when applied figuratively to wit. ACID is sharp, cutting, biting, perhaps sour.

ALKALINE is another frequently marked mislead. ALKALINE compounds contain sodium, potassium, or lithium. They neutralize acids to form salts, and turn red litmus paper blue, and so are the opposites of acids.

ASTRINGENTS are medicines, which bind together the parts of the body. E. Chambers says: 'They stand naturally opposed to LAXATIVES. They only differ from what are called STYPTICS, in degree of efficacy'.

897. *TRUCULENCY*, truculency (*trŭk'-ū-lĕn-sĭ*) *n.* Fierceness, savageness of manner, ferocity, barbarous appearance. Though some select SERVILITY, an opposite, TRUCULENCY is so little known that answers as to its meaning range widely, suggesting that they are guesses rather than misunderstandings of the word.

TRUCULENCY and TRUCULENCE come from the Latin *truculentus*, fierce, savage, from *trux, trucis*, fierce, wild. The ending -ENCE, from Latin, makes a noun from an adjective which ends in -ENT. Thus the adjective TRUCULENT, as: 'A TRUCULENT man', becomes the noun TRUCULENCE, ferocity, fierceness. TRUCULENCY, ending in Y, is a modern version, differing in no way except sound from the pleasanter TRUCULENCE. Use this last unless rhythm demands the extra syllable.

898. *HUDIBRASTIC*, hudibrastic (*hū-dĭ-brăs'-tĭk*) *adj.* Mock heroic, satirical, burlesque, quixotic. HUDIBRAS (*hū'-dĭ-brăs*), with the s pronounced, is a satire, written by Samuel Butler and published in 1663, against the Puritans. Although the whole is done in verse, and 20 per cent select BLANK-VERSE as the meaning of HUDIBRASTIC, MOCK-HEROIC is closer.

> 'For he was of that stubborn crew
> Of errant saints, who all men grant
> To be the true church militant —
> Such as do build their faith upon
> The holy text of pike and gun'.

The name HUDIBRAS comes from a member of the Round Table, Sir Hugh de Bras. HUDIBRAS is one of:

'That sect whose chief devotion lies
In odd perverse antipathies;'
'Who prove their doctrines orthodox
By apostolic blows and knocks;
Call fire and sword and desolation
A godly thorough reformation,
Which always must be carried on,
And still be doing, never done;
As if religion were intended
For nothing else but to be mended'.

899. *DEMESNE*, demesne. Of the pronunciation Phyfe says: (*dē-mān'* or *dē-mēn'*); The Century Dictionary says: (*dĕ-mēn'*) *n*. Estate, land holdings, manor house and land.
From the Latin *dominus*, lord, master, come the verb to DOMI-NATE, to control, rule without question, govern completely, and DOMINION, with the Latin *dominium*, both the right of ownership, authority to control, and the area ruled by a sovereign, territory under a government. The words DOMINION of Canada stress both the area and the right to control.

DEMESNE, which has survived through legal documents and legal terminology, is an Old French variation of *domaine*, right of ownership, power, dominion. The modern English word is DOMAIN (*dō-mān'*). *Demesne* should be used only of an important estate, a large area, as the land which belongs to the Lord of the Manor for his own use. This aspect of DEMESNE suggests the two misleads: HUNTING LODGE and LINEAGE, each selected by 12 per cent, and each characteristic of a large English estate.

900. *HARROWED*, harrowed (*hăr'-rōd*) *adj*. Tormented, harassed (v. b. 1121), distressed, much disturbed, bothered, afflicted, worried, troubled, agonized, racked, harried (v. b. 1463). Of the verb to HARROW, Nathan Bailey, 1721, says: 'To lay waste, ravage, or destroy'.

A HARROW, from Anglo-Saxon, with similar words in German, Icelandic, Swedish, and Danish, is a farming implement, a large flat platform with heavy spikes projecting below, dragged over rough ploughed ground to break up the lumps and smooth the surface. HARROWED, when used of persons, is figurative, to tear the person apart as a HARROW breaks up the clods.

HARROWED is thought by 33 per cent to mean TIRED, fatigued, exhausted, wearied. Strictly the state of being TIRED is the result of being HARROWED. One can be TIRED from other causes, as from a pleasant walk. HARASSED (hăr'-ăst), a synonym of HARROWED, means fatigued, exhausted, TIRED; but HARROWED is far stronger, almost torn to pieces, lacerated, as with a HARROW.

901. *SEDENTARY*, sedentary (sĕd'-ĕn-tā-rĭ) adj. Sitting, continuing in a seated position, applied to office work where there is no physical activity.

SEDENTARY comes from the Latin *sedens, sedentis*, the present participle of *sedere*, to sit, settle, the source of numerous words, some easily recognized as: SEDIMENT, lees, dregs, material which settles to the bottom in a liquid; SEDIMENTARY, rock formed of matter which settles in this way; and SEDATE, quiet, composed, serene, serious; as well as SESSION, a sitting together to discuss and decide, from *sessus*, the past participle of *sedere*, to sit.

ITINERANT (ĭ-tĭn'-ĕ-rănt) means traveling from place to place, wandering, strolling, as: 'An ITINERANT preacher'. SEDENTARY is used almost entirely of work, as: 'The SEDENTARY life of a scholar', or 'A SEDENTARY occupation', work done sitting down.

902. *PECULATION*, peculation (pĕk-ū-lā'-shŏn) n. Originally embezzling public money, stealing, pilfering, using for one's self money entrusted to one's care; Nathan Bailey says: 'Robbing or cheating the public'.

To 29 per cent PECULATION means GAMBLING. SPECULATION, differing from PECULATION by only a single letter, is GAMBLING. SPECULATION, from the Latin *speculatus*, the past participle of *speculari*, to watch, observe, spy out, from *specere*, to see, was once observing, inspecting, but is now investing money at a risk with hope of gain, and so GAMBLING.

PECULATION, without the s at the beginning, comes from the Latin *peculari*, to defraud the public, embezzle. This comes in turn from *peculium*, property, from *pecus, pecoris*, cattle.

Of PECULATION E. Chambers says: 'The crime of embezzling public money, by a person who has the management, receipt, or custody thereof. The Julian law among the Romans punished this crime with death, in a magistrate, and with deportation or banishment in a private person; and prosecuted even on the criminal's heir'.

903. *DETRITUS*, detritus (*dē-trī'-tŭs*) *n.* Loose fragments of rock, gravel, sand, drift.

DETRITUS comes from the Latin *detritus*, a rubbing away, from *deterere*, to rub away, a combination of *de*, away, and *terere*, to rub, the source of TRITE, worn thin by use, and DETRIMENT, prejudice, hurt, disadvantage.

DETRITUS is a geological term for loose fragments of rock. DRIFT is DETRITAL material which has come from a distance, or which is piled up on bed rock.

904. *CUSP*, cusp (*kŭsp*) *n.* The horn of a crescent, point formed by the meeting of two curves.

The Latin *cuspis* means not only a point, but also a spear, javelin, lance; and this may lead 16 per cent to select SHAFT as the meaning of CUSP. The first definition of SHAFT in the Century Dictionary is: a long slender rod forming the body of a spear or lance; also, the spear or lance itself, another illustration of the incredible way in which old meanings survive in the popular mind.

The word CUSP appears in architecture, mathematics, and many sciences, for some sort of spear-shaped projection, a point made by the joining of two curves. In astronomy either pointed end of the crescent moon is a CUSP. In mathematics the pointed space between two curves which meet is a CUSP. In architecture the decorative points around the inside edge of an arch, formed by the coming together of small half circles, are CUSPS. A LOBE is a rounded projection; a CUSP, pointed. An ANGLE is formed by the meeting of two straight lines; a CUSP, by the meeting of two curves.

905. *PRIVATION*, privation (*prī-vā'-shŏn*) *n.* The absence of that which is needed for comfort, defect of something necessary, want, destitution, penury, poverty, distress, necessity.

PRIVATION, from the Latin *privatio, privationis*, a taking away,

comes from the Latin verb *privare*, to deprive, strip, rob. PRIVA-
TION is robbing one's self.

Both PRIVATIONS and DEPRIVATIONS (*dĕp-rĭ-vā'-shŏnz*) are
going without comforts. DEPRIVATIONS are imposed by others;
PRIVATIONS are imposed by one's self, on one's self.

To 27 per cent PRIVATION means ECONOMY. ECONOMY comes
from the Greek οἶκος (*oikos*), household, and νέμειν (*nemein*),
to manage. ECONOMY is household management, intelligent saving. The word means care in spending, voluntarily depriving
one's self of something which might be enjoyable. ECONOMY
rarely suggests serious need. PRIVATION is almost suffering, a
needless going without.

906. *CLOTURE*, cloture (*klō'-tūr*) *n.* The Century Dictionary
  says: 'The same as CLOSURE'; in legislation, the closing of
a debate, cutting off discussion.
CLOTURE is the French word for the action of closing applied
to the closing of a debate in the French Assembly.

The English CLOSURE (*klō'-zūr*) comes from the Latin *clausus*,
the past participle of *claudere*, to close. The French spelling
CLOTURE is now used in the restricted sense of closing a par-
liamentary discussion, putting a stop to a long drawn out political argument.

To 22 per cent CLOTURE means DEBATE, a confusion of terms
belonging to the same situation, the second step in learning.
The technical term CLOTURE is the procedure employed when a
DEBATE becomes a FILIBUSTER. A small group can discuss, argue,
DEBATE indefinitely, and CLOTURE is the accepted method of
bringing such a DEBATE to a close.

907. *DISTICH*, distich (*dĭs'-tĭk*) *n.* A couplet, verse of two
  lines, of the same length, often riming. The big Oxford
gives the snappiest definition: 'A couple of lines of verse, usually
making complete sense, and riming'.
The popular mislead is TWO-PANELS, clearly suggested by TRIP-
TYCH, directly from the Greek τρίπτυχον (*triptychon*), literally threefold, from τρι- (*tri*), three, as in TRICYCLE, and πτυχη
(*ptyche*), a fold. A TRIPTYCH (*trĭp'-tĭk*) is a group of three
painted panels, hinged side by side, sometimes an altar-piece.

DISTICH, by analogy, might easily mean TWO-PANELS, especially when TRIPTYCH is misspelt with I, triptich. But DISTICH, correctly spelt with I, comes from a different Greek source: δι- (di-), two, and στίχος (stichos), line, row, verse.

STICH (stĭk), a general term for a single line of verse, appears in the better known ACROSTIC, a verse in which the first letters of the lines, taken in order, form a name or motto. An ELEGIAC (ĕ-lē'-jĭ-ăk) is a DISTICH in which the first and second lines differ in accent. A STANZA is the next largest arrangement of lines, a group of DISTICHS or couplets. DISTICH is a technical term in poetry for two lines of verse.

908. *FUNNEL*, funnel (fŭn'-nĕl) n. Smoke-stack, the channel of a chimney through which smoke ascends, used especially in steamships and locomotives, an iron chimney for a furnace. Another meaning of FUNNEL is a hollow cone with the point down, used for pouring liquid into a bottle or other container with a small opening. This leads 23 per cent to select SIEVE as the meaning of FUNNEL. A SIEVE is much like a STRAINER, but used for dry powders, not liquids. Although the Century Dictionary gives FILTER as a meaning of FUNNEL, the purpose of a FILTER is the separation of particles from a liquid. A FUNNEL, in this sense, may be used to hold FILTER-PAPER; but the purpose of a FUNNEL is primarily to aid in pouring liquids.

Etymologists trace FUNNEL through the Latin *infundibulum*, a funnel, also the hopper of a mill, to *infundere*, to pour in.

E. Chambers, 17th edition, says: 'FUNNEL of a chimney, the shaft or smallest part of the chimney from the waist upward'. Palladio, the architect of Verona, Italy, orders that: 'The FUNNEL be raised three to five feet above the roof that it may carry the smoke clear from the house'.

909. *CHANCERY*, chancery (chăn'-sĕ-rĭ) n. Specifically the office of the chancellor, where records are filed. In England, the highest court of justice next to Parliament. In the United States, a court of equity.

From the Latin *cancelli*, a lattice railing, come the semi-legal term CHANCELLOR, originally a doorkeeper who stood at the lattice railing inclosing the judgment seat, and CHANCERY, the office of the CHANCELLOR; and the religious term CHANCEL, the enclosed space in a church surrounding the altar, the sanctuary. This leads 56 per cent to choose the word CHURCH as a synonym of CHANCERY. To CHANT, from the Latin *cantare*, to sing, is to celebrate in song; and a CHANTRY is a church or chapel endowed for the maintenance of one or more priests to sing mass daily for the soul of the donor.

E. Chambers, 1728, starts with Nathan Bailey's definition of CHANCERY, 1721, and enlarges upon it: 'The grand court of equity and conscience instituted to moderate the rigor of the other courts that are tied to the strictest letter of the law. The court examines fraud, combinations, trusts, secret uses, to soften the severity of common law, and rescue people from oppression, to relieve them against cheats, unfortunate accidents, breaches of trust, etc.'

910. *MITER*, miter (*mī'-ter*) *n.* Head-dress, also spelt MITRE, an ecclesiastical head-dress worn by bishops.
MITER comes from the Latin *mitra*, from the Greek μίτρα (*mitra*), at first a belt, girdle, and then a head-band, turban.

Bailey says of MITER: A bonnet or turbant; attire on the head with labels hanging down, worn by bishops; and of LABELS: 'Ribbands hanging down on each side of a MITRE'.

MITRED ABBOTS are such governors of monasteries who have obtained the privilege of wearing the MITER, RING, GLOVES, and CROSIER STAFF of a BISHOP.

E. Chambers says of MITER: Spelt MITRE; a pontifical ornament worn on the head by bishops and certain abbots on solemn occasions.

911. *DEVOIR*, devoir (*dĕv-wāhr'*) *n.* Duty, service, civility, an act of respect, attentions due to another, as: 'To pay one's DEVOIRS to another', or 'We paid our DEVOIRS'.
DEVOIR, a French word, from the infinitive *devoir*, to owe, comes from the Latin *debere*, to owe, the source of the English DEBT, that which one owes, and DEBIT, again the amount owed.

A GREETING, the popular mislead, is a salutation. To GREET, directly from Anglo-Saxon, is to address formally, salute, hail, accost. DEVOIR, in the sense of noticing another with respect, is close to GREETING, but DEVOIR has a sense of owing something not included in GREETING. GREETING is, however, too close as a mislead, and will be removed in revision.

912. *INCONDITE*, incondite (*ĭn'-kŏn-dīt* or *ĭn-kŏn'-dīt*) *adj.*
    Badly put together, ill constructed, unpolished, rude. Thomas Carlyle says: 'Ineloquent and INCONDITE', badly spoken and poorly constructed.

INCONDITE, so seldom encountered, seems hardly worth the effort of learning; but, despite, this, 40 per cent of a high vocabulary group select the correct meaning UNPOLISHED, more than mark correctly apparently easier words.

INCONDITE, from the Latin *inconditus*, starts with the privative *in-*, not, followed by *conditus*, put together, from *condere*, to put together. A CONDIMENT is a relish, seasoning, spicy sauce, used with food to give flavor. This comes from the Latin verb *condire*, to spice, season, preserve fruit in wine, perhaps the same as *condere*, to put together. From the past participle *conditus* comes the English CONDITE, to preserve with sugar, salt, and spices, as, from Jeremy Taylor, 1613 to 1667: 'CONDITED or pickled mushrooms'.

From *condere*, to put together, come the verb to ABSCOND, a combination of *abs*, away, and *condere*, to put, and so to hide one's self, flee, escape, run off, lie concealed; also RECONDITE, put away, hidden, secret, and so figuratively abstruse, occult, mystical, deep, mysterious; and finally INCONDITE, starting with the privative *in-*, and so not put away, not orderly, not well put together, rough, crude, unpolished.

Of the pronunciation of RECONDITE, Fowler comments, in his Modern English Usage: 'The old pronunciation: (*rĭ-kŏn'-dīt*) is maintained by some scholarly persons, but (*rĕk'-ŏn-dīt*) is now used'. The Century Dictionary gives (*ĭn-kŏn'-dīt*) first, but the word should probably be accented on the first syllable to agree with RECONDITE.

913. *REFURBISHED*, refurbished (*rē-fer'-bĭsht*) *adj.* Polished
    up, furbished anew, refinished.
To FURBISH, from Anglo-Saxon, to rub, scour, polish, burnish, clean, renew, renovate, was once used for polishing by rubbing,

making resplendent the metal of helmets and other war equipment.

To FURNISH, to provide, supply, give, so much like FURBISH, comes from a different source. The word BROWN, the color, a dark reddish yellow, goes directly back to an Anglo-Saxon word from which comes the French *brunir*, the source of the English BURNISH, which ought to mean make brown but which has come to mean make glow, almost make burn brightly, and so practically the same as FURBISH.

To 49 per cent REFURBISHED means SECOND-HAND, compared with only 42 per cent who choose POLISHED, ideas closely associated. SECOND-HAND means received from some previous owner, not original, not new. SECOND-HAND furniture may be old, broken-down, dilapidated. To make it salable, it must be REFURBISHED, repolished. New furniture may be FURBISHED, polished. Only SECOND-HAND furniture can be REFURBISHED.

914. *DEBOUCH*, debouch (*dē-boosh'*) v. To emerge, issue, pass out, exit from a narrow opening.

DEBOUCH is French, a combination of *de-*, from, and *boucher*, to stop up, from *bouche*, mouth, from the Latin *bucca*, cheek.

Two misleads equally popular, selected by 25 per cent each, are BLOCKED and CELEBRATED. A DEBAUCH (*dē-bawch'*) is a wild CELEBRATION; and the similarity of DEBAUCH and DEBOUCH leads easily to the selection of CELEBRATE as the meaning of DEBOUCH.

A crowd cannot DEBOUCH unless it has already been checked. A crowd may LEAVE, EXIT, or DISPERSE; but in order to DEBOUCH it must have been BLOCKED by some sort of narrow exit through which it has been compelled to pass. An army, held up by a narrow mountain pass, can then DEBOUCH onto the plain.

915. *HIGGLER*, higgler (*hĭg'-glĕr*) n. A tricky bargainer, close huckster, one who sells for as much as he can get.

To HACK is to chop at random, roughly, crudely, awkwardly, without skill. The frequentative, HACKLE, by a slight change in pronunciation, became HAGGLE, to chop unskillfully, hack roughly, and also to bargain in a petty way, cavil, chaffer tediously, make difficulties. One of several variations is HIGGLE, the verb, and so HIGGLER for the person who HIGGLES.

916. *GUSTATION*, gustation (*gŭs-tā'-shŏn*) *n.* Tasting, the act of tasting, savoring, relishing.

To 21 per cent GUSTATION means VOMITING, almost an opposite and suggested perhaps by the word REGURGITATION, from the Latin *re-*, and *gurgitare*, to flood, pour back, surge back.

GUSTATION comes from the Latin *gustare*, to taste, and *gustus*, taste, relish. From the same source comes GUSTO (*gŭs'-tō*), zest, relish, keen enjoyment, appreciative taste.

917. *FLEDGED*, fledged (*flĕdjd*) *adj.* Feathered, having the wings developed for flight, able to fly, furnished with feathers, and so figuratively, developed, matured.

To 15 per cent FLEDGED means GRACED. To GRACE is to adorn, embellish, decorate. Of FLEDGED Bailey said: 'To be well covered with feathers as young birds are when they begin to fly'.

918. *DOSSAL*, dossal (*dŏs'-săl*) *n.* A hanging of silk, satin, damask, cloth of gold, at the back of an altar, and sometimes at the sides of the CHANCEL.

A church may have different DOSSALS of different colors for specific festivals. In Spanish and Latin the corresponding word may mean CANOPY. The word comes from DORSAL, pertaining to the back, because the DOSSAL is usually hung back of the altar.

The popular mislead selected by 27 per cent is COAT-OF-ARMS.

919. *PECCANT*, peccant (*pĕk'-kănt*) *adj.* Sinning, guilty, offending, bad.

The mislead TREACHEROUS is chosen by 25 per cent in preference to SINNING as a synonym of PECCANT.

PECCANT, from the Latin verb *peccare*, to offend, sin, transgress, is an adjective; PECCANCY, badness, the noun; and PECCANTLY, corruptly, the adverb. A PECCADILLO, directly from the Spanish *pecadillo*, the diminutive of *pecado*, is a petty crime, small sin.

920. *DODDERING*, doddering (*dŏd'-der-ĭng*) *adj.* Shaking, trembling, tottering, dithering, quivering, vibrating.

To 46 per cent DODDERING means INCOMPETENT, from the Latin *competere*, to be fit. INCOMPETENT, starting with the negative

IN-, means not fit, incapable, not adequate, ineffective, an idea included in the modern use of DODDERING, and perhaps too close for a mislead.

DODDERING comes through an old English word which meant to shiver. Today SHIVER means shaking with cold; while DODDER-ING suggests shaking with old age.

921. *TOUT*, tout (*towt*) v. (In pronunciation TOUT rimes with OUT and ROUT, not with ROUTE.) To look about for cus-tomers, solicit employment, specifically in modern racing slang to spy out the movements of race-horses at training.
To 42 per cent TOUT means BOAST OF and to another 36 per cent PROCLAIM. The verb to TOUT combines the two in almost equal proportions.

Of the noun a TOUT, the Slang Dictionary by John Camden Hotten, 1869, says: 'An agent in the training districts, on the look-out for information as to the condition and capabilities of those horses entering for a coming race'.

From Slang and Its Analogies, compiled by John S. Farmer and W. E. Henry, in seven volumes, 1903, comes: 'The verb to TOUT is to canvass for custom as do hotel, coach, or steamer servants, to solicit employment as does a guide, or to spy out special information concerning horses in training'.

922. *PHILISTINE*, philistine (*fĭ-lĭs'-tĭn* or *fĭ'-lĭs-tĭn*) adj. Com-monplace, contented, ordinary, of inferior culture, lacking in taste, of indifferent aesthetic refinement.
The word PAROCHIAL (*pă-rō'-kĭ-ăl*) is sometimes used in much the same way for one whose interests are limited to one's own parish. The BIGOTED, INTOLERANT person has opinions; the PHIL-ISTINE has none.

PHILISTINE, called COMMONPLACE by 36 per cent, is thought by 26 per cent to mean LIMITED. The PHILISTINES were a war-like people who inhabited the coast of Palestine about 1200 B.C. and harassed the Israelites for several centuries. The word is used today for a commonplace person, a matter-of-fact indi-vidual upon whom one can look down, a satisfied person, un-aware of his own lack of culture, one who is not only COMMON-PLACE but LIMITED.

923. *NUMISMATICS*, numismatics (*nū-mĭs-măt'-ĭks*) *n.* The
science of coins and medals, their history, classification,
and artistic qualities.

NUMISMATICS comes from the Greek νόμισμα (*nomisma*), a
coin, piece of money, anything approved for usage; plus the
Greek ending -ICS, which designates a science or art. Though the
derivation applies only to pieces of metal sanctioned for circulation, NUMISMATICS has come to include medals, made in much
the same manner as coins, but not for circulation.

Several words beginning with NUM- deal with numbers, as
NUMEROLOGY, a study of numbers as affecting life, and these no
doubt lead 38 per cent to select PROBABILITIES, the mathematical
chance of something happening, as the meaning of NUMIS-
MATICS, compared with 36 per cent who select COINS.

PHILATELY (*fĭ-lăt'-ě-lĭ*), from the Greek φίλος (*philos*), love,
is the enjoyment of collecting postage stamps. NUMISMATICS
is the parallel collecting of coins.

924. *GRAMINIVOROUS*, graminivorous (*grăm-ĭ-nĭv'-ō-rŭs*)
adj. Grass-eating, feeding on grass, as oxen, sheep, and
horses.

GRAMINIVOROUS comes from the Latin *gramen, graminis*, grass,
and *vorare*, to eat, devour, swallow. Thus CARNIVOROUS, from
the Latin *caro, carnis*, flesh, is meat-eating, as lions, tigers,
wolves, and eagles, as distinct from HERBIVOROUS, feeding on
vegetables, and INSECTIVOROUS, insect-eating. GRANIVOROUS (*gră-
nĭv'-ō-rŭs*) is feeding on seeds, as birds, and distinct from
GRAMINIVOROUS, eating grass.

From the same *vorare*, to eat, devour, and *omnis*, all, comes
OMNIVOROUS, which leads 25 per cent to select OVER-EATING as a
synonym of GRAMINIVOROUS. OMNIVOROUS, all-devouring, is eating food of every kind indiscriminately as pigs, hippopotami,
and perhaps man himself, almost an opposite of GRAMINIVOROUS,
eating grass and almost nothing else.

925. *COZENED*, cozened (*kŭz'-ěnd*) *v.* Cheated, defrauded,
sponged on, deceived, beguiled, tricked, treated dishonestly.
Originally COZENED was identical in form with COUSIN. Though
now a COUSIN is specifically the son or daughter of an uncle or

aunt, a COUSIN was once any relative further removed than brother or sister; and this made it easy for one to claim to be a cousin and so to ask favors which a relative might expect. This leads 24 per cent to select FAVORED as the meaning of COZENED. To FAVOR is to befriend, help, assist, patronize, treat with partiality, give support to. COZENED is cheated into helping someone who claims to be a COUSIN.

After giving BUBBLE as a synonym of COZEN, Nathan Bailey, 1721, continues: 'An exchange alley bubble, a scheme projected for the carrying on of a manufacture, insurance, or other pretended beneficial project, never designed to be carried on, but calculated for the meridian of Exchange Alley, to wipe the unwary and eager of their money, and keep the stockjobbers out of worse employment, if worse there be'.

926. *BALUSTER*, baluster (*băl'-ŭs-tĕr*) *n*. A small upright post
    used in a series to support a rail.
BALUSTER comes through the French from the Italian *balaustro*, a small pillar, and so from the Greek βαλαίστων (*balaiston*), the flower of the wild pomegranate tree, suggesting that BALUSTERS are not straight posts, but often beautifully carved.

Of another word, BANISTER, the Oxford Dictionary says: a corruption of BALUSTER; and continues: though condemned by Nicholson as improper, and by Stuart as 'vulgar', the term has now acquired general acceptance. Thus Walter Scott says: 'Holding hard on the BANISTERS'; and Sheridan, 1775, in the Rivals: 'He comes down stairs thumping the BANISTERS all the way'; and Wilkie Collins, 1860, in The Woman in White: 'He held fast by the BANISTERS, as he descended the stairs'. But the BANISTERS are still slender upright posts supporting the handrail.

The BALUSTRADE, through the French from the Italian *balaustrata*, strictly a barrier, is a combination of a horizontal rail resting on a series of upright BALUSTERS.

Despite the fact that a majority select RAIL, the BALUSTER is strictly the POST and not the RAIL.

927. *HONORARIUM*, honorarium (*ŏn-ō-ră'-rĭ-ŭm*) *n*. The
    plural is HONORARIA. Fee, gratuity, compensation, payment
for services rendered.

HONORARIUM, from the Latin *honorarium,* a present given on being admitted to a post of honor, is the neuter of *honorarius,* honorary, from *honor,* honor.

Surprisingly often, usage gives a remarkably accurate picture of a word. With PROFESSIONAL-FEE and AWARD both included among the five choices as synonyms of HONORARIUM, the population tested divide evenly between the two, 38 per cent for PROFESSIONAL-FEE and 36 per cent for AWARD. An English BARRISTER, one of the highest class of English lawyers, has no legal right to recover compensation for his services; he cannot maintain an action for his fee. Payment for his services is a GRATUITY, or more correctly, an HONORARIUM.

928. *LEGATE,* legate (*lĕg'-āt*) *n.* A representative, deputy, ambassador, person commissioned to represent a state in a foreign country.

To 49 per cent, half of those tested, LEGATE means LAWYER, an answer nearly correct; for LEGATE comes from the Latin *legatus,* a deputy, from *legare,* to send with a commission, from *lex, legis,* law. Of LAWYER, the Century Dictionary says: 'A general term, comprehending attorneys, counselors, solicitors, proctors, barristers, serjeants, and advocates'. Despite this list, and the derivation of the word, a LEGATE need not be a LAWYER.

According to Nathan Bailey, in his dictionary of 1721: 'A LEGATE is an ambassador sent by the Pope to a foreign prince. The most considerable are those whom the Pope commissions to take his place in councils'.

Of modern usage the Encyclopaedia Britannica says: 'A title now generally confined to the highest class of diplomatic representatives of the Pope, though still occasionally used in its original Latin sense, of any ambassador or diplomatic agent'.

929. *PLANGENT,* plangent (*plăn'-jĕnt*) *adj.* Beating, resounding, reverberating, clashing, noisy, dashing like waves.

PLANGENT comes from the Latin *plangens, plangentis,* the present participle of *plangere,* to beat, strike, also to beat the breast. From this same *plangere* come the verb to PLAIN, to lament, mourn, wail; the Latin noun *plaga,* a blow, shock, thrust, injury; and, from this, PLAGUE, a calamity, that which destroys.

To 25 per cent PLANGENT means JAZZY. Real JAZZ has in it something fundamental, recalling its African origin, and in this sense approaches PLANGENT.

Use PLANGENT with great care to mean a steady irresistible beating like waves against a rocky cliff.

930. *VORSPIEL*, vorspiel (fŏr'-shpēl) *n*. A prelude, overture, introduction, preface.

VORSPIEL is a German musical term meaning play beforehand, from *vor*, before, and *spiel*, play.

PRESENTATION is marked as a synonym by 20 per cent, the same number who underline the correct PRELUDE. PRESENTATION is an introduction to a person, or the introduction of a bill to an assembly. But the word is not used for a musical beginning. PRELUDE is an exact English equivalent of VORSPIEL, play beforehand. VORSPIEL should be used only in connection with German music.

931. *EPIGONE*, epigone (ĕ'-pĭ-gōn) *n*. One born after, successor, heir, offspring.

To 30 per cent EPIGONE means WRITE-UP, and to another 24 per cent POEM. An EPITAPH is an inscription on a tomb; while an EPIGRAM is a short poem also used as an inscription.

EPIGONE comes from the Greek ἐπίγονος (*epigonos*), literally born after, from ἐπί (*epi*), which ordinarily means upon, and -γονος (*-gonos*), born, the source of GENE. Although EPIGONE is used sometimes to mean IMITATOR, there is no such suggestion in the word, which means successor, heir, one who follows.

932. *KYLE*, kyle (kīl) *n*. A strait, channel, sound, a narrow body of sea water.

The word KYLE is wholly unknown, for answers to its meaning scatter almost evenly among the five choices of the vocabulary worksample and the selection of one seems pure luck.

A STRAIT is a channel connecting two large bodies of water, as the STRAIT of Gibralter between the Atlantic Ocean and the Mediterranean Sea; or the STRAITS of MAGELLAN, at the southern tip of South America, connecting the Atlantic and Pacific Oceans. A SOUND is a narrow channel of water between an island and the mainland, as: Long Island SOUND. A FRITH, spelt also FIRTH, is the opening of a river into the sea. These terms are used only in Scotland, as: The FIRTH of FORTH, and the FRITH of Clyde. KYLE appears in all three senses, as a FRITH, STRAIT, or SOUND.

933. *ORPHREY*, orphrey (ŏr'-frĭ) *n.* A kind of embroidery in gold, heavy ornamental border sometimes eight inches in breadth, reaching from the neck down, on an ecclesiastical vestment.

The real word is AURIPHRYGIA (*aw-rĭ-frĭ'-jăh*), from the Latin *aurum*, gold, and Phrygia, an ancient country in the center of Asia Minor where the Phrygians were famous for their skill in embroidering in gold. ORPHREY, sometimes called Phrygian work, is a shortened form of AURIPHRYGIA.

The misconception: BIRD-STATUE attracts 30 per cent compared with only 25 per cent who select RICH-EMBROIDERY. An OSPREY (ŏs'-prā), from the Latin *ossifragus*, literally a bone-breaker, from *os*, bone, and *frangere*, to break, is a bird of prey, a fish hawk. Another way in which OSPREY, the bird, has been spelt is ORFRAY, pronounced almost like the embroidered band. Also the embroidery has been spelt ORFRAY, revealing the same confusion between bird and embroidery still found in a vocabulary test.

ORPHREY is sometimes defined as the APPAREL of an AMICE. In the 10th century APPAREL was a simple fringe which in the 13th and 14th centuries became elegant embroidery. The AMICE was a large oblong piece of linen worn over the shoulders and pulled together at the neck in such a way that the gold embroidery, the ORPHREY, made a collar.

934. *RECUSANT*, recusant (rĕk'-ū-zănt, also pronounced rē-kū'-zănt) *adj.* Refusing obstinately, objecting, opposing; the corresponding noun is RECUSANCE (rĕk'-ū-zăns).

The adjective RECUSANT was applied to those who refused to attend Anglican divine service, the church of the crown, and who were persecuted. This may suggest UNHAPPY, miserable, wretched, especially as WRETCHED comes from an old German word meaning persecuted, banished, driven out.

RECUSANT is thought by 48 per cent, nearly half of those who have tried this vocabulary test, to mean HERMIT-LIKE. A RECLUSE (*rĕ'-klōos*) is a HERMIT, one who lives alone, a solitary person, monk. The corresponding adjective is also RECLUSE, spelt and pronounced in the same way, solitary, sequestered, shut up, retired from the world.

RECUSANT comes from the Latin, *recusans, recusantis*, the present participle of *recusare*, to reject, object, decline, refuse, from *re-*, back, and *causa*, a cause. To ACCUSE, from *accusare*, to call one to account, is to charge, indict, make an imputation against, from *ad-*, to, and *causa*, cause, reason, account, suit at law. In law a RECUSATION is the interposition of an objection for cause. To RECUSE is to refuse, reject as disqualified. RECUSANT, the adjective, is refusing in general.

935. *ABSTERGE*, absterge (*ăb-sterj'*) v. To wipe, wash away, clean by wiping.

A DETERGENT is something which wipes clean, scours, from the Latin *detergens, detergentis*, the present participle of *detergere*, a combination of *de*, off, and *tergere*, to scour, wipe clean.

The adjective TERSE, from *tersus*, wiped off, clean, neat, pure, the past participle of *tergere*, to wipe, rub off, dry, polish, originally meant literally wiped, rubbed smooth; and then more figuratively polished, refined; and from this comes the current meaning of neat, concise, compact.

The verb ABSTERGE is the Latin *abs*, off, and *tergere*, to wipe.

936. *ISSUE*, issue (*ĭs'-sū*) v. To come out, pass from within, go forth, proceed.

To EXIT, DEBOUCH, and ISSUE are three ways of going out. To EXIT, from the Latin *exire*, a combination of *ex*, out, and *ire*, to go, is just to go out and be forgotten. The noun, an EXIT, is a leaving. To DEBOUCH is used of a crowd, mob, army, or any large group which has been blocked by some narrow passage and is now pouring out into the open. To ISSUE is to go out with a purpose in mind to accomplish something. The noun, an ISSUE, is a result, conclusion, outcome, consequence. The implication in the word leads 32 per cent to select TOOK ACTION as the meaning of ISSUED.

937. *POSSET*, posset (*pŏs′-sĕt*) *n*. Beverage, a drink of hot
    milk, curdled with ale or wine, with sugar and spices
added.

The word POSSET goes far back in English to the year 1400.
Under POSSET Chambers, 1728, refers the reader to ZYTHOGALA,
which he says comes from the Greek ζῦθος (*zythos*), cerevisia,
a word of Gallic origin for beer, and γαλα (*gala*), lac, and
adds: a drink recommended by Sydenham. Thomas Sydenham
(*sĭd′-n-ăm*), an English physician, who lived from 1624 to 1689,
was surnamed: the English Hippocrates.

    'POSSET, called also BEER-POSSET, is an excellent mixture of hot
ale, milk, sugar, spices, and sippets.'

938. *MERETRICIOUS*, meretricious (*mĕr-ē-trĭsh′-ŭs*) *adj*.
    Wanton, libidinous; also showy, tawdry, vulgar, gaudy
but deceitful, alluring by false attractions.

MERETRICIOUS, belonging to a whore, comes from the Latin
meretrix, a prostitute, but is thought by 54 per cent, more than
half of those tested, to mean PRAISEWORTHY. MERITORIOUS is
deserving of reward, worthy of praise, possessing merit. MERE-
TRICIOUS, despite the similarity, is an exact opposite.

939. *FUCUS*, fucus (*fū′-kŭs*) *n*. A form of marine algae with
    no distinction between stem and leaf, seaweed.

SEAWEED and DRIFTWOOD, the popular mislead, both belong to
the sea, a confusion of words used in something of the same
situation, the second step in learning.

    The Latin word *fucus*, directly from the Greek φῦκος
(*phucos*), meant rock-lichen, which was used to make a red
dye; and FUCUS may still be the color red or purple.

940. *QUIDNUNC*, quidnunc (*kwĭd′-nŭnk*) *n*. A gossip, news-
    monger, tattletale, busybody.

The Latin *quid* means what, the neuter of *quis*, who; *nunc*
means now, so that the Latin *quid nunc* means: what now? In
English this has become one word, QUIDNUNC, a noun for the
person who is always asking what now? who is curious to know
what is going on next door. The word is used mostly in politics
and society.

Answers divide almost evenly among the four misleads with HAG slightly more popular. The Anglo-Saxon HAG was at one time a witch, and is now more often an ill-disposed old woman. A GOSSIP is a spiteful person gaining satisfaction from doing harm. A NEWSMONGER (*nūz'-mŏn-ger*) deals in news, sells it, much as a FISHMONGER sells fish. A QUIDNUNC may neither sell findings, nor use them maliciously, but is just curious to know what is going on.

941. *ABJURE*, abjure (*ăb-jūr'*) v. To renounce upon oath, withdraw formally, quit an opinion, repudiate, abandon with solemnity, retract, disavow, take back, disclaim, unsay, forswear the realm forever rather than come to legal trial.
According to E. Chambers, 1728, the noun ABJURATION is the act of denying or renouncing in a solemn manner, even with an oath; while according to Bailey, 1721, ABJURATION was a privilege anciently allowed to one who had committed a felony and betook himself to a sanctuary and there confessed his crime to the justice or the coroner; a sworn banishment.

ABJURE comes from the Latin *abjurare*, to deny on oath, a combination of *ab-*, from, and *jurare*, to swear, from *jus*, *juris*, law, right. From the same source come: PERJURE, CONJURE, and ADJURE.

To 30 per cent of those tested, ABJURE means UPHOLD. To UPHOLD is literally to hold up, elevate, support, sustain, maintain; and the connection with ABJURE seems too remote to mislead so large a percentage. To ADJURE is to charge, command earnestly, entreat, request, implore, enjoin, beg, beseech; also rarely to swear by, which might vaguely suggest UPHOLD.

To CONJURE (*kŏn'-jūr*), with the accent on the first syllable, is to summon by magic, bring about by enchantment, as to CONJURE up the devil; while the same word, accented on the second syllable, CONJURE (*kŏn-jūr'*), is to swear together, band together under oath, conspire, plot, and might suggest UPHOLD.

RECANT implies the adoption of an opposite belief, having found the former erroneous. RENOUNCE is the formal giving up forever of some opinion, profession, or pursuit, without turning to another. ABJURE suggests no other belief as does RECANT, but adds to RENOUNCE a swearing upon oath.

942. *SLEDGE*, sledge (*slĕdj*) *n.* Winter vehicle for use on
     snow, with runners instead of wheels. E. Chambers says:
'A kind of carriage without wheels, for the conveyance of
very weighty things'.

To 29 per cent, SLEDGE means FLATBOAT, and to another 14 per
cent MUD DIGGER, both misconceptions due probably to the
word DREDGE. DREDGE, from German, with similar words in
Dutch, Danish, and Swedish, comes ultimately from DRAG, to
pull, haul, tug, drag along by force. The verb to DREDGE is to
raise mud from the bottom of a harbor or river. The noun, a
DREDGE, is a MUD DIGGER, a shovel often on a FLATBOAT which
must move in shallow water.

    SLEIGH (*slā*) and SLED are doublets, both from the same
source, while SLEDGE is another form of SLED. All these are
snow vehicles on runners without wheels. Of SLEIGH the Century
comments: 'A bad spelling to conform with WEIGH, of what
should have been SLAY'. Another word, SLEDGE, directly from
Anglo-Saxon, is a heavy hammer.

943. *AGNOMICAL*, agnomical (*ăg-nŏm'-ĭ-kăl*) *adj.* Purpose-
     less, aimless, without fixed intention, with no set course,
pertaining to the absence of any clear direction.

AGNOMICAL comes directly from the Greek privative ἀ without,
and γνώμη (*gnome*), thought, purpose, judgment, intelligence.
In English a GNOME (*nōm*), pronounced (*nō'-mē*) in Latin,
is a brief saying, maxim, aphorism, saw. AGNOMICAL is literally
without judgment, lacking intelligence, but has come to mean
lacking a fixed purpose. From the same source comes GNOMON
(*nō'-mŏn*), the pointer on a sundial, the triangular metal indicator the shadow of which indicates the time; and in this sense
AGNOMICAL means without a pointer, with no indicator.

944. *PEDAGOGUE*, pedagogue (*pĕd'-ă-gŏg*) *n.* A teacher,
     instructor, professor, tutor, schoolmaster.

The word PEDAGOGUE comes through the Latin *paedagogus*,
from the Greek παιδαγωγός (*paidagogos*), originally a slave
or servant who took children to school and taught them on the
way. This Greek word is a combination of παῖς (*pais*), παιδός
(*paidos*), a boy, girl, child, and ἀγωγός (*agogos*), a guide,

conductor, also the act of teaching, from the verb ἄγειν (*agein*), to lead, conduct, guide. From the same παῖς (*pais*), παιδός (*paidos*), come PEDIATRICS, the treatment of children, and PEDIATRICIAN (*pĕ-dĭ-ă-trĭ'-shăn*), a specialist in the medical care of children.

SYNAGOGUE and DEMAGOGUE both come from ἄγειν (*agein*), to lead, guide. A SYNAGOGUE, starting with σύν (*syn*), together, is literally a leading together, assembly, congregation of Jews, and now also the place of coming together.

A DEMAGOGUE, starting with δῆμος (*demos*), people, was used at first in the pleasant sense for a leader of the people. Now the word DEMAGOGUE implies someone worshipped by the people to an unjustified extent; almost a demigod who is misleading them.

By derivation a PEDAGOGUE is a leader of children, a guide to boys and girls. But like DEMAGOGUE, the word PEDAGOGUE now carries a feeling of contempt. A PEDAGOGUE is dogmatic, narrow-minded, a meaning which shows more clearly in PEDANT, at first a teacher but now best described by J. R. Green in his History of The English People where, in discussing James I, he says: 'The temper of a PEDANT, a PEDANT's conceit, a PEDANT's love of theories, and a PEDANT's inability to bring his theory into any relation with actual facts'.

Those who have taken this form of the vocabulary test split almost equally between TEACHER and FOLLOWER as synonyms of PEDAGOGUE, one an opposite of the other. The Anglo-Saxon word to FOLLOW is to go along behind in the same direction, come after. The noun, a FOLLOWER, may be a disciple, the pupil of a master. A FOLLOWER is an attendant, one who accompanies a leader. A PEDAGOGUE may in time become dogmatic, conceited, narrow-minded, but he is a guide to children.

945. *CROONING*, crooning (*kroon'-ĭng*) adj. A low continued murmuring, soft humming, singing monotonously, moaning, lamenting.

To 45 per cent, nearly half of those tested, CROONING means LOVEMAKING. TO COO, an imitative sound, is to utter a low plaintive, endearing murmur characteristic of pigeons or doves in making love, to converse affectionately. CROONING, another im-

itative word, partly also from Scotch, differs slightly. It is more
monotonous, mournful, and lamenting.

946. *ANIMUS*, animus (*ăn'-ĭ-mŭs*) *n.* Hostility; originally in-
      tention, spirit, purpose, but today more often a hostile
character, almost anger, wrath, enmity, hatred, ill will, malignity, rancor, strong dislike, hate, and so ANIMOSITY.
ANIMUS is the Latin word for soul, mind, intellect, consciousness. Nathan Bailey, 1726, says: 'ANIMUS, the mind, the faculty
of reasoning; as distinguished from ANIMA, the being in which
that faculty resides'. The word ANIMOSITY, hostility, dislike,
goes far back in English to perhaps 1450. ANIMUS in English
first meant animating spirit, actuating feeling. ANIMUS, in the
sense of ANIMOSITY, is recent, not appearing in 1818, in Todd's
edition of Dr. Johnson's dictionary. ANIMUS is now an hostility
of mind which tends to break out into active hatred or enmity.

ANIMAL, as an adjective, frequently used in opposition to the
intellectual and spiritual, may lead 22 per cent to select LOW
INSTINCTS as the meaning of ANIMUS.

From Isaac Taylor, 1863: 'Almost every page affords an instance of an intense feeling, or, as we say, ANIMUS; this is the
word we use when a speaker or writer who is laboring to substantiate a defamation finds it more than he can do to repress
emotions that are not of the most amiable sort, and which he
does not choose to avow'.

947. *BROBDINGNAGIAN*, brobdingnagian (*brŏb-dĭng-nāg'-
      ĭ-ăn*) *adj.* Big, huge, enormous, gigantic.
In his Travels of Lemuel Gulliver, commonly known as Gulliver's Travels, Jonathan Swift invented the land BROBDINGNAG
(*brŏb'-dĭng-nāg*), an empire of giants, sixty feet and upward
in height, and the corresponding adjective BROBDINGNAGIAN.

How insignificant are our pursuits when tried by the standards of a mightier race. What is a lawyer but a hired liar, who
perverts the truth if he is an advocate, and sells it if he is a
judge? What is a legislator but a compound of idleness and vice?

This political and social satire, written by one of the great
masters of English prose, and finished in 1726, parallels his
religious satire of 1704: Tale of a Tub.

Among high-vocabulary adults the common misconception of BROBDINGNAGIAN is TINY, selected by 30 per cent, an exact opposite. LILLIPUTIAN (*lĭl-lĭ-pū'-shŏn*) is the word used by Swift to describe his imaginary kingdom of pygmies, six inches high.

948. *POSTERN*, postern (*pōs'-tern*) *n.* Back door, back gate, private entrance, small back way, a sally-port.

To 24 per cent POSTERN means BARRIER, defence, a confusion of ideas, closely associated, for a BASTION is a BARRIER, mound of earth faced with sod, standing out from a rampart. A POSTERN is sometimes in the side of a BASTION.

POSTERN comes from the Latin *posterus*, back, hinder (*hĭn'-der*), from *post*, after, as in P.M., POST MERIDIAN, after noon, and the source of POSTERIOR, situated behind, coming after, following in time, opposed to ANTERIOR.

According to Nathan Bailey, a POSTERN is: 'A back door, a small gate usually made in the flank of a BASTION, or in that part of the curtain descending into the ditch, whereby the garrison can march in and out unperceived by the enemy, another name for SALLY-PORT'.

949. *EXEGESIS*, exegesis (*ĕks-ē-jē'-sĭs*) *n.* Interpretation of a literary passage, explanation, exposition.

To 42 per cent EXEGESIS means DEPARTURE, more than twice as many as select INTERPRETATION. An EXIT, from the Latin *exitus*, a going out, the past participle of *exire*, to go out, from *ex-*, out, and *ire*, to go, is a way out, also any DEPARTURE, leaving, going. Also an EXODUS, from the Greek ἔξοδος (*exodus*), a combination of ἐξ (ex), out, and ὁδός (*hodos*), way, is a DEPARTURE, emigration, going out, as the EXODUS of the Israelites from Egypt under Moses.

EXEGESIS comes from the Greek ἐξήγησις (*exegesis*), interpretation, explanation, from ἐξ (*ex*), out, and ἡγεῖσθαι (*hegeisthai*), to lead, guide, and by derivation could easily mean a leading out, guiding out, but even in Greek meant an explanation and not a DEPARTURE. Of EXEGESIS, Bailey says: 'An explication, a figure in rhetorick, when that which was before delivered somewhat darkly, is afterwards in the same sentence rendered more intelligible'.

950. *CALIPH*, caliph (*kā'-lĭf*), also spelt CALIF. *n.* A title given
to the successor of Mohammed as head of the Moslem State,
successor, ruler.

CALIPH, from Arabic and Turkish words which mean to succeed, come after, follow, really means SUCCESSOR. To one who
thinks of CALIPH as meaning ruler, SHERIFF is a natural mislead,
chosen by 25 per cent. The word SHERIFF goes back to an Anglo-
Saxon word for SHIRE, used in England for districts of various
sorts and sizes. The SHERIFF was originally the chief civil officer
in a SHIRE.

KING, SOVEREIGN, PRESIDENT, and CHIEF are other words for
types of rulers. SULTAN is a Turkish and Arabic word for prince,
monarch, sovereign. SHEIK (*shēk*), another Turkish and Arabic
word for chief, is literally an elder, learned man. A CALIPH is
specifically a successor of Mohammed.

951. *INAMORATA*, inamorata (*ĭn-ăm-ō-räh'-täh*) *n.* A
woman with whom a man is in love, flame, loved one.

INAMORATA, an Italian word in which each syllable should be
enunciated, is the feminine of INAMORATO, a man in love. This
comes from the Latin *inamorari*, to fall in love, a combination
of *in-*, and the noun *amor*, love, from the verb *amare*, to love,
used in Latin grammars as the model of the first conjugation,
verbs ending in *-are*. From *amare*, to love, come AMIABLE,
friendly, kindly; AMITY, good will, understanding; and, through
the French *amour*, love, the English verb, to ENAMOUR (*ē-năm'-
ŏr*), to charm, captivate, inflame, fascinate, bewitch.

To 20 per cent INAMORATA means DESIRE. The verb to DESIRE
comes from the Latin *desiderare*, to long for, feel the want of,
perhaps from *de-* and *sidus, siderus*, a star, the source of SIDE-
REAL. The INAMORATA is the one desired, the object of the DESIRE.

952. *INDEFEASIBLE*, indefeasible (*ĭn-dē-fē'-zĭ-bl*) *adj.* Not
to be defeated, not to be overcome, perpetual (v. B. 442),
everlasting, permanent, that cannot be voided or set aside.

To 27 per cent INDEFEASIBLE means UNSPOKEN, not said, un-
uttered. The prefixes *in-*, from Latin, and *un-*, from Anglo-
Saxon, both mean not. Except for this there seems little in
common between INDEFEASIBLE and UNSPOKEN.

FEASIBLE (*fē'-zĭ-bl*), directly from the Latin *facĕre* (*fak'-ā-rā*), to do, make, a verb of the third conjugation ending in short -*ĕre*, and a part of countless English words, means capable of being done, practicable. DEFEASIBLE (*dē-fē'-zĭ-bl*), starting with the Latin privative *de-*, means capable of being undone, destroyed. INDEFEASIBLE, with a second negative in front of the DE-, means not capable of being undone, incapable of being destroyed, not to be defeated.

DEFEAT (*dē-fēt'*), a combination of the same Latin privative *de-*, not, and the same *facĕre*, to do, make, build, is to un-do, tear down, destroy.

DEFEASIBLE, which comes through French, applies to that which can be destroyed, or in legal terms annulled, voided, abrogated, wiped out. INDEFEASIBLE refers to that which cannot be defeated, annulled, voided, wiped out.

953. *EVANESCENCE*, evanescence (*ĕ-văn-ĕs'-sĕns*) *n.* Van-
    ishing, disappearance, fleeting, evaporating, gradual de-
parture, dissipation of mist.

At this point in this research, those tested divide evenly between BRIGHTNESS and VANISHING as synonyms of EVANESCENCE, 34 per cent, a third, voting for each. EFFULGENCE, from the Latin *effulgere*, to shine, is brightness, splendor, brilliance, lustre, radiance; and LUMINESCENCE, with the same last eight letters as EVANESCENCE, is the production of light.

But EVANESCENCE, from the Latin *evanescere*, to vanish away, comes from *e-*, out, and *vanescere*, to vanish, the direct source of the English verb to VANISH, to pass out of sight, fade away.

954. *SURREPTITIOUS*, surreptitious (*sŭr-rĕp-tĭ'-shŭs*) *adj.*
    Done by stealth, produced fraudulently, clandestine, un-
derhand, characterized by concealment.

SURREPTITIOUS is thought by 16 per cent to mean REPEATED. REPETITIOUS is REPEATED, characterized by tiresome repetition, from the Latin *repetere*, literally to attack once more, seek again, repeat, from *re-*, again, and *petere*, to attack, seek, the source of PETITION.

SURREPTITIOUS goes back to the Latin *surrepticius*, stolen, clandestine, from *surripere*, to take away secretly, a combination of *sub*, under, and *rapere*, to seize, snatch, the source of RAPA-CIOUS, grasping, seizing, and of RAPINE, plundering, snatching.

RAPINE (*răp'-ĭn*) is violent seizure, pillage, open plundering. The modern word SURREPTITIOUS has none of this feeling of violence but instead means secret, stealthy, and so fraudulent.

955, *LUCUBRATION*, lucubration (*lū-kū-brā'-shŏn*) *n*. La-borious study, deep thought, meditation; a written work resulting from such study or thought.

Lucubration is from the Latin, *lucubratio*, working by artificial light, ultimately from *lux*, *lucis*, light. Thus it is from the same root as LUCID, clear, shining, intelligible; LUCIFER, the light bearer, the fallen Archangel associated with Satan; and ELUCIDATE, to make clear or understandable.

The word LUCUBRATION evidently obtained its meaning in the days when to read or study after dark by candlelight or oil lamp was evidence of a deep dedication to learning. This idea remains in the expression 'to burn the midnight oil,' to study late at night.

LUCUBRATION is both the act of deep study and the result of such study, a learned essay or treatise. Today it is most often found in the plural, used humorously in reference to particu-larly pretentious or self-important literary works. Nathaniel Hawthorne refers to 'moldy and motheaten LUCUBRATIONS'.

956. *SUSPIRE*, suspire (*sŭs-pīr'*) *v*. To fetch a long deep breath, sigh.

SUSPIRE comes from the Latin *suspirare*, to breathe out, or to draw a deep breath, from *sub*, under, and *spirare*, to breathe, blow. To SPIRE, an obsolete verb, meant to breathe.

SPIRE appears in ASPIRE, CONSPIRE, EXPIRE, INSPIRE, PERSPIRE, RESPIRE, and TRANSPIRE. SUSPIRE is thought by 20 per cent to mean HOPE, and by 30 per cent to mean WITHDRAW. To ASPIRE is to HOPE. To RETIRE, from a totally different source, a combination of *re*, back, and the French *tirere*, to draw, pull, drag, is to WITHDRAW.

To TRANSPIRE is to exhale, pass out of the body in vapor, and from this has come to mean ooze out and so escape from secrecy, become generally known. The current use of TRANSPIRE to mean happen is called erroneous. Fowler says: 'The notorious misuse of this word consists in making it mean happen, or turn out, or go on. The legitimate meaning is to emerge from secrecy into knowledge, leak out, to become known by degrees.'

To RESPIRE is by derivation to breathe again, and so to enjoy breathing quietly after an effort; but the word has come to mean no more than to breathe normally.

To INSPIRE is to breathe into, put life into.

To EXPIRE is by derivation to breathe out, the opposite of INSPIRE, but has come to mean die, perish, come to an end, cease, terminate.

To SUSPIRE is the least used of this family and means not merely breathe but draw a long deep breath, sigh.

957. *DEBENTURE*, debenture (*dē-bĕn'-tūr*) *n.* A mortgage, note, written acknowledgment of a debt, an instrument under seal for the repayment of money, usually a large obligation of a corporation.

To 35 per cent DEBENTURES are SCRUPLES. A SCRUPLE is a doubt, hesitation closely connected with every borrowing of money, especially in a large sum.

DEBENTURE starts with the Latin word *debentur*, the third person plural of the present indicative passive of *debere*, to owe. The phrase *debentur mihi* means: There are owing to me.

958. *HUNKER*, hunker (*hŭng'-kĕr*) *v.* To squat, stoop, crouch. HUNKERED means crooked.

HUNKER is thought by 30 per cent to mean YEARN. To HANKER, from the Dutch, is to YEARN FOR, long for importunately, desire, want, crave. To HANK is a variation of HANG, and HANKER suggests hanging about.

HUNKER comes from the Icelandic word meaning to CROUCH, bend over. From the same source comes HUCKSTER, literally a CROUCHER, stooper, a pedlar bent over with his burden.

959. *KALE*, kale (*kāl*) *n.* Cabbage in Scotland, and, in general, any kind of greens, vegetable; or more specifically, a kind of cabbage with curved or wrinkled leaves, not forming a compact head like the common cabbage, and with a long stalk.

KALE is also called BORECOLE (*bōr'-kōl*), literally peasant's cabbage, from BOOR, a word used today for a countryman, rustic, peasant, and COLE, a term for cabbage in general.

In the first version of this vocabulary worksample both VEGETABLE and LEAVES were given as choices, and marked almost equally, with LEAVES slightly more popular. KALE is used occasionally for VEGETABLE in general, but more often for CABBAGE; and as KALE does not form a tight head, LEAVES is an excellent description.

960. *LABILE*, labile (*lăb'-ĭl*) *adj.* Unstable, transient, apt to slip.

LABILE, from the Latin *labilis*, apt to slip, liable to fall, comes from the Latin verb *labi*, the source of various English words, mostly through *lapsare*, to fall, stumble, the frequentative of *labi*, to slip, slide, fall. Thus to COLLAPSE, from *com*, together, is literally to fall together, to fall into a mass. A RELAPSE is a sliding back, slipping back, falling again. A LAPSE is a continued falling off, heard frequently in the phrase: a LAPSE of memory. This may, in some remote way, lead 40 per cent to believe that LABILE means UNKNOWN.

961. *ESPIAL*, espial (*ĕs-pī'-ăl*) *n.* Observation, seeing, scrutiny, the act of espying.

ESPIAL is thought by 50 per cent to mean TACTICS, a military term, the shifting of forces in battle, or the maneuvers of a navy in action.

ESPIONAGE (*ĕs'-pĭ-ō-năhj*), the systematic use of spies to learn the military secrets of another nation, directly from the French *espionnage*, through *espion*, a spy, from the Italian *espione*, also a spy, originally from the Latin *specere*, to see, look, is another military term closely connected with TACTICS. The corresponding modern verb is to SPY, with the same underhand implications.

The pleasant verb ESPY, to catch sight of, see from a distance, discover unexpectedly, discern, perceive, descry, goes directly back in English. ESPIAL, the noun, is the act of ESPYING, watching, observing, scrutinizing, with no secret, concealed, army implications.

962. *BALDACHIN*, baldachin (*băwl'-dă-kĭn*) *n.* A canopy of
    heavily embroidered cloth over the seat of an important
person; or a permanent, decorated covering supported by columns, over an altar in a church.

BALDACHIN comes from *Baldacco*, the Italian form of Bagdad,
a city which produces a rich cloth used for canopies. A BALDA-
CHIN may be a portable covering, or a fixed one over an isolated
altar, as in St. Peter's basilica in Rome. Or a BALDACHIN may be
of cloth over the chair of a church dignitary.

The mislead SANCTUARY (*săngk'-tū-ā-rĭ*), from the Latin *sanc-
tus*, holy, sacred, is that part of a church where the chief altar
stands. But the word may also be used for any consecrated spot.
With a fixed BALDACHIN over an isolated high altar, the spot may
be called a SANCTUARY. But SANCTUARY designates a location.

SANCTUARY has also come to mean a place of refuge for those
escaping from pursuit. In this respect a SANCTUARY and a BALDA-
CHIN are both shelters, but in different senses. A SANCTUARY is
a shelter from persecution; a BALDACHIN, an actual covering,
sometimes over an altar, over a religious relic, or over an important person.

963. *MUSKELLUNGE*, muskellunge (*mŭs'-kĕl-lŭnj*) *n.* A
    great pike, large fish of the Great Lakes area.

The MASKALONGE, as the Century Dictionary spells the name, or
MASKELUNGE as in the Encyclopaedia Britannica, are the largest
and finest of the PIKE, inhabiting the Great Lakes region of the
United States. The word is American Indian, Algonquin or
Chippeway, and means long-face or long-mask.

A PIKE is a long sharp-pointed weapon; and PIKE, the fish, is
so named for its long, sharp-pointed snout. The word PICKEREL,
the diminutive of PIKE, should mean small PIKE, as it did at one
time; but, except for the MUSKELLUNGE, all of the pikes of the
United States are now commonly called PICKEREL.

The first four letters MUSK, of perhaps the commonest spell-
ing, lead 16 per cent to select PERFUME as a synonym of MUSKEL-
LUNGE. MUSK, a strong-smelling substance secreted by the male
MUSK-DEER of Central Asia, is used as a PERFUME, with a power-
ful, penetrating, and persistent odor, the strongest of the
PERFUMES.

964. *PRIVILY*, privily (*prĭv'-ĭ-lĭ*) *adv.* Privately (v. B. 71),
       covertly, secretly (v. B. 3), cryptically, in a privy manner,
not openly, clandestinely (v. B. 707), not publicly. Read PRIVY
(v. B. 1395).

The doublets PRIVY and PRIVATE come from the Latin *privatus*,
private, individual, peculiar, personal, apart from the public,
the past participle of *privare*, to separate, from *privus*, single,
one's own. PRIVY is used by the British government to signify
PRIVATE in a formal manner, as: PRIVY PURSE, the private expenses of the sovereign.

       PRIVILY is thought by 19 per cent to mean OPENLY. PUBLICLY,
from the Latin *populus*, people, means OPENLY, an exact opposite
of the correct meaning of PRIVILY.

965. *LACHRYMOSE*, lachrymose (*lăk'-rĭ-mōs*) *adj.* Tearful,
       doleful, lugubrious, mournful, shedding tears.
H. W. Fowler says: 'The true spelling for all the words should
be LACRIM-, and it would be at least allowable to adopt it; but
the H and the Y are still usual'.

       To 15 per cent LACHRYMOSE means LAZY. LAZY, which goes
back to Old French, is slothful, sluggish, indolent, averse to
labor, disinclined to exertion. The confusion may be the word
LACKADAISICAL (*lăk-ă-dā'-zĭ-kăl*), listless, languid, sentimentally
woebegone, said to be a ludicrous extension of LACKADAY, alas
the day.

       LACHRYMOSE, or accepting the Century Dictionary spelling,
LACRIMOSE, and similar words in Spanish, Portuguese, and Italian, all come from the Latin *lacrimosus*, tearful, doleful, from
lacrima, tear.

966. *BELDAM*, beldam (*bĕl'-dăm*) *n.* Once a grandmother,
       now a hag, ugly old woman.
BELLADONNA, a doublet of BELDAM, is clearly a combination of
bella, beautiful, the feminine of *bello*, beautiful; and *donna*, lady,
from the Latin *domina*, the feminine of *dominus*, lord. The
plant BELLADONNA, literally a beautiful lady, received its name
because Italian ladies used it as a cosmetic. The plant and its
alkaloid are also used in medicine to relieve pain; and this leads
25 per cent to believe that BELDAM means REMEDY, cure, restora-

tive, specific, corrective, antidote. A BELDAM was once a fine lady, but the word came to be used ironically of a decrepit, ugly old woman, the only meaning of the word today.

967. *FEBRILE*, febrile (*fē'-brĭl*) *adj.* Marked by fever, feverish. FEVER is a temperature of the human body 3, 4, or 5 degrees higher than the normal 98 to 99 degrees fahrenheit. FEBRILE, paralleling the French *fébrile*, comes from the Latin *febris*, fever.

To 25 per cent FEBRILE means DYING, the most frequently marked mislead. The Latin *mors, mortis*, means death, and is the source of MORTAL, subject to death, and MORTGAGE, pledge unto death. FEVER and FEBRILE suggest death only indirectly. Neither word means DYING.

PYREXIA (*pī-rĕk'-sĭ-ăh*) is the Greek for FEVER, from πυρετός (*pyretos*), fever, from πῦρ (*pyr*), *fire*.

FEVER is Anglo-Saxon; FEBRILE, Latin; and PYREXIA, Greek; the order of difficulty of words from these three languages. Anglo-Saxon words as a whole are easy; Latin words more difficult; and Greek words still harder.

968. *CORBEL*, corbel (*kŏr'-bĕl*) *n.* A bracket, projection from the face of a wall to support something. In medieval architecture CORBELS were of stone and heavily carved.

The Latin *corvus* meant either raven or crow; and the Scotch CORBIE and CORBIN are still names for these two birds. The word CORBEL itself first meant raven or crow, but has come by some strange route to mean a support for a beam.

Given a choice between FIXTURE and BRACKET three times as many persons select the first. FIXTURE is a general term for anything FIXED, permanently attached. BRACKET is an accurate description of a CORBEL, a support which projects from the wall.

SHELF, the second most popular mislead, is very close, for like a SHELF, a CORBEL sometimes holds a statue or an ornament; but strictly the CORBELS are the BRACKETS under the SHELF, which support it.

GARGOYLES (*gahr'-goilz*) and CORBELS are both projections. A GARGOYLE juts out near the roof, a water spout for carrying rain away from the building. A CORBEL is a support.

969. *FLUMMERY*, flummery (*flŭm'-mĕ-rĭ*) *n.* A pudding, oatmeal, cooked combination of flour, eggs, and sugar. There are apparently two different words FLUMMERY, from different sources. One is a Welsh oatmeal, or any of various dishes made of flour, eggs, and sugar. Of the five choices in the vocabulary test, PUDDING is the nearest, selected by 50 per cent of the high-vocabulary group who have tried this form.

Another FLUMMERY means nonsense, foolishness, absurdities, agreeable humbug, empty compliments, and is perhaps more familiar than the first, although we have as yet no statistics.

970. *LAMELLATE*, lamellate (*lăm'-ĕl-lāt*) *adj.* Formed in layers, banded, stratified, stratiform.

There are two words, perhaps originally a mistake of some Roman: LAMELLA and LAMINA, both of which mean thin plate, leaf, layer. Occasional botanists and zoologists, who believe that two different words should not mean exactly the same thing, use LAMELLA (*lăm'-ĕl-lăh*) for thick plates, and LAMINA (*lăm'-ĭ-năh*) for thinner ones, a nice distinction. Both words retain their Latin plurals: LAMELLAE (*lăm'-ĕl-lē*) and LAMINAE (*lă'-mĭ-nē*). LAMELLATE and LAMINATE both survive.

LAYERED and PLATE-LIKE both appear in the vocabulary test, the first chosen by 50 per cent; the second by 30 per cent. Both are correct and one must be eliminated in the next revision.

971. *RAILLERY*, raillery (*răl'-lĕ-rĭ*) *n.* Good-humored pleasantry, banter, ridicule, jesting language, satirical merriment. Although the verb to RAIL means to speak bitterly, reproachfully, acrimoniously, to inveigh, from the Latin *radere*, to scrape, scratch, RAILLERY, directly from the French *raillerie*, jesting, mockery, has lost much of this unpleasant overtone, but still retains some, so that in one form where both BANTER and RIDICULE appeared as choices, 32 per cent selected the first, and 20 per cent the second. This is about the proportion of the two elements in the word.

In the next revision, where RIDICULE was removed, and REVILEMENT put in its place, 45 per cent of a slightly higher vocabulary group chose the last, compared with only 40 per cent for BANTER. REVILEMENT is much too strong; but there still exists in the popular mind some unpleasantness in the word RAILLERY, which is not so good-humored as dictionaries lead one to believe.

972. *CASTELLATION*, castellation (*kăs-těl-lā'-shŭn*) *n*. Battlements, crenellation, the indented top of a wall, formed by a series of rising square blocks with openings between through which soldiers fired shots.

To CASTELLATE originally meant to build a castle. Although CASTLE is pronounced with no T sound, CASTELLATE has the T. From this to CASTELLATE came to mean to build with battlements, with an indented parapet at the top of a wall formed by a series of rising members. In the same way CASTELLATION, originally the building of CASTLES, came to mean furnishing with battlements and now means a BATTLEMENT.

973. *FALCHION*, falchion (*făwl'-chŏn*) *n*. Although Webster in his first edition of 1828 includes no pronunciation of words, he does say of FALCHION: 'Is pronounced as in FALL'. A short broadsword; loosely: any sword.

FALCHION is from the Latin *falx, falcis*, sickle. The big mislead is CLUB, selected by 22 per cent. A BLUDGEON is a CLUB. Also a TRUNCHEON (*trŭn'-chŏn*), ending with the same sound as FALCHION, the diminutive of the French *trone*, trunk, stump, is a short staff, cudgel, CLUB.

A CLAYMORE was a two-edged, two-handed, heavy sword used in the Highlands of Scotland. SCIMITARS, CUTLASSES, and FALCHIONS are all short curved single-edged swords used for cutting and not thrusting. The SCIMITAR, spelt CIMITER by Webster and SIMITAR by Century, but SCIMITAR by the Encyclopaedic Dictionary, is of oriental design. The CUTLASS is a strong simple sword used at sea. The FALCHION is European.

974. *APOTHESIS*, apothesis (*ă-pŏth'-ĕ-sĭs*) *n*. The reduction of a fracture, the setting and restoration of a dislocated limb.

APOTHESIS, today strictly a medical term, comes from the Greek ἀπόθεσις (*apothesis*), to put back, a combination of ἀπό (*apo*), away, and τιθέναι (*tithenai*), to put, place, set.

The mislead SPURIOUSNESS is suggested by the word APOC-
RYPHA (*ă-pŏk'-rĭ-făh*), with the adjective APOCRYPHAL, any
writings of doubtful authenticity. APOCRYPHAL, spurious, fictitious, false, of doubtful authenticity, applies specifically to 14
books added to the Old Testament.

APOTHEOSIS (*ăp-ō-thē'-ō-sĭs*), differing in pronunciation, but
by only one letter, from APOTHESIS (*ă-pŏth'-ē-sĭs*), was the act
of elevating a Roman Emperor, at his death, to the level of the
gods, an excessive honor and so perhaps SPURIOUS.

975. *PROSELYTING*, proselyting (*prŏs'-ĕl-ĭ-tĭng*) *n.* Per-
    suading, attempting to convert a member of a group to
change his belief and join others.

PROSELYTE comes from the Greek προσήλυτος (*proselytos*),
a convert, literally one who has come over, a combination of
πρός (*pros*), to, toward, and ἐλθεῖν (*elthein*), to come. Today
a PROSELYTE is one who changes his party usually with no real
change in his belief; and to PROSELYTIZE or to PROSELYTE are
attempts to win PROSELYTES.

To 26 per cent PROSELYTING means TALKING. TALKING is a
general word for speaking and is certainly a part of PROSELY-
TING; but PROSELYTING is specifically attempting to gain a
convert.

976. *SCINTILLA*, scintilla (*sĭn-tĭl'-lă*) *n.* A spark, glimmer,
    minute particle, trace, tittle, tiny bit.

SCINTILLA is the Latin *scintilla*, spark, and the Italian *scintilla*,
with similar words in all of the Romance languages, those spoken
in regions at one time subject to Rome. These languages include
Italian, closest to Latin, French, Provençal, Spanish, Portuguese,
and Wallachian.

From the same source, by a roundabout course, comes TINSEL,
bits or strips of metal which sparkle in the light. A SCINTILLA
is really a spark, but has come to mean a tiny bit.

977. *ARBITRARY*, arbitrary (*ăhr'-bĭ-trā-rĭ*) *adj.* Using un-
    limited power, discretionary, capricious, unreasonable,
despotic, tyrannical, absolute in power, not governed by fixed
rules, with no external control.

At first ARBITRARY was the adjective for the noun ARBITER (*ahr′-bĭ-ter*), an umpire, referee, judge, and referred to those aspects of a decision not covered by rigid rules, and so uncontrolled, discretionary, subject to the individual judgment of the empire, determined by a tribunal as distinct from fixed rules; for the word comes from the Latin *arbitrarius*, pertaining to ARBITRATION, uncertain, from *arbiter*, an ARBITER, umpire, witness, judge, literally one who comes to see, a combination of *ad*, to, and *betere*, to come. From uncontrolled, it was only a step for the word to mean capricious, irresponsible, and then tyrannical, domineering, imperious.

To 36 per cent ARBITRARY means OPPOSING. ARBITRARY means DESPOTIC; but an ARBITRARY DECISION with which one agrees, a judgment in one's favor, rarely seems ARBITRARY. To give the impression of being ARBITRARY a decision must be in OPPOSITION to one's own wishes.

Although wrong answers to the meaning of ARBITRARY scatter, the second most popular, 16 per cent, is UNFAIR. Though an ARBITRARY decision may not be UNFAIR, the method of reaching it suggests UNFAIRNESS. Many final decisions must of necessity be ARBITRARY; but to make them seem FAIR greater care should be given to explaining how they were reached.

978. *CONY*, cony (*kō′-nĭ*) *n.* A rabbit, burrowing rodent, quadruped of the genus Lepus.

CONY comes by a long series of steps from the Latin *cuniculus*, a rabbit. The original pronunciation was (*kŭn′-ĭ*), still not incorrect.

The Latin *cornu*, horn, from which comes CORNET, CORNUCOPIA, and others, may lead to the frequent choice of HORN, as a synonym.

The most popular mislead, FARCE, comes from the French *farce*, stuffing for a fowl made of all sorts of ingredients. FARCE may be suggested by the word COMEDY, something like CONY in sound, or by the similarity of CONY and PHONY, a 20th century word, a combination of PHONE plus Y. PHONY means spurious, unsubstantial, without substance, like talks heard over the telephone. A FARCE in English is a comedy, differing from other comic dramatic compositions in its exaggerations and grotesqueness. The word was first used for a CANTICLE sung in a combination of Latin and French.

From CONY, which may also be spelt CONEY, comes the proper name CONEY, as in CONEY ISLAND.

979. *SETACEOUS*, setaceous (*sē-tā′-shŭs*) *adj*. Bristly, bristling, setiferous, setose, provided with bristles.

A SETA (*sē′-tah*) is a thick, stiff hair, a prickle, or a fine slender spine. SETACEOUS, from the Latin *seta*, a hair, bristle, stiff stout hair, means bristly.

The CRUSTACEANS, including lobsters, crabs, shrimps, and crawfish, are animals with shells, with crusts, and CRUSTACEOUS (*krŭs-tā′-shŭs*) means pertaining to a crust, like a shell; and easily leads to the selection, by 20 per cent, of ENCRUSTED as a synonym of SETACEOUS.

CETACEOUS, starting with C, means like a whale. SETACEOUS, pronounced the same but starting with S, means with bristles, prickly.

980. *SOJOURN*, sojourn (*sō′-jŭrn*) *n*. A dwelling for a time, living in a place as a temporary residence, the short stay of a traveler.

To 36 per cent SOJOURN means PILGRIMAGE, compared with only 24 per cent who select STAY. The two are closely related. A PILGRIMAGE is a journey, motion; a SOJOURN is a stay, but always the stop of a traveler, of one on a PILGRIMAGE.

SOJOURN, ADJOURN, JOURNAL, and the French word *jour*, day, are all related. A JOURNAL, from the French *jour*, day, is a daily paper. To ADJOURN is to put off, defer, stop a meeting, temporarily. To SOJOURN is to stop for a day, for a time, while on the way to somewhere else.

981. *AVATAR*, avatar (*ăv-ă-tăhr′*) *n*. The coming down of a god onto earth, descent of a deity, incarnation of a god, manifestation of a divine being, any remarkable appearance. AVATAR comes from India, a Hindu word which goes back to a Sanskrit word for descent. AVATAR is the descent of a deity to the earth, the incarnation of a god. From this AVATAR has come to mean a remarkable appearance of any kind.

The mislead SLAUGHTER-HOUSE is of course ABATTOIR (*ăh-băht-twăr'*), from a French word meaning to knock down, slaughter. ABATTOIR is today another word for SLAUGHTER-HOUSE. In another form of the vocabulary tests 36 per cent chose BEAST as the meaning of AVATAR, misled no doubt by the same ABATTOIR.

982. *CAVALIER*, cavalier (*kăv-ă-lēr'*) *adj.* Originally: knightly, brave, warlike; then the adjective came to mean gay, easy, sprightly; and finally haughty, disdainful, supercilious.

A CAVALIER, a French word from the Latin *caballus*, horse, was an armed horseman, a knight, a bold reckless gay fellow. From the same source comes CAVALCADE. Perhaps through envy of bravery, gaiety, knighthood, perhaps with no more than a confusion of opposites, complimentary words alter their complexion; but still for many persons retain their original sense. Given a choice between DISDAINFUL and IMPRESSIVE, 34 per cent select DISDAINFUL, but 62 per cent return to IMPRESSIVE, much closer to the original meaning.

983. *POTHER*, pother (*pŏth'-er*) *n.* Commotion, bustle, disturbance, fuss.

To 34 per cent a POTHER is a BUSTLE; to another 26 per cent, TRIFLING; and to 18 per cent, NOISE. All these elements play parts in the word POTHER. Even though some definitions include UPROAR, which justifies 18 per cent in marking NOISE, this is the smallest part of POTHER, which is motion with just enough NOISE to annoy.

The effect of POTHERING is TRIFLING, in comparison with a COMMOTION, justifying a quarter in selecting this choice. BUSTLE, a stir, commotion, ineffective fuss, with a great show of energy, is perhaps the best synonym; although a BUSTLE is both noisier and more effective than a POTHER.

984. *SUBTERFUGE*, subterfuge (*sŭb'-ter-fūj*) *n.* Craftiness, evasion, shift, trick, excuse, pretext, quirk, pretense, artifice used to escape; Bailey says a hole to creep out of.

SUBTERFUGE comes from the Latin *subterfugere*, to flee by stealth, escape secretly. The Latin adverb *subter* means below, beneath, under, and occasionally secretly as here. From the verb *fugere*, to flee, come not only SUBTERFUGE, but FUGITIVE, one who flees, deserter, runaway; and REFUGE, a place of safety to flee to, sanctuary, asylum, harbor, retreat, shelter for one who is fleeing, from *re-*, back, and *fugere*, to flee.

To 39 per cent, more than a third of those tested, SUBTERFUGE means SPYING. Both SPYING and SUBTERFUGE are secret. Both call for craftiness, tricks, shifts, evasions. SPYING, from the Latin *specere*, to see, look, is looking, seeing, discovering with the eye from a position of concealment. Bailey says: a SPY is one who clandestinely searches into the state of places or affairs. SUBTERFUGE is cunning in escaping, tricks used in fleeing, secrecy in running away.

985. *CANON*, canon (*kăn'-ŏn*) *n.* Law, rule; Bailey adds: 'Especially a church decree'; and Webster says: 'A rule of doctrine or discipline enacted by a council and confirmed by the sovereign, a regulation of policy'.

CANON goes directly back to an Anglo-Saxon *canon* which meant rule, and to a Latin *canon* with the same meaning. But even as the Greek κανών (*canon*) was often used for religious rules, SCRIPTURAL PASSAGE, in the vocabulary test as a mislead and selected by 39 per cent of high-vocabulary adults, compared with only 25 per cent who select RULE, the correct answer, is in reality correct and will be removed in the next revision. CHURCH SONG, another mislead in the test selected by 16 per cent, must also be taken out, for CANON, a Welch word for song, is used in music with exactly this meaning.

The phrase CANON LAW, defined in most large dictionaries as church law, religious rule, and which appears in the valuable book Thirteenth Greatest of Centuries by James J. Walsh, shows how easily words are misused, for CANON means law.

986. *DETENT*, detent (*dē-těnt'*) *n.* A catch, pawl, ratchet which prevents the backward motion of a ratchet wheel. From the Latin verb *tenere*, to hold, come *detinere*, to hold back, and from this DETENT, anything which checks, prevents motion, DETAINS, and such other words of the same type, as: CONTAIN, OBTAIN, and RETAIN.

DETENT is so little known that answers spread almost equally among the five choices, with no clear concentration on the right answer or any particular mislead. A DETENT is a hook which catches a tooth of a wheel and stops it from turning back.

987. *NISUS*, nisus (*nī'-sŭs*) *n.* Effort, endeavor, undertaking, attempt, striving. One of the synonyms given for this little-known word is CONATUS (*kō-nā'-tus*), equally unknown, from the Latin *conatus*, an effort, attempt, from *conari*, to attempt, try, undertake, strive after.

NISUS comes directly from the Latin *nisus*, effort. The confusion of a word with its opposite is the final step in learning, after acquiring both its sound and almost its meaning. For this unusual word NISUS, which should be unknown to everyone, the only two choices marked are EFFORT and LASSITUDE, exact opposites, selected by 32 per cent and 28 per cent respectively.

988. *ARROYO*, arroyo (*ahr-rō'-yō*) *n.* A rivulet, channel, water course, gully, often the dry bed of a stream.

A PAMPA (*păm'-pah*), a Spanish and Portuguese word, is a vast treeless plain, south of the Amazon River. Similar plains north of the Amazon are called LLANOS.

Alexander Humboldt, 1769 to 1859, a German naturalist and traveler who laid the foundations of physical geography and meteorology, used STEPPE and SAVANNA instead of PAMPA and LLANO. None of these sound enough like ARROYO to lead 25 per cent into believing that ARROYO, another Spanish and Portuguese word, means PLAIN. Originally an ARROYO was a stream for irrigation, but is now more often the dry bed of a stream.

989. *CHANGELING*, changeling (*chănj'-lĭng*) *n.* Ugly child, left by fairies in place of another; or according to Bailey: a fool or silly fellow or wench; or according to Webster, 1828, who quotes Johnson: 'It is said this word originated in a superstitious opinion that fairies steal children and put others that are ugly and stupid in their place'. In the highlands of Scotland babies are guarded until after their christening.

Among 27 high-vocabulary adults 5 mark SECOND-SON as a meaning of CHANGELING. One definition of SECOND reads: 'Next after the first in order, and so of second grade, perhaps inferior'. This may suggest CHANGELING, an inferior child.

From Reginald Scot, 1584, The Discoveries of Witchcraft, quoted in Oxford: 'They have so fraid us with elves, hags, changelings, incubus, Robin Goodfellows, and such other bugs that we are afraid of our own shadows'. An ELF, with the plural ELVES, is an imaginary being with magical powers who interferes capriciously in human affairs. A HAG, as used here, is a female evil spirit, goblin, or ghost. An INCUBUS is an imaginary being supposed to descend upon sleeping persons; while Robin Goodfellow is a sportive goblin of the 16th and 17th centuries believed to haunt the English country-side. A BUG, in this context, is a frightful walking specter.

Despite the quotation CHANGELING does not fit this group. A CHANGELING is the child changed, not the goblin or fairy who does the changing.

990. *SALVER*, salver (săl'-vĕr) *n.* A silver tray on which to present something; the Century Dictionary says a large and heavy tray, but the word is used more often as defined by Bailey: 'A piece of wrought plate to set glasses of liquor upon'. The Encyclopaedia Britannica, in their article on pewter, includes two photographs of round trays, each 17½ inches in diameter, both French, about 1550, which they call large SALVERS, one designed to match a EWER, pitcher.

Of 29 high-vocabulary adults, 4 select OINTMENT as the meaning of SALVER. SALVE (săhv), a word which goes directly back to Anglo-Saxon and is related to a Sanskrit word for butter, is a glutinous composition, medicament, substance, often slippery, applied to sores, an OINTMENT for anointing.

SALVER, from the Latin *salvare*, to save, the source of the English words SAVE and SAFE, was originally a special plate on which a small amount of food was served, to be tested by someone in advance and so protect the master from poison.

991. *SYLPH*, sylph (sĭlf) *n.* A slender woman. According to Paracelsus, whose real name was Theophrastus Bombastus von Hohenheim, a Swiss-German physician who lived from 1493 to 1541, called a quack, alchemist, occultist, some say be-

cause he was ahead of his time, a SYLPH is either a man or a woman, mortal, with no soul, an imaginary being of the air, half way between material and immaterial.

The word SYLPH is supposed to come from the Greek σίλφη (*silphe*), a kind of beetle, with the Greek ι changed to Y to make it look more mysterious and impressive. As SALAMANDER, an artificial made-up word, a lizard, supposed to live in fire, became a spirit of fire, so a SYLPH, originally a beetle, an insect, a flying creature, became a spirit of the air.

NYMPH was a real Greek word, one of a group of beautiful maidens eternally young, who presided over brooks, woods, and mountains, and the Y in NYMPH may have contributed to the Y in SYLPH.

Perhaps because of a confusion with NYMPH the word SYLPH has come to be applied figuratively to a graceful and slender girl. But if one knows the Greek meaning, beetle, insect, and the Paracelsian addition of no soul, the word is hardly complimentary.

The popular mislead, DESIGN, chosen by 28 per cent, seems hard to explain.

992. *NEATHERD*, neatherd (*nēt'-hĕrd*) *n.* One who looks after cattle, cares for them, attends them.

NEATHERD goes directly back to Anglo-Saxon, to a word for cattle including the ox and cow.

To 40 per cent NEATHERD means GYPSY. The GYPSIES are a distinct race of wanderers which first appeared in Europe in the 14th century, and in England two hundred years later. They are dark skinned, with black hair, and speak a Hindu dialect from Sanskrit. They are never SHEPHERDS or NEATHERDS, but wanderers, tinkers.

A SHEPHERD, selected by 18 per cent, but less than the correct synonym, is strictly one who attends sheep; although both sheep and CATTLE belong to the great family BOVIDAE (*bō'-vĭ-dē*), the hollow-horned ruminants.

Nathan Bailey, writing in 1721, makes a sharp distinction: 'NEATHERD is a keeper of neat-cattle'. Of NEAT Bailey continues: 'All kinds of beeves, as OX, COW, STEER, or HEIFER'. Of HEIFER, he says: 'A young cow'.

993. *GLACIS*, glacis (*glă'-sĭs* or *glă-sē'*, the French pronunciation) *n*. Any gentle slope toward a field, incline down
toward open country.

The French *glacis*, a slippery bank, and the English GLACIER,
both come from the Latin *glaciare*, to freeze, harden, and from
glacies, ice; and for this reason GLACIS is often a downward sloping ice field or surface of a GLACIER. ICEBERG, marked by 13 per
cent, and closely associated with GLACIS, is a floating mass of
detached ice, carried out to sea.

The mislead CREVASSE (*krĕ-văs'*), another French word related
to GLACIERS, is a break or fissure in the ice, almost an opposite.
A CREVASSE is a sharp, steep downward crack; a GLACIS is a
gentle slope.

994. *IMPUTRESCIBLE*, imputrescible (*ĭm-pū-trĕs'-sĭ-bl*) *adj*.
Not putrescible, not subject to putrefaction, incorruptible.
Start with the adjective PUTRID, in a state of decay, rotten, fetid,
corrupt, from the Latin *putridus*, with the same meanings. This
comes from the verb *putrescere*, to grow rotten, becoming
rotten, just beginning to be rotten. This Latin verb *putrescere* is
the inceptive form of *putrere*, to be rotten already. From the
present participle *putrescens*, *putrescentis* come: PUTRESCENT
and PUTRESCENCE, the condition of becoming rotten, corrupt.

Add to this the ending -IBLE, which means capable of, and
the word becomes PUTRESCIBLE, capable of decaying, of becoming corrupt.

Then as a final step start the word with the ·privative IN-,
which becomes IM- before what is called a LABIAL, P or B, and
the word becomes IMPUTRESCIBLE, incorruptible; long, awkward, almost unusable, but a great step ahead might be taken
if we could elect IMPUTRESCIBLE officials. Yet 24 per cent of
those persons we have tested believe that IMPUTRESCIBLE is
WICKED.

995. *AMPLITUDE*, amplitude (*ăm'-plĭ-tūd*) *n*. Breadth, extension in space, largeness, copiousness, extent, especially
width from side to side.

AMPLITUDE comes from the Latin *amplus*, large, a combination
of *am-*, standing for *ambi-*, around, about, and *-plus*, full. From

the same source come AMPLIFY (*ăm'-plĭ-fī*), to make bigger, AMPLIFICATION, the noun, and other recent technical terms, which lead 33 per cent to believe that AMPLITUDE means LOUD NOISE.

The Latin ending -TUDE creates abstract feminine nouns from adjectives, as: MAGNITUDE, from the Latin adjective *magnus*, great, large, grand, noble, important; LATITUDE, from the Latin *latus*, broad, strictly the distance from side to side, breadth, width, but in geography the distance up and down from the equator toward either pole; LONGITUDE, from the Latin *longus*, long, length, a distance measured around the earth parallel to the equator, technically the angle at the pole between GREEN-WICH and some other position; and finally ALTITUDE, which leads 16 per cent to believe that AMPLITUDE means HEIGHT. ALTITUDE is height. AMPLITUDE can be used for largeness in general but has come to mean width, breadth.

996. *PAROLE*, parole (*păh-rōl'*) *n.* Word of mouth, saying, language, text, statement, utterance, speech.

Among 29 high-vocabulary adults, 4 select IMPRISONMENT as the meaning of PAROLE. Today PAROLE, often in the phrase: 'On PAROLE', means the release of a prisoner on his word of honor before the expiration of his term of IMPRISONMENT, a meaning which goes back at least to Bailey, 1721: 'PAROLE is when a prisoner of war is permitted to go into his own country, or to his own party, upon his promise to return at the time appointed, if not exchanged'.

In the same group of adults, 7 others select ACT as the meaning of PAROLE. An ACT, in the legal sense, is the result of a public deliberation, the decision of some group or individual in authority. Release from IMPRISONMENT on PAROLE is an ACT. But PAROLE, from the Latin *parabola*, word, speech, through the French, still means word of mouth, utterance, statement.

997. *PROSCENIUM*, proscenium (*prō-sē'-nĭ-ŭm*) *n.* That part of the stage, in a theater, in front of the curtain, including the curtain and the frame which holds it.

PROSCENIUM is a Latin word, from the Greek προσκήνιον (*pro-scenion*), a combination of πρό (*pro*), before, and σκηνή (*scene*), tent, stage, scene. In the ancient theater the PROSCENIUM was the whole stage. Now the word is used mostly for the frame around the curtain.

The two popular misleads are BALCONY and ORCHESTRA-PIT, both parts of the theater, the second step in learning, placing a word in its correct environment.

998. *ANAMNESIS*, anamnesis (*ăn-ăm-nē'-sĭs*) *n.* Recollection, remembrance, reminiscence, recalling the past.

AMNESIA (*ăm-nē'-zĭah*), a loss of memory, and AMNESTY (*ăm'-nĕs-tĭ*), a complete forgetting of an offense which would ordinarily deserve punishment, treating a crime against the government as if it had not occurred, both come from the same combination of the Greek ἄ and the verb μνᾶσθαι (*mnasthai*), to remember.

From the Greek μνήμων (*mnemon*), mindful, from the same verb to remember, comes MNEMONICS (*nē-mŏn'-ĭks*), a system for improving the memory.

ANAMNESIS, from the Greek ἀνά (*ana*), back, and μνᾶσθαι (*mnasthai*), to remember, means remembering back; but the misleads and correct answer are chosen almost equally often, suggesting that ANAMNESIS is wholly unknown and should rarely be used.

999. *WHILOM*, whilom (*hwĭ'-lōm*) *adv.* Once, formerly, once upon a time.

WHILOM comes directly from Anglo-Saxon, with the flavor of Old English. Given a choice between LONG-LOST and FORMER as the meaning of WHILOM, 33 per cent select the first, compared with only 19 per cent for the second. FORMER is an adequate synonym for WHILOM; but, in the phrase: 'WHILOM friends', LONG LOST is a far more vivid expression for friends one once had, but with whom one has lost touch.

1000. *DAVIT*, davit (*dăv'-ĭt*) *n.* One of a pair of small derricks, used on shipboard to lower a rowboat to the water from the deck of a larger vessel.

The four-volume French dictionary, by Littré, 1873, suggests that DAVIT is the diminutive of DAVID, for many nautical terms are proper names, as Jack, and Billy, which occurs in BILLYBOY, a flat-bottomed barge of light draft. DAVIT appears in a treatise on English sea terms of 1626.

DAVITS work in pairs, like small derricks, with ropes and pulleys, each lifting the end of a small boat between them. They are sometimes fixed at the stern of a larger boat and lower a small rowboat to the water or raise it again to the deck. In larger vessels DAVITS are in pairs along each side, ready to lower lifeboats to the water.

The two misleads are BOAT and ANCHOR. A BOAT is the object lifted; the DAVITS are tools for lifting. An ANCHOR is lifted ordinarily by a CAPSTAN, a turning upright cylinder, about which a rope is wrapped. Both BOAT and ANCHOR are objects lifted; while DAVITS, DERRICKS, and CAPSTANS are mechanisms for lifting.

1001. *MENORAH*, menorah (*mĕ-nō'-răh*) *n.* A candelabrum, seven branched candlestick.

A SCONCE (*skŏns*) was once a dark lantern in which the light was hidden, from *absconsus*, the past participle of *abscondere*, to hide away, the source of ABSCOND, to run away and hide. Today a SCONCE is more often a wall candlestick.

A CANDELABRUM (*kăn-dĕ-lah'-brŭm*) is a branched candlestick which rests on a table, and like a MENORAH may hold seven candles, or sometimes fewer or more, but frequently grouped.

MENORAH is a Hebrew word for a branched candlestick, with seven candles in a line, one in the center and three on each side.

Despite the rarity of this word, it is answered correctly by a surprisingly large percentage of high-vocabulary persons, with TABLE-CLOTH and LAMP the two misleads.

1002. *CASSOWARY*, cassowary (*kăs'-sō-wā-rĭ*) *n.* A large ostrichlike bird, standing five feet high, inhabiting Australia. In looking up CASSOWARY in modern dictionaries, some descriptive terms are: STRUTHIOUS, STRUTHIFORM, RATITE, DROMAEOGNATHAUS, and TINAMOU.

Among 27 high-vocabulary adults, 6 select EMBANKMENT as the meaning of CASSOWARY. A CAUSEWAY (*kăwz'-wā*) is an EMBANKMENT, according to Ephraim Chambers, 1728: 'A massive construction of stones, fascines (*făs-sēnz*), bundles of sticks, and stakes; or an elevation of fat viscous earth well beaten; serving either as a road in wet marshy places or as a mole to retain the waters of a pond, or prevent a river from overflowing the lower ground.

'CAUSEWAY more usually denotes a common hard raised way, maintained and repaired with stones and rubbish.'

Nathan Bailey, a few years earlier, states more simply: 'CAUSE-WAY, a highway, a bank raised in marshy ground for foot-passage'.

'CASSOWARY, in ornithology,' again according to Ephraim Chambers, 1728: 'The name of an African bird of the ostrich variety, but not quite so tall though larger bodied; called also by many authors EMEU. Its legs are very long and robust; it has three toes on each foot, all placed before; it has the rudiments of wings, but they are very short. It has no tail. It is very common in Africa and is caught also in many parts of the East Indies.'

1003. *SEPT*, sept (*sĕpt*) *n.* A clan, tribe, sect, party, race, proceeding from a common progenitor: used of families in Ireland.

SEPT is thought to be a corruption of SECT, a party professing similar opinions.

Of 29 high-vocabulary adults 8 select SEVENTH SON as the meaning of SEPT. The Latin *septem* means seven. From this comes SEPTEMBER, the seventh month, when the months were named; for March was the first of the year, with, according to some, ten months, the two disagreeably cold months, January and February, not counting. Then, about the year 200 B.C. the beginning of the year was changed to January 1.

From Early History of Institutions by Sir Henry James Maine, whose Early Law and Custom, though published in 1882, should be familiar to every aspiring lawyer, comes: 'SEPT, the combined descendants of an ancestor long since dead'.

1004. *COIF*, coif (*kwăhf*) *n.* A skull cap fitting close to the head, made of leather for hunting, or lace for women, even trimmed with gold. The corresponding French word, also used in English, is CALOTTE (*kă-lŏt'*).

The COIF is always some sort of tight-fitting skull cap with no brim; but over the ages has been applied to various sorts of such head coverings. Recently, within the past hundred years, women have worn COIFs of fine lace. In the Middle Ages both men and women wore COIFs held in place by cords tied under the chin. Before the introduction of wigs in court, barristers wore COIFs.

The word COIF goes back through French probably to the German word for head, *kopf*. From the same source comes the French COIFFEUR, a hair dresser.

1005. *GENTILITY*, gentility (jĕn-tĭl'-ĭ-tĭ) *n*. Nobility fashionableness, stylishness.

From the Latin *gens* (jĕnz), *gentis*, family, race, nation, people, the source of the modern biological term GENE (jēn), come numerous words whose meanings overlap. Thus the GENTRY, which goes back to Middle English words meaning the behavior of a gentleman, is now a group of well-born people, in England, below the NOBILITY but of good position, well-bred, the upper middle class.

From the Latin *gentilis*, belonging to the same clan, having the same *gens*, race, family, comes GENTLE, once of good birth, well-born, belonging to the GENTRY as opposed to the NOBILITY; and then refined, respectable, and so gracious, kindly, and then mild, soothing, and so the noun GENTLENESS, kindness, tenderness, MILDNESS, this last selected by 25 per cent as the meaning of GENTILITY. But GENTILITY still means the quality of polite society, fashionableness, stylishness.

1006. *APPANAGE*, appanage (ăp'-păn-āj) *n*. Whatever belongs or falls to one's rank or station in life, inheritance, necessary patrimony, natural accompaniment.

Although 31 per cent concentrate on SURROUNDINGS, guesses as to the meaning ramble enough to show that APPANAGE is virtually unknown. Somewhat similar words as APPENDAGE, APPURTENANCE, ADJUNCT, and ACCESSORY, all suggest SURROUNDINGS. But APPANAGE has a different history for it comes from the Latin *appanare*, to furnish with bread, a combination of *ad*, to, and *panis*, bread, familiar in the Italian *pane* (*pah'-nā*), the Spanish *pan* (*pahn*), and the source of the English PANTRY.

Noah Webster in his first edition describes APPANAGE as: 'Lands appropriated by a prince to the maintenance of his younger sons as their patrimony; but on condition of the failure of male off-spring they were to revert to the donor or his heir. From the APPANAGE it was customary for the sons to take their surnames.'

In similar language the Oxford repeats: 'The provision made for the maintenance of the younger children of kings, princes, etc. It was originally a province.'

'Belinus had for his APPANAGE (as the French term it) Leogria, Wales, and Cornwall', the first quotation given in the Oxford from 1602.

1007. *BOSS*, boss (*bŏs*) *n.* A round swelling, protuberance, excrescence, hump, stud, knob; also a carved ornament in architecture.

Boss goes back to Middle English to the French *bosse*, hump, swelling, and then back probably to a German word for beat, strike. The word is occasionally used for an ornament in architecture and sculpture.

MOLDING, from the Latin *modulus*, a measure, is marked by twice as many as the correct answer CARVED ORNAMENT. A MOLDING, which the Century Dictionary spells MOLDING, without the U, while the English dictionaries spell the same word MOULDING, may make the connection between the wall and the ceiling. A MOLDING is long, the length of a room, or of a building. A BOSS is round. In sculpture a BOSS is a projecting mass to be carved later. BOSSES, round projections, sometimes occur at equal intervals in a MOLDING.

1008. *RETRORSE*, retrorse (*rē-trors'*) *adj.* Turned backward, directed back, retral.

RETRORSE, used mostly in such sciences as botany and zoology, is a contraction, sometimes known more elegantly in grammar as a SYNCOPATED form, this last from the Greek κόπτειν (*coptein*), to cut. RETRORSE comes from the Latin *retrorsus*, a contraction of *retroversus*, bent backward, turned back, a combination of *retro*, backward, and *versus*, the past participle of *vertere*, to turn, the source of numerous words with a clearer connection. Thus CONVERSE, REVERSE, INVERSE, turned end for end, and DIVERSE, all come through *versus*, from *vertere*, to turn. The corresponding verbs, as: to CONVERT, REVERT, INVERT, and DIVERT, come directly from the verb *vertere*, to turn, and not through the past participle.

RETRAL (*rē'-trăl*), an adjective directly from the Latin *retro*, backward, means back, hinder, caudal, toward the tail, posterior, the opposite of the equally unusual PRORSAL.

The popular mislead, selected by 20 per cent, is CONCEALED; with almost as many, 16 per cent, selecting INFLAMED. The unusual ANTRORSE, turned forward, is an opposite of RETRORSE, turned backward.

1009. *ADJUNCTION*, adjunction (*ăd-jŭnk'-shŏn*) *n.* Uniting, joining; legally: to join permanently one person's property with that of another, as building a house on land owned by someone else.

Words such as JOIN, JOINT, CONJOIN, DISJOIN, ENJOIN, and ADJOIN, to annex, attend, unite, also to be contiguous, in contact, all with the element -JOIN-, come to English through French; while JUNCTION, CONJUNCTION, INJUNCTION, DISJUNCTION, and ADJUNCTION, come directly from the Latin verb *jungere*, to join.

To 17 per cent ADJUNCTION means LEAVING. To DISJOIN, with the corresponding noun DISJUNCTION, is to separate, disunite, and suggests LEAVING. Also from a different source the verb to ADJOURN, to put off, refer to another day, suggests LEAVING.

E. Chambers gives the clearest discussion of ADJUNCTION: 'The act of joining or adding. All ADJUNCTIONS imply a subordination. Each ADJUNCTION is for the sake of a thing joined, not contrary-wise, as: clothes for the man, not the man for the clothes. Species of ADJUNCTION are by ADHESION, by APPOSITION, by ADJACENCY, by IMPOSITION, by ASSESSION, by ACCUBATION.'

1010. *CAIRN*, cairn (*kărn*) *n.* A small heap of stones set up as a landmark, pile of loose rocks as an indication on a mountain trail.

The technical term for a sepulchral mound, a burial place, a large hill of earth over a grave, containing stone weapons, bone implements, chests, and urns, is the Anglo-Saxon BARROW. In

Scotland and Wales stone BARROWS are known as CAIRNS, from Irish and Welch *carn*, rock.

Among high-vocabulary adults 30 per cent mark CAVE as a synonym of CAIRN. A CAVERN, sounding a bit like CAIRN, differs slightly from CAVE in having greater depth, and in being applied to natural hollows or chasms; but both CAVERNS and CAVES are hollow places in the earth, subterranean dens.

A CELL is essentially a sepulchral chamber or tomb, composed primarily of four, five, six or more upright megaliths, supporting a horizontal slab, which covers the whole space enclosed. Here are disposed the remains of the dead, or else urns containing their ashes. Then the polylith thus constructed is covered with a heap of stones or earth and is called a CAIRN, TUMULUS, GALGAL, MOUND, or BARROW. In time this superstructure may disappear, leaving exposed the original cell which is then called a CROMLECH or DOLMEN.

Today CAIRNS are small piles of a few stones used to mark a path over open ground.

1011. *METATHESIS*, metathesis (*mĕ-tăth'-ē-sĭs*) *n.* Transposing the letters of a word, interchanging two sounds or syllables.

To 33 per cent METATHESIS means PHILOSOPHY, and to another 22 per cent ABSTRACTION, both due probably to the word METAPHYSICS, a PHILOSOPHY and an ABSTRACTION. METAPHYSICS, beyond PHYSICS, is a supernatural science, the inward and essential nature of things.

METATHESIS, from the Greek μετά (*meta*), over, and τιθέναι (*tithenai*), to put, set, grammarians use for the interchange of two letters, two sounds, or syllables, as the transposition of the Anglo-Saxon *brid*, to the English BIRD. METATHESIS is also an interchange of sounds as between AX (*aks*) and ASK (*ask*).

1012. *LUNETTE*, lunette (*lū-nĕt'*) *n.* A small window, usually round or curved and in a vaulted roof.

The Latin *luna*, moon, the source of LUNAR and LUNATIC, affected by the rays of the moon, becomes *lune* in French. From this comes the diminutive LUNETTE. In architecture a LUNETTE is a window originally made by the intersection of a small vault with a larger one. From this the word has come to be used for any small round or curved window in or near the roof.

The popular misconception is OPERA-GLASSES, a confusion with the French word LORGNETTE, from the French *lorgner*, to see, spy, peek. A LORGNETTE is eyeglasses or OPERA-GLASSES held by a handle at the right.

1013. *FULMINATE*, fulminate (*fŭl'-mĭn-āt*) *v.* To explode with a loud noise, clash with detonations; according to Bailey, 1721; 'To thunder out, strike with a thunder-bolt, blast'; or figuratively, to issue threats, denunciate, menace.

Given a choice between DENOUNCE and EFFERVESCE as synonyms of FULMINATE 20 persons in a group of 27 high-vocabulary adults select EFFERVESCE, to bubble and hiss. EFFERVESCE comes from the Latin *fervēre*, which originally meant to boil, but came to mean ferment, glow, rage. EFFERVESCE used figuratively today may mean exhibit feelings that cannot be repressed or concealed, a meaning close to FULMINATE.

FULMINATE comes from the Latin *fulminare*, to hurl, strike with lightning, from *fulmen*, a thunder-bolt, from *fulgēre*, to shine, flash, the source of the word EFFULGENT, shining, bright, splendid.

Strictly FULMINATE should probably be reserved for the meaning given by Webster in his first edition, 1828: 'To thunder, also to detonate, make a loud or sudden noise or sharp crack, also figuratively to hurl papal thunder'.

1014. *STELE*, stele (*stē'-lē*) *n.* An upright slab or pillar bearing an inscription, burial stone, grave stone, also a mile-stone. Because STELE is so difficult, guesses as to its meaning scatter, high-vocabulary adults selecting TILED FLOOR, and others MOLD-ING, with no obvious reason for either.

STELE comes through the Latin *stela*, from the Greek στήλη (*stele*), an upright slab, pillar. According to the Encyclopaedia Britannica, a STELE is a non-structural pillar or vertical slab of stone, metal, or marble, set up for votive or commemorative purposes decorated with bas-reliefs or bearing inscriptions. The plural is STELAE. Inscriptions on STELAE go back 2500 years before Christ.

1015. *CENSORIOUS*, censorious (*sĕn-sō'-rĭ-ŭs*) *adj.* Fault-
finding, severely critical, carping, captious, hypercritical
(*hī-pĕr-crĭt'-ĭ-kăl*), apt to blame, addicted to censure, harsh in
commenting on others.

The word CRITIC comes through the Latin *criticus*, capable of
of judging, from κριτικός (*criticos*), fit for judging, from
κρίτης (*crites*), a judge, from the verb κρίνειν (*crinein*), to
separate, and so to judge. A CRITIC is skilled in judging, one
qualified to discern and distinguish both excellence and faults.

In ancient Rome the CENSOR was a political appointee whose
duty was to seek out the bad, heretical, immoral, subversive,
which could be fined, taxed, or made the cause of degrading,
and so make room for a friend. The CENSOR gained nothing by
discovering beauty, achievement, excellence. The CENSOR never
praised, that was not his function.

In selecting a synonym for CENSORIOUS 45 per cent underline
INTOLERANT, compared with only 25 per cent who prefer CARP-
ING. TOLERANT comes from the Latin *tolerare*, to endure, bear,
originally from a Sanskrit word which meant to lift. INTOLERANT
means making no effort to bear up under the circumstances, no
attempt to endure conditions, and so turning to unreasonable
criticisms. INTOLERANT and CENSORIOUS are often two aspects of
the same person; CENSORIOUS is specifically faultfinding.

1016. *FUSTIGATION*, fustigation (*fŭs-tĭ-gā'-shŏn*) *n.* Beating with a cudgel, clubbing, caning, flagellating.

To 25 per cent FUSTIGATION means INJUSTICE, perhaps because
of the word FRUSTRATION, from the Latin *frustrare*, to deceive,
trick, disappoint. INJUSTICE is FRUSTRATING, hopeless, in vain,
one can do nothing about it.

FUSTIGATION comes from the Latin *fustigare*, to beat to death,
from *fustis*, a club, cudgel, bludgeon.

1017. *CONUNDRUM*, conundrum (*kō-nŭn'-drŭm*) *n.* Anything which puzzles, enigma, question with a hidden
meaning, a riddle in which some odd resemblance is proposed
for discovery between unlike things; the answer involving a pun.

CONUNDRUM was originally slang, a made-up Latin word like
HOCUS-POCUS, or PANJANDRUM. CONUNDRUM goes back to 1600

when it meant whim, crotchet, maggot, conceit. Not until almost 1800 did it come to mean riddle, puzzling question, enigmatical statement. According to the Oxford Dictionary it was mentioned in 1645 as an Oxford term which originated in some university joke. To 30 per cent CONUNDRUM means PLOT, secret plan, stratagem, cabal; and to only 20 per cent RIDDLE.

1018. *POMADE*, pomade (*pō-mād'*) *n.* An ointment for the
    scalp, salve, unguent for the hair.
POMADE comes through the French *pommade*, from the Italian *pomata*, an ointment, from the Latin *pomum*, an apple, so called because POMADE was originally made from apples.

A LOTION, from the Latin *lavare*, to wash, is liquid. A COSMETIC, from the Greek κόσμος (*cosmos*), order, is a preparation to beautify the skin. MACASSAR and POMADE are both hair oils, popular in the first half of the 19th century.

POMADE is odorous, strongly perfumed; and this leads 30 per cent to select COLOGNE, compared with only 25 per cent who underline HAIR DRESSING.

1019. *RODOMONTADE*, rodomontade (*rō-dō-mŏn-tād'*) *n.*
    Empty bragging, vain boasting, thrasonical bullying, ranting, vaunting, bombast, fanfaronade.
The Italian *Rodomonte* is the name given to a brave but boastful leader of the Saracens against Charlemagne, in the imaginative poem Orlando Furioso, by Lodovico Ariosto, begun about 1503. Almost the same name appears earlier in Boiardo's Orlando Innamorato, where it is spelt Rodamonte.

The noun, a Rodomonte, literally one who rolls away mountains, comes from the Latin *rotare*, to roll away, and *mons*, mountains.

To 40 per cent of a high-vocabulary group, RODOMONTADE means ORATORY, compared with 55 per cent who prefer BRAGGING, a comment on ORATORY as that word is used today.

1020. *GRACILE*, gracile (*grăs'-ĭl*) *adj.* Slender, thin, lean,
    slight, gracefully slim.
Two Latin words *gratia* and *gracilis* had different meanings and have led to different groups of English words. From *gratia*,

esteem, agreeableness, with the plural *gratiae*, the Graces, come the Italian *grazia*, and the English GRACE, beauty of form, elegance of motion, and the adjective GRACEFUL, elegant.

From the Latin *gracilis*, which meant slender, slim, lean, come the Italian *gracile*, and the English GRACILE, which strictly means slender, thin, but which is certain to be influenced by GRACE and GRACEFUL, so that to 40 per cent GRACILE means RHYTHMIC.

1021. *EUPHRASY*, euphrasy (*ū'-fră-sĭ*) *n*. Delight, good cheer, cheerfulness.

EUPHRASY is thought by 30 per cent to mean HARMONY. EUPHONY (*ū'-fō-nĭ*), starting with the same Greek EU-, well, and accented on the same first syllable, means the quality of sounding well, HARMONY. But EUPHONY comes from φωνή (*phone*), voice, sound, the source of TELEPHONE. EUPHRASY comes from φρήν (*phren*), mind, the source of PHRENOLOGY, a study of the mind, as well as FRENZY, which has lost the original PH- in favor of F.

EUPHRASIA, the Greek εὐφρασία (*euphrasia*), delight, good cheer, is the technical term for the herb EYEBRIGHT, once used for eye diseases. EUPHRASY now means CHEERFULNESS.

1022. *EXOTERIC*, exoteric (*ĕks-ō-tĕr'-ĭk*) *adj*. External, open, popular, suitable for the general public, opposed to ESOTERIC.

Pantologia, a Cyclopedia of 1813, says: 'EXOTERIC, and ESOTERIC, terms denoting external and internal, and applied to the double doctrine of ancient philosophers: the one was public, or EXOTERIC; the other secret, or ESOTERIC. The first was that which they taught openly to the world, the latter was confined to a small number of disciples.'

To 48 per cent EXOTERIC means STRANGE, obviously the word EXOTIC, from the Greek ἐξωτικός (*exoticos*), foreign, alien, heathen, and so STRANGE.

EXOTERIC comes from the Greek ἔξω (*exo*), outside, through ἐξωτερικός (*exoterikos*), external, belonging to the outside. But EXOTERIC has come to mean for the outside world, in suggestion an opposite of EXOTIC, an exact opposite of ESOTERIC, literally inner, applied to scientific writings of Aristotle and in this sense to the secret teaching of Pythagoras.

1023. *JEREMIAD*, jeremiad (*jĕr-ĕ-mī'-ăd*) *n*. Lamentation, utterance in grief, complaining tirade.

Jeremiah, one of the great prophets, lived from 629 B.C. to about 580. In the Lamentations of Jeremiah, a book of the Old Testament, he prophesied evils to come because of the sins of the nation. The word JEREMIAD suggests that the grief is unnecessarily great and that its expression is tediously drawn out.

1024. *ACULEATE*, aculeate (*ă-kū'-lē-āt*) *adj*. Furnished with a sting, as bees and wasps, sharp, pointed, prickly, thorny.

The Latin *acer*, sharp, leads to a group of words which mean sharp to the taste, as ACID; and to another group which mean sharp-pointed. Thus from *acus*, needle, pin, comes ACUTE, sharp, ending in a point, as: 'An ACUTE angle'; and from the diminutive of *acus* comes *aculeus*, a sting, prickle, spine, and so ACULEATE, thorny, prickly.

The popular mislead, selected by 20 per cent, is RELAXING. Two unusual words: ACCUMBANT and ACCUBATION mean leaning back at meals, lying down while eating.

1025. *ADHIBIT*, adhibit (*ăd'-hĭb-ĭt*) *v*. To use, apply, employ, administer as a remedy, put into practical operation.

The Latin *habere*, to have, hold, becomes *hibere* in most compounds. Thus to PROHIBIT, from the Latin *prohibere*, is to stop, check, forbid, usually by authority. To INHIBIT, from the Latin *inhibire*, is to hold back, check, stop, restrain, almost intangibly, figuratively, not with the acknowledged authority of PROHIBIT.

These two words lead 30 per cent to select BLOCK-OUT as the meaning of ADHIBIT, an exact opposite when used in the phrase: 'ADHIBIT the light'. To ADHIBIT, from the Latin *adhibitus*, the past participle of *adhibere*, to hold toward, apply, is to use, apply, administer a remedy, in the same positive direction as EXHIBIT, to show, expose to view.

1026. *ADSCITITIOUS*, adscititious (*ăd-sĭ-tĭ'-shŭs*) *adj*. Added from without, acquired, derived, not intrinsic, supplementary, additional, not essential.

ADSCITITIOUS comes from the Latin *adscitus*, derived, assumed, foreign, the past participle of *adsciscere*, to take knowingly to one's self, appropriate, adopt, a combination of *ad*, and *sciscere*, to seek to know, from *scire*, to know, the source of SCIENCE, knowledge.

This derivation from *scire*, to know, leads 35 per cent to select WELL KNOWN as the meaning of the unusual ADSCITITIOUS, the same number as prefer SUPPLEMENTAL, and just as correct if one judges by origin only. But knowledge, information, comes from the outside, is added, external, as compared with an aptitude, a born characteristic, native gift; and the word ADSCITITIOUS has come to designate this aspect of knowledge, its derived quality, stressing its acquisition.

ADVENTITIOUS has much the same suggestion, except that ADVENTITIOUS means coming from the outside by luck, by chance; while ADSCITITIOUS implies acquired, added consciously.

1027. *FASTUOUS*, fastuous (*făs'-tū-ŭs*) *adj*. Proud, haughty, arrogant, supercilious, an obsolete word seldom used today.

FASTUOUS comes from the Latin *fastus*, pride, haughtiness, disdain, arrogance, disgust, from the same source as FASTIDIOUS, a pleasanter modern word with something of the same meaning, difficult to please, discriminating, hard to suit.

FASTUOUS is thought by 30 per cent to mean CRITICAL, a correct answer which must be removed from the test.

1028. *VOUCHSAFE*, vouchsafe (*vowch-sāf'*) *v*. To permit, grant, bestow; properly two words, literally to guarantee as safe, assure, secure.

The verb to VOUCH comes through French from the Latin *vocare*, to call, summon, the source of VOCATION, one's calling, the task to which one is called; and ADVOCATE, literally a person called to the bar to act as a counsel. To VOUCH was once to call witness, and so to declare, affirm, assert; or sometimes, from opposing points of view, to confirm, be surety for.

SAFE comes from the Latin *salvus*, whole, safe, unharmed, secure, the direct source of SALVAGE and SALVATION, and the verb to SAVE.

To 35 per cent VOUCHSAFE means DRAW UP. To DRAW UP, printed as two separate words, may be to arrange in order, sometimes in preparation for action. The figurative use: 'To draw up an answer' suggests planning it. To VOUCHSAFE an answer has come to mean almost to give, but with a suggestion of condescension, of deigning, stooping, to give an answer; to some extent an opposite of preparing an answer.

Perhaps the difficulty is the word ATTEST, used in the vocabulary test, an exact synonym, but difficult. To ATTEST is to testify to, bear witness to, and VOUCHSAFE is one of its meanings.

1029. *BARATHRUM*, barathrum (*băr'-ă-thrŭm*) *n.* A rocky pit, outside the walls of ancient Athens, into which criminals were thrown.
MARKET-PLACE, underlined by 30 per cent, compared with only 14 per cent who select PIT, is the popular mislead. BARATHRUM is so difficult a word that the selection of MARKET-PLACE seems pure chance. It is however overwhelmingly the popular answer and there must be some reason. The AGORA (*āg'-ō-răh*), from ἀγορά (*agora*), was the MARKET-PLACE in ancient ATHENS. BARATHRUM comes from βάραθρον (*barathron*), pit, gulf.

1030. *IMBRICATE*, imbricate (*ĭm'-brĭ-kāt*) *v.* To lap one over another, like tiles or shingles.
To 11 per cent: 'IMBRICATED tiles' are GLAZED. To GLAZE is to cover, usually toward the end of baking, with a smooth, shiny, transparent, often water-proof surface. GLAZING applies to each individual tile; IMBRICATE, to the manner of laying tiles.

In boat building the corresponding term is CLINCHER-BUILT, where each board or plate overlaps the one below, as opposed to CARVEL-BUILT, flush-jointed, with no overlapping. IMBRICATE, from the Latin *imbrex*, *imbricis*, hollow tile, gutter tile, partile, applies to laying tiles, and similar designs, but not to the overlapping of long boards.

1031. *CHRYSALIS*, chrysalis (*krĭ'-să-lĭs*), with the rarely heard plural CHRYSALIDES (*krĭ-săl'-ĭ-dēz*) *n.* Baby insect, pupa (*pū'-pah*) of a butterfly or moth, envelope, nymph, aurelia (*aw-rē'-lyah*), a form which butterflies, moths, and many other insects, assume when they abandon the caterpillar state, and before their wings develop.

To 32 per cent CHRYSALIS means FLYING MOTH. The CHRYSALIS
is specifically that stage of development before maturity, before
the wings develop, when FLIGHT is impossible, actually the stage
during which the wings are developing, during which there is
no motion.

First comes the LARVA, from the Latin *larva*, ghost, specter,
the early form of any animal when unlike its parents, as the
tadpole is the LARVA of the frog; the caterpillar, the LARVA of
the butterfly or moth.

Then comes the CHRYSALIS, fastened to a twig, motionless;
and finally the FLYING MOTH.

CHRYSALIS comes through the Latin *chrysallis*, from the Greek
χρυσαλλίς (*chrysallis*), the gold-colored sheath of a butterfly,
from the Greek χρυσός (*chrysos*), gold, the source of CHRY-
SANTHEMUM, the golden flower.

From E. Chambers: 'CHRYSALIS, a term used by modern
writers of natural history of insects in the same sense of NYMPHA
or AURELIA. The word seems to imply a peculiar yellow or
golden color but this is purely accidental.'

1032. *SCIOLISM*, sciolism (*sĭ'-ō-lĭzm*) *n.* Superficial knowl-
       edge, unfounded pretense to profound learning, shallow
knowledge, a smattering of education.
SCIOLISM comes from the Latin *sciolus*, a diminutive signifying
little, from the verb *scire*, to know, understand, plus the suffix
-ISM, added to form nouns signifying the practice or teaching
of a subject. From the present participle *sciens, scientis*, knowing, skilled, comes the English SCIENCE, and such adjectives as
OMNISCIENT, knowing all, and PRESCIENT, knowing beforehand.

Of 29 high-vocabulary adults, 9 mark ERUDITION (*ĕr-ū-dĭ'-
shŭn*) as the meaning of SCIOLISM. SCHOLARSHIP (*skŏl'-ăhr-shĭp*)
is learning, ERUDITION, an opposite of SCIOLISM, superficial
knowledge. In his Thirteenth, Greatest of Centuries, the physician and author James Walsh writes: 'The foolish tirades of
modern SCIOLISTS, who have often expressed their wonder that
these scholars of the Middle Ages did not devote themselves to
nature study, are absurd.' Of SCIOLISTS, Webster, 1828, says:
'One who knows little or who knows many things superficially;
a smatterer'.

1033. *PROROGUE*, prorogue (*prō-rōg'*) *v.* To prolong, discontinue for a time, defer, extend, protract.

Of the noun PROROGATION Nathan Bailey says: 'A deferring or putting off especially of a session in Parliament to a certain time appointed by the King in which case all bills passed in either of the houses that have not had royal assent must begin a-fresh at the next meeting; but not so in an adjournment'.

ADJOURNMENT is an act of an assembly, by virtue of its own authority. PROROGATION is an act of the authority which called the assembly together, and the group does not meet again until summoned by the same authority.

PROROGUE comes from the Latin *prorogare*, to prolong, protract, extend, a combination of *pro-*, forth, and *rogare*, to ask, the source of INTERROGATE (*ĭn-tĕr'-rō-gāt*), to ask, question, and PREROGATIVE (*prē-rŏg'-ă-tĭv*), once long ago asked to vote first and so today a special privilege.

To TERMINATE, selected by 7 per cent of high-vocabulary adults, is probably as close to the meaning of PROROGUE as the intended answer EXTEND. To TERMINATE is to stop, end, cancel, close, and suggests finality, almost dissolution. To EXTEND is to go on with. To PROROGUE is to stop temporarily but not finally.

In the same group another 7 per cent select OUTLINE as a meaning of PROROGUE, a choice more difficult to understand. A PROLOGUE, which differs from PROROGUE by only a single letter, although an INTRODUCTION, preface, or speech before a play, hints at what is coming and may suggest OUTLINE.

Sir William Blackstone, who wrote his Commentaries on the Laws of England in 1768, says: 'PROROGUE is to continue the Parliament from one session to another; an ADJOURNMENT is a continuance from day to day'.

1034. *BOWDLERIZED*, bowdlerized (*bōd'-lĕr-īzed*) *adj.* Expurgated, censored, purified, omitting from an author's writings those passages considered offensive or indelicate.

PRIVATELY-PRINTED, chosen three times as often as the correct answer, usually means paid for personally by the author, sometimes because no commercial publishing house will assume the risk. Sir Walter Scott printed privately through the Ballantyne Press, his poems and essays in ten volumes, and lost so heavily that he was forced to write his novels to pay off his debts. Henry Adams printed several of his books privately in small editions, partly because he wanted them to be individual expressions which he feared might be commercialized.

BOWDERLIZED is an eponym, from Thomas Bowdler, who published in 1818 an expurgated edition of Shakespeare.

1035. *GROTESQUE*, grotesque (*grō-tĕsk'*) *adj*. Wild, fantastic, whimsical, strange, odd, ludicrous, extravagant.

GROTESQUE goes back through the French *grotesque*, spelled in the same way, with Italian, Spanish, and Portuguese words meaning odd, ludicrous, to the Italian *grotta*, a subterranean cavity, natural cavern, often an artificial construction made for recreation.

To 80 per cent GROTESQUE means HORRIFYING. HORROR, from the Latin *horrere*, to bristle, shake with fear, be terrified, is fright, shock, dread; and the corresponding adjective HORRID is dreadful, shocking, offensive, abominable, frightful, awful, dire, revolting. Of the three words: FANCIFUL, FANTASTIC, and GROTESQUE, the last is the strongest, but not so extreme as HORRIFYING. FANCIFUL is odd, but still pleasing. FANTASTIC is more extreme; while GROTESQUE carries FANCY still further to the unnatural, incongruous, absurd.

E. Chambers: 'A wild whimsical figure or design of a painter, ridiculous, extravagant, and even monstrous; wildly pleasant in a person's dress, discourse, etc. Masquerade habits are the more valued, the more GROTESQUE they are'.

1036. *ADULATION*, adulation (*ăd-ū-lā'-shŏn*) *n*. Servile admiration, excessive praise, exaggerated compliments, feigned devotion; Nathan Bailey, 1721, says: 'Servile flattery; praise in excess and beyond what is merited; high compliments'.

ADULATION comes from the Latin *adulatus*, the past participle of *adulare*, to fawn upon, as a dog. Of the first twenty-seven high-vocabulary examinees, twenty chose WORSHIP, obviously a confusion of ADULATION with ADORATION, the act of paying honors to a divine being, a profound reverence, worship paid to God, homage to one in high esteem. High-vocabulary examinees, expecting words to be easy, go rapidly at the beginning of a test and often make careless errors. In the first version of this work-sample, ADULATION appeared as the third item. Because of the mistakes, ADULATION in the revision became 139, toward the end, among difficult words where high-vocabulary examinees were more careful, only 42 per cent selecting WORSHIP, in place of the correct answer, FLATTERY.

1037. *INTERCALATE*, intercalate (*ĭn-tĕr'-kăl-āt*) v. To insert an extra day in the calendar, to interpose (*ĭn-tĕr-pōz'*), interpolate (*ĭn-tĕr'-pō-lāt*); Bailey, 1721, says: 'INTERCALATION (*ĭn-tĕr-kă-lā'-shŏn*) is a putting of a day into the month of February in leap year'.
Of 28 high-vocabulary adults, 7 select GATHER as the meaning of INTERCALATE. To COLLATE, from the Latin *com-*, together, and *latus*, the irregular past participle of *ferre*, to carry, bring, is to bring together, GATHER, lay together and compare. A COLLATION is a meal, originally a repast of monks after reading a collection of lives of the saints.
INTERCALATE, a technical term, is a combination of the Latin *inter*, between, and *calare*, to call, the source of the English CALENDAR, a tabulation of days and weeks for the year.
The rotation of the earth on its own axis, with one of its faces sometimes toward the sun and sometimes in shadow, makes day and night. The same earth, moving around the sun, makes the year. The earth turns on its axis approximately 365 times each year, but not exactly — more nearly 365 ¼; so that every fourth year it is necessary to INTERCALATE an extra day, called an INTERCALARY (*ĭn-ter'-că-lā-rĭ*) day. Every fourth year has 366 days.
But this is just a bit too much, so that every hundred years, the last year of each century, which should be a leap year, is not; as 1900, which should have been a leap year, was not, and the year 2000, again, will not be a leap year.

1038. *HAGIOLOGY*, hagiology (*hă-jĭ-ŏl'-ō-jĭ*) n. The branch of literature which deals with the lives of saints, legends of the saints.
HAGIOLOGY comes directly from the Greek ἅγιος (*hagios*), sacred, and -λογία from λέγειν (*legein*), to speak.

The mislead is DEMONISM. Today the word DEMON means devil, an evil spirit, and DEMONISM means a belief in DEMONS, as thus defined. But the Greek word δαίμων (*daimon*) meant a god or goddess, a deity not of the highest rank. The change in meaning came because the Christians believed that all pagan deities were evil.

1039. *QUIDDITY*, quiddity (*kwĭd'-dĭ-tĭ*) *n*. That which distinguishes one thing from another, substantial form, inner nature, essence.

QUIDDITY comes from the Latin *quid*, meaning what, so that QUIDDITY means the whatness of something. The popular mislead, RELEVANCE, is selected by the same number of persons as ESSENTIAL-NATURE, considered correct. The adjective RELEVANT means to the purpose, applicable, pertinent, from the Latin *relevare*, to lift up, and so help, assist. A RELEVANT fact helps in making a decision. RELEVANCE is the connection of something outside with the matter under discussion, an obvious relationship of some second idea to the first. RELEVANCE calls for two distinct entities, and is the association between the two. QUIDDITY is the inner nature of one thing itself.

1040. *WIMPLE*, wimple (*wĭm'-pl*) *n*. A woman's head-cloth of silk or linen, formerly worn out of doors and so folded as to envelop the head, chin, sides of the face, and neck. Still used by nuns.

In the test phrase: 'A woman's WIMPLE', the popular mislead is FAINT CRY, clearly the word WHIMPER (*hwĭm'-per*), a low cry, plaintive sound. The word WIMPLE goes back to 1100.

1041. *AGONISTIC*, agonistic (*ăg-ŏn-ĭs'-tĭc*) *adj*. Combative, striving to overcome in argument, aiming at effect, strained, polemical, forensic, contending, competitive, argumentative.

To 30 per cent AGONISTIC means UNBELIEVING. Agnostic (*ăg-nŏs'-tĭk*), from the Greek ἄγνωστος (*agnostos*), unknown, a combination of the Greek privative ἀ, and γνωστός (*gnostos*), known, means disclaiming any knowledge of God, and so UNBELIEVING.

AGONISTIC, from the Greek ἀγωνιστής (*agonistes*), means contending for a prize. In Greek, ἀγών (*agŏn*) was a contest for a prize and from this comes AGONIST, one who contended for a prize in public games, champion. From the same source come: AGONY, ANTAGONIST (*ăn-tăg'-ō-nĭst*), one who contends against another; PROTAGONIST (*prō-tăg'-ō-nĭst*), one who contends in favor, usually of a cause; as well as the adjective AGONISTIC, enjoying contending.

1042. *FULSOME*, fulsome (*fŏŏl'-sŭm*) *adj.* Full, plump, fat; gross, disgusting, cloying; also offensive from excess of praise. According to Webster, 1828, FULL and FOUL are the same; and 'in the United States the compound *fullsome* takes its significance from FULL, in the sense of cloying, satiating, while in England FULSOME is predominantly foulness'.

Of the pronunciation Fowler — English Usage — says: 'The Oxford English Dictionary recognizes only (*fŭl-sŭm*), not (*fŏŏl-sŭm*)'.

FULSOME, a combination of FULL and -SOME, an Anglo-Saxon suffix as in WHOLESOME, TROUBLESOME, LONESOME, MEDDLESOME, means rather full, pretty full.

Of 27 high-vocabulary adults 13 select AWKWARD as the meaning of FULSOME. Of AWKWARD Noah Webster, 1828, says: 'Wanting dexterity in the use of the hands and of instruments; unready, not dexterous; bungling; untoward'. To FUMBLE is to manage awkwardly; and this word, which comes immediately after FULSOME in the dictionary, may suggest AWKWARD.

Of FULSOME, Nathan Bailey, 1721, says: 'Nasty, noisome, distasteful, loathsome, luscious' in the sense of over-sweet, cloying; and Webster adds 'nauseous, offensive'.

1043. *CORDITE*, cordite (*kōr'-dīt*) *n.* Gunpowder, smokeless powder, a combination of nitroglycerin and gun cotton introduced in 1889.

The misconception ROPE PILE may be selected because CORDITE was made in the form of a CORD, which suggested its name; or because of the word CORDAGE (*kōr'-dāj*), ropes in general, and so a ROPE PILE. The suffix -AGE is French, but originally from Latin, added to make collective nouns, as BAGGAGE and CORDAGE.

1044. *OBUMBRATE*, obumbrate (*ō-bŭm'-brāt*) *v.* To darken,
      shade, cloud, overshadow.

In astronomy UMBRA, with the plural UMBRAE (*ŭm'-brē*), is
the total shadow in, for example, an eclipse, complete blackness,
compared with the PENUMBRA (*pĕn-ŭm'-brah*), a partial shadow,
grayness, starting with the Latin *paene*, almost.

From the Latin *umbra*, shade, comes the Italian *ombrella*, the
diminutive of the Italian *ombra*, and so the English UMBRELLA,
only recently associated with rain. The UMBRELLA originated in
the Far East, in very remote times, as a sun protection; and was
used in ancient Greece for the same purpose.

From *umbra* comes also ADUMBRATE, to cast a shadow, now
used figuratively to mean FORESHADOW, throw a shadow ahead,
and also sketch vaguely, give a shadowy idea.

OBUMBRATE, a combination of OB, over, and *umbrare*, to
shade, shadow, is to overshadow, darken. To ILLUMINATE,
chosen by 16 per cent as a synonym of OBUMBRATE, is an
opposite.

1045. *APORIA*, aporia (*ă-pō'-rĭ-ă*) *n.* Doubt, puzzlement,
       anxiety, uneasiness; in rhetoric: a doubting or being at a
loss where to begin, or what to say on account of the variety
of matter.

Among 29 high-vocabulary adults 7 select the mislead
CEREMONIOUS ERROR as the meaning of APORIA. A CEREMONY
was at first a religious RITE; and the adjective CEREMONIOUS
means formal, punctilious as to outward behavior, elaborately
polite, following prescribed rules, solemn in manner.

APORIA comes directly from the Greek ἄπορος (*aporos*), in
doubt, a combination of the privative ἀ and πόρος (*poros*),
a way, passage, the source of POROUS, full of PORES, tiny holes,
openings, perforations, apertures.

From as far back as 1589 comes: 'APORIA, or the doubtful.
So called because oftentimes we will seem to cast perils, and
make doubt of things when by a plain manner of speech we
might affirm or deny'.

A century later Ephraim Chambers says: 'APORIA, from
απόρεω, I doubt, in rhetoric, denotes a state of wavering,
wherein the orator appears undetermined whether to say a

thing or not: Shall I speak out or hold my tongue'. Aporetic, inclined to raise objections, is the corresponding adjective.

1046. *BALDRIC*, baldric (*bŏl'-drĭk*) *n.* A belt worn diagonally from shoulder to hip, supporting a sword or horn, richly ornamented war girdle.

Baldric goes back through Old French, perhaps to the same source as belt, which was once spelt *balt*.

William J. Rolfe in his notes at the back of Much Ado About Nothing says: 'A baldrick was a belt, girdle, or sash, sometimes a swordbelt; generally passed round one side of the neck and under the opposite arm. Turberville, in his book of Hunting, 1611 edition, gives a figure of a huntsman with his horn hanging from a baldrick worn in that way'. The Rolfe edition of Shakespeare, used by Kittredge and so stamped as a final authority, binds each play separately in a small, thin, reddish brown volume.

To 34 per cent baldric means wig, perhaps because of the first four letters bald.

Among adults another 28 per cent select dagger as the meaning of baldric. None of the usual types of dagger: stiletto, poniard, dirk, sound like baldric; but a bodkin was originally a small dagger and, in the 1300's, a dagger was often attached to the swordbelt, and this may lead to the association.

1047. *SICCATIVE*, siccative (*sĭk'-kă-tĭv*) *n.* A dryer, any material added to an oil paint to hasten its drying. Turpentine is a common dryer or siccative. Dryer is the common term used by painters.

Siccative comes from the Latin *siccare*, to dry, from the adjective *siccus*, dry. From the same source comes the verb to desiccate (*dĕ'-sĭk-kāt*), to dry up. To desiccate is to deprive of moisture. The de- at the beginning, which is so often negative, in this instance intensifies the meaning.

The mislead moisture, wetness, dampness, from the Latin *mustus*, new, fresh, is selected by 30 per cent, almost as many as dryer, the synonym of siccative. This confusion of siccative with its exact opposite, moisture, which seems so incredible to one who knows the word, is the fourth and final step which those take who are learning a new word.

1048. *REEVE*, reeve (*rēv*) *n.* An old English official of high rank with local jurisdiction under the king, a steward, bailiff, business agent, overseer, greeve.

John Richard Green, in his popular Short History of the English People, which appeared in 1877 in four volumes, writes: 'The royal REEVES were officers dispatched to levy the royal revenues and administer royal justice'.

A few years later, 1883, in The Conquest of England, Green adds: 'A lord who has so many men that he cannot personally have all in his own keeping was bound to set over each dependent township a REEVE, not only to exact his lord's dues, but to enforce his justice within its bounds'.

In his encyclopaedia of 1728 Ephraim Chambers says: 'The REEVE of a church is the guardian of it, or the church-warden. So SHIRE-REEF is the SHERIFF, or guardian of a county; and PORT-REEVE, the warden of a port or haven'.

Among 18 high-vocabulary adults 8 select FARM-HAND as a synonym of REEVE, an opposite of the correct answer, the fourth and last step in learning.

1049. *AQUAEMANALE*, aquaemanale (*ăk-kwă-mă-nā'-lē*) *n.* Ornamental pitcher, elaborate ewer, metal water carrier; often made in the shape of a grotesque animal.

The two misleads are COOLER and CANAL, both suggested by *aqua*, water, at the beginning of AQUAEMANALE. Also an AQUAE-DUCT, from the same Latin *aqua*, water, and *ductus*, pipe, conveyance of any kind, from *ducere*, to lead, convey, may be a CANAL, channel.

AQUAEMANALE comes from the Latin *aquae*, the genitive of *aqua*, and *manale*, a pitcher, ewer, from *manare*, to flow, trickle, drip.

An AQUAEMANALE was originally any sort of pitcher for pouring water over the hands during meals, and is still used for this purpose. These pitchers then came to be made in the form of grotesque animals with a faucet at the front. The original pitchers go back to Roman times but the strange shapes are often 14th century, and the term is now limited to these curious metal pitchers of copper or silver, most of which are now museum pieces.

1050. *VILIPEND*, vilipend (*vil'-ĭ-pĕnd*) v. To hold of slight
    value, deprecate, depreciate, slander, disparage, treat
contemptuously.

The Latin *vilis* first meant of small value, paltry, of low price,
almost worthless; but the English VILE has come to be used more
strongly for depraved, shameful, contemptible, foul. VILIFY,
from the same Latin root *vilis*, vile, and *facere*, to make, is to
slander, defame, calumniate, malign, and so to make of little
value. Use a rare word of this sort precisely or not at all.

There are two Latin verbs: *pendĕre*, to weigh, balance, and
pendēre, to hang, be suspended. From these come the adjective
PENDENT, hanging; and the verbs to IMPEND, to hang over one's
head; DEPEND, to hang on to someone or something; to SUSPEND,
literally to hang, but now used to mean stop temporarily, discontinue, as: to SUSPEND operations; to APPEND, to attach; and
EXPEND, weigh out. In the unusual word VILIPEND, *pendĕre* is
used in the last sense of weighing, and suggests weighed out
carefully and found to be of little value.

The misconceptions scatter in such a way as to show almost
complete ignorance of the word.

1051. *MARGENT*, margent (*mähr'-jĕnt*) n. A gloss, note,
    scholium, marginal comment, explanation in the margin
of a book.

The MARGIN, from the Latin *margo, marginis*, edge, brink,
bounds, is a bounding space, border. MARGENT is MARGIN plus
what is called an UNORIGINAL T which appeared from somewhere, no one knows quite where. The same sort of T occurs
at the end of TYRANT.

Of 28 high-vocabulary adults 7 select COAT-OF-ARMS as the
meaning of MARGENT. Look up COAT-OF-ARMS and you will soon
realize why back in the 1500's there were dictionaries which
dealt only with the technical terms of heraldry. Technically, a
COAT-OF-ARMS is a complete ACHIEVEMENT, that is a design,
originally on a shield, including both crest and motto. ARGENT,
much like MARGENT in sound, means silver, and is one of the
two important TINCTURES in addition to the FURS.

A MARGENT is a note or annotation added to the text and
written or printed in the MARGIN.

1052. *RIMY*, rimy (*rī'-mĭ*) *adj*. Frosty, covered with hoar-
frost, with RIME.

To 30 per cent RIMY means EATEN AWAY. The verb to ERODE, and
the past participle ERODED, come from the Latin *e-*, out, off, and
rodere, to gnaw, the source of RODENT, a gnawing animal.
ERODED means EATEN AWAY, gnawed into. To GRIND is to wear
down, smooth by friction, whet, and so in a sense EAT AWAY;
and GRIME, differing from RIME by only a single letter, is dirt,
soil, possibly the result of GRINDING, although the word comes
from Scandinavian words meaning streak, stripe, spot, smut.

HOAR, from Anglo-Saxon, means white, or sometimes gray
with age, as in the adjective HOARY. HOAR-FROST is white frost.
RIME, also from Anglo-Saxon, is white frost, hoar-frost, con-
gealed vapor, frozen dew.

1053. *INTARSIA*, intarsia (*ĭn-tăhr'-zĭ-ăh*) *n*. A wood inlay
done in Italy during the Renaissance.

Three types of inlay are: MOSAIC, MARQUETRY, and INTARSIA.
MOSAIC (*mō-zā'-ĭk*) is designs, figures, pictures, made of small
thin colored stones called TESSERA, each about a quarter of an
inch square. MARQUETRY (*măhr'-kĕt-rĭ*), from the French
marque, a mark, spot, is much the same, but of softer material
such as wood, though ivory and tortoise shell are also employed.
Both MOSAIC and MARQUETRY are thin veneers which cover the
surface.

INTARSIA, from the Italian *intarsiare*, to inlay, from *tarsia*,
inlaid work, mosaic woodwork, is thin pieces of wood of various
colors set into a heavy wood background.

STAINED-GLASS, the most frequently chosen mislead, and
INTARSIA are types of art not far distant in time. Much of the
greatest STAINED-GLASS is 13th century; while INTARSIA was first
done in Venice in ivory in the 14th century. But the misleads
TILES and FOOT are nearly as attractive, suggesting that INTARSIA
is a difficult word and the choices as to its meaning are largely
guesses.

1054. *FULIGINOUS*, fuliginous (*fŭ-lĭj'-ĭ-nŭs*) *adj*. Sooty, of
the color of soot, deposited by smoke, pertaining to
smoke, dusty.

To 28 per cent FULIGINOUS means TAINTED, a correct answer, but not the one intended. TAINTED, which now means corrupted, poisoned, spoiled, comes through the French from the Latin *tinctus*, color, dye, tinge, hue, stain, and the verb *tintere*, to dye, color; and TAINTED in English originally meant colored, tinted. FULIGINOUS means not only SOOTY but has the suggestion of blackish, sooty in color.

FULIGINOUS, from the Latin *fuliginis*, comes from *fuligo*, soot, now an English word FULIGO (*fū-lĭ'-gŏ*), soot, a black substance formed by incomplete combustion, by smouldering.

To another 12 per cent FULIGINOUS means MISTY. MIST is water vapor, particles of water, tiny droplets of water held in the air. FULIGO is particles of soot.

1055. *PLASHY*, plashy (*plăsh'-ĭ*) *adj.* Watery, wet, moist, marshy, full of puddles.

PLASHY, which goes back to Dutch, German, and Scandinavian words with much the same meaning, is thought by 34 per cent to mean NOISY. The verb to SPLASH starts with s, not originally a part of the word, added at the beginning to strengthen the meaning. Of the noun a SPLASH, the Century Dictionary says: 'A NOISE from water dashed about'; so that NOISY would be a correct answer to SPLASHY. But PLASHY, without the s, is gentler, quieter, not so NOISY.

1056. *BELVEDERE*, belvedere (*bĕl-vĕ-dēr'*) *n.* Open gallery, loggia, covered balcony with a view, upper story of a building open to the air, or, especially in France and Italy, a summer house on an eminence, lantern or cupola on a roof.

BELVEDERE is the Italian word *belvedere*, spelt in the same way, but pronounced (*bĕl-vĕ-dā'-rā*), literally a beautiful view, from *bel*, beautiful, and *vedere*, to see, the source of VISION, and VIEW. E. Chambers, who spells the word with i, BELVIDERE, following the Latin verb *videre*, says: 'An Italian term denoting a fine prospect. The name is more peculiarly given to a pavillion on top of a building or an eminence, in the manner of a platform in a garden sustained by a terrace wall, or a massive mound of turf contrived for the sake of commanding a large and beautiful view.'

To 34 per cent BELVEDERE means TOWER. A BELL-TOWER is a CAMPANILE (*kăm-pă-nē'-lä*), another Italian word which may lead to the confusion. A TOWER is high and often built primarily for the view which it gives, a confusion of words from the same situation. A BELVEDERE is almost any place with a beautiful view, except perhaps a TOWER, probably because the word TOWER implies a view without calling it a BELVEDERE.

1057. *SLOUGH*, slough (*slŏw*) *n.* Soft, muddy ground, deep and small quagmire, marsh, swamp, mire, reedy pool.

The two popular misleads are SAILING VESSEL and CHANNEL. A SLOOP is a small fore-and-aft rigged sailing vessel with one mast. A SCOW is a flat-bottomed boat, a freighter or barge, used for transporting mud or freight. The combination of SCOW, pronounced like SLOUGH, and SLOOP, with the same first letters, seems to attract many away from the correct answer.

A SLUICE is an artificial runway for water and this may draw others to CHANNEL.

Two words, spelt alike but pronounced differently, are SLOUGH pronounced like COW, directly from Anglo-Saxon, meaning a marsh or swamp; and SLOUGH, pronounced like CUFF, MUFF, and TOUGH. This sort of SLOUGH is the skin of a snake, and the verb to SLOUGH is to cast off its skin.

A SWAMP, the broadest word, is usually with trees but too wet for pasturage. A BOG is treacherous with decaying vegetation. A QUAGMIRE is the worst kind of BOG. A MARSH is water at times, as when the tide is high. A SLOUGH is small in extent but deep mud and with no vegetation. John Bunyan in his Pilgrim's Progress talked of the Slough of Despond.

1058. *FACTIOUS*, factious (*făk'-shŭs*) *adj.* Given to party strife, critical, carping, captious, fault-finding, dissenting, cavilling, underhand, forming factions.

AUTHORITATIVE, selected by 45 per cent, nearly half, is almost an opposite, certainly in suggestion. AUTHORITY may be conferred by a vote of the people or by someone or some group above, or acquired by learning or achievements. A FACTION has no AUTHORITY. Many FACTIONS work to destroy AUTHORITY; and FACTIOUS implies fighting AUTHORITY.

A PARTY is a group with aims and ideals in common, working for what it believes to be the good of the state; FACTION, from the Latin *factio, factionis*, a doing, from *facere*, to do, is a small destructive group within a PARTY, with no civic purpose, sometimes with its own private goal in mind, but mostly working against the general trend, critical, secret, dissenting, dissatisfied with itself and so destructive of others. A FACTION is always an unpleasant group.

The adjective FACTIOUS, rarely seen, includes all the obnoxious qualities of a FACTION.

FACTITIOUS (*făk-tĭ'-shŭs*), made, manufactured, artificial, the opposite of FICTITIOUS, and FACTIOUS should be kept separate in spelling, pronunciation, and meaning.

1059. *MACERATE*, macerate (*mă'-sĕ-rāt*) v. To soften, separate the parts by soaking in a liquid, steep in order to extract solubles.

MACERATE comes directly from the Latin *macerare*, to soften.

To MASTICATE, from the Latin *masticare*, to chew, grind with the teeth, leads 40 per cent to select CHEW as the meaning of MACERATE, compared with only 30 per cent who prefer SOFTEN, the correct answer.

The object of STEEPING is the resulting liquid. One STEEPS tea, and then discards the tea leaves. One MACERATES in order to soften the substance and then discard the liquid.

1060. *LOOBY*, looby (*loo'-bĭ*) n. An awkward fellow, lout, lubber, gawk, lummox, zany, clownish person.

Those who have taken this vocabulary test split evenly between LOUT and STAID-PERSON as synonyms of LOOBY. STAID is the past participle of the verb to STAY. A STAY, the noun, is a prop, support. To STAY is to prop up, support, sustain, hold up, even to steady. A STAID PERSON is sober, grave, steady, sedate, regular, not wild, not flighty, as: an elderly STAID PERSON. Does this steadiness come only with age? What happens to all of the young LOUTS, LOOBIES, and LOBS?

LOUT comes from an Anglo-Saxon word meaning stooping, bent over. Stand up straight if you do not want to be a LOUT. LOOBY and LOB (*lŏb*) are both provincial English for bumpkin.

1061. *GORGONIZE*, gorgonize (*gŏr'-gŏn-īz*) *v.* To petrify, turn to stone.

To 27 per cent GORGONIZE means EAT RAVENOUSLY. To GORMANDIZE is to eat greedily, devour food voraciously.

A GORGON, from the Greek γοργός (*gorgos*), grim, terrible, fierce, was a female monster with a head covered with writhing serpents, a sight so horrible that anyone who saw a GORGON turned to stone. There were three GORGONS, sisters, of which MEDUSA is the best known.

To another 27 per cent to GORGONIZE means to DAZZLE. To DAZZLE is to overpower with brilliance, confuse with bright lights. To DAZZLE and to GORGONIZE are both to render incapable, DAZZLE by light, GORGONIZE by horror.

1062. *INSPISSATE*, inspissate (*ĭn-spĭs'-sāt*) *v.* To thicken a liquid by evaporation, condense, boil down.

INSPISSATE comes from the Latin *in-*, and *spissare*, to thicken, from *spissus*, dense, thick, compact, close.

THINNED-OUT, an exact opposite, is selected by 50 per cent compared with only 15 per cent who select THICKENED. IN-, at the beginning of most words, means not, as INCOMPLETE, not complete; INACCURATE, not accurate; and INTEMPERATE. Unless one knows this particular word, INSPISSATE should mean not thickened, not condensed, and so THINNED-OUT. But here, the initial IN- adds little. Originally this sort of IN- meant clearly in, as INBRED, INBORN; then came to intensify the meaning; but today is often of no value. SPISSATED and INSPISSATED both mean thick. Know this word, but use the Anglo-Saxon THICK or THICKENED.

1063. *BARTIZAN*, bartizan (*băhr'-tĭ-zăn*) *n.* A fortification, tower, small projecting turret often at a corner where two walls meet.

BARTIZAN does not appear in the Gentleman's Dictionary of the Military Arts of 1705 and seems to have originated with Sir Walter Scott's lines:

        ' . . . on battlement and bartizan
           Gleamed axe, spear, and partisan'.

Two popular misleads each marked by the same number of examinees as the correct answer are WALL and NOBLEMAN. BART is a contraction or abbreviation of BARONET, an inferior BARON.

WALL, the second mislead, and BARTIZAN are closely associated, for a BARTIZAN juts out from a WALL like a small fortified balcony.

1064. *GYRE*, gyre (*jīr*) *n*. A circle, ring, revolution, wheel.

To 8 per cent of high-vocabulary examinees GYRE means LEGGIN. An unusual verb to GYVE (*jīv*), to chain, manacle, shackle, fetter, may suggest LEGGIN, this last probably a misspelling in the vocabulary test of LEGGING, though LEGGIN is actually an obsolete form of LEGGING.

The noun GYRE, from the Latin *gyrus*, a circle, ring, circuit, comes in turn from the Greek γῦρος (*gyros*), a circle, ring. From the same Greek comes the verb to GYRATE, to turn round, whirl, rotate; the technical term GYROSCOPE; and the noun, a GYRATION, a revolution, wheeling, whirling, rotation.

1065. *MALEFACTION*, malefaction (*măl-ē-făk'-shŏn*) *n*. An evil deed, offense, crime, heinous wrong-doing, fault, violation, transgression, misdemeanor.

MALEFACTION, from the Latin *male*, ill, and *facere*, to do, is thought by 40 per cent to mean DISSATISFACTION, discontent, displeasure, annoyance, distaste. The verb to SATISFY, from the Latin *satis*, enough, and *facere*, to make, is to make amends, originally to a creditor.

A MALEFACTOR (*măl-ē-făk'-tor*) is the person, culprit, felon, convict, evil-doer. MALEFACTION is the act. BENEFACTION, a kindness, a good deed, is an exact opposite of MALEFACTION.

1066. *DECIMATE*, decimate (*děs'-ĭ-māt*) *v*. To reduce by one tenth, select by lot and put to death one tenth of a captured army.

The Anglo-Saxon word TITHE (*tīth*, with the TH pronounced as in THE) was one tenth of one's annual income paid as a tax, usually in support of the church. The Latin *decimus*, the source of DECIMAL, was also a tenth. From this comes the verb *decimare*, with the past participle *decimatus*, to select one tenth in payment. To DECIMATE originally meant to take a tenth part but has come to mean to destroy a large number.

Given a choice between REDUCE and RUIN as meanings of
DECIMATE 32 per cent select the first, and 62 per cent the second,
RUIN. By derivation DECIMATE means reduce by one tenth, and
the word should continue to mean REDUCE, perhaps by a large
number, but not RUIN.

1067. *MINION*, minion (*mĭn′-yŏn*) *n.* One who stoops to gain
favor, toady, toadeater, sycophant, fawning parasite.

To 28 per cent MINION means ESTATE, compared with 32 per
cent who select SERVILE-CREATURE. ESTATE, from the Latin *status*,
state, condition, the immediate source of the English word
STATE, may mean condition, rank, position, or land owned, and
so DOMINION. Despite the similarity of MINION and DOMINION,
a DOMINION is a territory under a single ruler, land subject to
control, domains, from the Latin *dominus*, lord.

MINION, with an entirely different background, comes from
the French *mignon*, darling, favorite, and still earlier from
German. From this beginning, MINION came to mean stooping
to gain favor, and so a servile intriguer.

1068. *SHIBBOLETH*, shibboleth (*shĭb′-bō-lĕth*) *n.* Watch-
word, password, countersign, parole by which to distinguish friend from foe.

This Hebrew word SHIBBOLETH, which actually means either
ear of corn or stream, was used by the judges of Israel to distinguish the fleeing Ephraimites, who could not pronounce SH,
from the Gileadites (*gĭl′-ē-ă-dīts*).

In the massacre of the French residents of Sicily, on Easter
Monday, 1282, the French were recognized because they could
not pronounce the Italian word *ciceri*.

Answers to the meaning of SHIBBOLETH divide between 40
per cent for PRETENDER and 32 per cent for CALL WORD; almost
everyone places SHIBBOLETH in its correct environment but does
not distinguish the test from the person tested.

1069. *SERENDIPITY*, serendipity (*sĕ-rĕn-dĭp′-ĭ-tĭ*) *n.* The accidental discovery and sagacious recognition of something
valuable while looking for something else, good fortune, chance
finding and understanding.

To 40 per cent SERENDIPITY means PEACEFULNESS. SERENITY (sĕ-rĕn'-ĭ-tĭ) is calmness, peace, tranquility, PEACEFULNESS.

Horace Walpole, a statesman, whose brilliant letters covered the years 1735 to 1796, first used the word SERENDIPITY in his letter of 1754, to Horace Mann, stationed in Florence as an envoy in the service of King George II. Here he refers to 'A silly fairy tale', published in Venice in 1557 by Michele Tramezzino, under the title: 'Peregrination of the Three Sons of the King of Serendip, translated from the Persian Language into Italian by M. Christoforo Armeno'.

The late Justice Benjamin N. Cardozo wrote: 'Like many of the finest things of life, like happiness and tranquility and fame, the gain that was most precious was not the thing sought, but one that came of itself in the search for something else'.

Almost every day everyone encounters an opportunity, a chance. Few have the wisdom, the sagacity, to grasp those which lead ahead in the right direction. SERENDIPITY is a combination of accident and sagacity.

1070. *HOMILY*, homily (hŏm'-ĭ-lĭ) n. A short sermon, familiar discourse made to the people, exposition of scripture, plain interpretation of a particular passage.
A HOMILY, from the Greek ὁμιλία (*homilia*), discourse, lecture, instructions, sermon, is expected to affect the heart and so differs from EXEGESIS, a critical explanation.

To 65 per cent a HOMILY is a SAYING, nearly three times as many as select SERMON. A SAYING, a maxim or adage, may also be something said or spoken; and in this sense a HOMILY may be a SAYING. But a HOMILY may also be a carefully written short sermon, as the HOMILIES of Clement I, about 95 A.D., one of the early bishops of Rome.

According to Ephraim Chambers: HOMILY originally signified a conference or conversation; but the word has since been applied to an exhortation, or sermon, delivered to the people. Discourses delivered in the church took these denominations to intimate that they were not harangues or matters of ostentation and flourish, like those of profane orators, but familiar and useful discourses as of a master to his disciples or a father to his children.

1071. *ANALOGUE*, analogue (ăn'-ă-lŏg) *n.* Something hav-
    ing agreement with something else, which corresponds
in certain aspects.

ANALOGUE is thought by 30 per cent to mean SOLUTION. This
may be the word ANALYSIS, directly from the Greek ἀνάλυσις
(*analysis*), a separation into parts, so important a step toward
SOLUTION that the Greek word is sometimes defined as the
SOLUTION of a problem. By another 20 per cent ANALOGUE is
thought to mean OPPOSITE. An ANTONYM is an OPPOSITE, frequently the OPPOSITE of a SYNONYM.

ANALOGUE comes through the Latin *analogus*, from the Greek
ἀνάλογος (*analogos*), conformable, proportional, a combination
of the prefix ANA-, from the Greek ἀνά (*ana*), which sometimes means throughout, according to, and LOGUE, from the
Greek λόγος (*logos*), ratio, proportion.

The familiar adjective ANALOGOUS means similar, like, corresponding, resembling. For the noun ANALOGUE the vocabulary
test gives CORRESPONDENCE, which is not really correct. An
ANALOGY is a likeness between two things, their agreement, resemblance, correspondence, relationship. An ANALOGUE is the
object which corresponds, not the relationship; it is one of the
two things which are ANALOGOUS.

In contrasting a HOMOLOGUE with an ANALOGUE the Century
Dictionary cites the wing of a bird and the wing of a butterfly
which differ in structure and history, and are not therefore
HOMOLOGUES; but, since they are both used for flight, they are
ANALOGUES.

1072. *ANTIPHONAL*, antiphonal (ăn-tĭf'-ō-năl) *adj.* Respon-
    sive singing, sung alternately with the choir divided into
two parts, each singing alternate verses of a psalm or anthem,
opposed to HOMOPHONY, from the Greek ὁμόφωνος (*homo-
phonos*), unison in music.

From Ephraim Chambers comes one of the clearest descriptions:
'ANTIPHONALLY, in respect of church music, imports as much as
alternately or anthem-wise. The Greeks have a method of
singing ANTIPHONALLY where-in two persons sing together, and
then are silent, and succeeded by two others, who sing awhile
and then are silent and so on.'

ANTIPHONY is the answer made by one choir to another, when the psalm or anthem is sung between the two. ANTIPHONY sometimes denotes a species of PSALMODY, wherein the congregation, being divided into two parts, repeats the psalms, verse for verse alternately. In this sense ANTIPHONY stands contradistinguished from SYMPHONY, derived from the Greek σύν (syn-), together, and φωνή (phone), sound, tone, voice, where the whole congregation sings together.

ANTIPHONY differs from RESPONSORIUM, because in this latter the verse is spoken by only one person, whereas in the former, the verses are sung by the two choirs alternately.

The original ANTIPHONAL singing in the western churches is referred to the time of Saint Ambrose, about the year 374. That father is said to have first introduced it into the church of Milan in imitation of that custom of the Eastern church, where it appears to have been of greater antiquity, probably introduced at Antioch, between the year of Christ 347 and 356.

To 42 per cent ANTIPHONAL means UNACCOMPANIED. Both UNACCOMPANIED and ANTIPHONAL refer primarily to the voice. UNACCOMPANIED means without instrumental support. ANTIPHONAL means responsive, one choir answering another.

1073. *DISSEMBLING*, dissembling (*dĭs-sĕm'-blĭng*, Phyfe says: not *dĭz-zĕm'-blĭng*) *adj.* Disguising, covering, hiding, pretending, concealing, cloaking, giving a false impression, masking under a deceptive manner.

To 47 per cent DISSEMBLING means TAKING APART, obviously a confusion of DISSEMBLING with DISASSEMBLING, the first of the four steps in learning, a confusion of words similar in sound, but different in meaning.

To ASSEMBLE is to bring together, put together, specifically fit together the parts of a machine. To DISASSEMBLE is to TAKE APART.

To RESEMBLE (*rē-zĕm'-bl*), to look like something else, comes from the Latin *simulare*, to be like, from *similis*, like, the source of the English SIMILAR, alike in certain ways. From the same source comes DISSEMBLE. Although the Latin privative *dis-* and *similis*, like, ought to mean not like, DISSEMBLING has come to mean pretending to be not like, feigning to be different.

1074. *ASSONANCE*, assonance (*ăs'-sō-năns*) *n.* Correspond-
     ence, harmony, agreement, pun, paronomasia (*pă-rō-nō-
mă'-zē-ah*), resemblance of sounds.
ASSONANCE, from the Latin *assonare*, to sound, correspond to,
comes from *ad*, to, and *sonare*, to sound. From the same source
comes DISSONANCE, want of harmony, disagreement, clashing.
ASSONANCE, in general, is no more than a resemblance of sounds.
Technically it consists of the same vowel sounds with different
consonants, as: PENITENT and RETICENCE.
     CONSONANCE and ASSONANCE both mean agreement. CONSO-
NANCE suggests a pleasant, agreeable harmony; while ASSONANCE
is more apt to be unpleasant. Thus from E. Chambers: 'Asso-
NANCE, in rhetoric and poetry, is a term used where the words of
a phrase or a verse have the same sound or termination and yet
make no proper rhyme, sometimes disagreeable to the ear,
usually vicious in English'. Of the corresponding adjective
ASSONANT, Skeat says: 'Such words as FAMOUS, SAILOR, NEIGHBOR,
etc. may be used as ASSONANT.'

1075. *IRREFRAGABLE*, irrefragable (*ĭr-rĕf'-rā-gă-bl*) *adj.*
     Undeniable, irrefutable (*ĭr-rĕf'-ū-tă-bl*), incontrovertible,
unanswerable, indisputable, unquestionable, indubitable, incapable of being broken down.
To REFRACT, from *fractus*, the past participle of *frangere*, to
break, is to bend, as rays of light going from one substance to
another. This leads 22 per cent to select UNBENDABLE as the
meaning of IRREFRAGABLE. FRAGILE is easily broken, and the
Latin *refringere* is to break into pieces, and these lead another
22 per cent to mark STRONG as the meaning of IRREFRAGABLE.
     REFRAGABLE (*rĕf'-ră-gă-bl*), from the Latin *refragari*, to op-
pose, resist, gainsay, is capable of being resisted. IRREFRAGABLE,
starting with the Latin *in-*, not, which becomes IR- before an R,
is not to be broken down, as: 'IRREFRAGABLE evidence', or 'An
IRREFRAGABLE argument'.

1076. *PAVONIAN*, pavonian (*pă-vō'-nĭ-ăn*) *adj.* Like a pea-
     cock, vain and gaudy, showing off.
The modern Spanish word for peacock is *pavoreal* (*pă-vō-rā-
ahl'*) and in biology the Latin PAVO is the genus to which the pea-

cock belongs. In something of the same way SIMIAN (*sĭm'-ĭ-ăn*), from the genus SIMIA, means ape-like; and EQUESTRIAN, horse-like, pertaning to horses. BOVINE (*bō'-vĭn* or *bō'-vĭn*), from the Latin *bos, bovis,* ox, is made in the same way from the genus Bos, to which the ox belongs; and BOVINE is a popular mislead for PAVONIAN, perhaps because BOVINE is used figuratively for slow, heavy, stolid, inert, dull, an opposite of PAVONIAN, vain, colorful.

The ending -INE, added to the Latin genus, the biological group to which an animal belongs, makes an adjective used in literature, as VULPINE (*vŭl'-pīn*), pertaining to a fox, and so cunning, crafty; LUPINE, wolf-like, wolfish, ravenous; CANINE, dog-like; and EQUINE, horse-like. PAVONINE (*păv'-ŏ-nīn*) sometimes occurs instead of the more elegant PAVONIAN.

1077. *CANARD,* canard (*kăn-ard'*) *n.* An absurd statement, fabricated story, hoax, broadside.

To 40 per cent CANARD means JOKE, and to another 35 per cent HOAX, intended as the correct answer. JOKE, HOAX, and CANARD overlap. A JOKE, through Dutch, Danish, and German, from the Latin *jocus,* is a jest, for amusement, often a word or picture. A HOAX is a practical JOKE, something done, often involving action. A CANARD has more the suggestion of lying, cheating. The French *canard* is a duck and occurs in the phrase: Vendeur de canard a moitie, one who half sells a duck, cheater, and this may lead to the English CANARD, a HOAX, JOKE, fabricated story but with a gain in mind.

1078. *AMBUSH,* ambush (*ăm'-bŏosh*) *n.* Lying in wait, for the purpose of attacking.

To 68 per cent AMBUSH means ATTACK. The ATTACK is the assault, falling upon the enemy, the beginning of hostilities. The AMBUSH is not the ATTACK, but lying concealed in order to ATTACK by surprise.

AMBUSH comes through the French, from the Latin *in,* in, and *boscus,* wood, bush. AMBUSH is the wood where soldiers hide themselves, waiting privily to surprise, catch, or intrap the enemy; or sometimes the body of men ready to rush out upon or inclose an enemy unawares.

1079. *PREENED*, preened (*prēnd*) *v.* Arrayed, trimmed, dressed, put in order, as a bird fixes its plumage with its beak.

PREENED goes directly back to Anglo-Saxon, a variant of PRUNE, to trim, as to PRUNE a tree.

E. Chambers says of PREENING: The action of birds, cleaning, composing, and dressing their feathers, to enable them to glide more easily through the air.

1080. *BESOM*, besom (*bē'-zŏm*) *n.* A broom, bunch of twigs tied together and used in sweeping.

Both SHOVEL and PITCH-FORK are selected more often, as meanings of BESOM, than the correct answer BROOM. All three: SHOVEL, PITCH-FORK, and BROOM have long handles.

Like many household words, BROOM, BESOM, and SWEEP are Anglo-Saxon. A BROOM is named for the BROOM plant, with long slender stems of which BROOMS are made. A BRUSH is smaller. A BESOM is really a bunch of TWIGS or small sticks tied together and used as a BROOM. One still occasionally sees BESOMS used in sweeping streets.

1081. *COMMINATION*, commination (*kŏm-mĭ-nā'-shŏn*) *n.* A threat of punishment, denunciation, anathema, threat of vengeance.

To 30 per cent COMMINATION means BLENDING. To COMMINGLE, starting with the same six letters, is to mix together, and so BLEND.

An ALLIANCE, the second most frequently marked mislead, chosen by 25 per cent, is a union by agreement, a COMBINATION, differing from COMMINATION by only a single letter. PRAISE, an opposite of the correct answer, is third most popular; while DENUNCIATION, the correct answer, has been chosen by no one.

COMMINATION comes from the Latin *com*, with, and *minari*, to threaten, and also to jut out, the source of MENACE, a threat; MINATORY, menacing, threatening; as well as EMINENT, jutting out in a figurative sense.

The COM- at the beginning of COMMINATION adds little to the meaning of the word, but is the reason for the misunderstandings. Use the simple word MENACE.

1082. *ARGILLACEOUS*, argillaceous (*ahr-jĭl-lā'-shŭs*) adj.
Resembling clay, applied to earth which contains a large
amount of clayey matter.
Bricks are made of CLAY. In the tiny hamlets of Mexico near a
CLAY PIT, a small child gathers an armful of CLAY which looks
like soft gray mud, exactly enough for six bricks, rarely missing by a spoonful, squeezes the CLAY into six molds, smoothes
the top, removes the mold and leaves the bricks to dry in the
sun. In the United States machines duplicate the same process.
Pottery plates, jugs, and other table utensils are made of the
same clay. Sculptors use it. ARGILLACEOUS is the adjective and
means pertaining to the kind of white clay used by potters,
brick makers, and sculptors.
ARGILLACEOUS comes from the Latin *argillaceus*, from *argilla*,
white clay. The English word ARGIL (*ăhr'-jĭl*), potter's clay,
comes from the Greek ἀργός (*argos*), white; and this leads 20
per cent to select SILVER as the meaning of ARGILLACEOUS. The
French ARGENT means SILVER or something resembling SILVER and
comes from the Greek ἄργυρος (*argyros*), and this in turn
from ἀργός (*argos*), white, the source of ARGIL, white clay.

1083. *BARBARA*, barbara (*băhr'-băh-răh*) n. The simplest
     kind of syllogism.
A SYLLOGISM is a kind of formal logical reasoning in which a
conclusion follows from two premises. There was a time when
SYLLOGISMS grew so elaborate that according to Samuel Butler,
writing in Hudibras:
> 'He'd prove a buzzard is no fowl,
> And that a lord may be an owl;
> He'd run in debt by disputation,
> And pay with ratiocination.
> All this by syllogism, true
> In mood and figure he would do'.

A BARBARA is a SYLLOGISM all three of whose statements are
affirmative, as the much quoted: 'All men are mortal. He is a
man. Therefore he is mortal.' The word BARBARA was invented
in about 1250, at a time when disputations were in fashion, when
great universities were being founded at Bologna and Padua,
and this sort of formal thinking was in vogue.

The frequent misconception is FORTIFICATION, selected by
30 per cent. A BARBICAN is an outwork projecting beyond the
walls of a fortress or castle, where troops can be stationed to
attack the flank of those attacking.

1084. *ALARY*, alary (*ā'-lah-rĭ*) *adj.* Wing-shaped, winged,
    with wings, relating to wings.
The word WING goes back to Icelandic, the Anglo-Saxon being
fether, and the Latin *penna*. ALA (*ā'-lah*), with the plural ALAE
(*ā'-lē*), is the Latin *ala*, wing, and appears in the sciences as a
noun to mean wing, or something like a wing in shape and
position. From the Latin *ala* comes the English AISLE, used in
architecture for the passage each side of the nave in a church,
and parallel to it. From *ala* come also ALATE, winged, furnished
with wings; ALAR (*ā'-lahr*), which also means pertaining to
wings; and ALARY, from the Latin *alarius*, from *ala*, wing.
    The misleads scatter with no concentration on any one mis-
understanding.

1085. *DOGGEREL*, doggerel (*dŏg'-ger-ĕl*) *n.* Trivial verse,
    burlesque poetry, loose, irregular measure with little
sense, comic rhythm.
Of those tested 20 per cent say DOGGEREL means FIXED-BELIEF.
A DOGMA is a FIXED-BELIEF, settled opinion, principle held as
being established, authoritative doctrine, tenet, precept.
    Of DOGGEREL Bailey says: rhyme, pitiful poetry, paultry
verses.

               Lucy Locket
               Lost her pocket
               Kitty Fisher found it.
               Nothing in it
               Nothing in it
               But the binding round it.

    Oxford says of DOGGEREL: Comic or burlesque verse of irregu-
lar rhythm; trivial or undignified verse.
    LIMERICK, a word which came into existence just before
1900, named for LIMERICK in Ireland, was invented for the
rimes of Edward Lear, who published his Book of Nonsense
in 1846. Ogden Nash designates his own creations as DOGGEREL:

Why then do you fritter away your time
on this DOGGERAL?
If you have a sore throat you can cure it
by using a good goggeral;
while those of Edward Lear are LIMERICKS.

1086. *LEGERDEMAIN*, legerdemain (*lĕj-er-dĕ-mān'*)   *n.*
Sleight of hand, magic, prestidigitation (*prĕs-tĭ-dĭ-jĭ-tā'-shŏn*), trick depending on dexterity, deceptive adroitness, the employment of pure manual dexterity without mechanical apparatus.

To 15 per cent LEGERDEMAIN means BOOKKEEPING. A LEDGER (*lĕj'-er*), a word of confused and doubtful background, often in the past spelt with no D, is an important book in accounting, BOOKKEEPING, showing at the left money spent, and at the right money received. Of LEGER-BOOK, Bailey says: 'Belonging to notaries and merchants'.

LEGERDEMAIN comes from the French *léger de main*, light of hand. JUGGLING, sometimes included under LEGERDEMAIN, is ordinarily pure skill, with no trick; whereas LEGERDEMAIN adds to skill the impression of a trick. LIGHT-FINGERED, in a complimentary sense, delicate, dexterous, may also designate the pick pocket, petty thief, shop lifter. Although card-sharpers employ tricks of LEGERDEMAIN, the word itself has retained its pleasant meaning of amazing, professional, tricks depending on dexterity developed by continuous practice.

1087. *BARGHEST*, barghest (*băhr'-gĕst*) *n.* Goblin, specter in
the form of a dog, bear, or other animal; also a gnome, kobold, demon, elf, sprite, hobgoblin, Robin Goodfellow; fairy, fay, sylph, jinn, genie, vampire, poltergeist.

A BARGE (*băhrj*) may be an elegantly decorated boat, often flat-bottomed, now towed by a tug, but in ancient times propelled by oars; and BARGE may suggest ROMAN-BOAT, selected by 30 per cent as the meaning of BARGHEST, considerably more than the correct answer GOBLIN.

A WERWOLF, directly from Anglo-Saxon and starting with *wer*, man, is a man in the form of a wolf, usually an evil spirit. A LYCANTHROPE (*lī-kăn'-thrōp*) is also a man-wolf, but from the Greek λύκος (lycos), wolf, and ἄνθρωπος (anthropos), man. BARGHEST, a word from Scotland and the north of England, is a man in the form of a dog.

1088. *BARROW*, barrow (băr'-rō) n. Originally a little hill, mound of earth; now technically a tumulus, ancient heap of stones piled over a grave.

To 41 per cent BARROW means WOODEN CASK, a confusion of the difficult BARROW with the easier BARREL, words similar in sound, the first step in learning. A BARREL (băr'-rĕl), which goes back through Middle English to Old French, with similar words in many languages, is a CASK made of wooden staves, round, but flat at both ends.

BARROW, which goes directly back to an Anglo-Saxon word for mountain, and BARROW in WHEELBARROW, also Anglo-Saxon, although spelt the same, are different words. The last was originally a flat form carried between poles by two men. BARROW meaning a hill denotes a mound of earth raised by art; according to Chambers supposed to have been a Roman tumulus or sepulcher. Today some are believed to date back to the Stone Age, before metal was known.

1089. *FILLIP*, fillip (fĭl'-lĭp) n. Quick jerk, jerk of the finger against the ball of the thumb, smart tap, sudden stroke, anything which tends to arouse or excite.

To 31 per cent, nearly a third, FILLIP means DISTURBANCE. A DISTURBANCE is a disorder, agitation, commotion, interruption of peace, violent change. The word comes from the Latin *dis-*, apart, and *turbare*, to throw into disorder, the source of TURBU- LENT.

FLAP, FLOP, FLIP, and FILLIP are intimately associated, may all be variations of the same word. A FLAPPING may be annoying, DISTURBING; but a FILLIP is a jerk of the thumb and finger as in tossing a coin with one's thumb or nail.

1090. *BACCIVOROUS*, baccivorous (băk-sĭv'-ōr-ŭs) adj. Eat- ing berries, berry-eating, living on berries.

The rarely occurring word BACCIVOROUS comes from the Latin *bacca*, berry, and *vorare*, to eat, swallow, devour.

GLUTTONOUS, selected by 25 per cent, is almost as popular as the correct answer, due to VORACIOUS (*vō-rā'-shŭs*), greedy in eating, ravenous, devouring much, from the same *vorare*, to eat, plus the ending *-acious*, which intensifies every word to which it is attached.

INSECTIVOROUS means living on insects; CARNIVOROUS, from *caro*, flesh, living on meat, meat-eating; and HERBIVOROUS, literally eating herbs, is living on grass and vegetation in general. BACCALAUREATE is a combination of *bacca*, berry, and *laurus*, laurel; and if one knows the Latin *bacca*, berry, BACCIVOROUS is obviously berry-eating, living on berries.

1091. *APOCRYPHAL*, apocryphal (*ă-pŏk'-rĭ-făl*) *adj.* Spurious, doubtful, fictitious, false, pseudo, mythical, fabulous, supposititious, not genuine, uncanonical; or according to Ephraim Chambers: 'Something dubious that comes from an uncertain author on which much credit cannot be reposed'.

To 41 per cent APOCRYPHAL means REVELATORY. The book of REVELATIONS of St. John the Divine, the last book of the New Testament, is also called the APOCALYPSE, easily confused with APOCRYPHAL, the first step in learning a difficult word.

APOCALYPSE comes from the Greek ἀπό (*apo*), from, off, away, and καλύπτειν (*calyptein*), to cover; so that the APOCALYPSE is the uncovering, disclosure, REVELATION.

APOCRYPHAL comes from the Greek ἀπό (*apo*), from, off, away, and ἀπόκρυφος (*apocryphos*), hidden, from the verb κρύπτειν (*cryptein*), to hide, conceal, the source of CRYPT and CRYPTIC. APOCRYPHAL means hidden, unknown, doubtful, and applies specifically to those books included in the Septuagint and Vulgate versions of the Old Testament which were not originally written in Hebrew and not counted genuine by the Jews, and which, at the Reformation, were excluded from the Sacred Canon by the Protestant party as having no well-founded claim to inspired authorship.

1092. *PRODIGAL*, prodigal (*prŏd'-ĭ-găl*) *adj.* Extravagant, spending money, lavish, profuse, riotous, wasteful, squandering, consuming unnecessarily; a characteristic of the SPENDTHRIFT.

PRODIGAL, from the Latin *prodigus*, wasteful, comes from *prodigere*, to squander, a combination of *pro*, forward, and *agere*, to drive.

WANDERING, the popular misinterpretation, results from the parable of the PRODIGAL SON, Luke xv, 11-32.

According to Roman law if a man by notorious PRODIGALITY was in danger of wasting his estate he was committed to the care of curators or tutors.

1093. *DUENNA*, duenna (*dū-ĕn'-năh*) *n*. The chief lady in waiting on the Queen of Spain.

DUENNA, from the Latin *domina*, mistress, the feminine form of *dominus*, master, has come to mean any elderly woman in charge of a younger one; governess, chaperone.

To 25 per cent DUENNA means ENEMY; and to another 20 per cent BEAU, with only one person selecting CHAPERONE.

1094. *CASQUE*, casque (*kăsk*) *n*. A helmet of any kind, skull, headpiece, armor to cover the head.

To 40 per cent CASQUE means BARREL. This is spelling, not vocabulary. CASK, spelt with K, is a general term for a PIPE, HOGSHEAD, BUTT, or BARREL; and both CASK, barrel, and CASQUE, helmet, come directly from the French *casque*, which may mean either BARREL or HELMET.

To another 38 per cent CASQUE means ARMOR, spelt ARMOUR by the English. ARMOR protects the whole body. The CASQUE or helmet is that part of the ARMOR which protects the head.

Edward Phillips, nephew of John Milton, in his dictionary of hard words of 1696, says merely: 'CASQUE, a helmet'.

1095. *SUSURRANT*, susurrant (*sū-sŭr'-rănt*) *adj*. Murmuring, sighing, soughing (*sōw'-ĭng* or *sŭf'-ĭng*), whispering, rustling, humming, an imitative word.

SUSURRANT is thought by 20 per cent to mean REFRESHING. The verb to SUSTAIN and the noun SUSTENANCE both start with the same first letters as the rare SUSURRANT, and may suggest REFRESHING.

SUSURRANT comes from the Latin *susurrans*, *susurrantis*, the present participle of *susurrare*, to murmur, whisper, hum, buzz.

1096. *QUISLING*, quisling (*kwĭz'-lĭng*) *n.* A person who un-
      dermines his own country from within, traitor.
QUISLING is an eponym from the name Vidkun Quisling, a pro-
Nazi leader in Norway, who lived from 1887 to 1945, a fifth
columnist.

Misleads scatter, with 20 per cent each for the two most
popular.

1097. *LEGERITY*, legerity (*lĕ-jĕr'-ĭ-tĭ*) *n.* Agility, nimbleness,
      lightness.
LEGERITY comes from the French *leger*, light, perhaps originally
from the Latin *levis*, light, the source of LEVITY (*lĕv'-ĭ-tĭ*), lightness of spirit, but used now to mean too light in the handling
of serious affairs.

To 30 per cent, more than select the correct answer AGILITY,
LEGERITY means LEGAL DOCUMENTS. LEGALITY is right, lawful-
ness, conformity to law.

The French *leger* appears in LEGERDEMAIN (*lĕj-ĕr-dē-mān'*),
literally, lightness of hand, a word used for tricks which depend
on motions of the hand. The unusual word LEGERITY is lightness,
nimbleness, which does not have trickery, deception, as its goal.

1098. *UKASE*, ukase (*ū-kās'*) *n.* A legislative order from the
      Russian government.
UKASE, with similar words in French, Spanish, Portuguese, and
German, goes directly back to Russian.

To 30 per cent of high-vocabulary adults, UKASE means DIS-
COMFORT.

1099. *EMBRANGLE*, embrangle (*ĕm-brăng'-gl*) *v.* To en-
      tangle, snarl, mix, ensnare, intermix, enmesh, disorder,
mix confusedly.
To 20 per cent EMBRANGLE means ENTICE, probably because of
the word ENVEIGLE (*ĕn-vē'-gl*), now ordinarily written IN-
VEIGLE, meaning to lead astray by blinding, mislead by deception, lure, cajole, ENTICE into a violation of duty.

To BRANGLE, probably a variation of WRANGLE, is to squabble,
dispute, contend noisily. To EMBRANGLE, though a combination
of EM- and BRANGLE, has no sense of squabble, but means en-

tangle, as: 'Inextricably EMBRANGLED'. EMBRANGLEMENT is the noun and means ENTANGLEMENT.

1100. *ERUBESCENT*, erubescent (*er-ū-běs'-sěnt*) *adj.* Growing red, blushing.
To 30 per cent ERUBESCENT means INDIFFERENT, an opposite, certainly in suggestion.
RED is Anglo-Saxon. From the same source come RUST and RUDDY. RUBY is Latin from *rubere*, to be red; and from this come RUBICUND, RUFOUS, and RUSSET. RUBESCENT, from *rubescere*, means growing red, becoming red, and so blushing.

1101. *PUBERULENT*, puberulent (*pū-běr'-ū-lěnt*) *adj.*
Downy, woolly, finely pubescent, covered with fine, short, soft hair.
PUBERULENT comes from the Latin *pubes*, grown up, of mature age, and also downy.
To 25 per cent PUBERULENT means ROUGH, an opposite, certainly in suggestion.
Other words for hairy are: VILLOUS; HIRSUTE (*běr-sūt'*), shaggy, rough, bristling; STRIGOSE; LANATE (*lā'-nāt*), from the Greek λῆνος (*lanos*), wool; and the noun LANUGO (*lā-nū'-gō*), a coat of delicate, soft hairs.

1102. *VITREOUS*, vitreous (*vĭt'-rē-ŭs*) *adj.* Resembling glass, consisting of glass, glassy, crystalline, hyaline, hyaloid.
VITREOUS comes from the Latin *vitreus*, pertaining to glass, from *vitrum*, glass, from *videre*, to see. Unlike the Latin *vesper*, evening, which leads to almost no other English words, the verb *videre* forms the base of several dozen, some easily recognized, as: EVIDENT; others influenced by the past participle *visus*, as: VISION and VISIBLE; and others, as VITREOUS and VITRIOL, still more remote. VITRIOL, another name for sulphuric acid, was so called because of the glassy appearance of some of its compounds. VITREOUS means like glass, resembling glass.
The popular misleads are METALLIC and VEGETABLE, each selected by 16 per cent, the first almost correct, for VITREOUS does not suggest transparent like glass, but more often like glass in appearance and structure, hard and glassy.

1103. *PEREGRINE*, peregrine (*pĕr'-ĕ-grĭn*) *adj*. Foreign, strange, alien, not native.

PEREGRINE, from the Latin *peregrinus*, a foreigner, stranger, comes from *pereger*, to pass through a land, from *per*, through, and *ager*, lane, field. The word PILGRIM is an offshoot, the original PEREGRIN becoming *pelegrin*, then *pelegrim*, and so PILGRIM, not in fact so clearly as this, but by devious steps. PILGRIMAGES, journeys made by PILGRIMS, under difficulties, to distant sacred places, play parts in many religions. Benares, on the Ganges, is the goal of PILGRIMS in India; and Mecca the goal of Mohammedans.

In the United States, the word PILGRIM applies to those who founded Plymouth, Massachusetts, in 1620, where it is said that the first child born was named PEREGRINE.

The original word PEREGRINE is almost out of existence, and is called SEACOAST as often as FOREIGN.

1104. *CERIFEROUS*, ceriferous (*sē-rĭf'-ĕ-rŭs*) *adj*. Producing wax.

CERIFEROUS comes from the Latin *cera*, wax, which occurs unchanged in Spanish and Italian, and *ferre*, to bear, carry. The ending -FEROUS, meaning bearing, producing, appears in CONIFEROUS, bearing cones; GRANIFEROUS, producing grains; GRAMINIFEROUS, producing grass; and BACCIFEROUS, producing berries.

1105. *BATTUTA*, battuta (*băt-too'-tăh*) *n*. A beat used in keeping time.

Grove's Dictionary of Music defines the phrases: A BATTUTA and A TEMPO, from the Latin *ad*, to, and *tempus*, time, as musical directives, used in recitatives, to return to the original and strict time after acceleration or retardation.

From the same Italian come BATTER, to beat, strike with repeated blows, pound violently; and the unusual BATTUE (*băt-tū'*), a method of hunting where beaters drive game from cover for huntsmen to shoot at ease. From this, BATTUE has come to mean indiscriminate slaughter.

The seldom seen BATTUTA, from the Italian *battere*, to beat, is a musical term, so that NOTES, selected by 30 per cent, and DISCORD, by another 30 per cent, are in the same general area.

1106. *TURBARY*, turbary (*tĕr'-bă-rĭ*) *n.* The right of digging
     turf on another man's land, also a peat moor.
To 40 per cent of high-vocabulary adults TURBARY means HEAD-
DRESS. A TURBAN, with similar words in German, Swedish,
Danish, Turkish, and Arabic, comes from Persian and Hindu
and is a Moslem HEAD-DRESS.
    The word TURF goes back to Anglo-Saxon; while TURBARY
comes from the Latin *turba*, turf.

1107. *FACTOTUM*, factotum (*făk-tō'-tum*) *n.* Handy one
     who does everything, anyone hired to do all kinds of
chores, one who fags; Bailey says: 'One who manages all affairs
in a family'.
The word FACTOTUM, from the Latin *facere*, to do, make, as in
FACTORY, a place where things are made, and *totum*, all, the
whole, means one who does everything, a man of all sorts of
work.
    To 22 per cent FACTOTUM means SPECIALIST. The adjective
SPECIAL from the Latin *species*, a kind, sort, means peculiar, individual, distinct from other kinds, not general; and a SPECIALIST
is one who devotes himself to a particular branch of a subject,
an exact opposite of FACTOTUM.

1108. *ALGETIC*, algetic (*ăl-gĕt'-ĭk*) *adj.* Producing pain, pain-
     ful, inflicting suffering; also related to pain.
Compared with 24 per cent who mark the correct PAINFUL,
54 per cent prefer SWAMPY, suggested by ALGAE (*ăl'-jē*), the
plural of ALGA, the Latin word for seaweed. Under ALGAE the
Century Dictionary discusses a dozen related words, while
giving no more than a two-line definition of ALGETIC. Thus an
ALGIST is an authority on ALGAE, and the unusual adjective ALGAL
(*ăl'-găhl*) means pertaining to the ALGAE. ALGETIC looks like the
adjective for ALGAE, but instead comes from the Greek ἀλγεῖν
(*algein*), to have pain.

1109. *FACETIAE*, facetiae (*fă-sē'-shĭ-ē*) *n.* Witty sayings, hu-
     morous writings, witticisms.
FACETIAE, the plural of the Latin *facetia*, jest, wit, witticism,
comes from the adjective *facetus*, witty.

To 15 per cent FACETIAE means FABRICATIONS, from the Latin *fabricatio, fabricationis,* a making, building, construction, from *fabricari,* to make. A FABRICATION may be anything made, built, constructed, or may be an invention of the imagination, fiction, figment, fable, false representation of the truth.

JOLLY, JOVIAL, MIRTHFUL, MERRY, all suggest a continuous flow of contagious good humor. FACETIOUS implies witty, clever, often with no real mirth or merriment. FACETIAE are the kind of remarks, clever sayings, witty writings, produced by the FACETIOUS person.

1110. *EPERGNE,* epergne (*ā-pārn'*) *n.* Centerpiece, ornament for the center of a dining table, containing several small dishes for fruit, candy, nuts; sometimes merely decorative.

To 29 per cent EPERGNE means SLEEVE ORNAMENT, compared with only 19 per cent who choose CENTERPIECE. An EPAULET (*ĕp'-aw-lĕt*), also spelt EPAULETTE, is a SHOULDER PIECE showing military rank, called sometimes a SHOULDER-KNOT.

EPERGNE is the French word *épargne,* which has, however, an entirely different meaning, thrift, economy. The French word for EPERGNE is *surtout* (*sūr-tŏo'*).

1111. *ACOLYTE,* acolyte (*ăk'-ō-līt*) *n.* An attendant, assistant, helper, follower; in the Roman Catholic church, an altar boy, strictly one formally ordained.

To 37 per cent ACOLYTE means NOVICE, the third step in learning, a confusion of words close in meaning but which, for accuracy, should be distinguished. A NOVICE, from the Latin *novus,* new, is a beginner, inexperienced person, new to the circumstances, one who has newly entered a religious order.

ACOLYTE comes from the Greek ἀκόλουθος (*acoloythos*), a follower, attendant. In the Roman Catholic church the ACOLYTE is immediately below the sub-deacon, an inferior church servant, technically the fourth and highest of the minor orders, directly under a deacon, and so not a NOVICE. The duties of an ACOLYTE are to light the candles and carry the bread and wine for the Eucharist. In one instance seven ACOLYTES walked before the Pope to the altar. Today the word ACOLYTE is used loosely for an attendant, assistant.

1112. *GRIFFIN*, griffin (*grĭf′-fĭn*) *n.* An imaginary animal,
with the head and wings of an eagle, and body of a lion.
The word goes back through Middle English, with similar
words in Spanish, French, and Italian, perhaps originally to
Greek. The GRIFFIN, which appears on ancient coins, was supposed to watch over gold mines and hidden treasure.

The SPHINX, also, had the body of a lion, but a human head,
in Greek mythology usually a woman's head.

The important mislead, underlined by 19 per cent, is BUFFALO.
The correct word is BISON (*bī′-sŏn*) for the heavy wild ox which
ranged over the United States in great herds, but is now almost
extinct.

1113. *PAWKY*, pawky (*paw′-kĭ*) *adj.* Humorously sly, arch,
cunning, smart.
A POKE is a lazy person, dawdler, familiar in the phrase SLOW-
POKE. POKY (*pō′-kĭ*) means slow, dull, stupid, which leads 50
per cent to select LAZY as the meaning of PAWKY. The difference
in pronunciation is much the same as that between WALK and
WOKE, or between CAUGHT and COAT. PAWKY is a little-known
Scotch word. A PAWK is a wile, good-humored pleasant trick,
stratagem, artifice, manœuver; and PAWKY means subtle, crafty,
cunning, sly, artful.

Words of this kind, such as ARTFUL, SLY, CLEVER, SMART, as
they became more common, gain an unpleasant suggestion of
too clever, too cunning; but PAWKY, perhaps because it is
Scotch, perhaps because it is so little used, has retained its feeling of good-humored cleverness.

1114. *BARRATOR*, barrator (*băr′-ră-tŏr*) *n.* A briber, simonist, one who either sells or buys a public office, or sometimes more generally any dishonest person in a position of
authority.
To a large majority BARRATOR means ATTORNEY. A BARRISTER is
a counselor or advocate allowed to plead at the bar, from BAR
plus the ending -STER, added to indicate an occupation, as GAME-
STER, SONGSTER, TEAMSTER. This ending goes directly back to
Anglo-Saxon and was used originally of women, as in SPINSTER,
one who spins.

ATTORNEY, used loosely for LAWYER, is a combination of the Latin *ad*, to, and TURN. An ATTORNEY is literally one who acts in the place of another, one to whom authority has been turned over.

The word BARRATOR, with its counterparts BARRAT, fraud, deception, and BARRATRY, is perhaps related to the English BARTER, to sell, and goes back to many languages. BARRATRY is the selling or buying of a state office. A BARRATOR may be a judge who takes a bribe, or anyone who buys or sells dishonestly, or the master of a ship who commits any fraudulent act in his management; and more recently a lawyer who stirs up others to litigation.

A SIMONIST and a BARRATOR both sell fraudulently. SIMONY (*sĭm'-ō-nē*) is specifically trafficking in sacred things, buying and selling church offices, ecclesiastical preferment. The word comes from Simon Magus who wished to buy the gift of the Holy Ghost. BARRATRY is selling public office.

1115. *FAGGING*, fagging (*făg'-gĭng*) v. Toiling, performing menial services, working until faint with weariness, laboring to exhaustion.

The noun, a FAG, is a laborious drudge; while the verb to FAG is to labor hard, work till tired. Completely FAGGED OUT means tired, exhausted.

The FAG-END, the end of a strip of cloth fastened to the loom in weaving and often imperfect, is different though perhaps from the same remote origin as the verb to FAG, to droop from weariness, fail, grow feeble.

To 40 per cent FAGGING means LOAFING. To LAG is to move slowly, fall behind, and so in a way to LOAF, to idle away the time, dawdle, lounge about, dally, an exact antonym of FAG, to work until exhausted, a confusion of opposites, the last stage of learning.

1116. *APOSTASY*, apostasy (*ă-pŏs'-tă-sĭ*) n. The abandonment of a belief, desertion, renunciation, forsaking, departure from principles.

To 24 per cent APOSTASY means CONVERSION, a confusion of two words close in meaning, near the last step in learning. CONVER-

SION may be changing from one religion to another, from one party to another, usually from something found false to something else regarded as true. CONVERSION emphasizes embracing the new; whereas APOSTASY emphasizes deserting the old.

APOSTASY, which Bailey spells APOSTACY, comes from the Greek ἀπό (apo), from, off, away, and στῆναι (stenai), to stand, is a falling away from the true religion. An APOSTATE is a backslider, deserter, renegade. The difference betwixt an APOSTATE and a HERETIC is that the latter abandoned only a part of his faith, whereas the former renounced the whole.

1117. *CLAQUE*, claque (*klăk*) *n.* A group of persons hired to
     clap vigorously at a mediocre theatrical performance and
so to stimulate general applause.
To CLACK (*klăk*), with similar words in numerous languages, is probably imitative, a word made up to sound like the sound itself. To CLACK is to make a sound which is sharp and quick, or a series of such sounds. From this, or from the same beginnings, come the French verb *claquer*, to clap, applaud, and so at the start of the 19th century, the CLAQUERS, still with the French accent on the last syllable, a highly organized group of hired clappers. The custom dates back to Nero, who is said to have had 5000 soldiers applaud his performances.

A CLIQUE (*klēk*), another French word, is a closely associated group, set, party, coterie, and this leads to the common misconception CLOSE FRIEND.

1118. *PULLULATE*, pullulate (*pŭl'-lū-lāt*) *v.* To come forth,
      bud, sprout, germinate, shoot out.
Even in the revision of this vocabulary test, both GERMINATE and SPROUT remained as synonyms. Both are correct, GERMINATE marked twice as often as SPROUT. One should be removed in the next revision.

The unusual PULLULATE, which goes back to the year 1600, comes from the Latin *pullulatus*, the past participle of *pullulare*, from *pullulus*, a young animal or, of plant life, a sprout, the diminutive of *pullus*, a young animal, the source of *pullet*, a young hen, almost directly from the French *poulette*, a chick, young hen, the diminutive of *poule*, a hen.

1119. *VIXENLY*, vixenly (*vĭks'-ĕn-lĭ*) *adj.* Ill-tempered, snarling, cross, quarrelsome, scolding, irritable, petulant, irascible.

To the Anglo-Saxon *fix*, with the same meaning as the present FOX, was added the feminine ending -*en*, so that FIXEN became a female FOX. The F changed to V and the word became VIXEN, a female FOX.

To 58 per cent the adjective VIXENLY means CRAFTY, cunning, more than twice as many as select ILL-TEMPERED, the dictionary meaning. The unusual noun FOXERY, the behavior of a FOX, means cunning, wiliness, and the adjectives FOXY and FOXISH mean cunning, tricky, CRAFTY. But the female form of the word has never meant CRAFTY. Instead the noun a VIXEN is a scold, termagant, quarrelsome woman.

1120. *LACUNA*, lacuna (*lă-kū'-nah*) *n.* Gap, hollow, hiatus, pit. The plural is LACUNAE (*lă-kū'-nē*).

LACUNAE means GAPS to only 5 per cent, compared with 24 per cent who select INSECT EGGS, and another 24 per cent who select BUTTERFLIES, these last two probably because of the word LARVAE. A LARVA is the early form of any animal which, during its development, differs radically from its parents.

Architects use LACUNAR (*lă-kū'-nahr*), ending in R, to mean a recess in a ceiling, sunken compartment, coffer, common in Renaissance buildings.

LACUNA, without the R, and HIATUS are synonyms. HIATUS (*hī-ā'-tŭs*), a cavern, comes from the Latin *hiatus*, the past participle of *hiare*, to yawn. LACUNA, a doublet of LAGOON, comes from the Latin *lacuna*, a ditch, hollow, hole, pit, cavity, pond, from *lacus*, a cistern, basin, lake.

1121. *BASILIC*, basilic (*bă-sĭl'-ĭk*) *adj.* Kingly, royal, sovereign.

BASILIC, through the French and Latin, directly from the Greek βασιλικός (*basilicos*), kingly, royal, comes from βασιλεύς (*basileus*), king. From the same source comes BASILICA, once a covered porch from which the king declared justice in Athens. Then, before the Christian era, a more elaborate hall of justice. Today a title conferred by the Pope on selected churches such as St. Peter's in Rome.

The mislead FORTIFIED is marked by more people than the correct answer. In medieval FORTIFICATION a BARBICAN was the outwork of a castle, from which attackers could be taken in the flank.

1122. *PUNDIT*, pundit (*pŭn'-dĭt*) *n.* Learned Brahman, who knows Sanskrit; today any scholar, learned man, savant. To 42 per cent PUNDIT means JOKER compared with only 24 per cent who choose SCHOLAR, a confusion of PUNDIT with PUNSTER. A PUN is a play on words, use of the same word in two different senses, or two words pronounced alike or nearly so.

PUNDIT comes from the Hindu word *pandit*, meaning a learned man, teacher, perhaps still earlier from Sanskrit.

It is not easy to explain just where to use PUNDIT. A SCHOLAR is one still learning. A SAVANT is one who already knows. PUNDIT started with the precise meaning of one versed in Sanskrit, and the word should be used today with a knowledge of its background.

1123. *SKIRL*, skirl (*skerl*) *v.* To make a shrill noise, scream, emit a sharp, keen note, utter a piercing, high-pitched sound, as of the Scottish bagpipes. To 56 per cent SKIRLED means EDDIED, compared with only 23 per cent who select SCREAMED as the meaning. To WHIRL, TWIRL, and SWIRL, the last differing from SKIRL by only a single letter, are all to turn round rapidly in EDDIES, rotate, revolve, wheel, spin as in a circling EDDY.

The adjective SHRILL, which like SWIRL goes back to Dutch and German, means piercing, high-pitched, sharp, keen. From this, or at least from the same source, come the Scotch SHIRL, meaning shrill, and SKIRL, which describe sounds, not motions.

1124. *ARCANA*, arcana (*ăhr-kā'-nă*) *pl. n.* Secrets, mysteries, hidden meanings. ARCANUM, the singular, is sometimes the great unknown secret of nature. Answers to ARCANA scatter almost equally among the five choices of the vocabulary test, MYSTERIES, the correct answer, attracting an average number, with VAULT and RUSTIC more popular.

ARCADIA (*ahr-kā'-dĭ-ăh*) was a mountain area in ancient Greece, so that ARCADIAN means pastoral, rural, simple, pleasant, and this similarity in sound may lead to the selection of RUSTIC as the meaning of ARCANA.

ARCANUM (*ahr-kā'-nŭm*), the singular, used ordinarily in the plural, ARCANA, is the Latin neuter of *arcanus*, hidden, closed, the source of the easier but still difficult ARCANE (*ahr-kān'*), secret, private, hidden, mysterious, esoteric. The Latin *arcanus* comes in turn from the verb *arcere*, to shut in, keep, enclose, the source of ARK, a chest, box, bin, receptacle; and one who knows this derivation might with justice select VAULT, a place in which to guard valuables, as a meaning of ARCANA.

ARCANA was used for the great unknown which the alchemists sought to uncover, and so is sometimes used for an elixir, secret remedy, sovereign cure.

1125. *EREMITE*, eremite (*ĕr'-ē-mīt*) *n*. Hermit, one who lives in the wilderness in solitude.

EREMITE, a doublet of HERMIT, comes from the Greek ἐρημίτης (*eremites*), a hermit, from ἐρημία (*eremia*), a wilderness, desert, solitude.

To 24 per cent EREMITE means DISCIPLE. With similar words in Spanish, Portuguese, Italian, French, and Anglo-Saxon, a DISCIPLE is a learner, scholar, pupil, follower, adherent.

To another 21 per cent EREMITE means HERETIC, a non-believer, one who holds a doctrine opposed to accepted beliefs. A HERMIT, similar in sound to HERETIC, is one who lives alone and so an EREMITE.

Of EREMITE Chambers says: 'A devout person retired into solitude to be more at leisure for prayer and contemplation and to disencumber himself from the affairs of the world'.

1126. *STERTOROUS*, stertorous (*ster'-tō-rŭs*) *adj*. Snoring, producing a deep snoring sound.

STERTOROUS is thought by 44 per cent to mean VERY LOUD. STENTORIAN means VERY LOUD, for STENTOR was a Greek herald in the Trojan War with a voice as loud as that of fifty other men. STERTOROUS, much like STENTORIAN in appearance, comes directly from the Latin *stertere*, to snore, and means snoring.

1127. *CORBIE*, corbie (*kor'-bĭ*) *adj*. Stepped back, pertaining
     to the top of an end wall, which rises by a series of steps
on each side.

CORBIE is the Scottish word for crow or raven, the diminutive
of *corb*, raven, from the Latin *corvus*. CORVINE, an adjective,
means pertaining to the family of birds which includes the
crow, raven, and jay.

SERRATED, marked by 32 per cent, compared with only 30 per
cent who select STEPPED, comes from the Latin *serra*, saw, and
means having sharp teeth, notched, jagged, like the edge of
some leaves, close in suggestion to CORBIE. Serrated suggests
sharp points sticking up with no horizontal surface.

A CORBIE GABLE is a stepped GABLE, the end of a building where
the wall at the top steps up, each step a horizontal level surface,
on which a raven might land.

1128. *GLOZING*, glozing (*glōz'-ĭng*) *n*. Deceiving, falseness,
     untrue flattery.

Three separate words, one from Greek, another from Icelandic,
and a third more directly from Anglo-Saxon, should be un-
tangled. The noun a GLOSS (*glŏs*), from the Greek γλῶσσα
(*glossa*), is a short explanation, scholarly remark, note written
in the margin of a book. The verb to GLOSS is to explain, translate,
make clear. Like many learned terms both noun and verb have
come to suggest a false explanation, artful comment, misleading remark. But this suggestion of falseness should be reserved
for GLOZE.

Another noun GLOSS, perhaps from Icelandic, is a superficial
lustre, smooth surface, polished; and so the verb to GLOSS over,
put on a fair face, extenuate, smooth over.

Still a third Anglo-Saxon verb, to GLOZE (*glōz*), has been used
to mean explain, to GLOSS, and also to chatter, wheedle, coax,
flatter, and so to deceive, make plausible, specious. Although
GLOZE and GLOSS are confused historically and by dictionaries, a
GLOSS should be a marginal note and GLOZING should mean deceitful flattery.

To 32 per cent GLOZING means ENTRANCING, compared with
30 per cent who prefer DECEIVING. ENGROSSING, all-absorbing,
is ENTRANCING, for to ENTRANCE, a combination of EN- and

TRANCE, is to put into a TRANCE, make insensible, and from this put into an ecstasy, enrapture, ravish with delight. Perhaps also GLOZING, false flattery, may delight, ENGROSS, ENTRANCE.

1129. *SINEWY*, sinewy (*sĭn'-ū-ĭ*) *adj.* Vigorous, muscular, robust, strong, brawny, of the nature of a SINEW (*sĭn'-ū*).
To 51 per cent SINEWY means THIN, compared with only 17 per cent who select VIGOROUS, two words often correctly applied to the same person. A SINEWY person is rarely FAT; but a THIN person may be emaciated, even sickly, for THIN means slender, slim, lean, spare, meager, not fat, not plump.
    SINEWY, from SINEW, a cord or tendon, directly from Anglo-Saxon, means muscular, strong, brawny.

1130. *PURBLIND*, purblind (*per'-blind*) *adj.* Dim-sighted, seeing obscurely, nearly blind, almost without sight.
PURBLIND comes from two Middle English words, *pur*, completely, quite, and *blind*. PURBLIND ought to mean thoroughly blind, but has come to mean almost blind, seeing obscurely.

1131. *CATECHUMEN*, catechumen (*kăt-ē-kū'-mĕn*) *n.* Neophyte, novice, novitiate, apprentice, student, learner, tirocinium, a pupil studying the rudiments of Christianity.
CATECHUMEN comes from the Greek verb κατηχεῖν (*catechein*), to instruct, a combination of κατά (*kata*), down, where the modern meaning is not really down, and ἠχέιν (*echein*), to sound, or ἠχό (*echo*), the source of the English ECHO, suggesting the give and take of questions and answers.
    The word CATECHUMEN was used largely of religious pupils, and this may lead to the selection of the mislead CHURCH-GARMENT. A CHASUBLE is a CHURCH-GARMENT of brocade, heavily embroidered, hanging down from the shoulders front and back, with no sleeves, put on over the head.
    A CASSOCK, though originally a great military coat, is another CHURCH-GARMENT, a long robe, reaching to the feet, buttoned in front, and held at the waist by a cord.
    CATECHISM, and the corresponding verb to CATECHIZE, are teaching by asking questions, receiving answers, and then offering explanations based on the answers. With a correct answer,

no time is wasted, no explanation is needed. With each wrong answer, a teacher sees immediately the difficulty and straightens out the misunderstanding. A CATECHISM is not an examination, but direct, rapid, individual instruction. A CATECHUMEN is a pupil who learns under this method of teaching.

1132. *DETRUDE*, detrude (*dē-trūd'*) *v.* To thrust down, push out, force to a lower position.

Numerous everyday words come from the Latin *trudere*, to thrust, and its past participle *trusus*. To INTRUDE is to thrust one's way in where one is not wanted, with the noun INTRUSION. This verb INTRUDE leads to the selection by a few of INTERRUPT as the meaning of DETRUDE. To PROTRUDE is to thrust out, stick out, jut out, and refers ordinarily to something solid, as a rock that PROTRUDES, with PROTRUSION as the noun. To EXTRUDE is to push out under pressure a relatively soft substance which flows.

DETRUDE, which starts with the Latin *de-*, down, by derivation means to thrust down, push down, but the word is not used often enough to have acquired any clear implication.

1133. *CORUSCATING*, coruscating (*kŏr'-ŭs-kā-tĭng*) *adj.*
Sparkling, flashing, gleaming, lightning, glittering, bursting with light, emitting vivid flashes of light; the Century says: 'As the reflection of lightning by clouds, or moonlight on the sea'. To 29 per cent CORUSCATING means SLANDEROUS. A SLANDER is a false report intended to injure the reputation of another, an aspersion. SLANDEROUS means hurtful, harmful, scathing, defamatory, calumnious, malicious, scandalous. The word CORRODING means burning, biting, searing, and may lead this large percentage into selecting SLANDEROUS as a meaning of CORUSCATING.

CORUSCATING comes from the Latin *coruscatus*, the past participle of *coruscare*, to move quickly, glitter, flash, sparkle, scintillate, vibrate, gleam.

Of CORUSCATION, which Bailey spells with two R's: CORRUSCATION, he says: 'A flash of lightning or a seeming sparkling fire which appears often at night, a glittering'. And E. Chambers adds: 'Glittering, flashing, a gleam of light emitted from anything. The term is chiefly used for a flash of lightning, nimbly darting down from the clouds in time of thunder'.

1134. *SPECIOUS*, specious (*spē′-shŭs*) *adj*. Pleasing to the eye,
    superficially fair, apparently right, plausible, beguiling,
ostensible, sophisticated, seemingly just.

Like CLEVER, which sometimes means overly clever, tricky,
crafty, to be doubted, SPECIOUS, from the Latin *speciosus*, good-
looking, beautiful, from *species*, form, figure, beauty, has come
to mean a bit too beautiful, and so to be distrusted.

Of 29 high-vocabulary adults, 19 select CLEARLY WORTHLESS
as the meaning of SPECIOUS. SPECIOUS is neither CLEAR nor
WORTHLESS, but appearing sound at first view, and to be questioned further, plausibly, superficially fair.

1135. *GRAMINEOUS*, gramineous (*grăm-ĭn′-ē-ŭs*) *adj*. Be-
    longing to the great herbaceous family, resembling vege-
tation on which cattle feed, pasturage.

GRAMINEOUS comes from the Latin *gramineus*, from *gramen*,
grass, one of the most important families in the vegetable kingdom, known as GRAMINEAE (*gră-min′-ē-ē*). GRAMINIVOROUS is
feeding on grass, subsisting on grass, which is from *gramen*,
grass, and *vorare*, to eat, devour.

The popular mislead marked by 35 per cent is CEMENT, com-
pared with only 5 per cent who select the correct answer,
GRASS-LIKE. GRANULAR, composed of grains, may suggest
CEMENT.

1136. *EXORDIUM*, exordium (*ĕks-ōr′-dĭ-ŭm*) *n*. The begin-
    ning of anything, principally the introduction to a speech
or writing, foreword, preface.

A FOREWORD, both parts from Anglo-Saxon, is nothing but a
word said beforehand. An INTRODUCTION, from *intro*, within, and
ducere, to lead, leads on in, and may mean little more than an
INTRODUCTION to a person. A PREFACE, from the Latin *prae*,
before, and *fari*, to say, is more personal than INTRODUCTION,
giving something about the author.

An EXORDIUM, from the Latin *exordiri*, to lay out the warp
before weaving, from *ex*, out, and *ordiri*, to begin to weave,
lays the foundation for what follows.

To 30 per cent EXORDIUM means COURT-APPEAL, more than
select the correct answer, SPEECH INTRODUCTION.

1137. *NESCIENCE*, nescience (*nĕsh'-ĭens*) *n.* Ignorance, lack of knowledge, almost stupidity, dullness.

SCIENCE is comprehension, an understanding of what is happening, knowledge, or more precisely knowing, ending in -ING, from the Latin *sciens, scientis*, the present participle of *scire*, to know.

CONSCIENCE, again from the present participle, once meant with knowledge, but now means moral judgment applied to one's self, thinking clearly about one's deeds; and CONSCIOUS, more directly from the infinitive *conscire*, and not through the present participle, now means with knowledge, and so awake, alive, not asleep. UNCONSCIOUS is of course without knowledge, with no awareness of what is going on.

PRESCIENCE, from *prae*, before, and *scire*, to know, is knowledge in advance, foreknowledge, almost foresight.

NESCIENCE is without knowledge, not knowing, and so ignorant. The adjective NESCIENT, ignorant, uninformed, not cognizant, destitute of knowledge, appeared in Ephraim Coles' tiny Dictionary of 1717.

Compared with only 10 per cent who, in a vocabulary test, select IGNORANCE as the meaning of NESCIENCE, 45 per cent underline WITCHCRAFT, a supernatural power, believed to be possessed by the witch and given by the devil, sometimes a gift of foresight, and in this sense almost an opposite of NESCIENCE.

1138. *INCORPOREAL*, incorporeal (*ĭn-kŏr-pō'-rē-ăl*) *adj.* Immaterial, not having a physical nature.

A CORPSE, from the Latin *corpus, corporis*, was originally a living body, the physical frame. The adjective CORPORAL (*kŏr'-pŏ-răl*) means pertaining to the body, as CORPORAL punishment, physical, bodily punishment. The Latin verb *corporare*, to make into a body, has become in English INCORPORATE, to form into a body. A CORPORATION is a body, a group set up legally to act as an artificial person.

The adjective CORPOREAL, as contrasted with CORPORAL, suggests not spiritual, perhaps not mental. When given a choice between INSUBSTANTIAL and DREAM-LIKE, as synonyms of INCORPOREAL, four times as many select the latter, which is probably a more suitable definition than INSUBSTANTIAL.

1139. *EPITHET*, epithet (*ĕp'-ĭ-thĕt*) *n*. An adjective which ascribes character; Bailey, 1721, says: 'A word expressing the nature and quality of another word to which it is joined'; or from Webster, 1828, 'An adjective expressing some real quality of the thing to which it is applied'.

Of 28 high-vocabulary adults 5 select TOMB-INSCRIPTION and 5 others HUMOROUS-PHRASE as the meaning of EPITHET. An EPITAPH, from the Greek ἐπί (*epi*), over, and τάφος (*taphos*), tomb, is an inscription on a tomb or monument in honor or in memory of the dead. From Ephraim Chambers, 1728, comes: 'The EPITAPHS of the present day are crammed with fulsome compliments never merited'.

An EPIGRAM, from the Greek ἐπί (*epi*) and γράφειν (*graphein*), to write, according to Bailey is 'a short witty poem, playing upon the fancies and conceits, which arise from any kind of subject'. This no doubt leads to the selection of HUMOROUS-PHRASE as a meaning of EPITHET.

EPITHET comes from the Greek ἐπίθετον (*epitheton*), epithet, a combination of ἐπί, on, to, beside, and τίθημι (*tithemi*), to place, set. An EPITHET is an adjective applied to, set beside, a noun. Dr. Johnson says: 'The word EPITHET is used improperly for phrase, expression, as when Shakespeare says: "Suffer love! A good EPITHET".'

1140. *NIMB*, nimb (*nĭm*) *n*. Halo, nimbus, circle, star, or other shape, characteristic of a saint and painted behind his head.

To 39 per cent NIMB means EDGE. LIMB, which comes through the French, Portuguese, and Italian, from the Latin *limbus*, border, edge, fringe, is used in astronomy for the edge of the sun or moon.

NIMB comes from the Latin *nimbus*, a rain cloud associated with NEBULA; and in religion a cloud surrounding a saint. A HALO is circular but seen in perspective as if floating horizontally just above the top of the head. A NIMB is a circular disc or other shape behind a head parallel to the canvas or surface of the painting and so seen round. An AUREOLA (*ăw-rē'-ō-lăh*) is an oval emanation surrounding a whole body. A GLORY is a combination of an AUREOLA and a NIMB or NIMBUS.

1141. *ENTHYMEME*, enthymeme (*ĕn'-thĭ-mēm*) *n.* An inference from likelihoods, rhetorical syllogism; Bailey,
1721: 'An imperfect syllogism, where either the major or minor
proposition is wanting, as being easily to be supplied by the
understanding'. Webster, 1828, in his first edition, gives the
clearest meaning: 'In rhetoric an argument consisting of only
two propositions, an antecedent and a consequence deduced
from it; as, we are dependent, therefore we should be humble.
Here the major proposition is suppressed; the complete syllogism would be, dependent creatures should be humble; we are
dependent creatures; therefore we should be humble'.

ENTHYMEME, a combination of the Greek ἐν (*en*), in, and
θυμός (*thymos*), mind, is so unusual a word that answers of
even high-vocabulary adults scatter widely with little indication
of an intelligent guess as to its meaning.

1142. *EPIDICTIC*, epidictic (*ĕp-ĭ-dĭk'-tĭk*) *adj.* Displaying the
skill of a speaker, rhetorical, demonstrative, opposed to
judicial.
EPIDICTIC comes from the Greek ἐπιδεικνύναι (*epideiknunai*),
to display, show, exhibit, a combination of ἐπί (*epi*), upon, and
δεικνύναι (*deiknunai*), to show, point out. From this comes the
Latin *dicere*, to say, tell, the immediate source of perhaps a hundred English words such as: DICTION, DICTIONARY, and PREDICT.
Directly from the Greek, and not through Latin, come only a
few, two of which are: APODICTIC and EPIDICTIC.

Of 27 high-vocabulary adults 14 select INCONTESTABLE, indisputable, clear, as the meaning of EPIDICTIC. APODICTIC means
evident beyond contradiction, capable of being established, a
term introduced by Aristotle. EPIDICTIC is almost an opposite,
purely rhetorical, affording pleasure.

1143. *MYOPIC*, myopic (*mī-ŏp'-ĭk*) *adj.* Short-sighted, near-
sighted, brachymetropic, affected with MYOPIA (*mī-ō'
pē-ă*).
The noun MYOPIA comes from the Greek μυοπία (*myopia*),
from μύειν (*myein*), to close, and ὤψ (*ops*), ὠπίς (*opis*)
eye, literally therefore to close the eye. HYPERMETROPIC (*hī-
pĕr-mĕ-trŏp'-ĭk*), far-sighted, is the opposite of MYOPIC.

1144. *DELITESCENT*, delitescent (*dĕl-ĭ-tĕs'-sĕnt*) *adj.* Concealed, lying hid.

DELITESCENT comes from the Latin *delitescens, delitescentis*, the present participle of *delitescere*, to lie hid, a combination of *de*, away, and the inceptive verb *latescere*, from *latere*, to lie hid, the source of LATENT, so that DELITESCENT really means beginning to lie hidden, starting to be concealed.

The misleads PUBLIC, OVERDUE, and LEGAL all attract more examinees than HIDDEN, the correct meaning, showing that the word DELITESCENT is practically unknown.

1145. *TURBOT*, turbot (*tĕr'-bŏt*) *n.* A flatfish, a close relation of the halibut.

To 30 per cent of high-vocabulary adults TURBOT means PHEASANT. The PHEASANTS (*fĕz'-ăntz*) are birds; the TURBOT, a fish. Some varieties of PHEASANTS have long colorful tails, though of course not so gorgeous as the peacock, which belongs to the same family.

The word TURBOT comes through Irish, Gaelic, and Welsh from the Latin *turbo, turbinis*. From the Latin source *turbo*, which meant top, in the sense of a spinning top, comes the modern word TURBINE, a wheel turned by water or by steam, which generates power.

The TURBOT belongs to the same flatfish family as the HALIBUT but is smaller. HALIBUT is said to be an abbreviation of holy flounder because the fish was eaten on holy days. The HALIBUT occasionally weighs 300 to 400 pounds compared with the TURBOT's 30 to 40 pounds. Both are colored on one side and white on the other, and both have their two eyes on one side of the head.

From Pantologia, a Cyclopaedia of 1813, comes: 'The PLEURONECTES are the flat-fish, a genus, head small, eyes spherical, both on the same side of the head, and near each other; mouth arched, jaws unequal, toothed.

'This genus embraces the TURBOT, sole, halibut, plaice, flounder, pearle, and whiff. These swim constantly obliquely and reside at the bottom of the water.'

The word PLEURONECTES (*plŏŏ-rŏ-nĕk'-tēz*) is the Greek πλευρά (*pleura*), side, plus νήκτης (*nectes*), a swimmer.

Pantologia continues: 'There are twenty-nine species, seventeen with both eyes on the right side of the head and twelve with both eyes on the left.'

Of the TURBOT: 'The species is excellent food. The skin is entirely destitute of scales. The eyes are on the left side.'

TURBOT fisheries extend on the North of England and Holland. These fishes are most successfully caught by hook and line.

1146. *PLY*, ply (*plī*) *v.* To offer with persistence, press upon, continue to present.

To PLY, from the Latin *plicare*, to fold, which originally meant to fold, bend, shape, mold, has come to be used in various ways and as parts of numerous words. To REPLY (*rē-plī'*), literally to fold back, is to turn back, return, respond, give back an answer.

The verb to PLY is thought by 55 per cent to mean TEMPT, and by 35 per cent to mean SUPPLY; with the real meaning between the two, in about these percentages. To PLY is to force something upon another, again and again, against the other's better judgment, and real desires.

1147. *POSIT*, posit (*pŏz'-ĭt*) *v.* To affirm, present as a fact, lay down as a principle, assume as real, postulate.

When looked for, the Latin verb *ponere*, to place, put, and its past participle *positus*, are found in countless English words. The verb to COMPOSE is to put together, place together. A POSITION is a place. To DEPOSIT, starting with the Latin *de-*, down, is to put down, place, lay down, and this no doubt suggests DELIVER, to the 25 per cent who select this as the meaning of POSIT, affirm.

1148. *ENCAENIA*, encaenia (*ĕn-sē'-nĭ-ăh*) *n.* A celebration of the founding of a city, ceremonies commemorating the consecration of a church.

To 40 per cent the rare word ENCAENIA means DEGREE, a step-up; for DEGREE comes from the Latin *gradus*, a step. But the same DEGREE occurs in education as a title conferred on the completion of a course of study or in recognition of outstanding achievement.

Although in early times in Greece ENCAENIA, ἐνκαίνια (*encainia*), was a celebration in honor of the founding of a city, a feast of consecration, its recent use, by the University of Oxford, is a festival in June in honor of the founders and benefactors, and may easily suggest DEGREE. ENCAENIA is a celebration in honor of the founding of a city, a church, university, or some similar institution.

1149. *DEIPNOSOPHIST*, deipnosophist (*dīp-nŏs'-ō-fĭst*) *n.* One who converses learnedly at dinner.

DEIPNOSOPHIST comes from the Greek δειπνοσοφιστής (*deipnosophistes*), the singular of Δειπνοσοφισταί (*Deipnosophistai*), the name of a book by Athenaeus, literally Learned Men at Dinner, in which a number of learned men discourse on literature and other matters. The Greek is a combination of δεῖπνον (*deipnon*), dinner, and σοφιστής (*sophistes*), a learned man, the source of the word SOPHIST.

DEIPNOSOPHIST is thought by 50 per cent to mean CULTIST, correct certainly in implication, for a CULT is a relatively small selected group with an ideology of their own, usually religious. Or the same word CULT may designate the belief rather than the group. According to the Century Dictionary, a CULTIST is specifically one of a school of Spanish poets who imitated the pedantic affectation and labored elegance of Gongora y Argote, a Spanish writer of 1561 to 1626.

There should be more DEIPNOSOPHISTS. Too many dinners lack learned conversation.

1150. *POACHY*, poachy (*pō'-chĭ*) *adj.* Swampy, marshy, muddy, damp, slushy, wet and soft; used of land.

To 60 per cent of high-vocabulary adults POACHY means WORTHLESS compared with only 10 per cent who select the correct meaning SWAMPY.

There are three verbs to POACH; the first is to stab, pierce, and also to tread, and from this to make slushy by frequent treading, also to be damp, muddy, marshy, swampy. The second verb POACH is to encroach on another person's property, killing his game, to trespass. The third verb to POACH is to cook by breaking the shell of an egg and dropping the egg into hot water.

From the first of these three verbs comes the unusual adjective POACHY, which means wet and soft, land into which the feet of cattle sink easily.

1151. *HYSON*, hyson (*hī'-sn*) *n.* A Chinese tea from early pluckings.

To 27 per cent of high vocabulary adults HYSON means HERBS, compared with only 10 per cent who select CHINESE TEA, the correct answer. HERB comes from Latin through Old French and according to the Century Dictionary should be pronounced without the H; although HERBACEOUS, and HERBARIUM, which come more recently from the Latin and not through Old French, should be pronounced with the H, a delicate distinction, and HERB is correct either with or without the H. An HERB is a plant in which the stem dies back to the ground each year. TEA is a shrub, three to six feet high, with a woody stem, which does not die back annually. HYSON in Chinese means blooming spring.

1152. *QUINCY*, quincy (*kwĭn'-sē*) *n.* A rowboat.

The popular mislead for QUINCY is TIGHTWAD, chosen by 55 per cent. TIGHT, used colloquially, means close-fisted, covetous, avaricious, parsimonious, niggardly, and so STINGY, perhaps near enough to QUINCY in sound to suggest TIGHTWAD as a mislead.

A QUINSY, spelt with s, is a sore throat, tonsilitis, from the Greek κυνάγχη (*cynagche*), a sore throat; and so 20 per cent select SORE THROAT as the meaning of QUINCY, spelt with a c. Some persons are good spellers, enough to suggest the existence of a spelling aptitude, perhaps independent of vocabulary. Spelling tests and vocabulary tests should be developed independently of each other, if this is possible.

A DORY is another type of small boat, usually flat bottomed and frequently used by fishermen working from a larger vessel.

1153. *SYNERGETIC*, synergetic (*sĭn-ĕr-jĕt'-ĭk*) *adj.* Working together, cooperating; the word is used for the working together of muscles or bodily organs. The noun is SYNERGY (*sĭn'-ĕr-jĭ*).

This unusual word is answered correctly by more than three quarters of a high-vocabulary group who have tried this form of the vocabulary worksample, probably because of SYN- at the beginning, which means together, and which appears in SYNONYM, in SYNAGOGUE, and as SYM- in SYMPHONY and SYMPATHY.

SYNERGETIC, the Greek συνεργητικός (*synergeticos*), is a combination of σύν (*syn*), together, and ἔργειν (*ergein*), to work.

1154. *NONCE*, nonce (*nŏns*) *n*. Time being, for the immediate present, for once, for that time only. The Century Dictionary calls NONCE: 'A word of no independent status'.
The Anglo-Saxon ONE means single, unity, alone, definitions more difficult than the simple ONE, in such a phrase as: 'ONE apple', or 'ONE person'. ONCE is ONE plus the Anglo-Saxon possessive ending -*es*, misspelt -CE, in HENCE, WHENCE, TWICE, and ONCE. ONCE ought to mean one time, on a single occasion; but in the phrase: 'I ONCE did it' suggests the past, and ONCE is sometimes wrongly defined as formerly, in the past. The same ONCE even occasionally implies the future.

NONCE is ONCE plus N, which originally belonged to the word before, so that THEN ONCE became THE NONCE; and NONCE, which should mean for the one occasion only, has come, like ONCE, to suggest both past and future. Webster, 1828, even defines NONCE as purpose, intent, design, so that of 28 high-vocabulary adults 8 select FUTURE and 5 PAST as meanings of NONCE, the second step in learning, the confusion of words used often in the same situation.

1155. *DIRE*, dire (*dīr*) *adj*. Dreadful, awful, frightful, calamitous, disastrous, woeful, terrific, destructive, dismal.
DIRE comes directly from the Latin *dirus*, fearful, awful, dreadful; from the Greek δείδειν (*deidein*), to fear.
Given a choice between FEARFUL and THREATENING as meanings of DIRE, 19 out of 28 high-vocabulary adults select THREATENING. Of THREATENING Webster, 1828, says: 'Menacing, indicating something impending, declaring a purpose to inflict evil on a person or country'. FEARFUL and THREATENING are so close as hardly to be distinguishable; but THREATENING describes pur-

pose, while FEARFUL is more appearance, and indicates the effect
on the beholder. Both THREATENING and DIRE cause fear,
THREATENING by the intent of that which THREATENS, DIRE by
appearance. THREATENING applies to the future, to something
which has not yet happened. DIRE may be used in describing a
past experience or event.

1156. *AGONIC*, agonic (*ā-gŏn′-ĭk*) *adj*. Not forming an angle,
    without angles.
AGONIC comes directly from the Greek ἄγωνος (*agonos*), without an angle, a combination of the Greek privative ἀ-, without,
and γωνία (*gonia*), angle, which appears in the middle of TRIG-
ONOMETRY, literally three-angled measurements, a science constructed on the triangle with its three angles.

A CLOISTER is a covered walk, or arcaded way around the
inner court in many monasteries, convents, and religious buildings; CLOISTERED may mean shut up in a CLOISTER, solitary, retired from the world. But it is hard to see why CLOISTERED
should be selected as a meaning of AGONIC.

AGORAPHOBIA, a dread of open spaces, starts with the same
three letters as AGONIC; and CLAUSTROPHOBIA, the opposite, is the
dread of confined places and may suggest CLOISTERED.

The so-called AGONIC LINE goes north through North Carolina,
Virginia, Ohio, and Lake Erie, and is the line on which a mag-
netic compass points to the true pole, with no angle between
the compass reading and true north.

1157. *ACCIPITRAL*, accipitral (*ăk-sĭp′-ĭ-trăl*) *adj*. Hawk-like,
    pertaining to birds of prey.
ACCIPITER (*ăk-sĭp′-ĭ-ter*), the Latin word for birds of prey,
especially for the common hawk, comes from the Latin *acci-
pere*, to take, seize, from *capere*, to take, seize, hold. In compounds, the A of *capere* may change to I, as in RECIPIENT, from
recipere, to receive, from *capere*, to hold.

The popular mislead is of course BACK OF THE HEAD. OCCIPITAL
means pertaining to the BACK OF THE HEAD. ACCIPITRAL is hawk-
like.

Under ACCIPITRES, The Cyclopaedia Pantologia says: 'The
first order of the Linnean class, Birds: The original character-

istics being: bill somewhat hooked downwards, the upper mandible dilated near the point, or armed with a tooth; nostrils open; legs short, and strong; feet formed for perching, having three toes forwards and one backwards; claws hooked and sharp pointed; body muscular; flesh tough and not fit to be eaten; food, the carcasses of other animals, which they seize and tear; nest in high places; eggs about four; female larger than the male; they live in pairs.'

1158. *PRIGGISH*, priggish (*prĭg'-gĭsh*) *adj.* Conceited, affected, precise, narrow-minded, overly nice. PRUDISH is the same sort of adjective applied to a woman who affects rigid correctness.

Of such adjectives as PROUD, HAUGHTY, and ARROGANT, PRIGGISH is the only one which implies no just claim to an exalted position.

To 42 per cent PRIGGISH, a word of unknown origin, means NARROW. NARROW-MINDED is a phrase used in most definitions of PRIGGISH. To another 28 per cent PRIGGISH means CONCEITED, another word which appears in many dictionaries in definitions of PRIGGISH. A PRIG is perhaps a combination of the two.

Though exquisite apparel is not ordinarily implied by PRIGGISH, as it is by FOPPISH, Steele in the Tatler, Number 77, says: 'A cane is part of the dress of a PRIG'. The noun PRIG is used in provincial England for a small pitcher, and like a small pitcher, the mind of a PRIG holds but little.

1159. *PROTEAN*, protean (*prō'-tē-ăn*) *adj.* Changeable, variable, iridescent, assuming different shapes, pertaining to PROTEUS, a sea god who could change his shape at will.

A CHAMELEON (*kă-mē'-lē-ŏn*) is a lizard with the gift of changing the color of its skin to match his environment. CHAMELEONIC (*kă-mē-lē-ŏn'-ĭk*) is the awkward adjective.

To 34 per cent PROTEAN means NATURAL, more than mark the correct answer VARIABLE.

1160. *SOBRIQUET*, sobriquet (*sō-brĭ-kā'*) *n.* A nickname, word used instead of the real name, sometimes an abbreviation, shortened form, nome de plume, cognomen, fanciful appellation.

A PSEUDONYM is an assumed name, pen name, nom de guerre, taken by an author to hide his real name. A SOBRIQUET is always a pleasant nickname.

To 30 per cent a SOBRIQUET is a SIGN. A SIGN is often a gesture; a SOBRIQUET is always a word, name.

Because of his victory over the Indians near the Tippecanoe River in Northern Indiana, in 1811, William Henry Harrison, in 1841, became the 9th president of the United States under the slogan TIPPECANOE & Tyler Too. TIPPECANOE might almost be called an AGNOMEN (ăg-nō′-mĕn), a fourth name given anciently to a Roman because of some outstanding achievement.

1161. *DELICT*, delict (dē-lĭkt′) n. A misdemeanor, offense, transgression, crime.

DELICT comes from the Latin *delictus*, a fault, offense, the past participle of the verb *delinquere*, to fail, offend, be wanting, a combination of *de-*, and *linquere*, to leave, the source of DELINQUENT. A DELINQUENCY, a shortcoming, offense, misdeed, is a milder term than CRIME. A CRIMINAL, one who commits a CRIME, is a culprit, transgressor, evildoer, malefactor, a stronger term than DELINQUENT. A DELICT is a slight offense which does not immediately affect the public, but which implies an obligation to make atonement.

To 46 per cent DELICT means FAULT and to another 28 per cent TRANSGRESSION, both relatively mild and equally correct answers.

1162. *APOPEMPTIC*, apopemptic (ăp-ō-pĕmp′-tĭk) n. Valedictory, sending away, farewell; Webster, 1828: 'Denoting a song or hymn among the ancients, sung or addressed to a stranger on his departure from a place to his own country'. APOPEMPTIC, sending off, dismissing, comes from the Greek ἀπό (apo), off, and πέμπειν (pempein), to send.

To 25 per cent APOPEMPTIC means RANTING. To RANT, from Old German words meaning noise, is to declaim violently, speak noisily. To 5 per cent APOPEMPTIC means WELCOMING, an opposite of the correct answer. But APOPEMPTIC is so unusual that the scattering of answers is largely chance.

VALEDICTORY (văl-ē-dĭk′-tō-rĭ), the synonym given in numerous dictionaries, comes from the Latin *vale*, farewell, the present imperative of *valere*, to be well, and *dicere*, to say. VALEDICTORY is literally saying farewell, and so an exact synonym for APOPEMPTIC.

1163. *SEIZIN*, seizin (*sē'-zĭn*) *n.* Possession of a house, completion of the ceremony of feudal investiture, ownership of a freehold.

Of 36 high-vocabulary adults, 10 select CONDEMNATION and 7 others REDEVELOPMENT as meanings of SEIZIN. The application to land of the word REDEVELOPMENT is recent, and involves the taking, seizing of privately owned land and its sale to private investors. The legal process of SEIZING land either for public purposes, a road, or public building, or for REDEVELOPMENT is called CONDEMNATION.

The verb to SEIZE (*sēz*), which goes back to Old French, but not apparently to Latin, is to lay hold of, grasp, clutch, take possession of violently. SEIZURE (*sē'-zūr*) is the noun, the act of taking, grasping, seizing.

SEIZIN, almost identical in sound with SEIZING and from the same source, is technical, going back to feudal days, and means actual possession. From Bailey, 1721, restated by Webster one hundred years later: 'SEIZIN is of two sorts. SEIZIN in fact or deed is actual or corporal possession. SEIZIN in law is when something is done which the law accounts possession, as when land descends to an heir, but is not yet entered on'.

1164. *BACULUS*, baculus (*băk'-ū-lŭs*) *n.* A long staff upon which worshippers were allowed to lean during lengthy religious services, a kind of crutch.

The common misconception of this unusual word is DRAW-BRIDGE. In the 14th Century, a DRAWBRIDGE, which led across the moat around a fortified castle, could be drawn up, from the inside, in such a way as to cover the entrance. A PORTCULLIS, somewhat similar in sound to BACULUS, and thought by many to be the DRAWBRIDGE, is a heavy gate which slides up and down in vertical grooves.

BACULUS comes from the Latin *baculum*, staff, stick, scepter. From the same source come BACTERIUM, a micro-organism, better known in the plural, BACTERIA, and BACILLUS, a tiny rod.

1165. *RECREANT*, recreant (*rēk'-rē-ănt*) *n.* One who yields in combat, coward, unfaithful wretch, a mean-spirited person.

RECREANT, a combination of the Latin *re*, again, and *credere*, to believe, has come to mean one who changes his belief, literally one who owns himself beaten.

Ephraim Chambers writes: 'RECREANT was so reproachful a term that Glanville would not describe it'. Ranulf de Glanville, in about 1175, during the reign of Henry II, compiled perhaps the first coherent code of English law.

Of 28 high-vocabulary adults, 5 select COWARD as the meaning of RECREANT, compared with 11 who prefer THIEF, and 7 UN-BELIEVER. All three are reproachful words. A MISCREANT was originally and by derivation an UNBELIEVER, but has come to mean a scoundrel, detestable villain, and this no doubt leads to the selection of THIEF as a synonym of RECREANT.

Of RECREANT, Bailey in the sixth edition of his dictionary says: 'A fainthearted or cowardly fellow'; while Webster gives: 'One who yields in combat and cries craven; one who begs for mercy; hence a mean-spirited, cowardly wretch'.

1166. *BODKIN*, bodkin (*bŏd'-kĭn*) *n.* A small pointed instrument of steel, bone, or ivory, for piercing holes in cloth, a blunt needle, with an eye, for drawing thread, cord, tape, or ribbon through a loop or hem.

Among high-vocabulary adults 34 per cent select CORSET as the meaning of BODKIN. A BODICE, the plural of BODY, and once spelt BODIES, is a CORSET, a waistcoat worn by women, quilted, with whalebone or stays.

BODKIN, related to Celtic, Gaelic, and Irish words, was originally a small dagger, stiletto, or punch.

1167. *LYNCEAN*, lyncean (*lĭn-sē'-ăn*) *adj.* Sharp-sighted, keen-eyed, lynx-eyed.

LYNCEAN comes through the Latin from the Greek λύγκειος (*lygceios*), from λύγξ (*lygx*), lynx. A LYNX is a wildcat, with long legs and a short tail.

CUNNING, selected by 30 per cent, is attributed to the FOX. SHARP-SIGHTED, selected only half as often, is reputed to characterize the LYNX, and the phrase LYNX-EYED means keen eyed, sharp sighted, with acute vision.

1168. *AGATHISM*, agathism (*ăg'-ă-thĭzm*) *n.* Optimism, the doctrine that all things tend toward ultimate good.

To 40 per cent AGATHISM means DISBELIEF, twice as many as select OPTIMISM, the correct answer. This misconception is obviously the word AGNOSTIC, a combination of the Greek privative ἀ-, not, and γνωστός (*gnostos*), known, the same word which leads so many to think that an AGAMIST, a non-marrier, is an UNBELIEVER.

AGATHISM is almost the only word which comes from the Greek ἀγαθός (*agathos*), good.

1169. *LITTORAL*, littoral (*lĭt'-tŏr-ăl*) *adj.* Coastal, pertaining to the shore of the sea or great lakes, situated on a river.

LITTORAL and LITERAL, though pronounced practically the same, have widely different backgrounds and modern meanings. LITERAL (*lĭt'-ĕr-ăl*), according to the letter, expressed in letters, following letter by letter, and so exact, comes from the Latin word for letter, sometimes spelt with one T and sometimes with two, *litera*, or *littera*, the source of the French *lettre* and the Spanish *letra*, as well as the English LITERARY and LITERATURE. This word LITERAL leads 20 per cent to select EXPRESSED as the meaning of LITTORAL, in the phrase: 'LITTORAL Trade'.

LITTORAL, now spelt with two T's though in the past it has sometimes been spelt with one, the French *littoral*, the Spanish and Portuguese *litoral*, and the Italian *litorale*, all come from the Latin *litoralis*, belonging to the seashore, from *litus*, *litoris*, seashore, coast, shore of a lake, also the bank of a river.

1170. *EPICEDIUM*, epicedium (*ĕp-ĭ-sē'-dĭ-ŭm*) *n.* Funeral song, dirge, elegy, lamentation, verses in praise of the dead; an unusual word which the Oxford calls: not naturalized.

Among 27 high-vocabulary adults 11 select PLATFORM as the meaning of EPICEDIUM. A PODIUM, ending in the same last four letters, literally a small foot, the diminutive of the Greek πούς (*pous*), ποδός (*podos*), foot, was originally a raised platform which surrounded the arena in ancient amphitheatres.

An ELEGY is a funeral oration. An EPICEDIUM, from the Greek ἐπί (epi), and κῆδος (kedos), sorrow, care, is a funeral song.

1171. *HEBDOMADAL*, hebdomadal (hĕb-dŏm'-ă-dăl) *adj.* Weekly, occurring each week, appearing every seven days.

HEBDOMADAL comes from the Greek ἑβδομάς (hebdomas), ἑβδομάδος (hebdomados), seven, a week, from ἑπτά (hepta), seven. The prefix HEPTA, meaning seven, appears in HEPTARCHY, a government by seven, already discussed, apparently an easier word, and in the technical terms of many sciences, as HEPTANE in chemistry, with seven carbon atoms, and HEPTAGONAL, with seven angles; between HEXAGONAL, from ἕξ (hex), six, and OCTAGONAL, from ὀκτώ (octo), eight.

ABDOMINAL, pertaining to the abdomen, much like HEBDO-MADAL in sound, may suggest MEDICAL, the popular choice underlined three times as often as the correct synonym WEEKLY.

MONTHLY is second in popularity, with WEEKLY the least frequently marked of all five choices. DIURNAL means daily, happening every day. MENSUAL (mĕn'-sū-ăl) is monthly; HEBDOMADAL is WEEKLY.

1172. *ALEATORY*, aleatory (ă'-lē-ă-tō-rĭ) *adj.* Of or pertaining to chance or gambling; depending upon a contingent event; unpredictable.

ALEATORY comes from the Latin *aleator*, gambler, originally from *alea*, die, the singular for dice. The Latin word is best known from Caesar's famous statement, 'Alea iacta est,' 'The die is cast;' said to have been uttered when he crossed the Rubicon in defiance of the Roman Senate.

ALEATORY has expanded beyond this literal reference to dice; in English it now means unpredictable, as random and as dependent on chance as the throw of dice. In law, ALEATORY contracts are those in which the obligations and the performance are dependent on an uncertain event over which the contracting parties have no control, such as insurance contracts, lottery agreements and annuities.

A bizarre modern art form is referred to as 'ALEATORY music.' In this form of composition, the notes to be played depend on chance, not the composer. In general, ALEATORY is used to describe anything which cannot be foreseen or which is left to luck, such as 'the ALEATORY aspects of life'.

1173. *LING*, ling (*lĭng*) *n*. Common heather, a low-growing plant, with tiny purple or white flowers, which covers almost every heath in Britain.

LINGO, from the Latin *lingua*, tongue, speech, the source of LINGUAL, leads 32 per cent to select LANGUAGE as the meaning of LING. LINGO is a strange, foreign-sounding kind of LANGUAGE unintelligible to ordinary men, as the LINGO of science, or of medicine; a specialized terminology.

LINK, a ring or any one of the solid pieces of which a chain is made, leads another 20 per cent to select CHAIN as the meaning of LING.

HEATHER, a low-growing plant, the correct answer, chosen by only 12 per cent, comes directly from the word HEATH; while LING, a rare term for Scotch HEATHER, comes from Icelandic, Danish, Swedish, and Norwegian words for heath, desolate uncultivated land, usually in Great Britain, in which shrubs grow wild with LING, HEATHER, and FURZE. FURZE is an Anglo-Saxon word for a low spiny shrub with small yellow flowers, also called GORSE and WHIN.

1174. *IMP*, imp (*ĭmp*) *v*. To strengthen, mend, implement, extend, enlarge; in falconry to graft feathers onto a wing to improve its powers of flight.

Of 27 high-vocabulary adults, 11 believe that IMP, an unusual word directly from Anglo-Saxon, means WALK-AWKWARDLY. To LIMP, also from Anglo-Saxon, is to WALK-AWKWARDLY, haltingly, because of lameness.

According to Bailey, 1721: 'IMPING (in falconry): the inserting a feather in the wing of a hawk in the place of one that is broke, as: "To IMP a feather in a hawk's wing", to add a new piece to an old broken stump'.

In his dictionary of a century later Webster says: 'To graft, also to lengthen, extend, enlarge by something inserted; a term originally used by falconers who repair a hawk's wings by adding feathers'.

1175. *APPARITOR*, apparitor (*ăp-păr'-ĭ-tŏr*) *n.* A servant, messenger, aide, attendant who carried out the orders of a Roman magistrate, a beadle in a university, a pursuivant to a herald, also the lowest officer in a religious or ancient civil court. From the Latin verb *apparere*, with the past participle *apparitus*, to attend, wait upon, serve, appear, come two sets of modern terms, one meaning appear and the other to serve. An APPARITION, which in Latin meant an attendant, one who serves, is now an appearance, the act of appearing, becoming visible. This leads to the selection of GHOST as the meaning of APPARITOR, far more popular than the correct answer, SERVANT. A GHOST, directly from Anglo-Saxon, is an APPARITION, phantom, appearance of a human specter. APPARITOR is used occasionally for one who appears, an appearer, but not in the sense of an abnormal appearance such as a GHOST.

APPAREL is clothing, raiment, with similar words in many languages, perhaps originally from Latin. An APPARITOR might easily be one who makes clothes, and so a TAILOR, another popular mislead. But APPARITOR is never used in this way.

In Roman history both APPARITORS and LICTORS were attendants to magistrates. The LICTOR carried the FASCIS (*făsh'-ĭs*), a bundle of sticks, a sign of authority. APPARITOR was a more general term for a public servant who waited on a magistrate.

1176. *BATHOS*, bathos (*bā'-thŏs*) *n.* A ludicrous descent in writing from the elevated to the commonplace, anticlimax, a sinking in style.
To 42 per cent BATHOS means SORROW. Numerous words differ by a single letter as: CAT, RAT; DOG, HOG; SALLY, DALLY. PATHOS, from the Greek πάθος (*pathos*), suffering, misery, feeling, is an emotion of pity, compassion, sadness, sympathy, SORROW. BATHOS is from the Greek βάθος (*bathos*), depth.

TURGIDNESS, BOMBAST, FUSTIAN, and BATHOS are all used uncomplimentarily of writing. TURGID is swollen, high-sounding, with needless inflated words. BOMBAST was once a soft material used to stuff garments, as the shoulder padding in a coat. A BOMBASTIC style is today stuffed-up ranting, but not so empty as TURGID. Like BOMBAST, FUSTIAN is a material, a heavy coarse cloth. Now the word may characterize writing filled with extravagant expressions. BATHOS belongs to the same family but is more difficult to describe. It is mock-heroic: 'The depth into which one falls who overleaps the sublime'.

1177. *CREBRITY*, crebrity (*krĕb'-rĭ-tĭ*) *n.* Frequency, close succession, near occurrence, oftenness, recurrence.

CELEBRITY, renown, fame, leads easily to the selection, by 30 per cent, of DIGNITY, nobleness, worthiness, as the meaning of the rare word CREBRITY.

CREBRICOSTATE (*krē-brĭ-kŏs'-tāt*), from the Latin *creber*, close, frequent, and *costa*, rib, is used in CONCHOLOGY, the science of shells, to mean with ridges set close together. Similarly CREBRISULCATE (*krē-brĭ-sŭl'-kāt*), from *sulcus*, furrow, means with furrows close together.

The adjective CREBROUS means near together, frequent, often. The noun may be either CREBRITUDE or CREBRITY, frequentness, oftenness.

1178. *DOXY*, doxy (*dŏk'-sĭ*) *n.* Mistress, sweetheart, paramour, wench, moll, usually in a bad sense. Bailey says: 'She beggar, a trull'; Webster, 1828: 'A prostitute'.

Of 28 high-vocabulary adults 9 select BELIEF as the synonym of DOXY. ORTHODOXY (*ŏr'-thō-dŏk-sĭ*), from the Greek ὀρθός (*orthos*), straight, correct, right, and δόξα (*doxa*), opinion, belief, is opinion regarded as correct, soundness of belief, in conformity with the accepted. HETERODOXY (*hĕt'-ĕ-rō-dŏk-sĭ*), from the same Greek δόξα (*doxa*), is heresy, a doctrine contrary to the Scriptures, or contrary to those of an established church. In these words -DOXY comes from the Greek; while the English DOXY by itself is Dutch or German slang for mistress.

Various quotations involve all three words, perhaps the first by Bishop Warburton about 1750: 'ORTHODOXY is my DOXY — HETERODOXY another man's DOXY'; and from Carlyle, nearly a hundred years later, 1837: 'ORTHODOXY or My-DOXY and HETERODOXY or Thy-DOXY'.

1179. *EXPATIATION*, expatiation (*ĕks-pā-shĭ-ā'-shŏn*) *n.* Elaborating on a subject, wandering around without restraint, copiousness, expansion, digression, amplification.

Three words, in appearance much alike: EXPATIATION, EXPIA-
TION, and EXPATRIATION, seem easily confused. Among 27 high-
vocabulary examinees, 14 mark ATONEMENT as the meaning of
EXPATIATION. EXPIATION (*ĕks-pĭ-ā'-shŏn*), the second of these
three similar words, from the Latin *ex*, out, and *piare*, to appease,
propitiate, from *pius*, pious, devout, is ATONEMENT, reparation,
satisfaction for a wrong.

Of the same 27 adults, 5 mark BANISHMENT as the meaning of
EXPATIATION. EXPATRIATION (*ĕks-pā-trĭ-ā'-shŏn*), the third of
these three similar words, from the Latin *ex*, out, and *patria*,
one's native land, fatherland, from *pater*, father, is BANISHMENT.
Of EXPATRIATION, Webster, 1828, says: 'More generally the
forsaking of one's own country, with the renunciation of allegiance and with the view of becoming a permanent resident and
citizen in another country'.

EXPATIATION, from the Latin *expatiatus*, the past participle of
expatiari, to go out of the way, wander, digress, a combination
of *ex*, out, and *spatiari*, to take a walk, from *spatium*, space,
originally meant wandering, roving at large, moving in space
without limits; enlarging in discourse or writing; copiousness in
argument, amplifying in language. Of the verb to EXPATIATE,
Bailey, in his dictionary of 1721, says: 'To enlarge on a subject,
to wander abroad'.

1180. *COMMENDAM*, commendam (*kŏm-mĕn'-dăm*)   *n.*
    Religious office, ecclesiastic benefice, church living held
temporarily.
COMMENDAM comes from the Latin *commendere*, to entrust,
give in trust. The verb to COMMEND (*kŏm-mĕnd'*) is to give in
charge, deliver with confidence. A COMMENDAM is a church
office given by the crown to a qualified person to hold until a
proper person is provided, often applied to a living held by a
bishop after he has ceased to perform the duties.

A COMMENDATOR (*kŏm'-mĕn-dā-tŏr*) is the person who holds
a church office temporarily. The practice of holding an ecclesiastical benefice IN COMMENDAM, the usual expression, was condemned by the Council of Constance in 1417 and again by the
Council of Trent in 1563 and was prohibited by the Church of
England in 1836.

1181. *PELLICLE*, pellicle (*pĕl'-lĭ-kl*) *n.* Thin skin, cuticle, film,
    scum, crust; according to Bailey, 1721: 'A little skin, a
film or fragment of membrane'.

Of 28 high-vocabulary adults, 11 select SEED VESSEL as a synonym of PELLICLE; and 7 others, LEAF STALK. A FOLLICLE is a
SEED VESSEL; according to the Century Dictionary, a FOLLICLE
is 'A single CARPEL, DEHISCENT only by the VENTRAL SUTURE'.
FOLLICLE is the diminutive of the Latin *follis*, a money bag,
also a wind bag, and so a bellows, an attempt to describe the
appearance of this SEED VESSEL. PERICARP (*per'-i-kahrp*) is another technical term for SEED VESSEL and may add to the confusion.

A PEDICEL (*pĕd'-i-sĕl*), a division of the PEDUNCLE (*pē-
dŭng'-kl*), is a single stalk supporting one flower only, the stem
of a single flower; while the PEDUNCLE, an inclusive word, may
support a cluster.

PELLICLE comes from the Latin *pellicula*, a small skin, the
diminutive of *pellis*, skin, hide, the source of PELL, a noun used
in English for the skin of a beast, hide, and PEEL, the skin of
fruit. The more familiar PELT, another word for the skin of an
animal with the hair still on, comes apparently from an entirely
different source. A PELLICLE is a little skin, thin tissue. MEM-
BRANE, the correct answer in the vocabulary test, is a thin,
pliable, expansive, structure of the body, from the Latin *membrana*, skin, from the Greek μεμβράνα (*membrana*), parchment.

1182. *AGGLUTINATE*, agglutinate (*ăg-glū'-tĭ-nāt*) *v.* To
    stick, unite, join, attach, fasten, glue together.
Nearly everyone who has taken this worksample chooses GATH-
ER TOGETHER as the meaning of AGGLUTINATE, compared with
only 12 per cent who select the correct answer. This may be
the result of confusion with the word AGGLOMERATE (*ăg-glŏ'-
mĕ-rāt*), to collect, bring together, collate, from the Latin
glomus, a ball. To AGGLOMERATE is to GATHER TOGETHER into a
ball. The nouns, a CONGLOMERATION and the simpler CONGLOM-
ERATE, and the verb, to CONGLOMERATE, to gather together into
a ball, are more familiar.

The verb AGGLUTINATE comes from the past participle of the
Latin verb *agglutinare*, from the noun *gluten*, paste, glue.

Despite the overwhelming popularity of the answer GATHER TOGETHER the derivation of AGGLUTINATE contains nothing which suggests this. To AGGLUTINATE is to stick together, join, fasten.

1183. *DEHISCE*, dehisce (*dē-hĭs'*) *v.* To burst open; originally to yawn, gape.

The noun DEHISCENCE, the adjective DEHISCENT, and occasionally the verb to DEHISCE, are all used in botany for the opening of a seed pod to release the seeds. At first DEHISCE meant to gape, yawn, for the word comes from the Latin, *dehiscere*, to gape, yawn, a combination of *de-*, off, and *hiscere*, to gape, the source of the English HIATUS, opening, aperture, gap, chasm, identical with the Latin *hiatus*, the past participle of *hiare*, to yawn.

To 40 per cent DEHISCE means to WILT, droop, fade, wither, grow limp, compared with only 20 per cent who prefer the correct meaning BURST OPEN.

1184. *SCHOLIUM*, scholium (*skō'-lĭ-ŭm*) *n.* Marginal note, annotation, commentary, explanatory remark, gloss, brief exposition, short comment; among mathematicians: an observation subjoined to a demonstration. Bailey adds: 'A remark made, as it were, by the by, on any proposition before treated of'. SCHOLIUM comes from the Greek σχόλιον (*scholion*), interpretation, commentary, from σχολή (*schole*), a learned discussion, dissertation, disputation, lecture; also a place for discussion, a school room.

Of 29 high-vocabulary adults, 11 select TREATISE, and 7 CLASS-ROOM, both meanings of σχολή, the source of SCHOLIUM. A TREATISE, from *tractare*, to handle, manage, treat, is a written composition, involving more form than an essay, and certainly more than a SCHOLIUM, a mere note, short comment.

Several words ending in -IUM mean ROOM, as TEPIDARIUM, a heated room in the ancient Roman baths, and FRIGIDARIUM, a cold room; so that SCHOLIUM might logically be a SCHOOL-ROOM, CLASS-ROOM, but even in Greek σχόλιον (*scholion*) meant a note, comment, interpretation. The plural is SCHOLIA.

1185. *CORACLE*, coracle (*kor'-ă-kl*) *n.* A British boat made like a basket, nearly as broad as it is long. To this the Encyclopaedic Dictionary, 1883, adds: 'It is light and capable of being carried on the shoulders of one man'.

According to Bailey, 1721: 'A CORACLE is a sort of small boat used by fishermen in the River Severn'; or from Webster, 1828, quoting Johnson: 'A boat used in Wales by fishermen, made by covering a wicker frame with leather or oil-cloth'. Wales is the country in the West of England to which the ancient Britons fled, when Britain was invaded by the Saxons.

Francis Palgrave, in his history of the Anglo-Saxons, writes: 'The Cymric Britons (an early name for the Welsh), though they lived on an island, had no vessels or boats except CORACLES, framed of slight ribs of wood, covered with hides. These frail barks are still used by the Welshmen on the Wye', a river in Wales which joins the Severn.

The word CORACLE is so little known that guesses as to its meaning range widely.

1186. *INFUSION*, infusion (*ĭn-fū'-shŏn*) *n.* A liquid in which special plants have been soaked or heated in order to extract their flavor. Tea is an INFUSION.

INFUSION comes from the Latin *infundere*, to pour in, with the past participle *infusus*.

The popular mislead, DISTURBANCE, selected by 40 per cent, is clearly the word CONFUSION, from the Latin *com*, together, and the same past participle *fusus*, of *fundere*, to pour. A CONFUSION is a pouring together of all sorts of things. From the same Latin verb *fundere*, and its past participle *fusus*, come the verb to FUSE, the noun FUSION, AFFUSE, EFFUSE, INFUSE, PERFUSE, and PROFUSION. An EFFUSION is an outpouring, a flowing forth, an extravagant display of feeling. INFUSION may be the act of pouring in; or it may be the liquid extract made by steeping, soaking a plant in liquid.

1187. *FANE*, fane (*fān*) *n.* An ancient temple, church, place consecrated to religion.

Among 28 high-vocabulary adults, 10 select SERVANT and 8 others OVERLORD as the meaning of FANE. Of THANE, Bailey, 1721, says: 'A nobleman, a magistrate, a freeman', and this no doubt leads to the marking of OVERLORD. But a THANE, from a Saxon word meaning to serve, was originally a SERVANT, then an attendant on the king, and so an important person.

But FANE comes from the Latin *fanum,* sanctuary, temple, from *fari,* to speak in the sense of dedicate. From *fans, fantis,* the present participle of *fari,* come INFANT, literally not speaking, a child too young to talk, and an INFANTRY, originally a boy page to a knight. FANE, meaning an ancient temple, is a difficult word, and this confusion in sound of FANE and THANE is the first step in learning.

1188. *CORINTHIANIZE,* corinthianize (*cor-ĭn'-thĭ-ăn-īz*) *v.*
          According to dictionaries: to debauch; according to the public: to embellish.

From CORINTH, a city on the isthmus of Corinth, at the heart of ancient Greece, noted for its magnificence and licentiousness, comes CORINTHIANIZE. Given a choice between EMBELLISH and DEBAUCH as synonyms, 42 per cent select the first and only 10 per cent the second. Sometimes a manufactured word is popular enough to gain an independent meaning. But CORINTHIANIZE seldom appears and until this verb, manufactured from the name of a city with two characteristics, becomes more thoroughly established the reader has a right to interpret it either way. In this instance, led perhaps by the CORINTHIAN column and its elaborate capital, four times as many interpret CORINTHIANIZE as meaning EMBELLISH.

1189. *ALGORISM,* algorism (*ăl'-gōr-ĭsm*) *n.* The mathematics of Arabic figures, art of computation, now commonly called arithmetic, numbers, notation.

The word ALLEGORY comes from the Greek ἀλληγορία (*allegoria*), the discussion of one subject under the guise of another, a combination of ἄλλος (*allos*), other, and ἀγορεύειν (*agoreuein*), to speak, from ἀγορά (*agora*), the market place where speaking was done. An ALLEGORY is today the treatment of one subject in terms of another, a kind of writing which demands INTERPRETATION on the part of the reader; and this may lead to the underlining of INTERPRETATION as the meaning of ALGORISM.

The word ALGORISM comes from the proper name of an Arabian mathematician, who lived in the 9th century and whose work was translated into Latin in the 13th century, whose name, written in Latin, Algoritmi, came to be applied to ARITHMETIC much as EUCLID was used for GEOMETRY.

1190. *ETHNARCH*, ethnarch (*ĕth'-nark*) *n.* The governor of a province, viceroy in ancient Greece.

ETHNARCH is the Greek ἐθνάρχης (*ethnarches*) written in Roman letters, from ἔθνος (*ethnos*), a nation, people, race, and ἄρχειν (*archein*), to rule, govern. From this last comes MONARCH, one who rules alone, from μόνος (*monos*), alone; while from ἔθνος (*ethnos*) comes ETHNIC, pertaining to races, or sometimes to a nation; and from this ETHNOLOGY, the science of races, study of the mental and physical differences of mankind, and the basic principles of human guidance; and ETHNOGRAPHY, a description and classification of races of man. This last may lead 40 per cent to decide on HISTORIAN as the meaning of ETHNARCH, governor, ruler, especially if one thinks of the literal meaning of ETHNOGRAPHY, writing about races.

1191. *PARAPET*, parapet (*pă'-ră-pĕt*) *n.* A wall rising breast high, rampart, enceinte (*ŏn-sănt'*).

PARAPET comes directly from the Italian *parapetto*, a breastwork, a combination of *parare*, to guard, and *petto*, breast, from the Latin *pectus*, breast. A PARAPET is breast high. From the Latin *parare*, to guard, come PARASOL, to guard against the sun, from the Latin *sol*, sun; and PARACHUTE, ending in the French *chute*, a fall, from the Latin *cadere*, to fall.

To 12 per cent PARAPET means TRENCH. In the fortifications of the Middle Ages a RAMPART was a mound of earth taken from the ditch or TRENCH, and heavy enough to withstand cannonshot. On top of the RAMPART was the PARAPET, a breast-high wall.

1192. *HUSTINGS*, hustings (*hŭs'-tĭngs*) *n.* A temporary platform from which a candidate speaks, a stand constructed for a political campaign.

HUSTINGS, from Anglo-Saxon, may be a public meeting, council, court, but may also be a stage, built for a political campaign, from which a candidate addresses the people.

To 24 per cent HUSTINGS means DEMANDS, probably because of some connection with the original meaning of HUSTINGS, a court, council, public meeting.

A ROSTRUM was an elevated place in the Roman forum, for orations, pleadings, and funeral speeches. PODIUM is more general, a small stand for any speaker or even for a music conductor. A HUSTINGS is specifically for a political campaign.

1193. *SALLY*, sally (săl'-lĭ) v. To dash out, spring forth, leap out, burst out, set out briskly. The corresponding noun, a SALLY, is a sudden rushing forth of troops, sortie.

To 30 per cent SALLY, dash out, means LOITER, to linger, delay, an exact opposite. To DALLY is to linger, LOITER, delay. To SALLY, from the Latin *salire*, to leap, jump, is to jump out energetically.

To ISSUE is to go out. To EMERGE is to come into view from concealment. To SALLY is to dash out, leap out.

1194. *EPIPHANY*, epiphany (ĕ-pĭf'-ă-nĭ) n. The appearance of a deity on earth, manifestation, avatar, apparition of a divine person.

The word EPIPHANY comes from the Greek ἐπιφάνεια (*epiphaneia*), the feminine singular, meaning appearance, manifestation, apparition, from ἐπιφανής (*epiphanes*), appearing suddenly, a combination of ἐπί (*epi*), and φαίνειν (*phainein*), to show, the source of PHANTASM and FANCY.

Among the ancient Greeks, EPIPHANY was a festival commemorating the appearance of a god on earth. Today EPIPHANY is a Christian festival, on January 6, celebrating the manifestation of Christ to the Gentiles by the Magi.

Given a choice between VISION and APPEARANCE as synonyms of EPIPHANY, 28 per cent select the first, and 24 per cent the second. A VISION may be something supernatural, seen in the mind, or something actually seen with the physical eye, and is probably a slightly better answer than the cold-blooded APPEARANCE.

1195. *QUONDAM*, quondam (kwŏn'-dăm) adj. Former, once, prior, heretofore, of old, having been, at one time in the past.

To 40 per cent QUONDAM means QUESTIONABLE, uncertain, doubtful, suspicious, disputable, liable to question, compared with
only 24 per cent who select FORMER. The confusion is probably the word QUANDARY (*kwahn'-dā-rĭ*), a state of perplexity,
uncertainty, puzzlement, hesitation, a QUESTIONABLE situation.

Though the word QUONDAM suggests QUESTIONABLE to nearly
half of those who have tried this vocabulary worksample, QUON-
DAM is the Latin word for formerly, and should continue to
mean: once upon a time.

1196. *ADVERT*, advert (*ăd-vert'*) *v.* To turn the attention to,
        remark on, allude to, refer to, hint at, take notice of.
ADVERT comes from the Latin *advertere*, to turn toward, regard,
notice, a combination of *ad*, to, and *vertere*, to turn, the source
of CONVERT, INVERT, DIVERT, SUBVERT, and AVERT. This last misleads 46 per cent of adults into selecting AVOID as the meaning
of ADVERT, compared with only 8 per cent who select NOTICE,
the correct answer. To AVERT (*ă-vert'*) is to keep off, divert,
prevent the occurrence of something evil, ward off, oppose,
and so AVOID.

To ADVERTISE was once to notice, observe, take note of; and
then came to mean inform, announce, proclaim, promulgate.

To ADVERT to, REFER to, ALLUDE to, HINT at, are in order of
diminishing intensity or directness. To HINT at is indirect, hardly
noticeable. To ALLUDE to is casual, by derivation to play upon.
To REFER to is direct, plain. To ADVERT is not only direct and
plain, but sudden, abrupt, so as to catch and hold the listener's
attention.

1197. *ETIOLATE*, etiolate (*ē'-tĭ-ō-lāt*) *v.* To whiten, blanch,
        grow white by the absence of natural coloring matter.
ETIOLATE, used mostly in horticulture of plants, sometimes in
pathology of persons, comes directly from the French *étioler*,
to blanch, by a roundabout process from the Latin *stipula*, straw.

Of 29 high-vocabulary adults 13 select ENLARGE as the meaning of ETIOLATE. To DILATE, from the Latin *dilatare*, to spread
out, a combination of *dis*, apart, and *latus*, the past participle of
ferre, to carry, is to expand, distend, ENLARGE, extend in all
directions.

To BLEACH is to make white by a chemical process. To BLANCH is to grow white by a natural process. To ETIOLATE is to turn white usually by the exclusion of light, as to ETIOLATE celery by piling dirt around it as it grows.

1198. *IRENICON*, irenicon (*ī-rĕn'-ĭ-kŏn*) *n*. A plan to promote peace, scheme designed to gain peace.

To 20 per cent an IRENICON is a SATIRE, suggested no doubt by the word IRONY. SATIRE, SARCASM, and IRONY are various ways of ridiculing present conditions. IRONY is an expression which means the opposite of what it seems to say, intending the opposite of what is stated. SARCASM is direct, bitter, severe. SATIRE is more elaborate than SARCASM, not so bitter, and not so direct.

The Greek proper name Εἰρήνη (*Eirene*), which in English becomes IRENE (*ī-rē'-nē*), was the personification of peace and quiet, directly from the Greek εἰρήνη (*eirene*), peace. IRENIC (*ī-rĕn'-ĭk*), the adjective, used mostly in theology, means peaceful, pacific, quieting, pertaining to peace, promoting peace. The opposite is POLEMIC, from the Greek πολεμικός (*polemicos*), warlike, from πόλεμος (*polemos*), war. POLEMICS is offensive, ecclesiastical controversy, the practice of arguing. The adjective POLEMICAL, used also in theology, means controversial, disputative. POLEMIC may be a noun and mean disputant, controvertist, or may be an adjective.

The noun IRENICS (*ī-rĕn'-ĭks*) is peaceful theology; IRENICON, a plan or scheme for peace.

1199. *OTIOSE*, otiose (*ō'-shĭ-ōs*) *adj*. Idle, indolent, futile, ineffective, lazy, unemployed, inactive, at rest.

Among 29 high-vocabulary adults, 5 select SHOWING OFF as the meaning of OTIOSE, the popular misconception. OSTENTATIOUS (*ŏs-tĕn-tā'-shŭs*), where the -TIO has the same SH sound, from the Latin *ostentus*, a show, parade, is making a public display, SHOWING-OFF from vanity, boastful presentation of endowments in a gaudy light.

OTIOSE comes from the Latin *otiosus*, at ease, having leisure, from *otium*, leisure, ease, rest. From the same source comes NEGOTIATE, with the same -oti- in the middle, literally, not at ease.

Given a choice between INACTIVE and PHLEGMATIC as synonyms of OTIOSE, 14 per cent select the first and 12 per cent the second.

1200. *GNOMON*, gnomon (*nō'-mŏn*) *n.* Time indicator, the triangular projecting piece on a sun-dial, which by its shadow shows the hours of the day. The early GNOMONS used for astronomical purposes were vertical pillars or OBELISKS. GNOMON comes from the Greek γνώμων (*gnomon*), a judge, interpreter, one who knows, from γνῶναι (*gnonai*), to know. From this come IGNORANT, without knowledge, and the noun IGNORANCE; as well as IGNORE, not to know, and IGNOMINY, literally without a name.

A GNOMON is thought by 64 per cent of those who have taken this vocabulary form, more than half, to be a DWARF, a confusion of GNOMON with GNOME. A GNOME is a saying, saw, maxim, a word taken apparently by Paracelsus for one of his imaginary beings, and so today a grotesque DWARF, small person.

Despite the fact that only one tenth, 11 per cent, mark time-indicator, GNOMON is a technical term for the arm of a sun-dial which casts the shadow, which in turn indicates the time.

1201. *PALMARY*, palmary (*păl'-mă-rĭ*) *adj.* Worthy of receiving the palm, distinguished, preeminent, conspicuous. PALM (*pahm*), pronounced with no L sound, goes back through French, Spanish, and Italian to the Latin *palma*, the palm of a hand. From this comes PALMISTRY, the art of telling fortunes by certain lines or marks on the palms of the hands. This leads 10 high-vocabulary adults in a group of 29 to underline ASTROLOGICAL as the meaning of PALMARY.

PALMARY comes from PALM meaning a leaf of the PALM-TREE, so named because the leaf resembles the palm of the hand in shape. In ancient Rome a leaf of the palm-tree was a symbol of victory, a custom which survives today in PALM SUNDAY, the commemoration of Christ's triumphal entry into Jerusalem. PALMARY means deserving of receiving the PALM.

Another 6 high-vocabulary adults select COMMONPLACE, an exact opposite; but PALMARY is so unusual that most answers are guesses.

1202. *EPITOME*, epitome (*ē-pĭt'-ō-mē*) *n.* Abridgment, summary, abstract, compendium, digest.

Among 29 high-vocabulary adults 24 choose ACME as the meaning of EPITOME. ACME, from the Greek ἀκμή (*acme*), is the top, highest point, utmost, maturity, perfection, prime; among physicians, the crisis of a disease, its utmost violence.

Of EPITOME, Nathan Bailey says: 'An abridgment, abstract, or short draught of a book'; and in his first edition, 1828, Noah Webster agrees: 'An EPITOME is an abridgment: a brief summary or abstract of any writing; a compendium containing the substance or principal matters of a book'. Ordinarily the Laboratory accepts the consensus of opinion of high-vocabulary examinees as the current meaning of each word. But in this instance all dictionaries and the derivation of the word are so unequivocal that, despite the overwhelming majority for ACME, we have kept to the historical definition.

EPITOME, from the Greek ἐπί (*epi*), upon, and τέμνειν (*temnein*), to cut, comes from τόμος (*tomos*), a cutting, piece, section, part of a book, volume, the source of TOME, ATOM, and ANATOMY. Also even these same high-vocabulary readers recognize the verb to EPITOMIZE as meaning shorten, abridge, abstract in a summary the principal matters in a book, contract into a narrower compass. An EPITOME is a summary.

1203. *BROWSE*, browse (*browz*) *v.* To eat, nibble, graze, consume, feed on tender shoots.

To 41 per cent BROWSED means WATCHED, compared with only 25 per cent who select ATE, the past tense of EAT. To WATCH is to keep vigil, be awake, notice carefully, observe, be attentive, keep a sharp look-out. One hears so often of BROWSING among books, looking for interest, that one forgets the real meaning of the word.

The noun BROWSE, from the Old French word for BUD, sprout, twig, tender shoot, properly denotes the food which deer find in young copses, continually sprouting anew, the tips of branches that shoot forth early in the spring whereon cattle feed. Although the verb to BROWSE means to feed on tender shoots, graze, knapping or nibbling at the tips of young sprigs, herbs, and grass, it has come to suggest moving about looking for food, as an animal moves about a pasture, and so to move among books WATCHING for something of interest.

1204. *PERORATION*, peroration (pĕr-ōr-ā'-shŏn) n. Concluding part of an oration, recapitulation, summary. The PROLOGUE is the beginning, the PERORATION the ending.

PER-, almost always translated as through, sometimes has this literal meaning, as in PERFORATE, to bore through. But sometimes PER- means through to the end as in PERFECT (per-fĕkt'), to make to the end, carry through to completion. From this, PER- comes to mean end, as in PERORATION, the last part of an ORATION.

To 36 per cent PERORATION means EULOGY (ū'-lō-jē), a confusion of words close in meaning and often used in the same situation. Both are formal. A EULOGY is always high praise, from the Greek εὖ (eu), good, well, and λέγειν (legein), to speak. An ORATION, from orare, to speak, is an inspired, prepared speech on almost any subject. A EULOGY may be written or spoken; an ORATION is always spoken, though it may be published later. Of PERORATION, E. Chambers says: 'The epilogue or last part of an ORATION; wherein, what the orator had insisted on through his whole discourse is urged afresh with greater vehemence and passion'. The PERORATION consists of two parts, one the recapitulation, wherein the substance of what was discussed throughout the whole speech, is collected briefly and cursorily, and, two, summed up with new force and weight, to move the passions. The PERORATION was Cicero's masterpiece: here that great orator not only set his judges and auditors on fire, but even seemed to burn himself.

The passions to be raised in the PERORATION are various: in a panegyric: love, admiration, emulation, joy; in an invective: hatred, contempt; in a deliberation: hope, confidence, fear.

1205. *AGNATE*, agnate (ăg'-nāt) n. A descendant who traces his relationship exclusively through males.

COGNATE means allied by blood, related in origin, connected by birth, of the same family, and comes from the Latin cognatus, a combination of co-, together, and gnatus, an old form of natus, born, the past participle of nasci, to be born. From natus come also NATIVE, NATAL, and NATION.

AGNATE, from the same source, means connected through males only, a descendant through fathers.

INNATE, an adjective from the same *natus*, born, with no corresponding noun, means inborn, not acquired, inherited, and this leads easily to BORN-TRAITS, the common mislead, marked by 29 per cent, compared with only 11 per cent who select the correct MALE-LINE.

1206. *SUBORN*, suborn (*sŭb-ōrn'*) *v.* To bribe, procure unlawfully, also to give false testimony, induce a witness to perjure himself.

SUBORN comes from the Latin *sub*, under, and *ornare*, to furnish, equip, adorn, the source of ORNAMENT, ORNATE, and ADORN. Although SUBORN has in the past been used in English to mean furnish, equip, adorn, Walter W. Skeat, 1882, gives the meaning of the Latin *subornare* as to furnish or supply in an underhand way or secretly, and translates *sub* as under, secretly. SUBORN should always have this secret, underhand implication.

Of SUBORN E. Chambers says: SUBORNATION, a secret or underhand preparing, instructing or bringing in a false witness; or corrupting or alluring a person to do such a false act.

H. W. Fowler in Modern English Usage includes SUBORN in his list of formal words, and would like the simple BRIBE used more often in its place.

1207. *INDITE*, indite (*ĭn-dīt'*) *v.* To write, compose, put into words.

To 61 per cent INDITING is POINTING OUT, compared with only 16 per cent who select WRITING. The connection goes far back. To INDICATE is to POINT OUT, show, from the Latin *in-*, and *dicare*, to declare, say, originally to point. DITE, directly from the Latin *dictare*, to dictate, is the frequentative of *dicare*. To DITE is to write, although the word is now obsolete and replaced by INDITE, unusual but still in good standing.

To INDICT, where the C is modern to imitate the Latin, was once to write, but is now to charge formally with a crime, accuse. To INDITE is to compose, or, Bailey says: 'To dictate the matter of a letter or other writing', but now more often to do the writing one's self.

1208. *ACAULESCENT*, acaulescent (*ăk-ō-lĕs'-sĕnt*) *adj.*
    Without a stem, with no apparent stalk.
ACAULESCENT, from the Latin *caulis*, a stalk, stem, familiar in
CAULIFLOWER, starts with the Greek privative *a-*, not, and ends
with the Latin -ESCENT which suggests just beginning, starting,
as ADOLESCENT, just beginning to be an adult; CONVALESCENT,
starting to get well; and OBSOLESCENT, almost OBSOLETE, starting
to get out of use.
    ACAULESCENT applies to plants in which the stem is apparently
absent.

1209. *RIPARIAN*, riparian (*rī-pā'-rĭ-ăn*) *adj.* Pertaining to the
    bank of a river, situated on the bank of a river.
To 40 per cent RIPARIAN means CIVIL, from the French *civil*, and
Latin *civilis*, belonging to a citizen, from *civis*, a citizen. To
another 25 per cent RIPARIAN means RESTORED. To REPAIR, from
re-, again, and *parare*, to get, prepare, is to RESTORE, renovate,
put back into good condition.
    RIPARIAN, from the Latin *riparius*, belonging to the bank of
a river, from *ripa*, bank, from the same source as RIVER, should
be used strictly of a river bank, and not the sea-shore.

1210. *PIPPIN*, pippin (*pĭp'-pĭn*) *n.* A kind of tart apple.
    The word PIPPIN, as the name for a kind of tart apple, is
older and more important than one realizes. Shakespeare used it
in Henry IV and Merry Wives. It appears in Minsheu, Guide
into the Tongues, 1627; and in Cotgrave, 1611. Skeat in his
discussion quotes Wedgwood: 'An apple raised from the PIP
or seed'.

1211. *QUOTIDIAN*, quotidian (*kwō-tĭ'-dĭ-ăn*) *adj.* Daily,
    diurnal, occurring every day.
The English QUOTA (*kwō'-tă*) is the Italian *quota*, a share, proportion, part, assignment, from the Latin *quota*. This in turn
is the feminine of *quotus*, how many, of what number, from
quot, how many, as many as. A QUOTA is a share, a proportional
part, as: 'They never once finished their QUOTA', their share.
    A QUOTIENT (*kwō'-shĕnt*) is a proportion, the number of
times one number goes into another, the result of dividing. This

leads 24 per cent to select DIVISIONAL as the meaning of QUOTI-
DIAN. DIVISIONAL means pertaining to a DIVISION of land, or a
DIVISION of the army; but DIVISIONAL is not ordinarliy used of
the mathematical process of DIVIDING.

QUOTIDIAN, from the Latin *quotidianus*, daily, starts with the
same Latin *quot*, as many as, and ends with *dies*, day. From *dies*
come DIARY (*dī'-ă-rĭ*), a daily record; and DIURNAL (*dī-ĕr'-năl*),
happening every day. DAY and DAILY are Anglo-Saxon, not
Latin.

QUOTIDIAN means daily, happening every day. SEPTAN (*sĕp'-
tăn*) means happening every seventh day, every week; while
MENSUAL means happening every month; and ANNUAL, happening every year. Still another 20 per cent mark YEARLY as the
meaning of QUOTIDIAN, daily.

1212. *DISSIMULATION*, dissimulation (*dĭs-sĭm-ū-lā'-shŭn*)
          n. Feigning, pretending, deceit, hypocrisy, duplicity, con-
cealment of reality.
DISSIMULATION comes from the Latin *dissimulare*, to dissemble,
conceal, pretend, a combination of the privative *dis-* and *similis*,
like, the source of SIMILAR, RESEMBLE, and DISSEMBLE, to give a
false impression.

To DISSEMBLE is to pretend that a thing which is, is not. To
SIMULATE is to pretend that a thing which is not, is, as to SIMU-
LATE friendship. To DISSIMULATE is to hide the truth under some
other appearance.

DISSIMULATION is thought by 30 per cent to mean DIFFERENCE.
SIMILAR means resembling, almost the same; while SIMILARITY,
the noun, is likeness, resemblance. DISSIMILAR is unlike; and
DISSIMILARITY is unlikeness, and so DIFFERENCE. But DISSIMULA-
TION, almost the same in sound, is pretending, hiding the truth.

1213. *CALCINE*, calcine (*kăl'-sĭn*) *v.* To convert into lime by
          the action of heat.
CALCINE comes from the Latin *calx, calcis*, lime. CALCINATION
is the formation of lime.

The verb to CALCINE goes back to ALCHEMY, to 1400, to burn
in the fire to a CALX or friable, powdery substance. It was
thought by the ALCHEMIST to be a purifying process.

1214. *THERSITICAL*, thersitical (*thĕr-sĭt'-ĭ-kăl*) *adj.* Grossly abusive, scurrilous, foul-mouthed.

THERSITICAL is thought by 24 per cent to mean SANCTIMONIOUS, an exact opposite. SANCTIMONIOUS originally meant SACRED, saintly, holy, but has come to mean making a show of SANCTITY. The ending -MONY is the Latin -*monia*, which added at the end makes a noun, as: CEREMONY, PARSIMONY, MATRIMONY, TESTIMONY, ACRIMONY. Add to this the Latin suffix -OUS, and the noun becomes an adjective.

Thersites (*Thĕr-sĭ'-tēz*) was a scurrilous character in Homer's Iliad (II 212), the ugliest man in the Greek camp before Troy, a railing demagogue, but a relative of Diomedes, the Greek hero.

1215. *INANITION*, inanition (*ĭn-ă-nĭ'-shŭn*) *n.* Emptiness, exhaustion from lack of nourishment, starvation, also mental starvation.

Among high-vocabulary adults, 60 per cent select LAZINESS, as the meaning of INANITION, as opposed to STARVATION, scored as correct. INANIMATE, from the Latin *in*, not, and *anima*, life, breath, vital principle, is lifeless, and suggests sluggishness, slothfulness, indolence, habitual aversion to labor. LAZINESS is thought of as a disinclination to work, but may be due to INANITION.

INANITION comes from the Latin *inanire*, to make empty, with the past participle *inanitus*, from *inanis*, empty. From the same source comes INANE, a combination of the Latin privative *in*, and *anis*, a word of unknown origin. INANE means empty but has come to mean without intelligence, void of sense, silly, senseless. INANITION is the state of being INANE; but INANITION stresses emptiness more than lack of intelligence.

1216. *MISOPEDIA*, misopedia (*mĭs-ō-pē'-dĭ-ah*) *n.* Child-hatred, an extreme dislike of children, aversion to children.

To 35 per cent MISOPEDIA means FOOT-TROUBLE. Numerous words come from the Latin *pes*, *pedis*, foot, as PEDAL, and PEDESTRIAN, walking on foot; but -PEDIA at the end of MISOPEDIA comes from the Greek παῖς (*pais*), παιδός (*paidos*), child, boy or girl, pronounced like the Latin *pes*, *pedis*, foot. From the Greek come PEDIATRICIAN, which ends with the Greek ἰατρεία (*iatreia*), medical treatment, and PEDAGOGUE, from παῖς (*pais*), παιδός (*paidos*), child, and ἄγειν (*agein*), to lead, guide.

From the Greek μισεῖν (*misein*), to hate, come MISOGYNY, hatred of women; MISOGAMY, dislike of marriage; and MISO- PEDIA, dislike of children.

1217. *ATRABILIOUS*, atrabilious (ă-tră-bǐl'-ǐ-ŭs) *adj*. Melancholy, sad, unhappy, hypochondriacal, splenetic.

The Greek physician, Hippocrates, 460 to 357 B.C., conceived four humors: blood, black bile, yellow bile, and phlegm. ATRABILIOUS comes from the Latin *atra*, the feminine of *ater*, black, and *bilis*, bile. The single noun BILE, a bitter, yellow liquid, secreted by the liver, is used for ill nature, peevishness; while the adjective BILIOUS (bǐl'-yŭs), from the Latin *biliosis*, full of BILE, means cross, testy, choleric.

Although answers scatter, showing that ATRABILIOUS is beyond most of those who have taken the worksample, 40 per cent concentrate on HOSTILE, misled perhaps by BELLICOSE, warlike, pugnacious, from the Latin *bellum*, war, perhaps because BIL- IOUS means cross, peevish. But ATRABILIOUS is sad, melancholy, rather than BELLICOSE, hostile.

1218. *VALETUDINARY*, valetudinary (văl-ĕ-tū'-dĭ-nă-rĭ) *adj*. Sickly, infirm, weak, invalid, delicate, seeking to recover health.

To 40 per cent of high-vocabulary adults VALETUDINARY means GRADUATING, compared with only 10 per cent who select SICK. The VALEDICTORY (văl-ĕ-dĭk'-tō-rĭ) comes from the Latin *vale-dictus*, the past participle of *valedicere*, to say farewell, a com- bination of *vale*, farewell, the imperative of *valere*, to be well, strong, and *dicere*, to say. As an adjective, VALEDICTORY means bidding farewell, taking leave, and as a noun is the farewell oration spoken at graduation. The VALEDICTORIAN (văl-ĕ-dĭk- tō'-rĭ-ăn) is the student who pronounces the oration at the GRADUATING exercises.

VALETUDINARY, and the more used VALETUDINARIAN, which may be either an adjective or a noun, come from the Latin *valetudinarius*, sickly, in bad health, from *valetudo*, *valetudinis*, sickness, which come, strangely, from *valere*, to be strong.

1219. *INCUBUS*, incubus (*ĭn'-kū-bŭs*) *n.* Imaginary demon,
    preternatural being, vampire, barghest (*bähr'-gĕst*),
nightmare, also sometimes heavy burden.
INCUBUS, directly from the Latin *incubus* which meant nightmare, comes from the Latin verb *incubare*, to lie upon, a combination of *in*, and *cubare*, the source of CUBICLE (*kū'-bĭ-kl*),
not just a little room, but specifically a little bedroom. From the
same *incubare* come INCUBATOR, INCUBATION, and the verb to
INCUBATE, to sit upon, brood, and so hatch eggs, produce by
hatching. These lead directly to the popular mislead, HATCHERY,
marked by 35 per cent, compared with only 10 per cent who
select NIGHTMARE. The word INCUBUS, although from the same
source as INCUBATE, has come to have the specific meaning
vampire, demon.

1220. *HEATH*, heath (*hēth*) *n.* Open uncultivated land, deso-
    late in character, waste land overgrown with shrubs.
HEATH is thought by 44 per cent to mean MOUND. This is probably the word HEAP, directly from Anglo-Saxon, a pile, stack,
mass of things gathered together on top of one another.
    HEATH, also from Anglo-Saxon, where the original sense was
open uncultivated land, is marked by 30 per cent as FARM LAND.
A HEATH is always uncultivated and so not FARM LAND.
    Another 6 per cent selected DESERT as the meaning. A DESERT
is usually sandy, and the word emphasizes almost complete lack
of water. WASTE, wild, barren land without habitation, is a
better one-word synonym.
    HEATHER, a low-growing evergreen shrub, called also HEATH,
is characteristic of a HEATH.

1221. *BINNACLE*, binnacle (*bĭn'-nă-kl*) *n.* A thick water-
    proof housing on a ship's deck to hold a compass.
In this vocabulary item, 22 per cent select CASE, compared with
16 per cent in favor of COMPASS. Strictly the BINNACLE is the
CASE in which the compass is kept, fitted with lights for night
reading. The word comes from the Latin *habitaculum*, a little
dwelling.
    Another 22 per cent select CROW'S NEST as the meaning of
BINNACLE: while 24 per cent choose PEAK. A PINNACLE, the same

except for the first letter, is a PEAK, the sharp-pointed top of a mountain, or in architecture a sharp-pointed ornament.

A BINNACLE is a COMPASS CASE.

1222. *CURMUDGEON*, curmudgeon (*ker-mŭj'-ŏn*) *n.* An avaricious churl, miser, niggard, a penurious, stingy, close-fisted, parsimonious fellow.

BRACE, marked by 36 per cent, is the popularly accepted meaning of CURMUDGEON. LARGE CLUB, chosen by another 26 per cent, is obviously a confusion of CURMUDGEON with BLUDGEON, a heavy stick often loaded at one end.

MISER, selected by only 22 per cent, comes from the Latin *miser*, wretched, unfortunate, miserable, sick, worthless, the source of MISERY, and MISERABLE. From this word MISER has come to mean one who behaves as if he were MISERABLE but who in reality hoards money.

A CUR, probably of Scandinavian origin, is a worthless dog, an outcast, or sometimes an ill-natured man, despicable fellow. MUDGEON is an unusual word for a grimace, wry face, grotesque look. Though the literal translation of CURMUDGEON is CUR-FACED, and all of the definitions are unpleasant, the word is used only of someone who, despite his faults, one really at heart respects.

1223. *LUBBERLY*, lubberly (*lŭb'-ber-lĭ*) *adj.* Clumsy, awkward.

The noun, a LUBBER, goes back through Middle English and, like many nautical terms, to Dutch and German. A LUBBER, a word used by sailors, is a heavy, clumsy fellow, dolt, a member of the crew with no seamanship. A LUBBERHEAD is a stupid-fellow. A LUBBER'S HOLE is a hole next to the mast used by LUBBERS and greenhorns as an easy way up. The unusual noun LOB means a dull, sluggish person, a lout; also the last person in a race. To LOB in tennis is to hit a slow ball over the head of an opponent.

Given a choice between SLOW and MASSIVE as synonyms of LUBBERLY, 38 per cent select the first and 22 per cent the second, and this is about the degree to which the two ideas enter the word LUBBERLY.

1224. *PECTORAL*, pectoral (*pĕk'-tō-răl*) *n.* A pendant, ornament worn on the breast, locket hanging from a necklace.
To 46 per cent PECTORAL means SHOULDER BLADE, compared with only 11 per cent who mark PENDANT. SCAPULA (*skăp'-ū-lah*), directly from the Latin *scapula*, shoulder, is the technical term for the SHOULDER BLADE; Bailey says: 'The hinder (*hĭn'-dēr*) part of the shoulder, a broad bone of triangular figure'.

PECTORAL, relating to the breast, from the Latin *pectus, pectoris*, the breast-bone, at one time meant a breastplate, armor to protect the breast, but is now an ornament worn on the breast; Chambers says: 'In the Romish Church, bishops and regular abbots wear a PECTORAL cross, a little cross of gold hanging from the neck down to the breast'.

1225. *OBSEQUIES*, obsequies (*ŏb'-sē-kwēs*) *n.* Funeral rites, ceremonies for the burial of the dead.
To 63 per cent OBSEQUIES means FLATTERERS, four and one-half times as many as select FUNERAL RITES. There are two words: OBSEQUY, spelt and pronounced alike. One comes from the Latin *obsequium*, compliance, yielding, obedience, from *obsequi*, to comply with, yield, literally to follow upon, from *ob-*, and *sequi*, to follow. From this comes OBSEQUIOUS, submissive to the will of another, slavish, servile, dutiful, compliant, cringing, fawning, sycophantic, ready to obey, careful to please, and so OBSEQUIOUS.

The word OBSEQUY, with the plural OBSEQUIES, comes from the Latin *exsequiae*, funeral rites. OBSEQUIES are funeral solemnities, ceremonies performed at the burials of eminent personages, being the last devoirs rendered to the deceased.

1226. *MADDER*, madder (*mad'-der*) *n.* Pigment, dyestuff, coloring matter.
In the first form of this vocabulary worksample, where by mistake both PIGMENT and DYE were included as choices, 47 persons selected PIGMENT, and only 11 per cent DYE, though the latter was called correct. PIGMENT and DYE are synonymous. Both are substances which give color.

MADDER is a plant which yields a valuable red or crimson dyestuff.

1227. *INVEST*, invest (*ĭn-vĕst'*) *v.* To surround with troops,
     encircle, beleaguer, hem in so as to prevent escape; the
same word now means place money at interest or with the hope
of profit.

INVEST comes from the Latin *investire*, to clothe, cover, dress,
attire, a combination of *in*, and *vestire*, to dress, from the Latin
vestis, clothing, the source of VEST, VESTMENT, VESTRY, and
TRAVESTY, literally a dressing over in different clothes, disguising. To INVEST was originally to dress, clothe, cover, the opposite
of DIVEST, strip, uncover, take away.

From the original cover, comes this derived meaning of hem
in, surround with troops, as: 'The town was INVESTED'. OCCU-
PIED, marked by nearly everyone, many more than select the
correct answer, SURROUND, may be the word INFEST, which
originally meant attack, but which has come to mean overrun,
almost OCCUPY.

The two misleads, SURRENDERED and OCCUPIED, are both close
to the military meaning of INVESTED. INVESTING a town, surrounding it with troops, cutting it off from communication,
is a final step toward OCCUPYING it, actually entering and taking
it over. Also INVESTING a town, surrounding it, is just preliminary to the town's SURRENDER, giving up.

1228. *PERUKE*, peruke (*pĕ-rūk'*) *n.* A man's wig.
     A PERUKE is a wig, but as many persons select BEARD and
ROBE as WIG, 24 per cent each for BEARD and ROBE compared with
20 per cent for WIG. The PERUKE came into fashion as early as
1550 as a small wig to cover a bald spot. Then one hundred years
later, between 1650 and 1725, it grew heavy and elaborate. The
PERUKE survived in Great Britain in the wigs worn by barristers,
judges, Speaker of the House of Commons, and the Lord
Chancellor.

1229. *PERSPICUOUSLY*, perspicuously (*per-spĭk'-ū-ŭs-lĭ*)
     adv. Plainly, clearly, lucidly, transparently, intelligibly.
To 39 per cent PERSPICUOUSLY means INTELLIGENTLY. INTELLI-
GIBLY means clearly, plainly, PERSPICUOUSLY. Both PERSPICU-
OUSLY and INTELLIGIBLY apply to that which is produced as:
'He writes PERSPICUOUSLY', clearly; or, 'He writes INTELLIGIBLY'.

But INTELLIGENT and INTELLIGENTLY apply to the person trying to understand, as 'He reads INTELLIGENTLY', with understanding. Possibly the word PERSPICACIOUS adds to the confusion, for PERSPICACIOUS means quick-sighted, quick-witted, INTELLIGENT.

Of the noun PERSPICUITY (*per-spĭ-kū'-ĭ-tĭ*), from *perspicere*, to see through, a combination of *per*, through, and *specere*, to see, Ephraim Chambers says: 'Clearness or plainness in writing or speaking, a principal excellence of style to which all the ornaments and beauties of speech ought to give way, as it is necessary to render a discourse intelligible, and form one of the constituent parts of elegance. Three ways in which the PERSPICUITY of a composition may be violated are: by obscurity, ambiguity, and unintelligible expression.'

1230. *FACULTATIVE*, facultative (*făk'-ŭl-tā-tĭv*) *adj*. Conferring the power of doing, occasional, incidental.

Ordinarily -IVE, added to a verb, makes it an adjective. Here it is added to the noun FACULTY. FACULTY, from the Latin *facultas*, *facultatis*, capability, ability, skill, means power to perform an action, ability, talent, reason, memory, aptitude, natural gift. This leads 12 persons in a group of 29 high-vocabulary adults to select INHERITED as the meaning of the adjective. Many FACULTIES, gifts, aptitudes are INHERITED, received from ancestors; and according to The Century Dictionary FACULTATIVE first meant conferring a FACULTY. But INHERITED means specifically received from ancestors, not acquired by study, practice, or hard work, whereas FACULTATIVE has drifted in an almost opposite direction.

FACULTY may also mean a selected group upon whom a FACULTY has been conferred and so a group of professors. This leads another 15 examinees to select INSTRUCTIVE as the meaning. While GIFTED, TALENTED, ENDOWED all mean with FACULTIES in the original sense, there is no adjective for the FACULTY of a college, and FACULTATIVE might easily go in this direction as INSTRUCTING is the popular meaning.

But for many years FACULTATIVE has had the exact but unusual meaning of conferring the power of doing or not doing, rendering optional, and so finally having the power to perform but exercising it only occasionally or failing to exercise it, an opposite of OBLIGATORY.

1231. *BASILISK*, basilisk (*băs'-ĭ-lĭsk*) *n.* Dragon, cockatrice,
    imaginary serpent, fabulous creature, lizard; its breath
and even a sight of it were fatal.
BASILISK comes through the Latin from the Greek βασιλίσκος
(*basiliskos*), a little king, also a kind of serpent, the diminutive
of βασιλεύς (*basileus*), a king.
    To 38 per cent BASILISK means TEMPLE, the popular mislead.
A BASILICA (*bă-sĭl'-ĭ-kah*), from the same Greek βασιλεύς, was
originally, several hundred years before Christ, a building in
Athens in which the king declared justice. Later, in Rome, when
the same building was used for Christian worship, the word
BASILICA became nearly synonymous with CHURCH.
    To another 36 per cent BASILISK means TALL MONUMENT,
suggested of course by OBELISK, a tall square column, with a
pointed top, sometimes seventy or more feet in height. OBELISK
comes from the Greek ὀβελίσκος (*obeliskos*), a painted pillar,
the diminutive of ὀβελός.
    A COCKATRICE and a BASILISK are apparently the same.

1232. *CACHINNATE*, cachinnate (*kăk'-ĭn-nāt*) *v.* To laugh
    loudly, inmmoderately, and continuously, without suffi-
cient reason. The noun CACHINNATION is loud continued laughter.
Compared with the simple Anglo-Saxon LAUGH, the words
CACHINNATE and CACHINNATION, said to be imitative, from the
Latin *cachinnare*, also to laugh loudly, are as unpleasant as the
sounds they name. Use LAUGH except for unpleasant laughter.
Other kinds of LAUGHTER are: CACKLE, GAGGLE, GIGGLE, and
CHUCKLE.
    The mislead SPIT is perhaps because of the equally long word
EXPECTORATE, which ends with the same letters.

1233. *ILLATION*, illation (*ĭl-lā'-shŏn*) *n.* An inferring from
    premises, inference, deduction, conclusion.
To INFER is to draw a tentative conclusion from facts, to form
an opinion, to believe as the result of reasoning. INFERENCE is
the corresponding noun, the opinion reached, the conclusion
drawn.
    But *latus*, the past participle of the verb *ferre*, to carry, bear,
bring, and *inlatus*, which becomes *illatus*, is the past participle

of *inferre*. From this *illatus* comes ILLATION, and inference, deduction drawn from premises, conclusion based on reasoning from observation.

Another pair of English words, the first from *ferre* and the second from *latus*, are TRANSFER and TRANSLATE.

To 20 per cent, one fifth of those who have taken this vocabulary test, ILLATION means MANEUVER. To ELUDE is to avoid by artifice, evade by trickery, while the noun ELUSION is an evasion, escape by stratagem, and this may lead to the selection of MANEUVER as the meaning of ILLATION. But ELUDE, spelt with one L, and ELUSION, as well as ALLUDE, DELUDE, ILLUDE, to deceive by false hopes, and LUDICROUS, all come from *ludere*, to play. An ILLATION, from *latus*, is not an ALLUSION or ILLUSION, but an inference drawn.

1234. *VIDUITY*, viduity (*vĭ-dū'-ĭ-tĭ*) *n.* Widowhood, the condition of having lost a husband by death.

To 55 per cent VIDUITY means EMPTINESS. VACUITY, much like VIDUITY in sound and spelling, from the Latin *vacuus*, empty, is emptiness, vacancy, vacant space, a vacuum, and may lead to the selection of EMPTINESS.

Also VIDUITY comes from the Latin *vidua*, a widow, which as an adjective may mean lacking, and so lacking a husband. From *viduus*, lacking, comes the English VOID, empty, all of which may contribute to the selection of EMPTINESS.

WIDOW and WIDOWHOOD are Anglo-Saxon; VIDUITY is Latin and means WIDOWHOOD. Both VIDUITY and WIDOWHOOD come probably from the same Sanskrit source, perhaps as far back as 2000 B.C.

1235. *THURIBLE*, thurible (*thĕr'-ĭ-bl*) *n.* A censer, a metal vessel, hanging from three chains, in which incense burns before the altar, ornamental receptacle for holding smouldering incense, any container designed to contain material which burns slowly and gives off a sweet pleasant odor.

INCENSE (*ĭn'-sĕns*), the noun, accented on the first syllable, from *incensus*, the past participle of the Latin verb *incendere*, to kindle, inflame, set on fire, is an aromatic gum or sweet smelling substance producing a pleasant fragrance when burned. A

CENSER, from the same Latin, contains hot charcoal on which odoriferous powders are sprinkled.

The Century Dictionary says: 'THURIBLE is the technical ecclesiastical term for CENSER', for the two are identical, CENSER, directly from the Latin, THURIBLE from the Greek, through the Latin *thuribulum,* a censer, from *thus thuris,* frankincense, from the Greek θύος (*thuos*), incense.

The earliest ancient Egyptian THURIBLES were bowl-shaped, with a handle like a ladle. Those of the Greeks and Romans were small beautifully decorated braziers, open dishes of bronze. Today THURIBLES more often hang from three slender chains.

To 24 per cent THURIBLE means CROSS, words used in the same environment, the second step in learning; but the misconceptions scatter, suggesting that the word is wholly unknown to most persons, as are many words of Greek origin.

1236. *COMATOSE,* comatose (*kŏm'-ă-tōs*) *adj.* Morbidly drowsy, lethargic, resembling a COMA, deeply sleepy, somnolent, in a state of STUPOR.

A COMA, from the Greek κῶμα (*coma*), is a deep sleep, a state of unconsciousness, from which one cannot be roused.

In the first form of this worksample, both SOMNIFEROUS (*sŏm-nĭ'-fĕ-rŭs*) and TORPID were included, the first selected by 50 per cent, and the second by 20 per cent. TORPID, though used of animals in the natural sleep of hibernation, is a closer synonym of COMATOSE. Those who select the first, probably know the meaning of COMATOSE; but SOMNIFEROUS, from the Latin *somnus,* sleep, and *ferre,* to bring, when used correctly, means bringing on sleep, producing drowsiness, soporific, as: 'A SOMNIFEROUS potion'. SOMNOLENT (*sŏm'-nō-lĕnt*) is the adjective which means sleepy, a synonym of COMATOSE.

1237. *BURSARY,* bursary (*ber'-sā-rĭ*) *n.* Today the treasury of a college; but once a grant to a college student to help with his room and board, a scholarship.

BURSE and PURSE are fundamentally the same word. Both are bags usually to hold money. Both come from the Greek βύρσα (*bursa*), a hide, skin. A PURSER is often the paymaster of a ship, in charge of keeping accounts and dispensing money.

From BURSE comes the BOURSE, the STOCK EXCHANGE of Paris. A CASHIER is one in charge of cash, handling routine money transactions. A BURSAR is the treasurer of a college, often with great authority; and BURSARY may be the place in which a BURSAR works.

The original meaning of BURSAR was the college student who received an allowance for his subsistence; and a BURSARY was the sum paid.

VAULT, marked by 30 per cent, and PURCHASE, by 24 per cent, both connected with money, are selected more often than the unusual meaning GRANT.

1238. *TELEOLOGICAL*, teleological (*tē-lē-ō-lŏj'-ĭ-kăl*) *adj.*
Pertaining to the doctrine of final causes, relating to the philosophy of a designed existence, of the theory of a tendency toward a purposeful end.

The Greek τῆλε (*tele*) means afar, distant, as in TELEPHONE, a sound at a distance, and TELESCOPE, literally distant view; while another Greek word τέλος (*telos*), with the genitive τέλεος (*teleos*), at the beginning of TELEOLOGICAL, means end, completion, final.

Given a choice between FUTURE-ORIENTED and PURPOSEFUL as synonyms of TELEOLOGICAL, 32 per cent select the first, and 20 per cent the second. Both are implied in TELEOLOGICAL.

The opposite of TELEOLOGICAL is sometimes given as MECHANICAL; and this purposeless aspect of a MECHANICAL world disturbs many thoughtful people.

1239. *WAFT*, waft (*wăft*) *v.* To carry through the air, drift, move through a buoyant medium.
To WAVE, to move to and fro, sway back and forth, flutter, undulate, fluctuate, comes directly from the Anglo-Saxon *waftam*. The past is WAVED, but may also be WAFT. Even though WAFT is already a past tense of WAVE, it has become so much a separate verb that one encounters WAFTED.

To 28 per cent WAFTED means PERMEATED, passing through a substance, penetrating the pores, pervading; and to another 24 per cent ROOTED, an exact opposite, because WAFTED means carried along as if by a wave.

1240. *APODICTIC*, apodictic (*ă-pō-dĭk'-tĭk*) *adj.* Provable, demonstrable, incontestable.

The second part of this word comes obviously from *dicere*, to say, the source of DICTATE, to give orders, command with authority; and DICTUM, a pronouncement, positive assertion. The question is, does APO- at the beginning, from the Greek ἀπό (*apo*), from, away, off, negative the assertion, or add to it positively. To 38 per cent APODICTIC means GROUNDLESS, without foundation, the best guess based on the derivation, unless one knows that the word has come to mean capable of being demonstrated, and so provable.

1241. *CICERONE*, cicerone (*sĭs-ĕ-rō'-nē*; the Italian pronunciation is *chē-chä-rō'-nä*) *n.* A museum guide, leader of a tour, docent, conductor of a traveling group.

The word comes directly from the proper name CICERO, the Roman statesman and orator who lived from 106 to 43 B.C. This leads 48 per cent to select ORATOR as the meaning of CICERONE, a correct interpretation except that the adjective CICERONIAN (*sĭs-ĕ-rō'-nĭ-ăn*) now refers to CICERO and his orations; while the word CICERONE has come to signify specifically a GUIDE, especially one in Italy who conducts parties through museums, talking on art, or who accompanies them on more extended expeditions.

1242. *COMESTIBLE*, comestible (*kō-mĕs'-tĭ-bl*) *n.* An edible, esculent, eatable, article of food, anything fit to be eaten.

To 24 per cent COMESTIBLE means HOUSEHOLD, establishment, usually the whole family, including anyone who lives in the house more or less permanently.

To another 30 per cent COMESTIBLE means FEAST. An EDIBLE is anything fit to eat, from the Latin *edere*, to eat. The COM-, at the beginning, intensifies the meaning. A FEAST is a grand, rich meal; its food is more than just EDIBLE; yet the selection of FEAST rather than EDIBLE can certainly be understood.

1243. *CONFITURE*, confiture (*kŏn'-fĭ-tūr*) *n.* Jam, comfit, sweetmeat, confection (*kŏn-fĕk'-shŏn*).

CONFITURE comes from the Latin *confectura*, a compound of

com, together, and *facere*, to make. A CONFECTION is the modern word for sweetmeat made of sugar.

A CONDIMENT is also something put together, from the same *com* or *con*, together; but a CONDIMENT is sharp, spicy, a relish, seasoning; a CONFITURE is always sweet.

To COMFORT (*kŭm'-fert*) comes from the Latin *com-*, together, and *fortis*, strength, and once meant to strengthen, fortify, give strength. A COMFORTER, something which COMFORTS, a thick, stuffed, quilted bedcover, leads 16 per cent to select QUILT as a meaning of CONFITURE.

COMFIT and COMFORT are two of the rare words in which the Latin *con-* has been changed in English to COM-. A COMFIT (*kŭm'-fĭt*) is also a sweet, a bonbon, fruit preserved in sugar, from *confectus*, the past participle of *conficere*, to put together, prepare. CONFITURE is archaic, rarely seen today.

1244. *HABILIMENT*, habiliment (*hă-bĭl'-ĭ-mĕnt*) *n.* Almost
           always in the plural: HABILIMENTS. A garment, vestment, or, in the plural, clothing, raiment, garb.

CUSTOMS, as the meaning of HABILIMENTS, attracts 30 per cent, and the two words have much in common. A COSTUME is a dress, garb, something worn, usually something characteristic of a period or sometimes of a nation. COSTUMES, starting with CO and ending with UME, are HABILIMENTS.

CUSTOMS, the word which appears in the vocabulary test, starting with CU and ending in OM, are habitual practices, habits, usages, the ordinary way of acting, defined sometimes as HABITUDES of a community; and it is easy to confuse HABITUDES with HABILIMENTS.

HABITUDE is customary mode of feeling, manner of acting, way of living. HABITUDE is the French *habitude*, from the Latin *habitudo*, condition, appearance, from *habitus*, the past participle of *habere*, to have, hold, keep.

HABILIMENTS, clothing, also through French from, *habiller*, to dress, clothe, through *habile*, able, ready, comes from the same Latin *habere*, to have, hold, the source of a dozen English words with different and distinct meanings.

CUSTOMS and HABITUDES are ways of doing things. COSTUMES and HABILIMENTS are things to wear.

1245. *BRAVURA*, bravura (*brah-voŏ'-rah*) *adj*. Spirited, brilliant, florid, displaying power.

To 49 per cent BRAVURA means BRILLIANT; and to another 27 per cent DARING. BRAVURA is an Italian word meaning bravery, daring, spirit, from the adjective *bravo*, brave, used as a noun in English, BRAVO, for a bandit, daring villain. In music, BRAVURA means BRILLIANT, spirited; so that the word combines the two ideas of BRILLIANCE and DARING.

1246. *ACCRESCENT*, accrescent (*ăk-krĕs'-sĕnt*) *adj*. Increasing, growing, accruing.

To 20 per cent ACCRESCENT, growing, means HEALTHY, and GROWING certainly suggests HEALTH. But ACCRESCENT comes from the Latin *accrescere*, to grow, a combination of *ad*, to, and *crescere*, to grow.

The verb to INCREASE, to add to, make greater, bigger, enlarge; the CRESCENT moon, the growing moon; an ACCRETION, an increase, addition; and to DECREASE, literally to grow down, all come from the same source, *crescere*, to grow.

1247. *EUTAXY*, eutaxy (*ū'-tăk-sē*) *n*. Good order, well managed, neat placement in sequence.

EUTAXY comes from the Greek εὐταξία (*eutaxia*), good arrangement, a combination of εὖ, well, and τακτός (*tactos*), arranged in order, regulated. Eu-, at the beginning, means well, as in EUPHONY, sounding well; and EUTAXY, well arranged, placed in good order. From τακτός comes TACTICS, in the military sense, moving forces about, usually secretly, as opposed to long range planning, called STRATEGY, and this may suggest, to 50 per cent, SLOW-MOVEMENTS as the meaning of EUTAXY, though the success of TACTICS usually depends on speed.

EUTAXY means RIGHT ORDER, an answer thus far marked by no one.

1248. *RECUSANCY*, recusancy (*rĕk'-ū-zăn-sĭ*) *n*. Obstinate refusal, denial, opposition, rejection, protesting against.

RECUSANCY comes from the Latin *recusare*, to reject, object, a combination of *re*, back, and *causa*, a cause, the source of ACCUSE. To RECUSE (*rē-kūz'*) is to reject, refuse.

The popular mislead, selected by 30 per cent, is TEMPERANCE, with no one as yet selecting OBSTINATE REFUSAL as the meaning.

1249. *SUBFUSC*, subfusc (*sŭb-fŭsk'*) *adj.* Brownish, tawny, duskish, swarthy, moderately dark, tinged with gray.

The unusual adjective SUBFUSC, and the more usual FUSCOUS, both come from the Latin *fuscus*, dark, swarthy, tawny, dusky, and mean dark brown, tinged with gray. To OBFUSCATE (*ŏb-fŭs'-kāt*), from *ob-*, to, and the same Latin *fuscus*, is to darken, obscure, and so confuse, bewilder.

The adjective SUBFUSC is misinterpreted by 35 per cent as ABANDONED, deserted, forsaken. Instead SUBFUSC means somewhat dark, as: 'The University statute requires the wearing of black or SUBFUSC clothing'.

1250. *ANTIMACASSAR*, antimacassar (*ăn-tĭ-mă-kăs'-săhr*) *n.* An ornamental covering for the back of a chair and the arms of a sofa to protect them from Macassar oil used on the hair; a tidy.

MACASSAR was a heavy oil, from Macassar, used by men in the 1800's. Of MACASSAR, John Mason Good, in his Encyclopaedia of 1813, writes: 'A seaport of the island of Celebes, the king of which is in alliance with the Dutch. The houses are of wood, and built upon piles, to preserve them from inundations, for which reason they must be entered by ladders'. The Celebes are north of Australia and south of the Philippines. Macassar oil had not yet become popular enough for him to mention it.

ANTE-, ending in E, means before, in front of; ending in I, ANTI-, means against. ANTIMACASSAR is against MACASSAR.

By 60 per cent an ANTIMACASSAR is called a BIB, twice as many as mark TIDY. A TIDY, the Anglo-Saxon word TIDE, time, season, has come to mean the covering for the back of a chair, or for its arms, and is an exact synonym of ANTIMACASSAR. A BIB is for children; an APRON for adults; while TIDIES and ANTIMACASSARS are for furniture.

1251. *CADUCITY*, caducity (*kă-dū'-sĭ-tĭ*) *n.* A tendency to fall or decay, the period of declining life, senility, feebleness, weakness.

CADUCITY comes from the Latin, *caducus*, falling, from *cadere*, to fall. From this root come also: CADENCE, a falling of the voice in reading or speaking; DECADENT (*dē-kā'-dent*), deteriorating, going down, falling away; DECAY, falling into an inferior position; ACCIDENT, from *accidere*, a combination of *ad*, to, and the same *cadere*, to fall, anything which befalls unexpectedly; and OCCIDENT, the region of the falling sun, the West. CADUCITY is any tendency to fall, decline.

Those who have taken this vocabulary test divide evenly among the four misleads, with no one marking SENILITY as the meaning of CADUCITY.

1252. *DESINENCE*, desinence (*dĕs'-ĭ-nĕns*) *n*. Ending, close, termination, inflectional suffix, formative addition to a word root which gives it grammatical meaning.

DESINENCE is thought by 20 per cent to mean TIMBRE, probably because of the word DISSONANCE, from the Latin *dis*, apart, and *sonus*, a sound, discord, harshness, jarring of sounds, a combination of unrelated tones. TIMBRE (*tĭm'-br* or *tăm'-br*) is that quality of a tone which, because of its overtones, differentiates it from other tones of the same pitch.

DESINENCE comes from the Latin *desinens*, *desinentis*, closing, the present participle of *desinere*, to cease, close, end, a combination of *de*, off, and *sinere*, to leave.

1253. *LATERITIOUS*, lateritious (*lăt-ĕ-rĭsh'-ŭs*) *adj*. Like bricks, of the color of bricks.

LATERITIOUS, usually spelt LATERICEOUS but pronounced the same, comes from the Latin *latericius*, consisting of bricks, from *later*, a brick, or brick tile.

To 67 per cent LATERITIOUS means SIDE, with no one thus far marking BRICK RED. The Latin *latus*, *lateris*, means SIDE, and from this comes the English LATERAL, on the side, at the side, as in QUADRILATERAL, four-sided, and COLLATERAL, which has come to mean a combination of secondary, subordinate, and strengthening.

LATERITIOUS comes from an entirely different Latin word, but one almost identical in appearance: *later*, LATERIS, meaning brick, or brick tile.

1254. *HYPOGEAL*, hypogeal (*hĭ-pō-jē'-ăl*) *adj*. Subterranean, underground, beneath the surface of the earth.

The prefix HYPO-, the Greek ὑπό (*hypo*) in Roman letters, means under, below, as opposed to HYPER-, over, above. HYPO- appears in chemistry for a series of compounds each with one less oxygen atom than the series above.

The suffix -AL at the end makes an adjective. The -GE- in the middle is the Greek γῆ (*ge*), γαῖα (*gaia*), the earth, ground. From this comes GEOGRAPHY, literally writing about the earth, GEOLOGY, studying the earth, and GEOMETRY, measuring the earth. HYPOGEAL belongs to botany, applying to plants which germinate underground.

1255. *EMBACLE*, embacle (*ĕm-băk'-ĕl*) *n*. The accumulation of broken ice in a river; an ice-jam.

An EMBACLE, from the French *embâcle*, is formed during very cold winters in rivers and other waterways by the gradual piling-up of drift-ice. If the river swells and lifts free this mass of ice, it can float downstream and cause considerable damage to bridges and boats.

A DEBACLE, from the French *débâcle*, in its original meaning is the break-up or dispersion of this mass of ice, as in the spring thaw, and the sudden, violent rush of water which this can cause; hence, any sudden downfall or collapse. EMBACLE, which has not developed such a useful secondary meaning, is much less common in English than its companion word DEBACLE.

1256. *OSCITANT*, oscitant (*ŏs'-ĭ-tănt*) *adj*. Yawning, gaping, sleepy, drowsy, dull, sluggish.

The verb to OSCITATE (*ŏs'-sĭ-tāt*), to yawn, gape with sleepiness, appeared in the Imperial Dictionary, published in Glasgow, in 1850, based on Noah Webster's American Dictionary of 1828, and in turn the basis of the Century Dictionary of 1891.

OSCITANT is the Latin *oscitans, oscitantis*, the present participle of *oscitare*, to yawn, gape, open the mouth wide, a combination of *os*, with the Latin plural *ora* (*ō'-rah*), the mouth, and *ciere*, to put into motion. From *citare*, to cause to move, excite, the frequentative of *ciere*, come the verbs to EXCITE, and INCITE, stir up, arouse, both suggesting motion.

To 20 per cent OSCITANT means INVIGORATED, a translation of the Latin, but an exact opposite of OSCITANT, as that word is used in English.

1257. *MORDANT*, mordant (*mŏr'-dănt*) *adj*. Biting, caustic, keen, acrid, severe, and, figuratively, sarcastic.

To 40 per cent MORDANT means GLOOMY, compared with only 12 per cent who select CAUSTIC. MORBID (*mŏr'-bĭd*) is GLOOMY, from the Latin *morbidus*, sickly, diseased, from *morbus*, diseased. MORBUS in English means diseased, as CHOLERA MORBUS. MORBID in English is not only diseased, sickly, unhealthy, but applied mentally suggests a depression of spirits, and so GLOOMY.

MORDANT comes from the Latin *mordens, mordentis*, the present participle of *mordere*, to bite, also to sting, smart. From this verb *mordere*, to bite, come by steps the past participle *morsus*, and the neuter *morsum*, a bit, and so MORSEL, a bite, mouthful, fragment, small piece, and MUZZLE, once spelt MORSEL, the snout or mouth of an animal, and also a contrivance to put over the mouth or snout to keep the animal from biting. Directly from the verb *mordere* comes MORDANT, biting in the sense of an acid; used as a noun in etching for a substance which bites into and eats away metal.

1258. *PATULOUS*, patulous (*pă'-ū-lŭs*) *adj*. Spreading, gaping, open, patent, expanded, having a wide aperture.

The marking of the five choices seems pure chance, with less concentration on the correct OPEN than on any of the others.

PETAL, part of a flower, comes from the Greek πέταλον (*petalon*), a leaf, the neuter of πέταλος (*petalos*), outspread, flat, broad. From the same original source comes the Latin *patere*, to lie open, with the present participle *patens, patentis*, lying open, and so public, and from this PATENT, open, an opposite of COVERT, concealed. From the same *patere*, to lie open, comes the Latin *patulus*, lying open, and so PATULOUS, used in botany to mean spreading, expanded.

1259. *SUBSUME*, subsume (*sŭb-sūm'*) *v*. To state a case under a general rule, name an object as belonging to a class under consideration.

To 26 per cent SUBSUMED means ADDED, perhaps because of the letters SUM in the word SUBSUME; for the English noun a SUM comes from the Latin *summa*, with two M's, and not from *sumere*, to take.

To RESUME, from the Latin *re*, again, and *sumere*, to take, is to take up again. To ASSUME is to undertake, take upon one's self, as: 'To ASSUME a responsibility'. Though ASSUME may mean take for granted without proof, PRESUME, to accept beforehand, take for granted in advance, infer as probable, should be used for this meaning.

To SUBSUME, starting with the Latin *sub*, under, prefixed to *sumere*, to take, is used in logic to mean take a particular example under a general heading. William Fleming, in his Vocabulary of Philosophy, says: 'Thus if one were to say: "No man is wise in all things", and another to respond: "You are a man", this proposition is a SUBSUMPTION under the former'.

1260. *MAGNILOQUENT*, magniloquent (*măg-nĭl'-ō-kwĕnt*) adj. Pompous, bombastic, grandiloquent, writing in a lofty style.

LOCUTION, from *loquens, loquentis*, the present participle of *loqui*, to speak, is the act of speaking, form of speaking: ELOQUENT is speaking out well. MAGNILOQUENT, from the Latin *magnus*, great, lofty, is speaking in a grand manner, an exact synonym of GRANDILOQUENT.

With both POMPOUS and LOFTY as choices in the vocabulary test, 60 per cent prefer the first, and 18 per cent the second, LOFTY. The word LOFTY may be complimentary, of high character, exalted rank; or it may mean superficially elevated, and so POMPOUS, MAGNILOQUENT. Both POMPOUS and MAGNILOQUENT are invariably uncomplimentary.

1261. *PRISTINE*, pristine (*prĭs'-tĭn*) adj. Pertaining to the earliest period, primeval, original, primitive, former, previous.

In the test phrase: 'The PRISTINE state', the word is thought by 34 per cent to mean PERFECT, the popular misconception. PERFECT comes from the Latin *perfectus*, finished, a combination of *per*, through, and *facere*, to make, and by derivation means carried through to completion and so lacking in nothing, complete. But PERFECT is also used to mean unblemished, without a defect. In Macbeth, Shakespeare uses 'PRISTINE health'; and Symonds says 'PRISTINE state of happiness', where the word in both instances can be misinterpreted to mean complete, PERFECT, and even the highest vocabulary examinees mark PERFECT, practically as often as ORIGINAL, as the meaning of PRISTINE. But PRISTINE means ORIGINAL, and not PERFECT.

By only 18 per cent is PRISTINE thought to be PRIMITIVE, compared with 48 per cent who select INNOCENT, pure, virtuous, blameless, guiltless, also simple, naive. PRIM means stiffly precise, demure, neat, formal, and may suggest INNOCENT.

PRIMARY, PRIOR, PRIME, PRIMITIVE, PRISTINE, PRIMEVAL, PRIMORDIAL, and PRIMAL, are all associated, and all by derivation mean first, going before. PRIMARY and PRIME mean first in time, first in order of importance; PRISTINE, from the Latin *pristinus*, early, original, means primitive, belonging to the beginning, but is always complimentary, and this aspect of the word may contribute to the selection of INNOCENT as the meaning.

1262. *WEN*, wen (*wĕn*) *n*. A benign tumor of small size, wart, cyst.

WEN is thought by 38 per cent to mean DEPRESSION, hollow, hole, cavity. This may be the word DEN, a hole in a mountain side, or it may be a confusion of opposites, for a WEN is a swelling, small protuberance, abnormal elevation on the skin containing a fatty greasy substance.

1263. *SCION*, scion (*sī-ŏn*) *n*. A child, offspring, descendant, son or daughter.

SCION should be spelt *sion*, without the C, which was wrongly inserted in the 17th century in the belief that SCION comes from the Latin *scindere*, to cut, the source of SCISSORS, spelt correctly with the C. SCION comes in fact from the Latin *secare*, to cut, the source of SECTION, a division, part cut off, and of SCYTHE, a long, curving blade, with a sharp edge, and a handle for mowing, a word which should also be spelt with no C. A SCION is a twig, branch, sprig, shoot, literally a twig cut to graft on another tree. From this SCION has come to mean OFFSPRING.

To 30 per cent SCION means BENEFICIARY, compared with only 18 per cent who select CHILD. A SCION, offspring, child, is apt to receive something in a will, but a BENEFICIARY may also receive something from a trust or even from an insurance company.

To another 24 per cent, SCION means NOBLE ONE. SCION is too elegant a word to apply to an ordinary child, and suggests the offspring of a royal family.

1264. *CHATOYANT*, chatoyant (*shă-toi'-ănt*) *adj.* Changing color, lustrous, iridescent, shimmering.

Both CHATOYANT and IRIDESCENT add color to SHIMMERING. The verb to SHIMMER, from Anglo-Saxon, is to shine faintly with a changing light. Dictionaries define SHIMMERING as tremulous, trembling, shaking. SHIMMER, although selected by 45 per cent as the meaning of CHATOYANT, lacks color.

IRIDESCENT, spelt with one R, from IRIS, goddess of the rainbow, through the Latin *iris*, and the Greek ἴρις (*iris*), the rainbow, is shimmering with rainbow colors.

CHATOYANT, the French chatoyant (*shăt-oi-yăn'*), the present participle of *chatoyer*, to change lustre like the eye of a cat, comes from the French *chat*, cat, and is a combination of SHIMMERING and CHANGING-COLOR, this last selected as a synonym by only 12 per cent.

1265. *KERMIS*, kermis (*kĕr'-mĭs*) (usually spelt kermess) *n.*

A country celebration, fair, festival in honor of the founding of a church, with entertainment; any annual fair, especially for charitable purposes.

The Encyclopaedia Britannica spells this word KERMESSE, and adds: also KERMIS and KERMESS, equivalent to 'KIRKMASS', a mass said on the anniversary of the founding of a church, in honor of the patron saint of the community. KERMIS, with similar words in Polish, Russian, and Lithuanian, all come from the Dutch and Flemish word *kermis*. In the Low Countries and Northern France, a KERMIS is now a country fair, with dancing, sports, and feasting.

The selection of choices scatter, showing almost complete ignorance of the word.

1266. *ESCULENT*, esculent (*ĕs'-kū-lĕnt*) *adj.* Edible, fit for
    food, eatable.

To 40 per cent of better-than-average examinees ESCULENT
means JUICY, a confusion with SUCCULENT (*sŭk'-kū-lĕnt*),
JUICY, full of juice, from the Latin *succulentus*, full of juice,
from the verb *sugere*, to suck.

EAT is Anglo-Saxon, but related words appear in numerous
languages, from Icelandic to the Greek ἔδειν (*edein*), to eat.
ESCULENT comes from the Latin *esculentus*, good to eat, eatable,
from *esca*, food, which comes probably from *edere*, to eat, the
source of EDIBLE, fit to be eaten.

1267. *PROTOCOL*, protocol (*prō'-tō-kŏl*) *n.* The minutes of
    a transaction, original copy of any treaty, draft of pro-
ceedings signed by friendly powers, record of the agreements
in a conference signed by the parties, as: 'The representatives of
all the powers signed the PROTOCOL'.

PROTOCOL comes from πρωτο (*proto*), first, and κόλλα (*colla*),
glue. PROTOCOLLUM, πρωτόκολλον, was a term used in ancient
jurisprudence for the first leaf of a book, the fly-leaf, wherein
was the mark of the paper or parchment; also the first minute,
draught, or summary of an act to be passed, which the notary
drew up, to be afterwards enlarged at leisure.

In medieval Latin and the Romance languages, especially
French, the same word PROTOCOL is applied to the etiquette
observed by the head of the state in official ceremonies.

1268. *CAREERING*, careering (*kă-rēr'-ĭng*) *v.* Running, rac-
    ing, moving forward rapidly; colloquially, to tear ahead.
The verb to CAREER is to run rapidly as in a race. The noun,
a CAREER, was originally a race course, the grounds on which a
race was run, hence a path or way.

The most commonly marked mislead is SAUNTERING, walking
slowly, wandering idly, selected by 24 per cent. CAREERING is
almost an opposite, to run fast on a definite course.

To another 18 per cent CAREERING means SWAYING. To CAREEN
is to tip a ship on one side so as to examine the bottom. From
this CAREEN has come to mean lean on one side, and this may
suggest SWAYING.

1269. *ZARF*, zarf (*zarf*) *n*. An ornamental metal holder for a
hot coffee cup, to prevent burning the fingers.

ZARF is thought by 40 per cent to mean INSIGNIA. A MARK,
somewhat like ZARF in appearance, is an emblem, symbol, IN-
SIGNIA. By another 32 per cent ZARF is thought to mean SCEPTER,
a staff or wand carried in the hand as an emblem of power.

The term ZARF comes directly from the Arabic, and is a term
used throughout the LEVANT.

1270. *PALFREY*, palfrey (*pawl'-frē*) *n*. A small saddle-horse,
woman's saddle-horse.

PALFREY comes through similar words in French, Spanish, and
Italian, perhaps originally from the Greek παρά (*para*), beside,
suggesting an extra horse.

To 24 per cent PALFREY means MENIAL, servile. The adjective
PALTRY, much like PALFREY in sound and appearance means
trifling, petty, insignificant, and from this has come to suggest
contemptible, mean, close to servile, MENIAL.

To another 36 per cent, PALFREY means DWARF, midget,
pygmy. A PALFREY is a small horse, larger than a PONY, and
not small enough to be a DWARF.

A letter from Barry Weaver, in answer to a request for more
information, states: 'In a broad but definite sense, the cowgirls
at the Will Rogers Memorial Rodeo at Claremore were riding
PALFREYS in the barrel race.

'Among the many subdivisions of riding horses and saddle
horses are some called QUARTER HORSES. Registered by the
American Quarter Horse Association these specifically were
the ones being ridden by those cowgirls. They can be red,
brown, or gray in color. Their name comes from their speed
in quarter-mile horse races. They are always a mixed breed
including Arabian, thoroughbred, and often sorrel riding stock.
MUSTANGS (degenerated Spanish horses gone wild in the American Southwest) and PINTO ponies or PINTOS (small spotted horses
often used by Navajo and some Indians) are strains of riding
stock which had an early but mediocre influence on the development of top QUARTER HORSES.

'DRAFT-HORSE would contrast with PALFREY as would CHARGER
and of course CLYDESDALE, a breed of draft-horse.'

1271. *LUBRICIOUS*, lubricious (*lū-brĭ'-shŭs*) *adj*. Slippery, smooth; or figuratively, glib, voluble, uncertain.

LUBRICIOUS comes from the Latin *lubricus*, slippery, deceitful, from the verb *lubricare*, the source of LUBRICATE, to make slippery, greasy, smooth with grease.

1272. *BILLINGSGATE*, billingsgate (*bĭl'-lĭngz-gāt*) *n*. Ribaldry, blackguardism, profane language, scurrilous abuse.

BILLING'S GATE was one of the old gates of the city of London. Near it was a fish market, noted for its foul language.

To 28 per cent BILLINGSGATE means HARD WORK; and to another 21 per cent, LETTER WRITING.

1273. *TRUDGEN*, trudgen (*trŭd'-jĕn*) *n*. In swimming the double over-arm stroke.

A TRUNCHEON (*trŭn'-chŏn*) is a cudgel, short staff, CLUB, this last underlined by 55 per cent as the meaning of TRUDGEN.

The TRUDGEN stroke, more commonly called the TRUDGEN, was named for J. TRUDGEN, whose great swimming speed popularized the stroke in England in 1873. Though TRUDGEN learned it in South America, it was described in 1825 by a writer on swimming who called it the thrust.

As the Encyclopaedia Britannica says: TRUDGEN kept on the chest and lifted the upper part of his body out of the water, at each stroke, and at each swing of the arms pulled himself forward, a considerable swirl of water occurring as each movement was finished. The arms were brought forward sideways, each completing a circle on each side of the body and the head kept completely above water.

1274. *CACHET*, cachet (*kă-shā'*) *n*. An official seal, stamp, distinguishing mark.

To 32 per cent CACHET means HIDING PLACE. A CACHE (*kăsh*) is a hiding place, a place of concealment. Both CACHE and CACHET come from the French *cacher*, to hide. CACHE was introduced by Canadians called voyageurs (*vwŏ-yah-zherz'*) who worked for the Hudson's Bay Company, an enterprise which began in 1670 with a grant from Charles II, and lasted a hundred years or more.

CACHET is not Canadian, but a word used in French history, in the phrase: *Lettre de* CACHET, a letter, under seal, from the King, ordering the life imprisonment of someone who had fallen into his displeasure.

In philately, a CACHET is the name or slogan of a company stamped or printed on an envelope.

1275. *EDACIOUS*, edacious (*ē-dā'-shus*) *adj.* Given to eating, voracious (v. b. 1517), ravenous, rapacious, greedy, consuming.

EDACIOUS is derived from the Latin *edere*, to eat, devour, and by transference to inanimate objects: devouring, destroying, consuming. From this same root comes EDIBLE, capable of being eaten, and from the past participle of *edere, esum*, comes the stronger ESURIENT, hungry, greedy, and ESCULENT, suitable for use as a food, a synonym for EDIBLE. Indeed, the Anglo-Saxon derivation of our common word eat and the related German *essen* may share a common ancestor with the Latin in the Sanskrit *adakas*.

Ovid, noted Roman poet, in his Metamorphoses wrote: *Tempus edax rerum*, time, the devourer of things. This analogy to time's EDACITY, its rapaciousness, ravenous consuming, has been echoed by James Russell Lowell in his reference to an early landmark of American revolutionary history: 'Concord Bridge had long since yielded to the EDACIOUS tooth of Time,' and by modern humorist and essayist Clifton Fadiman: 'Time may have its EDACIOUS way even with those who deal in absolute truths.'

1276. *TESTATOR*, testator (*tĕs-tā'-tōr*) *n.* One who makes a will.

In legal terminology, a TESTAMENT is specifically a will, the disposition of property to take effect at death. The word comes directly from the Latin *testamentum*, the publication of a will.

To TESTIFY is to give evidence, bear witness, declare solemnly, from the Latin *testari*, to be a witness, testify, attest. Today a TESTIFIER is a witness, one who gives testimony. A TESTATOR is one who makes a will. A TESTATRIX is a female TESTATOR, a woman who makes a will.

1277. *CONTUMACIOUS,* contumacious (*kŏn-tū-mā'-shŭs*) *adj.* Headstrong, resisting authority, stubbornly disobedient, rebellious, insolent.

To 34 per cent CONTUMACIOUS means SCORNFUL, compared with only 14 per cent who select RESISTING. CONTEMPTUOUS means SCORNFUL, disdainful, but another word CONTUMELIOUS (*kŏn-tū-mē'-lĭ-ŭs*), much closer to CONTUMACIOUS in sound, also means insolent, rude, haughtily offensive, CONTEMPTUOUS; with CONTUMELY, insolence, contemptuousness, overbearing language, abusive speech, as the corresponding noun.

STUBBORN is negative, not listening to advice. OBSTINATE is active, continuing in one's own direction. CONTUMACIOUS, from the Latin *contumax, contumacis,* stubborn, insolent, perhaps connected with *contemnere,* to despise, combines haughtiness, insolence, contumely, with rebellion, headstrong resistance.

1278. *THAUMATURGY,* thaumaturgy (*thaw'-mă-ter-jĭ*) *n.* Doing something wonderful, magic, legerdemain, performing miracles, conjuring, wonderworking.

THAUMATURGY comes from the Greek θαυματουργός (*thaumatourgos*), wonderworking, starting with θαῦμα (*thauma*), θαῦματις (*thaumatis*), a wonder, miracle. The Greek θέρμη (*therme*) means HEAT, as in THERMOMETER and THERMAL, and this no doubt leads 30 per cent to believe that THAUMATURGY means HEAT TREATMENT. To another 34 per cent THAUMATURGY means TECHNIQUE, method of execution, manner of performing, mechanical manipulation. LEGERDEMAIN, SLEIGHT OF HAND (*slīt ov hănd*), and CONJURING, all depend upon TECHNIQUE. THAUMATURGY is more miraculous, performing miracles, working wonders of a higher level.

1279. *GIGMANIC,* gigmanic (*gĭg-măn'-ĭk*) *adj.* With limited ideas, without culture, commonplace, philistine, matter-of-fact, satisfied, ignorant of one's own lack of culture.

Thomas Carlyle, who grew fond of the word, used GIGMAN, GIGMANITY, and GIGMANIA, as well as the adjective. It is said to come from Thurtell's trial, in which a witness said: 'I always thought him a respectable man'. 'What do you mean by respectable?'. 'He kept a gig'.

To 27 per cent GIGMANIC means EXTRAVAGANT, suggested no doubt by GIG, a one-horse chaise, a light carriage, with one pair of wheels, and drawn by one horse. Despite this, GIGMANIC means COMMONPLACE.

1280. *ADIAPHOROUS*, adiaphorous (*ă-dĭ-ă-fŏr'-ŭs*) *adj.* Indifferent, neutral, morally neither right nor wrong.

To DIFFER, in Latin, is *dis-*, apart, and *ferre*, to carry. In Greek, the same word is διά- (*dia-*), apart, and φέρειν (*pherein*), to carry. From this Greek φέρειν (*pherein*), or more correctly from φορεῖν (*phorein*), the frequentative, to carry, bear, bring, come a few scattered English words. Thus a SEMAPHORE, from σῆμα (*sema*), sign, is a sign, signal, to control bringing, carrying, a word applied to railway signals.

In Latin LUCIFER, *lux, lucis*, light, plus *ferre*, to carry, bring, is the morning star, bringer of light. In Greek, the same person is called PHOSPHOR, from light, and ending in the same PHOR. From the proper name PHOSPHOR come the chemical element PHOSPHORUS, as well as PHOSPHORESCENT.

DIAPHOROUS is carrying apart, in different directions, and so differing, having one's own individual point of view. ADIAPHOROUS, starting with the Greek privative *a-*, means not having an opinion, indifferent.

FIRM, selected by 28 per cent, compared with only 8 per cent for NEUTRAL, is an opposite at least in suggestion.

1281. *KERYGMA*, kerygma (*kĕ-rĭg'-măh*) *n.* Preaching, proclamation, herald. KERYTICS (*kĕ-rĭk'-tĭks*) is the science of preaching.

KERYGMA is the Greek κήρυγμα (*kerygma*) in Roman letters. The verb is κηρύσσειν (*keryssein*), to proclaim.

To 28 per cent KERYGMA means HUMILITY, and to another 16 per cent HOLINESS, both somewhat related, for KERYGMA is primarily Christian preaching.

1282. *MAUNDER*, maunder (*mawn'-der*) *v.* To speak with a beggar's whine, mutter foolishly, talk incoherently, drivel.

A MAUNDER was originally a beggar, from the Latin *mendicare*, to beg, the source of the English MENDICANT, a beggar.

Given a choice between BEG and FAWN as synonyms of MAUNDER, 28 per cent select each. MENDICANT is a pleasant word for BEGGAR, as in the phrase: 'MENDICANT friars'. To MAUNDER is to BEG, but always with something of the unpleasant suggestion contained in FAWN.

1283. *VATICINAL*, vaticinal (*vă-tĭs'-ĭ-năl*) *adj.* Prophetic, oracular, pertaining to predictions.

To 56 per cent VATICINAL means PAPAL, compared with only 8 per cent who prefer PROPHETIC. VATICINATION (*vă-tĭ-sĭ-nā'-shŏn*), a prophecy, prediction; VATICINATE (*vă-tĭs'-ĭ-năt*), to foretell, proclaim beforehand; and VATICINAL, all go back to the original Latin verb *vaticinari*, to predict, foretell, from *vates*, a seer, prophet, the source from which the VATICAN HILL obtained its name, long before the Papacy.

In Roman times, before Christianity, Vatican Hill was a residential area of villas and gardens. The VATICAN, on VATICAN HILL, is now the residence of the Pope, and this leads to the marking of PAPAL instead of the correct oracular, prophetic.

1284. *AFFLATE*, afflate (*ăf-flāt'*) *v.* To breathe on, inspire.

AFFLATE comes from the Latin *ad*, to, and *flare*, to blow. From the same source comes INFLATE, to blow up, swell, expand, which leads 15 per cent to select PUFFED UP as the meaning of AFFLATE; and DEFLATE, to remove the air from, which may lead another 11 per cent to select DEPRESSED.

The verb to AFFLATE, to inspire, the noun AFFLATION, inspiration, and AFFLATUS, impelling mental force, acting from within, power of expression, should be used more often, for there is perhaps no other word in the language to express the inner need for achievement.

1285. *SUCCUSS*, succuss (*sŭk-kŭs'*) *v.* To shake, agitate, fling about.

To 35 per cent SUCCUSS means ENCOURAGE, inspire, give heart to. The noun SUCCESS differs from SUCCUSS by only a single letter; and the verb to SUCCUSS might easily mean help a person to SUCCEED. A word of this sort is perhaps needed. One of the nearest is ENCOURAGE.

But SUCCUSS, and the corresponding noun SUCCUSSION, come from a different source, from the Latin *quatere*, to shake, shatter, with the past participle *quassus*, the source of DISCUSSION, PERCUSSION, and CONCUSSION, as well as the less familiar corresponding verbs. The noun DISCUSSION, debate, argument, comes from the Latin *discussus*, the past participle of *discutere*, to shake apart, break up, scatter, where the *qu-* of *quatere* changes to *cu*. A DISCUSSION is literally a shaking apart.

A PERCUSSION, from *per*, through and the same *quatere*, is hitting so as to shake; with the verb to PERCUSS. Drums are PERCUSSION instruments. A CONCUSSION is more violent.

To SUCCUSS is to shake violently, SUCCUSSION is the noun, a shaking, violent shock.

1286. *ENCOMIUM*, encomium (ĕn-kō'-mĭ-ŭm) *n*. A formal expression of praise, eulogy, commendation.

ENCOMIUM is thought by 34 per cent to mean ACHIEVEMENT, something done, deed, accomplishment. To ACHIEVE is to carry through, bring to a successful end. Praise, an ENCOMIUM, is given as the result of an ACHIEVEMENT. An ACHIEVEMENT is the deed; an ENCOMIUM, the reward.

A PANEGYRIC is praise only, often over-praise, exaggerated praise. EULOGY, from the Greek εὖ (*eu*), well, is just praise in general, even tempered with criticism. An ENCOMIUM is a celebration in honor of a great ACHIEVEMENT.

1287. *SOLECISM*, solecism (sōl'-ĕ-sĭzm) *n*. A grammatical error, gross deviation from correct speech, blunder, barbarism, impropriety, inconsistency; also breach of good manners. Ephraim Chambers, 1728, often gives the clearest understanding: 'A gross impropriety in speech, contrary to the use of language and the rules of grammar either in respect of declension, conjugation, or syntax. The word is Greek σολοικισμός (*soloikismos*), derived from Σόλοι, the Soli, a people of Attica who, being transplanted to Cicilia, lost the purity of their ancient tongue, and became ridiculous to the Athenians for their impropriety therein'.

Of 28 high-vocabulary adults, 7 select MONASTICISM as the meaning of SOLECISM. A MONASTIC is a monk, recluse, and MON-

ASTICISM is living the life of a monk, religious retirement from the world. Several words beginning with SOL- suggest this sort of living apart. SOLITUDE is remoteness from society, lack of companionship, loneliness. A SOLITARY is one who lives alone, an anchorite; and the unusual word SOLITAIRE (*sŏl-ĭ-tār′*) is a recluse, hermit.

To 38 per cent SOLECISMS are AMENITIES, compared with only 8 per cent who select ERRORS, the least frequently marked of the five choices. AMENITIES are the pleasantries of the situation, the agreeableness of the climate, affabilities of manner, as in the title: 'The AMENITIES of Book Collecting'.

From George Campbell, principal of Marischal College in Aberdeen, Scotland, in his Philosophy of Rhetoric, 1776, comes: 'In three different ways, purity may be injured. First, the words used may not be English. This fault hath received from grammarians the determination of BARBARISM. Secondly, the construction of the sentence may not be in English idiom. This hath gotten the name of SOLECISM. Thirdly, the words and phrases may not be employed to express the precise meaning which hath affixed to them. This is termed IMPROPRIETY'.

Such words as SYSTEMIZE, PROVEN, and HEFT, are BARBARISMS. 'Who did you see?' is a SOLECISM. 'There let him lay' is an IMPROPRIETY.

a-, 36
ab-, 592
abandon, v. 941, 652, 815
abandoned, adj. 1249
abandoned, v. 182
abandonment, n. 1116
abandons, v. 191
abasement, n. 264
abash, v. 656
abate, v. 274
abating, adj. 724
abattoir, n. 981
abbreviation, n. 1160, 592
abdicate, v. 652
abdomen, n. 71, 765
abdominal, adj. 1171
aberrant, adj. 592
ABERRATION, n. 592
ABET, v. 274
abetted, v. 274
ABEYANCE, n. 372
ABHOR, v. 69
abhorrence, n. 69
abhors, v. 69
abide, v. 353, 235
ability, n. 1230
ABJECT, adj. 239, 157, 17
abject, v. 56
abjectness, n. 239
abjuration, n. 941
ABJURE, v. 941, 815, 839, 427
-able, 267
abnormality, n. 574
ABODE, n. 235, 318
abode, v. 235
abolish, v. 600, 315, 412
abominable, adj. 69, 1035
abominate, v. 69
ABORTIVE, adj. 45
abrasion, n. 485
abridge, v. 1202
abridgment, n. 1202
abridgement, n. 592
ABROGATE, v. 600, 315, 193,
    412
abruptly, adv. 382, 657
abruptness, n. 657

ABSCIND, v. 768
ABSCOND, v. 271, 1001, 912
absolute, adj. 425
absolution, n. 651, 135
absolve, v. 452, 135
absorb, v. 51, 109
absorbed, adj. 722
absorbed, v. 51
absorbing, adj. 109
absorption, n. 413
abstemiousness, n. 529
ABSTERGE, v. 935
abstinence, n. 321
abstract, n. 1202
abstract, v. 1202
abstraction, n. 413, 1011
abstruse, adj. 912, 517
absurdities, pl. n. 969
abundance, n. 342, 789, 124, 715
abundant, adj. 78, 620
abundantly, adv. 1, 115
abuse, n. 552
abuse, v. 110, 1272, 355
abused, adj. 745
abusive, adj. 1214
abyss, n. 149
ac-, 284
ACATALEPSY, n. 786
ACAULESCENT, adj. 1208
acc-, 284
ACCEDE, v. 300
accelerate, v. 726, 588
acceleration, n. 726
accent, n. 11
ACCENTUATE, v. 11
accessory, n. 1006
accident, n. 1251
accidental, adj. 846
accipiter, n. 1157
accipitres, n. 1157
ACCIPITRAL, adj. 1157
acclivity, n. 637
ACCOLADE, n. 582
accommodate, v. 502
accommodation, n. 502, 419
accomplish, v. 300, 796, 443
accomplishment, n. 1286, 752

accordant, *adj.* 775
accordingly, *adv.* 670
accost, *v.* 911
accoutrements, *pl. n.* 158
ACCRESCENT, *adj.* 1246
accretion, *n.* 1246
accruing, *adj.* 1246
accubation, *n.* 1024
accumbant, *adj.* 1024
accumulate, *v.* 494, 251
accuracy, *n.* 385
accurate, *adj.* 9, 856
accurately, *adv.* 451
accusation, *n.* 655, 552, 466
accuse, *v.* 1248, 640, 1207, 934
-aceous, 725
ACETOUS, *adj.* 406
achator, *n.* 713
achieve, *v.* 269, 300, 796, 443
achievement, *n.* 1286, 269, 1051
aching, *adj.* 728
ACHROMIC, *adj.* 766
acid, *adj.* 896, 1024
acid, *n.* 58, 406
ACME, *n.* 58, 399, 1202
ACOLYTE, *n.* 1111
ACOUSTICS, *n.* 284
acqu-, 631
acquaint, *v.* 730
acquiesce, *v.* 266
acquire, *v.* 610
acquired, *adj.* 1026, 364
acquired, *v.* 293
acquires, *v.* 610
acquit, *v.* 452
acrid, *adj.* 371, 1257
acrimony, *n.* 1214
acrobat, *n.* 365, 580, 832
Acropolis, 832
acrostic, *n.* 907
act, *n.* 996
action, *n.* 229
active, *adj.* 735, 874, 638, 385
activity, *n.* 231, 385
ACULEATE, *adj.* 1024
acute, *adj.* 1024, 808
-ad, 93

adage, *n.* 1070
adamant, *n.* 541
ADAMANTINE, *adj.* 541
Adams, Brooks, 286
adapted, *adj.* 623
adapting, *n.* 671
add, *v.* 1246, 893
added, *adj.* 1026, 893
added, *v.* 1259
addition, *n.* 40, 8, 1246
additional, *adj.* 1026
addle, *n.* 893
addle, *v.* 893
ADDLED, *adj.* 893
address, *n.* 302, 818, 427, 634
address, *v.* 911, 302
adherent, *n.* 760, 1125
adhesive, *adj.* 803
ADHIBIT, *v.* 1025
ADIAPHOROUS, *adj.* 1280
adjacency, *n.* 116
adjective, *n.* 239
adjoin, *v.* 1009, 368
adjoined, *adj.* 524
adjourn, *v.* 815, 980, 1009
adjournment, *n.* 621, 1033
adjudge, *v.* 660
ADJUDICATE, *v.* 660
adjunct, *n.* 40, 10, 1006
ADJUNCTION, *n.* 1009
ADJURE, *v.* 815, 460, 941
adjust, *v.* 283, 515
adjusted, *adj.* 113
adjusting, *n.* 671
administer, *v.* 1025
admiration, *n.* 1036
admire, *v.* 759, 129
admired, *v.* 129
admiringly, *adv.* 36
admission, *n.* 652
admittance, *n.* 74
admonition, *n.* 273, 460, 806
ado, *n.* 702
adolescent, *adj.* 1208
ADORATION, *n.* 42, 187, 1036, 25
adore, *v.* 54, 42
adorn, *v.* 376, 759, 163, 917, 1206

amalgams, *pl. n.* 176
amateur, *n.* 767
AMATORY, *adj.* 192
amazing, *adj.* 538
ambassador, *n.* 928
amber, *adj.* 587
ambiguous, *adj.* 121, 517
ambition, *n.* 255, 705
ambitious, *adj.* 109
amble, *v.* 70
ambry, *n.* 316
ambulatory, *n.* 70
AMBUSH, *n.* 1078, 249
amenities, *pl. n.* 1287
amerciament, *n.* 733
American College Dictionary, 237
amiable, *adj.* 67, 651, 951
AMICABLE, *adj.* 67
amice, *n.* 933
amity, *n.* 651, 951
amnesia, *n.* 324, 998, 651
amnesties, *pl. n.* 651
AMNESTY, *n.* 651, 998
amorous, *adj.* 192
amount, *n.* 345, 715, 911
ampere, *n.* 680
AMPHORA, *n.* 685
amphorae, *pl. n.* 685
ample, *adj.* 78
amplification, *n.* 1179, 995
amplify, *v.* 995
amplifying, *n.* 1179
AMPLITUDE, *n.* 995
amply, *adv.* 1, 115
AMPUTATE, *v.* 198
AMULET, *n.* 453
amuse, *v.* 515
amused, *adj.* 515
amuses, *v.* 109
amusing, *adj.* 553
amusing, *v.* 91
ana-, 1071
anaesthesia, *n.* 771
anaesthetic, *adj.* 771
analogous, *adj.* 1071
ANALOGUE, *n.* 1071
analogy, *n.* 633, 1071

analysis, *n.* 1071
An American Dictionary of the English Language, 209
ANAMNESIS, *n.* 998
anarchy, *n.* 428
anathema, *n.* 1081
anatomy, *n.* 1202
Anatomy of Invertebrates, 180
-ance, 231, 647
ancestors, *pl. n.* 444
ancestry, *n.* 303
anchor, *n.* 1000
anchorite, *n.* 1287
ANCHOVY, *n.* 411
ancient, *adj.* 276, 442, 801
Andrew, 354
andro-, 751
ANDROCENTRIC, *adj.* 751
Andy, 354
anemia, *n.* 481
anew, *adv.* 36
angelic, *adj.* 287
angels, *pl. n.* 287
anger, *n.* 946, 756, 845, 891, 253
angle, *n.* 904, 729
angry, *adj.* 371
anguish, *n.* 485, 253
angular, *adj.* 729
animal, *adj.* 946
animal, *n.* 104, 365, 281, 599
animal-life, *n.* 694
animate, *v.* 721
animated, *adj.* 5, 797
animation, *n.* 317
animosity, *n.* 946, 99, 621, 779
ANIMUS, *n.* 946, 779
annals, *pl. n.* 337
annex, *n.* 40
annex, *v.* 1009
annexed, *adj.* 524
annihilate, *v.* 412
anniversary, *n.* 417
annotation, *n.* 1184, 1051
announce, *v.* 571, 543, 1196, 656
announcement, *n.* 155, 543, 470, 714
annoy, *v.* 754, 49, 203, 696, 102, 281, 360, 858, 628

appeasement, *n.* 575
appeasing, *n.* 810
APPELLATE, *adj.* 894
appellation, *n.* 650, 1160
append, *v.* 40, 46, 1050
APPENDAGE, *n.* 40, 1006
APPENDANT, *adj.* 524
appended, *adj.* 524
applaud, *v.* 81, 576
applauding, *adj.* 272
apple, *n.* 1210
applicable, *adj.* 1039, 623
apply, *v.* 1025
appoint, *v.* 689, 693, 228
apportion, *v.* 105
apposite, *adj.* 623
appraise, *v.* 345, 730, 297
appraisement, *n.* 345
appreciate, *v.* 576, 297
apprehend, *v.* 233, 53, 109, 786
apprehension, *n.* 253, 485, 523
apprentice, *n.* 1131
apprenticeship, *n.* 74
APPRISE, *v.* 730
approach, *n.* 171
approach, *v.* 171
appropriate, *adj.* 584, 589, 430, 623
appropriateness, *n.* 430
appropriation, *n.* 221
approximation, *n.* 116
appurtenance, *n.* 1006
apron, *n.* 1250
apt, *adj.* 391
aptitude, *n.* 260, 1230, 637
aptitudes, *pl. n.* 1230
aptly, *adv.* 391
aqu-, 631
aquaeduct, *n.* 1049
AQUAEMANALE, *n.* 1049
AQUAGE, *n.* 631, 21
AQUARIUM, *n.* 21
aquarius, *n.* 21
aquatic, *adj.* 21
aqueduct, *n.* 631, 21
Arab, 248
ARABESQUE, *adj.* 248
arabian, *adj.* 248

arbiter, *n.* 977
arbitrament, *n.* 675
ARBITRARY, *adj.* 977
arbitration, *n.* 977
arbitrator, *n.* 675
arbitrary decision, 977
arbitrement, *n.* 675
arborescent, *adj.* 877
arcade, *n.* 581
arcadia, *n.* 1124
arcadian, *adj.* 1124
ARCANA, *n.* 1124
arcane, *adj.* 1124
arcanum, *n.* 1124
arch-, 337
arch, *n.* 276
archae-, 276
archaeology, *n.* 276
ARCHAIC, *adj.* 276
archangels, *pl. n.* 287
archetype, *n.* 408
architect, *n.* 276, 337
architrave, *n.* 602
ARCHIVES, *pl. n.* 337
ardent, *adj.* 192, 797, 48
ardor, *n.* 216, 29, 48
ARDUOUS, *adj.* 48
area, *n.* 206, 847, 561, 608
areason, *v.* 655
argent, *adj.* 1082
argent, *n.* 883
ARGENTAL, *adj.* 883
Argentina, 883
argil, *n.* 1082
ARGILLACEOUS, *adj.* 1082
argot, *n.* 62
argue, *v.* 14, 825, 233, 279, 500, 531
arguing, *v.* 531
argument, *n.* 460, 818, 328, 1285
argumentative, *adj.* 842, 1041
aristocratic, *adj.* 511
arithmetic, *n.* 1189
ark, *n.* 1124
armada, *n.* 687
armadillo, *n.* 687
ARMOIRE, *n.* 316
armoires, *pl. n.* 316

armour, *n.* 1094
Arnold, Matthew, 16, 571
aromatic, *adj.* 445
arouse, *v.* 556, 721, 1256
arousing, *adj.* 721
arousing, *n.* 196
arraign, *v.* 655
ARRAIGNMENT, *n.* 655
arraiment, *n.* 163
arrange, *v.* 307, 1028, 515, 689, 223,
   163
arranged, *adj.* 177, 178, 375, 307
arrangement, *n.* 438, 163, 403
array, *n.* 163
array, *v.* 376, 163
arrayed, *adj.* 348
arrayed, *v.* 1079
arrayment, *n.* 163
arrest, *v.* 53, 786
arrive, *v.* 300
arrogant, *adj.* 1158
arrow-headed, *adj.* 807
ARROYO, *n.* 988
art, *n.* 322, 284
Arte of English People, 861
artful, *adj.* 322, 1113, 275, 557
artichoke, *n.* 411
article, *n.* 605
articulate, *v.* 543
artifice, *n.* 125, 1113, 110
artificial, *adj.* 119, 1058
artisan, *n.* 322
ascend, *v.* 702
ascendancy, *n.* 342
ascent, *n.* 637
ascribe, *v.* 105
ascription, *n.* 530
ash, *n.* 87
ask, *v.* 193, 1033, 528
askance, *adv.* 400
asked, *v.* 368
askew, *adj.* 491
askew, *adv.* 400
asking, *n.* 600
asking, *v.* 203
aslant, *adv.* 400
aspect, *n.* 446, 863, 331

asperge, *v.* 705
asperse, *v.* 705
ASPERSION, *n.* 705, 292, 1133
aspiration, *n.* 705
aspirations, *pl. n.* 705
aspire, *v.* 300, 956
ass, *n.* 41
assail, *v.* 63, 705
assailed, *adj.* 63
assault, *n.* 845, 1078
assault, *v.* 52
assaulted, *adj.* 52
assemblage, *n.* 403, 822, 207
assemble, *v.* 154, 202, 690, 1073
assemblies, *pl. n.* 798
assembly, *n.* 27, 427, 944
assent, *n.* 423
assents, *v.* 423
assert, *v.* 1028
assertion, *n.* 705, 330
asserts, *v.* 500
assess, *v.* 345
ASSESSMENT, *n.* 345
assessments, *pl. n.* 733
assets, *pl. n.* 345
assiduous, *adj.* 722
assign, *v.* 105
assist, *v.* 274, 196, 925, 513
assistant, *n.* 1111, 196, 205, 820, 315
assistant rector, 564
associate, *n.* 422, 468, 205
associate, *v.* 468
associated, *v.* 273
association, *n.* 410, 822, 273
ASSONANCE, *n.* 1074
assonant, *adj.* 1074
assuage, *v.* 334
assuaging, *adj.* 780
assume, *v.* 1147, 1259
assumption, *n.* 402
assurance, *n.* 138
assure, *v.* 1028
astonished, *adj.* 36, 515
astonishing, *adj.* 24
astounding, *adj.* 538
astray, *adv.* 53
ASTRINGENT, *adj.* 896

astringents, *pl. n.* 896
astrological, *adj.* 1201
asunder, *v.* 817
asylum, *n.* 318, 984
asylums, *pl. n.* 318
-ate, 93, 233
ate, *v.* 1203
athletic, *adj.* 580
atom, *n.* 1202
atonement, *n.* 575, 1179
ATRABILIOUS, *adj.* 1217
atrocious, *adj.* 220
attach, *v.* 1182, 893, 40, 1050
attached, *adj.* 524, 180
attachment, *n.* 25
attack, *n.* 204, 1078, 662
attack, *v.* 228, 281, 882, 1227, 52, 552
attacked, *adj.* 52
attacking, *adj.* 688
attain, *v.* 300, 443
attaint, *adj.* 256
attempt, *n.* 987
attend, *v.* 658, 1009
attendant, *n.* 232, 741, 760, 1111,
    1175, 196, 1187
attendants, *pl. n.* 1175
attention, *n.* 255, 621, 833, 43
attentions, *pl. n.* 911
attentive, *adj.* 644, 533, 638
ATTEST, *v.* 500, 839, 1028
attested, *adj.* 500
attests, *v.* 500
attire, *n.* 158, 163
attorney, *n.* 1114
attract, *v.* 140, 563
attractive, *adj.* 114, 285, 589, 5, 140
attribute, *n.* 105, 141
attribute, *v.* 105
attrition, *n.* 485, 770
audience, *n.* 60
auditor, *n.* 60
augmentation, *n.* 8
augur, *v.* 571
august, *adj.* 673
aureda, *n.* 1140
aurelia, *n.* 1031
auriphrygia, *n.* 933

Aurora, 843
Aurora Borealis, 843
auspicious, *adj.* 520
austerity, *n.* 431
Austin, Alfred, 117
authenticate, *v.* 500, 839
authoritative, *adj.* 230, 1058
authority, *n.* 534, 560, 342, 147, 1058
authorize, *v.* 147
autocrat, *n.* 489
automobile, *n.* 686
autumnal, *adj.* 764
auxiliaries, *pl. n.* 820
auxiliary, *n.* 820
avarice, *n.* 285, 533
avaricious, *adj.* 1152
avariciously, *adv.* 533
AVATAR, *n.* 981, 1194
AVER, *v.* 839
averse, *adj.* 359
aversion, *n.* 440
avert, *v.* 91, 1196
avid, *adj.* 533
AVIDLY, *adv.* 533
avoid, *v.* 91, 1196, 1233
awakening, *n.* 184
award, *n.* 582, 927
awe, *n.* 54
AWE, *v.* 527
awed, *v.* 527
awful, *adj.* 1155, 527, 1035, 69, 148
awkward, *adj.* 225, 1223, 491, 1042,
    479
awry, *adv.* 400
axiom, *n.* 878
Ayliffe, John, 806
azimuth, *n.* 58

babble, *n.* 62, 597
babble, *v.* 597, 606, 64
baccalaureate, *adj.* 1090
BACCALAUREATE, *n.* 417, 117
baccarat, *n.* 712
BACCHANALIA, *n.* 712
Bacchus, 712
bacciferous, *adj.* 1104
BACCIVOROUS, *adj.* 1090

baptise, *v.* 103
baptistery, *n.* 103
baptistry, *n.* 103
BAPTISM, *n.* 103
Baptists, 103
bar, *n.* 308, 1114
bar, *v.* 436, 686
BARATHRUM, *n.* 1029
BARBARA, *n.* 1083
barbarian, *n.* 132
barbarism, *n.* 430, 1287
barbarisms, *pl. n.* 1287
barbican, *n.* 1083, 1121
BARD, *n.* 213
bare, *v.* 686
BARED, *adj.* 686
bared, *v.* 686
bargain, *v.* 57, 279, 696, 915, 825
bargainer, *n.* 915
barge, *n.* 1087, 2, 1000, 1057
barge-board, *n.* 384
BARGHEST, *n.* 1087, 1219
bark, *n.* 795, 609, 37
BARKANTINE, *n.* 795
BARNACLE, *n.* 180
barnacles, *pl. n.* 180
barns, *pl. n.* 96
baron, *n.* 615, 1063
baronet, *n.* 1063
barrat, *n.* 1114
BARRATOR, *n.* 1114
barratry, *n.* 1114
barred, *v.* 686
barrel, *n.* 1088, 1094
barren, *adj.* 356, 893
barrier, *n.* 948
barrister, *n.* 1114, 927
BARROW, *n.* 1088, 150, 1010
barrows, *pl. n.* 1010
bart, *n.* 1063
barter, *n.* 825
BARTER, *v.* 57, 825, 1114
BARTIZAN, *n.* 1063
BASAL, *adj.* 708
basalt, *n.* 708
basaltic, *adj.* 708
base, *adj.* 7, 112, 157, 728

base, *n.* 708
baseness, *n.* 718
bashful, *adj.* 459
basic, *adj.* 490, 708
BASILIC, *adj.* 1121
basilica, *n.* 1121, 1231
BASILISK, *n.* 1231
basket, *n.* 106
BASTION, *n.* 420, 948
bat, *n.* 548
bath, *n.* 457
bathe, *v.* 457
BATHOS, *n.* 1176
baton, *n.* 331
batter, *v.* 1105, 825
battle, *v.* 233, 666
battledore, *n.* 548, 367
battlement, *n.* 972
battling, *adj.* 59
battue, *n.* 1105
BATTUTA, *n.* 1105
bawdy, *adj.* 804
bay, *n.* 739
bays, *pl. n.* 739
be-, 63, 291, 376
beadle, *n.* 1175
beads, *pl. n.* 595
beadshouse, *n.* 318
beadsmen, *pl. n.* 318
beaker, *n.* 625
beam, *n.* 742
bear, *v.* 443, 713
beard, *n.* 1228
bearish, *adj.* 459
beat, *n.* 1105
beat, *v.* 154, 274, 683, 825, 1105
beaten, *v.* 154
beatification, *n.* 514
beating, *adj.* 929
beau, *n.* 862, 1093, 354
beautification, *n.* 429
beautified, *adj.* 348
beautified, *v.* 363
beauty, *n.* 429, 771
becoming, *adj.* 589, 502
bed, *n.* 503, 383, 145, 130
bedcover, *n.* 1243

bedding, *n.* 503
bedeck, *v.* 376
bedeshouse, *n.* 318
bedesmen, *pl. n.* 318
bedim, *v.* 661
bedraggle, *v.* 291
bedraggled, *adj.* 291
bedspread, *n.* 834
bee, *n.* 63
beer, *n.* 63
beetle, *n.* 854, 991
before, *prep.* 177
beforehand, *adv.* 258
befriend, *v.* 925
beg, *v.* 815, 1282, 941, 369, 460, 824
began, *v.* 3
beggar, *n.* 1282
begging, *n.* 824
begin, *v.* 3
beginner, *n.* 74, 1111
beginning, *adj.* 169
beginning, *n.* 344, 1136, 399, 74, 1204, 867
beguile, *v.* 208, 293
beguiled, *adj.* 925
beguiled, *v.* 208
beguiling, *adj.* 1134
BEHEMOTH, *n.* 104
behind, *adv.* 585
behind, *n.* 380
behindhand, *adj.* 291
beholding, *n.* 237
being, *n.* 179, 209
BELATED, *adj.* 291
be late, 291
BELDAM, *n.* 966
beleaguer, *v.* 1227, 63
BELEAGURED, *adj.* 63
belfry, *n.* 559
belie, *v.* 571
belief, *n.* 402, 816, 1178, 268
belies, *v.* 571
belittling, *n.* 297
bell, *n.* 788
Belladonna, 966
belladonna, *n.* 966
bell-flower, *n.* 559

BELLICOSE, *adj.* 59, 1217
belligerent, *adj.* 59, 823
bellow, *n.* 37
bellowing, *adj.* 405
bell-tower, *n.* 559, 1056
bell-turret, *n.* 559
below, *adj.* 13
belt, *n.* 206, 1046, 713
beluga, *adj.* 668
beluga, *n.* 411
beluga caviar, 668
BELVEDERE, *n.* 1056
bench, *n.* 100
bend, *n.* 1146, 810, 469
benediction, *n.* 703, 18
benefaction, *n.* 1065
benefactor, *n.* 703
BENEFICE, *n.* 611, 1180
beneficence, *n.* 829
beneficent, *adj.* 322, 516
beneficiary, *n.* 1263
benevolence, *n.* 829, 42, 703
benevolent, *adj.* 516, 703
benighted, *adj.* 291
BENIGN, *adj.* 388, 322, 703
benignant, *adj.* 388
benignity, *n.* 388
BENISON, *n.* 703
bent, *adj.* 349, 72, 491
bent, *n.* 260, 637
bent, *v.* 469
benumbed, *adj.* 181
beret, *n.* 667
bernacle goose, 180
berry-eating, *adj.* 1090
berth, *n.* 383
beseech, *v.* 815, 824, 941
beset, *adj.* 63
beset, *v.* 63
besiege, *v.* 63
besieged, *adj.* 63
BESOM, *n.* 1080
besoms, *pl. n.* 1080
bespatter, *v.* 705
bestow, *v.* 105, 1028
betoken, *v.* 571
betraying, *adj.* 112

boviform, *adj.* 769
BOVINE, *adj.* 769, 871, 1076
bow, *v.* 266
BOWDLERIZED, *adj.* 1034
bowl, *n.* 21, 625
bowline, *n.* 303
bows, *pl. n.* 462
box, *n.* 383, 106, 1124
box-car, *n.* 314
boxing, *adj.* 579
boyish, *adj.* 41
Boyle, 392
brace, *n.* 1222
brachycephalic, *adj.* 532
brachymetropic, *adj.* 1143
bracket, *n.* 968, 548
brackets, *pl. n.* 968
bragging, *n.* 802, 1019
Brahman, 1122
braid, *n.* 335
braid, *v.* 335
branch, *n.* 1263
branching, *adj.* 877
branching, *n.* 441
brand, *n.* 784
branded, *adj.* 886
brandish, *v.* 784
brandy glass, 404
brangle, *v.* 1099
brass, *n.* 134
bravado, *n.* 802
brave, *v.* 823
brave, *adj.* 128, 982
bravery, *n.* 1245
bravo, *n.* 1245
BRAVURA, *adj.* 1245
bravura, *n.* 1245
brawl, *n.* 243, 556
brawl, *v.* 14
brawling, *adj.* 405
brawny, *adj.* 1129, 609
bray, *n.* 37
bray, *v.* 770, 802
BRAZEN, *adj.* 134, 370
breach, *n.* 469
breadth, *n.* 995
break, *n.* 469, 260

break, *v.* 306, 836, 768, 563
breaking, *n.* 204
break off, 513
break-up, *n.* 135
bream, *v.* 373
breastplate, *n.* 1224
breath, *n.* 219
breathe, *v.* 956
breathing, *n.* 705
breed, *v.* 699
bribe, *v.* 1206
bribed, *adj.* 256
briber, *n.* 1114
brick red, 1253
bridge, *n.* 462, 840
bridge-builder, *n.* 119
Bridges, Robert, 117
brief, *adj.* 9
briefly, *adv.* 382
brigand, *n.* 641, 795
brigantine, *n.* 795
bright, *adj.* 31, 1013, 664, 755
brightness, *n.* 953
brilliance, *n.* 1245, 953
brilliant, *adj.* 31, 1245
brinded, *adj.* 886
BRINDLED, *adj.* 886
brink, *n.* 384
brisk, *adj.* 5, 673
briskness, *n.* 649
bristling, *adj.* 979, 1101
bristly, *adj.* 979
brittle, *adj.* 65
broad, *adj.* 263
broad-headed, *adj.* 532
broadside, *n.* 1077
broadsword, *n.* 973
Brobdingnag, 947
BROBDINGNAGIAN, *adj.* 947
broil, *n.* 556
broils, *pl. n.* 14
broken, *adj.* 349, 306
broken bowl, 738
bromidic, *adj.* 407
brood, *n.* 525, 699
brood, *v.* 699, 1219
BROODING, *adj.* 699

Cardozo, Justice Benjamin, 1069

care, *n.* 120, 253

care, *v.* 686

cared, *v.* 686

CAREEN, *v.* 373, 1268

career, *n.* 1268

career, *v.* 1268, 373

CAREERING, *v.* 1268

care for, 564

carefree, *adj.* 114

careful, *adj.* 120, 450, 709, 533

carefully, *adv.* 61, 115, 120, 41, 533

careless, *adj.* 350, 804

carelessness, *n.* 9, 164

caress, *v.* 129

careworn, *adj.* 72, 279

cargo, *n.* 870

Carlyle, Thomas, 912, 1178

carmine, *adj.* 507

CARMINE, *n.* 692

carnelian, *n.* 505

carnivorous, *adj.* 872, 924, 1090

carouse, *n.* 712

carp, *v.* 734, 885

carping, *adj.* 1015, 1058

carping, *n.* 734

carping, *v.* 885

carriage, *n.* 70, 605, 1279

carrier, *n.* 713

carry, *v.* 713, 397

carton, *n.* 173

caruncle, *n.* 862

carved, *adj.* 883

carved ornament, 1007

carvel-built, *adj.* 1030

cascades, *pl. n.* 396

case, *n.* 1221, 618, 173

cashier, *n.* 1237

cask, *n.* 614, 1088, 1094

CASQUE, *n.* 1094

cassock, *n.* 1131

CASSOWARY, *n.* 1002

cast, *n.* 863

castellate, *v.* 972

CASTELLATION, *n.* 972

casting, *n.* 56, 505

castle, *n.* 972, 468

cat, *n.* 1176

cataclysm, *n.* 805, 549

CATACLYSMAL, *adj.* 805

catacomb, *n.* 150, 396

catafalque, *n.* 339

catalepsy, *n.* 580, 786

CATALEPTIC, *n.* 580

catalyst, *n.* 805

catamount, *n.* 886

CATARACT, *n.* 396

catastrophe, *n.* 396, 549, 805

catch, *n.* 986

catch, *v.* 81, 125

catechism, *n.* 1131

catechize, *v.* 1131

CATECHUMEN, *n.* 1131

caterer, *n.* 713

cathartic, *adj.* 780, 439

cattle, *n.* 992, 590, 700

CAUCUS, *n.* 493

caudal, *adj.* 237

caught, *v.* 1113

cauliflower, *n.* 1208

causal, *adj.* 1008

cause, *n.* 33, 635

causeway, *n.* 1002

CAUSTIC, *adj.* 371, 1257, 406

caution, *n.* 806, 120

cautious, *adj.* 120, 450, 533

cautiously, *adv.* 61, 645, 171

CAVALCADE, *n.* 66, 982

CAVALIER, *adj.* 982

cavalier, *n.* 982

cavalry, *n.* 66

cave, *n.* 336, 1010

CAVEAT, *n.* 806

caveman, *n.* 336

cavern, *n.* 474, 1120, 336, 1010, 528

cavernous, *adj.* 336

caverns, *pl. n.* 1010

caves, *pl. n.* 1010

caviar, *n.* 411, 668

CAVIL, *v.* 734, 279, 915

caviling, *adj.* 734, 1058

caviling, *n.* 734

cavity, *n.* 1262

-ce, 33, 172, 1154

cease, *v.* 513, 267, 636, 956

ceaseless, *adj.* 60

ceiling, *n.* 6

-ceive, 293

CELEBRATE, *v.* 669, 576, 909, 414, 914

celebrates, *v.* 669

celebrated, *v.* 914

celebration, *n.* 401, 1148, 1265, 551, 914

celebrity, *n.* 414, 669, 1177

CELERITY, *n.* 726

CELESTIAL, *adj.* 6, 287

celestial beings, 287

celestial hierarchy, 287

cell, *n.* 1010

cement, *n.* 1135

cemetery, *n.* 832

CENOTAPH, *n.* 861, 150

censer, *n.* 1235

censor, *n.* 1015

censored, *adj.* 1034

CENSORIOUS, *adj.* 1015

censurable, *adj.* 640

censure, *n.* 552, 705

censure, *v.* 733

cent, *n.* 136

centaurs, *pl. n.* 88

centenary, *n.* 136

centerpiece, *n.* 1110

centipede, *n.* 136

centralized, *adj.* 246

centre, *n.* 308

-centric, 751

CENTUPLICATE, *adj.* 136

century, *n.* 136

Century Dictionary, 36, 83, 92, 109, 117, 146, 148, 152, 187, 204, 210, 225, 232, 233, 255, 257, 282, 283, 335, 358, 377, 398, 439, 445, 458, 471, 475, 480, 496, 515, 539, 598, 616, 630, 738, 785, 799, 809, 868, 872, 904, 906, 912, 928, 942, 1055, 1133, 1154, 1235

ceremonies, *pl. n.* 1148

ceremonious, *adj.* 1045, 821

ceremonious error, 1045

ceremony, *n.* 227, 1045, 1214

CERIFEROUS, *adj.* 1104

certain, *adj.* 329, 121

certify, *v.* 500

CERULEAN, *adj.* 366

cessation, *n.* 32, 621

cesura, *n.* 32

cetaceous, *adj.* 979

ch-, 630

chafe, *v.* 696

chaff, *n.* 825, 696

chaff, *v.* 696

CHAFFER, *v.* 696, 279, 915

chafferer, *n.* 915

chaffing, *n.* 607

chain, *n.* 512, 719, 1173

chain, *v.* 1064, 201

chained, *adj.* 201

chainman, *n.* 512

chair-covering, *n.* 570

chaise, *n.* 1279

chalcedony, *n.* 505

CHALICE, *n.* 386

chalky, *adj.* 725

challenge, *v.* 823, 222

challenged, *adj.* 500

Chambers, Ephraim, 23, 42, 71, 72, 79, 80, 95, 96, 127, 142, 144, 145, 155, 165, 166, 247, 248, 249, 256, 263, 305, 308, 311, 331, 336, 337, 339, 340, 341, 347, 348, 349, 351, 358, 360, 361, 373, 392, 396, 411, 416, 419, 420, 424, 427, 453, 460, 485, 486, 498, 504, 508, 509, 528, 540, 548, 555, 556, 561, 564, 581, 582, 590, 600, 602, 608, 611, 624, 629, 633, 651, 652, 654, 662, 663, 671, 688, 704, 713, 717, 722, 723, 734, 745, 790, 805, 813, 815, 821, 824, 857, 867, 872, 881, 896, 902, 908, 909, 910, 937, 941, 942, 949, 1002, 1009, 1031, 1035, 1045, 1048, 1056, 1070, 1072, 1074, 1079, 1091, 1125, 1133, 1139, 1165, 1204, 1206, 1224, 1229, 1287

chameleon, *n.* 1159

chameleonic, *adj.* 1159

CHAMOIS, *n.* 365

concur, *v.* 732
concurrable, *adj.* 775
concurrence, *n.* 732
concurrent, *adj.* 732
concussion, *n.* 1285
condemn, *v.* 69
condemnation, *n.* 186, 1163
condensation, *n.* 592
condense, *v.* 1062
condign, *adj.* 338
condiment, *n.* 1243, 912
condite, *v.* 912
condition, *n.* 181, 1067
conditions, *pl. n.* 284
condolence, *n.* 471
conduce, *v.* 185
conduct, *v.* 185
conductor, *n.* 1241
cone, *n.* 908
Coney, 978
coney, *n.* 978
Coney Island, 978
confection, *n.* 1243
confederacy, *n.* 483
confer, *v.* 210, 684, 690
conference, *n.* 584
confidence, *n.* 484
confidentially, *adv.* 451
confine, *v.* 201, 494, 672, 719
confined, *adj.* 201, 672
confined, *v.* 208
confirm, *v.* 500, 556, 689, 1028
confirmed, *adj.* 500
CONFITURE, *n.* 1243
conflict, *n.* 352
conflict, *v.* 488, 666
conflicting, *adj.* 488, 666
conform, *v.* 531
confounded, *adj.* 49
CONFRERE, *n.* 422
confuse, *v.* 49, 515, 787, 1249
confused, *adj.* 515, 661, 49, 62, 149
confusion, *n.* 352, 593, 1186
congeal, *v.* 392
CONGLOMERATE, *n.* 50, 706, 1182
conglomerate, *v.* 50, 1182
conglomeration, *n.* 1182

CONGLUTINATE, *adj.* 706
congress, *n.* 427, 165
Congreve, William, 166
congruous, *adj.* 775
coniferous, *adj.* 1104
conjecture, *v.* 448
conjoin, *v.* 273, 368, 1009
conjugal, *adj.* 594, 207
conjugation, *n.* 207
conjunction, *n.* 1009, 273, 10
conjure, *v.* 448, 941
CONJURER, *n.* 448, 468
conjuring, *n.* 1278
connected, *adj.* 524, 112
connive, *v.* 274
connubial, *adj.* 594
conquer, *v.* 313, 222, 534
conquering, *n.* 207
conscience, *n.* 303, 1137
conscience-stricken, *adj.* 770
conscientiousness, *n.* 262
conscious, *adj.* 1137
conscription, *n.* 530
consent, *v.* 423
consenting, *adj.* 776
consents, *v.* 423
consequence, *n.* 33, 398, 627, 936
consequent, *adj.* 398
consequential, *adj.* 177
CONSEQUENTLY, *adv.* 670, 33
consider, *v.* 217, 258, 710, 278, 618,
    622, 660, 357, 75, 168, 882
considerately, *adv.* 61
considerateness, *n.* 703
consideration, *n.* 829, 41, 618, 703
considered, *v.* 278
considering, *v.* 618
consign, *v.* 601
CONSIGNEE, *n.* 601
consist, *v.* 513
consistent, *adj.* 775, 648
console, *v.* 294
consoling, *adj.* 780
consonance, *n.* 1074
CONSORT, *n.* 468
consort, *v.* 468
conspicuous, *adj.* 1201

conspicuously, *adv.* 451
conspire, *v.* 941, 956
constancy, *n.* 262
constant, *adj.* 60, 722
constellation, *n.* 200
constituent, *n.* 224
constituents, *pl. n.* 327
constituted, *adj.* 375
CONSTRAIN, *v.* 831, 184, 448
CONSTRAINT, *n.* 184, 831, 756
constrictive, *adj.* 896
consume, *v.* 1203
consuming, *adj.* 1092, 1275
consuming, *n.* 1275
CONSUMMATE, *adj.* 269
consummate, *v.* 269
consumptive, *adj.* 203
contact, *n.* 634
contagious, *adj.* 261
contain, *v.* 109, 443, 986
container, *n.* 614
contaminated, *adj.* 256
CONTEMPLATE, *v.* 217, 710, 618, 622,
    75, 168
contemplation, *n.* 372
contempt, *n.* 157, 621
contemptible, *adj.* 7, 157, 1270, 1050
contemptuous, *adj.* 1277
CONTEND, *v.* 658, 885, 823, 500, 531,
    1099
contending, *adj.* 85, 1041
content, *adj.* 296
content, *v.* 527
contented, *adj.* 922
contention, *n.* 423, 43
contentious, *adj.* 183, 842, 823, 579
contentiousness, *n.* 43
contest, *n.* 249
contest, *v.* 658, 500
contingency, *n.* 421
continuation, *n.* 627
continue, *v.* 353, 636, 235, 443
continuous, *adj.* 60
contort, *v.* 108
contortion, *n.* 458
CONTOUR, *n.* 608, 561
contour-line, *n.* 608

contra-, 89
contract, *n.* 202
contract, *v.* 563, 1202
contracted, *adj.* 896
contracting, *n.* 592
contraction, *n.* 44
contradict, *v.* 882
CONTRADISTINCTION, *n.* 89
contrary, *adj.* 881
contrast, *n.* 89
contribute, *v.* 105
contribution, *n.* 141
contrite, *adj.* 770
CONTRITION, *n.* 485
contrivance, *n.* 125, 447, 588, 310
contrive, *v.* 258, 310, 375, 515
control, *n.* 534, 147
control, *v.* 899, 147
controlled, *v.* 147
controlling, *v.* 147
controversial, *adj.* 531, 1198
controversy, *n.* 466, 1198
controvert, *v.* 531
contusion, *n.* 808
controvertist, *n.* 1198
CONTUMACIOUS, *adj.* 1277
contumelious, *adj.* 1277
contumely, *n.* 1277
CONUNDRUM, *n.* 1017
convalescence, *n.* 169
convalescent, *adj.* 139, 1208
convene, *v.* 202
convenient, *adj.* 502, 588, 589, 202
convention, *n.* 403, 427, 202
conversation, *n.* 584, 825, 597
converse, *adj.* 1008
conversion, *n.* 1116
convert, *n.* 191, 975
convert, *v.* 829, 91, 1008, 1196
convey, *v.* 713
conveyer, *n.* 713
conveyor, *n.* 713
convict, *n.* 1065
convivial, *adj.* 790
convocation, *n.* 403, 427
convulsion, *n.* 44
CONY, *n.* 978

coo, *v.* 945
cook, *v.* 1150
Cook, James, 211
cooked, *adj.* 619
cooler, *n.* 1049
Cooley, Thomas, 292
coop, *n.* 672
cooperating, *adj.* 1153
cooperation, *n.* 732
COPIOUS, *adj.* 78
copiously, *adv.* 1, 115
copiousness, *n.* 995, 1179
coppice, *n.* 598
copy, *n.* 627, 530, 78
copy, *v.* 810
CORACLE, *n.* 1185
CORBEL, *n.* 968
corbels, *pl. n.* 968
CORBIE, *adj.* 1127
corbie, *n.* 1127, 968
corbie gable, 1127
corbin, *n.* 968
cord, *n.* 540, 1129, 1043, 303
cordage, *n.* 1043
cordial, *adj.* 67
cordiality, *n.* 265
CORDITE, *n.* 1043
Corinth, 1188
CORINTHIANIZE, *v.* 1188
cork, *n.* 367
corn, *n.* 358
corn-cob, *n.* 358
corn-cobs, *pl. n.* 358
cornet, *n.* 978
CORNICE, *n.* 602
cornucopia, *n.* 78, 978
coronet, *n.* 234
corporal, *adj.* 1138
CORPORATE, *adj.* 394
corporation, *n.* 394, 1138
corporations, *pl. n.* 410
corporeal, *adj.* 1138, 394
corps, *n.* 144
corpse, *n.* 144, 394, 1138
CORPULENT, *adj.* 144, 394
corral, *n.* 614
correct, *adj.* 338, 856, 9

corrective, *n.* 966
correctness, *n.* 430
correct speech, 543
correspondence, *n.* 1074, 1071, 665
corresponding, *adj.* 1071
corroborate, *v.* 500, 839, 689
corroding, *adj.* 371, 1133
corrupt, *adj.* 994
corrupt, *v.* 164
corrupted, *adj.* 256, 1054
corrupting, *adj.* 858
corruption, *n.* 860, 224
corruptly, *adv.* 919
corsage, *n.* 250
corsair, *n.* 641
corset, *n.* 1166
CORTEGE, *n.* 250
CORUSCATING, *adj.* 1133
coruscation, *n.* 1133
corvine, *adj.* 1127
coryphee, *n.* 27
cosmetic, *n.* 1018
cosset, *n.* 678
COSSET, *v.* 678
costume, *n.* 163, 1244
costumes, *pl. n.* 158, 1244
cot, *n.* 822
COTERIE, *n.* 822, 1117
Cotgrave, Randle, 465
COTILLION, *n.* 486, 507
cottage, *n.* 822
cotter, *n.* 822
cotton-cloth, *n.* 94
cougar, *n.* 886
council, *n.* 403, 410, 1192, 427
councils, *pl. n.* 798
counselor, *n.* 1114
count, *v.* 693, 441
COUNTENANCE, *n.* 484, 446, 863
counterfeit, *adj.* 785
countermand, *v.* 600
COUNTERPANE, *n.* 834
counterpoint, *n.* 834
counterpoise, *n.* 835
countersign, *n.* 1068
counting, *n.* 441
countryman, *n.* 762, 615

county, *n.* 504
couplet, *n.* 907
couplets, *pl. n.* 907
courage, *n.* 216, 190, 779
courageous, *adj.* 350
course, *n.* 603
court, *n.* 614, 1192, 909, 642, 581, 382
court-appeal, *n.* 1136
court-appointed, *adj.* 315
courteous, *adj.* 114, 322, 388, 634, 776, 644
courteously, *adv.* 382
courtesy, *n.* 388, 537
courtly, *adj.* 382
courtyard, *n.* 614, 581, 642
cousin, *n.* 925
COVENANT, *n.* 202
covenanted, *adj.* 305
cover, *v.* 866, 376, 787, 1030, 1227
covered, *adj.* 525
covering, *n.* 358, 376, 800, 962, 1073, 1250, 618, 830, 859
coverlet, *n.* 800, 834
covert, *adj.* 344, 1258, 525
covert, *n.* 525
covertly, *adv.* 964, 451
COVETABLE, *adj.* 285
covetous, *adj.* 1152
covetousness, *n.* 285
COVEY, *n.* 525
cow, *n.* 743, 309, 674
cow, *v.* 656
coward, *n.* 1165
cowardly, *adj.* 157
cower, *v.* 734
COXCOMB, *n.* 862, 354
cozen, *n.* 925
cozen, *v.* 110, 578, 112, 293
COZENED, *v.* 925, 208
crab, *n.* 200, 370
Crabb, 48
crabbed, *adj.* 801, 200
crack, *n.* 98, 289, 455, 469, 474, 993, 260
craft, *n.* 110
craftily, *adv.* 645

craftiness, *n.* 984, 369
crafty, *adj.* 1113, 275, 557, 1134, 1076
craggy, *adj.* 674
crammed, *adj.* 502
crannies, *pl. n.* 455
CRANNY, *n.* 455
crass, *adj.* 364
crate, *n.* 173, 106
crating, *n.* 106
CRAVAT, *n.* 212
crave, *v.* 958
craving, *n.* 285
crawl, *v.* 26, 243, 702
crawled, *v.* 26
crazy, *adj.* 496
crazy-quilt, *n.* 834
crazy-work, *n.* 834
create, *v.* 310
created, *adj.* 536
creation, *n.* 162, 184, 867
crebricostate, *adj.* 1177
crebrisulcate, *adj.* 1177
crebritude, *n.* 1177
CREBRITY, *n.* 1177
crebrous, *adj.* 1177
credence, *n.* 816
CREDENDA, *n.* 816
credendum, *n.* 816
credential, *n.* 816
credit, *n.* 484, 816
creed, *n.* 816, 752
crenellation, *n.* 972
creep slowly, 26
CRESCENDO, *n.* 55
crescent, *adj.* 749, 55, 1246
cretaceous, *adj.* 725
CREVASSE, *n.* 474, 455, 993
crevice, *n.* 98, 289, 455, 469, 474, 149
crime, *n.* 687, 1065, 1161, 919
crimes, *pl. n.* 687
criminal, *adj.* 523
criminal, *n.* 1161
crimson, *adj.* 507
crimson, *n.* 692
cringe, *v.* 734

DEBACLE, *n.* 506, 1255
debar, *v.* 436, 51
debasement, *n.* 165
debasing, *n.* 499
debatable, *adj.* 75
debate, *n.* 466, 825, 906, 1285
debate, *v.* 233, 375
debating, *v.* 531
debauch, *n.* 914
debauch, *v.* 1188
DEBENTURE, *n.* 957
debentures, *pl. n.* 957
debit, *n.* 911
DEBONAIR, *adj.* 114
DEBOUCH, *v.* 914, 936
debt, *n.* 911
decadence, *n.* 630, 722
decadent, *adj.* 1251
decanter, *n.* 409
decapitation, *n.* 892
decay, *n.* 1251, 630, 722
deceased, *adj.* 10
deceit, *n.* 1212
deceitful, *adj.* 112, 643
deceive, *v.* 110, 495, 578, 112, 85, 293, 1128, 1233
deceived, *v.* 925
deceiving, *n.* 1128
decent, *adj.* 589
deception, *n.* 125, 1114, 57, 110
deceptive, *adj.* 758, 477, 557
decide, *v.* 660
DECIDUOUS, *adj.* 722
decimal, *adj.* 1066
DECIMATE, *v.* 1066
decision, *n.* 186, 312, 569, 799, 996, 202, 18, 135
decisions, *pl. n.* 569
deck, *n.* 376
DECK, *v.* 376, 163
decked, *adj.* 348
declaim, *v.* 165, 469, 1162
declamation, *n.* 431, 165
DECLAMATORY, *adj.* 616
declame, *v.* 616
declaration, *n.* 543, 616, 330
declaratory, *adj.* 616

declare, *v.* 660, 839, 1028, 1276, 543, 616
declares, *v.* 500
decline, *v.* 778, 637, 56, 165
DECLIVITY, *n.* 637
DECOLLATION, *n.* 892
decomposition, *n.* 135
decorate, *v.* 759, 917, 551, 163
decorated, *adj.* 348
decorated, *v.* 363, 551
decoration, *n.* 429, 158
decoy, *v.* 140
decrease, *n.* 8
decrease, *v.* 817, 1246
decree, *n.* 18, 186
dedication, *n.* 253
DEDUCE, *v.* 185
deduct, *v.* 185
deduction, *n.* 1233
deed, *n.* 850, 1286
deep, *adj.* 884, 722, 517, 912
deep orange, 692
deep-rooted, *adj.* 722
deer, *n.* 461
deface, *v.* 659
defamation, *n.* 705, 330
defamatory, *adj.* 292, 1133
defame, *v.* 1050
defeasible, *adj.* 952
defeat, *n.* 135
defeat, *v.* 288, 952
defeated, *v.* 266
defect, *n.* 260, 749
defector, *n.* 191
defence, *n.* 333, 948
defend, *v.* 228
defendable, *adj.* 568
defendant, *n.* 565
defends, *v.* 213
defense, *n.* 158, 830
defensible, *adj.* 568
defensive, *adj.* 688
defer, *v.* 1033, 638, 815, 980, 684, 690
deferring, *adj.* 638
deficient, *adj.* 4
defied, *v.* 823

depicting, *adj.* 616
deplete, *v.* 715, 174
deplore, *v.* 772
deponent, *adj.* 43
deposit, *v.* 278, 1147
depot, *n.* 320
depraved, *adj.* 1050, 579, 803
depravity, *n.* 718
deprecate, *v.* 1050
depreciate, *v.* 1050, 297
DEPRECIATION, *n.* 297
DEPREDATION, *n.* 681
depress, *v.* 319, 572
depressed, *adj.* 699, 17
depressed, *v.* 1284
depressing, *adj.* 218, 377
depression, *n.* 572, 1262, 92
deprivations, *pl. n.* 905
deprive, *v.* 768
depriving, *n.* 165
deputy, *adj.* 315
deputy, *n.* 315, 928
derangement, *n.* 592
Derby, 667
DERELICT, *n.* 182
deride, *v.* 607, 222, 288
deriding, *n.* 607
derision, *n.* 607
derisive, *adj.* 557
derived, *adj.* 1026
DERMATOID, *adj.* 83
derogation, *n.* 600
derrick, *n.* 1000
derricks, *pl. n.* 1000
DESCANT, *v.* 622
descend, *v.* 423, 165
descendant, *n.* 1205, 1263
descendants, *pl. n.* 444
descension, *n.* 423
descent, *n.* 637, 981, 423
describe, *v.* 326
description, *n.* 714, 530
descriptive, *adj.* 616
descry, *v.* 961
desert, *n.* 1220
deserted, *adj.* 1249
deserter, *n.* 191, 1116, 131, 984

desertion, *n.* 1116
deserts, *v.* 191
deserved, *adj.* 338
DESHABILLE, *n.* 593
desiccate, *v.* 1047
design, *n.* 991, 1051
design, *v.* 293
designate, *v.* 693
designation, *n.* 650
DESINENCE, *n.* 1252
desirable, *adj.* 285, 588
desire, *n.* 236, 384, 255, 705, 951,
      533, 285
desire, *v.* 958, 951
desires, *pl. n.* 705
desirous, *adj.* 533, 359
DESIST, *v.* 513, 636
desk, *n.* 343
despair, *n.* 92
desperate, *adj.* 7
desperation, *n.* 92
DESPICABLE, *adj.* 7, 112, 606
despise, *v.* 7
despite, *n.* 621
despoil, *v.* 130
DESPOILED, *adj.* 130
despoiling, *n.* 286, 681
despondency, *n.* 92
despondent, *adj.* 218
despotic, *adj.* 977
Desroches-Noblecourt, C., 432
destine, *v.* 689
destiny, *n.* 186
destitution, *n.* 905
destroy, *v.* 659, 357, 681, 952
destroyed, *adj.* 952
destruction, *n.* 873, 101, 137
destructive, *adj.* 612, 805, 1155, 858
desuetude, *n.* 740
detach, *v.* 25
detached, *adj.* 10
DETACHMENT, *n.* 25
detained, *adj.* 291
detains, *v.* 986
DETENT, *n.* 986
DETER, *v.* 102
deterge, *v.* 935

draw, *v.* 195, 509
drawbridge, *n.* 1164
drawing, *n.* 639
draw up, 1028
dread, *n.* 527, 1035
dreadful, *adj.* 220, 1155, 69, 527, 1035, 148
dream, *n.* 453
dream, *v.* 215, 54
dream-like, *adj.* 1138
dreamy, *adj.* 79
dreaming, *adj.* 215
dredge, *n.* 942
dredge, *v.* 942
dregs, *pl. n.* 679, 901
dress, *n.* 158, 1244
dress, *v.* 759, 163, 1227
dressed, *v.* 1079
drift, *n.* 603, 903
drift, *v.* 1239, 857
drifting, *v.* 857
driftwood, *n.* 939
drink, *n.* 424, 731, 790
drink, *v.* 566, 731, 110, 363
drinkable, *adj.* 790
drink-offering, *n.* 663
drip, *v.* 389
drive, *n.* 184
drive, *v.* 831, 196, 588, 235
drivel, *v.* 1282
drive-out, *v.* 304
driveway, *n.* 732
driving, *n.* 196
DROLL, *adj.* 553, 853
drollery, *n.* 20, 553
dromaeognathaus, *adj.* 1002
drone, *n.* 641
droop, *v.* 761, 1183
drooping, *adj.* 508, 481
dross, *n.* 679
drove, *v.* 235
drowsiness, *n.* 99
drowsy, *adj.* 79, 1236, 1256
drudge, *n.* 1115, 641
drug, *n.* 878
druggist, *n.* 131
drugs, *pl. n.* 878

drum, *n.* 788
drunkard, *n.* 731
drunken, *adj.* 181
drunkenness, *n.* 277, 181
dry, *adj.* 406
dry, *v.* 1047
dry-season, *n.* 843
Dryden, John, 6
dryer, *n.* 1047
dryness, *n.* 406
dub, *v.* 693
dubitable, *adj.* 329
DUBITATIVE, *adj.* 35
duckling, *n.* 39
duds, *n.* 163
due, *adj.* 338
duel, *adj.* 59
DUENNA, *n.* 1093
DULCET, *adj.* 546
dull, adj. 1256, 364, 553, 664, 1076, 871, 1113, 808
dull, *v.* 808
dullness, *n.* 99, 691, 1137
dump, *n.* 679
dunce, *n.* 862
dune, *n.* 455
dunes, *pl. n.* 455
dupe, *v.* 293
duped, *v.* 208
duplicate, *adj.* 136, 335
duplicate, *n.* 627
duplicate, *v.* 810
duplication, *n.* 810
duplicity, *n.* 1212
durable, *adj.* 280
dusk, *n.* 218
duskiness, *n.* 864
duskish, *adj.* 1249
dusky, *adj.* 864
dusty, *adj.* 1054
duties, *pl. n.* 733
dutiful, *adj.* 1225
duty, *n.* 911
dwarf, *n.* 1200, 1270
dwell, *v.* 235, 799, 175
dwelling, *n.* 799, 235, 980, 828
dye, *n.* 1226

dye, v. 363
dyestuff, n. 1226
dying, adj. 967

e-, 771
eager, adj. 797, 533, 48
eagerness, n. 29, 48
earlier, adj. 585, 588
earth, n. 389, 327
ease, n. 735
ease, v. 521, 556
easy, adj. 982
eat, v. 1203, 1266, 1275
eatable, adj. 1266
eatable, n. 1242
eat away, 1052
eaten away, 1052
eat ravenously, 1061
eating, n. 497
eating, v. 197
EBULLIENCE, n. 231
eccentric, adj. 751
ecclesiastic, n. 564, 856, 648
ecclesiastical, adj. 856
ecclesiastics, pl. n. 403
ECHELON, n. 438
echelons, pl. n. 438
echo, v. 1131
Echo, 264
echoing, adj. 690
economical, adj. 268
economically, adv. 115, 128
economics, n. 268
economist, n. 268
economize, v. 254, 268
economizer, n. 268
economizing, n. 254
economy, n. 905, 268, 798
ECTOMORPHIC, adj. 750
ECUMENICAL, adj. 798, 403
Ecumenical Council, 798
-ed, 459, 526
EDACIOUS, adj. 1275
edacity, n. 1275
eddied, v. 1123
eddies, pl. n. 1123
eddy, n. 819, 1123

eddy, v. 156
edge, n. 241, 384, 1140
edging, n. 384
edible, adj. 1266, 1275
edible, n. 1242
EDICT, n. 18
EDIFICATION, n. 868, 467
EDIFICE, n. 467, 868, 611
edify, v. 467, 868
edifying, adj. 868
Edinburgh Review of 1869, 225
editing, n. 783
educating, n. 467
education, n. 467
Education of Henry Adams, 274
-ee, 601
EFFACE, v. 659
effect, n. 181
effect, v. 796
effective, adj. 230, 796, 479
effectively, adv. 479
effectiveness, n. 479
effects, pl. n. 430
effervesce, v. 1013
effervescence, n. 231, 169
EFFETE, adj. 356
efficacious, adj. 796
efficacy, n. 385, 796
efficient, adj. 479
effigy, n. 752
effluent, n. 141
effort, n. 522, 987, 48
effulgence, n. 953
EFFULGENT, adj. 841, 1013
effuse, v. 787, 1186
effusion, n. 124, 1186
effusive, adj. 841
eggs, pl. n. 411
egocentric, adj. 751
egoism, n. 264, 829
egregiously, adj. 736
egress, n. 165
egress, v. 43
-ei-, 220
ejaculate, v. 239
EJACULATION, n. 17
eject, v. 56, 17

entire, *adj.* 798, 578, 327
entitle, *v.* 693
entrance, *n.* 74, 141
entrance, *v.* 1128
entrancing, *adj.* 1128
entreat, *v.* 815, 448, 824, 941
entreaty, *n.* 219
enumerate, *v.* 693
enveigle, *v.* 1099
envelope, *n.* 1031
envoy, *n.* 648
envy, *v.* 85
epaulet, *n.* 1110
epaulette, *n.* 1110
EPERGNE, *n.* 1110
ephemeral, *adj.* 280
EPIC, *n.* 311, 680
epicarp, *n.* 358
EPICEDIUM, *n.* 1170
epick, *n.* 311
epidemic, *n.* 261
epidermis, *n.* 83
EPIDICTIC, *adj.* 1142
EPIGONE, *n.* 931
epigram, *n.* 1139, 931
EPIPHANY, *n.* 1194
episcopal, *adj.* 119
epitaph, *n.* 861, 931, 1139
EPITHET, *n.* 1139
EPITOME, *n.* 1202
epitomize, *v.* 1202
epitomizing, *n.* 592
EPONYM, *n.* 680, 604, 118
eponyms, *pl. n.* 680
epopee, *n.* 311, 680
epos, *n.* 311
EQUABLE, *adj.* 133
equal, *adj.* 133, 338, 519
equal, *n.* 205
equality, *n.* 519, 665
equalness, *n.* 519
equate, *v.* 133
equestrian, *adj.* 1076
equine, *adj.* 1076
equip, *v.* 1206
equipment, *n.* 174
EQUITABLE, *adj.* 338, 133

equity, *n.* 133, 338, 523
equivalence, *n.* 519, 665
equivocal, *adj.* 121
-er, 508, 601
erase, *v.* 659, 330
EREMITE, *n.* 1125
ermine, *n.* 692
erode, *v.* 1052
eroded, *adj.* 1052
err, *v.* 53, 592
errant, *adj.* 592
error, *n.* 749, 592, 227
errors, *pl. n.* 1287
ERUBESCENT, *adj.* 1100
erudition, *n.* 1032
eruption, *n.* 101, 204
-es, 33
escape, *n.* 1233
escape, *v.* 271, 912
-escence, 169
-escent, 1208
escharotic, *adj.* 371
escritoire, *n.* 343
ESCULENT, *adj.* 1266, 1275
esculent, *n.* 1242
esoteric, *adj.* 653, 1022, 1124
ESPIAL, *n.* 961
espionage, *n.* 961
espy, *v.* 961
espying, *n.* 961
-esque, 248
essay, *n.* 328, 704, 837, 955
essays, *pl. n.* 704
ESSENCE, *n.* 209, 1039
essential, *adj.* 209
essential-nature, *n.* 1039
establish, *v.* 689, 228, 747
established, *adj.* 280, 747
established, *v.* 228
establishment, *n.* 1242, 273
estate, *n.* 899, 1067, 828, 446, 484
esteem, *n.* 42, 54
esteemed, *v.* 129
estimate, *n.* 317
estimate, *v.* 345, 730, 297
estival, *adj.* 764
esurient, *adj.* 1275

exedra, *n.* 812
EXEGESIS, *n.* 949, 1070
exemplar, *n.* 408
exercised, *adj.* 304
exert, *v.* 147
exhalations, *pl. n.* 240
exhale, *v.* 956
exhaust, *v.* 279, 715
exhausted, *adj.* 356, 508, 1115, 279, 120, 900
exhausting, *v.* 279
exhaustion, *n.* 628, 120, 169
exhedra, *n.* 812
exhibit, *n.* 247
exhibit, *v.* 247, 175, 1025
exhibition, *n.* 486, 66, 247, 331
exhilarate, *v.* 317
exhilarated, *adj.* 326
EXHILARATION, *n.* 317
exhort, *v.* 460, 576
EXHORTATION, *n.* 460, 273
EXHUMATION, *n.* 499
exigency, *n.* 421
exile, *n.* 574
exist, *v.* 636, 513
exit, *n.* 613, 949, 936
exit, *v.* 914, 936
exodus, *n.* 403, 949
exogen, *n.* 547
exogenous, *adj.* 547
exorbitant, *adj.* 460
EXORCISE, *v.* 304
exorcised, *adj.* 304
EXORDIUM, *n.* 1136
EXOTERIC, *adj.* 1022
exotic, *adj.* 1022
expand, *v.* 817, 1197, 326, 1284
expanded, *adj.* 1258
expandedly, *adv.* 451
expansion, *n.* 1179
expatiate, *v.* 1179
EXPATIATION, *n.* 1179
expatriation, *n.* 575, 1179
expected, *adj.* 332
expecting, *v.* 70
expectorate, *v.* 1232
EXPEDIENT, *adj.* 588

expedient, *n.* 588
expedients, *pl. n.* 588
expedite, *v.* 588
expedition, *n.* 204
expeditiously, *adv.* 61
expel, *v.* 304
expelling, *n.* 56, 683
expend, *v.* 13, 40, 46, 725, 1050
expending, *v.* 13
expenditure, *n.* 342
expensive, *adj.* 725
experienced, *adj.* 776
experiences, *pl. n.* 162
experimentally, *adv.* 171
expert, *adj.* 479
EXPIATION, *n.* 575, 357, 1179
expiatory, *n.* 439
expire, *v.* 956
explain, *v.* 122, 267, 554, 1128, 755
explained, *adj.* 122
explanation, *n.* 949, 1051, 1070, 1128, 267
explicable, *adj.* 554
explode, *v.* 1013
exploratory, *adj.* 772
explore, *v.* 501, 509, 772
expose, *v.* 1025
exposed, *adj.* 686
exposition, *n.* 949, 1184
expostulation, *n.* 247
expound, *v.* 622
expressed, *adj.* 1169
expression, *n.* 17, 194, 458, 863, 471
expressive, *adj.* 841
expressively, *adv.* 491
expulsion, *n.* 683, 575
expurgated, *adj.* 1034
exquisite, *adj.* 546
exquisite, *n.* 354, 862
extempore, *adj.* 332
extend, *v.* 1033, 1174, 600, 1197, 340, 658, 817
extent, *n.* 995
extenuate, *v.* 1128
exterior, *adj.* 585
external, *adj.* 1022, 585
extinct, *adj.* 10

extinguish, *v.* 661
EXTOL, *v.* 576, 272
extolling, *adj.* 272
extolling, *v.* 576
extraction, *n.* 303
extraneous, *adj.* 846
extraordinarily, *adv.* 736
extraordinary, *adj.* 538
extravagance, *n.* 231
extravagant, *adj.* 1035, 1092, 538,
    1279, 282, 845
extreme, *adj.* 891, 845
extricable, *adj.* 554
extricate, *v.* 554
extrinsic, *adj.* 846
extrude, *v.* 1132
extruded, *v.* 683
EXTRUSION, *n.* 683
exuberance, *n.* 342, 1, 153
exuberant, *adj.* 5, 1
EXUBERANTLY, *adv.* 1
exudation, *n.* 435
exult, *v.* 401
exultant, *adj.* 326
exultation, *n.* 401, 317
eye-bright, *n.* 1021
eye-glass, *n.* 462
eyeglasses, *pl. n.* 462

fable, *n.* 1109
fabric, *n.* 404, 467
fabricate, *v.* 683
fabrication, *n.* 1109
fabrications, *pl. n.* 1109
fabulous, *adj.* 1091
face, *n.* 446, 458, 484, 863
face, *v.* 659
FACETIAE, *n.* 1109
facetious, *adj.* 553, 853, 1109
facetiousness, *n.* 20
face value, 519
facial contortion, 458
faction, *n.* 1058
FACTIOUS, *adj.* 1058
factitious, *adj.* 752, 1058
factor, *n.* 224, 601
factors, *pl. n.* 327

factory, *n.* 1107
FACTOTUM, *n.* 1107, 39, 760
FACULTATIVE, *adj.* 1230
faculties, *pl. n.* 1230
faculty, *n.* 1230
fade, *v.* 1183
Fadiman, Clifton, 1275
fag, *n.* 1115, 760
fag, *v.* 1115
fag-end, *n.* 1115
fagged out, 1115
FAGGING, *v.* 1115
FAGOT, *n.* 480
fail, *v.* 227
failing, *adj.* 45
failing, *n.* 749
failure, *n.* 135, 227, 324
faint, *adj.* 508
faint cry, 1040
fair, *adj.* 338, 133, 977
fair, *n.* 1265
fairness, *n.* 133, 338, 523
fairy, *n.* 1087
faith, *n.* 262, 29, 132
faithfulness, *n.* 262
faithless, *adj.* 112, 797
faithlessness, *n.* 112, 262
FALCATE, *adj.* 749
FALCHION, *n.* 973
falcon, *n.* 749
fall, *n.* 630
fall, *v.* 488, 960
fallacious, *adj.* 477, 749, 726
fallacy, *n.* 749
fallen, *adj.* 432
false, *adj.* 112, 1091, 477, 643, 785,
    758, 974, 164, 330
falsehood, *n.* 262
falseness, *n.* 1128
falsify, *v.* 164
fame, *n.* 362, 1177
familiar, *adj.* 263
family, *n.* 303
family-tree, *n.* 162
famished, *adj.* 72
famous, *adj.* 220
fanatical, *adj.* 845

fancied, *adj.* 536
fanciful, *adj.* 22, 248, 1035
fancy, *adj.* 179, 1194
fancy, *n.* 738, 1035
fancy, *v.* 233
FANE, *n.* 1187
fanfaronade, *n.* 1019
Fannie Farmer's Boston Cooking-School Cook Book, 454
fantastic, *adj.* 22, 758, 1035, 179
fantasy, *n.* 179
far, *adj.* 686
farce, *n.* 978
farces, *pl. n.* 721
farcical, *adj.* 553
farewell, *n.* 1162
far-fetched, *adj.* 112
farm-hand, *n.* 1048
farming, *adj.* 143
farm land, 1220
farm-worker, *n.* 570
far-sighted, *adj.* 1143
farthermost, *adj.* 672
fascinate, *v.* 140, 951
fascine, *n.* 480
fascis, *n.* 1175
fashion, *n.* 354, 158
fashionableness, *n.* 1005
fashions, *pl. n.* 354
fasten, *v.* 1182, 447
fastened, *adj.* 706
fastidious, *adj.* 1027
FASTUOUS, *adj.* 1027
fat, *adj.* 144, 632, 1042, 394, 859, 1129
fatal, *adj.* 99
fate, *n.* 186
fatigue, *n.* 169, 120, 628
fatigue, *v.* 279, 431
fatigued, *adj.* 120, 900
fatiguing, *adj.* 218
FATUITY, *n.* 550
fatuous, *adj.* 550
fault, *n.* 469, 687, 1065, 1161, 227, 260, 749
faultfinding, *adj.* 1015
fault-finding, *adj.* 1058

faultfinding, *n.* 734
faultless, *adj.* 565
faults, *pl. n.* 687
faulty, *adj.* 749, 640
faun, *n.* 694
FAUNA, *n.* 694
favor, *n.* 333
favor, *v.* 925
favorable, *adj.* 388, 520
favored, *v.* 925
fawn, *n.* 1282
fawn-colored, *adj.* 609
fawner, *n.* 578
fawning, *adj.* 1225
fay, *n.* 1087
fealty, *n.* 187, 262
fear, *n.* 253, 527, 485
fear, *v.* 527
fearful, *adj.* 1155, 496, 69, 527, 148
fearlessness, *n.* 190
feasible, *adj.* 952
feast, *n.* 395, 497, 712, 1242, 551
feast, *v.* 551
feat, *n.* 752
feather, *n.* 201
feathered, *adj.* 917
feathers, *pl. n.* 851
feature, *n.* 484
features, *pl. n.* 446
FEBRILE, *adj.* 967, 203
fee, *n.* 927
feebleness, *n.* 1251
feed, *v.* 296, 1203, 274, 699
feeling, *n.* 471, 771, 617
feign, *v.* 624
feigning, *adj.* 1073
feigning, *n.* 1212
FEINT, *n.* 624
fell, *v.* 432
fellow, *n.* 468, 110
felon, *n.* 1065
felt, *n.* 229
fen, *n.* 674
fence, *n.* 830, 614
fences, *pl. n.* 830
fender, *n.* 228
-fer, 690, 696

fodder, *n.* 518
foil, *n.* 480
foil, *v.* 91, 288
foison, *n.* 124
FOIST, *v.* 495
foisting, *v.* 495
fold, *n.* 335, 672
fold, *v.* 335, 1146, 810
folded, *adj.* 335, 810
folding, *n.* 810
foliage, *n.* 248
follicle, *n.* 1181
follow, *v.* 509, 944
follower, *n.* 232, 741, 760, 1111, 1125, 944
following, *adj.* 398, 627, 177, 670
FONDLE, *v.* 129, 678
fondled, *v.* 129
fondling, *n.* 599, 742
fondness, *n.* 129
food, *n.* 699, 483
foodstuffs, *pl. n.* 96
fool, *n.* 862
fool, *v.* 110
fooled, *v.* 208
foolhardy, *adj.* 350, 7
foolish, *adj.* 391, 887, 41, 364
foolishly, *adv.* 160
foolishness, *n.* 550, 969
FOOLSCAP, *n.* 763
foot, *n.* 1053
footman, *n.* 232, 760
foot-trouble, *n.* 1216
fop, *n.* 354, 862
foppish, *adj.* 1158
forage, *v.* 210
foray, *n.* 204
forbear, *v.* 513
forbearance, *n.* 80, 779, 115
forbearing, *adj.* 776
forbid, *v.* 175, 1025
forbidden, *adj.* 211
force, *n.* 831, 836
force, *v.* 304, 1146, 172, 110
forced, *adj.* 112
forceful, *adj.* 148
forcing, *n.* 683

fore, *adj.* 585
FOREBODE, *v.* 571
forebodes, *v.* 571
foreboding, *n.* 253, 485
forefathers, *pl. n.* 444
forego, *v.* 267
foreign, *adj.* 846, 1103
foreknowledge, *n.* 1137
foremost, *adj.* 588
FORENSIC, *adj.* 747, 1041
forerunner, *n.* 419
forerunning, *adj.* 772
foresee, *v.* 713
foreseeing, *v.* 571
foreshadow, *v.* 571, 1044
foresight, *n.* 171, 1137
foresighted, *adj.* 450, 370
foresightedly, *adv.* 61
foretell, *v.* 571, 1283
forever, *adv.* 359
foreword, *n.* 1136, 344
forge, *v.* 495, 683
forgery, *n.* 495
forget, *v.* 217
forgetful, *adj.* 169
forgetfully, *adv.* 400
forgetfulness, *n.* 169, 324, 99, 400
forgetting, *n.* 651, 998
forging, *n.* 683
forgivable, *adj.* 86
forgive, *v.* 267, 452
forgiveness, *n.* 86, 267
forgotten, *adj.* 169
forlorn, *adj.* 294, 574
form, *n.* 1039, 354
form, *v.* 233, 283, 293
formal, *adj.* 1045, 1261
formation, *n.* 162, 438
former, *adj.* 1195, 1261, 999, 398
formerly, *adv.* 999, 1154
FORMIDABLE, *adj.* 148
formless, *adj.* 149
formulate, *v.* 293
forsaken, *adj.* 1249
forsaking, *n.* 1116
forswear, *v.* 941, 815

grudge, *n.* 621
grudgingly, *adv.* 115
gruesome, *adj.* 377
guarantee, *n.* 138
guarantee, *v.* 1028
guaranteed, *adj.* 500
guard, *n.* 741, 213
guard, *v.* 228
guarding, *adj.* 120
guess, *v.* 448
guide, *n.* 1241, 944
guide, *v.* 185
guiltless, *adj.* 565, 1261
guilty, *adj.* 919, 640
gulled, *v.* 208
gully, *n.* 988
gun, *n.* 514
gunpowder, *n.* 1043
GURU, *n.* 123
gust, *n.* 352
GUSTATION, *n.* 916
gusto, *n.* 916
gypsies, *pl. n.* 992
gypsy, *n.* 992
GYRATE, *v.* 15, 156, 1064
gyration, *n.* 1064
GYRE, *n.* 1064, 15
gyro-, 15
gyrocompass, *n.* 15
gyroscope, *n.* 1064
gyve, *v.* 1064
gyved, *adj.* 201

HABILIMENT, *n.* 1244, 593
habiliments, *pl. n.* 1244
habit, *n.* 158, 175, 573
habitation, *n.* 235, 799
habits, *pl. n.* 1244
habitual, *adj.* 203
habitude, *n.* 1244
habitudes, *pl. n.* 1244
hack, *v.* 915, 279
hackle, *n.* 851
hackle, *v.* 279, 915
HACKLES, *n.* 851
hackneyed, *adj.* 407, 139, 770
hag, *n.* 966, 940, 989

haggard, *adj.* 72, 279
HAGGLE, *v.* 279, 696, 915
haggling, *v.* 279
HAGIOLOGY, *n.* 1038
hail, *v.* 911
hair, *n.* 895, 979
hair-dresser, *n.* 1004
hair dressing, 1018
hairy, *adj.* 895
half-boiled, *adj.* 619
half-clad, *adj.* 593
half-day, *adj.* 167
half-dressed, *adj.* 593
half-month, *n.* 167
halibut, *n.* 1145
halo, *n.* 1140
halt, *n.* 32, 789
halted, *v.* 3
halter, *n.* 719
hammer, *n.* 854, 942
hammering, *n.* 683
handcuff, *n.* 201
handicap, *v.* 494
handily, *adv.* 479
handsome, *adj.* 589
handsomeness, *n.* 158
handwriting, *n.* 639
hang, *v.* 40, 1050
hanger-on, *n.* 760
hanging, *adj.* 107, 524, 1050
hangman, *n.* 760
hanker, *v.* 958
hankering, *n.* 285
happen, *v.* 772
happening, *n.* 229
happy, *adj.* 701
harangue, *n.* 431
harass, *v.* 228, 586, 754, 110, 203
harassed, *adj.* 49, 526, 900
HARBINGER, *n.* 419
harbor, *n.* 419, 984
harbor, *v.* 799
hard, *adj.* 48, 541, 686
hard-hearted, *adj.* 113
hard-of-hearing, *adj.* 391
hard-working, *adj.* 29, 638
harden, *v.* 159

hardened, *adj.* 113
harder, *adj.* 48
hardihood, *n.* 190
hardness, *n.* 134
hard work, 1272
harm, *v.* 831
harmful, *adj.* 796, 1133, 858
harmless, *adj.* 565
harmonious, *adj.* 67, 546, 775
harmony, *n.* 1074, 732, 1021
harried, *adj.* 900
harrow, *n.* 900
harrow, *v.* 900
HARROWED, *adj.* 900
harsh, *adj.* 801
harshness, *n.* 431
harvested, *v.* 154
hasten, *v.* 588
hastily, *adv.* 332, 657
hasty, *adj.* 350, 809
hat, *n.* 667, 691, 208
hatch, *v.* 699
hatchery, *n.* 1219
hatchet, *n.* 854
hate, *n.* 946, 99
hate, *v.* 69, 85, 500
hateful, *adj.* 220, 445
hatred, *n.* 946, 99, 440, 703
haughtiness, *n.* 802
haughty, *adj.* 982, 1027, 1158
haul, *v.* 942
haunt, *v.* 228
hawk, *n.* 749
hawk-like, *adj.* 1157
hay, *n.* 503
hazard, *n.* 630
haze, *n.* 396
he, *pron.* 63
head, *adj.* 246
head, *n.* 123, 765
head-cloth, *n.* 1040
head-dress, *n.* 234, 910, 1106
headland, *n.* 341, 474
headlong, *adj.* 350
headpiece, *n.* 1094
headstrong, *adj.* 350, 1277
heal, *v.* 735

health, *n.* 1246, 735
healthy, *adj.* 1246
heap, *n.* 1220, 50
heard, *v.* 60
hearing, *adj.* 284
heartiness, *n.* 265
heat, *n.* 1278, 48
HEATH, *n.* 1220, 1173
heathen, *n.* 270
heathenism, *n.* 270
heather, *n.* 1173, 1220
heat treatment, 1278
heave, *v.* 101
heavenly, *adj.* 6
heavily, *adv.* 657
heaving, *n.* 101
heavy, *adj.* 75, 144, 811, 240, 657,
    220, 364, 609, 1076, 101, 459
heavy-footed, *adj.* 545
HEBDOMADAL, *adj.* 1171
heckle, *v.* 203
heckling, *v.* 203
HECTIC, *adj.* 203
heed, *n.* 43, 120
heed, *v.* 617, 350, 357
heedful, *adj.* 120
heeding, *adj.* 617
heedless, *adj.* 350, 370, 804
heft, *v.* 1287
heifer, *n.* 992, 743
height, *n.* 995
HEINOUS, *adj.* 220, 445
heir, *n.* 931, 599
held, *v.* 201, 81
helical, *adj.* 879
helicoidal, *adj.* 879
helmet, *n.* 1094, 208
help, *v.* 274, 925, 686
helper, *n.* 1111, 196, 205, 820, 315
helpful, *adj.* 516
hemmed-in, *adj.* 63
hen, *n.* 437
HENCE, *adv.* 33, 1154
HENCHMAN, *n.* 760
-hend-, 325
hepta-, 1171
heptagonal, *adj.* 1171

heptane, *adj.* 1171
HEPTARCHY, *n.* 428, 1171
her, *pron.* 63, 592
herald, *n.* 419, 1281
herb, *n.* 1151, 1021
herbaceous, *adj.* 1151, 725
herbarium, *n.* 1151
herbivorous, *adj.* 924, 1090
herbs, *pl. n.* 1151
heresy, *n.* 1178
heretic, *n.* 132, 1116, 1125
heretical, *adj.* 531, 881
heretics, *pl. n.* 132
heretofore, *adj.* 1195
hermit, *n.* 1125, 934, 1287
hermit-like, *adj.* 934
heroic poem, 680
hesitant, *adj.* 35, 329
hesitation, *n.* 957, 1195
HETERODOX, *adj.* 881
heterodoxy, *n.* 1178
heterogeneity, *n.* 881
heterogeneous, *adj.* 50, 881
hew, *v.* 432
hewed, *v.* 432
hewing, *v.* 432
HEWN, *adj.* 432
hexagonal, *adj.* 1171
hiatus, *n.* 1120, 1183
hibernal, *adj.* 764
hidden, *adj.* 517, 653, 1091, 1124, 1144, 525, 912
hide, *n.* 830, 1181, 358
hide, *v.* 866, 97, 271, 1001, 1212, 912
hideous, *adj.* 875
hiding, *adj.* 1073
hiding, *v.* 97
hiding place, 1274
hiding-place, *n.* 249
hiemal, *adj.* 764
hieroglyphic, *n.* 604
hieroglyphics, *pl. n.* 604
higgle, *v.* 915
HIGGLER, *n.* 915
higgles, *v.* 915
high-colored, *adj.* 632
higher, *adj.* 588

high-pitched, *adj.* 1123
high-sounding, *adj.* 1176
highwayman, *n.* 641
hike, *n.* 336
hilarious, *adj.* 317
hilarity, *n.* 317
hill, *n.* 1088, 420, 455, 832, 150
hinder, *adj.* 585, 1008
hinder, *n.* 390
hinder, *v.* 102, 175, 288, 436, 494, 319, 686, 274, 588
hindered, *v.* 102
hindering, *adj.* 251
hindrance, *n.* 494, 251, 184
Hindu-priest, 542
hinge, *v.* 142
HINT, *n.* 380, 449, 470, 635, 806, 530
hint, *v.* 1196, 470, 723
hinted, *v.* 656
Hippocrates, 878
hippopotamus, *n.* 104
hire, *v.* 278
HIRELING, *n.* 39, 760
hirsute, *adj.* 1101
historian, *n.* 1190
historical document, 328
history, *n.* 444
hit, *v.* 81, 154, 415
hitting, *adj.* 488
hoar, *adj.* 1052
hoar-frost, *n.* 1052
hoary, *adj.* 1052
hoax, *n.* 125, 1077
hoax, *v.* 110
hobble, *v.* 254
hobbled, *v.* 254
hobbling, *v.* 254
hobgoblin, *n.* 88, 1087
hocus-pocus, *n.* 1017
hoe, *n.* 432
hog, *n.* 28, 1176
-hog, 595
hogshead, *n.* 1094
HOG-TIED, *adj.* 28
hoist, *v.* 101, 495
hold, *v.* 102, 175, 447, 443, 51, 81, 358

limber, *adj.* 735, 508
limberness, *n.* 481, 369
limerick, *n.* 1085
limit, *v.* 254
limitation, *n.* 184
limited, *adj.* 4, 38, 269, 922
limitless, *adj.* 38
limp, *adj.* 107, 508, 607
limp, *v.* 1174, 254
linage, *n.* 303
line, *n.* 237, 241, 303, 608, 865, 283, 689
LINEAGE, *n.* 303, 899
lineal, *adj.* 303
linear, *adj.* 177
-ling, 39, 599, 742
LING, *n.* 1173
linger, *v.* 353, 647, 1193
lingering, *adj.* 638
lingo, *n.* 1173, 62
lingual, *adj.* 1173
link, *n.* 1173, 851
Linnaeus, Carolus, 30
liquefy, *v.* 397
liquid, *adj.* 508, 176
liquor, *n.* 424, 731
liss, *n.* 735
LISSOME, *adj.* 735
list, *v.* 617
listen, *v.* 617
listening, *adj.* 617
listless, *adj.* 617, 965, 481
literal, *adj.* 1169
literary, *adj.* 1169
literary work, 605
literate, *adj.* 330
literature, *n.* 629, 1169
lithe, *adj.* 735, 508
lithesome, *adj.* 735
-lithic, 442
litigation, *n.* 842
LITIGIOUS, *adj.* 842
LITTER, *n.* 503, 130
littered, *adj.* 130
little necks, 595
LITTORAL, *adj.* 1169
liturgy, *n.* 842

live, *v.* 636, 235, 799
live in, 175
liveliness, *n.* 317, 649
lively, *adv.* 5
livid, *adj.* 169, 400
lizard, *n.* 1231, 1159, 991
llanos, *pl. n.* 988
load, *n.* 835, 870
loaf, *v.* 1115
loafing, *v.* 1115
loath, *adj.* 359
loathe, *v.* 69
loathsome, *adj.* 858
lob, *n.* 1223
lob, *v.* 1223
lobe, *n.* 904
lobs, *pl. n.* 1060
local, *adj.* 246
location, *n.* 273
locker, *n.* 316
locket, *n.* 46, 1224, 93
locution, *n.* 1260
lodge, *v.* 799
lodgement, *n.* 799
lodging, *n.* 235, 799, 419
lodgings, *pl. n.* 346
LODGMENT, *n.* 799
loftiness, *n.* 190
lofty, *adj.* 1260
-log-, 604
log, *n.* 252
loggia, *n.* 1056
logic, *n.* 818
loiter, *v.* 353, 647, 1193
loitering, *adj.* 638
loitering, *n.* 647
loneliness, *n.* 207, 1287
lonesome, *adj.* 735, 1042
long, *adj.* 48, 673
LONGANIMITY, *n.* 779
longed-for, *adj.* 285
longevity, *n.* 779
long-headed, *adj.* 532
longing, *n.* 255
longitude, *n.* 995
long-lost, *adj.* 999
loobies, *pl. n.* 1060

maraud, *v.* 498
MARAUDER, *n.* 498
marauders, *pl. n.* 387
marauding, *n.* 681
marble, *n.* 126
mare, *n.* 41
MARGENT, *n.* 1051
margin, *n.* 384, 1051
Marion, 73
MARIONETTE, *n.* 73
mark, *n.* 1269
mark, *v.* 794, 89, 509, 11
marketplace, *n.* 1029, 791, 747
marquetry, *n.* 1053
Marquis de Sade, 118
marriage, *n.* 207, 472
marriage song, 594
marring, *n.* 130
marsh, *n.* 1057, 674
marshalling, *n.* 125
marshland, *n.* 346
marshy, *adj.* 674, 1055, 1150
marsupial, *n.* 461
martial, *adj.* 59
MARVEL, *n.* 24
marveled, *v.* 129
marvelous, *adj.* 538
Mary, 73
Masefield, John, 117
mash, *v.* 154
maskalonge, *n.* 963
maskelunge, *n.* 963
masking, *adj.* 1073, 880
masquerade, *n.* 82
mass, *n.* 109, 227, 323, 340
massacre, *n.* 781
massacring, *adj.* 612
mass-book, *n.* 227
massive, *adj.* 75, 1223, 153
master, *n.* 417
masticate, *v.* 1059
mastodon, *n.* 104
mat, *n.* 307
mat, *v.* 307
material, *adj.* 394
materials, *pl. n.* 96
matins, *pl. n.* 464

matricide, *n.* 652, 487
matricula, *n.* 652
matriculate, *v.* 652
MATRICULATING, *n.* 652
matriculation, *n.* 652
matrimonial, *adj.* 594, 472
matrimony, *n.* 594, 1214
MATTED, *adj.* 307
matter-of-fact, *adj.* 1279
matured, *adj.* 917
maturity, *n.* 1202
MAUL, *n.* 854
maul, *v.* 65
maunder, *n.* 1282
MAUNDER, *v.* 1282
mausoleum, *n.* 150
maxim, *n.* 402, 878, 1070, 1200, 943
maximum, *adj.* 8
MEAD, *n.* 424
meadow, *n.* 631
MEAGER, *adj.* 4, 609, 1129
meagerly, *adv.* 115
meagerness, *n.* 4
meagre, *adj.* 4
meal, *n.* 497, 1242, 1037
mean, *adj.* 4, 7, 68, 112, 157, 239, 666, 728, 433, 1270
Meander, 215
meander, *v.* 215
MEANDERING, *n.* 215
meanness, *n.* 239
means, *n.* 588
measured, *adj.* 9
measures, *pl. n.* 588
meat-eating, *adj.* 924, 1090
mechanical, *adj.* 1238
meddlesome, *adj.* 644, 1042
meddling, *adj.* 644
medical, *adj.* 1171
medicament, *n.* 990
medicines, *pl. n.* 896, 685
MEDIEVAL, *adj.* 298, 779
meditate, *v.* 217, 258, 710, 168, 699
meditating, *adj.* 699
meditation, *n.* 258, 703, 955
medium, *adj.* 90
medley, *n.* 170

Mincheu, 893
mind, *n.* 622
mind, *v.* 357, 350
mine, *n.* 528
mingling, *n.* 865
mingling, *v.* 265
minimum, *adj.* 8
Mining Glossary, 323
MINION, *n.* 1067
miniscule, *adj.* 720
minor, *adj.* 8
minority, *n.* 8
minotaur, *n.* 88
minstrel, *n.* 213, 512
minus, *prep.* 8
minute, *adj.* 437, 8
miracle, *n.* 24, 538
miraculous, *adj.* 736
mire, *n.* 674, 1057, 893
mire, *v.* 674
mirth, *n.* 512
mirthful, *adj.* 553, 1109
mis-, 53
MISAPPREHEND, *v.* 53, 786
misapprehended, *v.* 53
misapprehends, *v.* 53
misbehavior, *n.* 301, 860
miscarriage, *n.* 135
miscellaneous, *adj.* 170, 214
mischance, *n.* 805
mischief, *n.* 845, 262
mischievous, *adj.* 261
misconduct, *n.* 301
miscreant, *n.* 1165
misdeed, *n.* 1161
misdemeanor, *n.* 1065, 1161
miser, *n.* 1222, 471
miserable, *adj.* 934, 574, 239, 1222, 471
miserly, *adj.* 68
misery, *n.* 1222
MISFEASANCE, *n.* 860, 301
misfortune, *n.* 805
misguide, *v.* 53
mishap, *n.* 805
misinterpret, *v.* 53
mislead, *v.* 53, 1099

misleading, *adj.* 477
misleads, *v.* 53
misled, *v.* 53
mismanagement, *n.* 860
misogamy, *n.* 1216
misogyny, *n.* 1216
MISOPEDIA, *n.* 1216
misquote, *v.* 164
misrepresent, *v.* 164
misrule, *v.* 53
miss, *n.* 227
miss, *v.* 227
MISSAL, *n.* 227
missal-book, *n.* 227
missile, *n.* 86
mission, *n.* 86
mist, *n.* 1054, 396
mistake, *n.* 749, 592
mistake, *v.* 53, 786
mistral, *n.* 843
mistress, *n.* 1178
mistrust, *v.* 69
misty, *adj.* 1054
misunderstand, *v.* 53, 786
misuse, *n.* 301
MITER, *n.* 910, 234
mitigate, *v.* 521, 113
mitigating, *adj.* 724
mitre, *n.* 234, 910
mitred abbots, 910
mix, *v.* 1099, 265, 1081, 397, 787
mixed, *adj.* 706, 881
mixing, *n.* 265
mixture, *n.* 176, 715, 706, 165
mixtures, *pl. n.* 715, 176
mizzenmast, *n.* 795
mnemonics, *n.* 998
moaning, *adj.* 945
moaning, *n.* 194, 219, 196
moat, *n.* 420
mobility, *n.* 803
mock, *v.* 607, 734, 288, 222
mock-heroic, *adj.* 898
mocking, *adj.* 607
mode, *n.* 671, 1244, 354
model, *n.* 408, 889
moderate, *v.* 521

mound, *n.* 244, 150, 288, 1220, 420, 1010

mount, *v.* 702, 307

mountainous, *adj.* 674

mourn, *v.* 357, 737, 586, 929, 219

mournful, *adj.* 565, 701, 965, 699

mourning, *n.* 194, 219

mouthful, *n.* 1257

move, *n.* 482, 295, 597, 70

movement, *n.* 44, 125

moving, *adj.* 809, 263

moving, *n.* 522

moving, *v.* 70

moving sullenly, 97

mud, *n.* 389, 674, 893

mud-digger, *n.* 942

muddle-brained, *adj.* 364

muddled, *adj.* 893

muddy, *adj.* 1150

mudgeon, *n.* 1222

muffled, *adj.* 319

MULCT, *v.* 733

mulcts, *pl. n.* 733

mule, *n.* 41

mulish, *adj.* 183, 41, 459

MULISHLY, *adv.* 41

mull, *v.* 258

multiplication, *n.* 810

mundane, *adj.* 717

MUNICIPAL, *adj.* 246

municipality, *n.* 246

muniments, *pl. n.* 337

murder, *n.* 487

murderer, *n.* 873

murderous, *adj.* 612

murmur, *v.* 761

murmuring, *adj.* 945, 1095

muscular, *adj.* 1129, 750, 723, 609

muse, *v.* 217, 710

music, *n.* 299, 512

musical, *adj.* 558

musical composition, 558

musical drama, 558

musician, *n.* 512

musing, *n.* 255

musk, *n.* 963

musk-deer, *n.* 963

MUSKELLUNGE, *n.* 963

mutable, *adj.* 643

mute, *adj.* 255

mutilate, *v.* 164

muzzle, *n.* 1257

muzzled, *adj.* 319

myopia, *n.* 1143

MYOPIC, *adj.* 1143

myrrh, *n.* 435

mysterious, *adj.* 267, 517, 1124, 912

mysteriously, *adv.* 736

mystery, *n.* 1124

mystic, *adj.* 653, 736

mystical, *adj.* 912

myth, *n.* 536

MYTHIC, *adj.* 536

mythical, *adj.* 1091, 536

myths, *pl. n.* 536

nadir, *n.* 58

nag, *v.* 754

naive, *adj.* 1261

naked, *adj.* 686

name, *n.* 1160, 650, 359

name, *v.* 693, 650

NAP, *n.* 492, 418, 497, 895

NARCISSISM, *n.* 264

Narcissus, 264

narcissus, *n.* 264

NARCOSE, *adj.* 181

narcosis, *n.* 181

narcotic, *adj.* 264

narcotic, *n.* 181

narcotize, *v.* 181

narrate, *v.* 690

narrative, *n.* 311, 633, 714, 680

narrow, *adj.* 1158

narrow-minded, *adj.* 1158

nascent, *adj.* 736, 472

NATAL, *adj.* 472, 364, 1205

nation, *n.* 1205

national, *adj.* 798

National Geographic, 283

native, *adj.* 433, 364, 472

native, *n.* 1205

natural, *adj.* 433, 472, 1159, 736

naturally, *adv.* 364, 645

non-conforming, *adj.* 531
non-equivalence, *n.* 665
nonfeasance, *n.* 301
non-marrier, 852, 1168
non-ruminant, *n.* 28
nonsense, *n.* 367, 969
noon, *adj.* 90
noon, *n.* 626
nose, *n.* 146
NOSEGAY, *n.* 146
not, *adv.* 325
notary, *n.* 856
notation, *n.* 1189
notch, *n.* 455
notch, *v.* 711, 279
notched, *adj.* 151, 1127
note, *n.* 957, 1051, 1184, 1128
note, *v.* 633
notes, *pl. n.* 1105
nothingness, *n.* 412
notice, *n.* 806, 43, 380
notice, *v.* 1196, 1203, 293
notify, *v.* 730
notion, *n.* 738, 179
nourish, *v.* 443
nourishment, *n.* 483, 497
novelty, *n.* 24
novice, *n.* 1131, 1111, 74
NOVITIATE, *n.* 74, 1131
now, *adj.* 433
now, *adv.* 309
noxious, *adj.* 858
noy, *v.* 858
NUANCE, *n.* 591
nuciferous, *adj.* 405
nuisance, *n.* 261
null, *adj.* 412
nullify, *v.* 412
NULLITY, *n.* 412
num-, 923
number, *n.* 224, 1211
number, *v.* 693, 441
numbers, *pl. n.* 1189
numbness, *n.* 691
numerate, *v.* 693
numerology, *n.* 923
numerous, *adj.* 620

NUMISMATICS, *n.* 923
nuptial, *adj.* 594, 472
nurseling, *n.* 742
nurture, *n.* 162
nut, *n.* 110
nymph, *n.* 1031, 991

o-, 400
oafish, *adj.* 251
oatmeal, *n.* 969
ob-, 400
obdurate, *adj.* 113
obdurately, *adv.* 41
obedience, *n.* 187
obeisance, *n.* 187
obelisk, *n.* 442, 1231, 773
obelisks, *pl. n.* 1200
obfuscate, *v.* 1249
object, *n.* 209, 239
object, *v.* 734, 513
objecting, *adj.* 934
objection, *n.* 247
objects, *pl. n.* 76
objurgation, *n.* 552
obli-, 400
obligatory, *adj.* 1230
oblige, *v.* 831, 184
OBLIQUELY, *adv.* 400, 491
obliquity, *n.* 400
obliterate, *v.* 659, 330
obliteration, *n.* 330
OBLIVESCENCE, *n.* 169
oblivion, *n.* 651, 169, 400
oblivious, *adj.* 169, 400
obliviously, *adv.* 400
obscene, *adj.* 804
obscure, *adj.* 218, 267, 517, 661, 400,
    736
obscure, *v.* 1249
obscurity, *n.* 756
OBSEQUIES, *n.* 1225, 177
obsequy, *n.* 1225
observance, *n.* 262, 43, 132
observances, *pl. n.* 663
observation, *n.* 961, 1184
observe, *v.* 669, 217, 1203, 1196, 414,
    293

Pinehurst, 598
pinion, *n.* 201, 707
pinion, *v.* 201
PINIONED, *adj.* 201
pinnacle, *n.* 399, 1221
PIOUS, *adj.* 29, 842
pipe, *n.* 1094
PIPPIN, *n.* 1210
piquancy, *n.* 225
pique, *n.* 756
piracy, *n.* 387
pirate, *n.* 795
pirates, *pl. n.* 387
pit, *n.* 518, 679, 1029, 1120, 528
pitch, *v.* 784
pitcher, *n.* 625, 1049, 1158, 990
pitch-fork, *n.* 1080
pitfall, *n.* 554
pitiful, *adj.* 606
pit-pan, *n.* 252
pittance, *n.* 29
pity, *n.* 471, 1176, 440, 29, 575
PIVOT, *v.* 142
placate, *v.* 810
placating, *n.* 810
placation, *n.* 810
place, *n.* 116, 1147
place, *v.* 1147, 163
plague, *n.* 360, 261, 929
plague, *v.* 228, 360, 281, 49
plagued, *adj.* 49
plaguing, *adj.* 261
plain, *adj.* 121, 122, 688
plain, *n.* 988
plain, *v.* 929
plainly, *adv.* 1229
plaint, *n.* 194, 565
plaintiff, *n.* 565
PLAINTIVE, *adj.* 565, 701
plait, *n.* 335
PLAIT, *v.* 335, 554
plaited, *adj.* 810
plaiting, *n.* 810
plan, *n.* 1017, 125
plan, *v.* 293, 658, 168
planet, *n.* 741
planetoid, *adj.* 83

planetoid, *n.* 83
PLANGENT, *adj.* 929
plangent, *n.* 461
planning, *adj.* 613
planning, *n.* 1247
plant, *n.* 1173, 1151, 547, 19
plantigrade, *adj.* 545
plant-life, *n.* 694
plant-like, *adj.* 970
PLASHY, *adj.* 1055
plataresque, *adj.* 883
plate, *n.* 625, 970, 990
platform, *adj.* 314
platform, *n.* 100, 1192, 127, 1170,
   812, 314
platitudinous, *adj.* 407
plausible, *adj.* 1134
play, *n.* 721, 704
play, *v.* 373
player, *n.* 512
playful, *adj.* 153
pleasant, *adj.* 67, 114, 277, 527, 688,
   20, 1124
pleasantness, *n.* 20
pleasantries, *pl. n.* 1287
PLEASANTRY, *n.* 20, 971
please, *v.* 527
pleased, *v.* 527
pleasing, *adj.* 277, 589, 429
pleasure-seeking, *adj.* 751
pleasure, *n.* 527
pleat, *n.* 335
pleat, *v.* 554
plebeian, *adj.* 157, 511
plebeian, *n.* 511
pledge, *v.* 278
plenary, *adj.* 578, 798
plenteous, *adj.* 78
plentiful, *adj.* 78, 620
plentifully, *adv.* 1, 115, 128
plenty, *adj.* 124
plenty, *n.* 342, 715, 578
pleonasm, *n.* 753, 361
pleonastic, *adj.* 361
plethora, *n.* 296
pleuronectes, *pl. n.* 1145
pliable, *adj.* 335

probingly, *adv.* 171
proceed, *v.* 936, 300
proceeding, *n.* 215, 229
process, *n.* 229
process, *v.* 229
processed, *adj.* 229
processes, *pl. n.* 229
procession, *n.* 66, 250
proclaim, *v.* 921, 543, 1196, 571
proclamation, *n.* 18, 1281, 407, 543
proclivity, *n.* 637
procrastinate, *v.* 647
procrastination, *n.* 638
procreation, *n.* 162
procure, *v.* 293
procured, *v.* 293
prod, *n.* 196
prod, *v.* 196
prodding, *n.* 196
PRODIGAL, *adj.* 1092, 538
prodigality, *n.* 538, 1092
PRODIGIOUS, *adj.* 538
prodigiously, *adv.* 736
prodigy, *n.* 538
produce, *v.* 310, 796
production, *n.* 162
productive, *adj.* 638
profane, *adj.* 717
profess, *v.* 624
profession, *n.* 427
professional-fee, *n.* 927
professor, *n.* 944
PROFFER, *v.* 684
proficient, *adj.* 684
profile, *n.* 608
profit, *n.* 590
profit, *v.* 684
profitable, *adj.* 588, 323
profligateness, *n.* 321
profound, *adj.* 517
profuse, *adj.* 78, 1092, 787
profusely, *adv.* 1
profusion, *n.* 342, 1186, 715
progenitor, *n.* 444
progenitors, *pl. n.* 444
progeny, *n.* 303, 444
prognosticate, *v.* 571

prognostication, *n.* 635
program, *n.* 242
progress, *n.* 165
progress, *v.* 43
prohibit, *v.* 436, 686, 175, 1025
prohibited, *adj.* 211
prohibition, *n.* 18
project, *v.* 340, 56
projectile, *n.* 239, 17
projecting, *adj.* 341
projection, *n.* 340, 341, 572
projections, *pl. n.* 1007
proletarian, *adj.* 511
proletarian, *n.* 511
prolixity, *n.* 753
prologue, *n.* 1204, 1033, 604
prolong, *v.* 1033
promenade, *n.* 732, 341, 608
prominence, *n.* 231
prominent, *adj.* 341
promise, *n.* 202, 138
PROMONTORY, *adj.* 341
prompt, *adj.* 638, 332
prompting, *n.* 236
promptly, *adv.* 61
promulgate, *v.* 1196
prone, *adj.* 849
pronounce, *v.* 11, 543
pronouncement, *n.* 1240
PRONUNCIAMENTO, *n.* 543
pronunciation, *n.* 62, 543
prop, *n.* 127, 320, 308, 1060
prop, *v.* 443
proper, *adj.* 338, 502, 588, 589, 430
property, *n.* 869, 430
prophecy, *n.* 155, 1283
prophesy, *v.* 571
prophetic, *adj.* 1283
propitiation, *n.* 810
propitious, *adj.* 520
proportion, *n.* 1211
proposal, *n.* 344
propose, *v.* 684
proposition, *n.* 344, 402
propriety, *n.* 430
prorogation, *n.* 1033
proud, *adj.* 1158

reward, *n.* 441, 582, 1286
reward, *v.* 452
RHETORIC, *n.* 199
rhetorical, *adj.* 616, 1142
rhythmic, *adj.* 1020
ribaldry, *n.* 1272
rich, *adj.* 620, 323, 78
Richardson, Charles, 268
rich-embroidery, *n.* 933
riches, *pl. n.* 342, 869
riddle, *n.* 1017
ride, *v.* 235
ridge, *n.* 288, 455, 555
ridicule, *n.* 607, 971, 825
ridicule, *v.* 288, 696
ridiculed, *adj.* 745
ridiculous, *adj.* 553
ridings, *pl. n.* 504
RIFE, *adj.* 620
riffraff, *n.* 804
rifling, *n.* 286
rift, *n.* 98, 289, 469
rift, *v.* 469
rigamarole, *n.* 367
right, *adj.* 338, 583, 491
right, *n.* 193, 1097, 338, 430, 755
righteous, *adj.* 29
right order, 1247
rigid, *adj.* 896
rigidity, *n.* 481
rigorous, *adj.* 896
RILL, *n.* 654
rime, *n.* 330, 626, 1052
RIMY, *adj.* 1052
rind, *n.* 358, 801, 830, 225
ring, *n.* 1064, 15, 1173, 910
riot, *n.* 506
riotous, *adj.* 1092
rip, *n.* 469
RIPARIAN, *adj.* 1209
RIPOSTE, *n.* 676
rise, *v.* 226
rising, *n.* 16, 101
risk, *n.* 630
rite, *n.* 103, 1045, 172
rive, *v.* 469
river, *n.* 141, 631, 1209, 105

rivers, *pl. n.* 327
rivulet, *n.* 654, 988
roar, *n.* 37
roaring, *adj.* 405
rob, *v.* 130
robbed, *adj.* 130, 745
robber, *n.* 498, 641
robbers, *pl. n.* 387
robbery, *n.* 221, 286, 52, 387
robbing, *n.* 286, 681
robe, *n.* 800, 1228, 1131
Robert of Sorbonne, 616
robust, *adj.* 128, 1129, 580
Rock, 514
rock, *n.* 50, 903, 706
rock-plant, *n.* 456
rock plants, *pl. n.* 180
rocky, *adj.* 341, 674
rod, *n.* 384, 1164
rode, *v.* 235
rodent, *n.* 416, 978, 1052
RODOMONTADE, *n.* 1019, 802
roe, *n.* 411, 668
rogation, *n.* 600
Rolfe, William J., 1046
roll, *v.* 707
rolled, *adj.* 473
roller, *n.* 707
rolling, *adj.* 263
Roman-boat, *n.* 1087
romp, *v.* 482
roof, *n.* 859
room, *n.* 799, 1184, 316
roomage, *n.* 501
roomy, *adj.* 502, 128
rooster, *n.* 862
rooted, *adj.* 613, 722
rooted, *v.* 1239
rope, *n.* 540, 117, 719, 303
rope pile, 1043
ropes, *pl. n.* 1043
Rosenthal, Gilbert, 355
Rosetta Stone, 807
rostrum, *n.* 100, 1192
rotate, *v.* 15, 1064, 1123
rotation, *n.* 1064
rotten, *adj.* 893, 994

slow-paced, *adj.* 545
slow-poke, *n.* 1113
slow-witted, *adj.* 364
sluggard, *n.* 641
sluggish, *adj.* 508, 638, 1256, 334, 657, 965
sluggishly, *adv.* 545
sluggishness, *n.* 99, 691, 1215
sluice, *n.* 314, 1057
sluiceway, *n.* 314
slumber, *n.* 32
slumberous, *adj.* 79
slushy, *adj.* 1150
sly, *adj.* 1113, 557, 275
smack, *v.* 81
small, *adj.* 437
small-headed, *adj.* 532
smallness, *n.* 789
smart, *adj.* 473, 1113
smartness, *n.* 64
smear, *v.* 759, 661
smell, *n.* 445, 260
smell, *v.* 566
smell-producing, *adj.* 690
smelly, *adj.* 445, 393
smile, *v.* 880
smiling, *adj.* 880
smirk, *v.* 880
SMIRKING, *adj.* 880
Smith, Charles J., 607
Smith, Joseph Lindon, 4
smoke, *v.* 727
smoke-stack, *n.* 908
smooth, *adj.* 1271, 695, 263, 294, 172
smooth, *v.* 1052, 1128
smoothness, *n.* 308
smothered, *adj.* 319
smudge, *v.* 661
snare, *n.* 125
snarl, *v.* 1099
snarled, *adj.* 307
snarling, *adj.* 1119
snatching, *n.* 954
sneak, *v.* 97
sneaking, *v.* 97

sneer, *v.* 288
sneering, *adj.* 557
snoring, *adj.* 1126
snout, *n.* 1257
snow vehicle, 942
soaked, *adj.* 426
sober, *adj.* 1060
soberness, *n.* 321, 529
SOBRIETY, *n.* 529, 321
SOBRIQUET, *n.* 1160
soft, *adj.* 475, 735, 1150
soften, *v.* 521, 1059, 397
softened, *adj.* 113
softening, *adj.* 724, 521
softness, *n.* 735
soil, *n.* 1052
soil, *v.* 291
soiled, *adj.* 291
SOJOURN, *n.* 980
sol-, 1287
solace, *n.* 294
sold, *v.* 501
soldier, *n.* 641, 110
SOLECISM, *n.* 1287, 777
solecisms, *pl. n.* 1287
solemn, *adj.* 1045
solemnize, *v.* 669
solicit, *v.* 921
solicitation, *n.* 219
solicitude, *n.* 253, 485
solid, *adj.* 415, 508, 640
SOLIPSISM, *n.* 777
solitaire, *n.* 1287
solitary, *adj.* 934, 1156
solitary, *n.* 1287
solitude, *n.* 207, 1287
solution, *n.* 1071, 176, 135
solutions, *pl. n.* 176
solve, *v.* 135
solved, *v.* 168
somber, *adj.* 218, 657
-some, 251, 735, 858
somniferous, *adj.* 1236, 79, 690
somnolent, *adj.* 1236
son, *n.* 1263
sonata, *n.* 93

spent, *adj.* 356
spherical, *adj.* 259, 27
sphinx, *n.* 88, 814, 1112
spinster, *n.* 1114
spin, *v.* 15, 1123
spine, *n.* 979
Spinoza, Benedictus, 268
spiral, *adj.* 879
spiral, *n.* 762
spire, *v.* 956
spirillum, *n.* 189
spirit, *n.* 216, 331, 510, 867, 1245, 5, 287, 162, 190, 536, 779
spirited, *adj.* 5, 1245
spiritless, *adj.* 508, 157
spiritual, *adj.* 536, 717, 123
spiritualistic seance, 77
spissate, *adj.* 415
spissated, *adj.* 1062
spit, *v.* 1232
spite, *n.* 621, 183
spiteful, *adj.* 183
splash, *n.* 1055
splash, *v.* 1055
splashy, *adj.* 1055
splendid, *adj.* 841, 1013
splendor, *n.* 953
splenetic, *adj.* 1217, 97
split, *n.* 469, 768
split, *v.* 469, 98
splitting, *n.* 98, 768
spoil, *v.* 893, 357, 130
spoiled, *adj.* 256, 893, 1054, 130
spoiling, *n.* 681
spoliated, *adj.* 130
sponge, *v.* 578
sponges, *v.* 578
spongy, *adj.* 674
sponsor, *n.* 676
spontaneously, *adv.* 539
sport, *n.* 20, 281
sport-coat, *n.* 667
sportive, *adj.* 853, 153
spot, *n.* 47, 865
spot, *v.* 794, 865
spots, *pl. n.* 865

spotted, *adj.* 47, 307, 794, 837
spouse, *n.* 468
spread, *v.* 349, 271, 326
spreading, *adj.* 1258
sprig, *n.* 1263
sprightliness, *n.* 649
SPRIGHTLY, *adj.* 5, 874, 982
spring, *v.* 482, 1193
spring-like, *adj.* 764
springing, *n.* 16
sprinkle, *v.* 705
sprinkled, *v.* 787
sprinkling, *n.* 103, 705
sprite, *n.* 1087, 5
sprites, *pl. n.* 88
sprout, *n.* 1203
sprout, *v.* 1118
spruce, *adj.* 473
spur, *n.* 236, 552
spur, *v.* 552
spurious, *adj.* 1091, 785, 974, 978
spuriousness, *n.* 974
spurn, *v.* 56
spurring, *n.* 196
spy, *v.* 961
spying, *n.* 984
squabble, *v.* 14, 1099
squall, *n.* 843
squandering, *adj.* 1092
squash, *n.* 84
squat, *v.* 958
squeezed, *adj.* 502
squirm, *v.* 108
stab, *v.* 1150
stable, *adj.* 280
stables, *pl. n.* 96
stack, *n.* 1220
staff, *n.* 320, 1164, 1269, 331, 409, 384, 973
stag, *n.* 743
stage, *n.* 100, 997, 1192
staggard, *n.* 743
staid, *adj.* 1060
staid-person, *n.* 1060
stain, *n.* 865
stain, *v.* 794

tortuous, *adj.* 723
torture, *n.* 781
torture, *v.* 195
toss, *v.* 784
totter, *v.* 597
tottering, *adj.* 920
touch, *n.* 634
touch, *v.* 35
touchable, *adj.* 688
touched, *adj.* 381
touching, *n.* 634
tour, *n.* 608
tout, *n.* 921
TOUT, *v.* 921
toward, *prep.* 238
tower, *n.* 559, 1056, 1063
town, *n.* 504, 246
towns, *pl. n.* 504
toxic, *adj.* 277
trace, *n.* 591, 976
trace, *v.* 509
track, *n.* 259, 370
tract, *n.* 206, 704
tractable, *adj.* 563
TRACTATE, *n.* 704
traction, *n.* 563
tractor, *n.* 563
trade, *n.* 394
trade, *v.* 57, 696
traffic, *v.* 57
tragedies, *pl. n.* 721
tragedy, *n.* 721
train, *n.* 66, 250
train, *v.* 563
trained, *adj.* 304
training, *n.* 162
trait, *n.* 105
traitor, *n.* 191, 1096
traitorous, *adj.* 112
trajectory, *n.* 239
trance, *n.* 1128
tranquil, *adj.* 388, 526
tranquility, *n.* 435, 526, 1069
tranquilize, *v.* 556
tranquilizing, *adj.* 724
transcription, *n.* 530

transfer, *v.* 397, 600, 601, 690, 1233
transform, *v.* 91
TRANSFUSE, *v.* 397, 787
transfusion, *n.* 397
transgressing, *v.* 460
transgression, *n.* 1065, 1161
transgressor, *n.* 1161
transient, *adj.* 960, 280
transit, *n.* 613
TRANSITORY, *adj.* 280, 722
translate, *v.* 1128, 690, 1233
transmission, *n.* 86
transmit, *v.* 86, 397
transmute, *v.* 91
transparent, *adj.* 240, 755
transparently, *adv.* 1229
transpire, *v.* 956
transport, *v.* 713, 397
transportation, *n.* 173
trap, *n.* 125
trash, *n.* 679, 804
trash collector, 232
trash collectors, 232
trashy, *adj.* 804
TRAUMA, *n.* 226
TRAVAIL, *n.* 522
travel, *n.* 522
traveling, *adj.* 613
traveling, *v.* 857
traveller, *n.* 295
travesty, *n.* 1227
tray, *n.* 990
TREACHEROUS, *adj.* 112, 919, 643
treachery, *n.* 112, 262
tread, *v.* 1150
treasonable, *adj.* 112
Treasure Island, 81
treasurer, *n.* 1237
treasury, *n.* 1237
treat, *v.* 129
treatise, *n.* 955, 328, 704, 1184, 837
treatises, *pl. n.* 704
tree, *n.* 889
trellis, *n.* 106
trembling, *adj.* 920, 1264
tremulous, *adj.* 1264